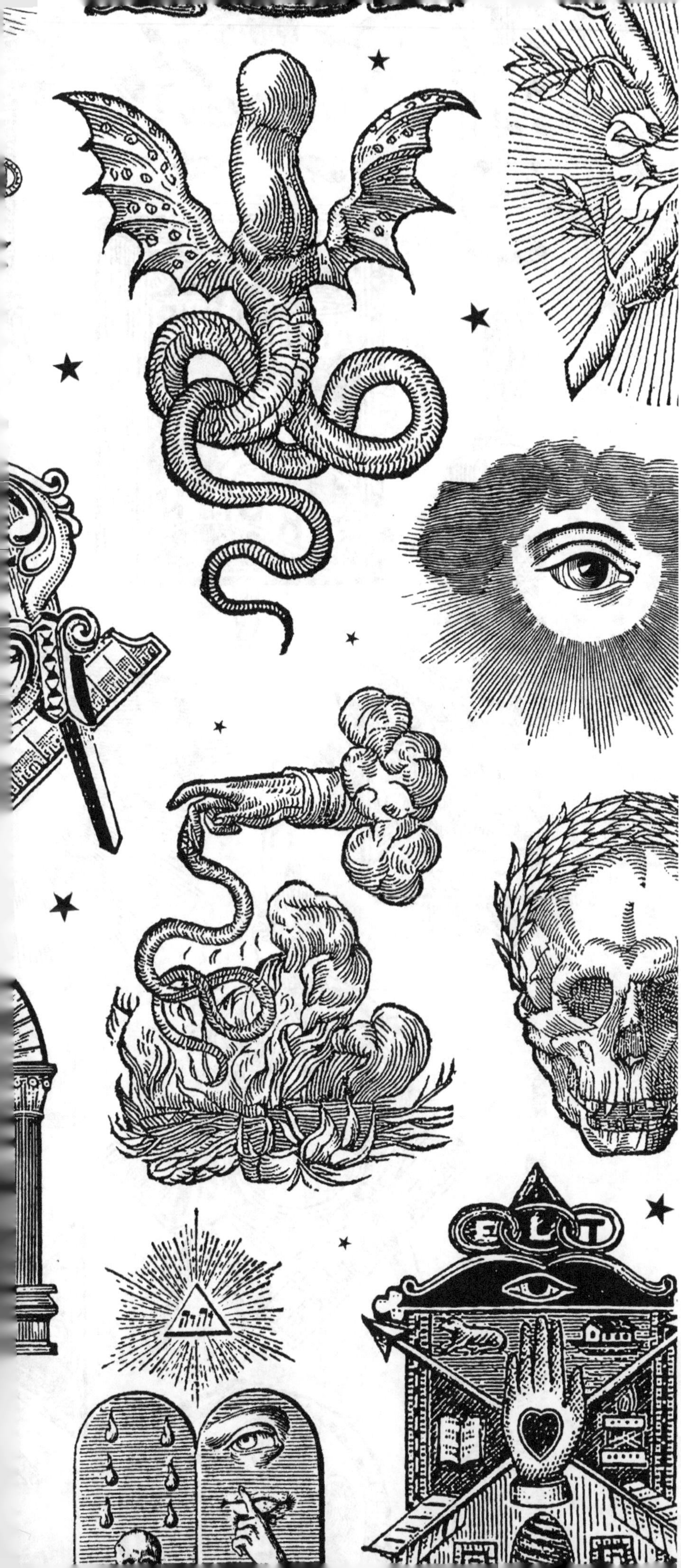

AF225222

SYMBOLS & EMBLEMS

AN IMAGE ARCHIVE FOR ARTISTS And DESIGNERS

EDITIONS Vault

INTRODUCTION

For centuries, symbols and emblems have served as the secret language of Western civilisation — vessels of meaning, power, and belief encoded in image and form. From the heraldic devices of medieval nobility to the allegorical woodcuts of Renaissance emblem books, these motifs have shaped the visual culture of artists, scholars, printers, and mystics alike.

Symbols & Emblems, an Image Archive by Vault Editions, is a celebration of this rich and enduring tradition. This collection brings together 1,047 meticulously restored woodcuts, engravings, and heraldic illustrations drawn from the great symbolic and emblematic traditions of Renaissance and early modern Europe. Skulls and serpents, mythological beasts and celestial bodies, shields and daggers, allegorical figures and printer's devices — the collection spans the full visual vocabulary of Western symbolic art, from the memento mori of the vanitas tradition to the intricate emblematic language of the Baroque period.

Whether you are a graphic designer seeking bold and timeless visual assets, a tattoo artist drawing on centuries of symbolic tradition, or simply a lover of historical art and ornament, this book offers an inexhaustible source of visual inspiration. Each image has been carefully selected and restored to ensure that the detail and character of these remarkable works are preserved and ready for modern use.

Additionally, we've included a unique download link granting access to all 1,047 images featured in the collection as high-resolution JPEG files, perfect for use in your art and design projects — allowing you to bring the symbolic power of five centuries of imagery into new and imaginative contexts.

Explore five centuries of symbolic art with *Symbols & Emblems, an Image Archive* by Vault Editions.

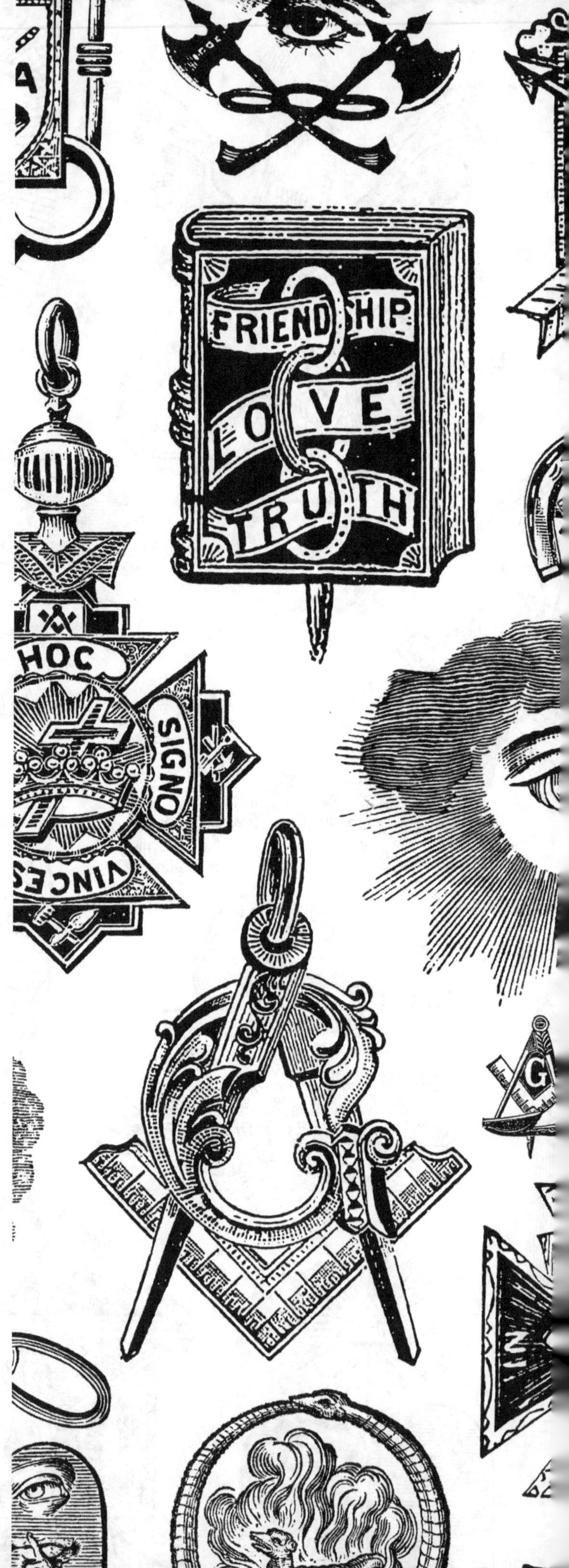

PREFACE

There is something about the symbol that has always exceeded its own meaning. Across cultures and centuries, emblems and devices have carried layers of significance that resist simple reading — encoded with belief, aspiration, warning, and wonder by the artists, scholars, and craftsmen who made them. They are images that ask something of the viewer, and artists have returned to them again and again, producing some of the most intricate and enduring visual work in the Western tradition.

This book was born from a fascination with that imagery and a desire to gather it into a single, usable archive. In curating this collection, I sought to bring together a wide range of subjects and traditions — the heraldic devices of medieval and Renaissance nobility, the allegorical woodcuts of the great emblem books, the memento mori and vanitas symbols of the Baroque period, the serpents and mythological beasts of classical tradition, and the printer's marks and ornamental devices that shaped five centuries of European visual culture.

Together, these 1,047 images trace a remarkable lineage of symbolic thinking, rendered in woodcut and engraving by craftsmen whose names are largely lost but whose skill speaks clearly across the centuries.

Symbols & Emblems, an Image Archive is a resource for the modern creative. Whether you are designing a book cover, building a collage, seeking references for your own illustrations, or working within the traditions of tattooing, heraldry, or ornamental design, this book is intended to inspire and support your work. With the included downloadable JPEG files, you can take these works beyond the page and into your own projects, giving new life to some of history's most compelling visual language.

It is my hope that this collection serves as a practical tool and an invitation to engage with a tradition that remains as vital and resonant as ever.

— *Kale James*

DOWNLOAD YOUR FILES

Downloading your files is simple. To access your digital files, please go to the last page of this book and follow the instructions.

For technical assistance, please email:
info@vaulteditions.com

Bibliographical Note

This book is a new work created by Vault Editions Ltd.

ISBN: 978-1-922966-78-0

01

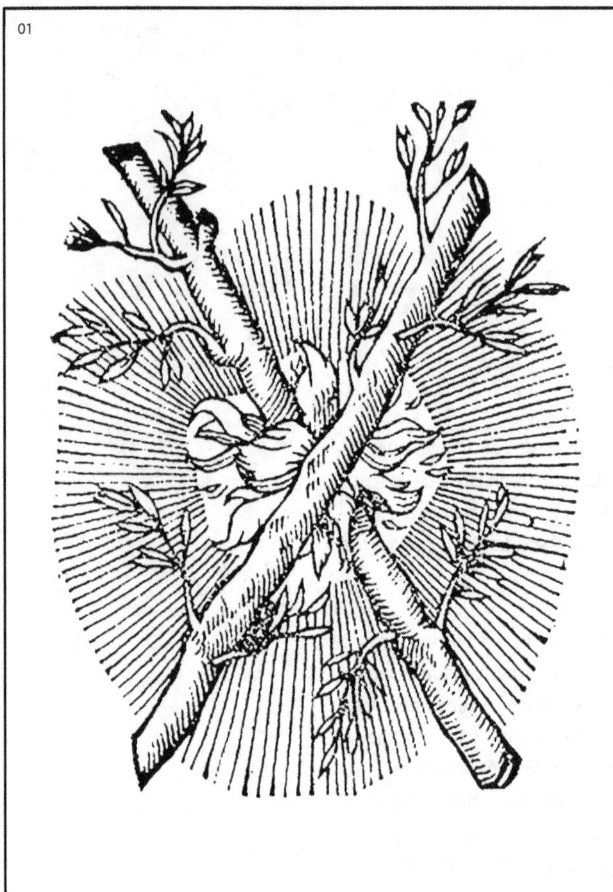

02

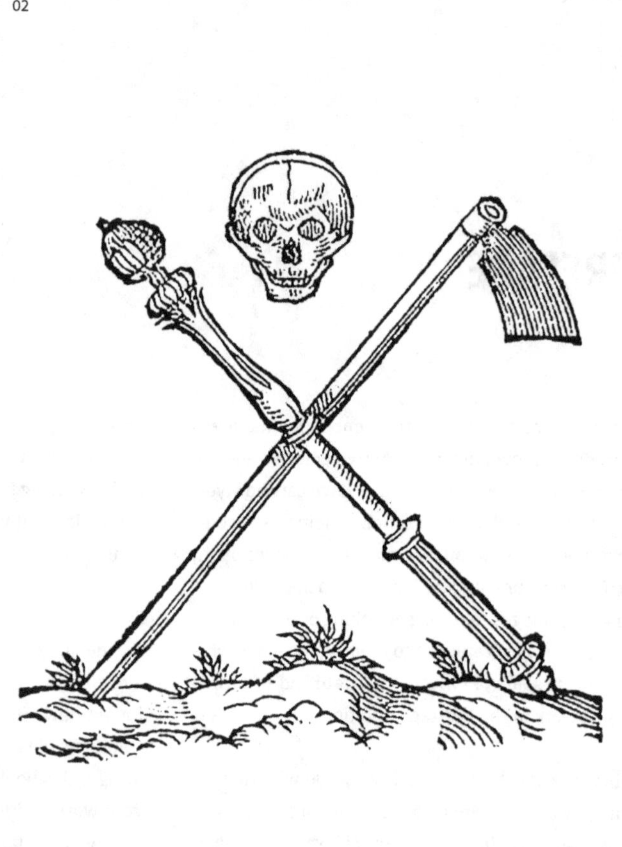

03

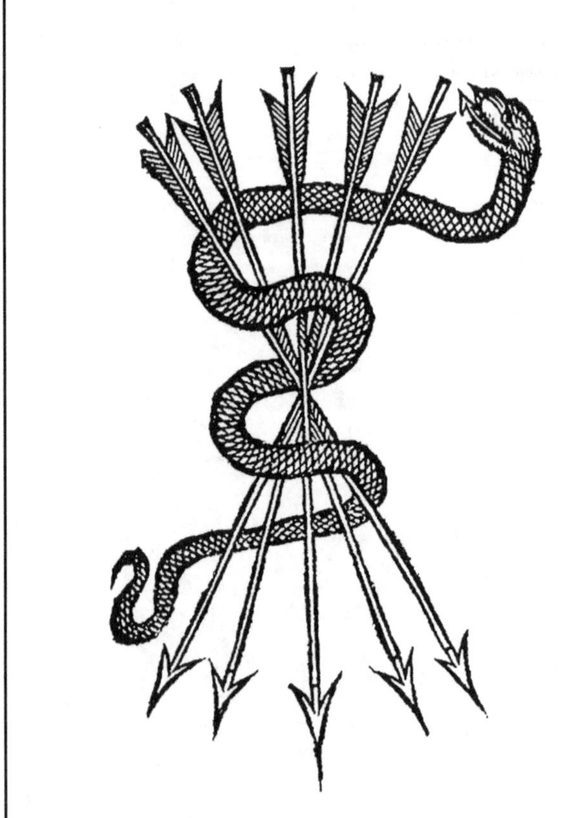

04

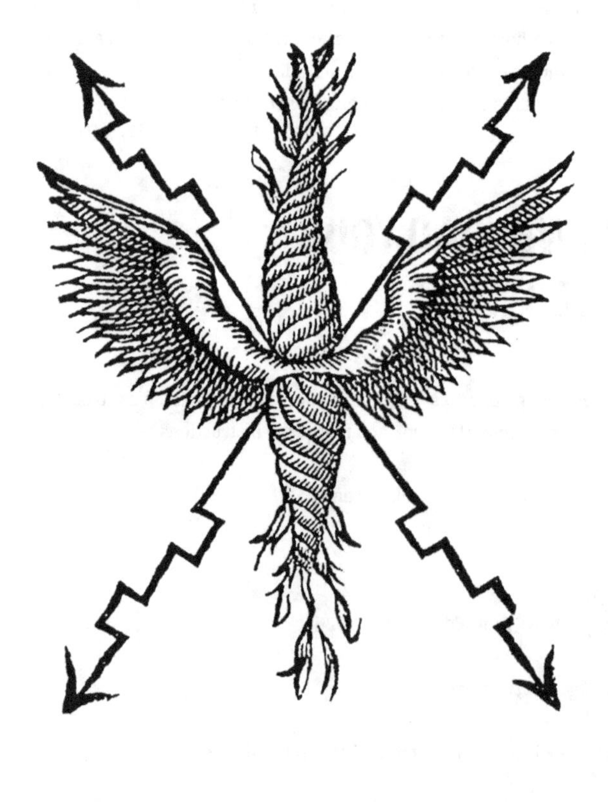

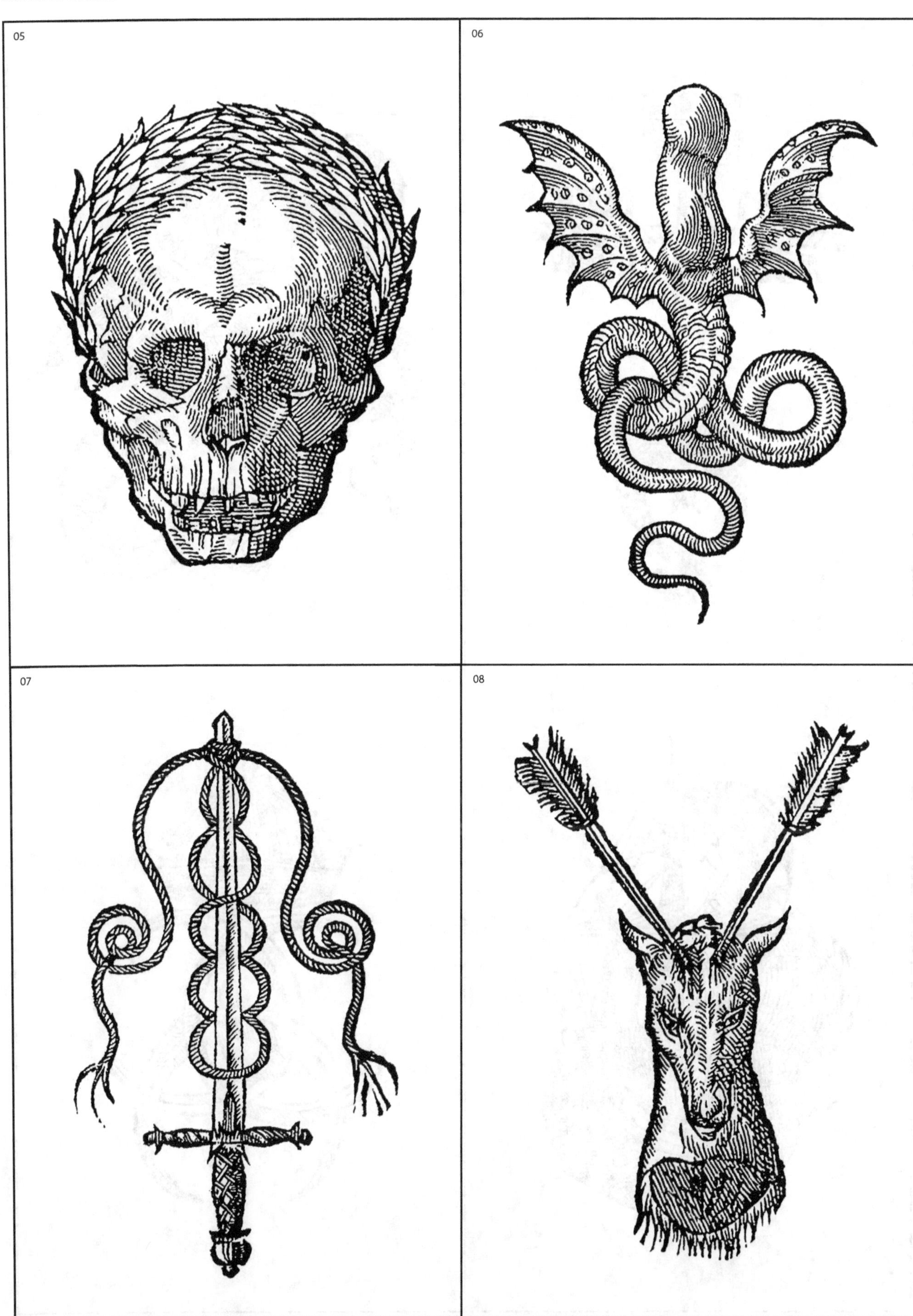

09
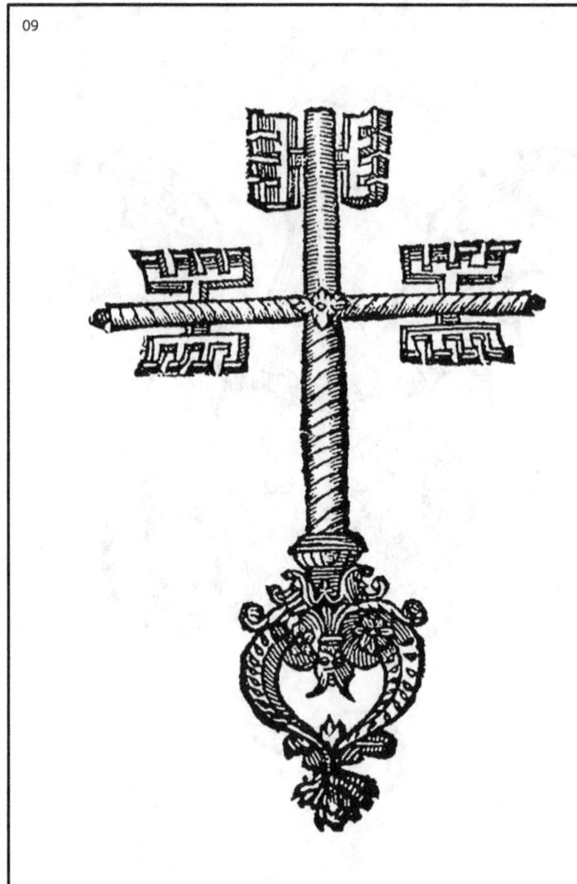

10
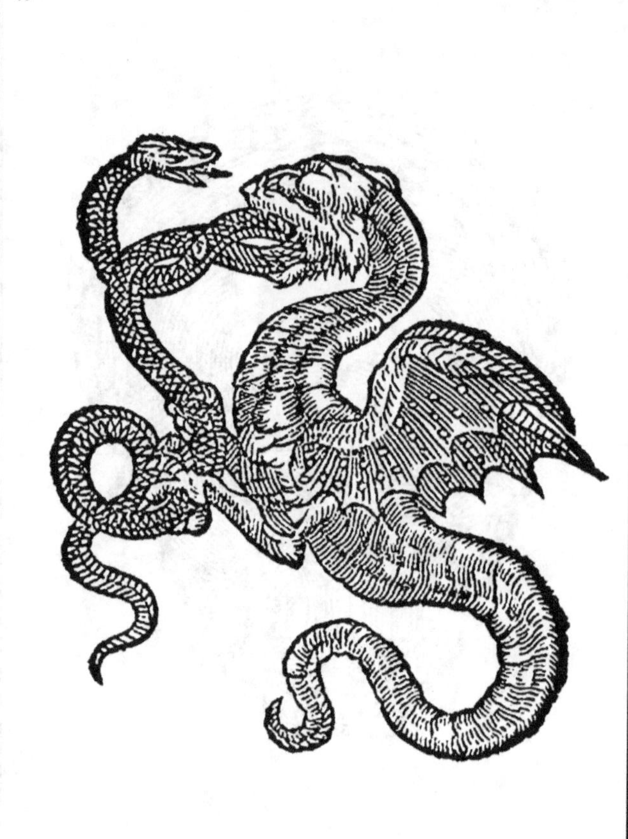

11
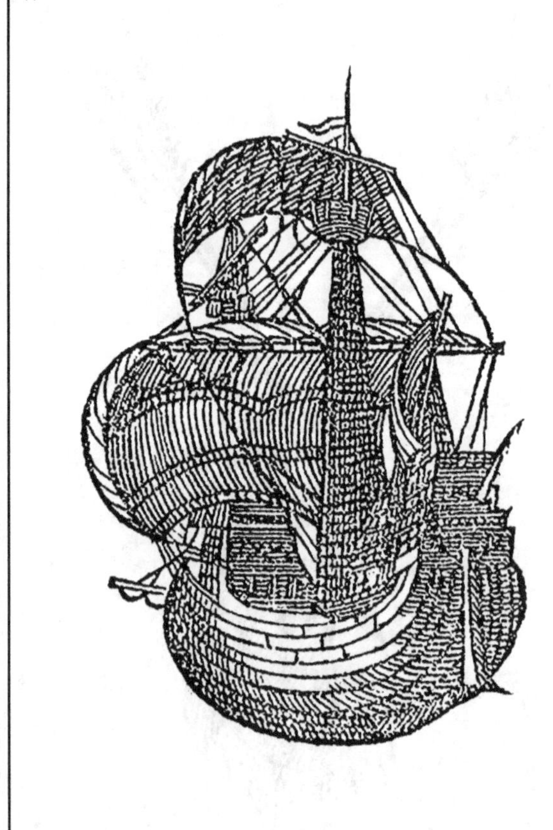

12
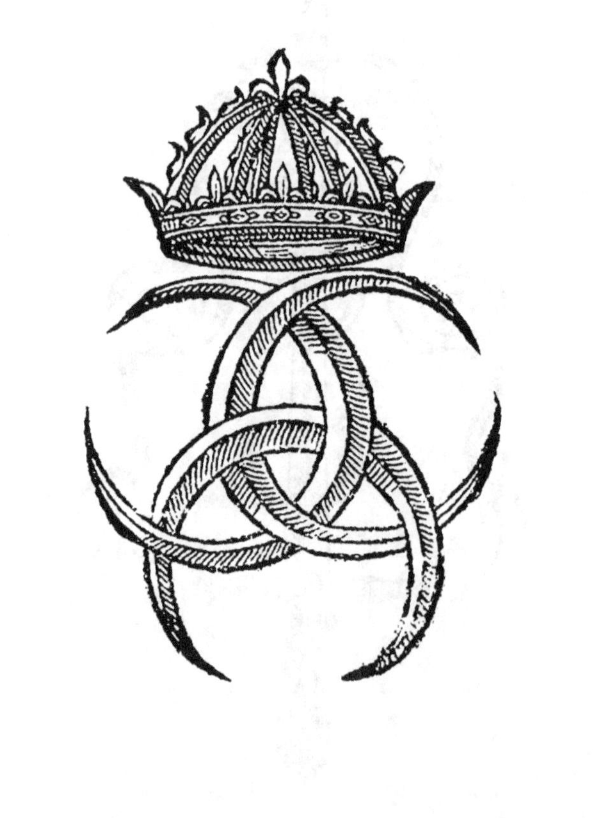

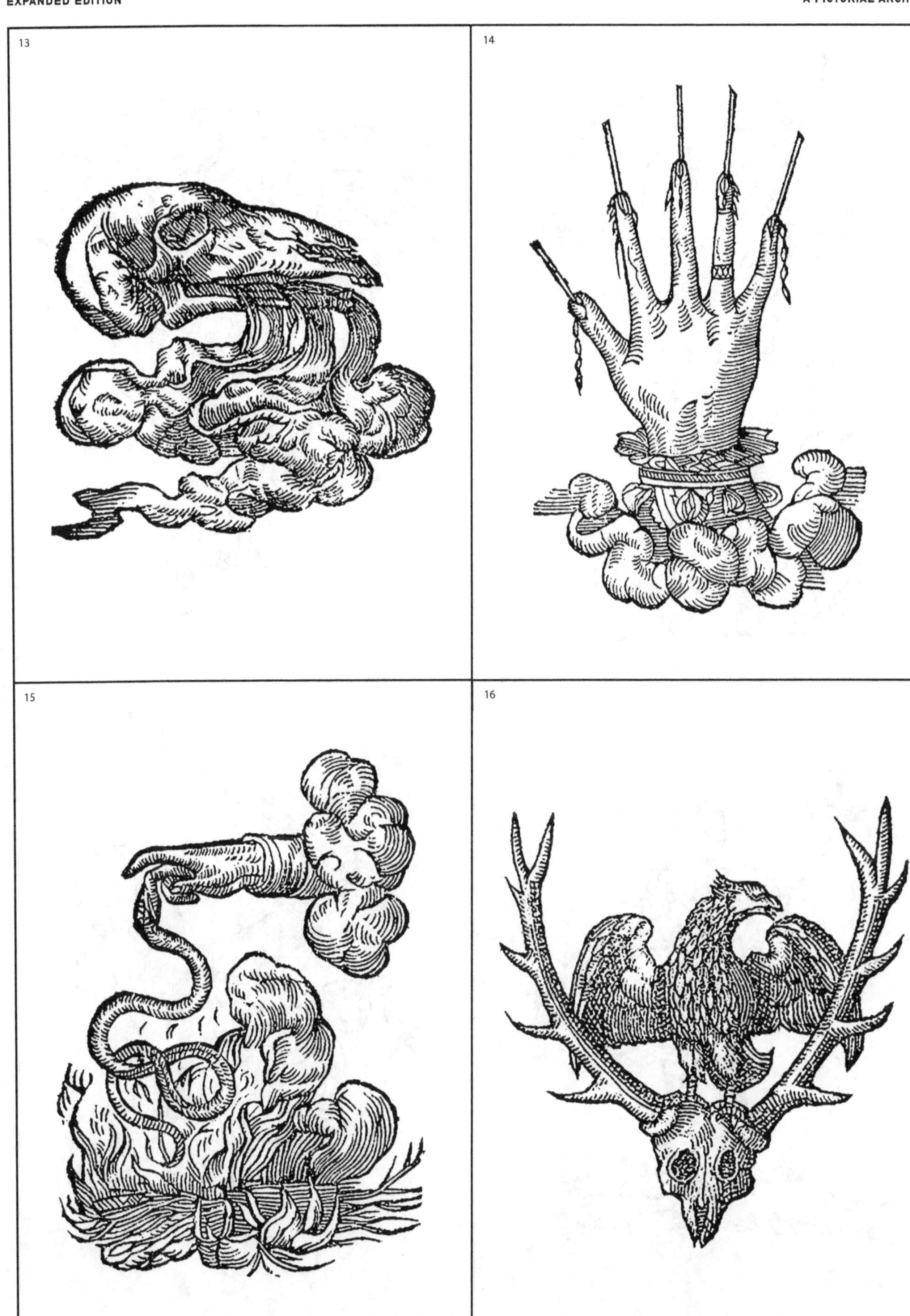

13

14

15

16

17

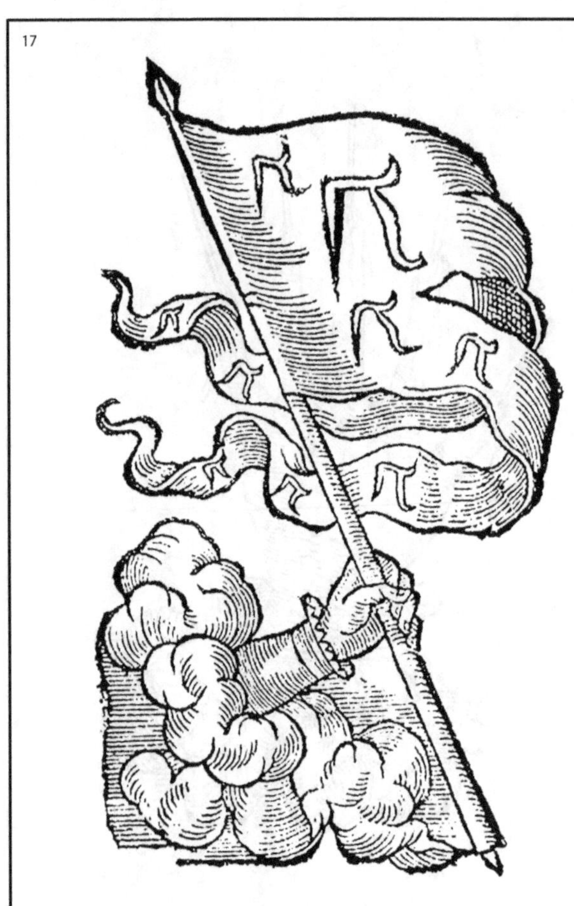

18

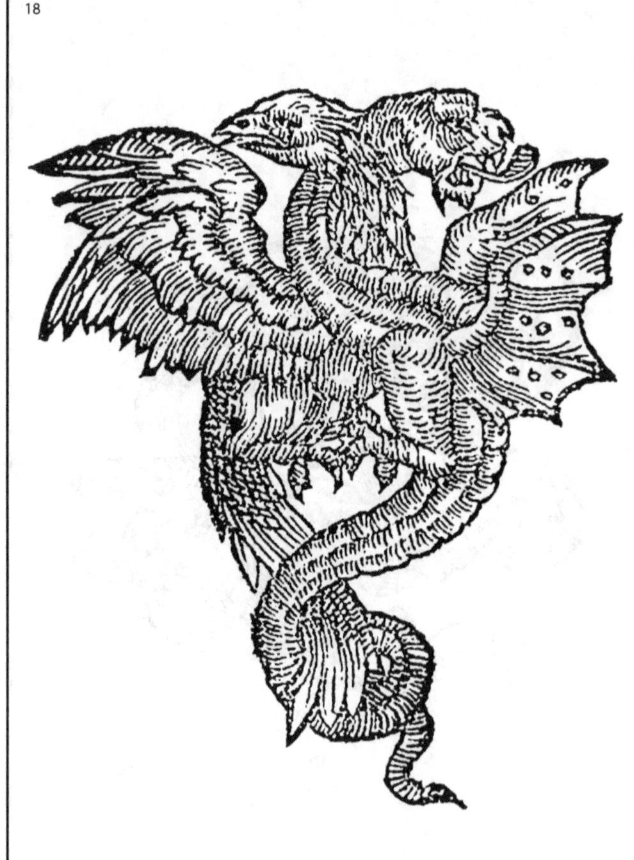

19

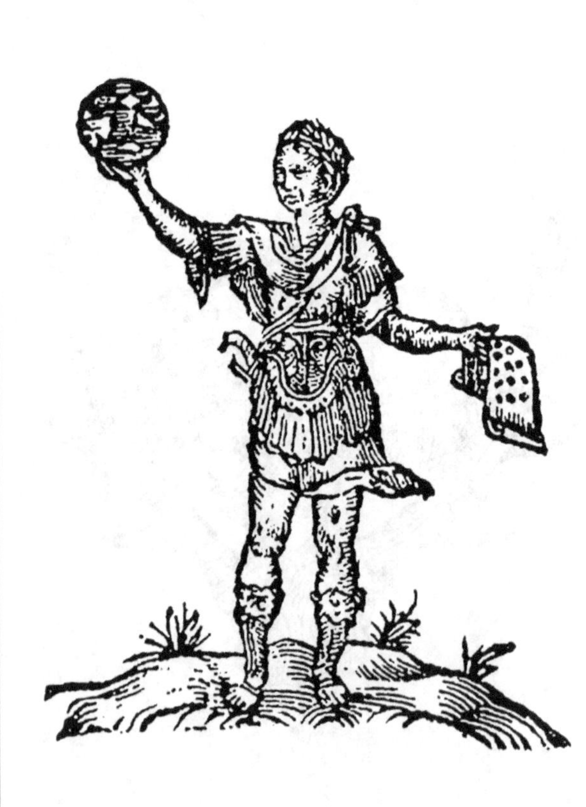

20

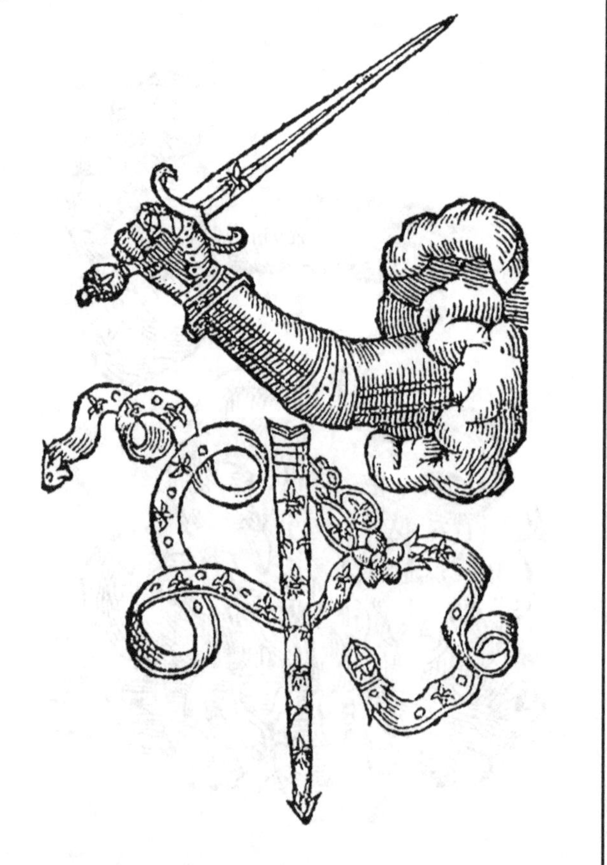

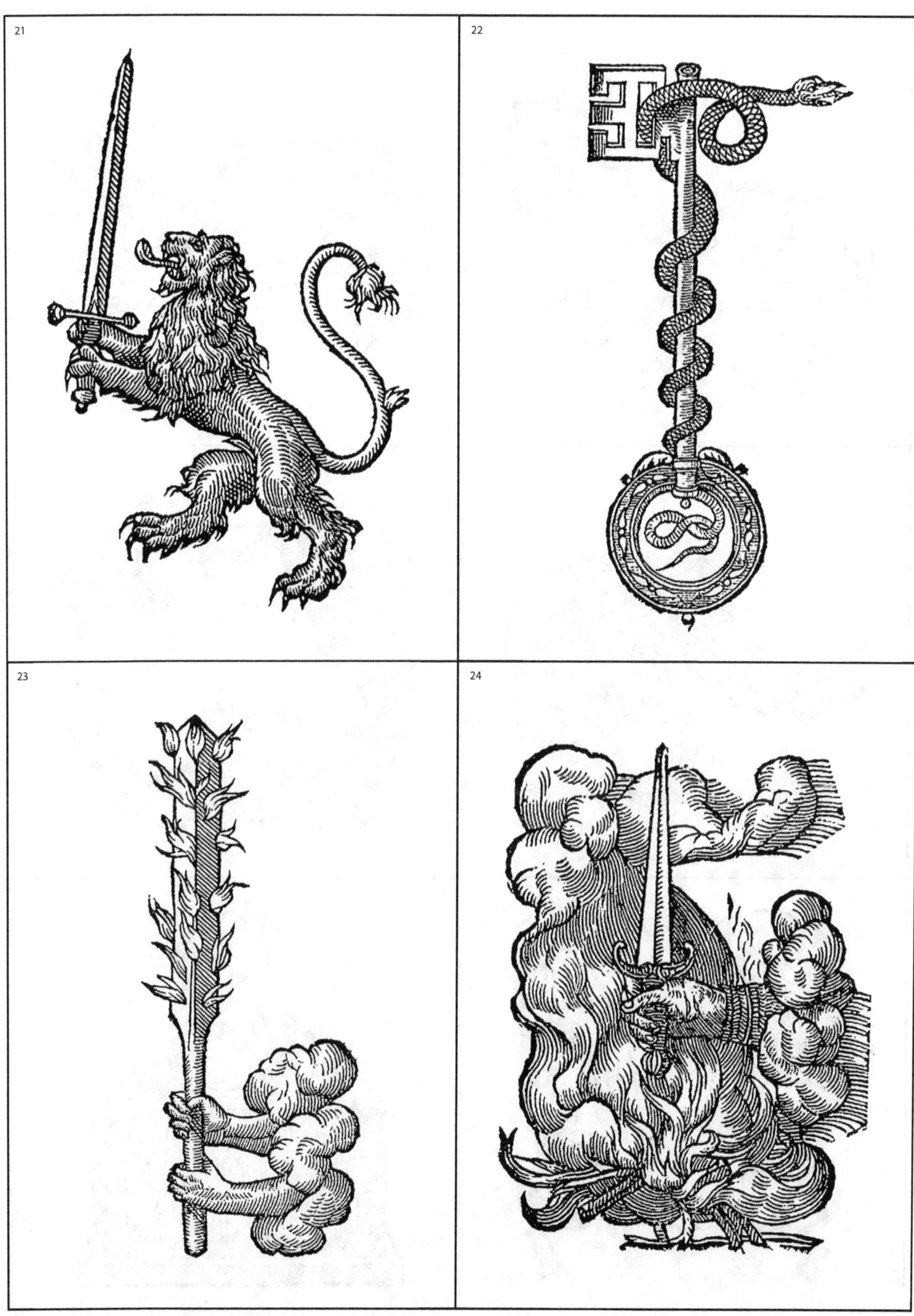

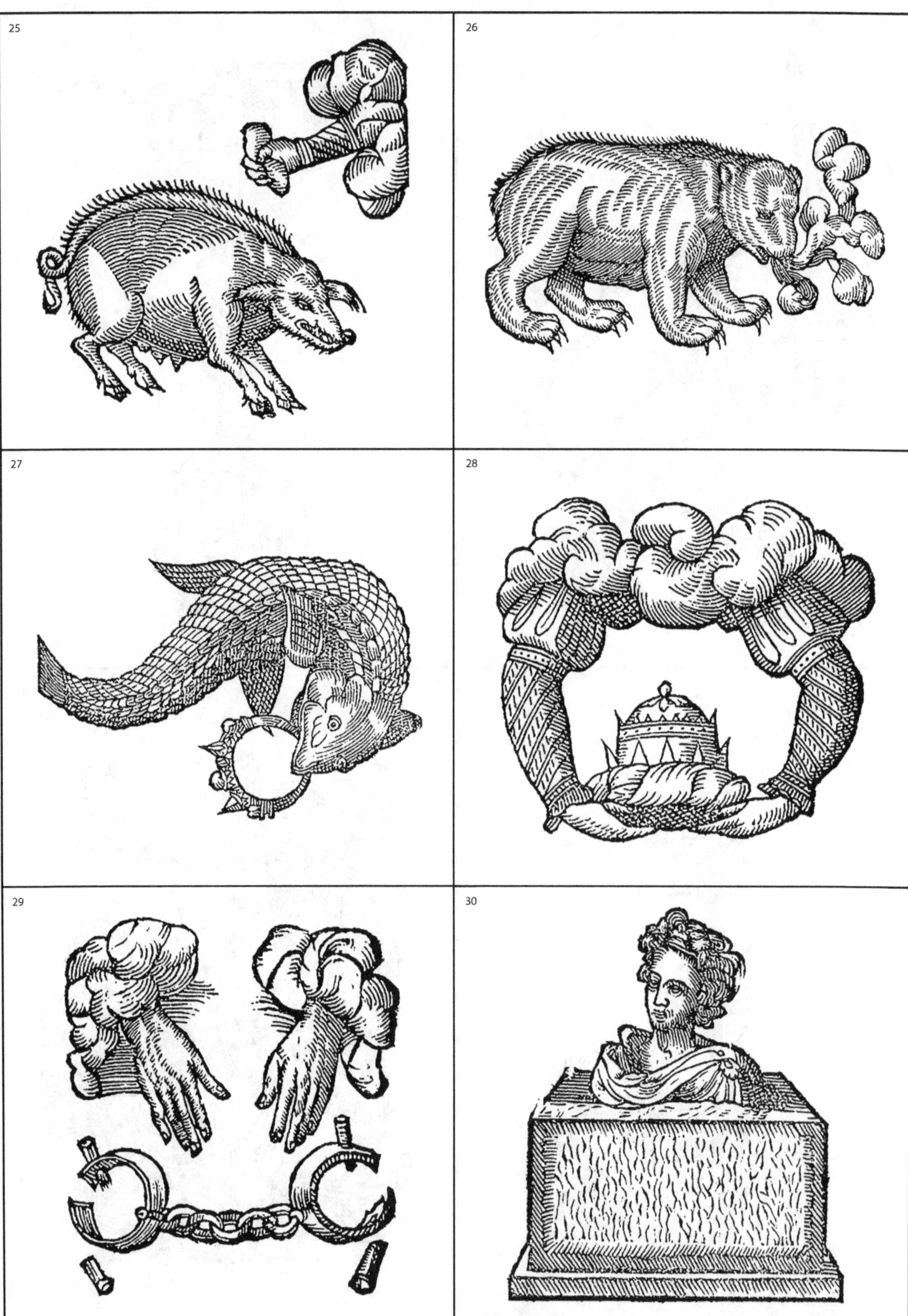

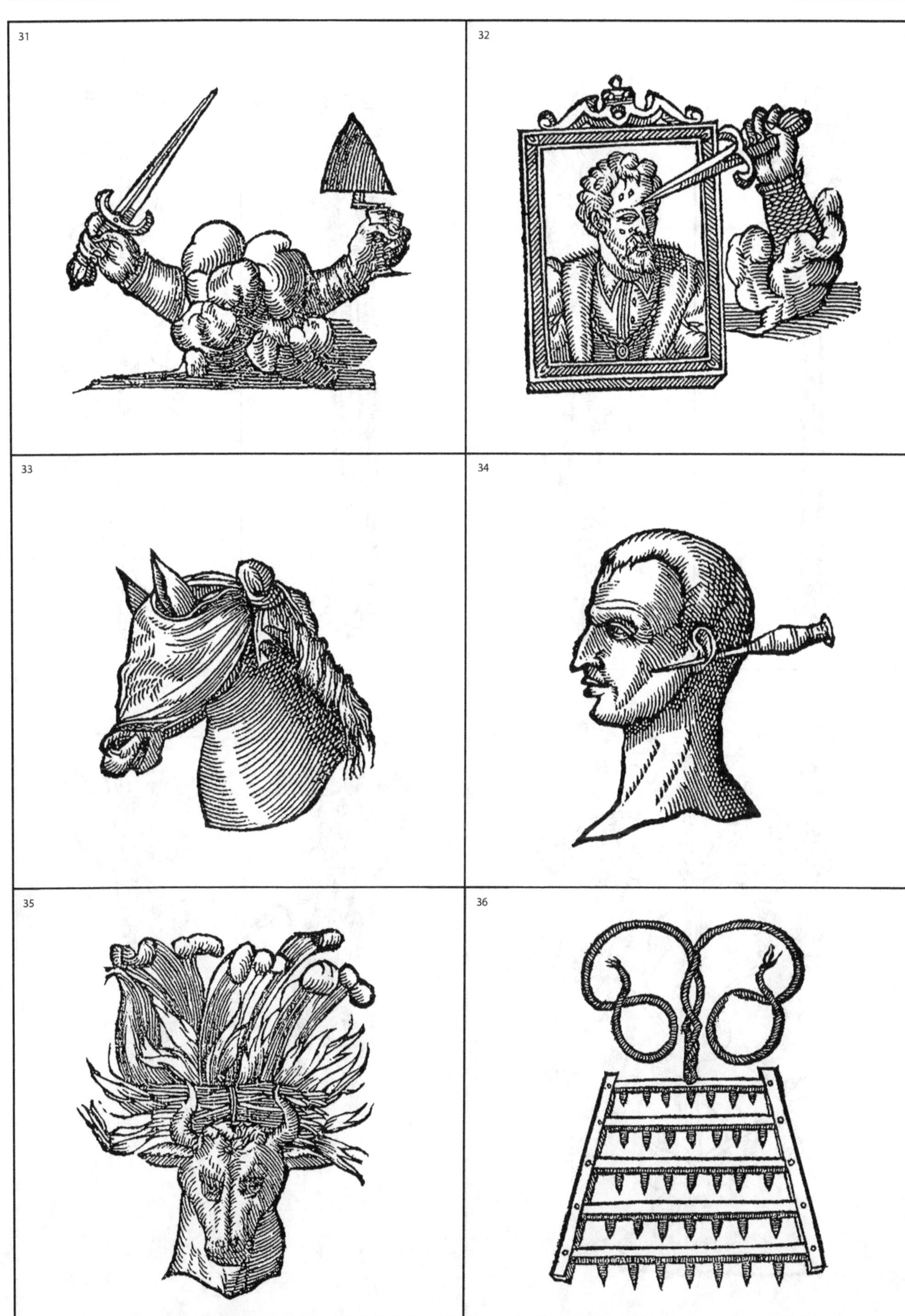

31
32
33
34
35
36

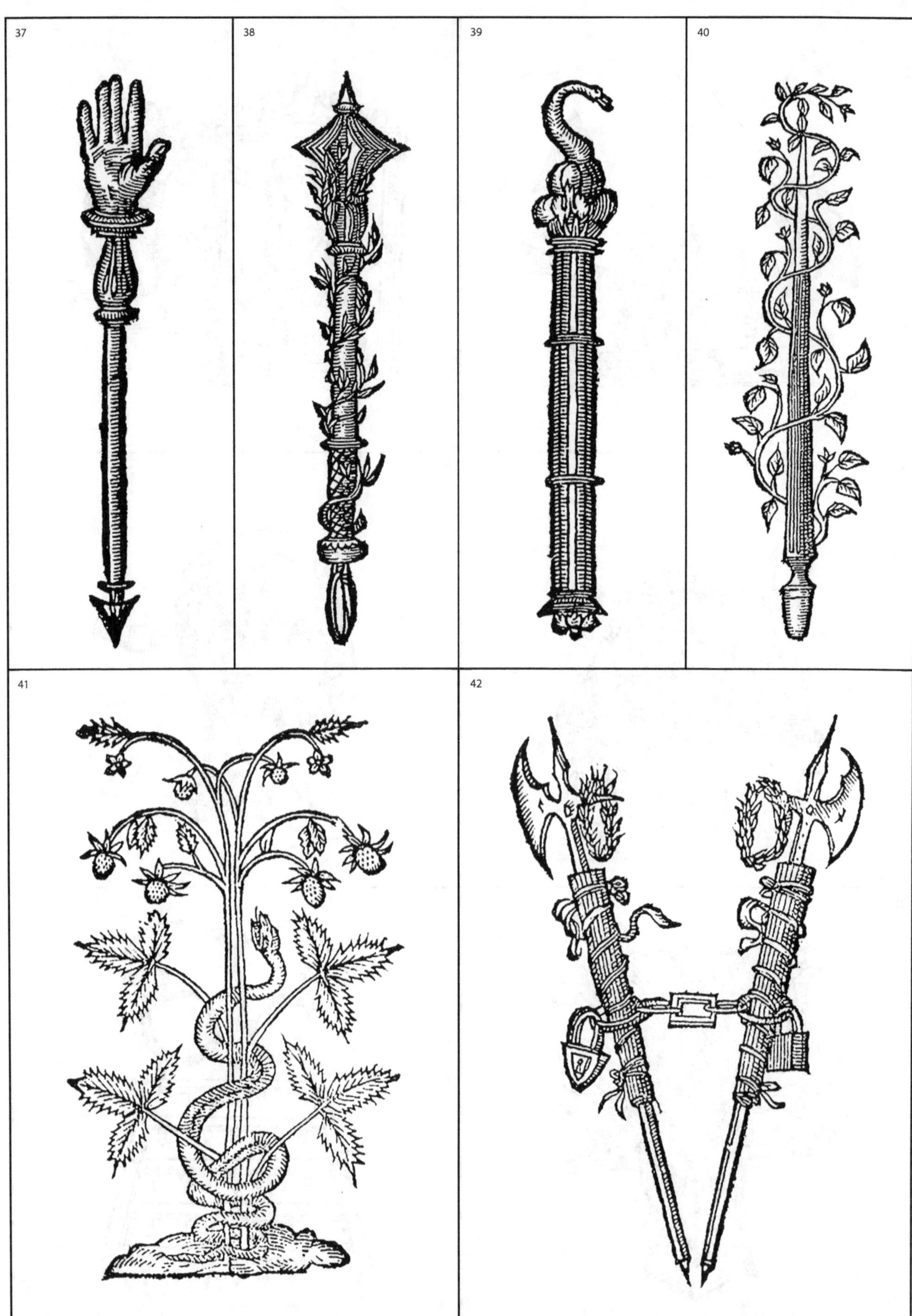

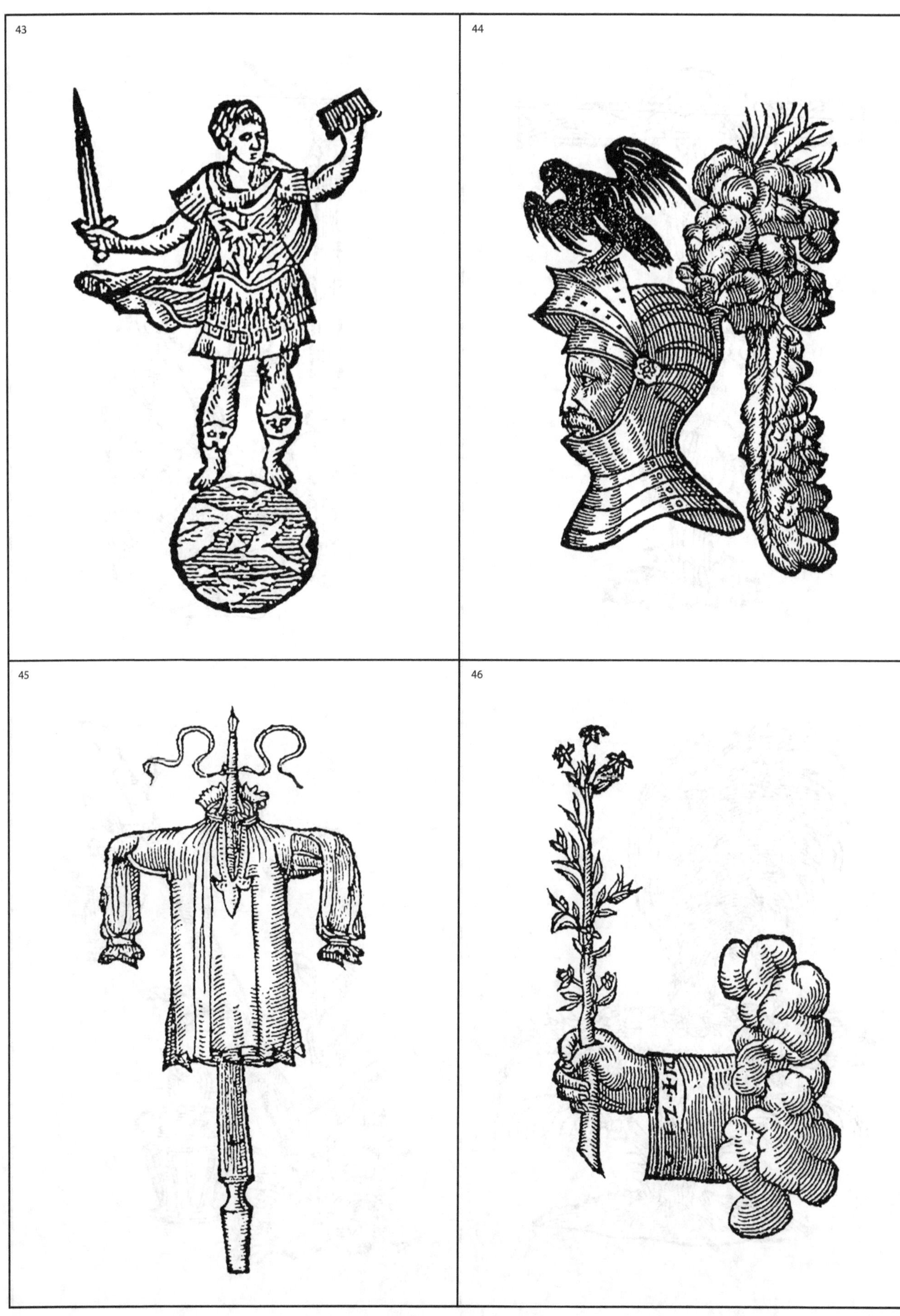

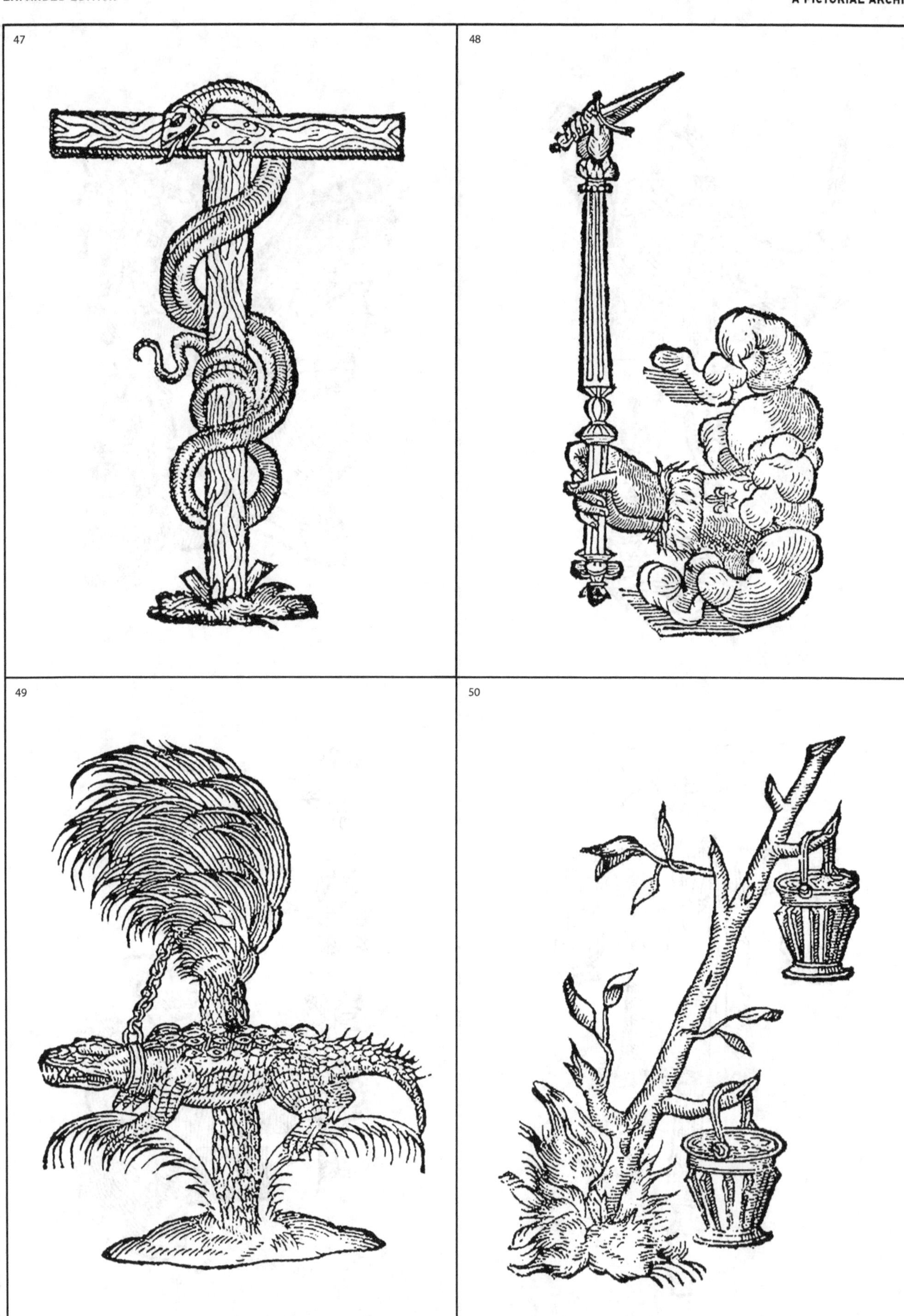

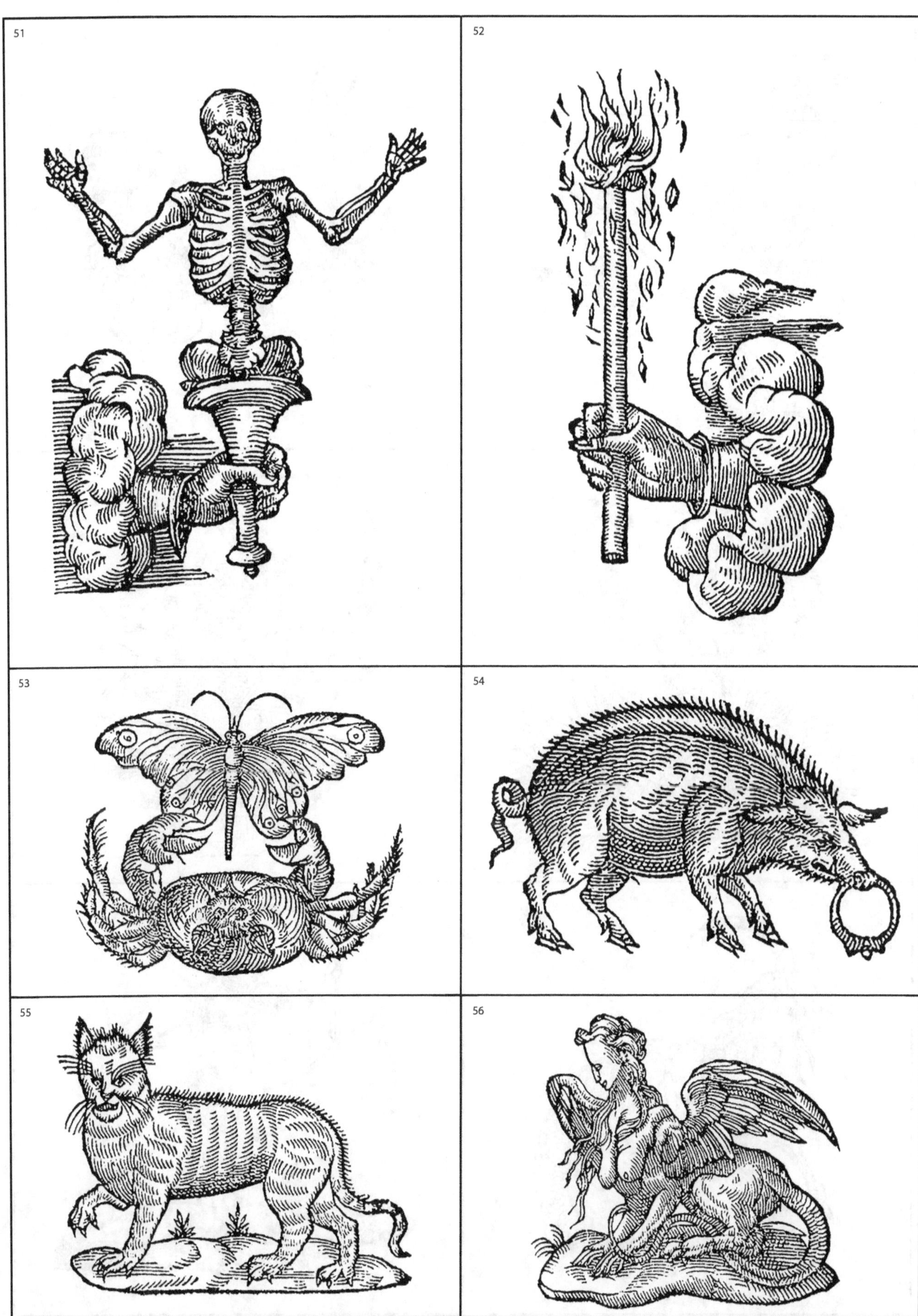

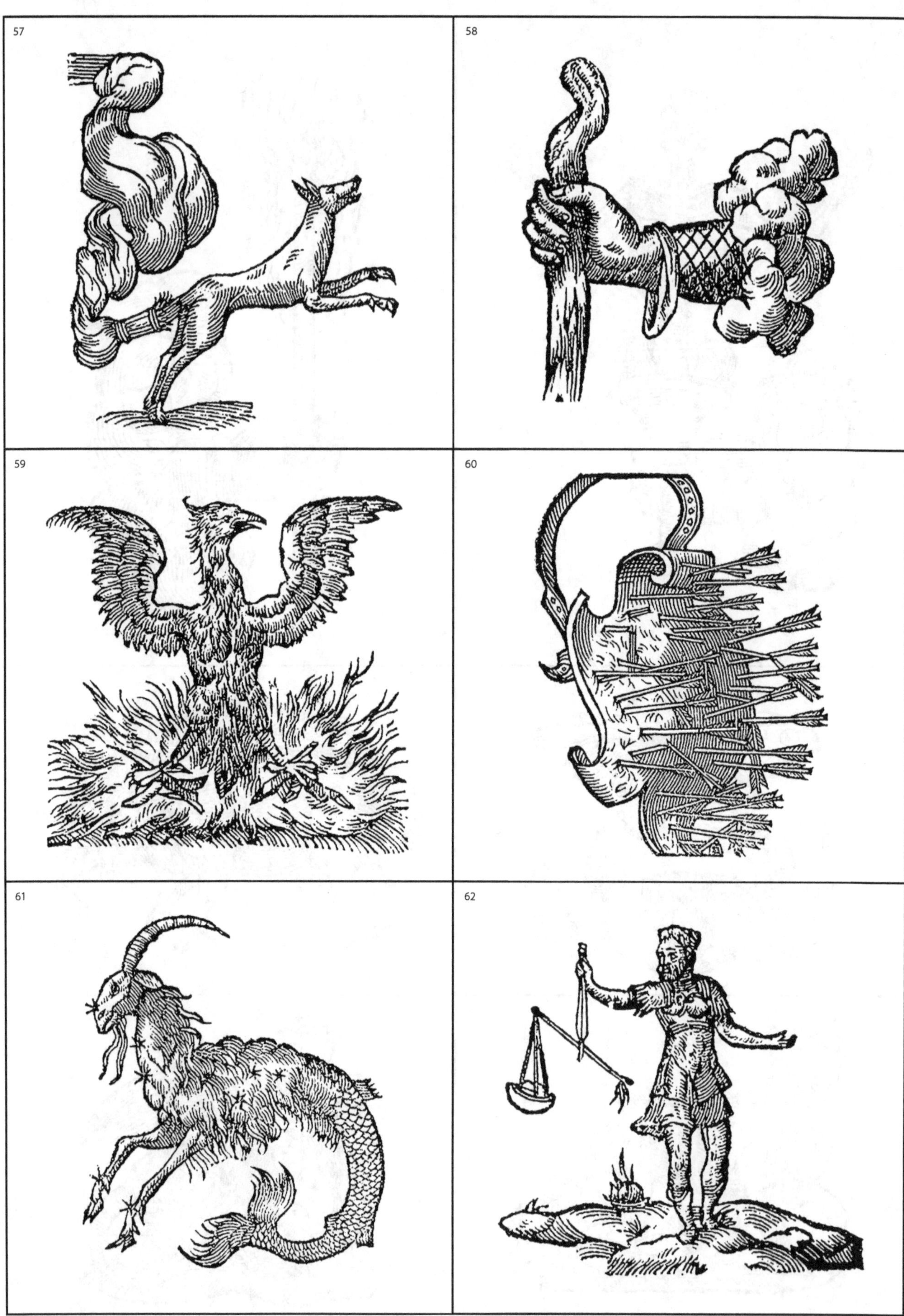

63

64

65

66

67

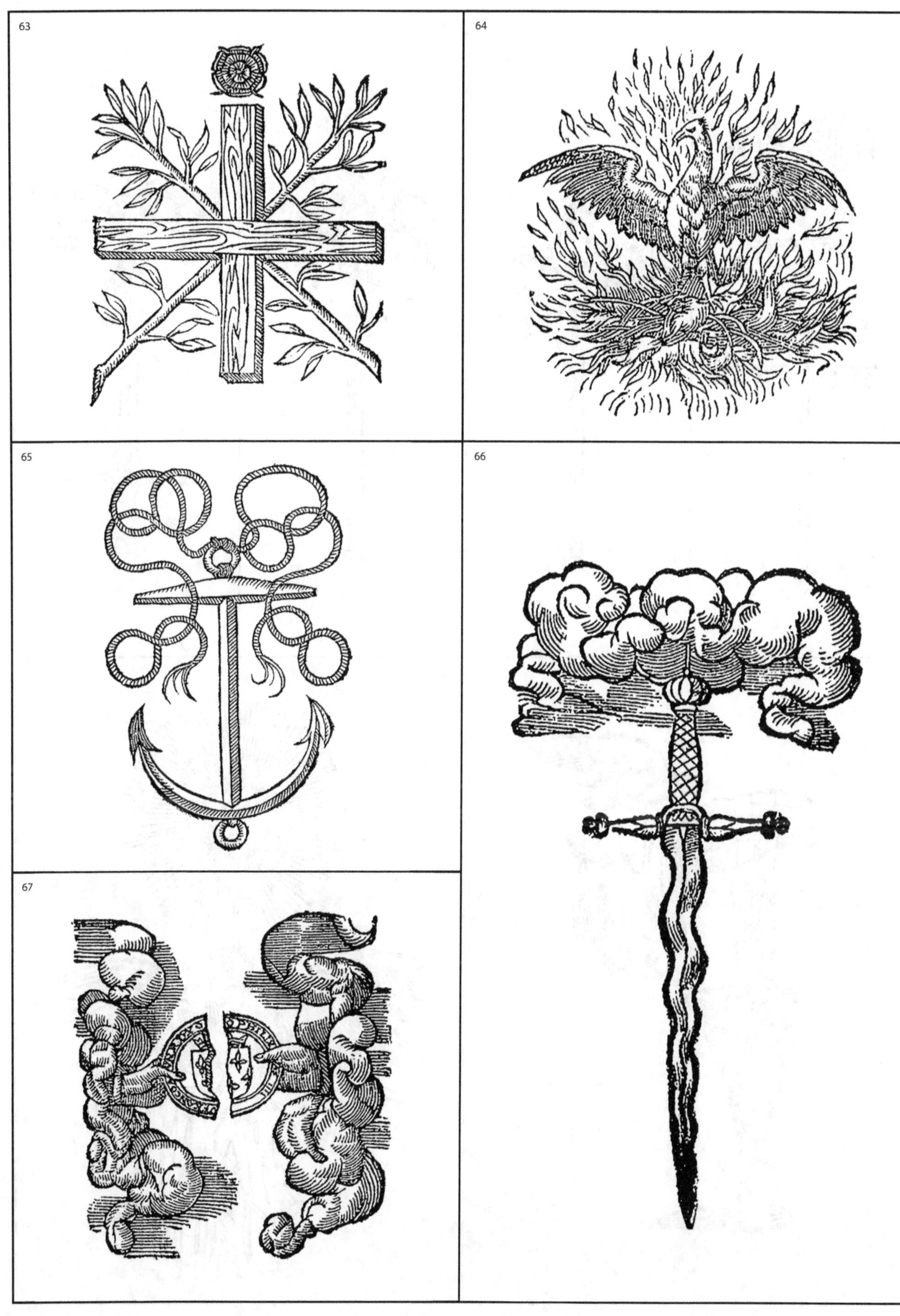

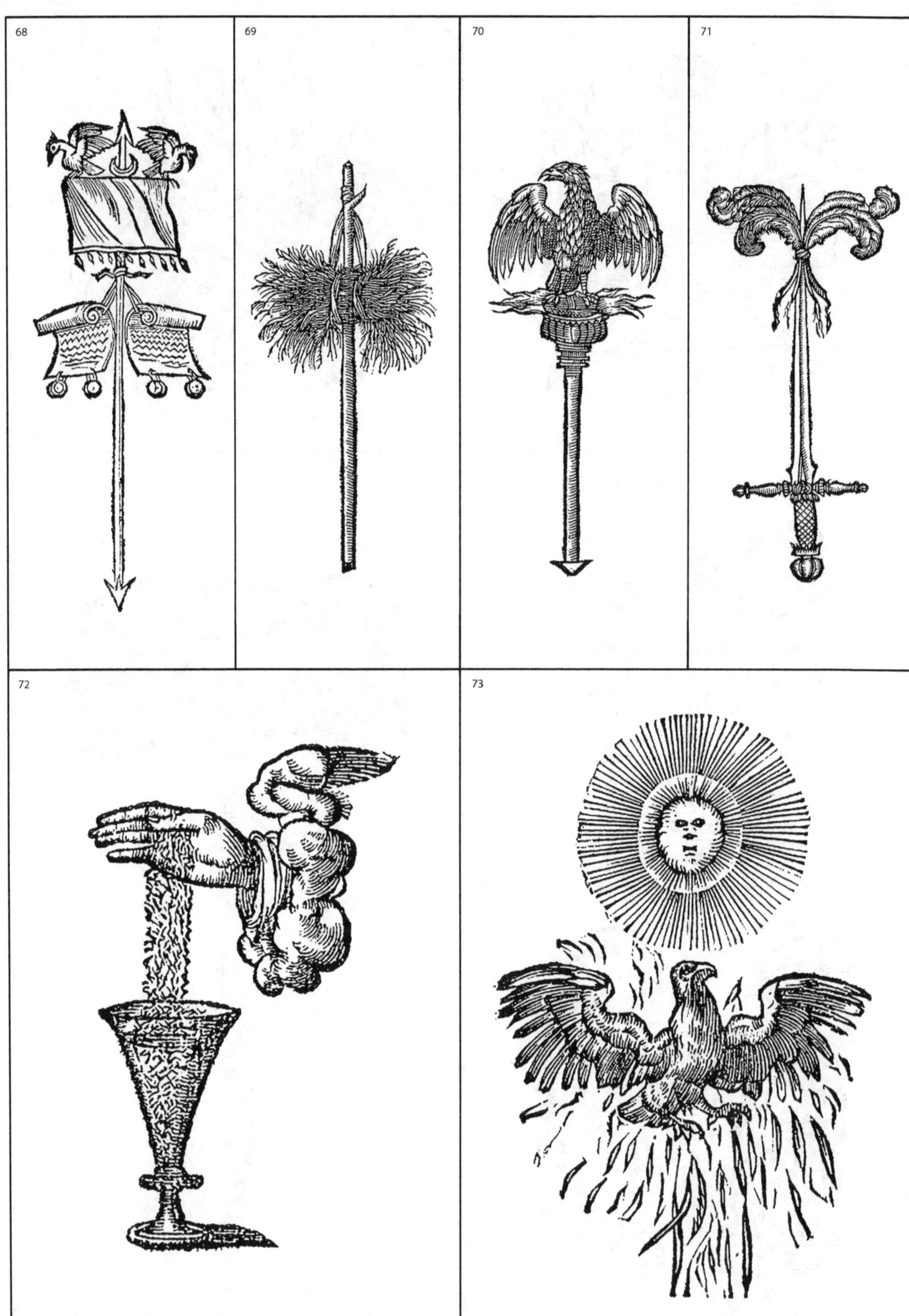

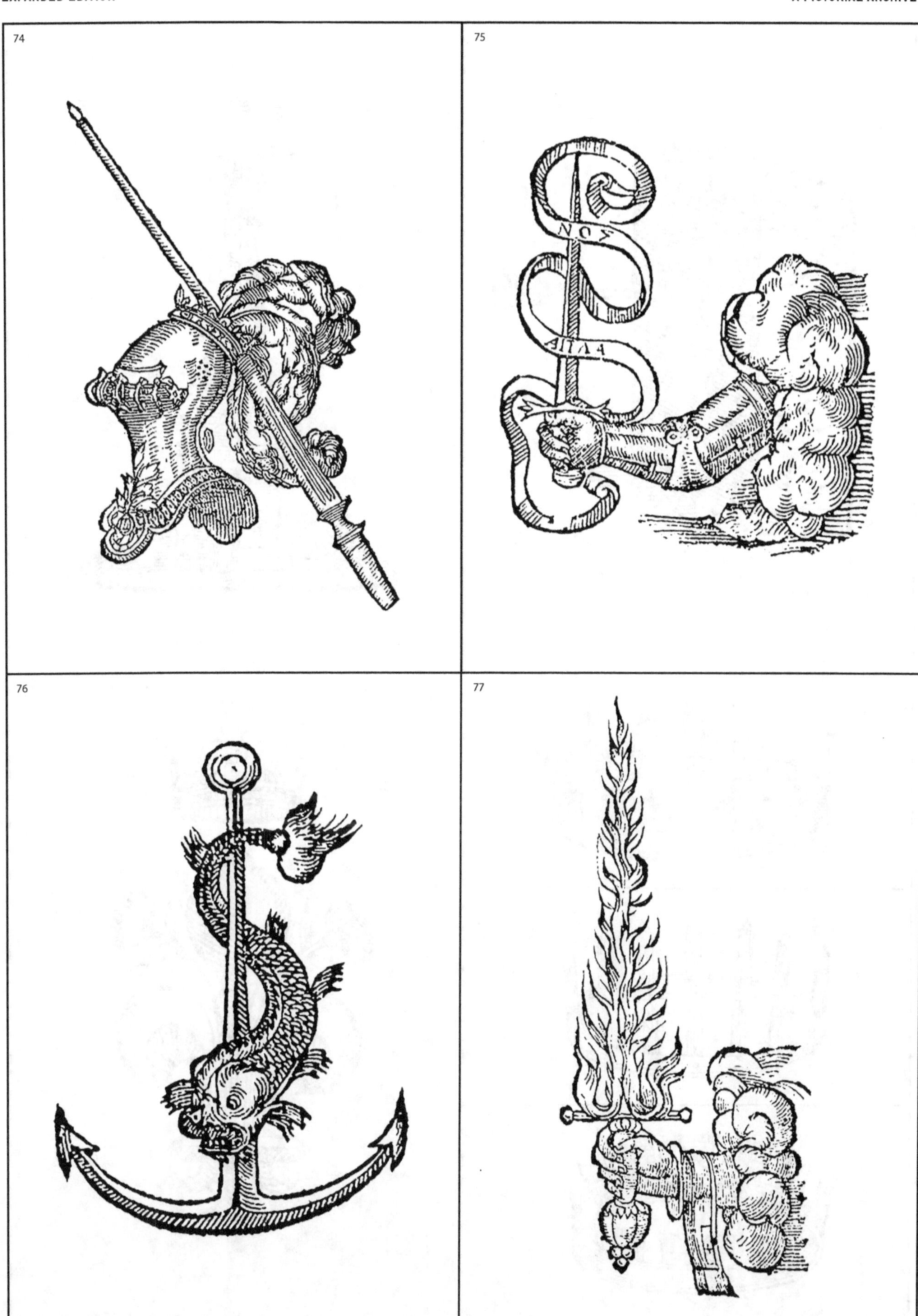

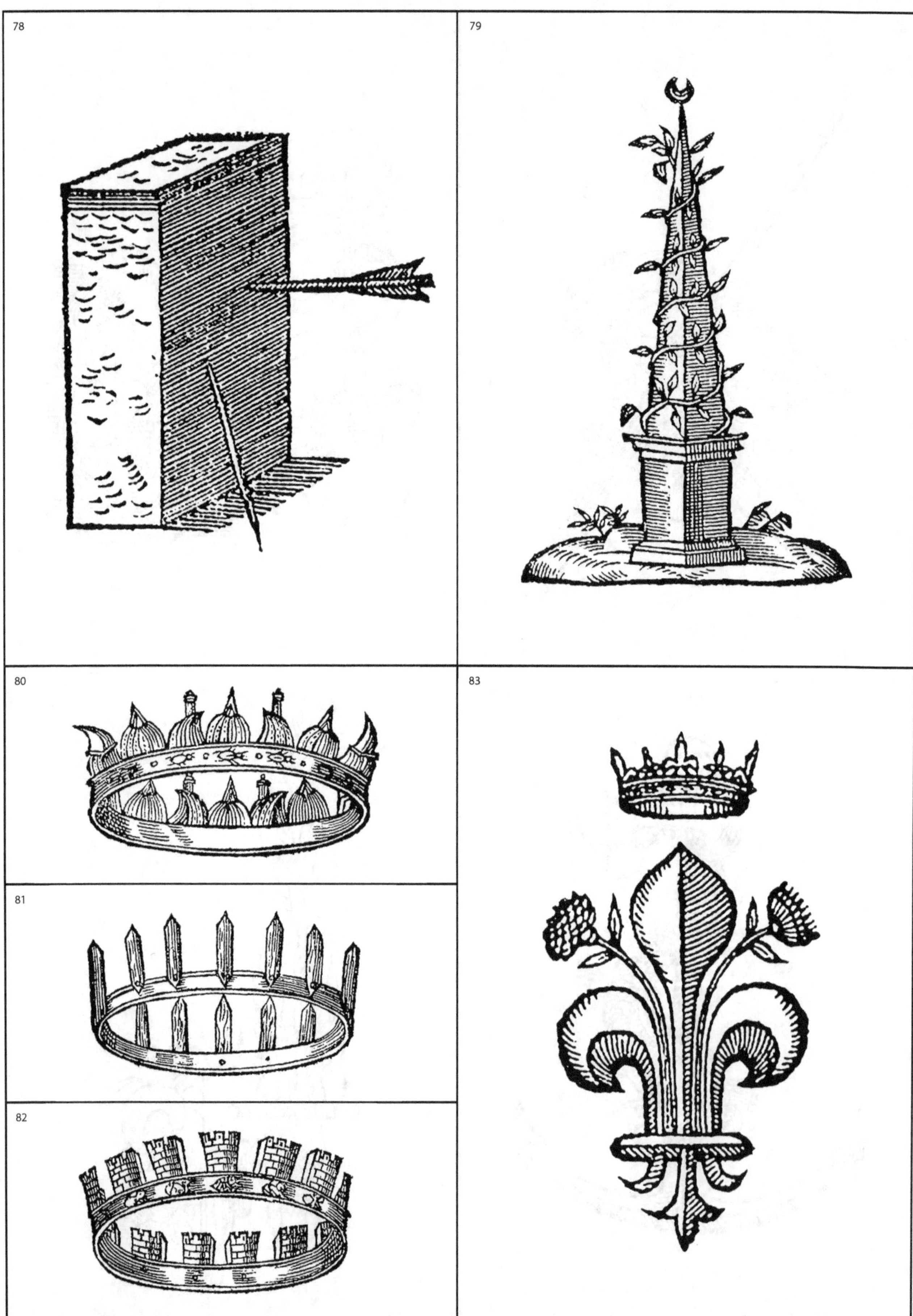

84

85

86

87

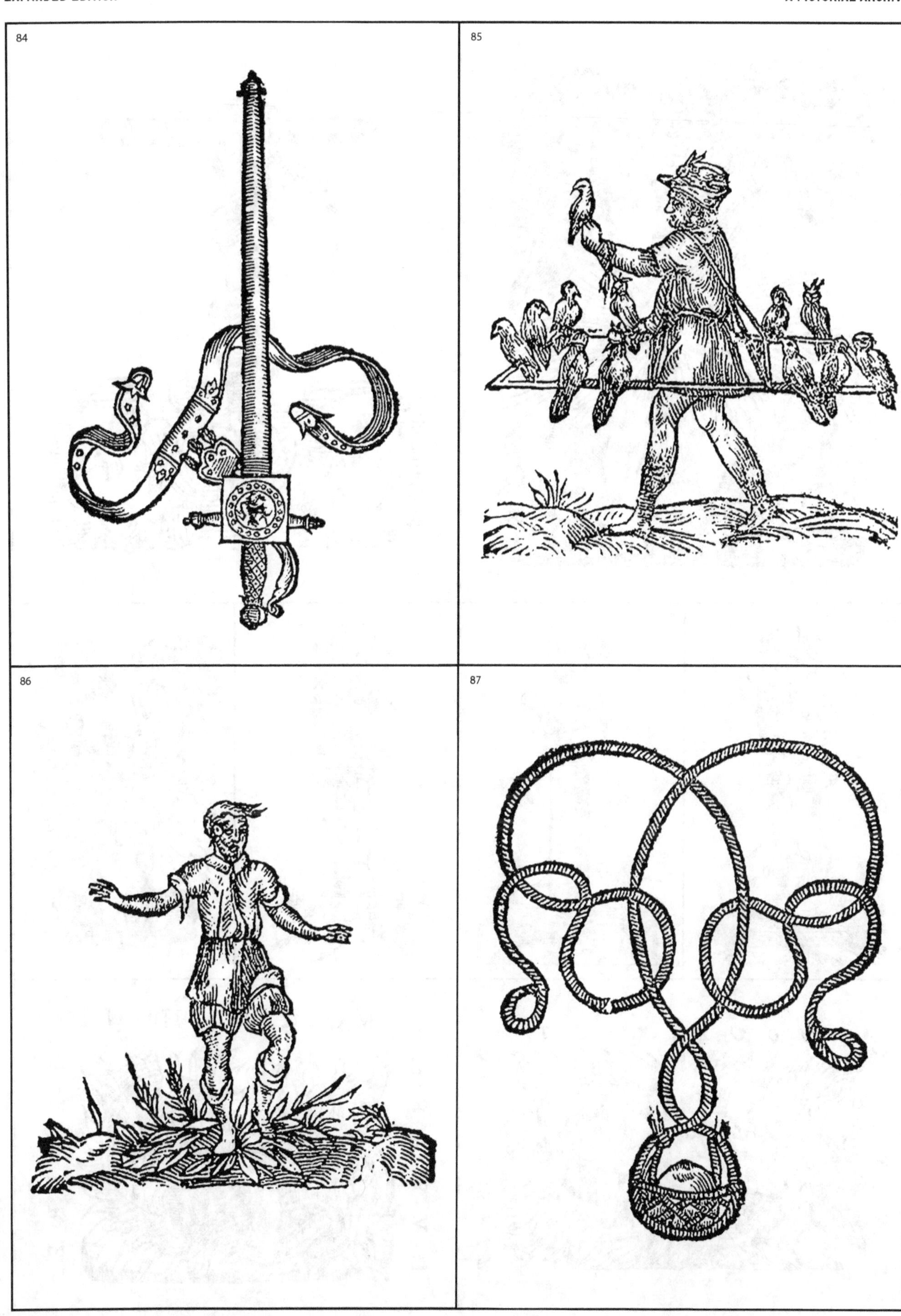

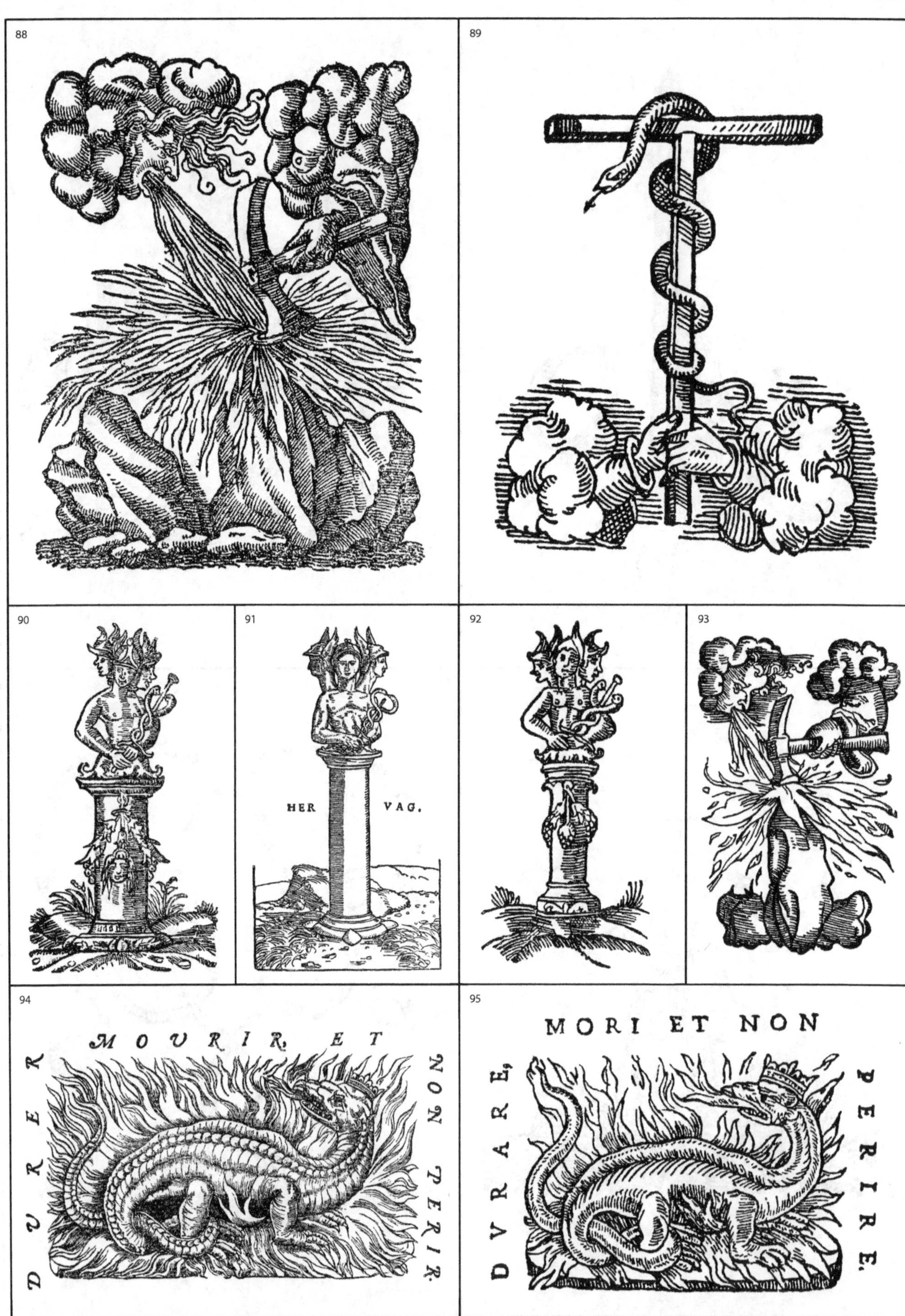
88
89
90
91
HER   VAG.
92
93
94
MOURIR ET
DURER
NON PERIR.
95
MORI ET NON
DVRARE,
PERIRE.

96

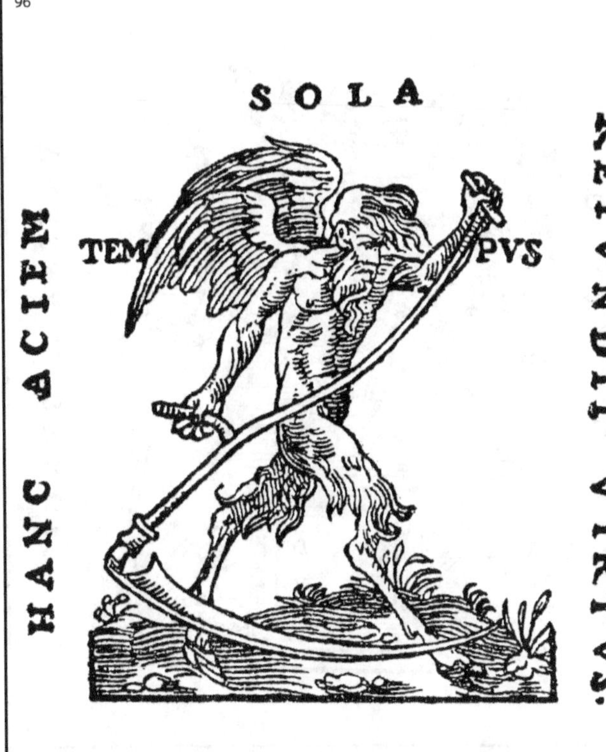

97

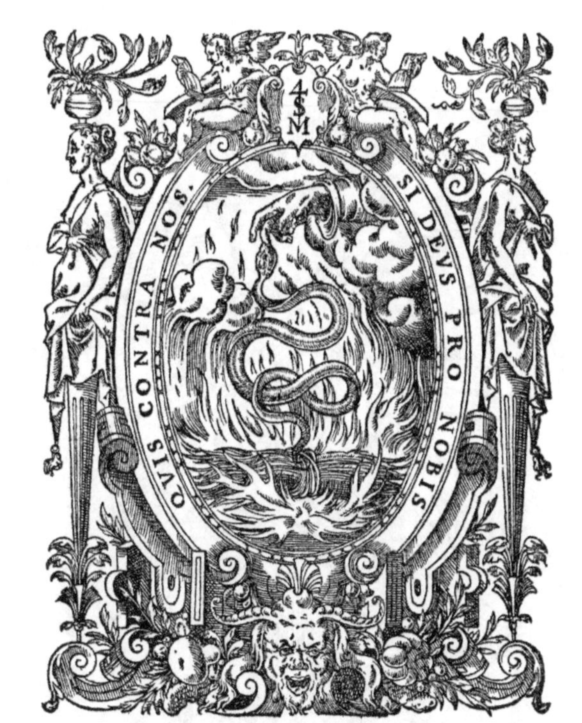

98

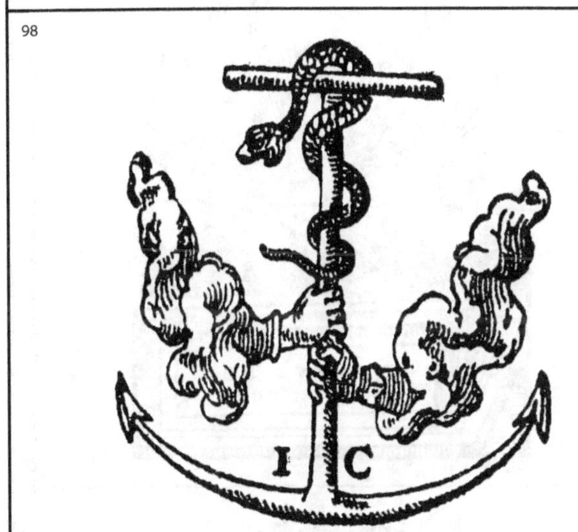

99

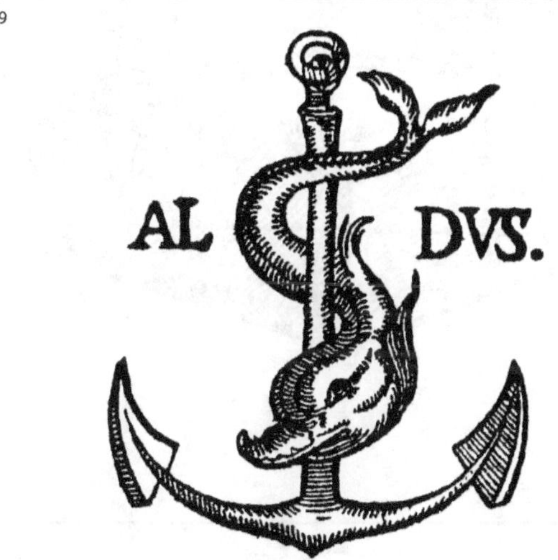

100

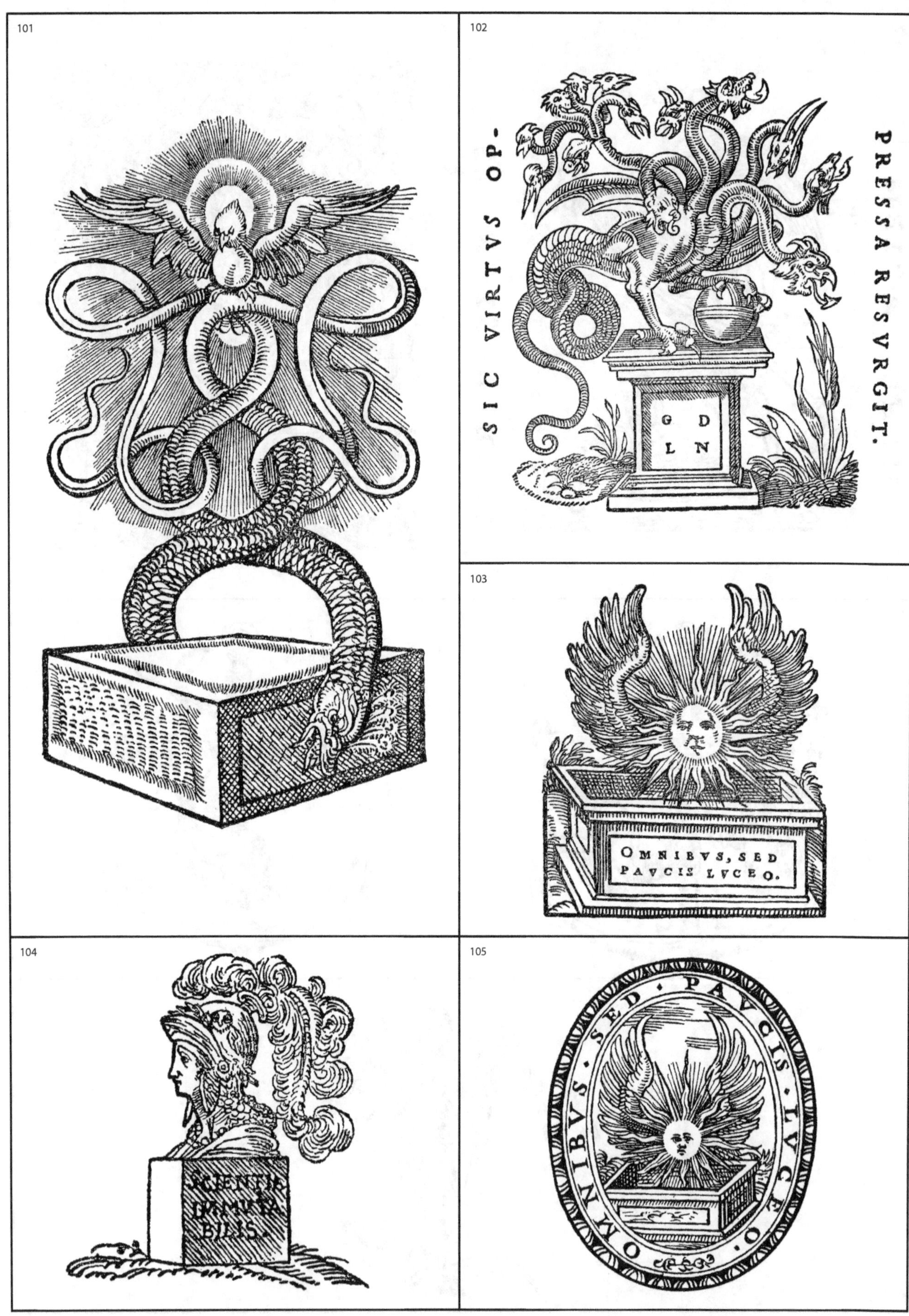
101
102
SIC VIRTVS OP-
PRESSA RESVRGIT.
G D
L N
103
OMNIBVS, SED
PAVCIS LVCEO.
104
105
OMNIBVS · SED · PAVCIS · LVCEO ·

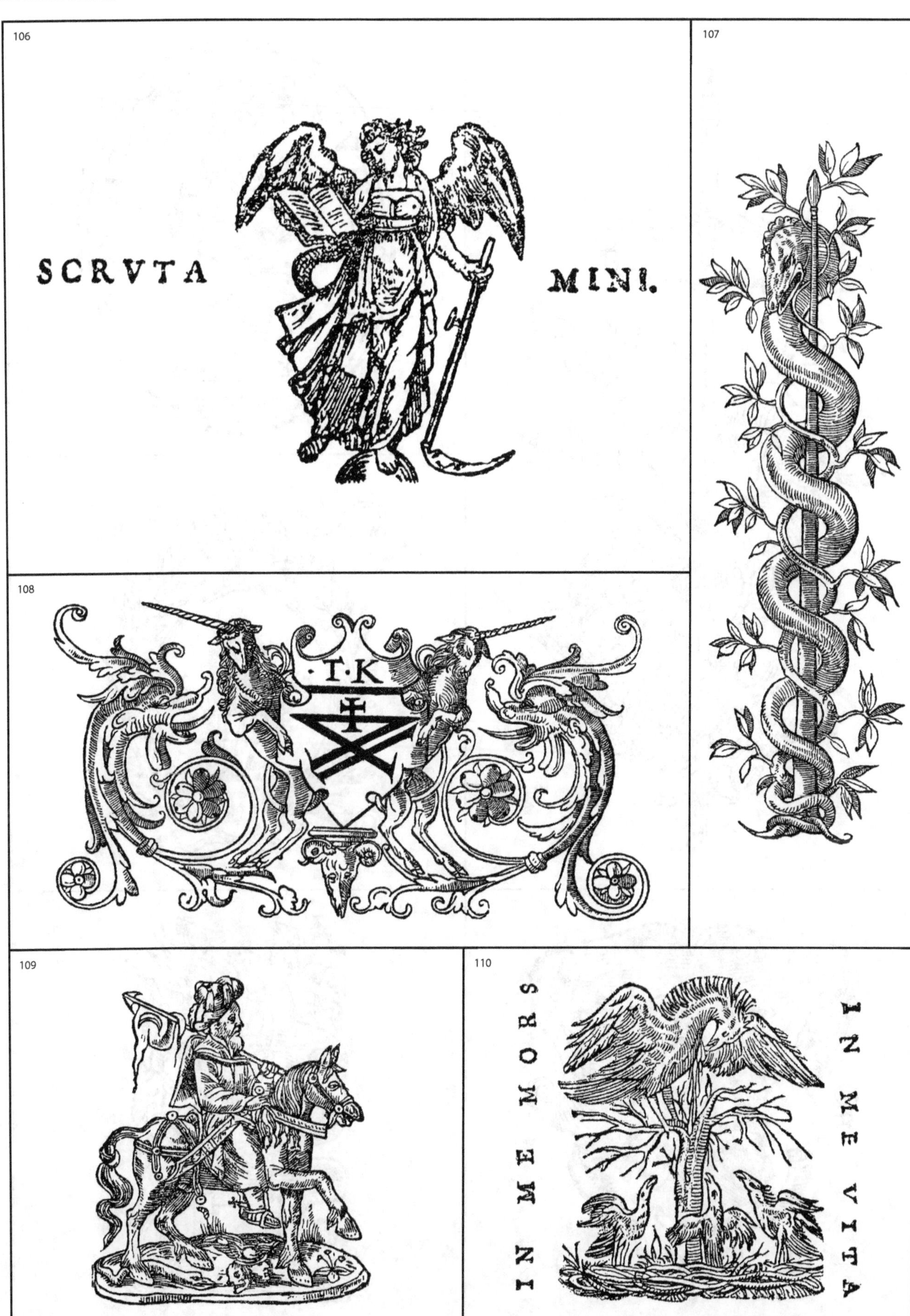
106
SCRVTA
MINI.
107
108
109
110
IN ME MORS
IN ME VITA

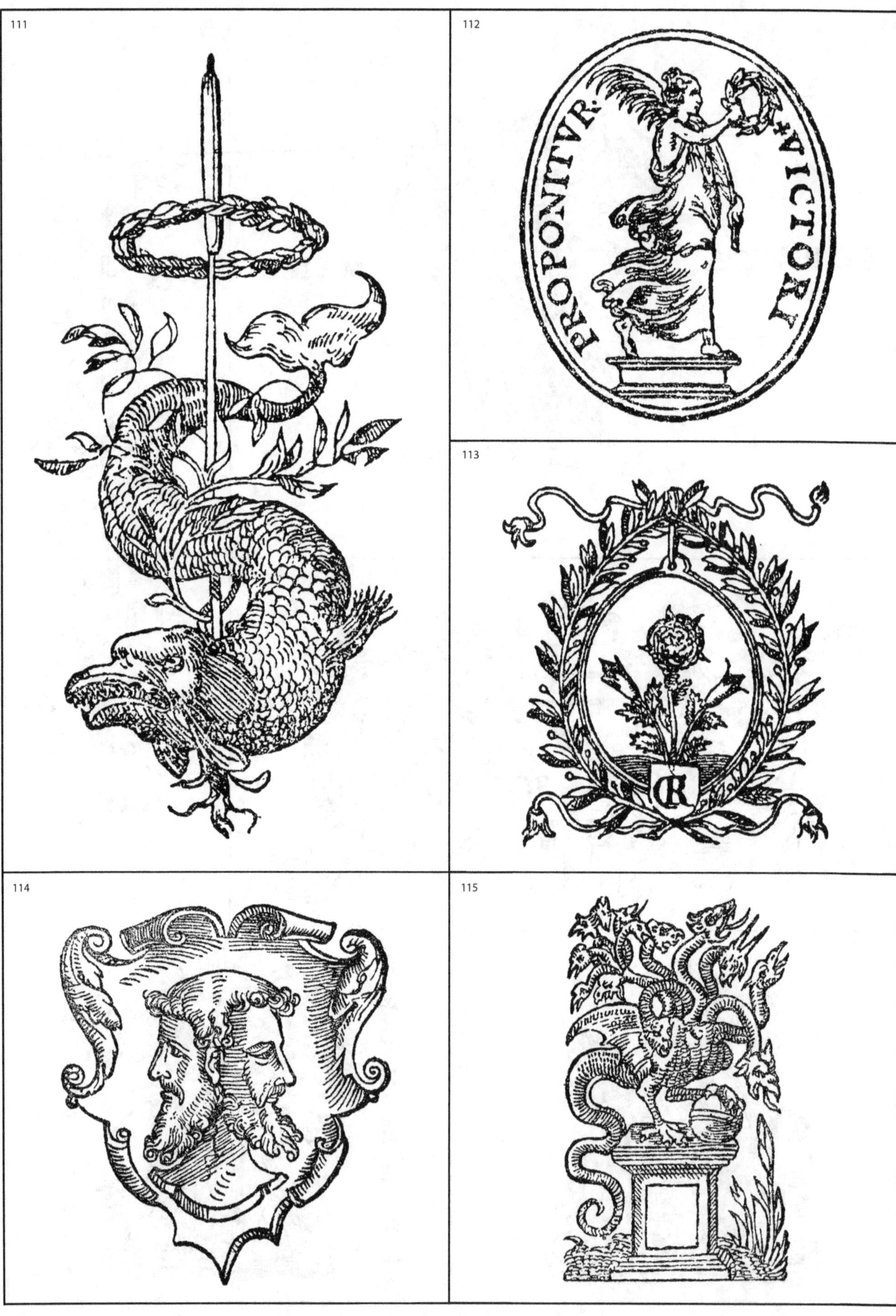
PROPONITVR.
+VICTORI

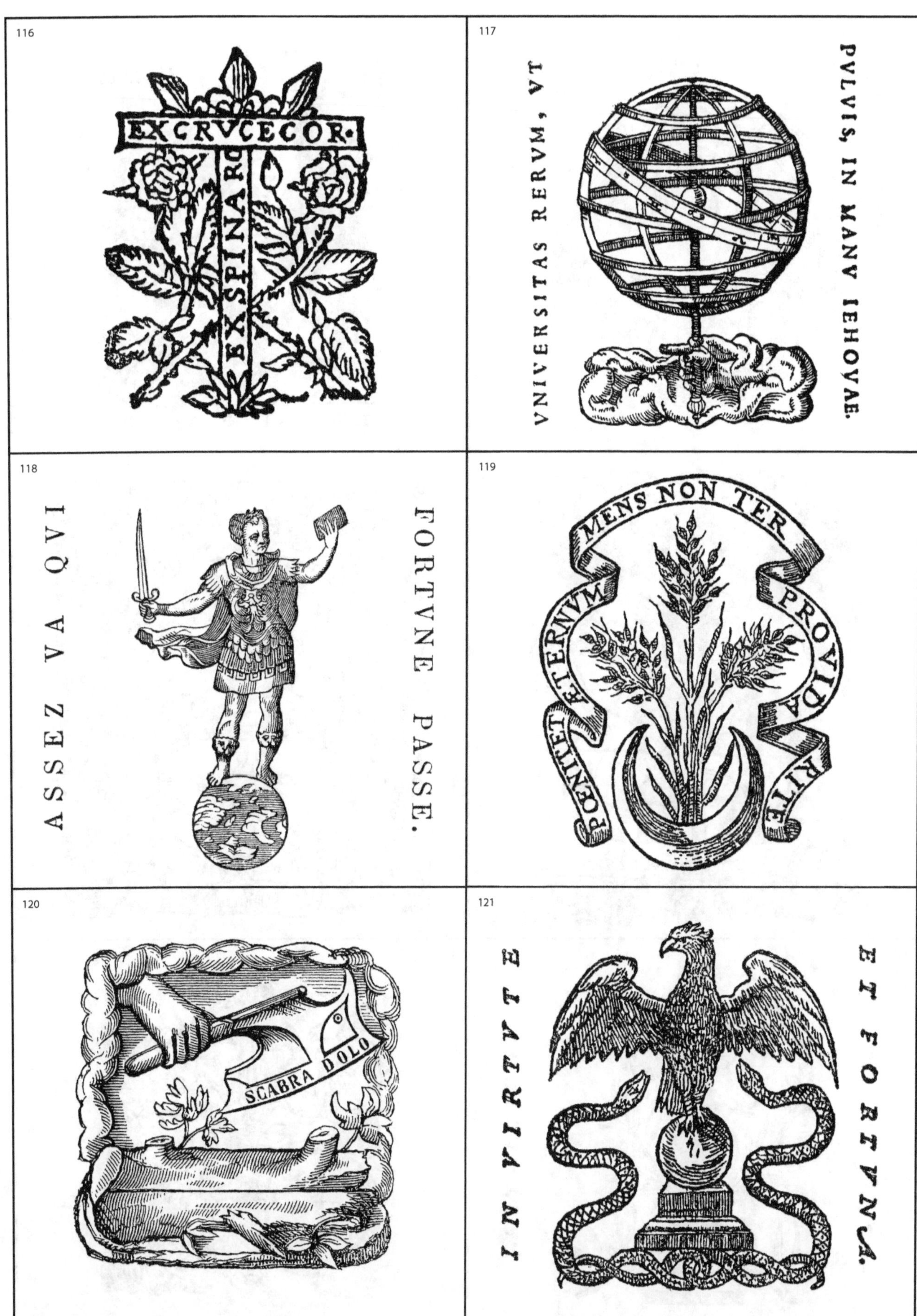
116
EXCRVCECOR·
EX SPINA RO...

117
VNIVERSITAS RERVM, VT
PVLVIS, IN MANV IEHOVAE.

118
ASSEZ VA QVI
FORTVNE PASSE.

119
MENS NON TER...
POENITET AETERNVM
PROVIDA... RITE

120
SCABRA DOLO

121
IN VIRTVTE
ET FORTVNA.

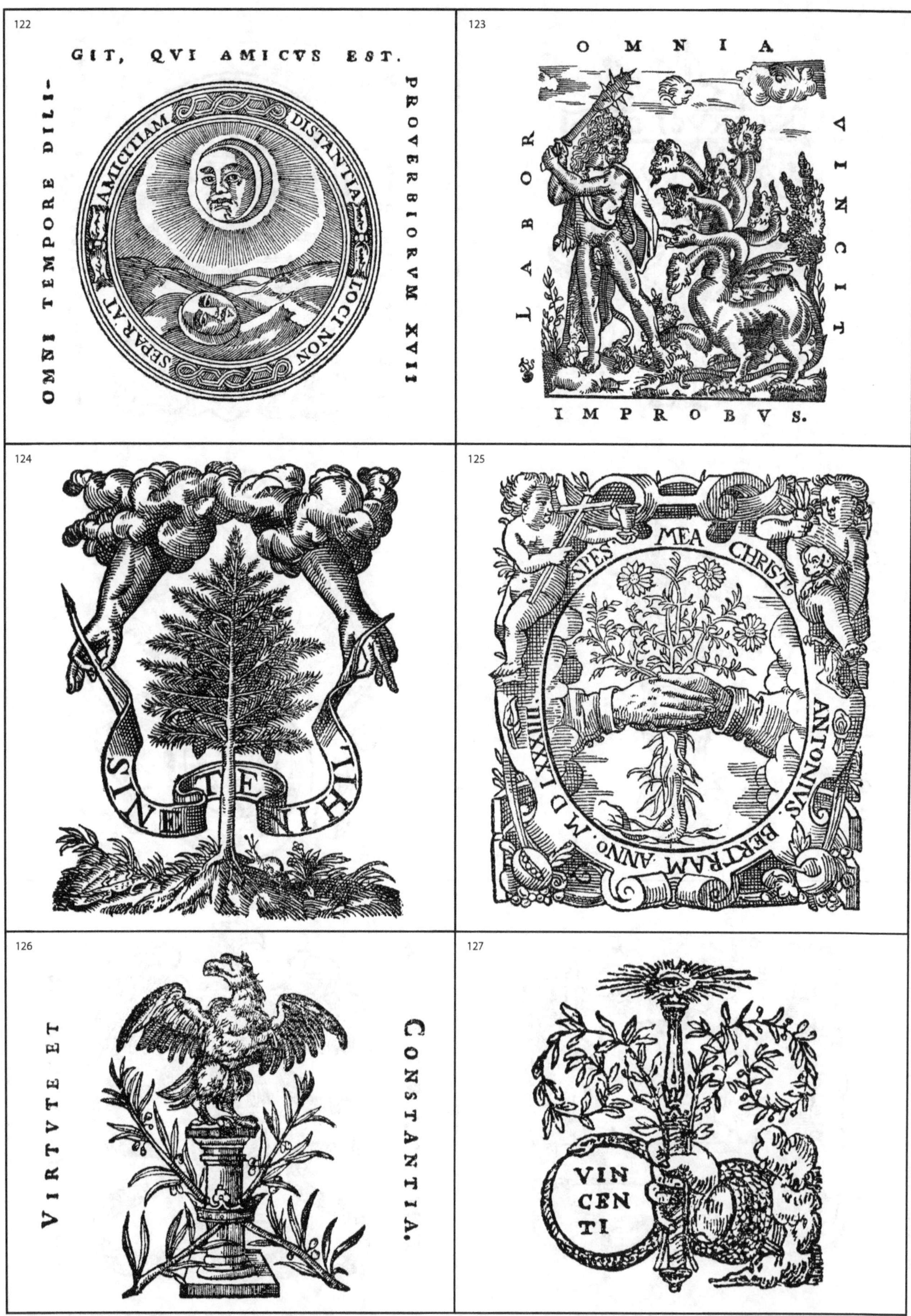
122
GIT, QVI AMICVS EST.
OMNI TEMPORE DILI-
PROVERBIORVM XVII
AMICITIAM DISTANTIA LOCI NON SEPARAT

123
OMNIA
LABOR
VINCIT
IMPROBVS.

124
SINE TE NIHIL

125
SPES MEA CHRISTVS
ANTONIVS BERTRAM ANNO M D LXXIIII.

126
VIRTVTE ET
CONSTANTIA.

127
VIN
CEN
TI

128

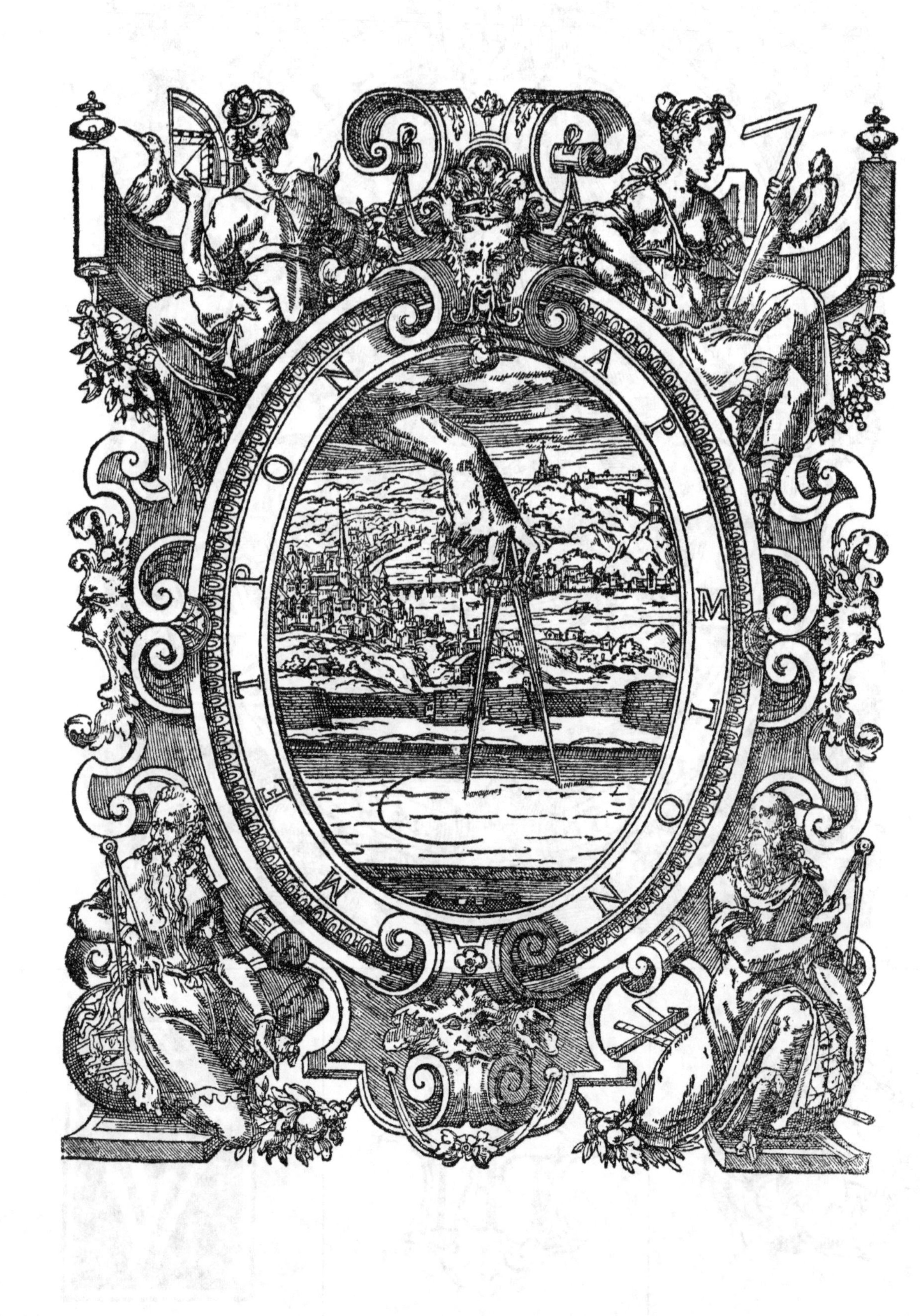

129
SIC LIMITE·
SVO SAPIENS GAVDET

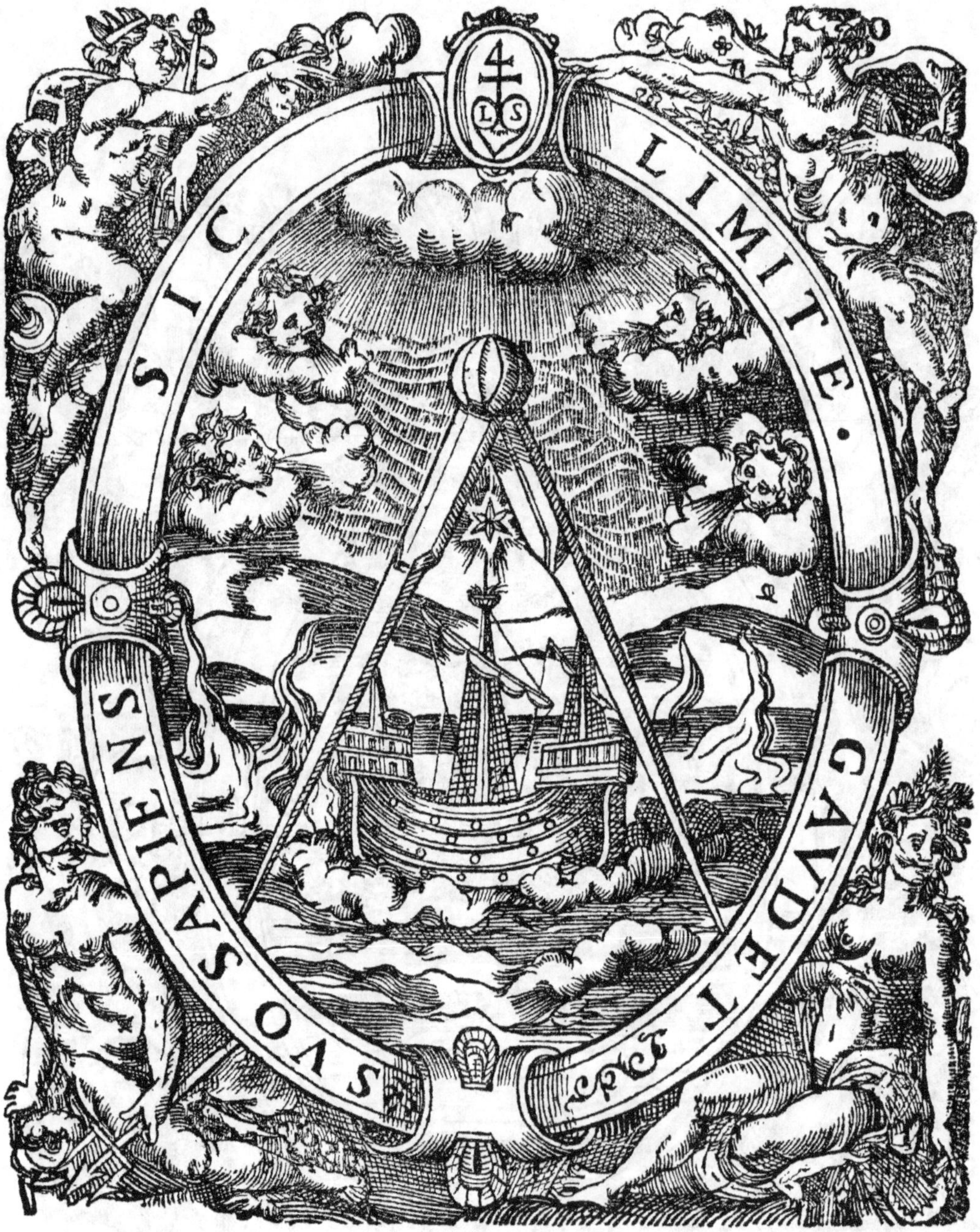

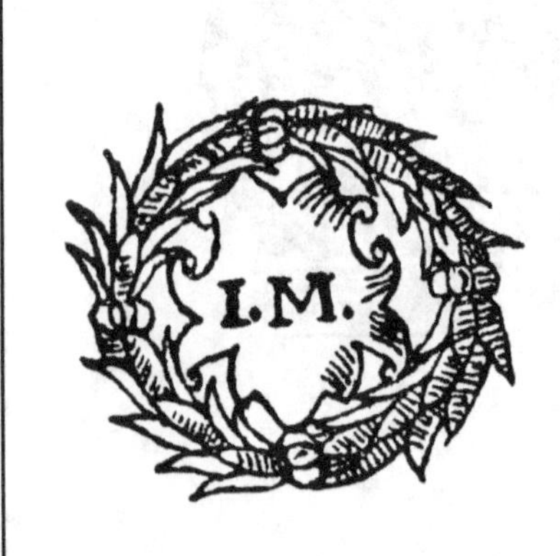
130
I.M.

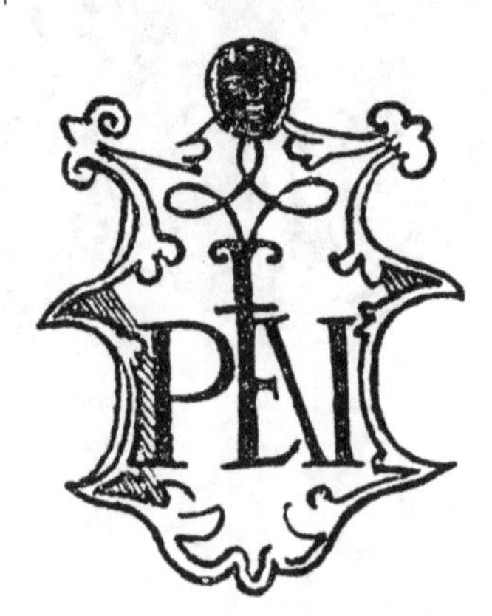
131
PAI

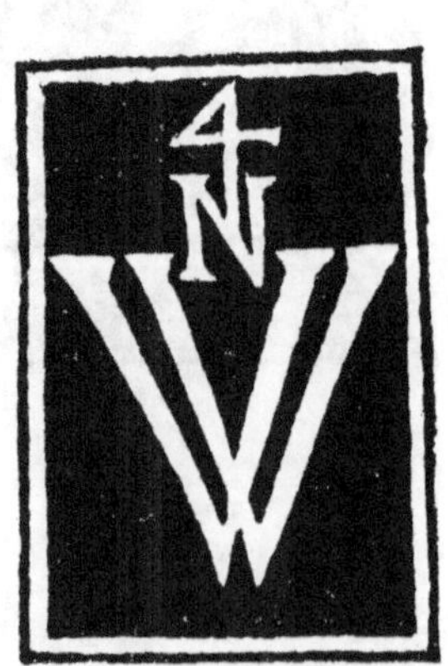
132
4
N
V

133

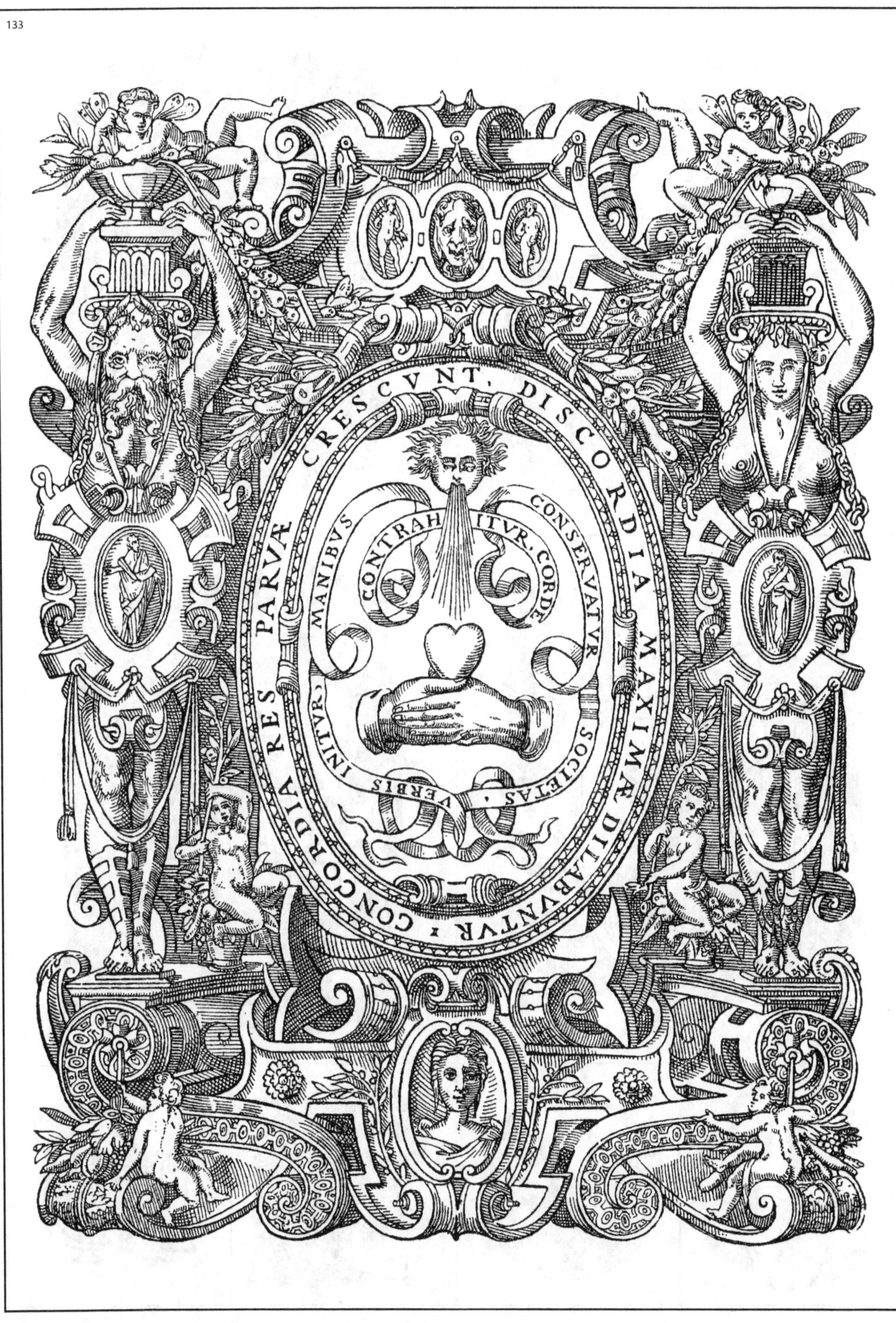
CRESCVNT, DISCORDIA MAXIMÆ DILABVNTVR : CONCORDIA RES PARVÆ
CONTRAHITVR, CONSERVATVR CORDE SOCIETAS · VERBIS INITVR MANIBVS

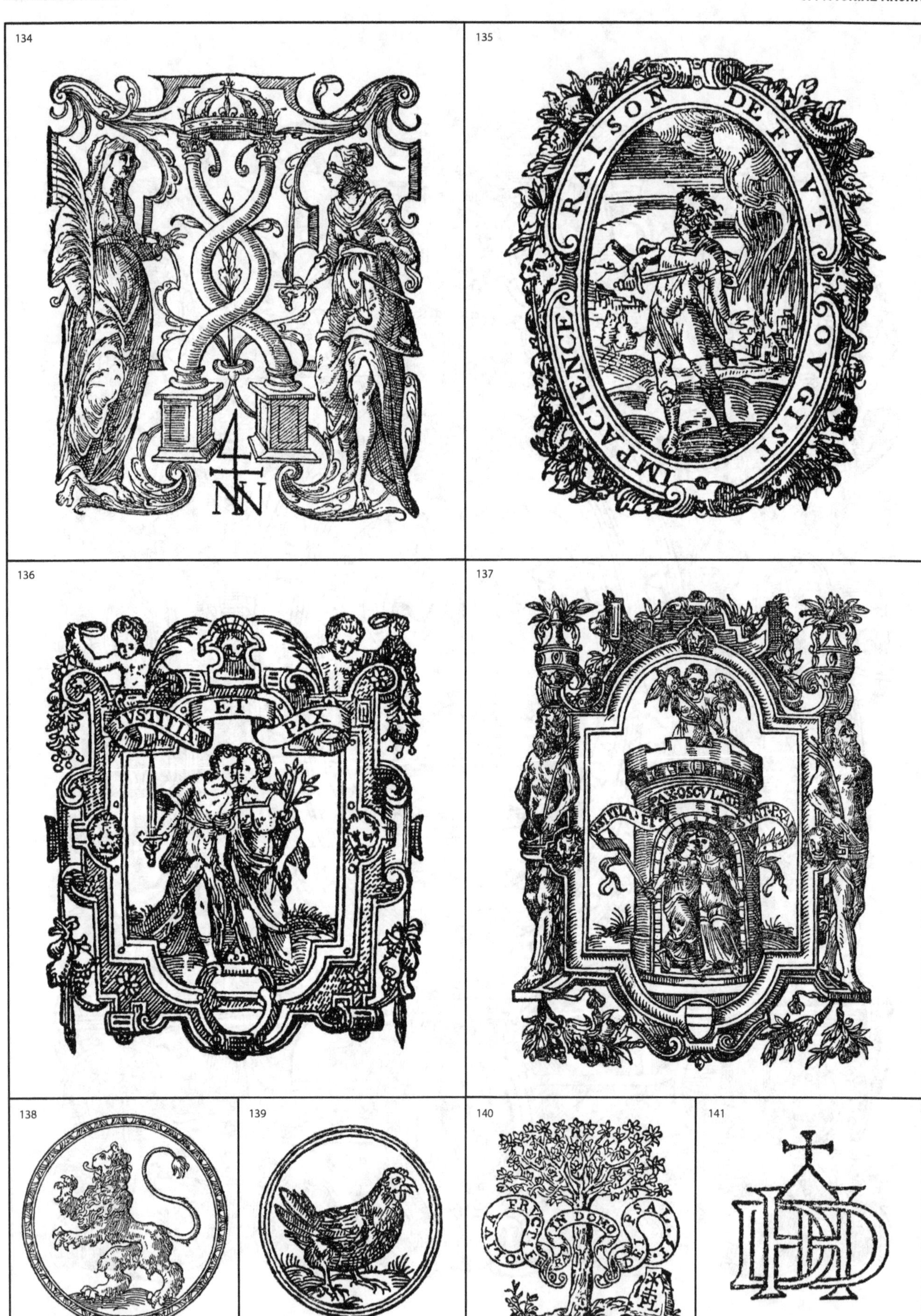

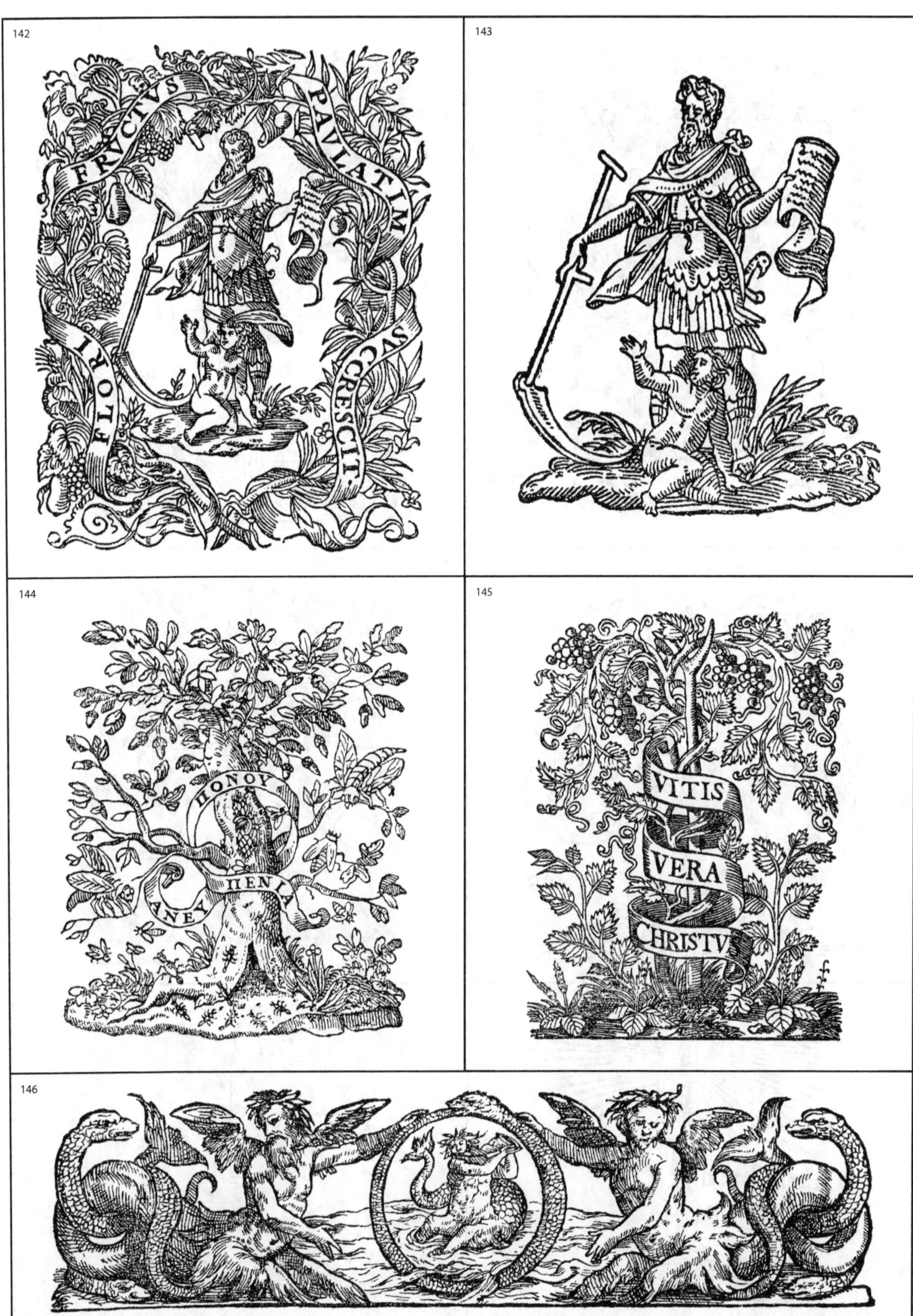
142
FRVCTVS
PAVLATIM
FLORVS
CRESCIT
143
144
HONOV
MEN
ANEY
145
VITIS
VERA
CHRISTV
146

147

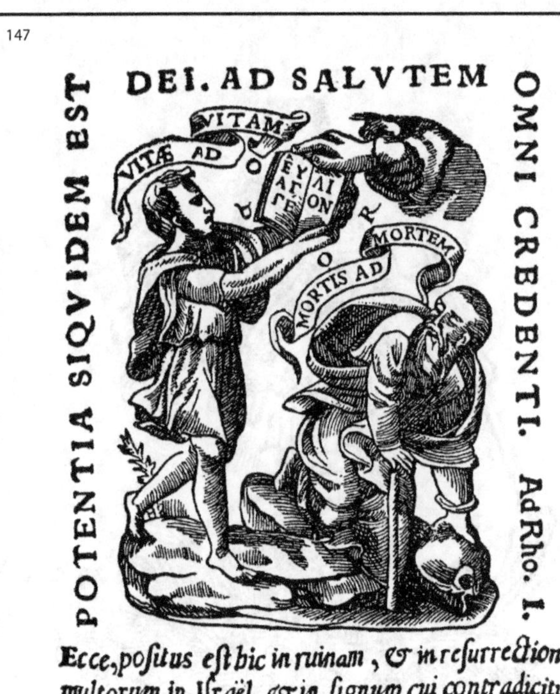

148

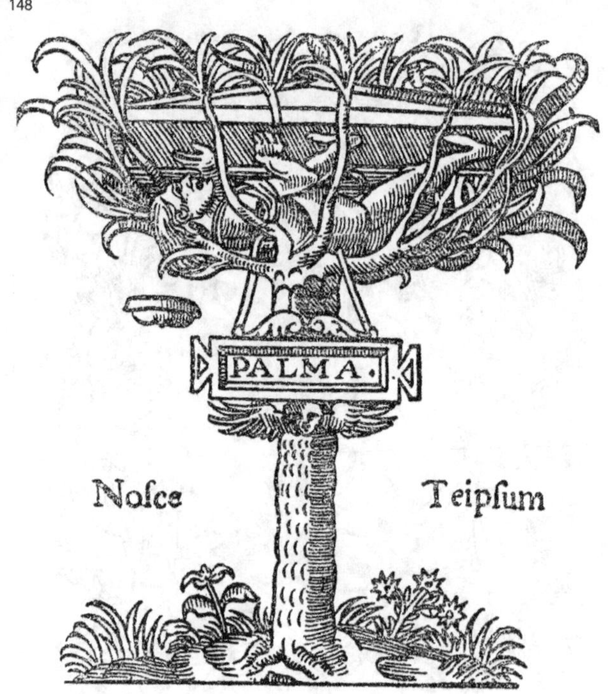

149

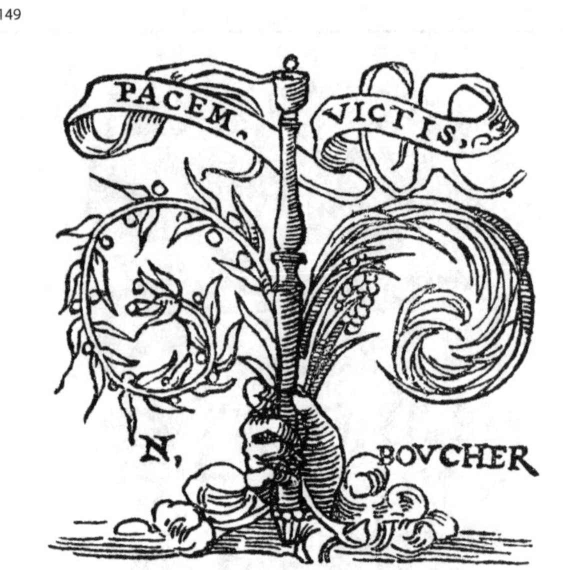

150

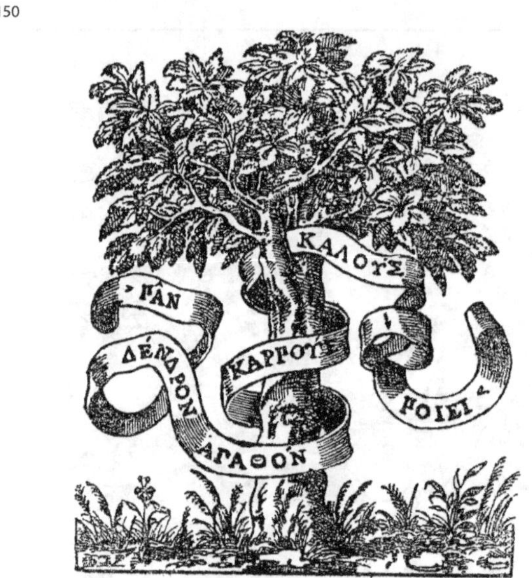

151

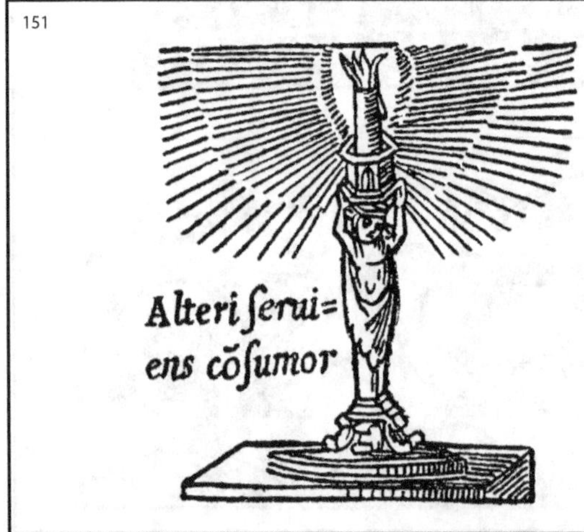

152

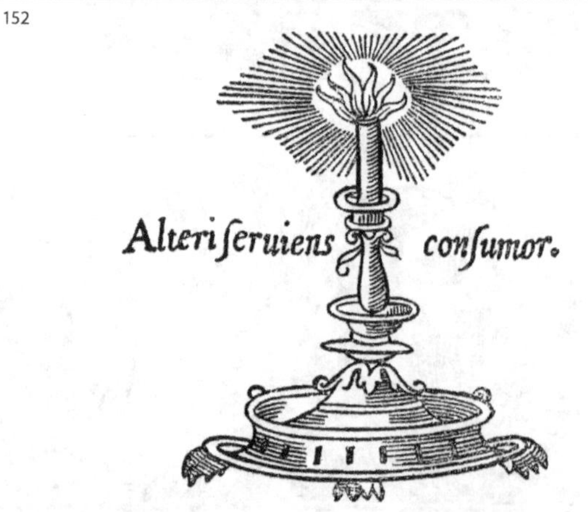

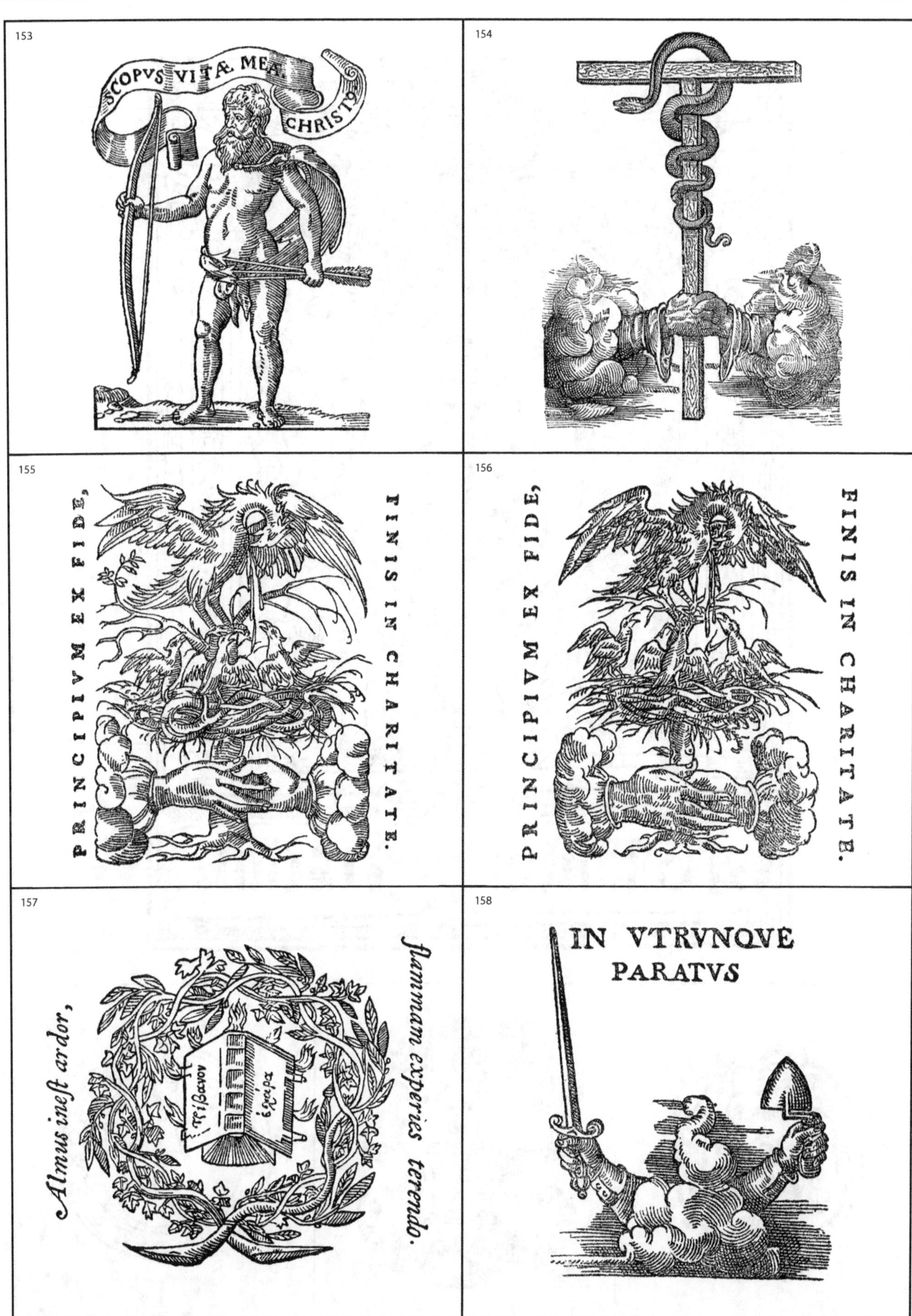
153
SCOPVS VITÆ MEA. CHRISTVS.

154

155
PRINCIPIVM EX FIDE,
FINIS IN CHARITATE.

156
PRINCIPIVM EX FIDE,
FINIS IN CHARITATE.

157
Almus inest ardor,
flammam experies terendo.

158
IN VTRVNQVE PARATVS

159

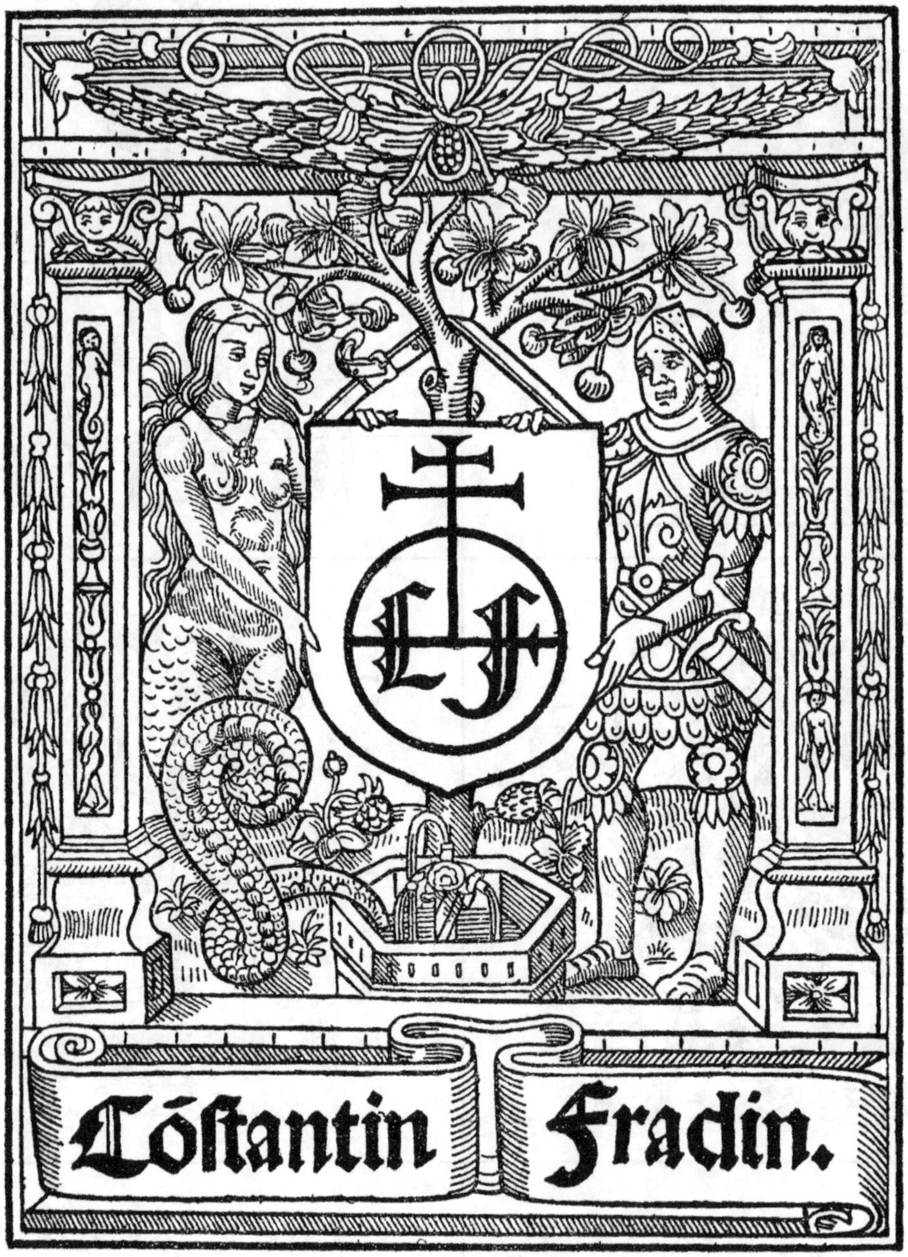

160

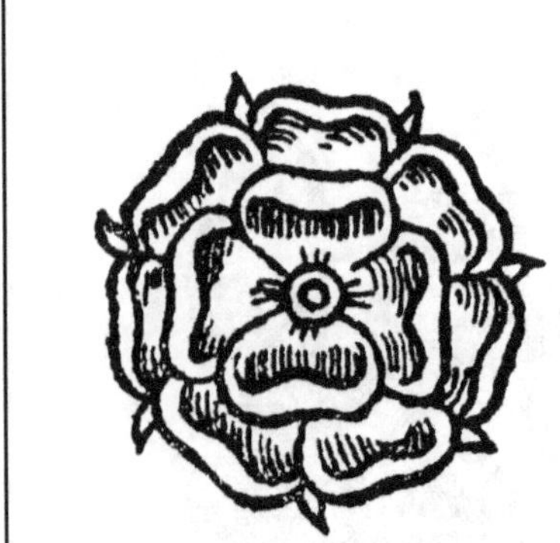

161

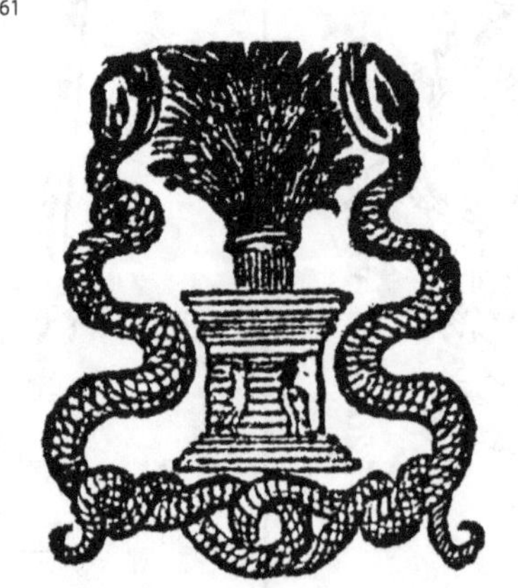

162

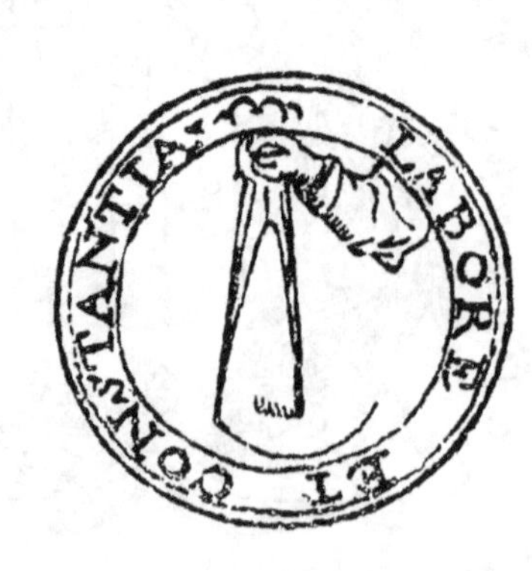

163

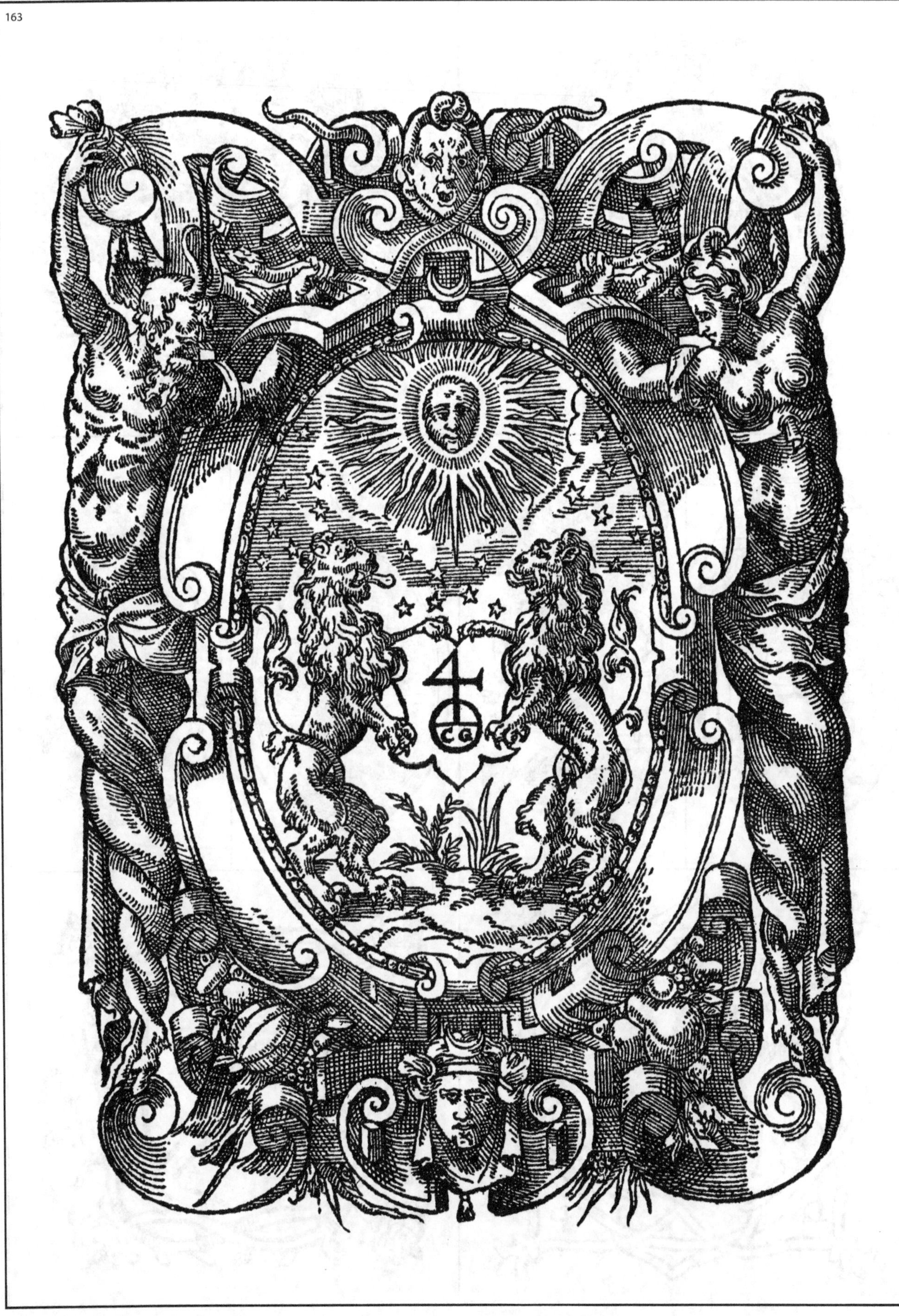

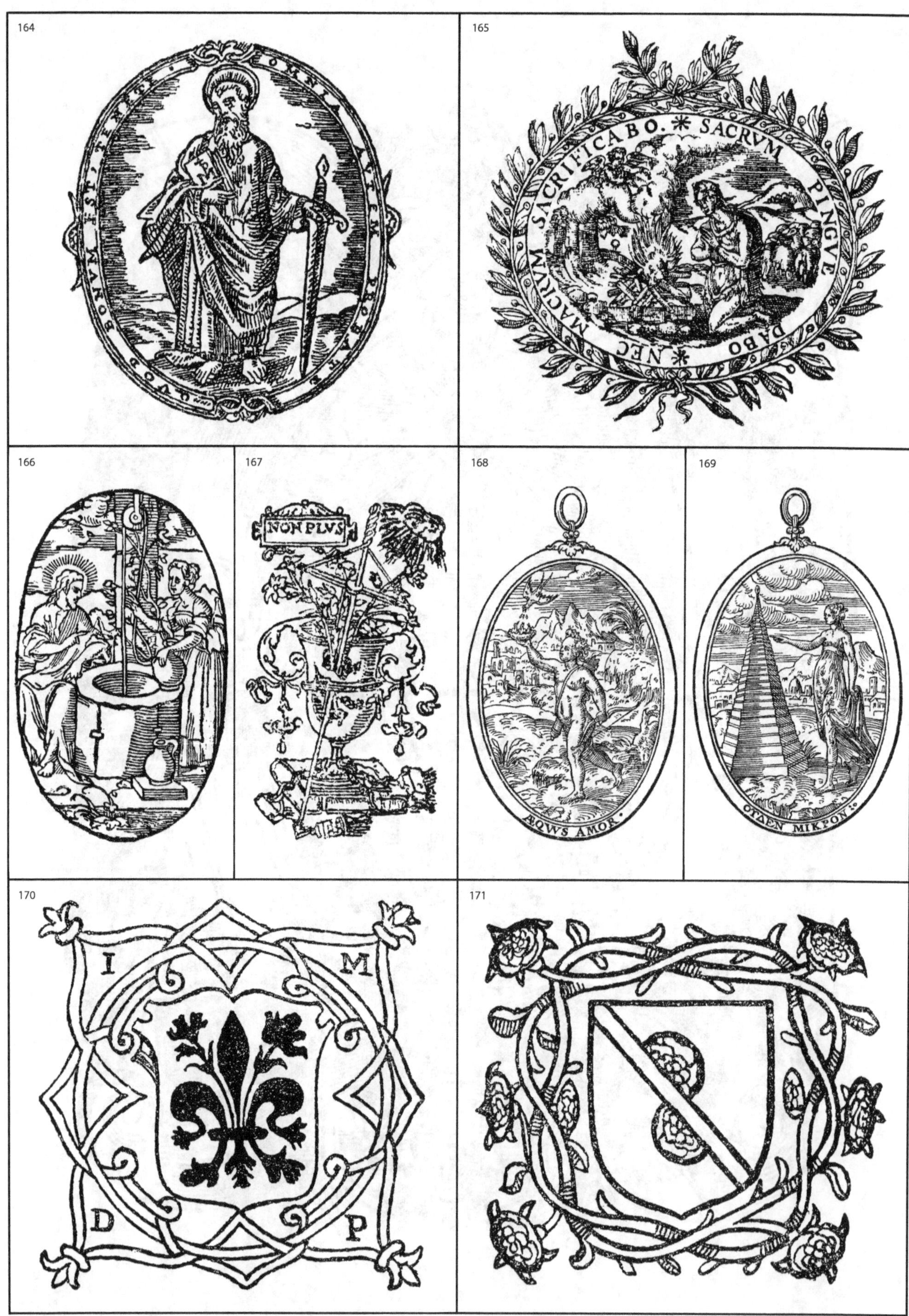
164
165
166
167
168
169
170
171
NON PLVS
AQWS AMOR
OYAEN MIKPON
I M
D P

172

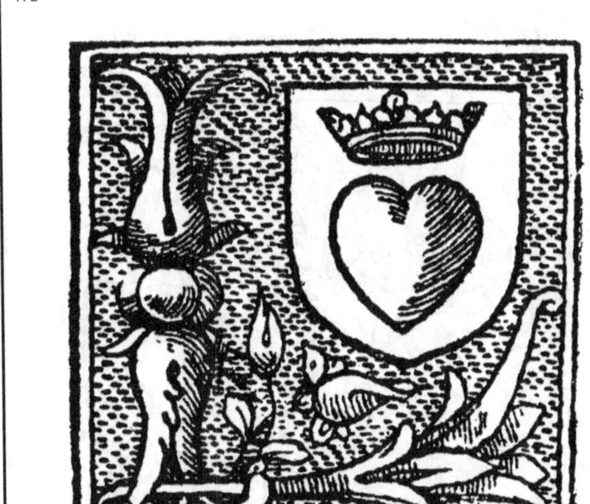

173

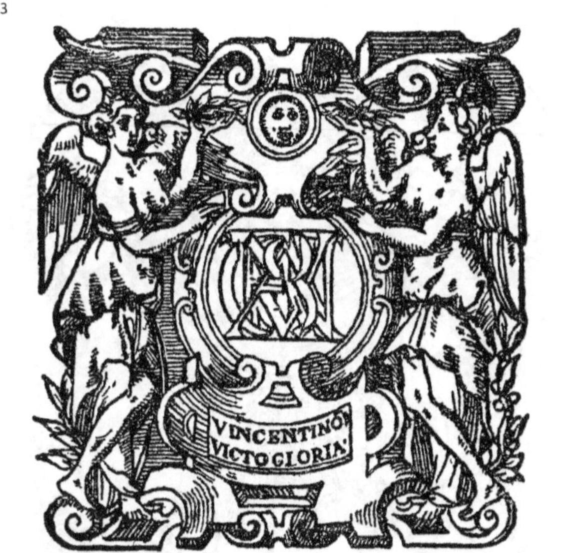

174

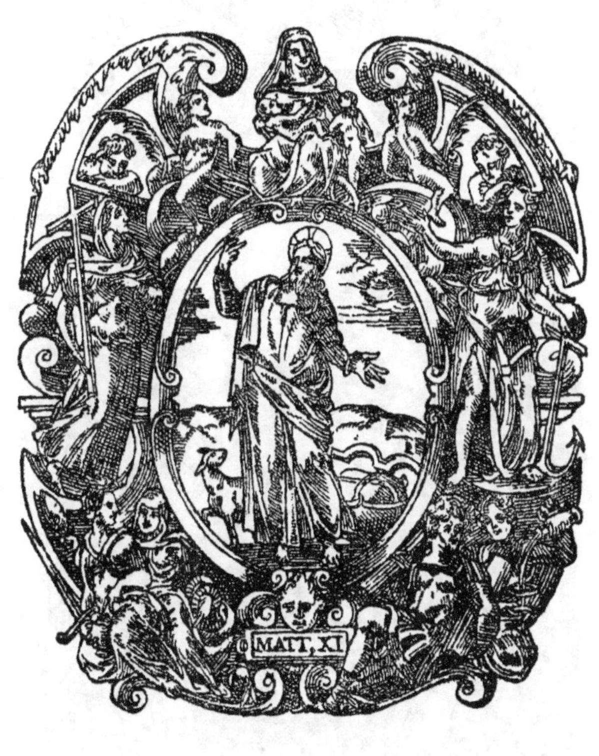

175

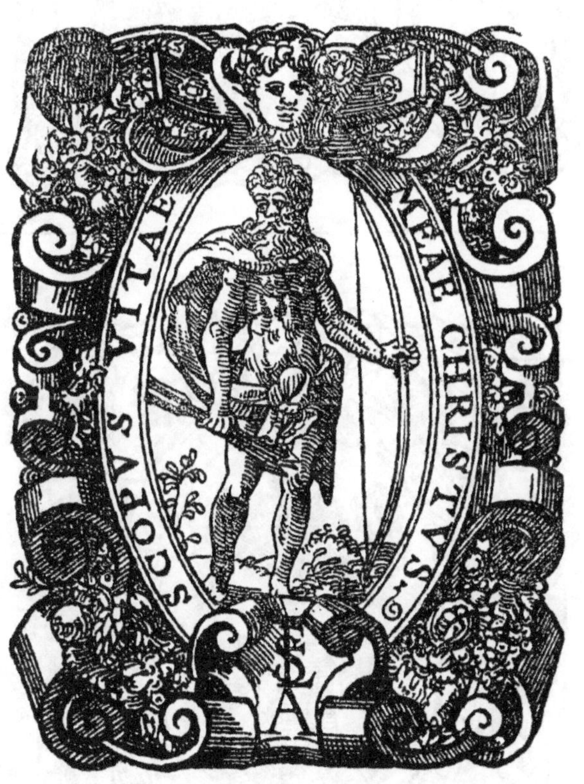

176

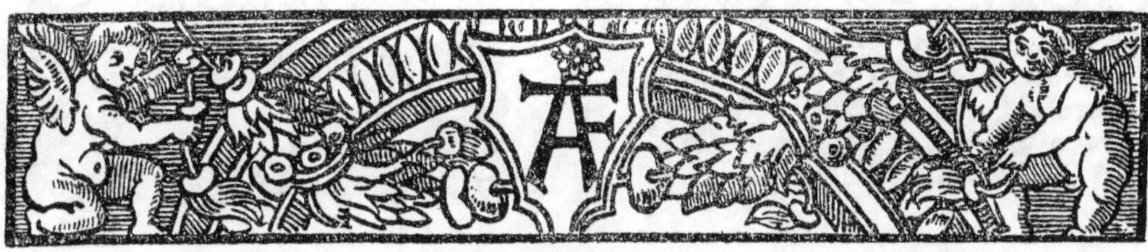

177

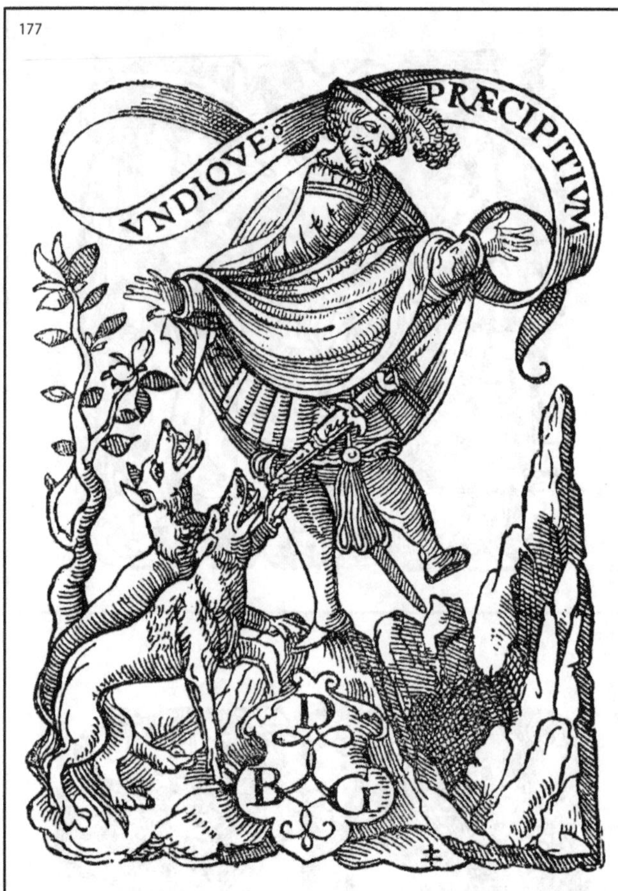

178

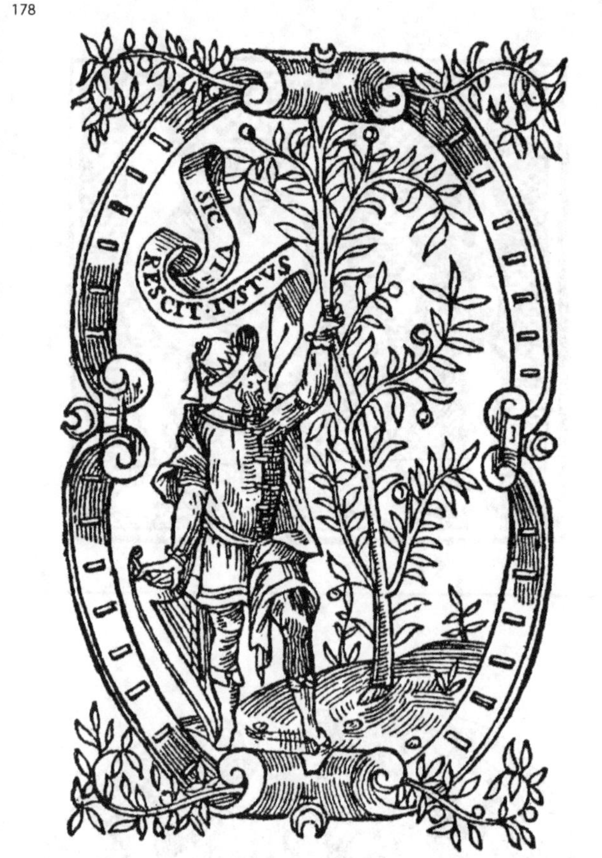

179

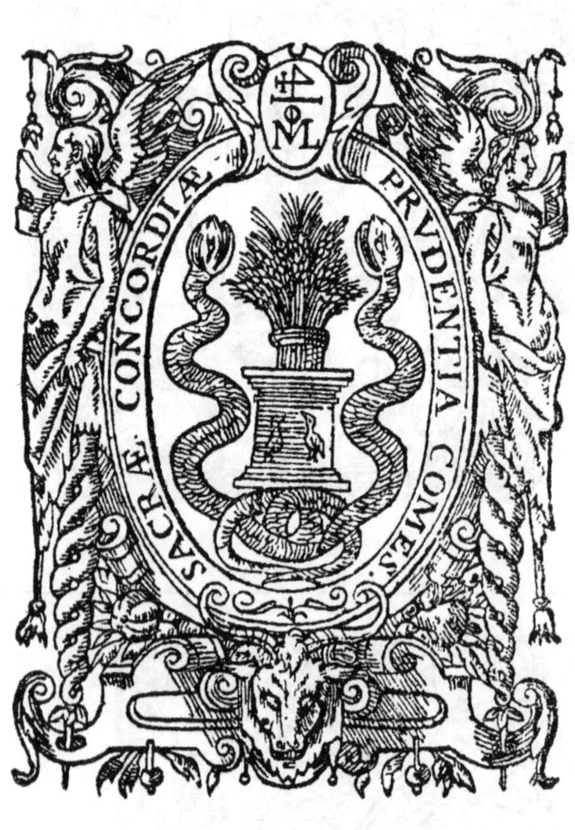

180

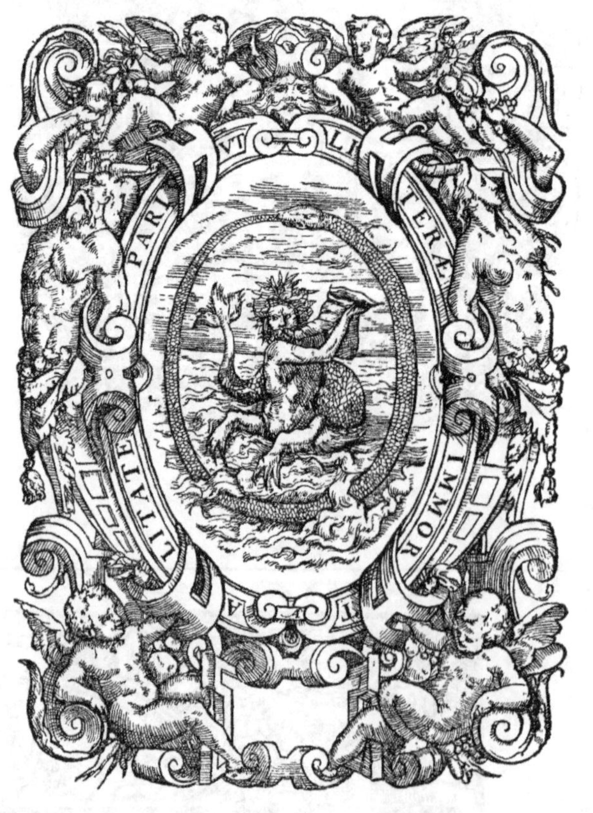

181

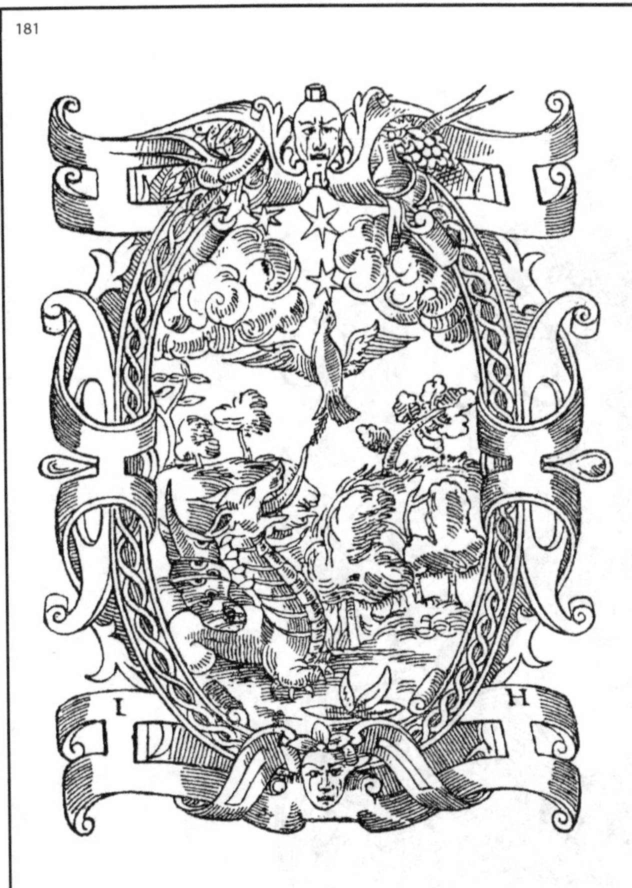

182

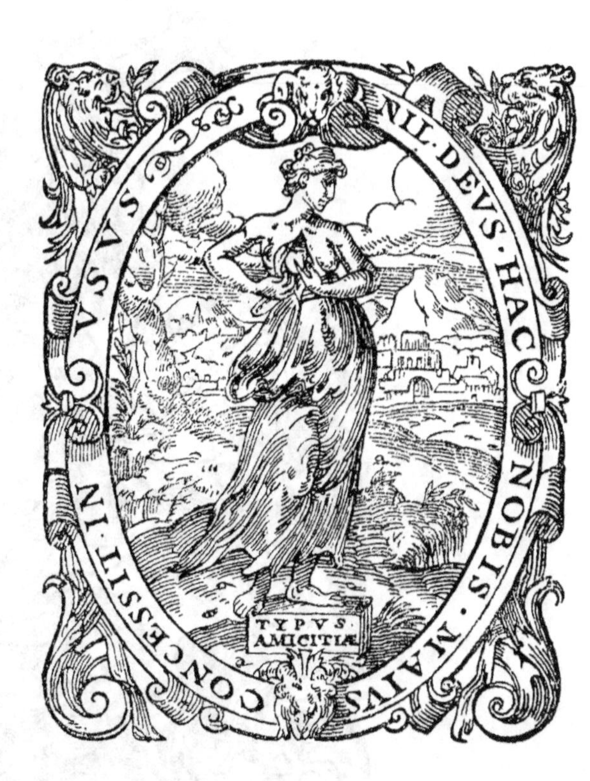

183

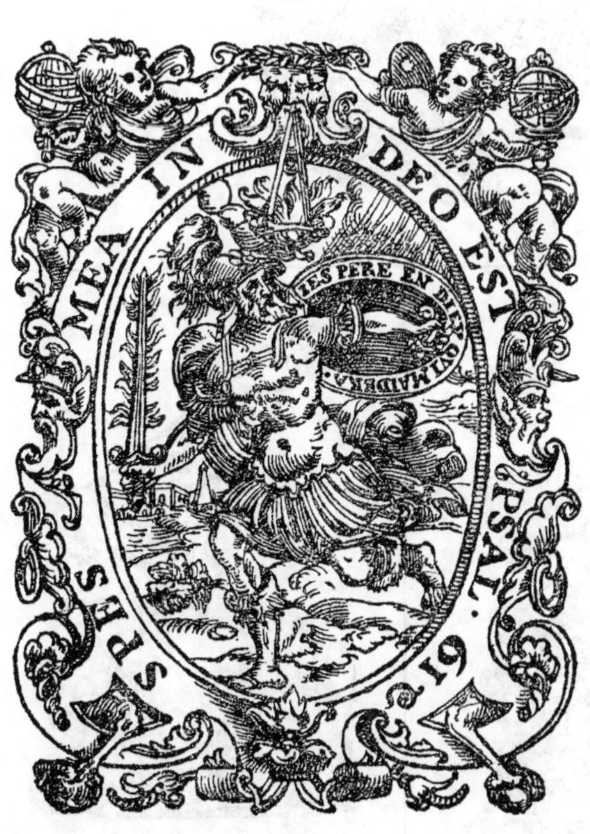

184

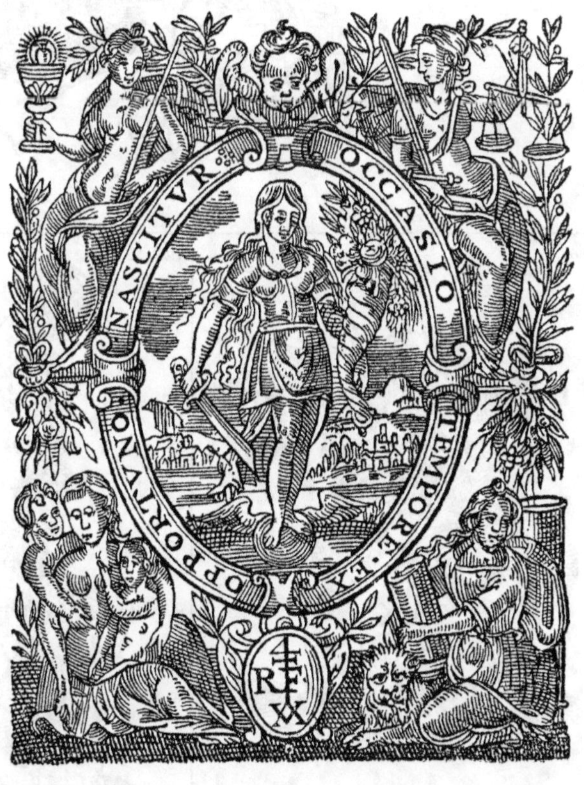

185

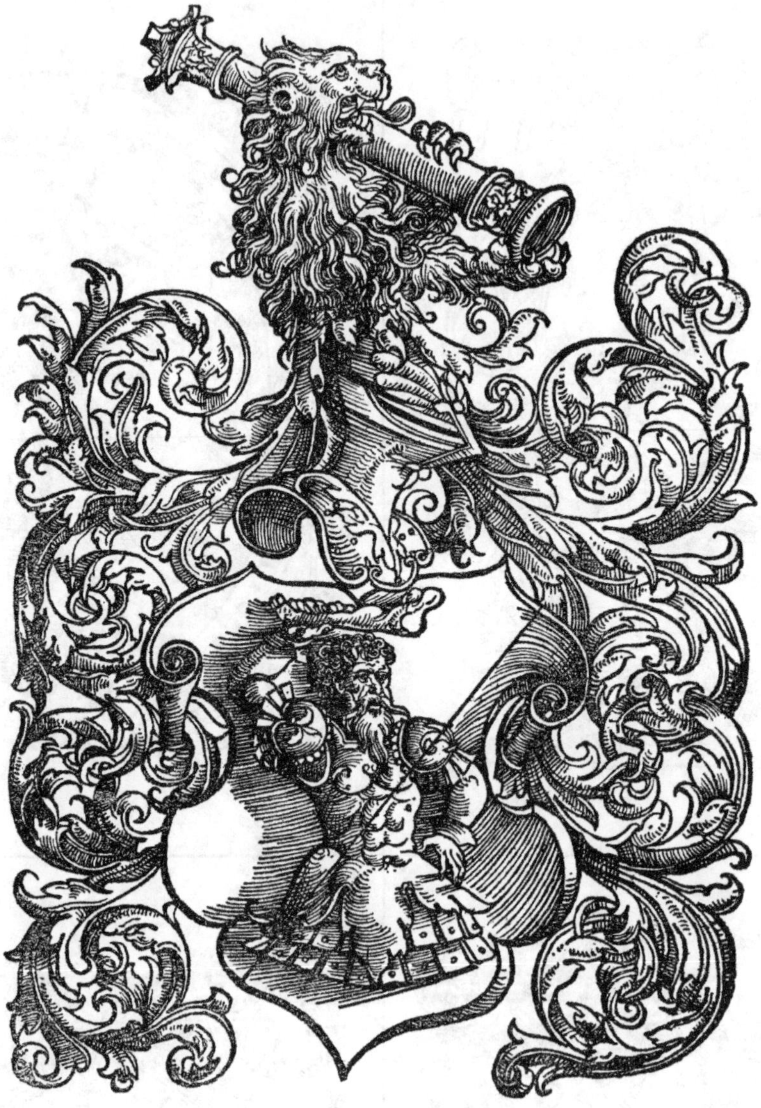

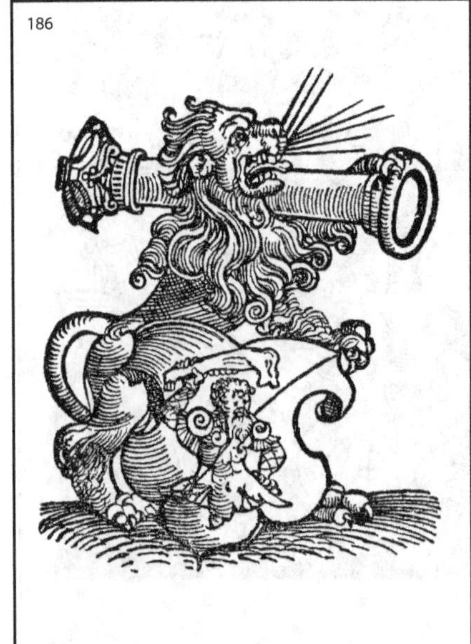

186

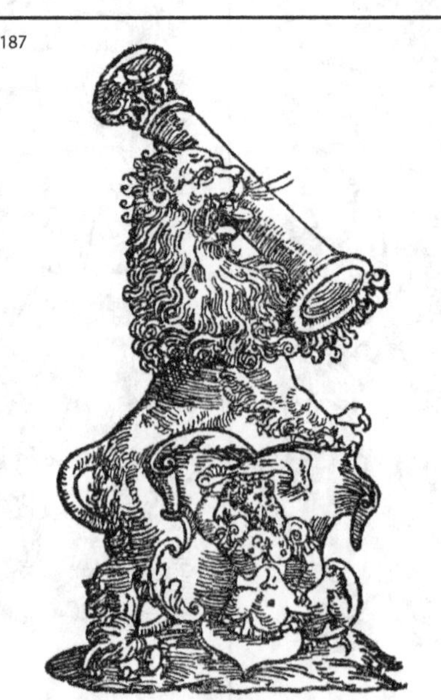

187

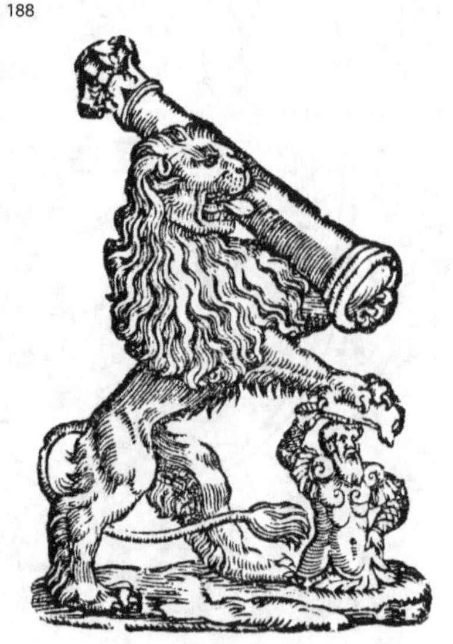

188

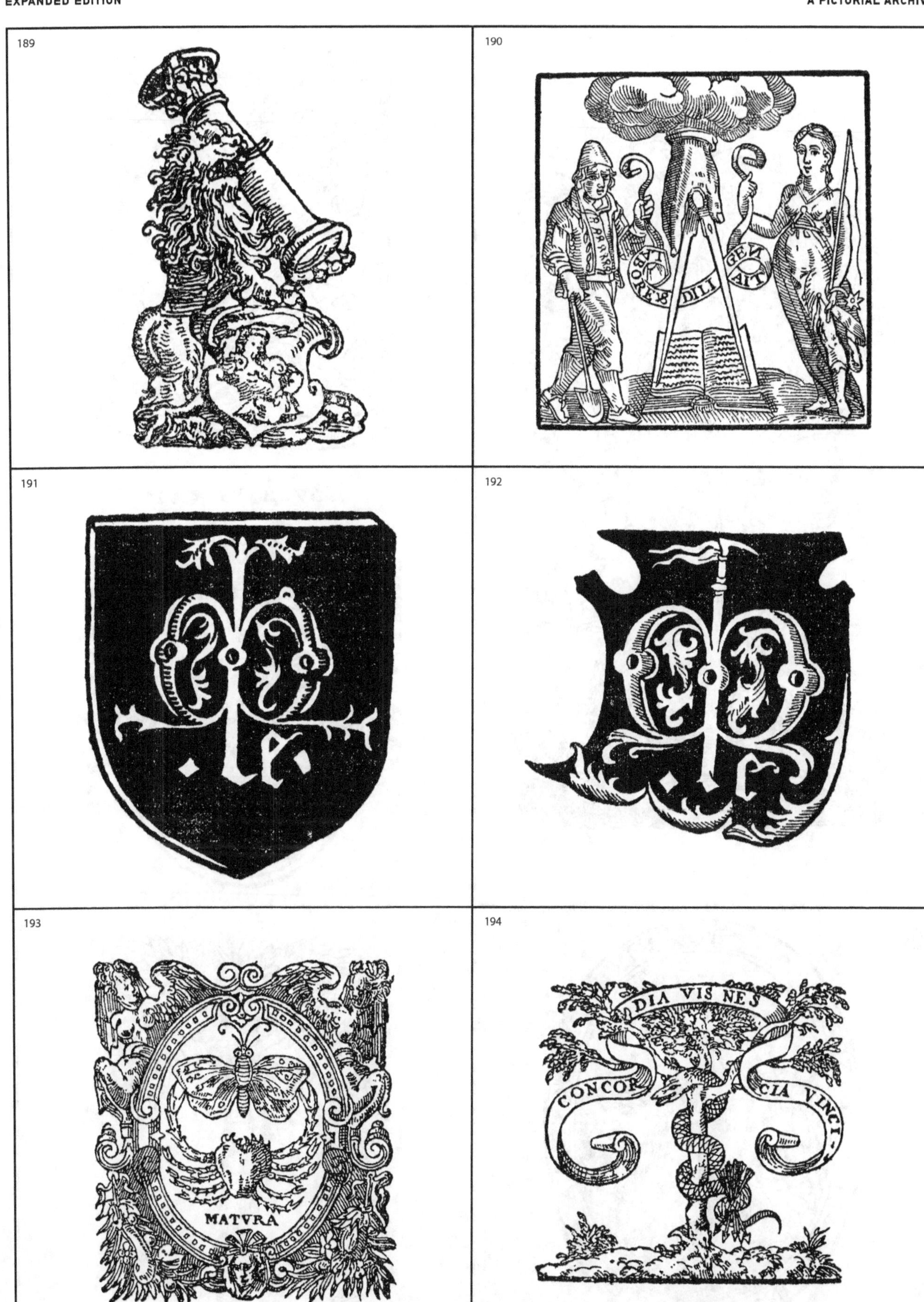
189
190
191
192
193
MATVRA
194
DIA VIS NE S
CONCOR
CIA VINCI

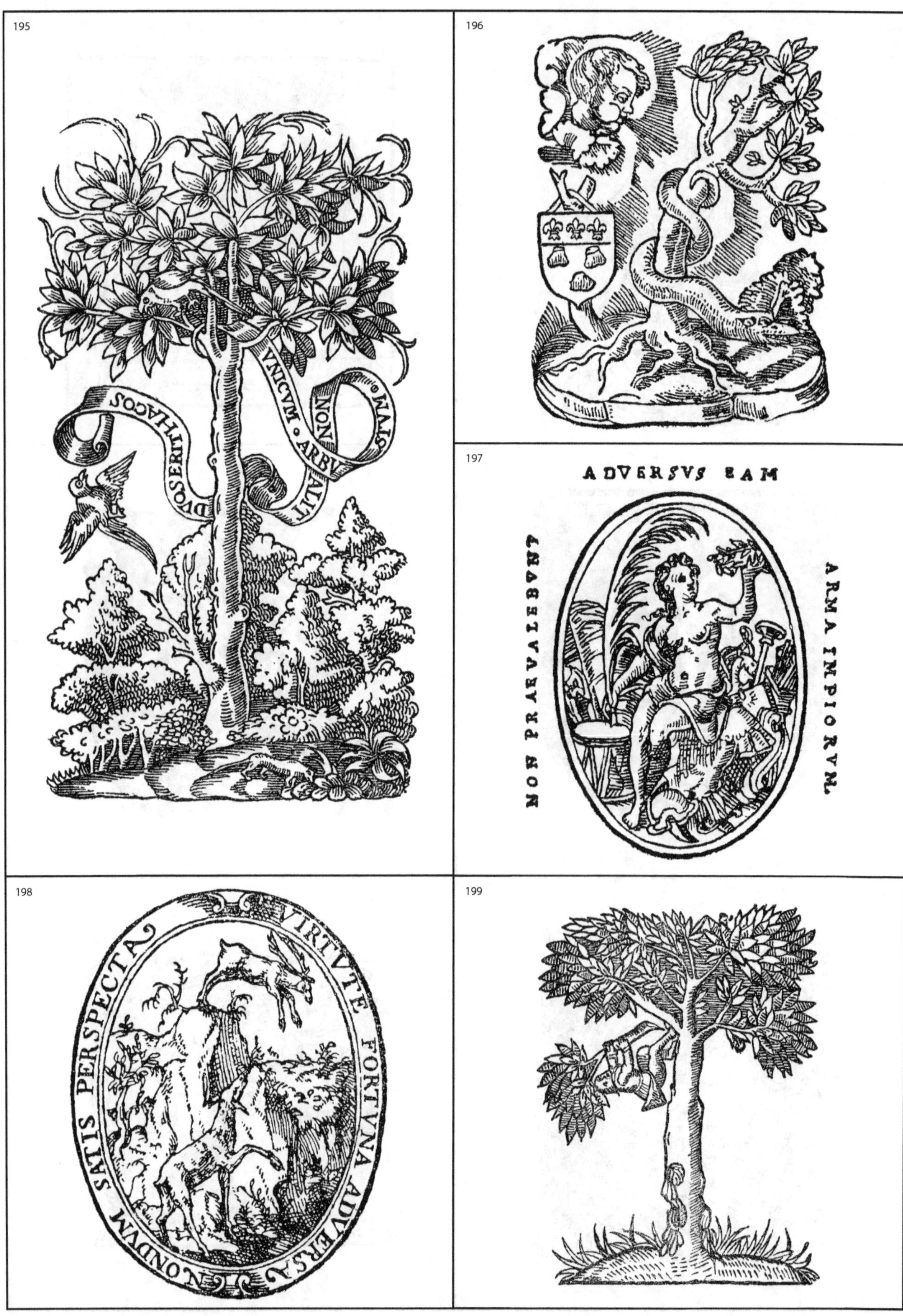
195
196
197
ADVERSVS EAM
NON PRAEVALEBVNT
ARMA IMPIORVM
198
VIRTVTE FORTVNA ADVERSA
NONDVM SATIS PERSPECTA
199

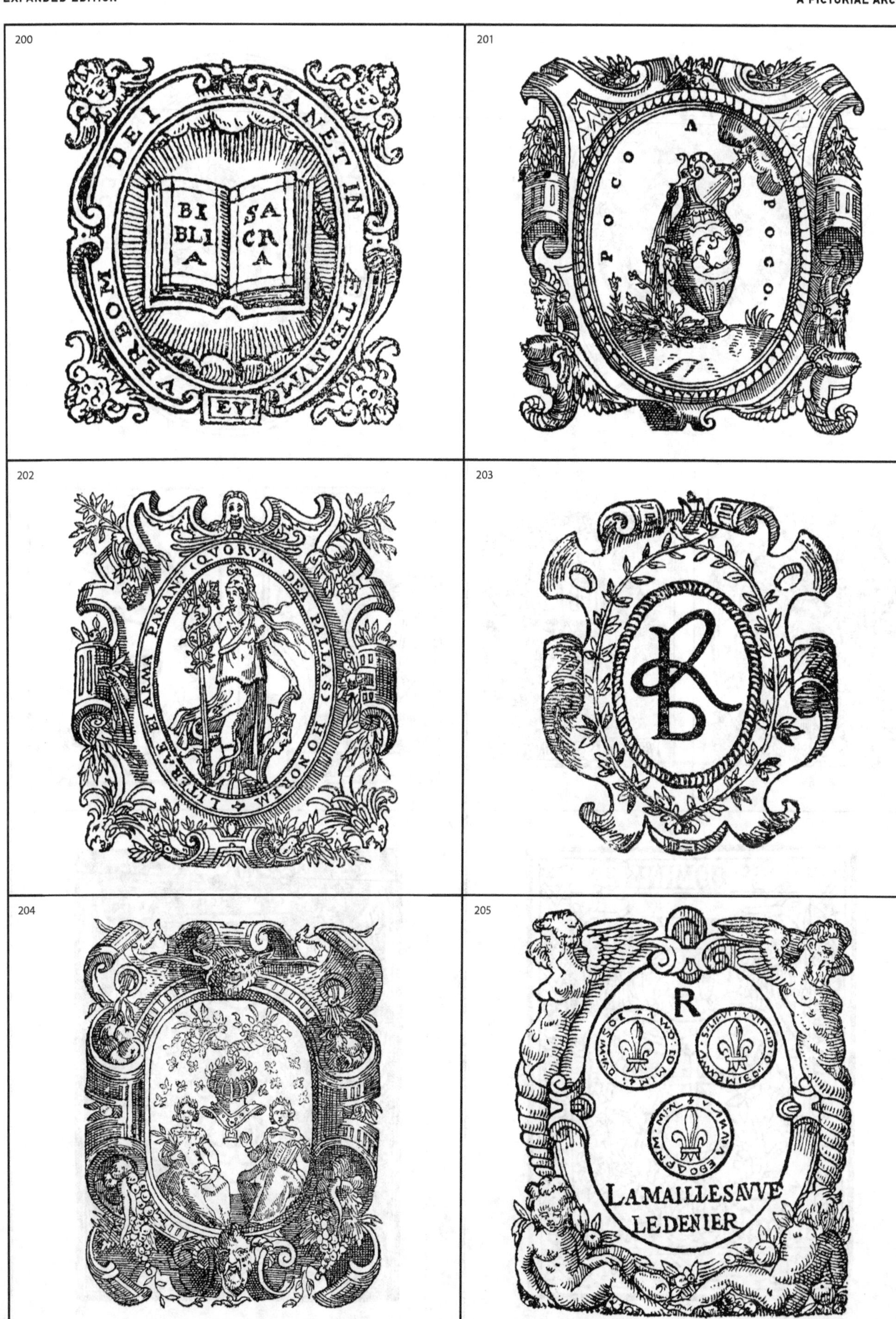

SYMBOLS & EMBLEMS

206

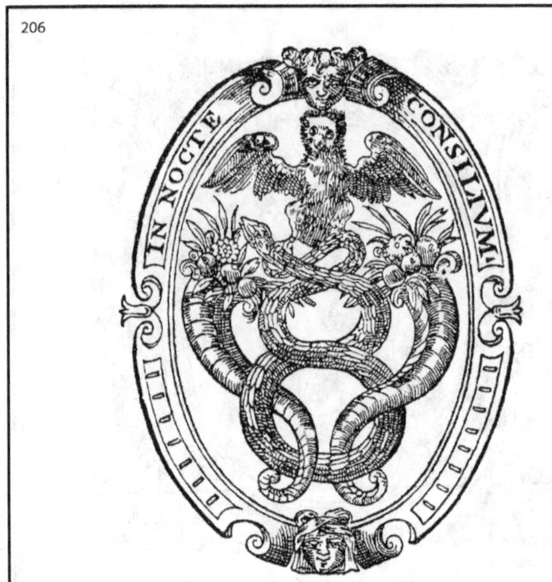

207

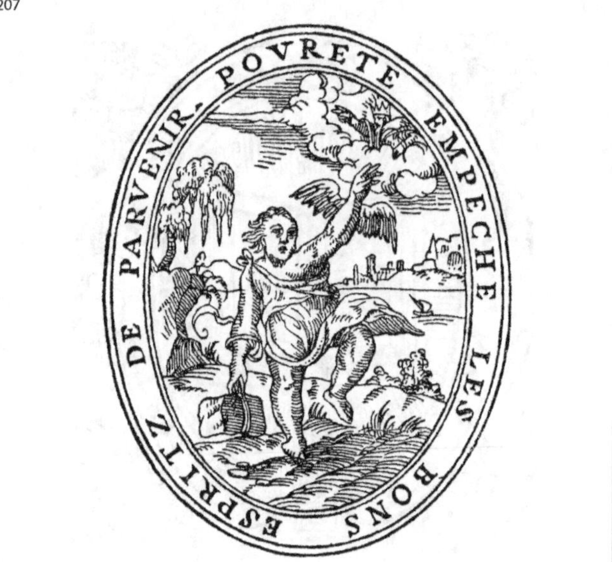

208

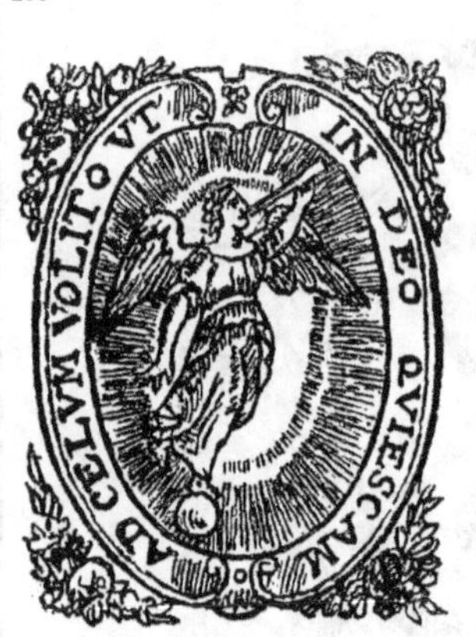

209

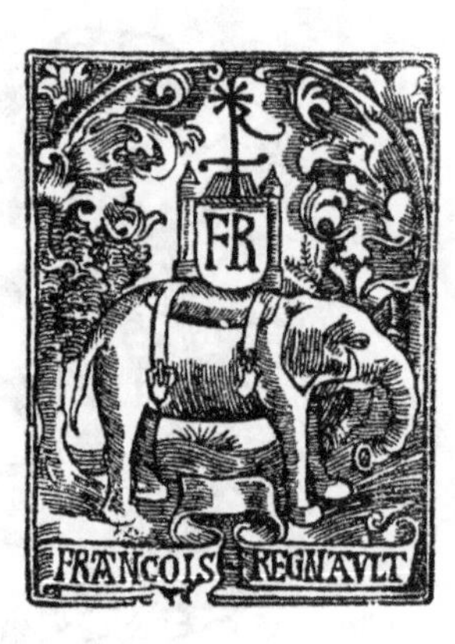

210

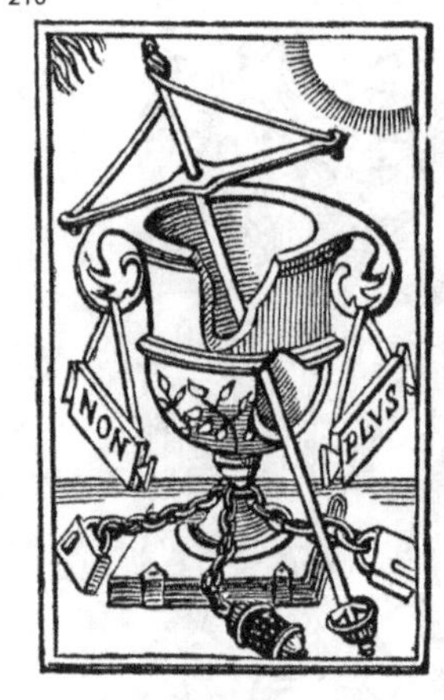

211

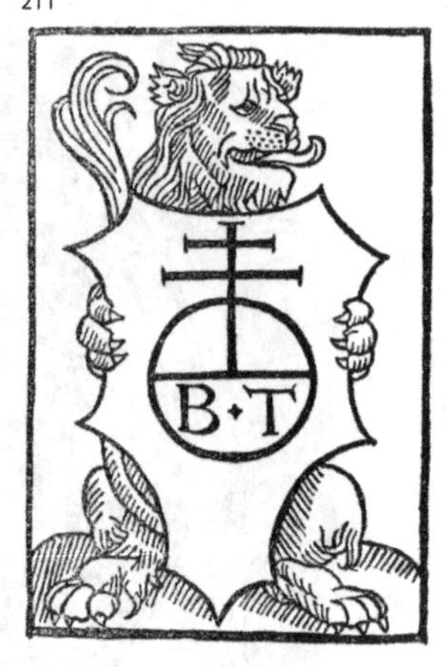

212

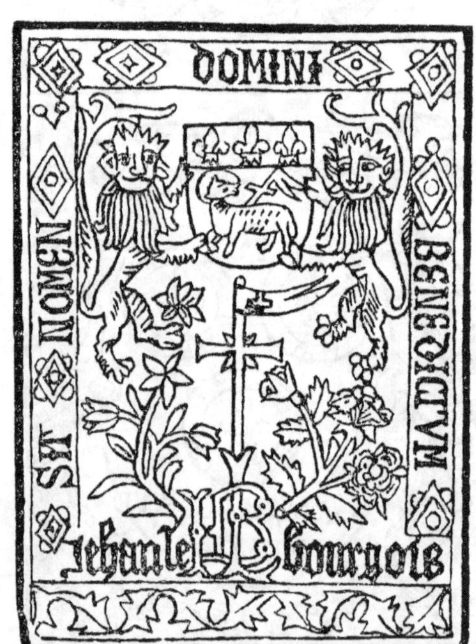

213

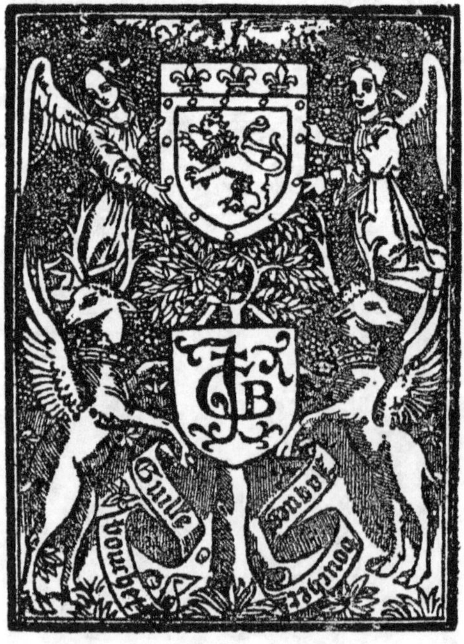

214

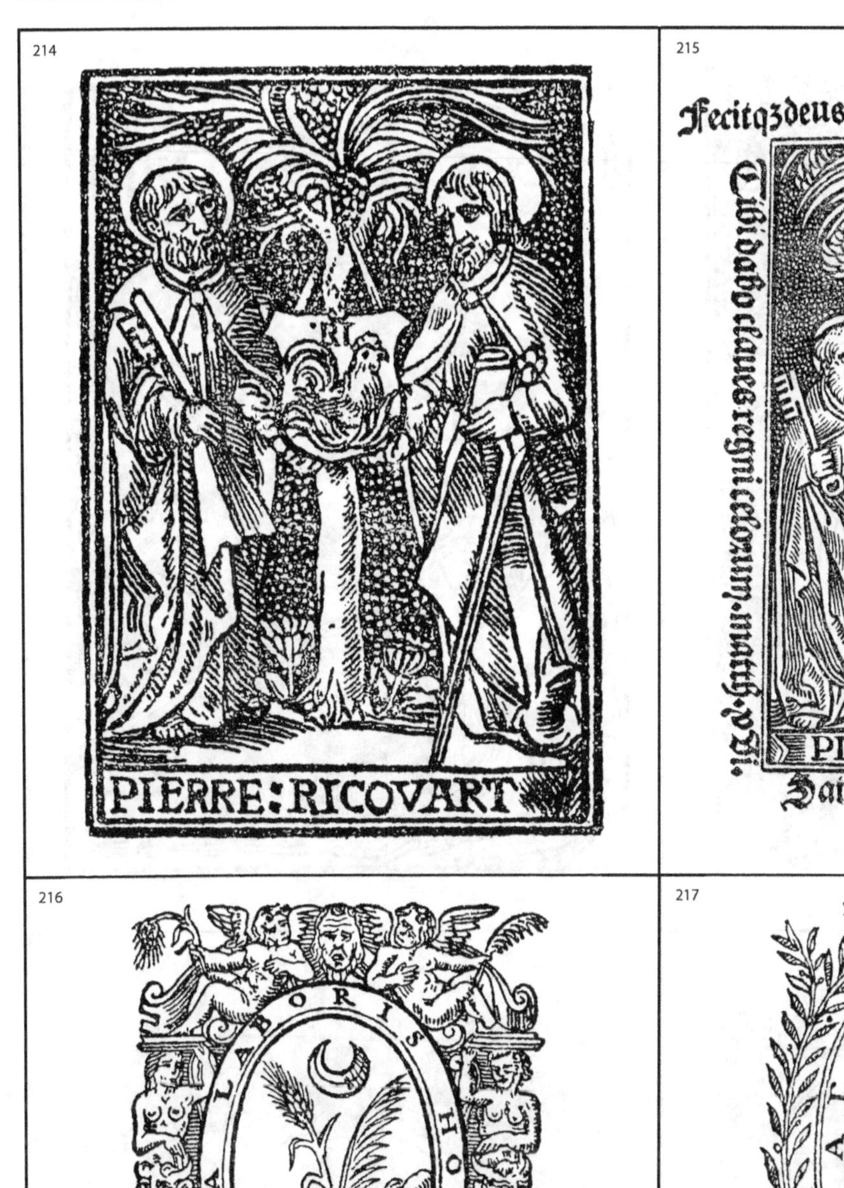

215

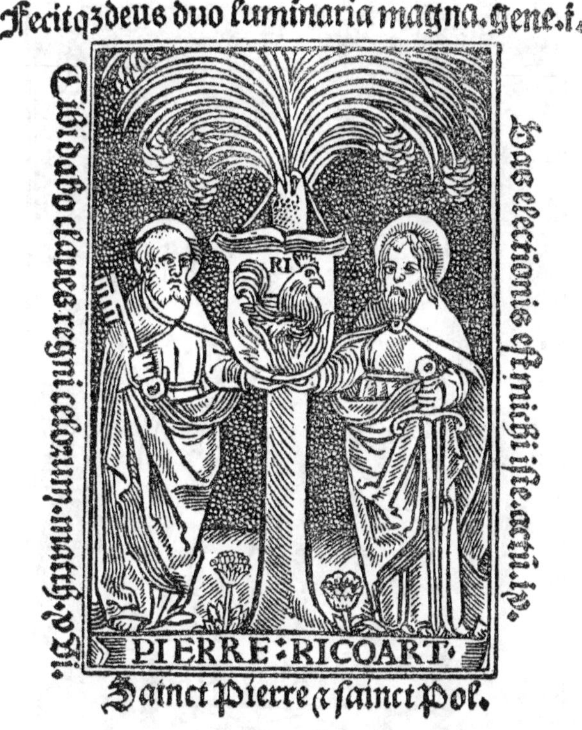

216

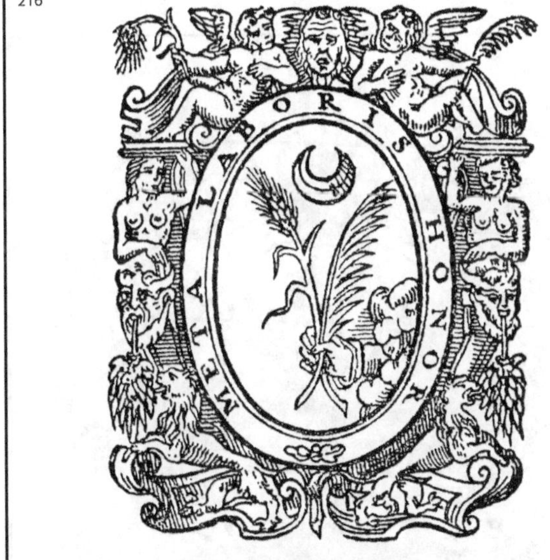

217

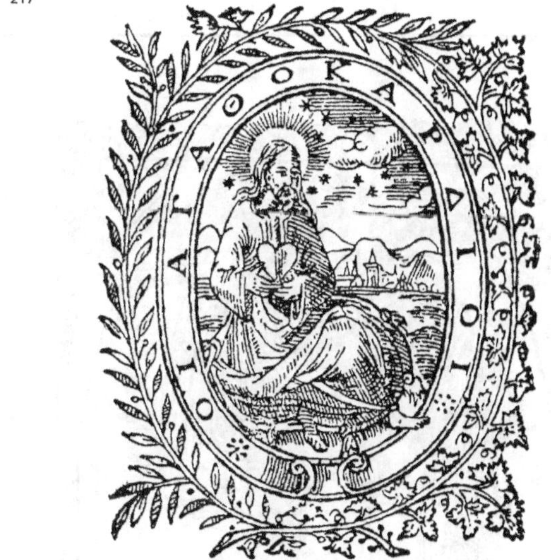

218

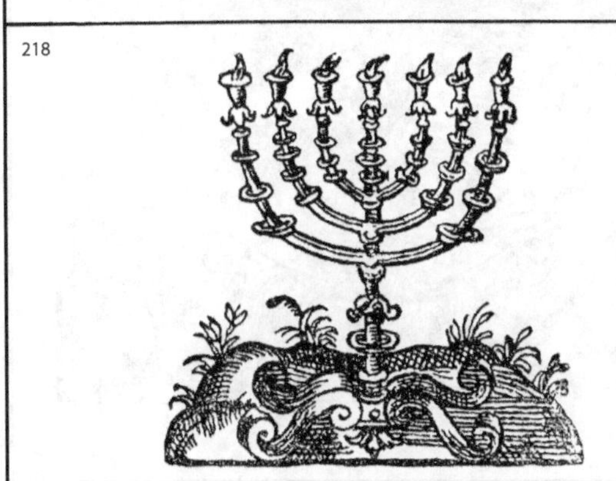

219

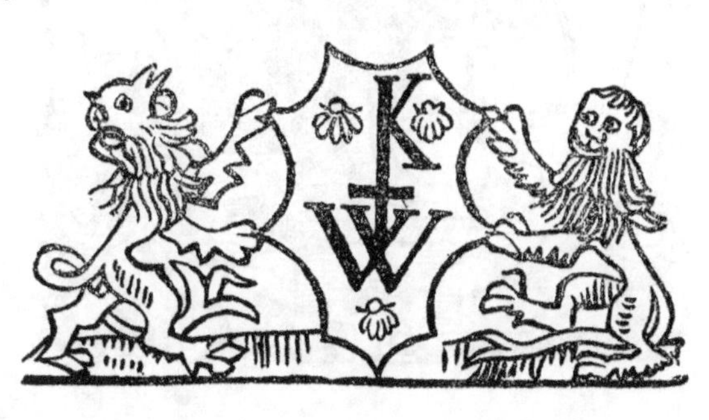

220

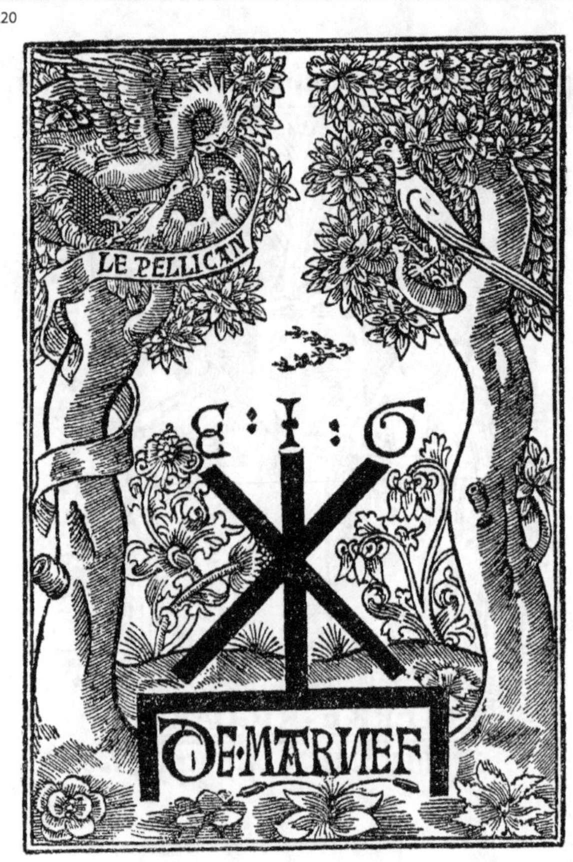

221

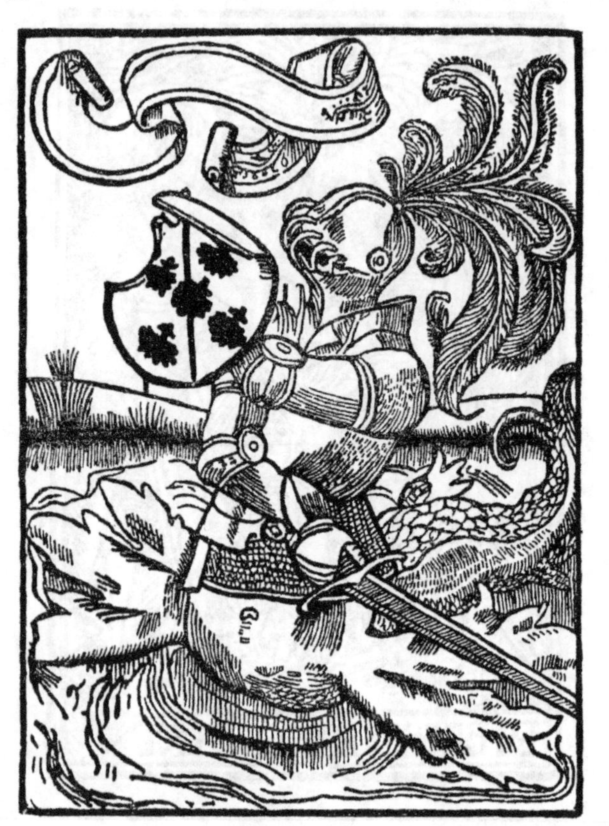

222

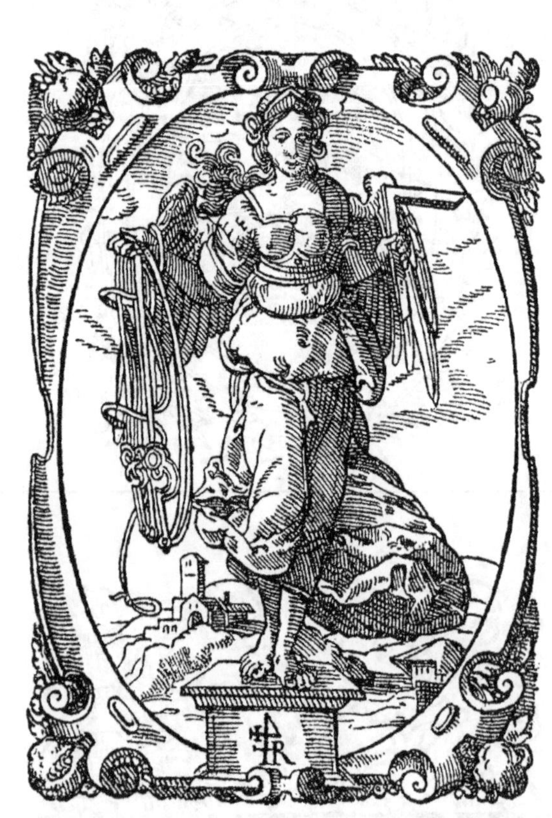

223

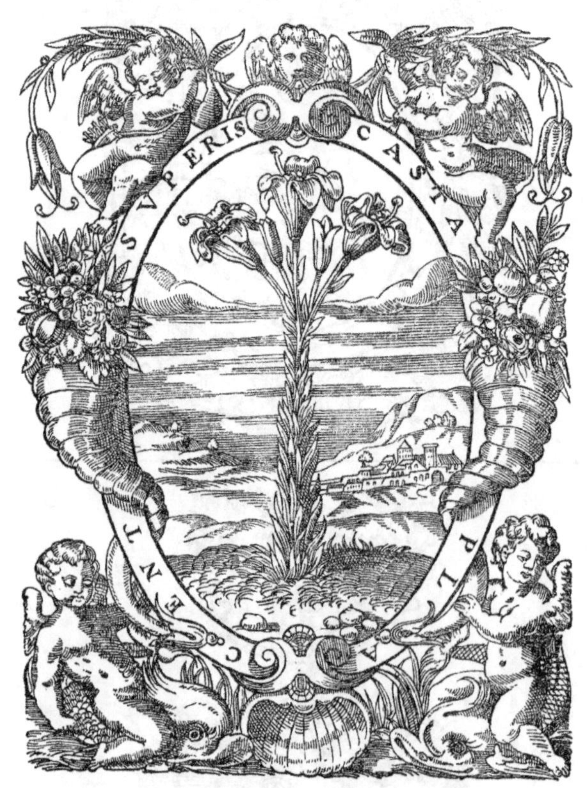

224

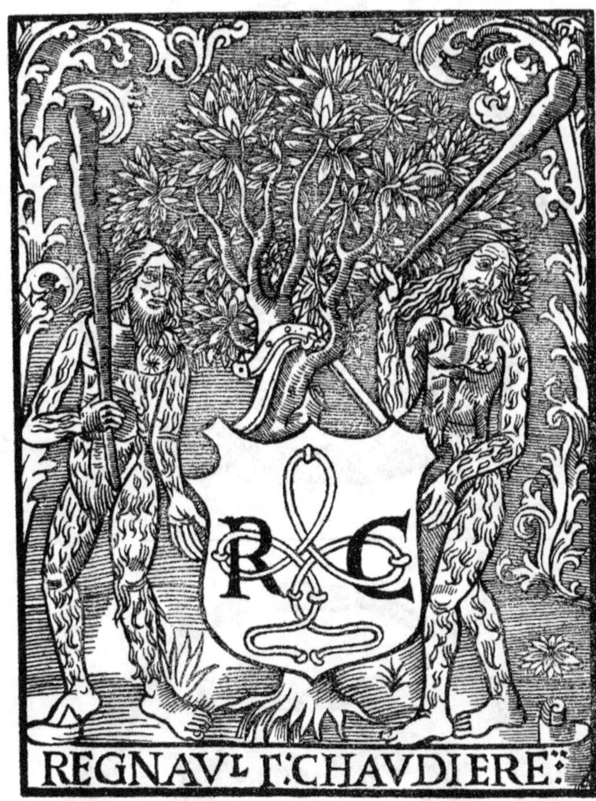

225

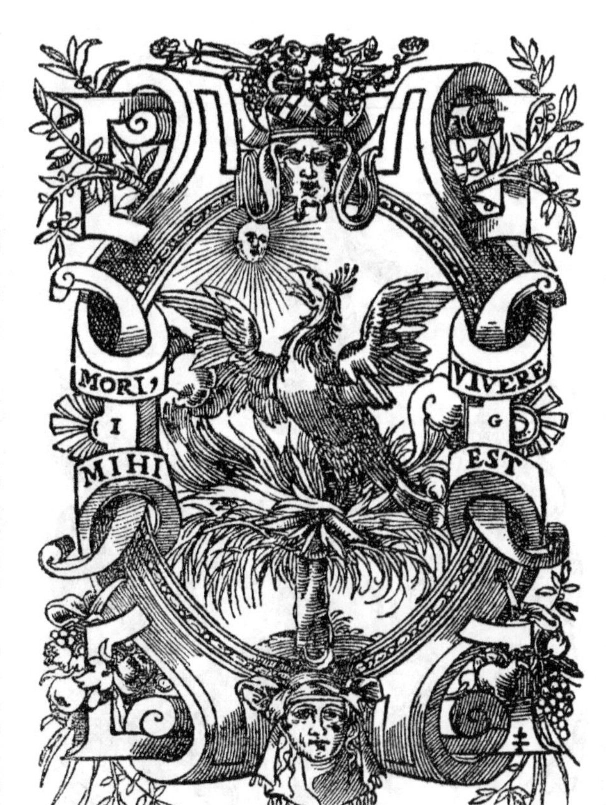

226

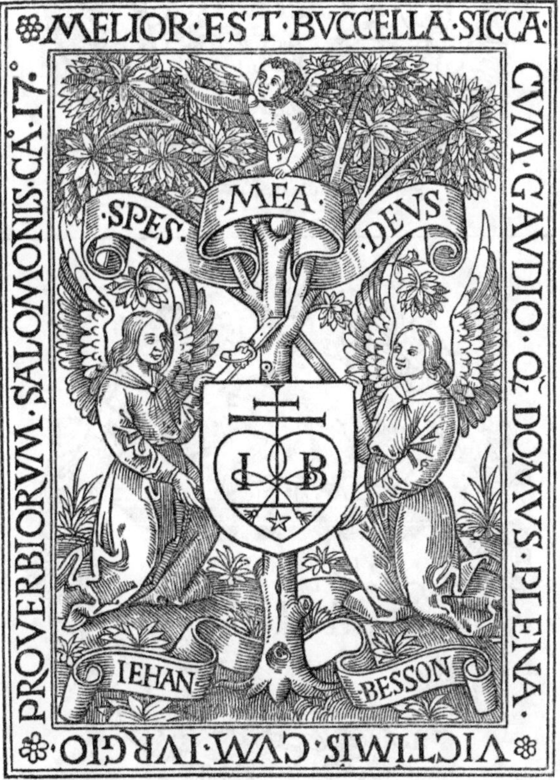

227

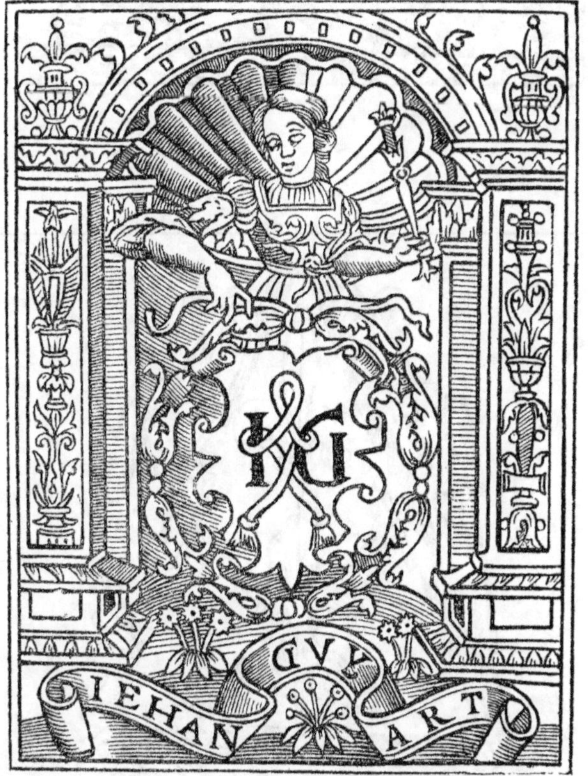

228

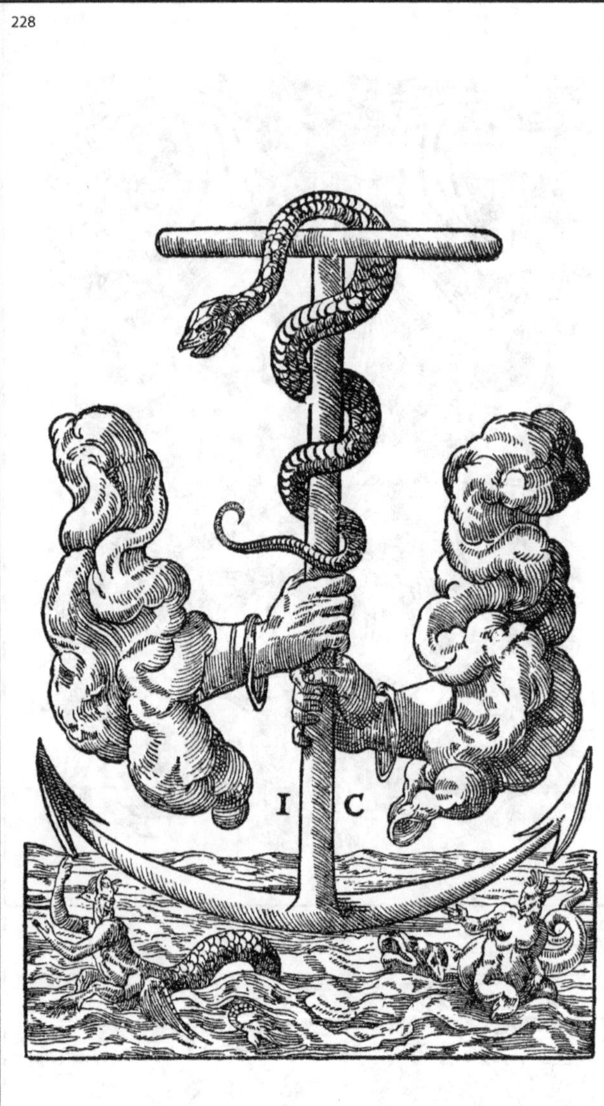

229

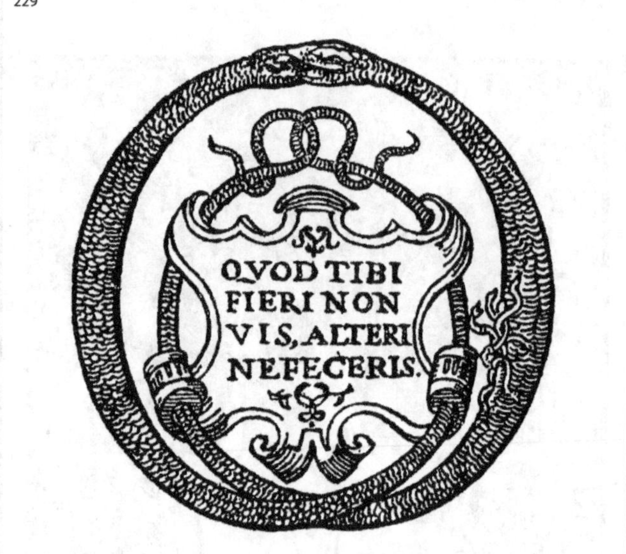

230

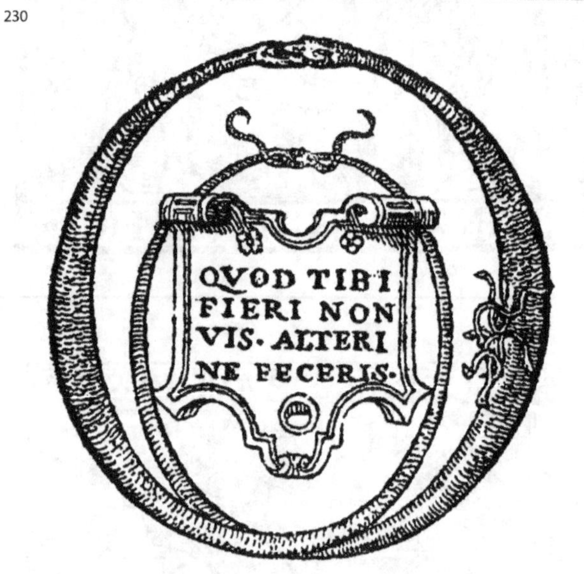

231

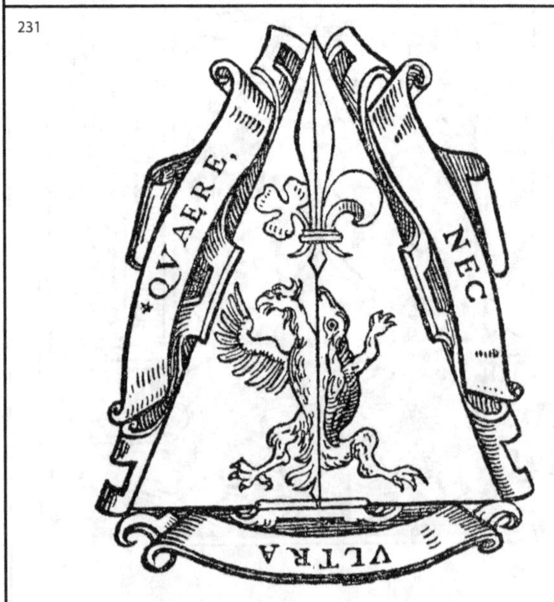

232

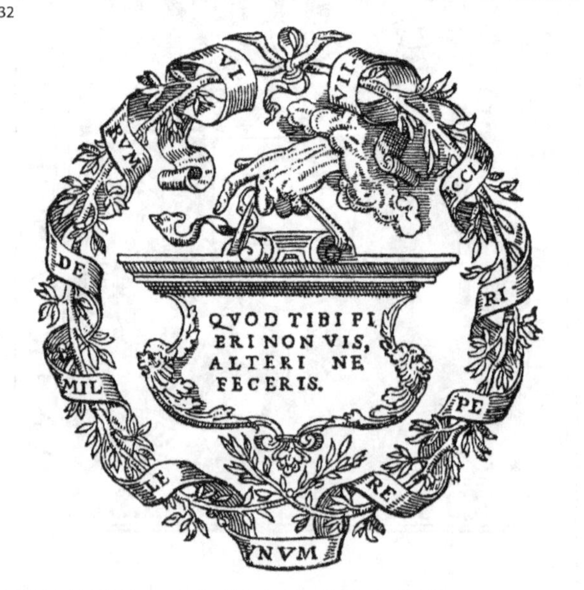

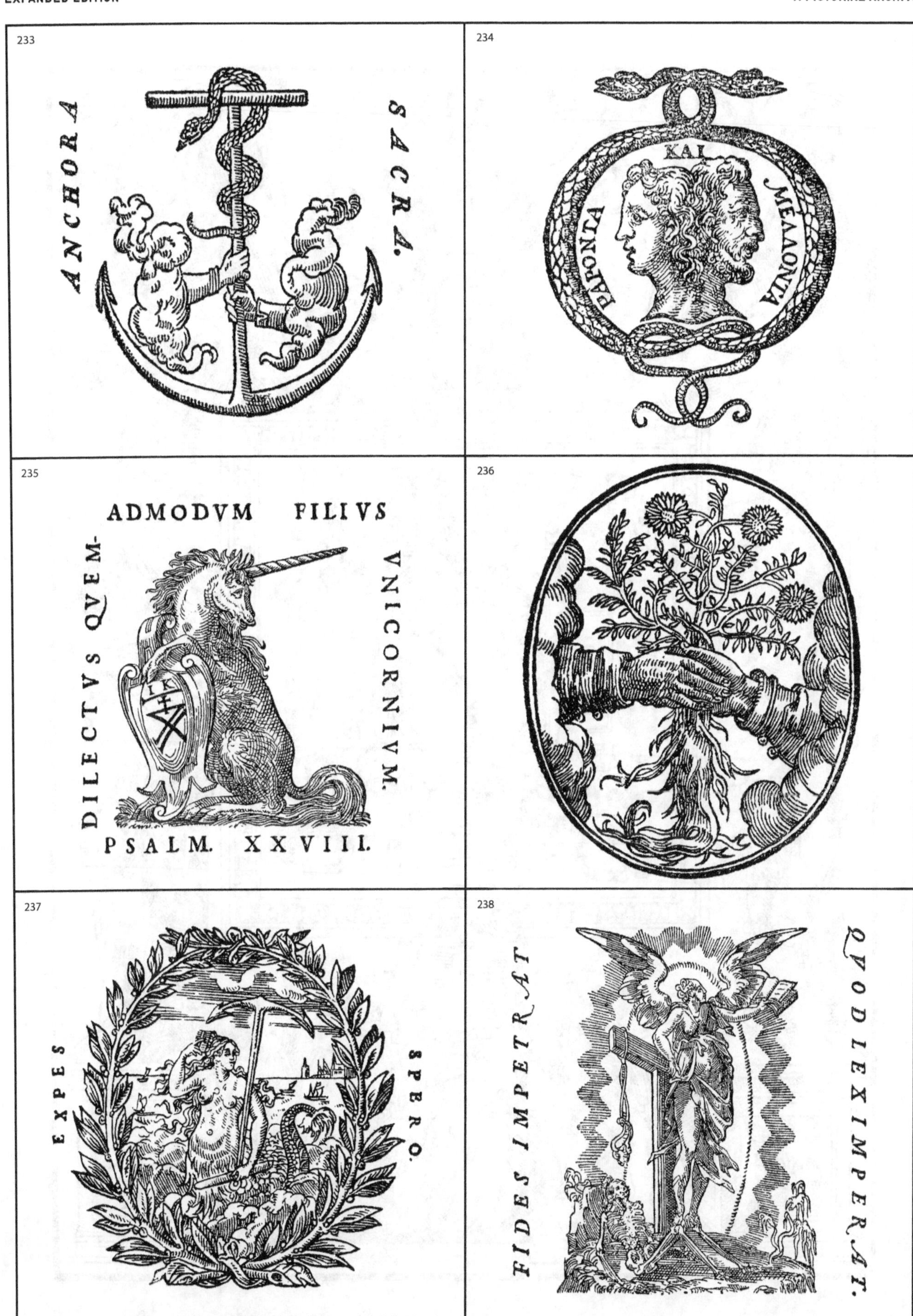
233
ANCHORA
SACRA.
234
PAΦONTA
KAI
MEΛΛONTA
235
ADMODVM FILIVS
DILECTVS QVEM-
VNICORNIVM.
PSALM. XXVIII.
236
237
EXPES
SPERO.
238
FIDES IMPETRAT
QVOD LEX IMPERAT.

239

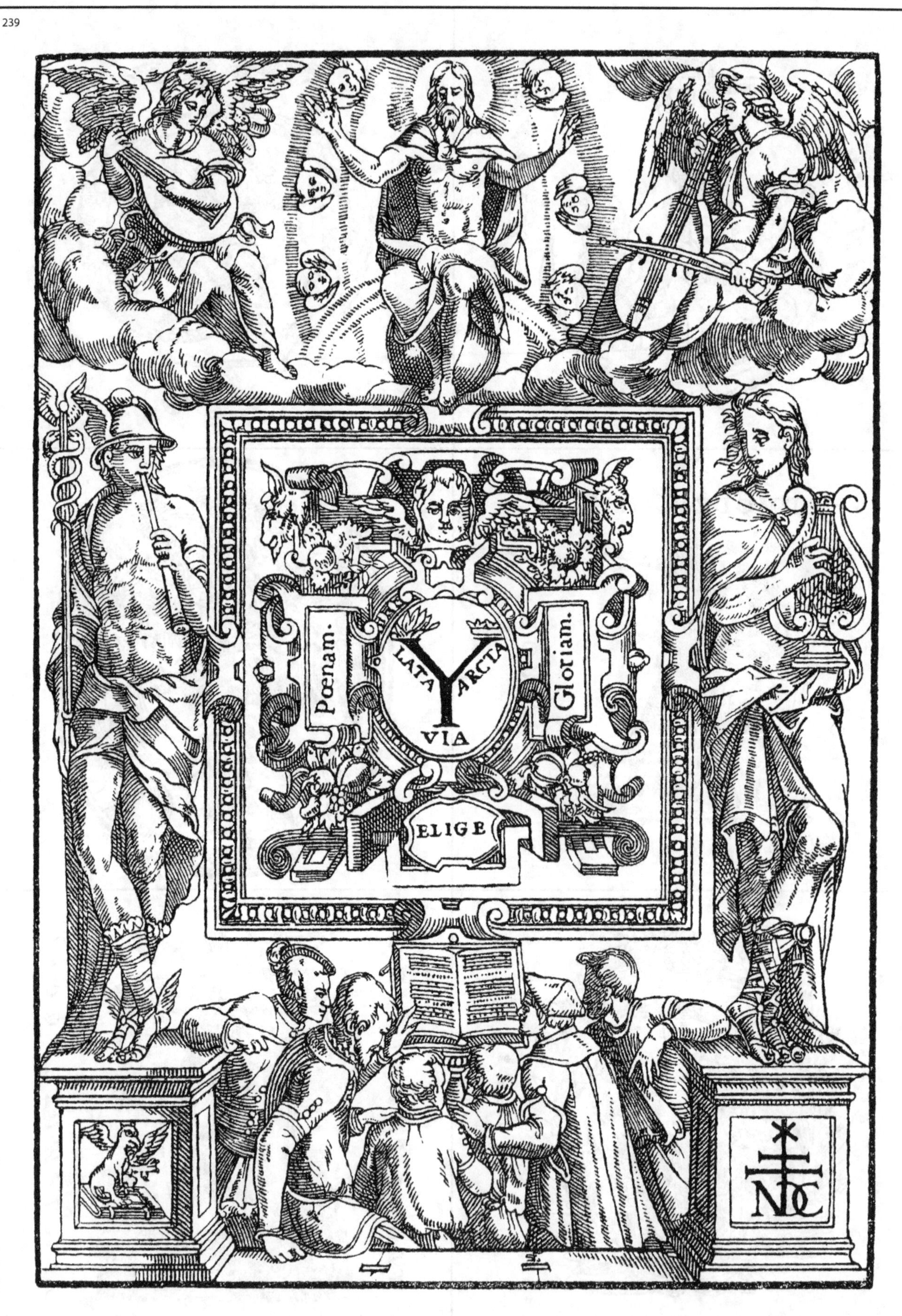

240

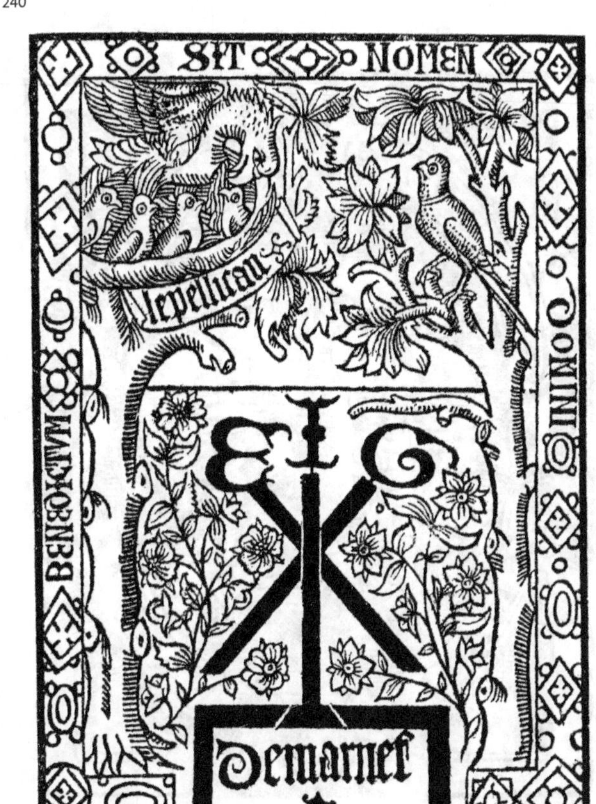

241

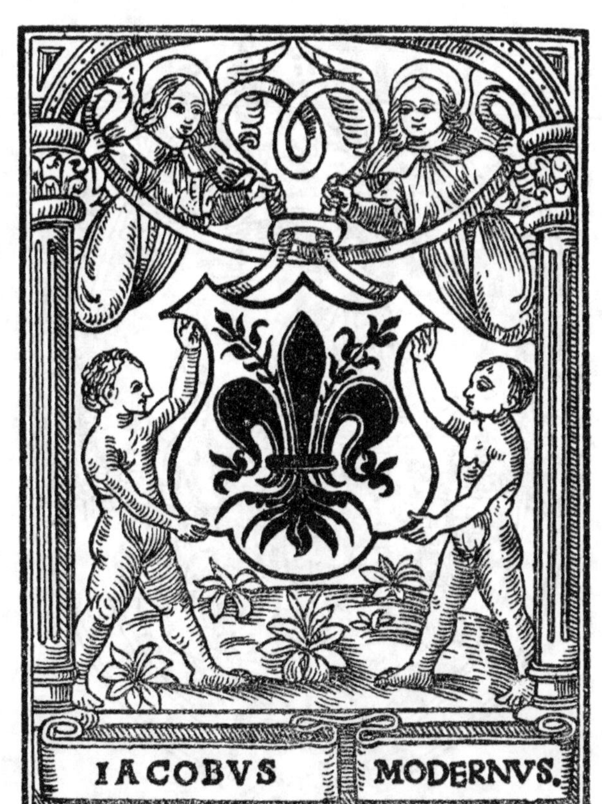

242

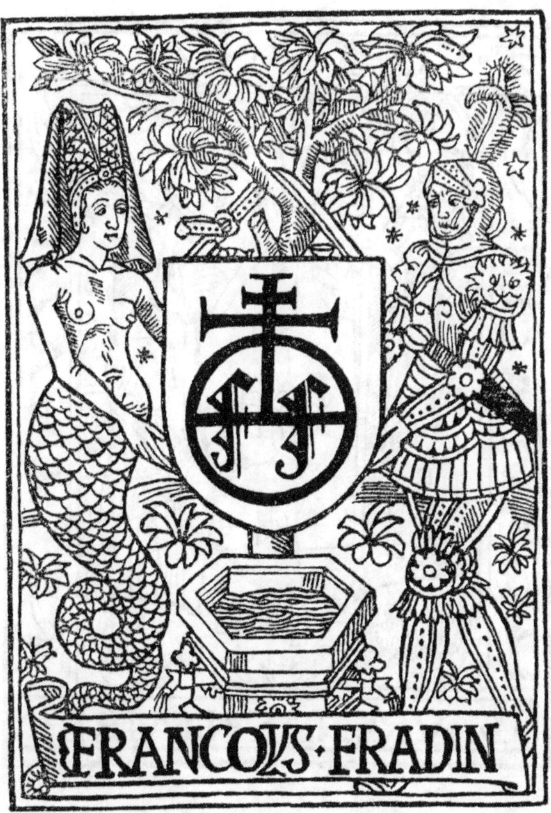

243

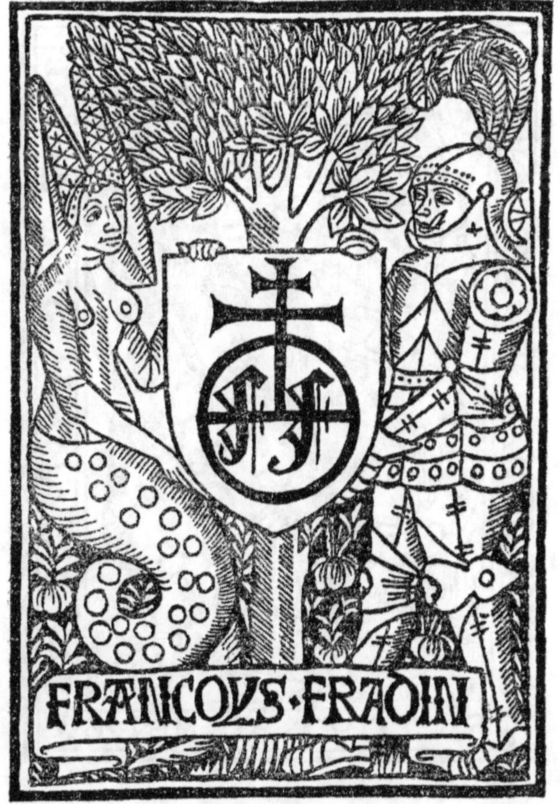

244

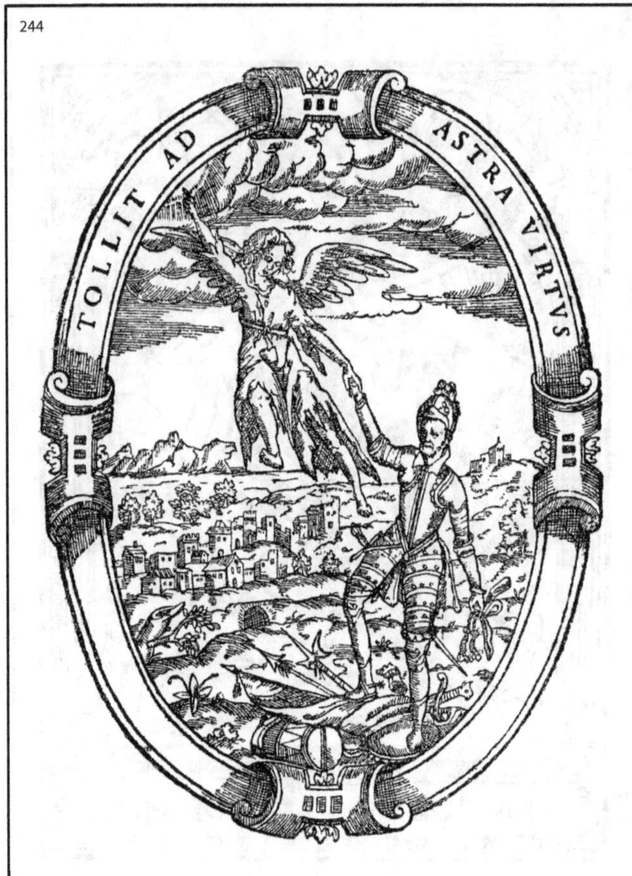

245

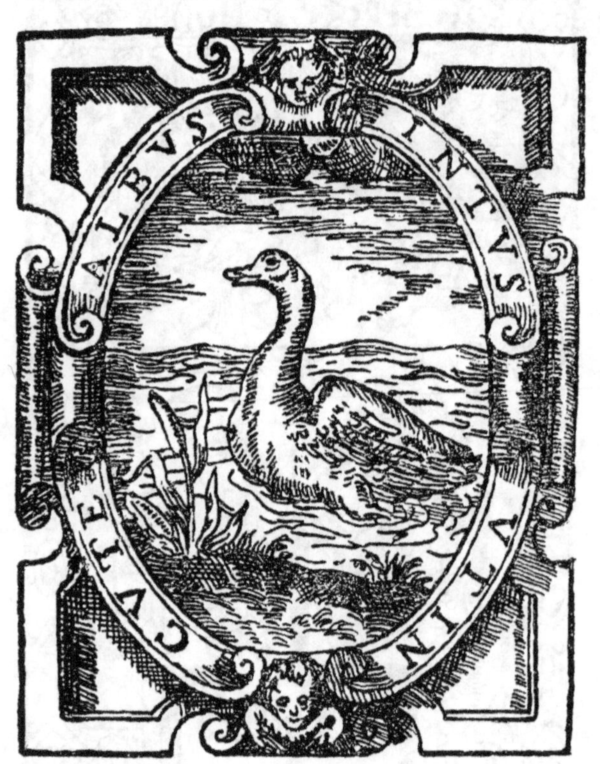

246

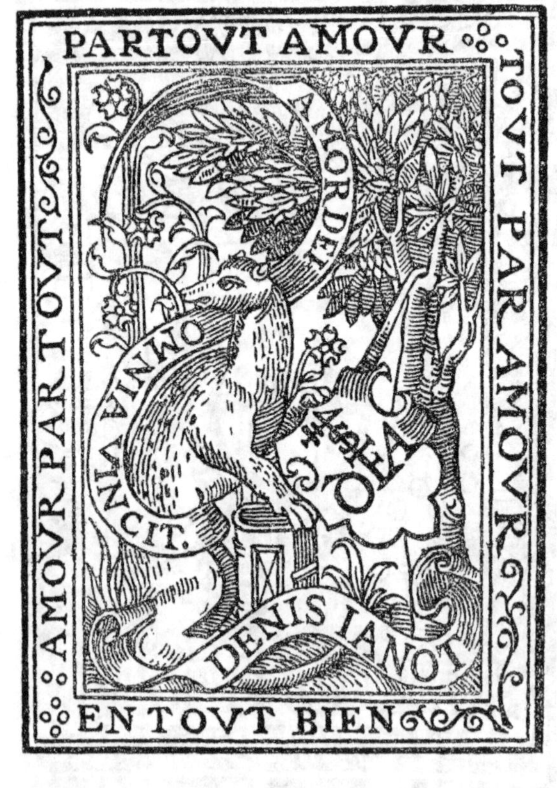

247

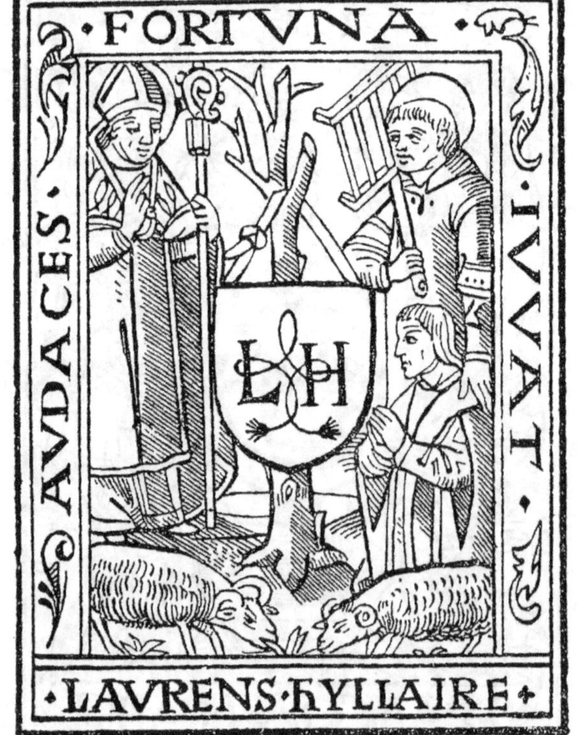

248

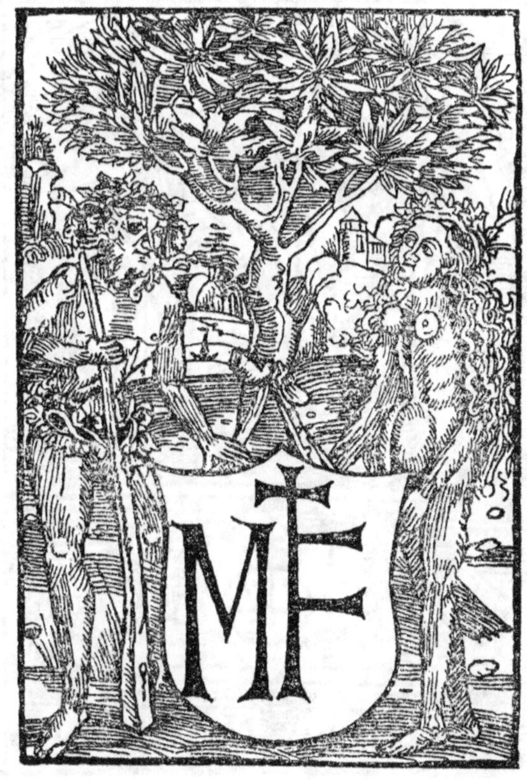

249

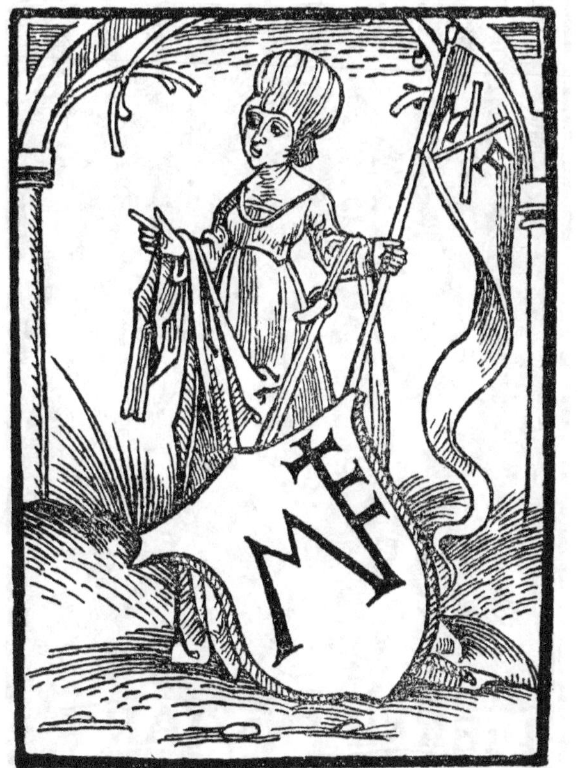

250

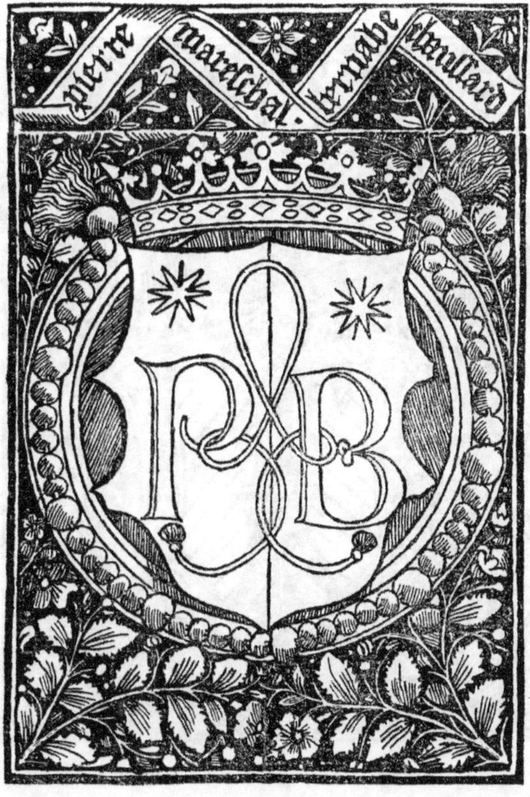

251

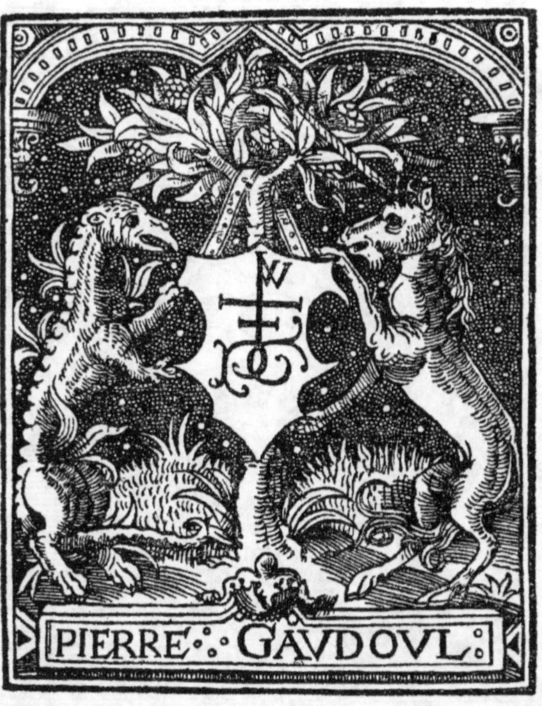

252

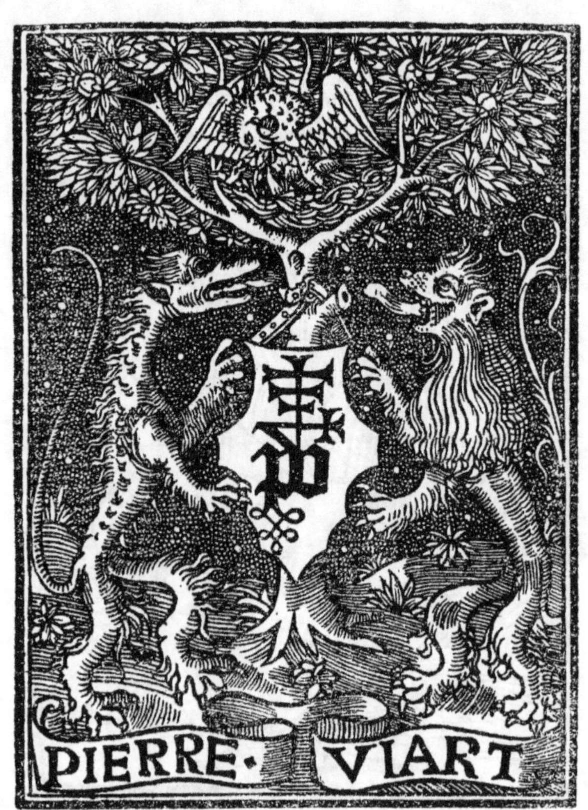

253

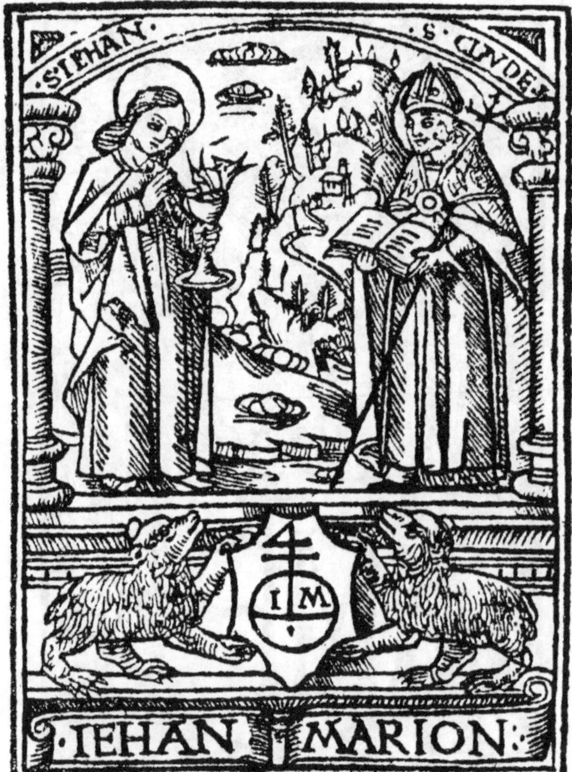

254

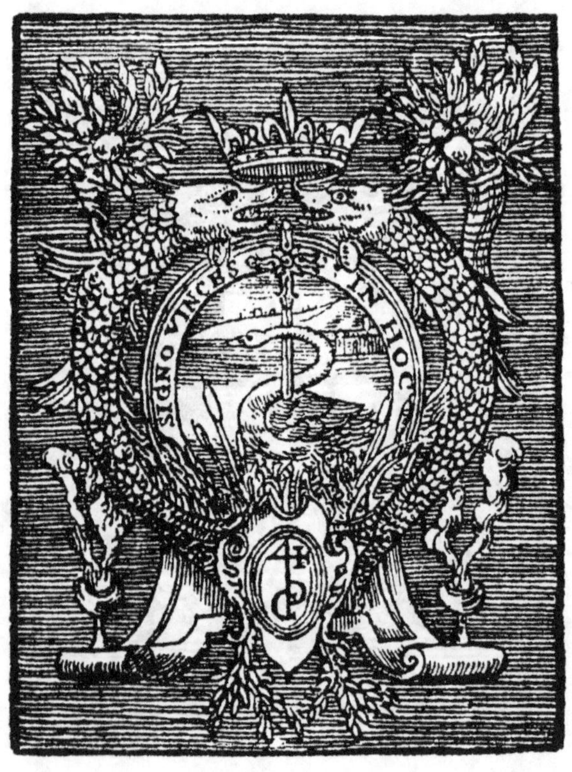

255

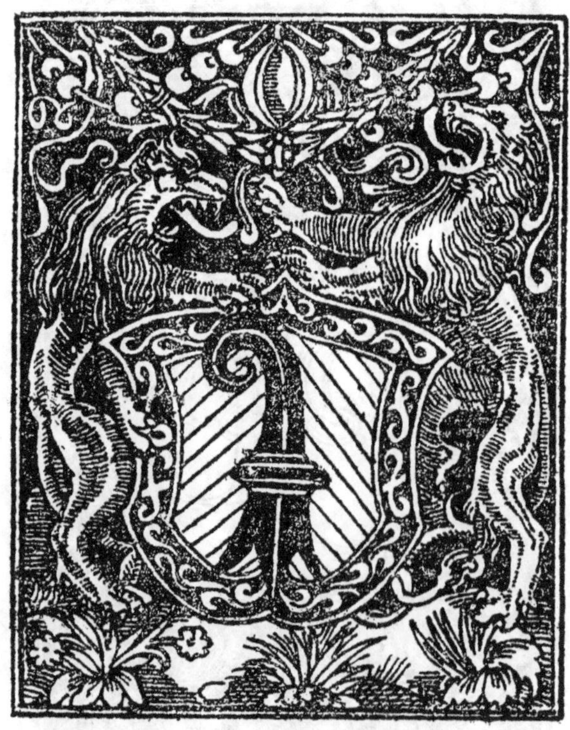

256

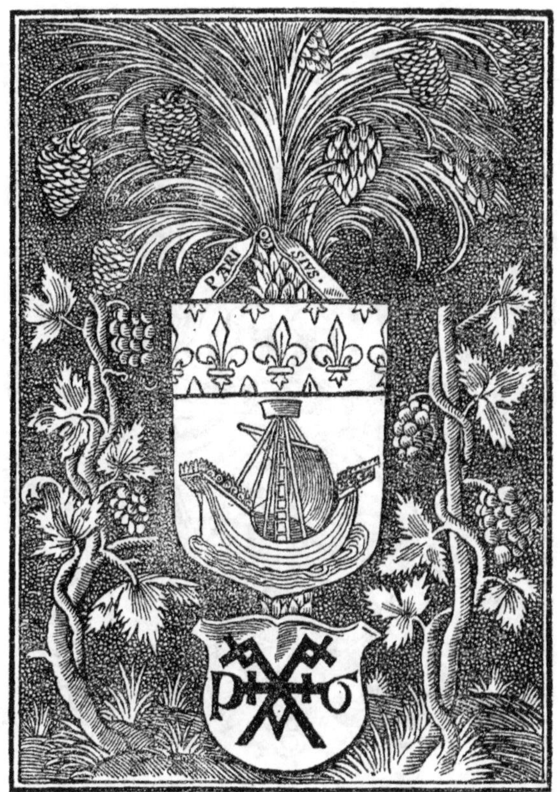

257

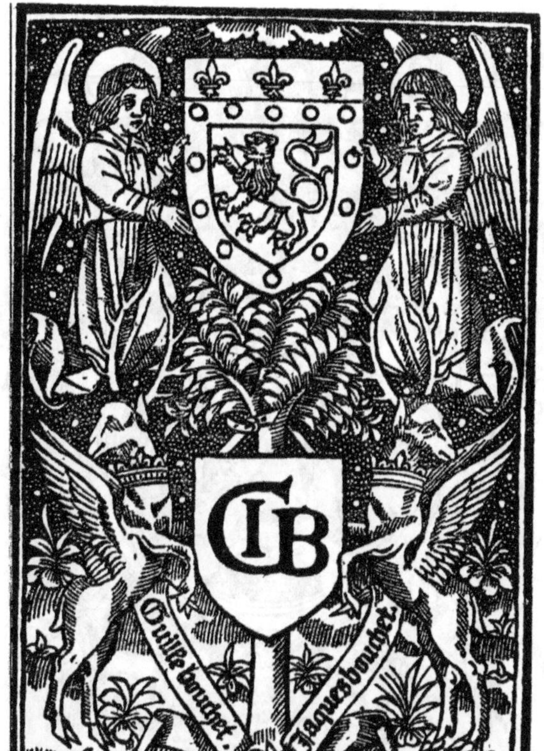

258

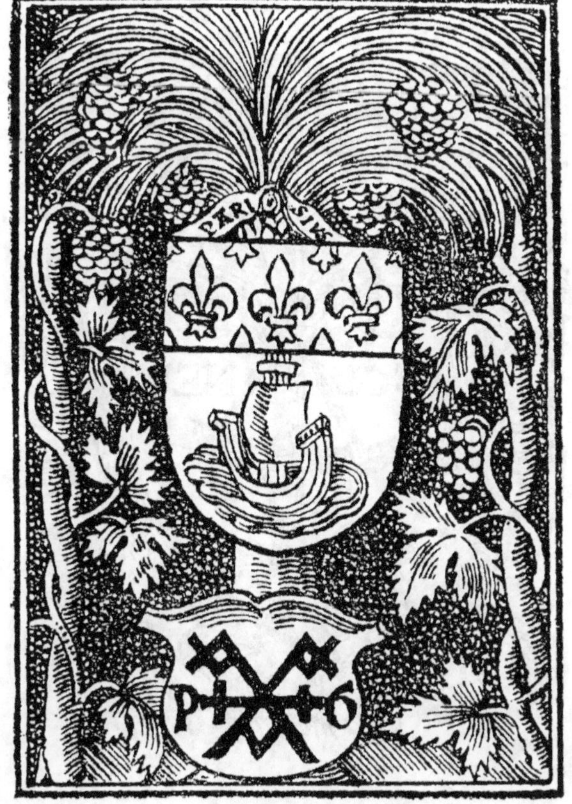

259

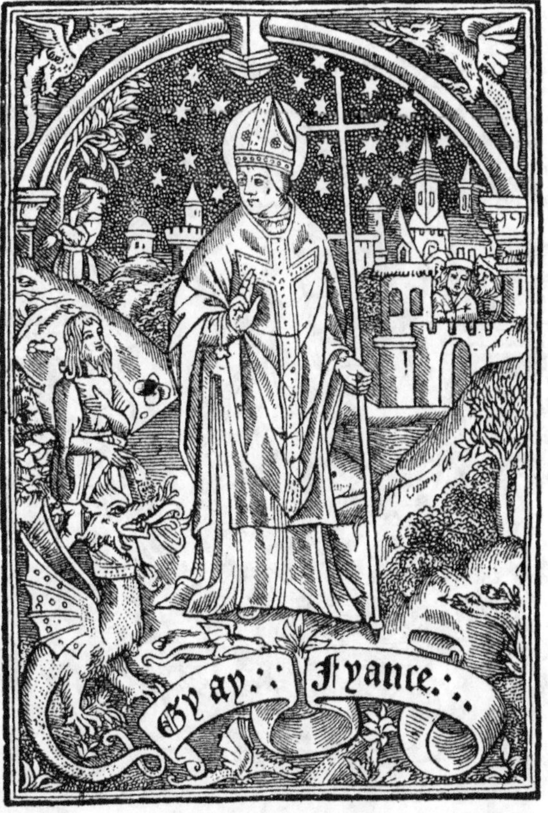

260

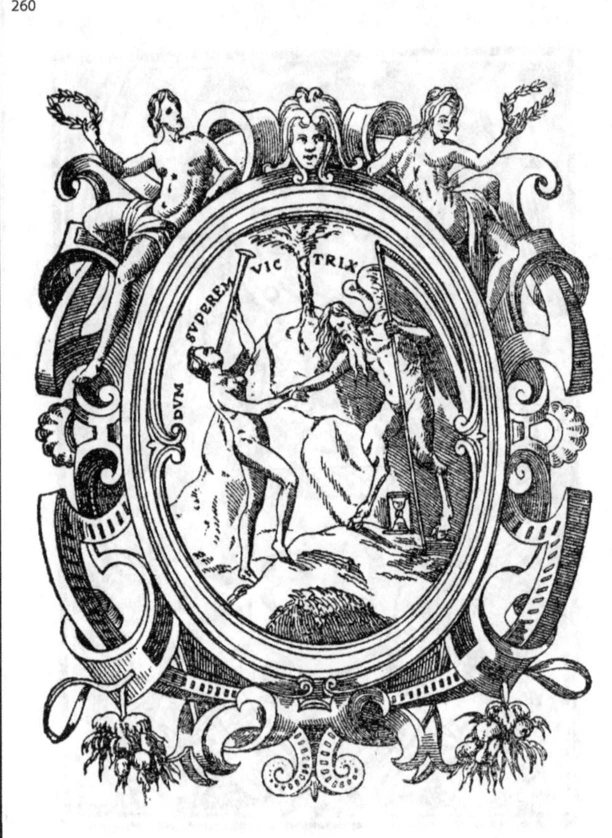

261

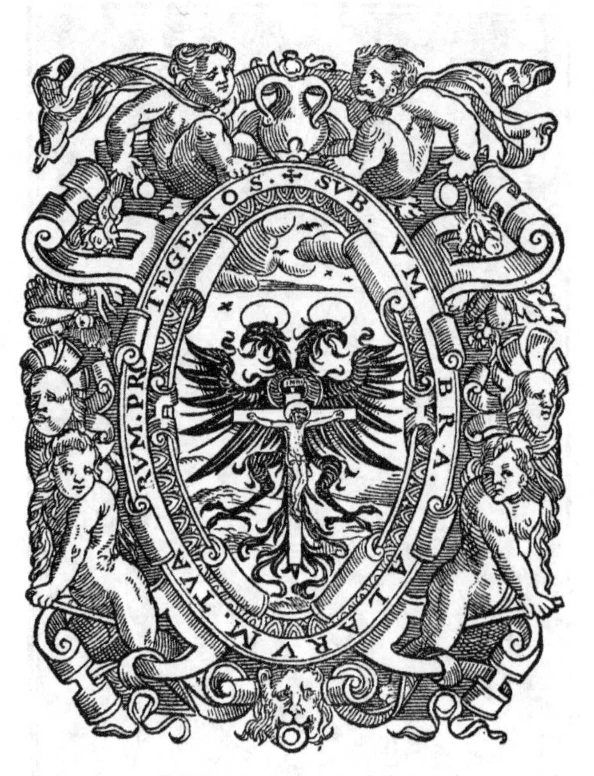

262

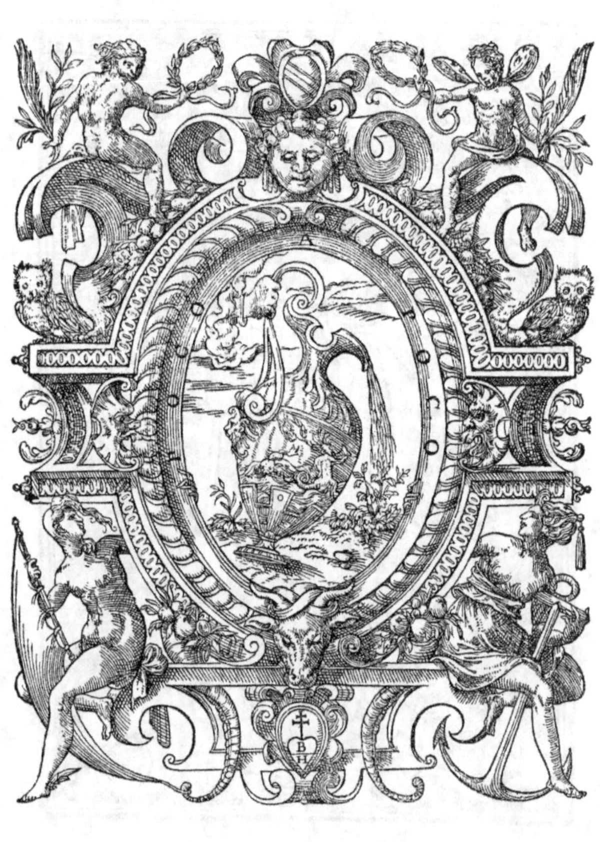

263

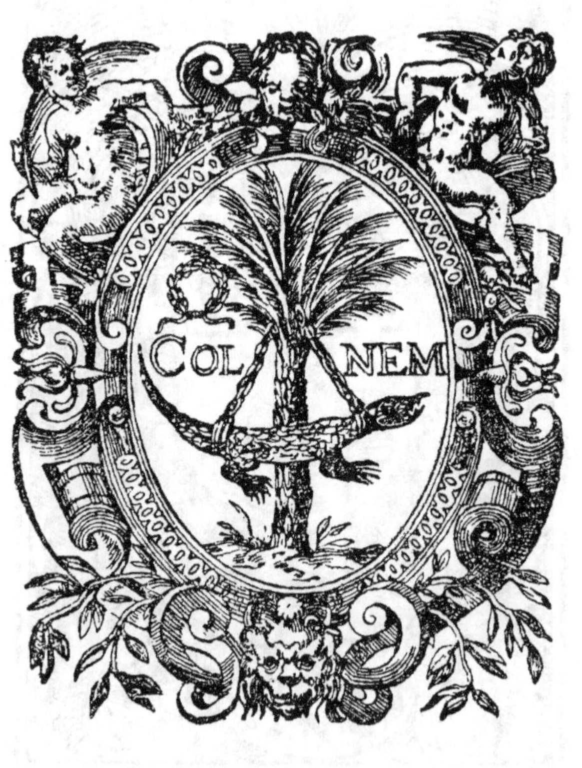

264

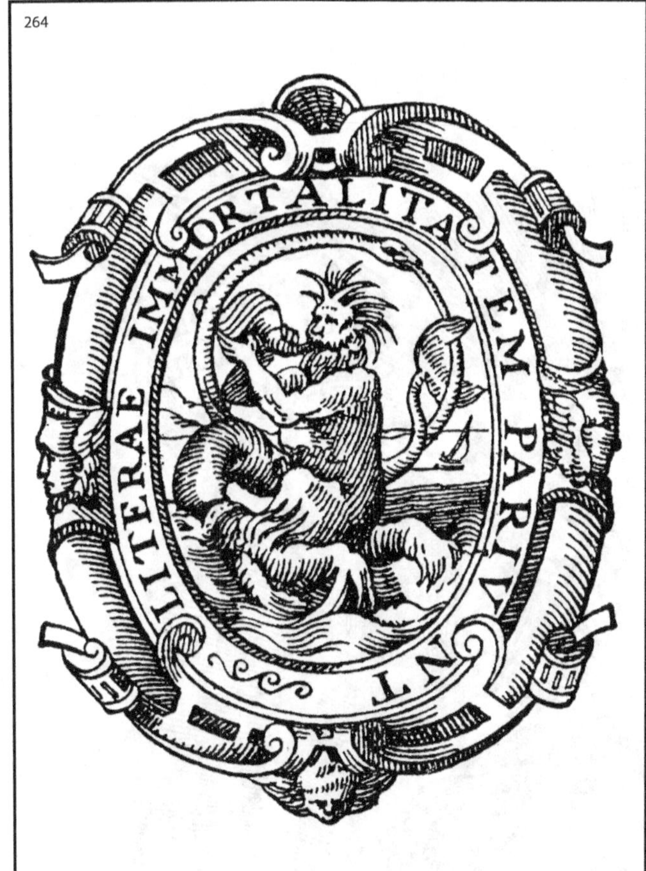

265

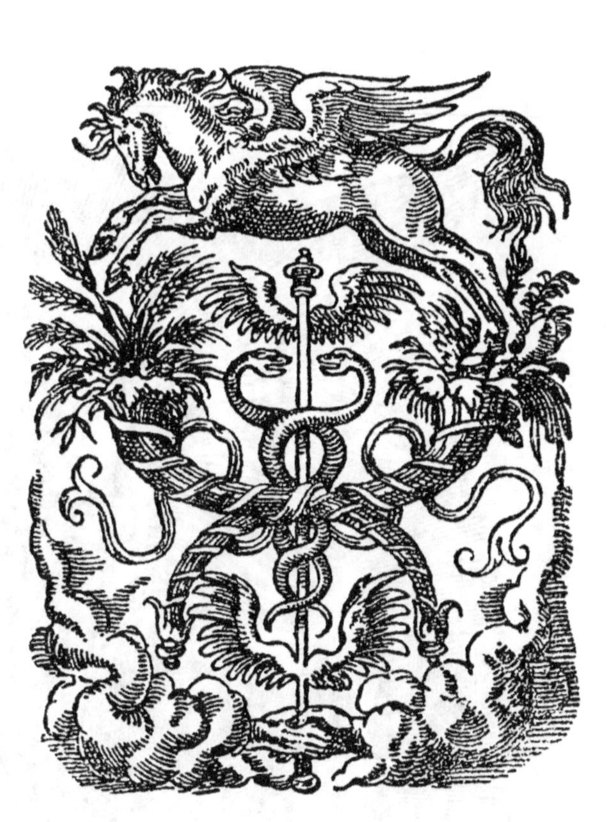

266

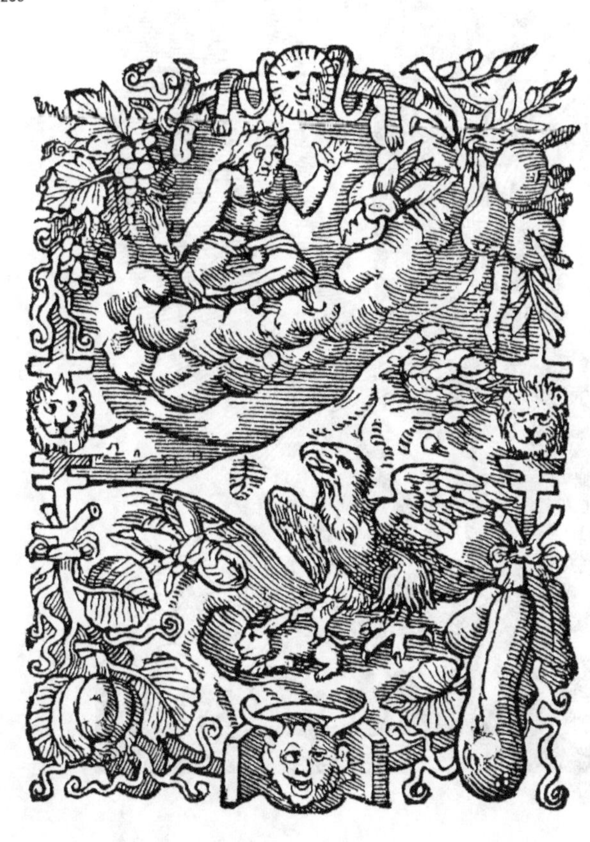

267

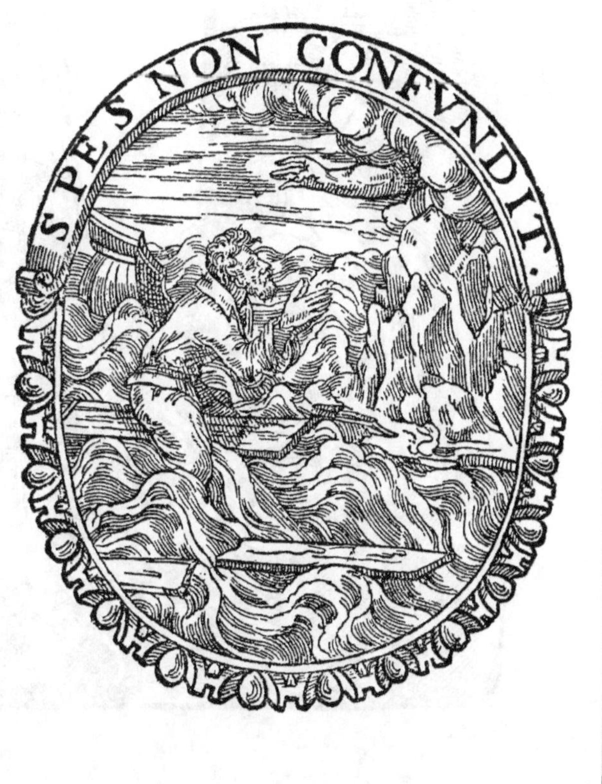

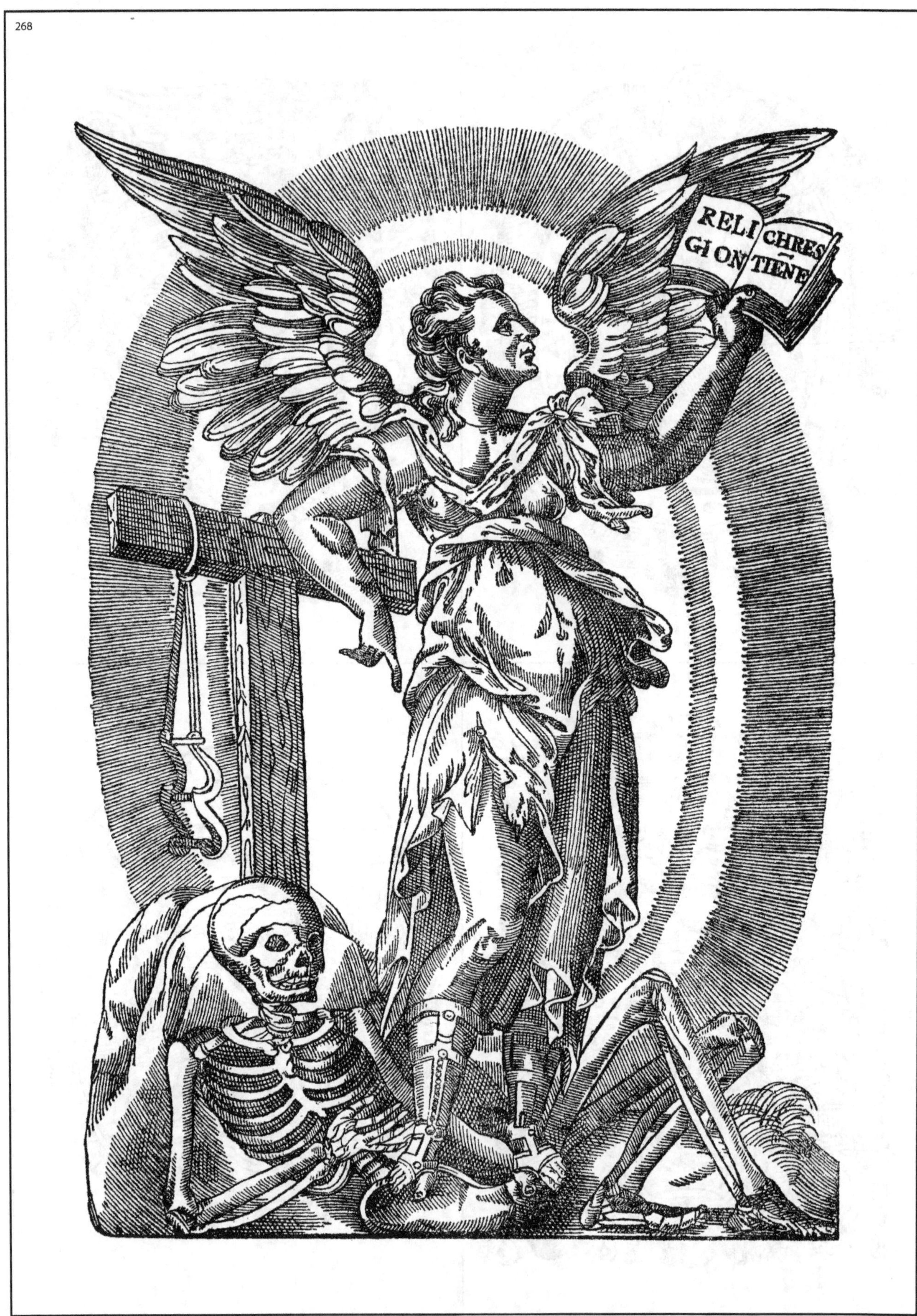

268
RELI CHRES
GI ON TIENE

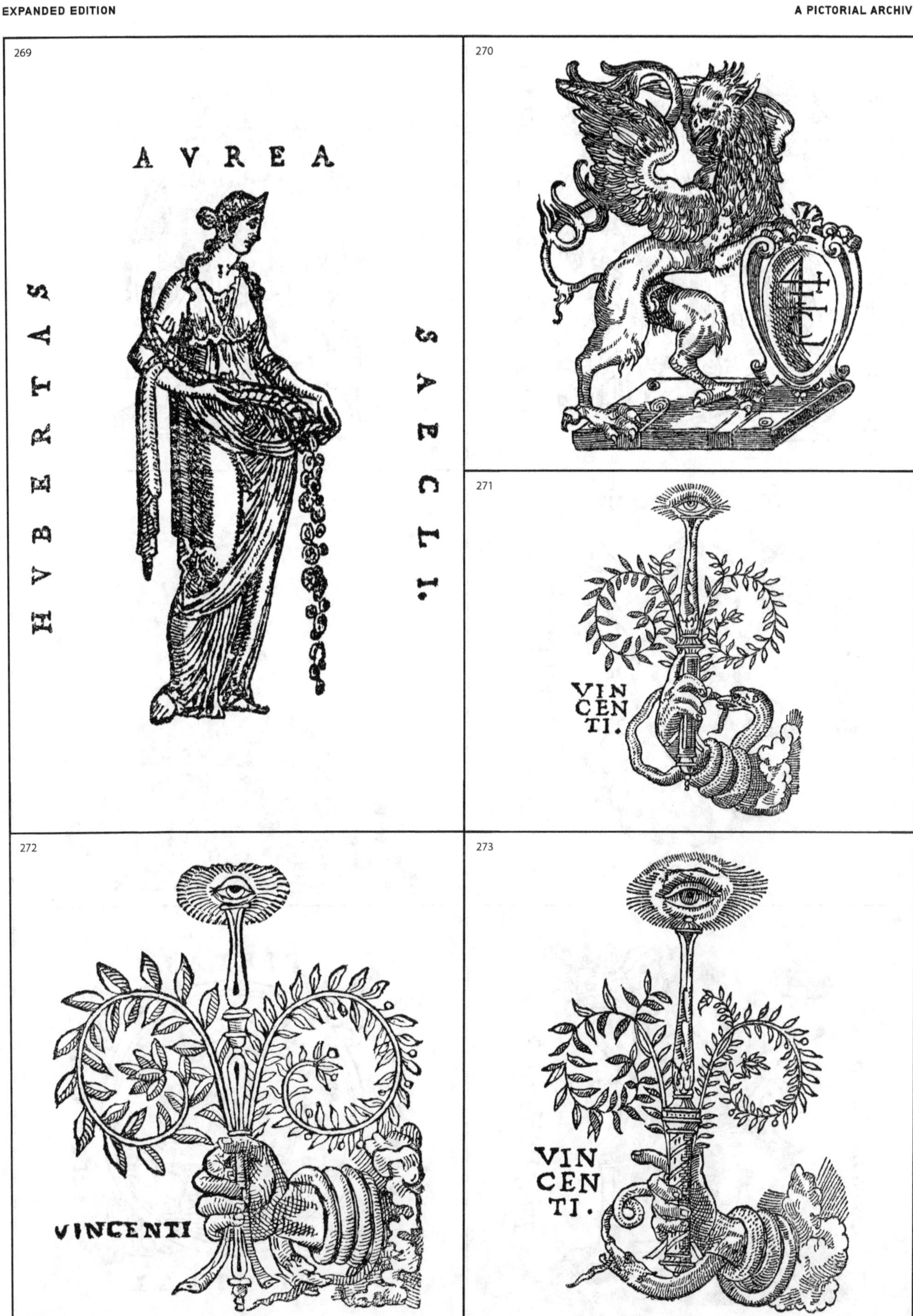

269
AVREA
HVBERTAS
SAECLI.
270
271
VIN
CEN
TI.
272
VINCENTI
273
VIN
CEN
TI.

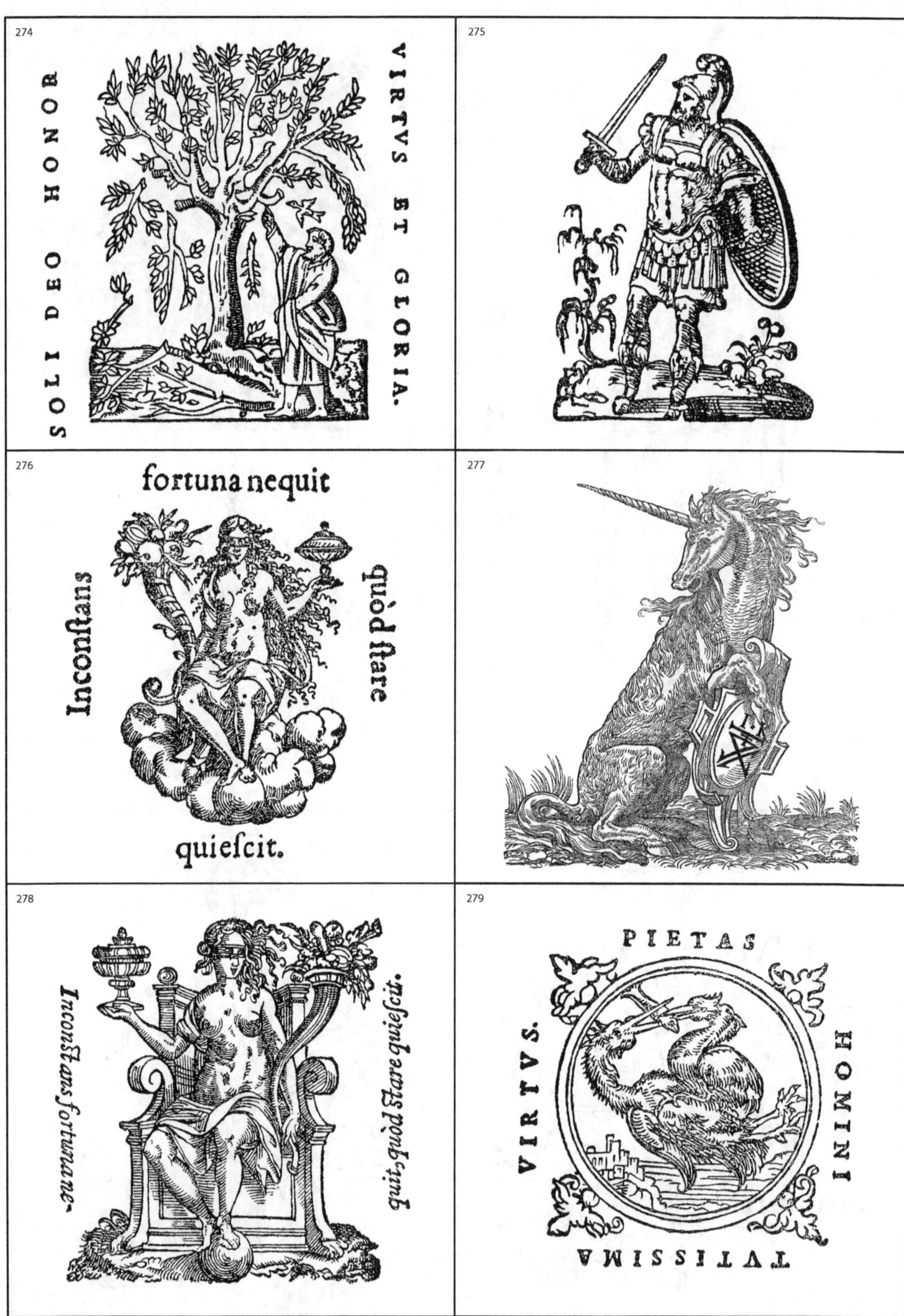
274
SOLI DEO HONOR
VIRTVS ET GLORIA.

275

276
fortuna nequit
Inconstans
quòd stare
quiescit.

277

278
Inconstans fortunae
quit quòd stare quiescit.

279
PIETAS
VIRTVS.
HOMINI
TVTISSIMA

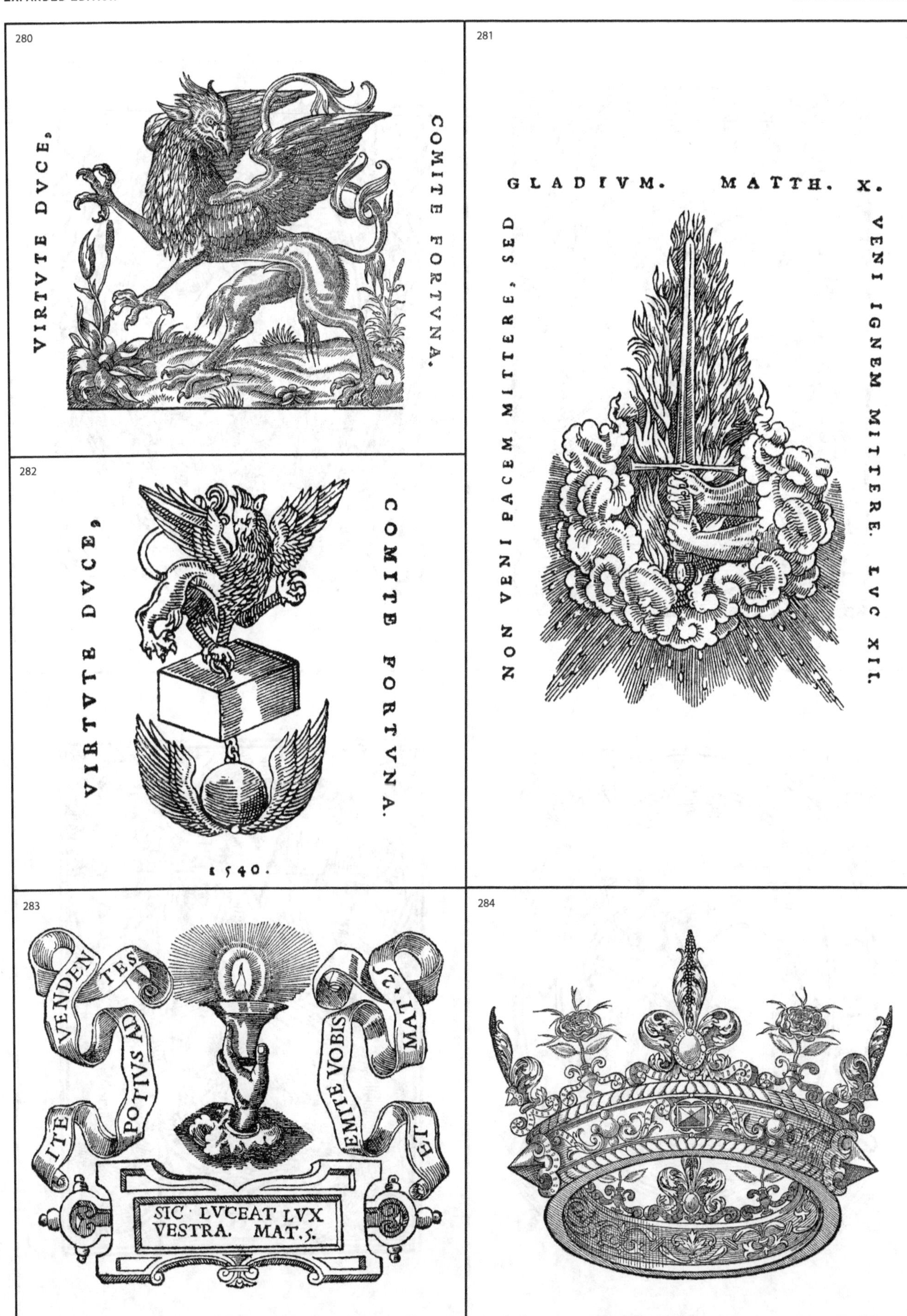

280
VIRTVTE DVCE,
COMITE FORTVNA.

282
VIRTVTE DVCE,
COMITE FORTVNA.
1540.

281
GLADIVM.   MATTH. X.
NON VENI PACEM MITTERE, SED
VENI IGNEM MITTERE. LVC XII.

283
VENDEN TES
ITE POTIVS AD
EMITE VOBIS
ET
MAT·25·
SIC · LVCEAT LVX
VESTRA.   MAT·5·

284

285

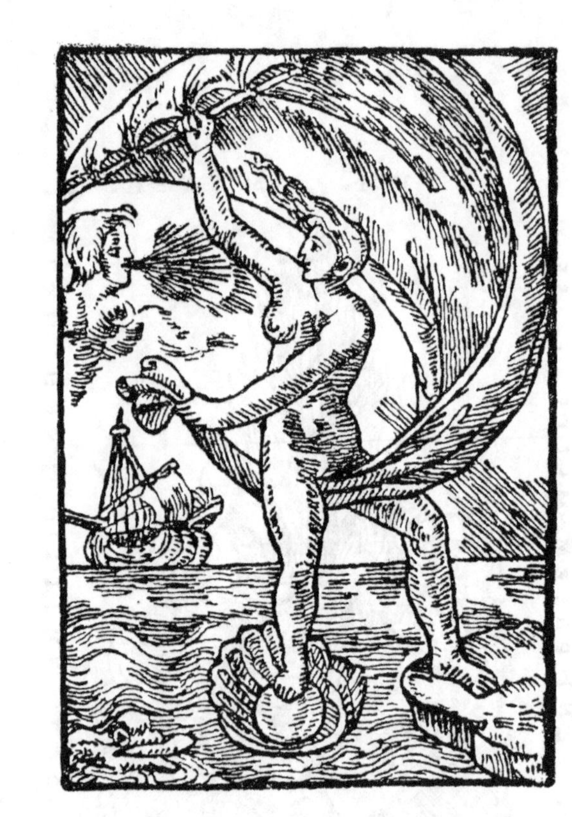

286

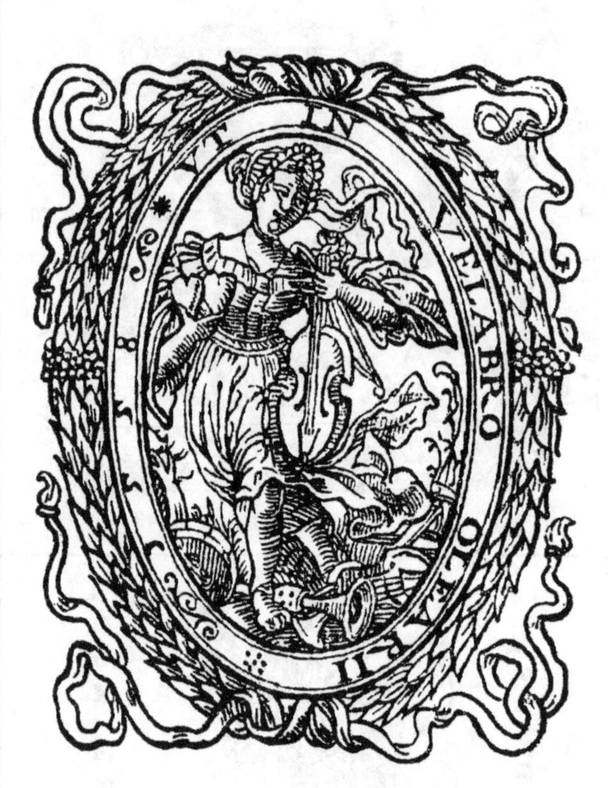

287

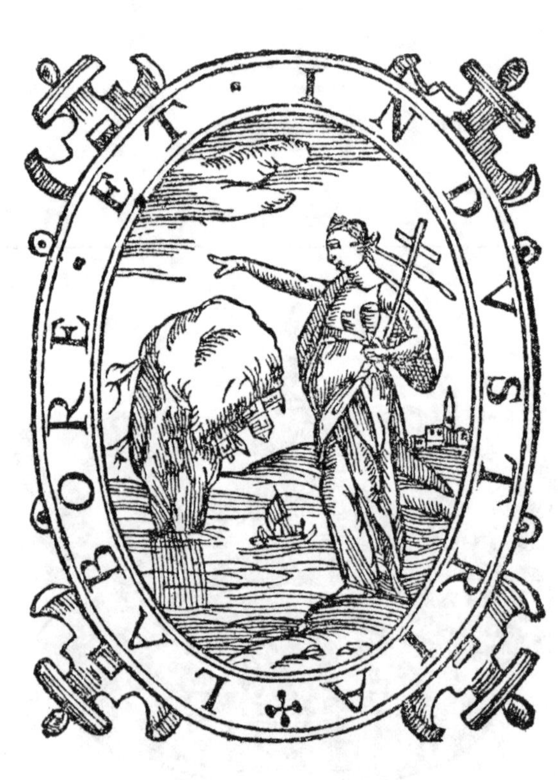

288

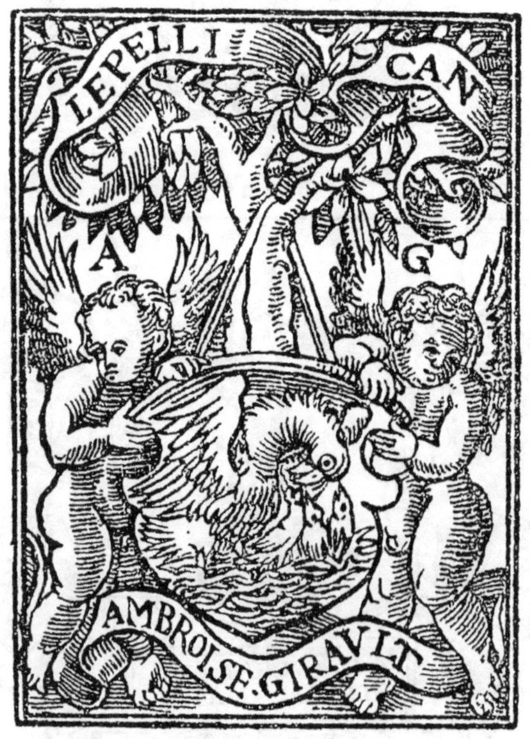

289

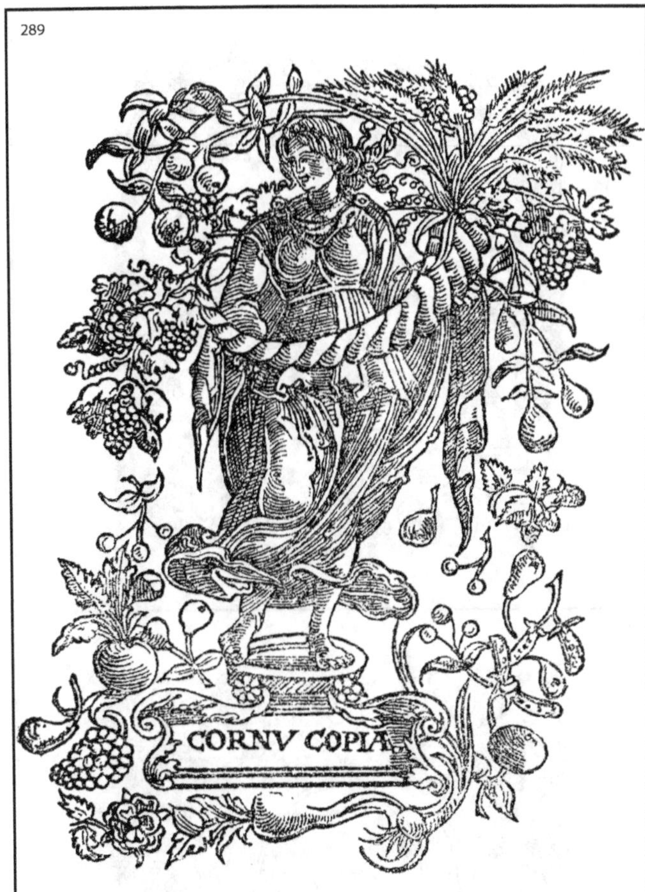

290

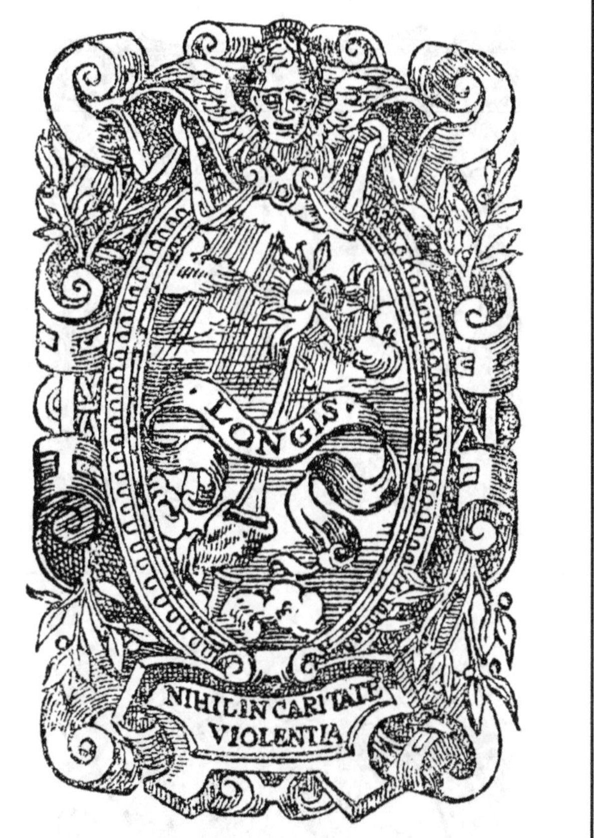

291

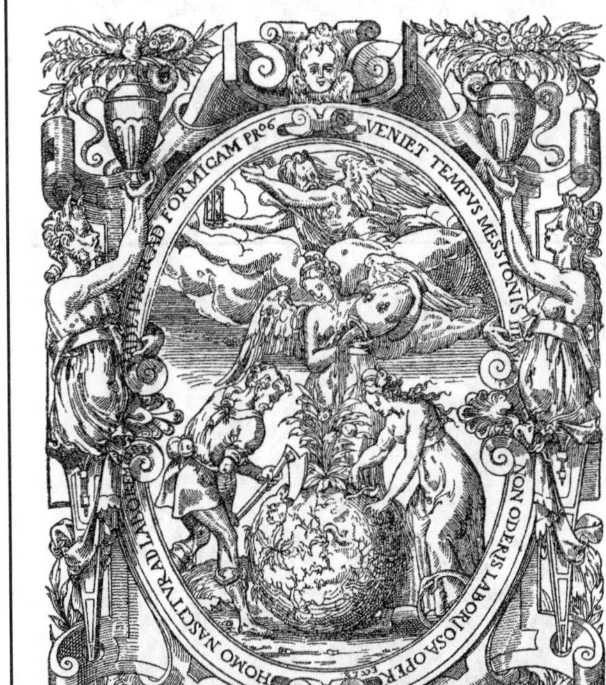

292

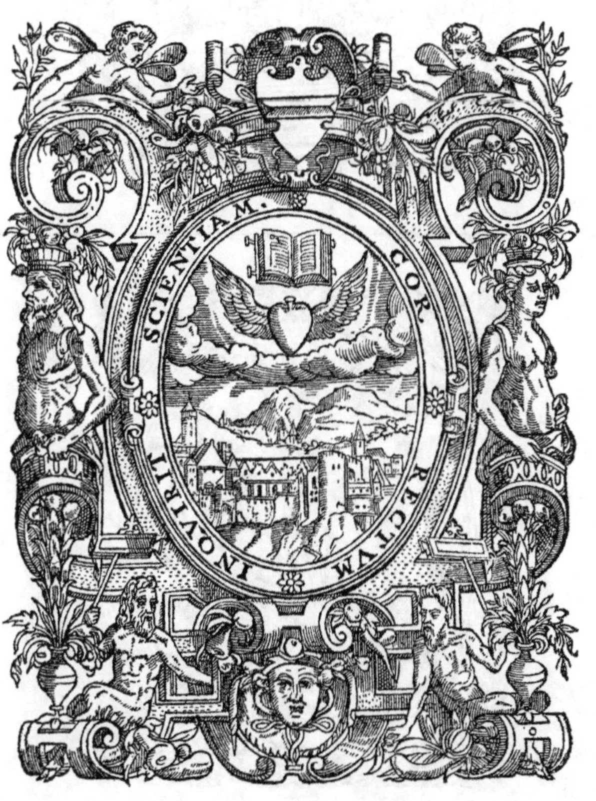

293

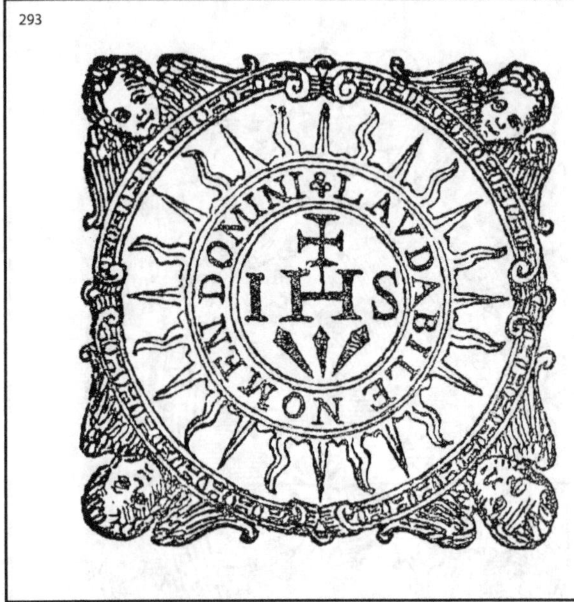

294

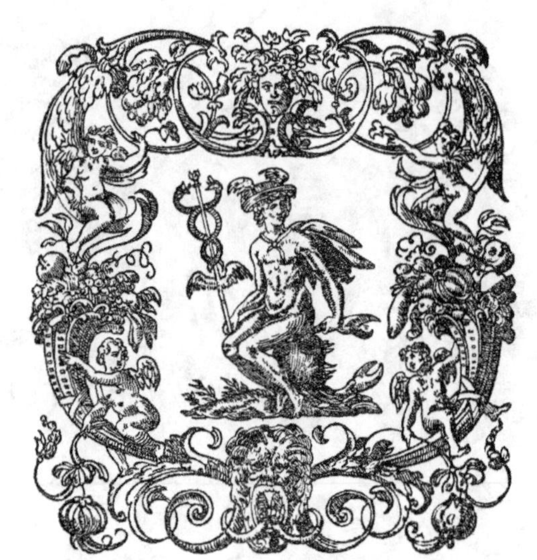

295

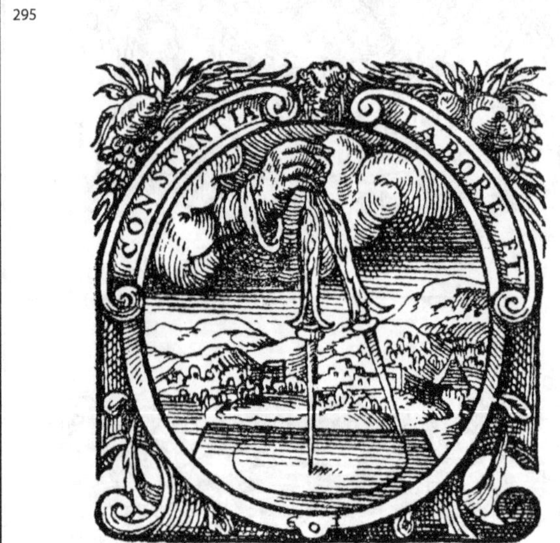

296

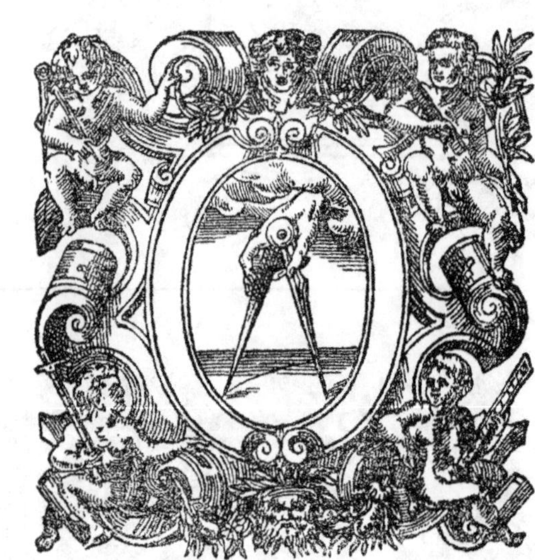

297

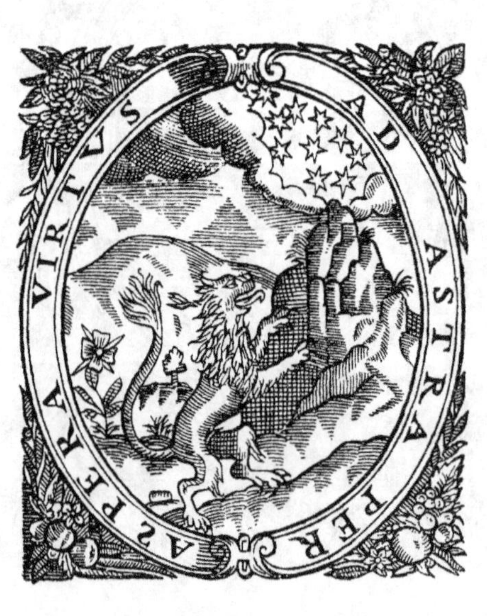

298

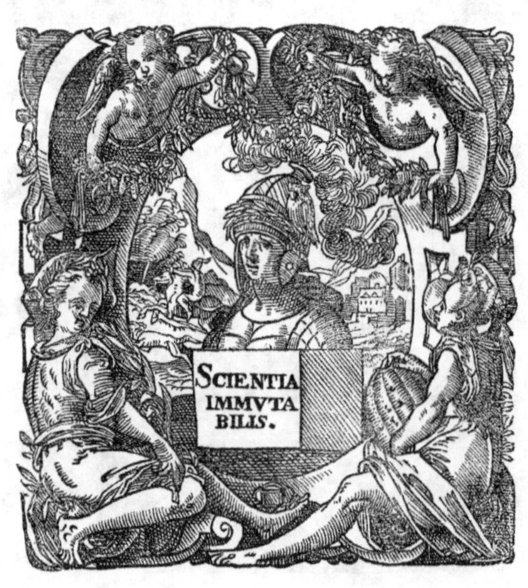

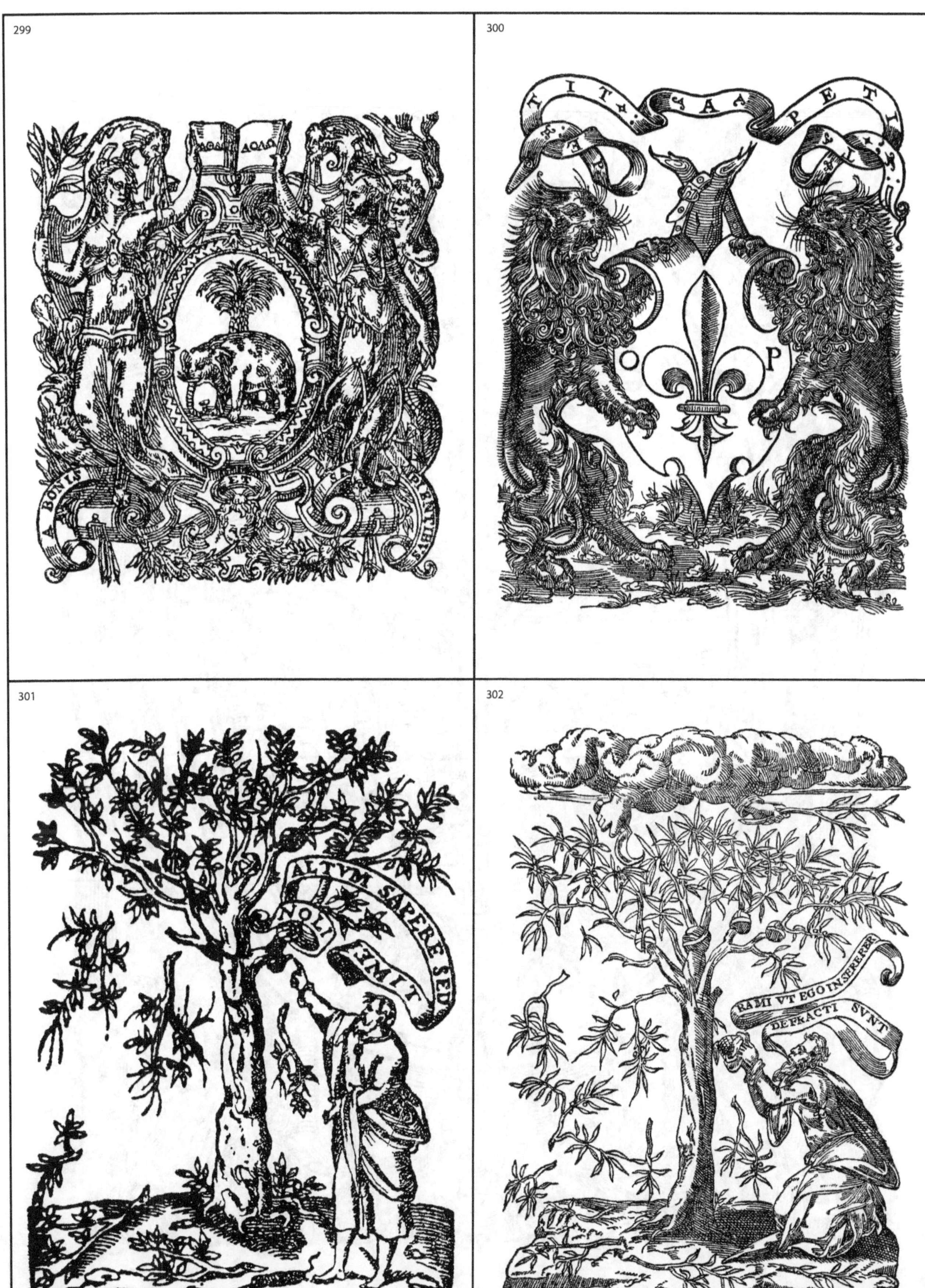

303

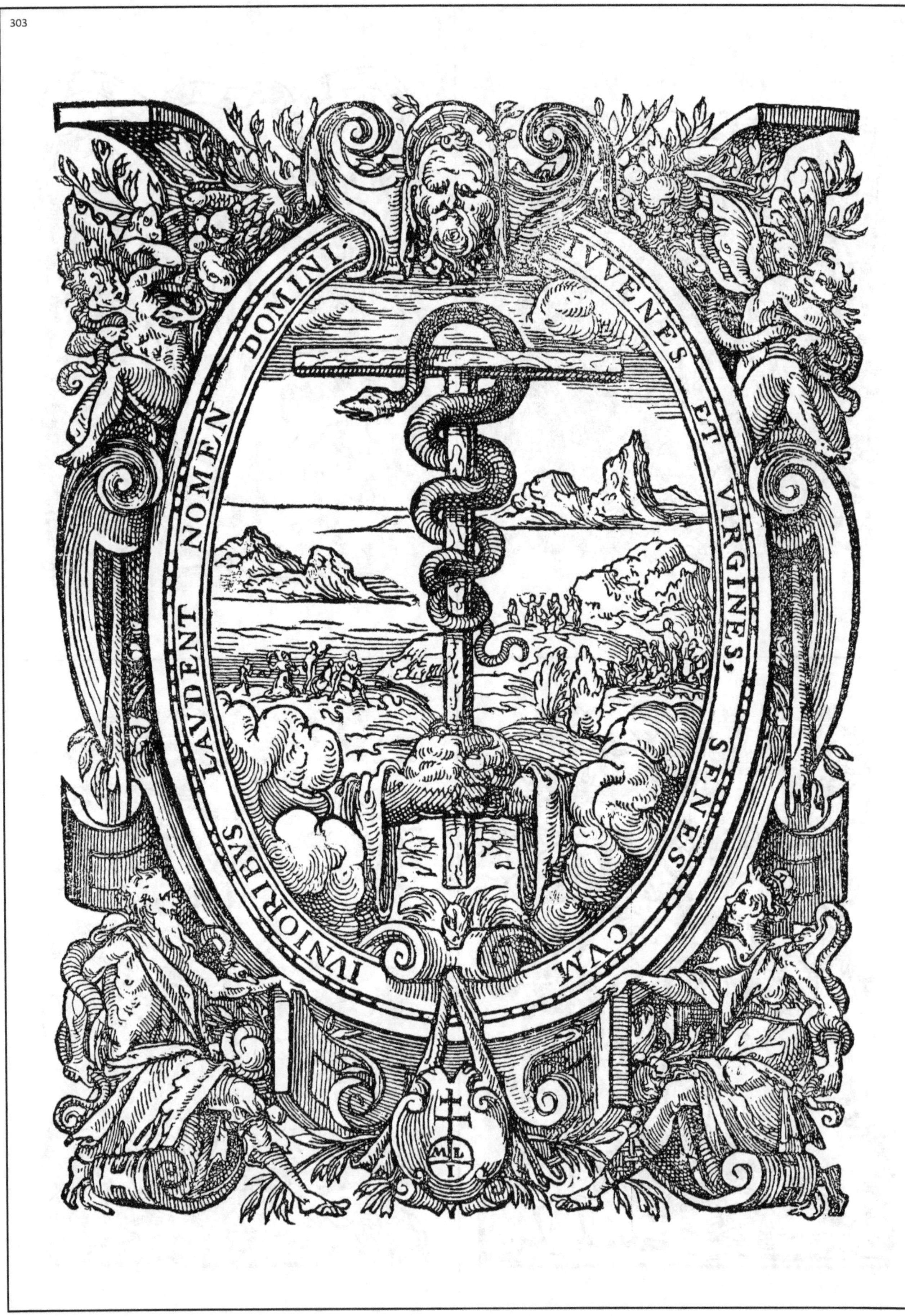
LAVDENT NOMEN DOMINI.
IVVENES ET VIRGINES, SENES CVM IVNIORIBVS

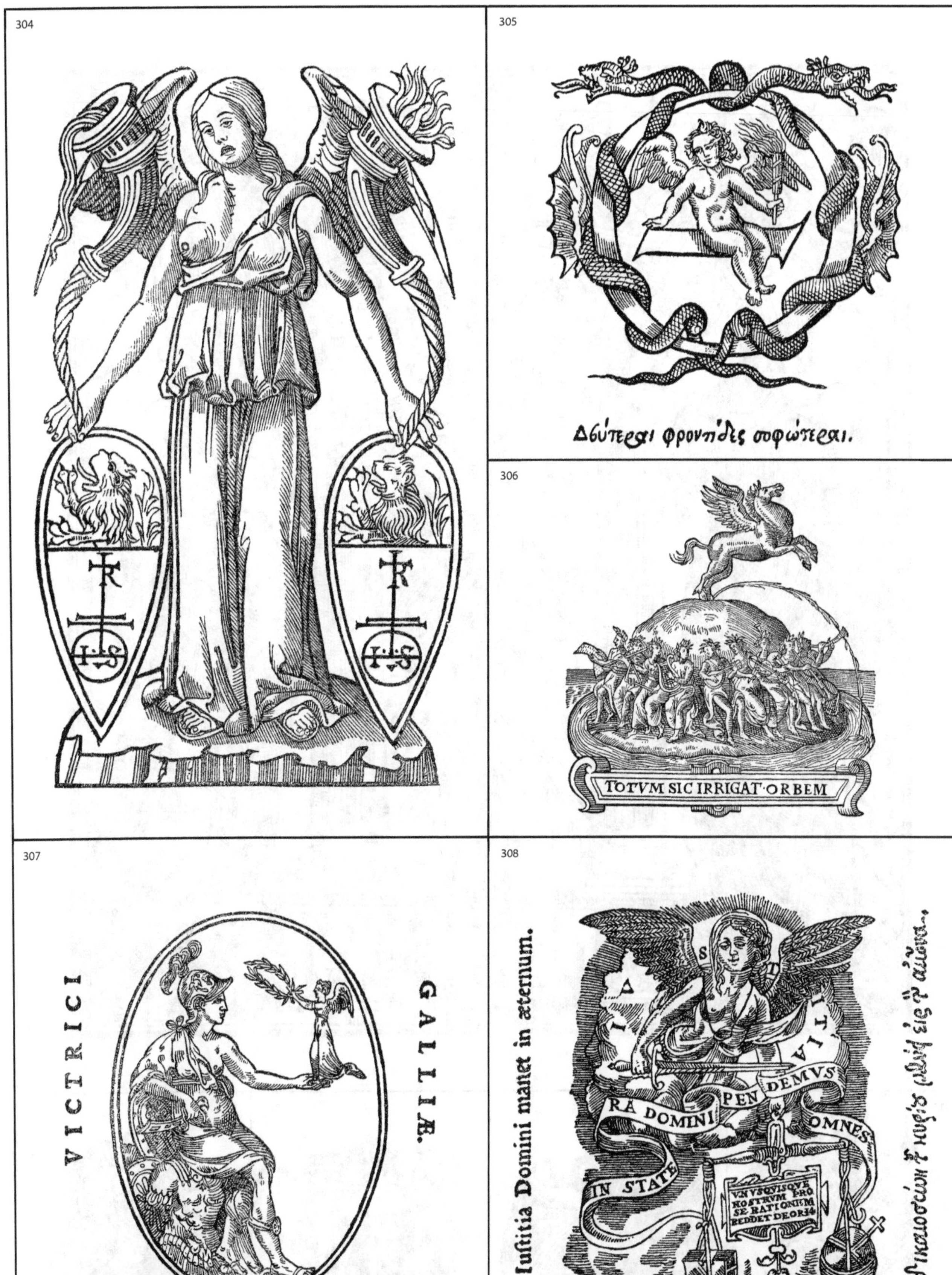
304

305

Δεύτεραι φροντίδες σοφώτεραι.

306

TOTVM SIC IRRIGAT·ORBEM

307

VICTRICI

GALLIÆ.

308

Iuſtitia Domini manet in æternum.

IA S
VLTI
TIA
PEN DEMVS
RA DOMINI
OMNES
IN STATE
VNVSQVISQVE
NOSTRVM PRO
SE RATIONEM
REDDET DEORV

309

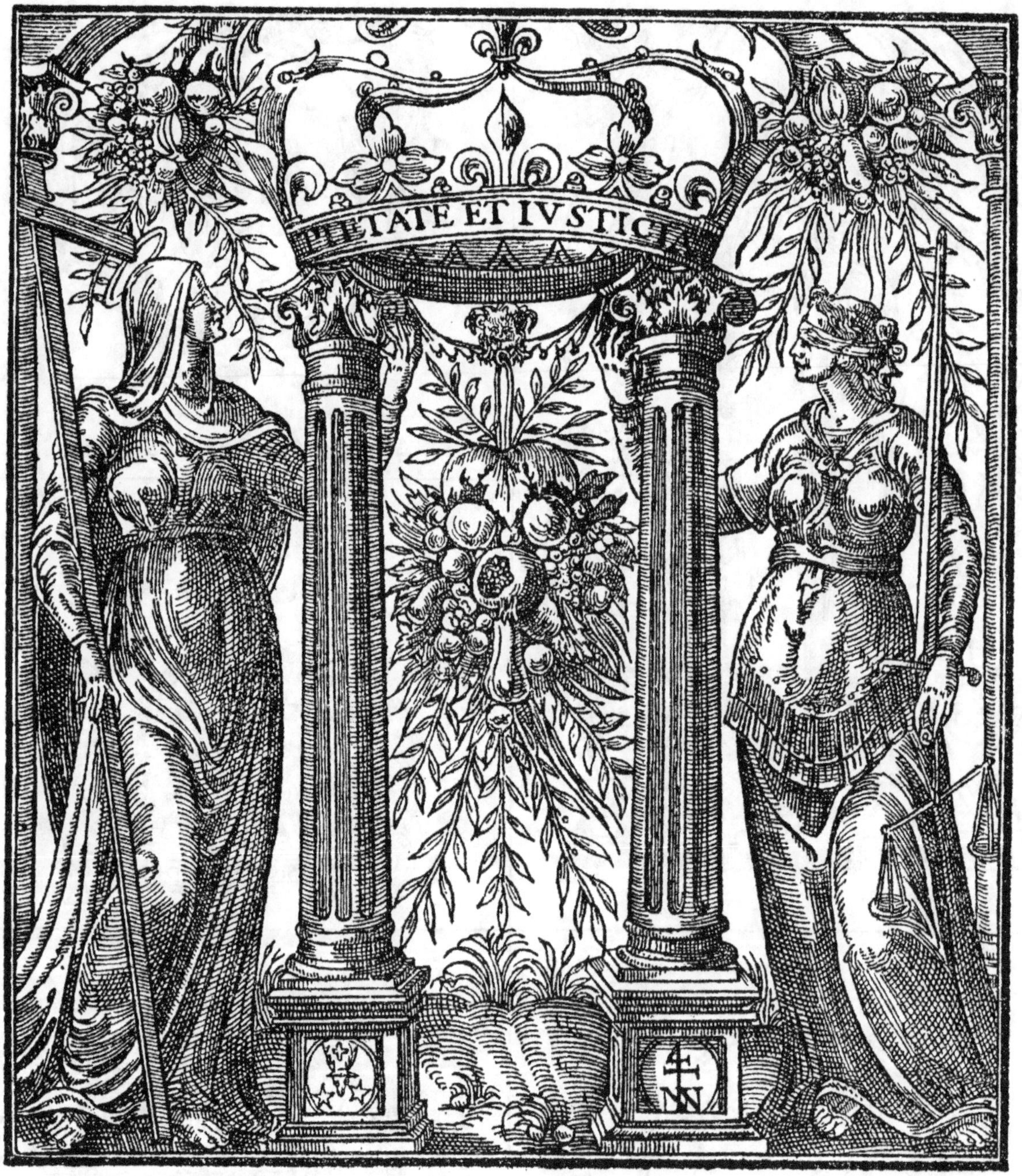

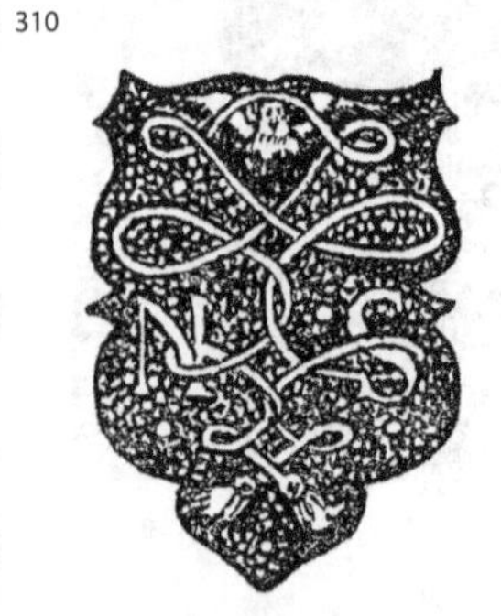

310

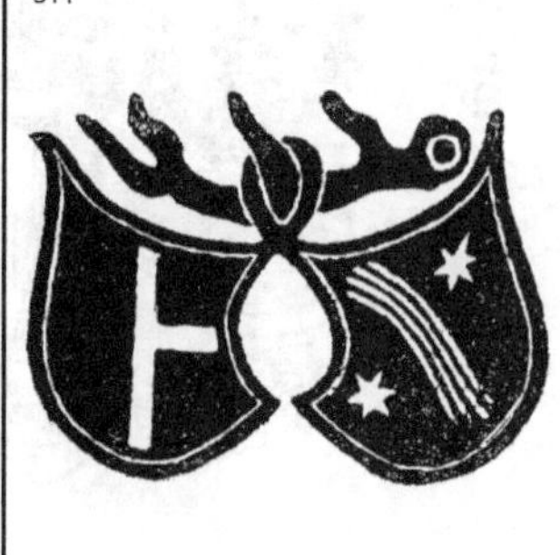

311

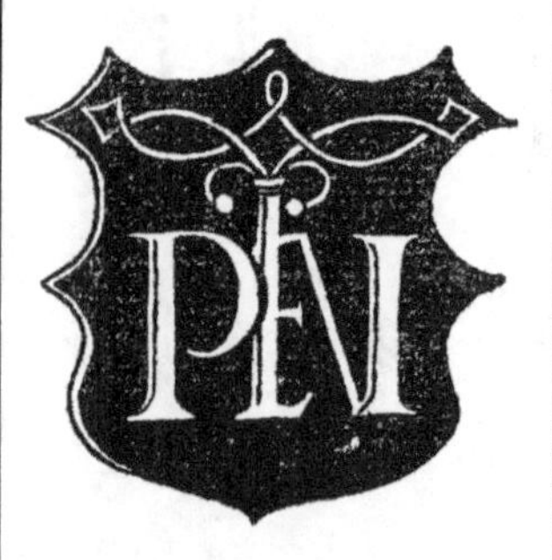

312

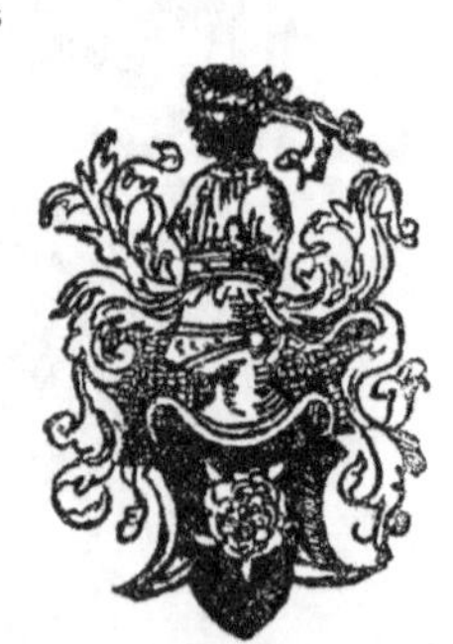

313

314

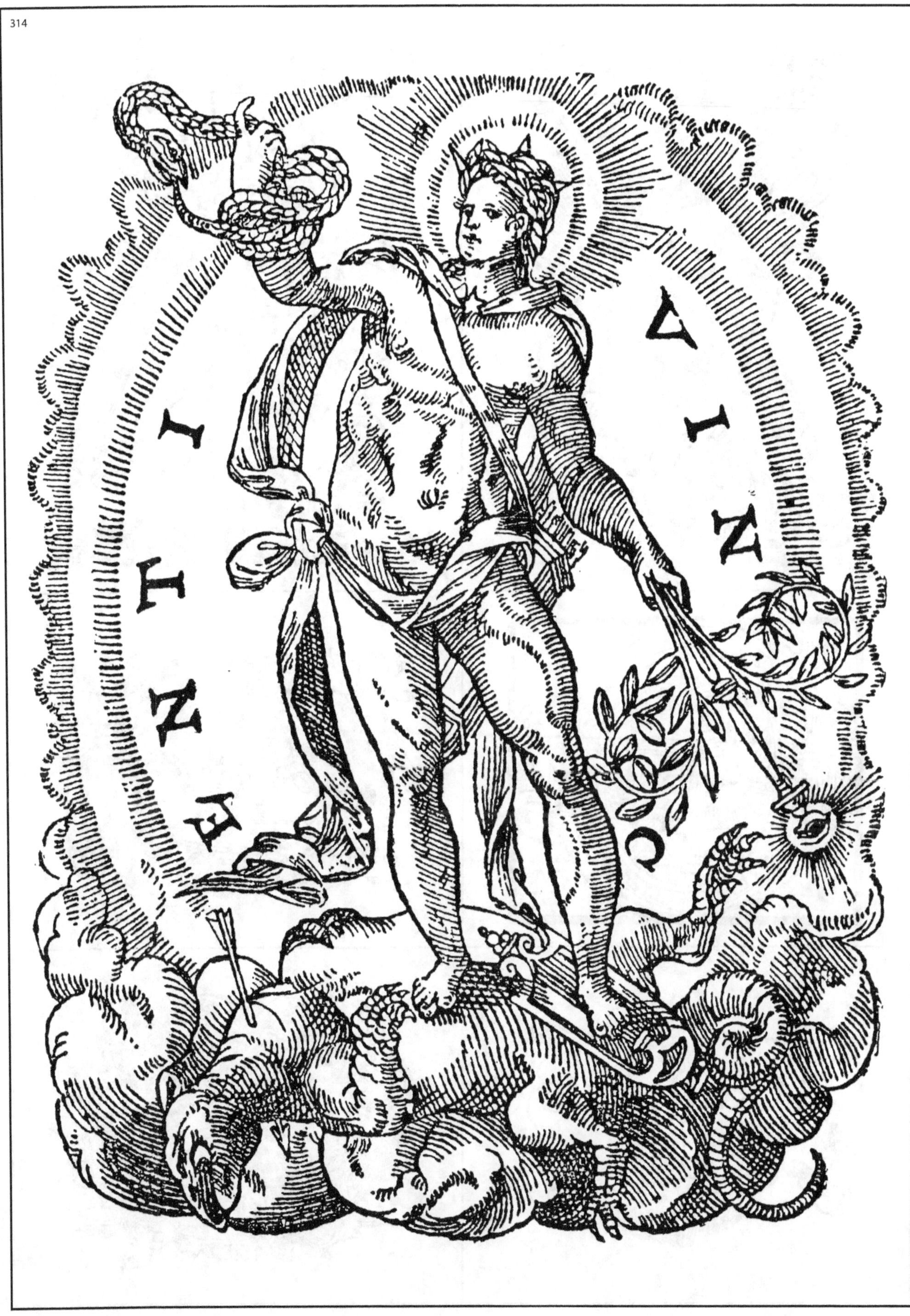

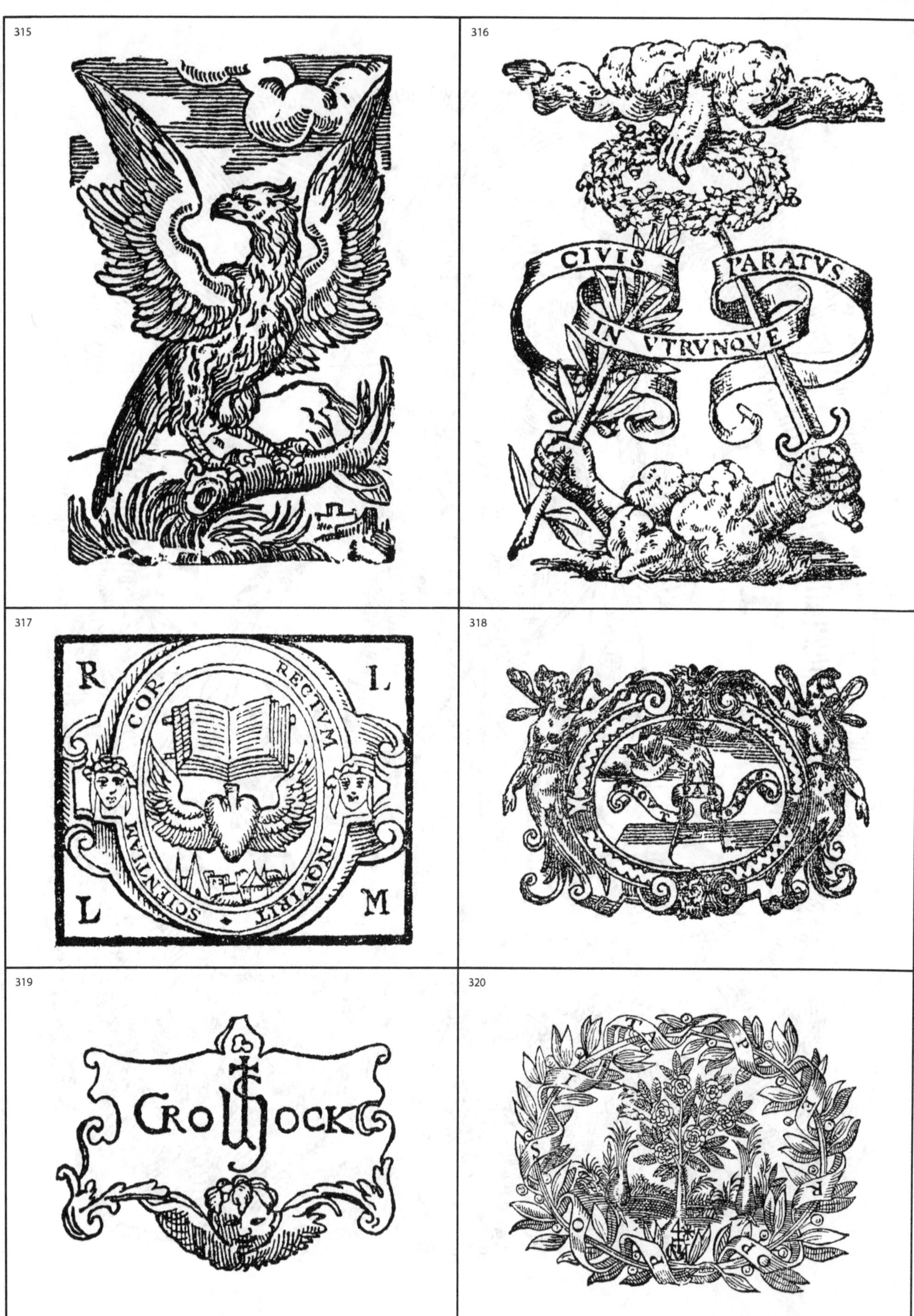
315
316
CIVIS PARATVS
IN VTRVNQVE
317
COR
RECTVM
SCIENTIA INVENIT
R
L
L
M
318
319
CroHock
320

321

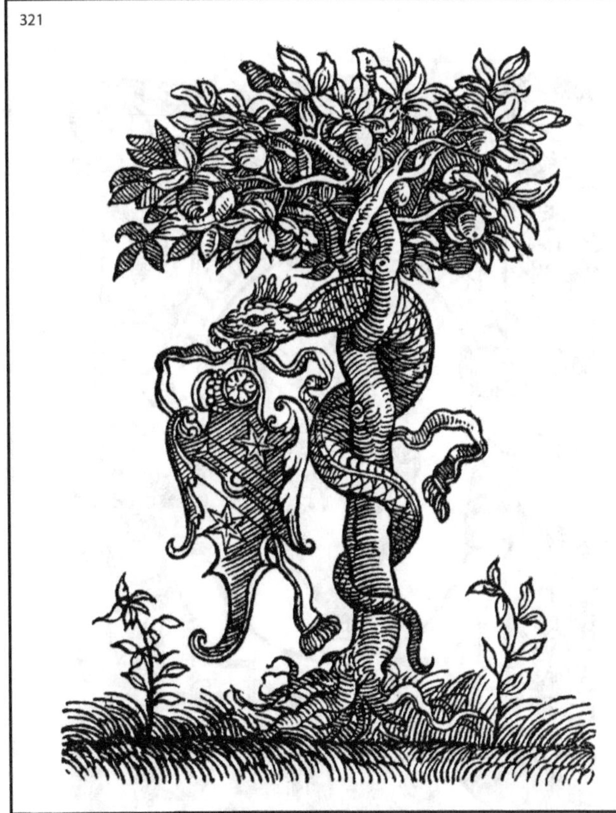

322

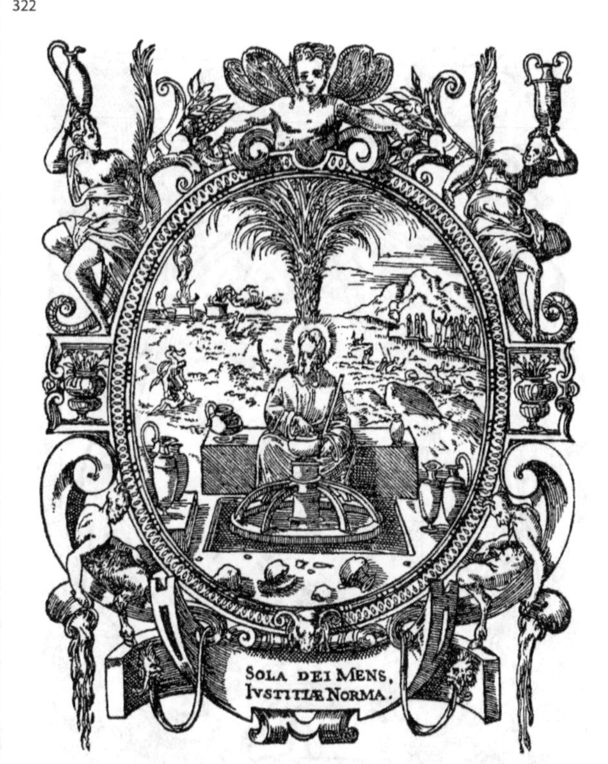

323

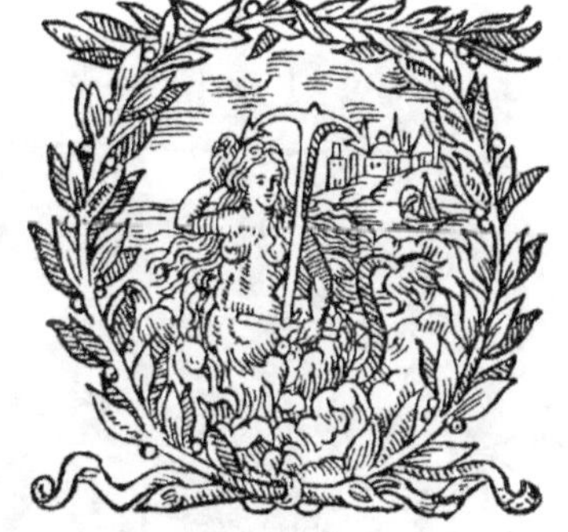

324

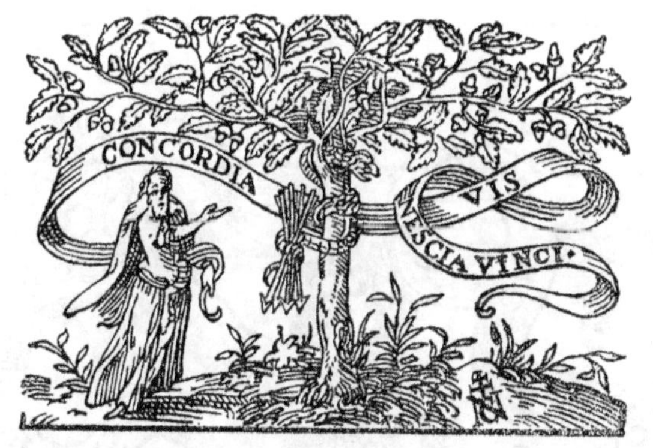

325

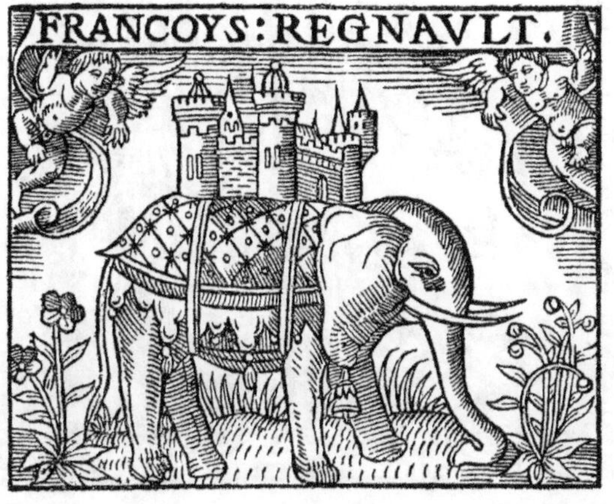

326

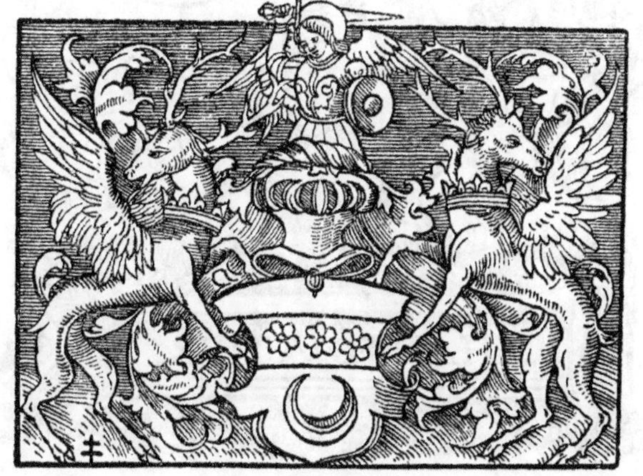

327

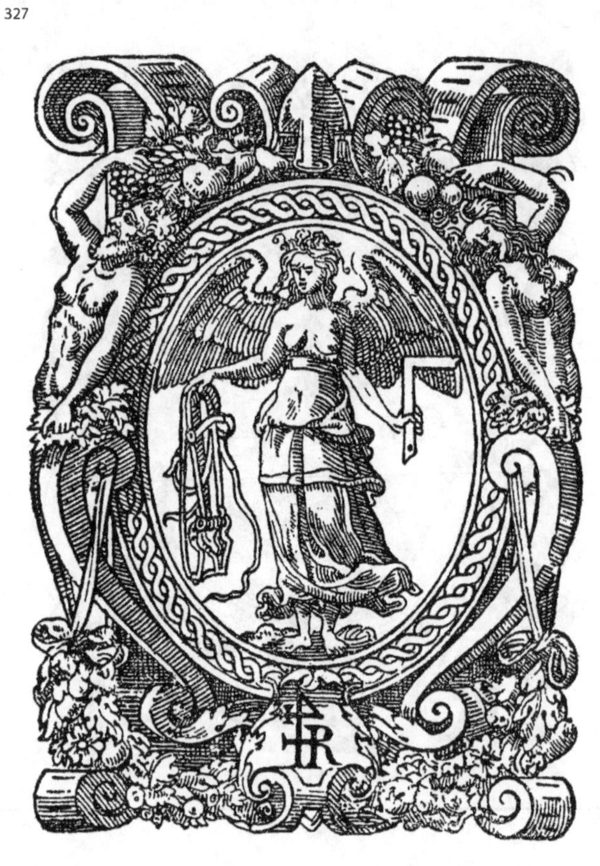

328

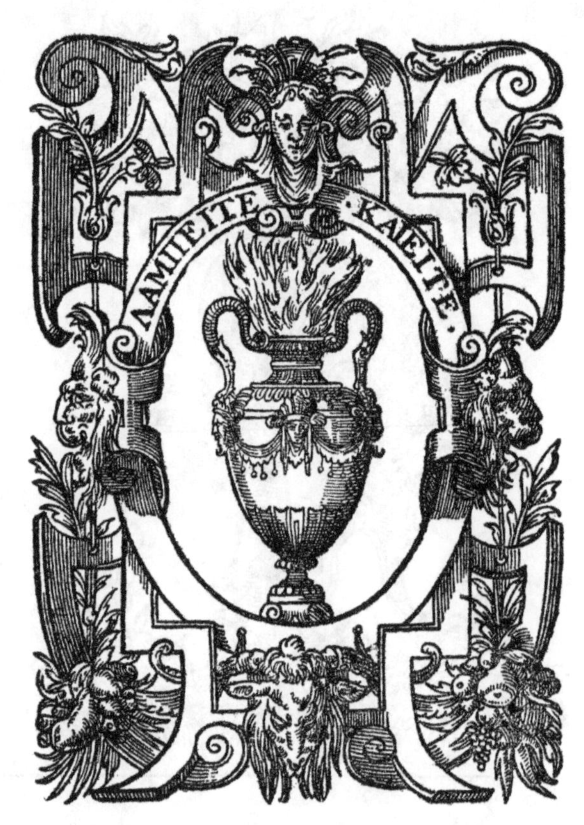

329

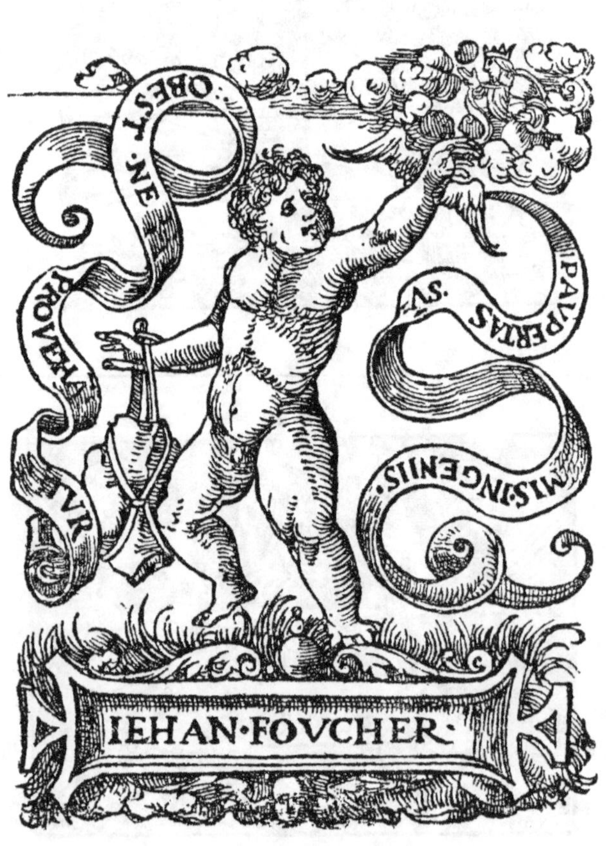

330

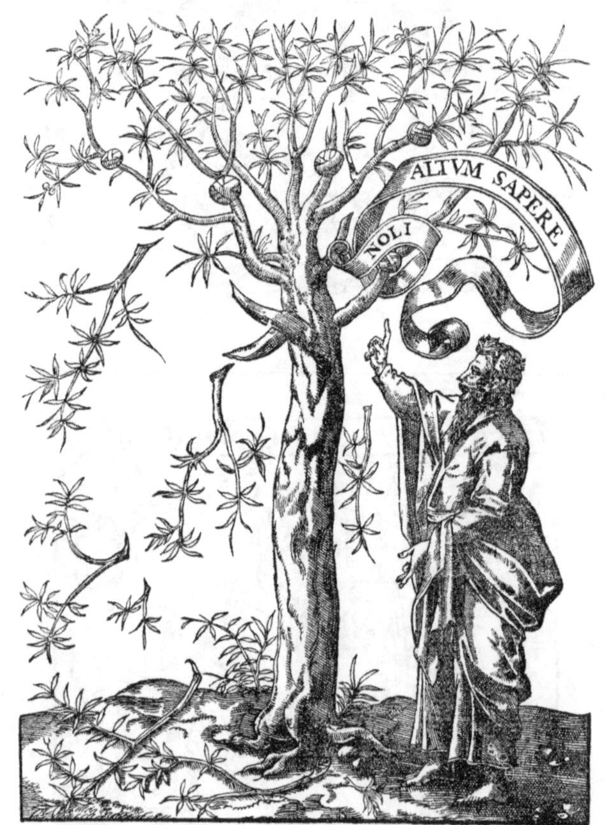

331

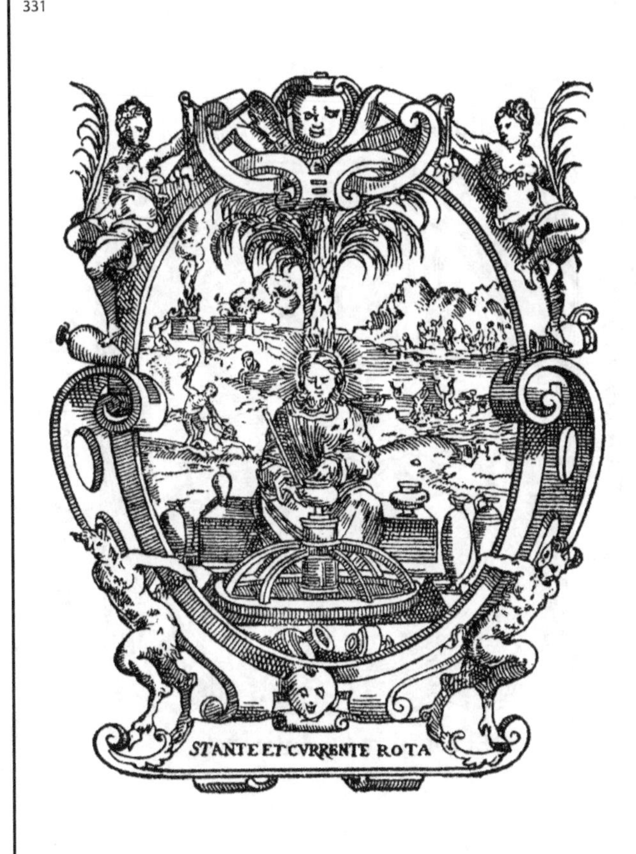

332

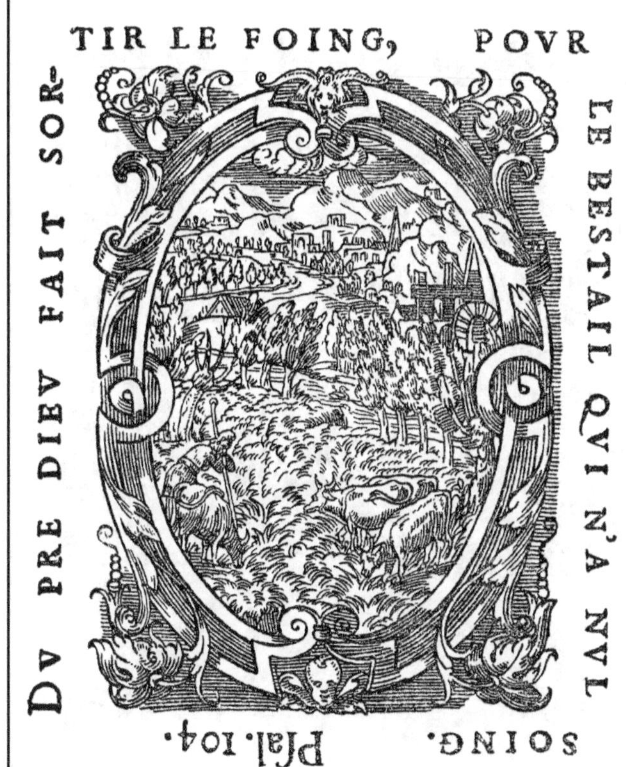

333

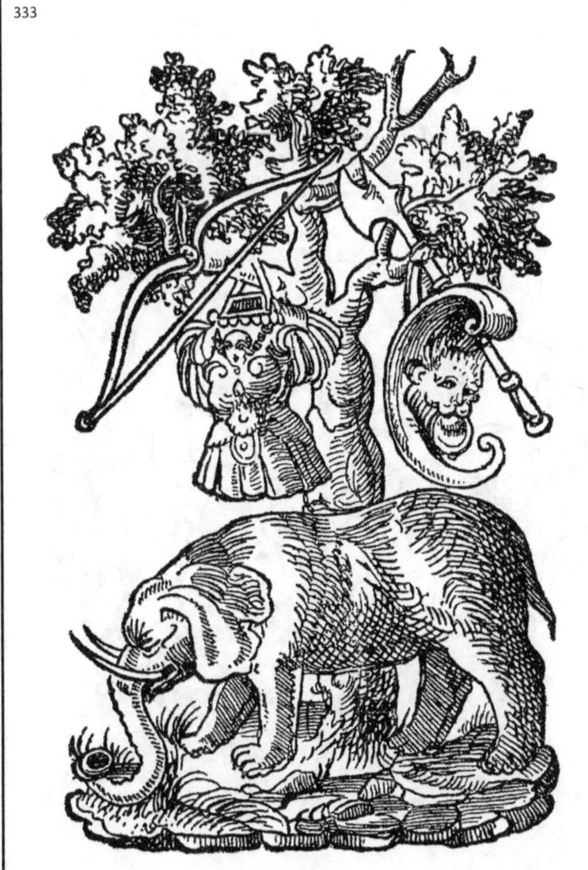

334

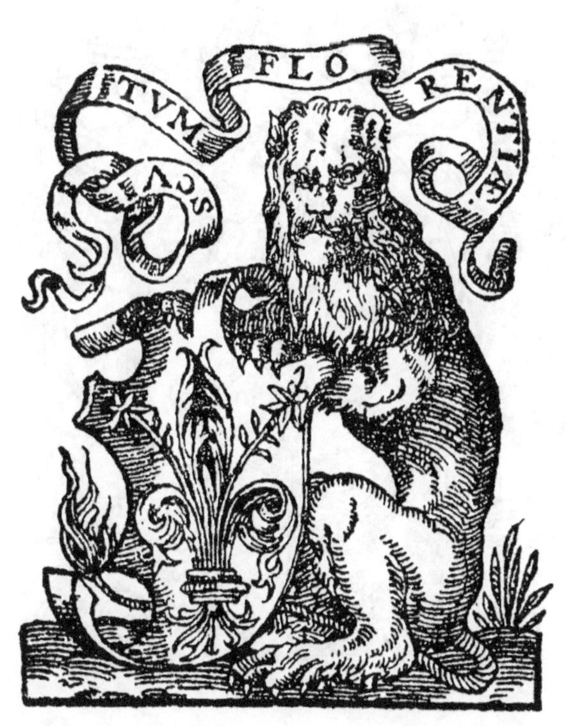

335

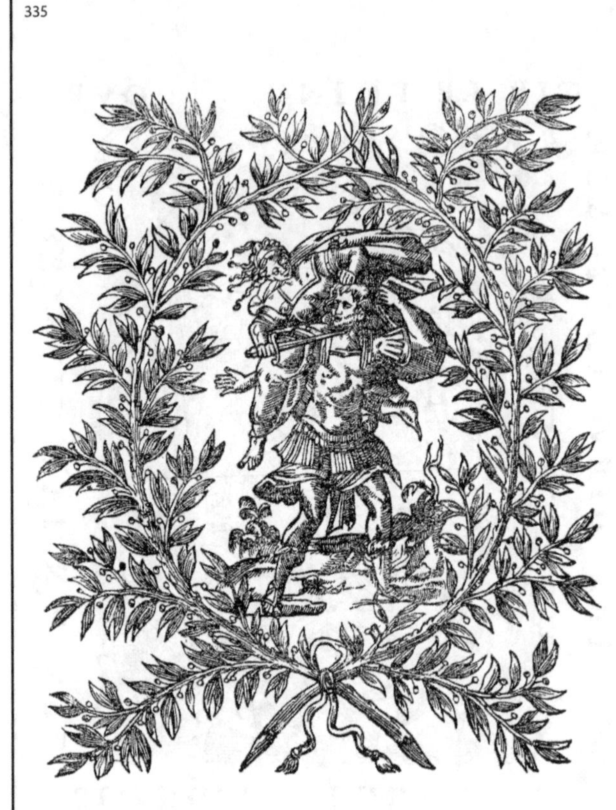

336

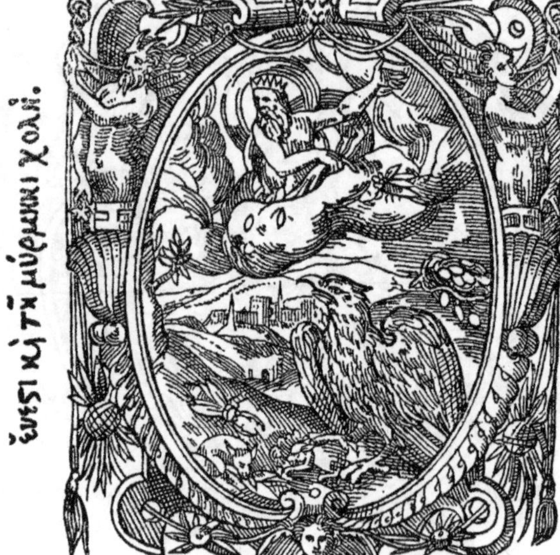

337

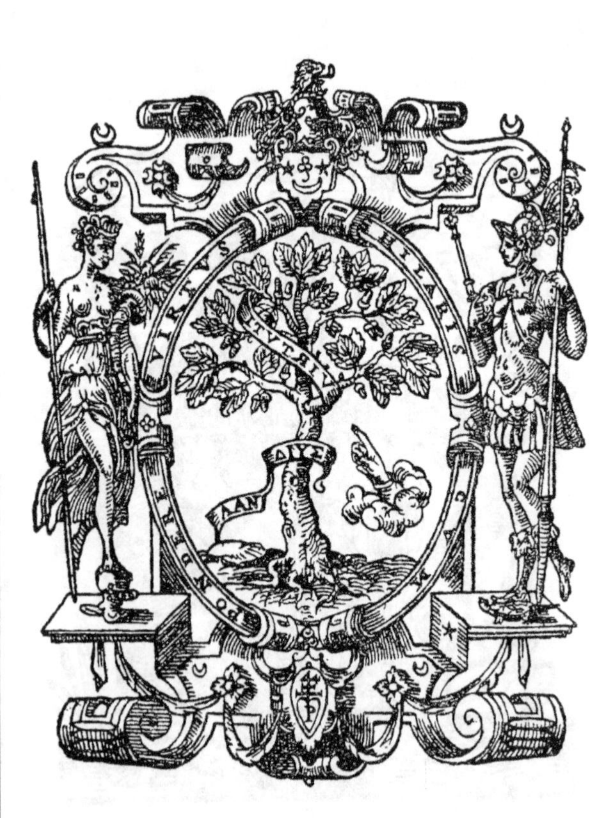

338

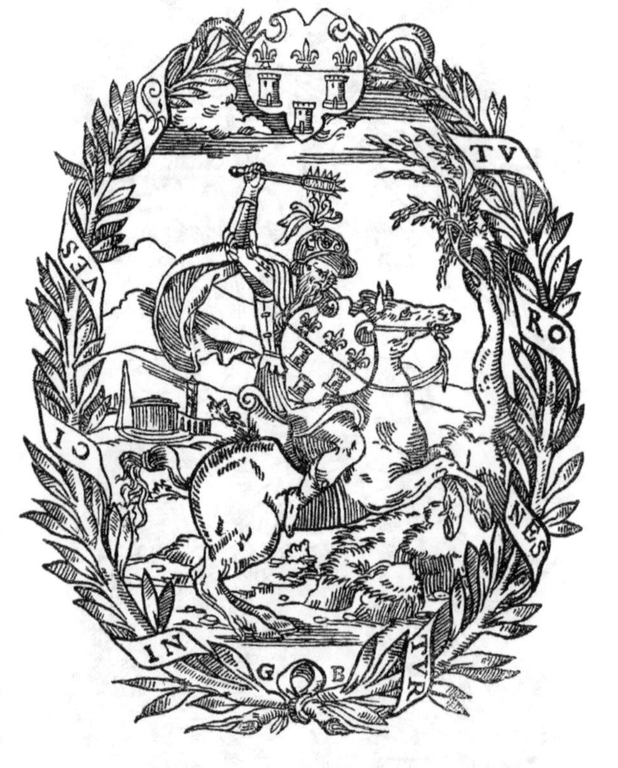

339

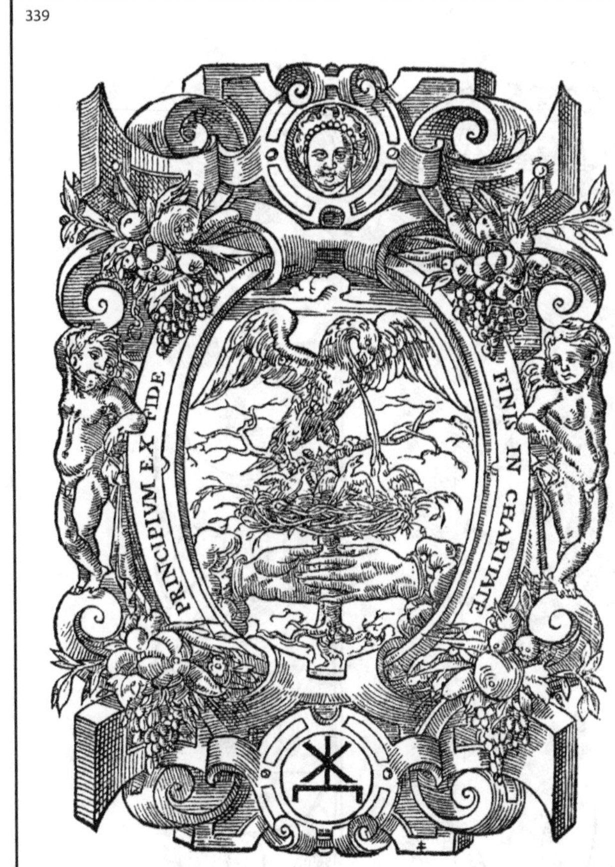

340

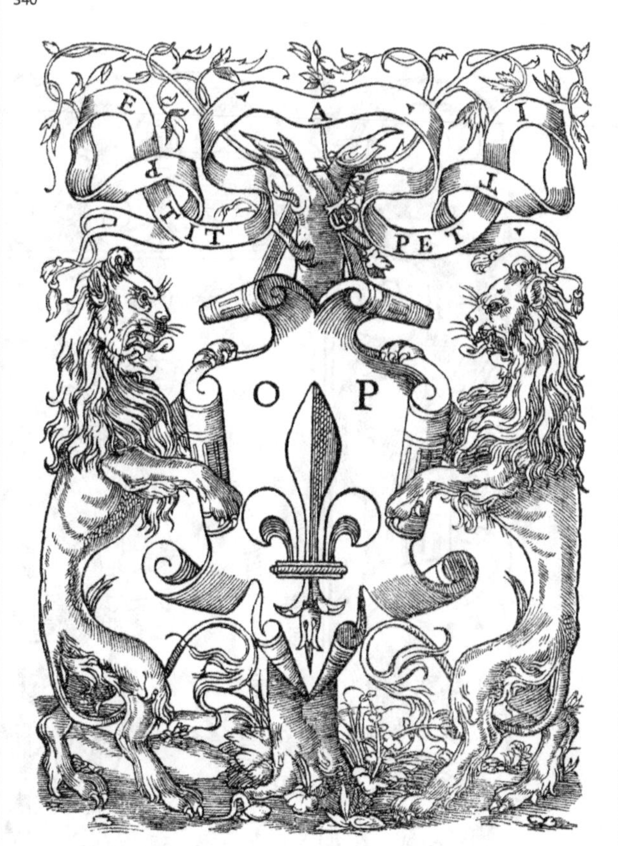

341

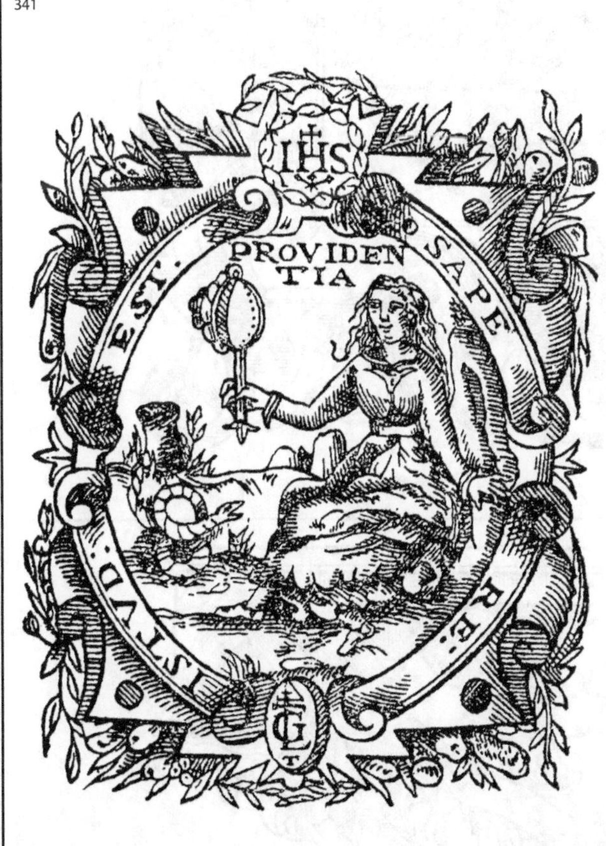

342

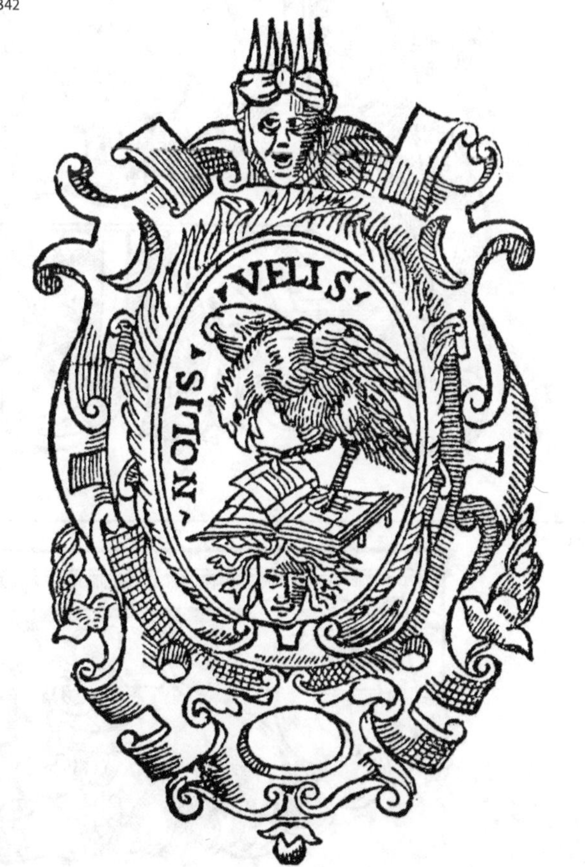

343

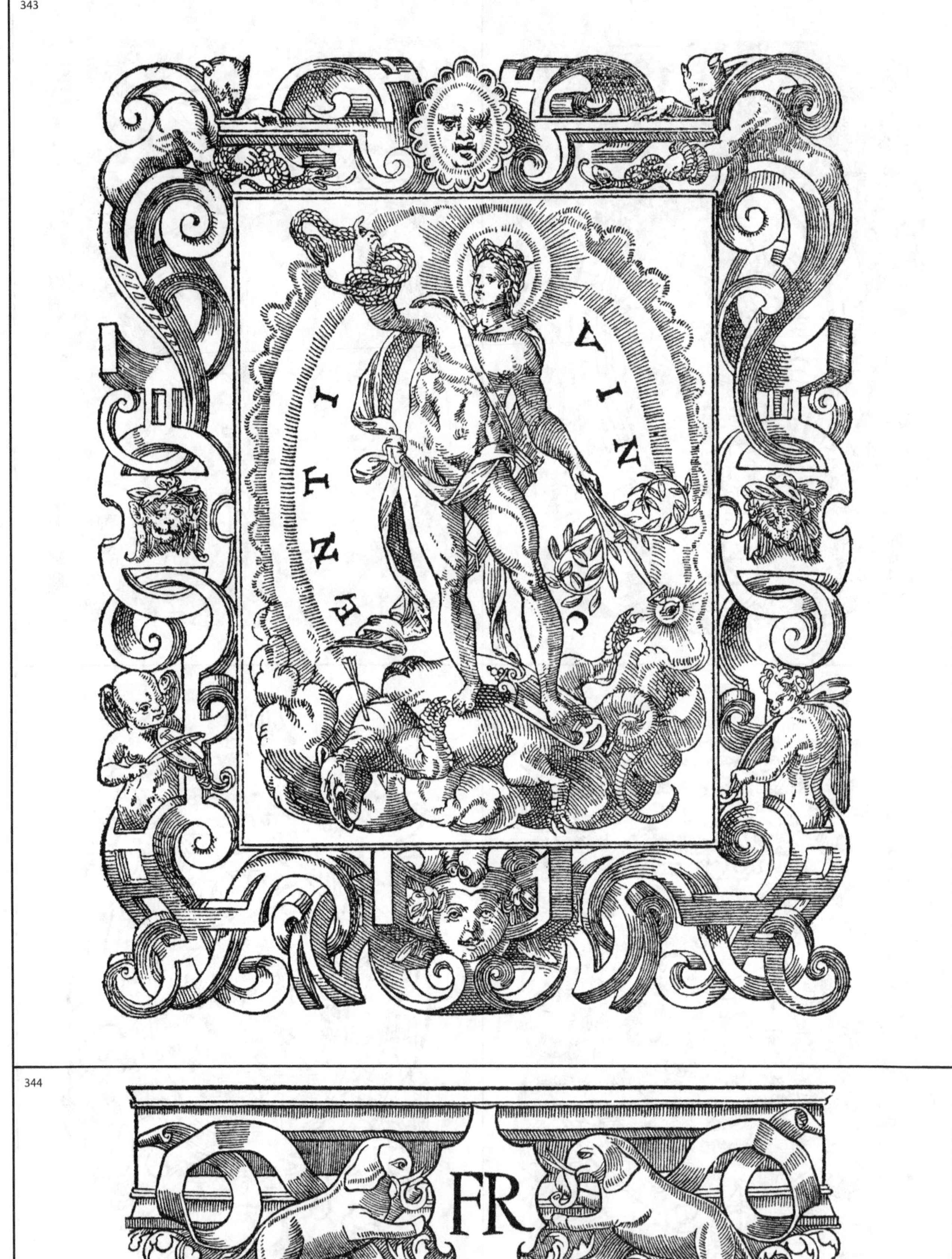

344

345

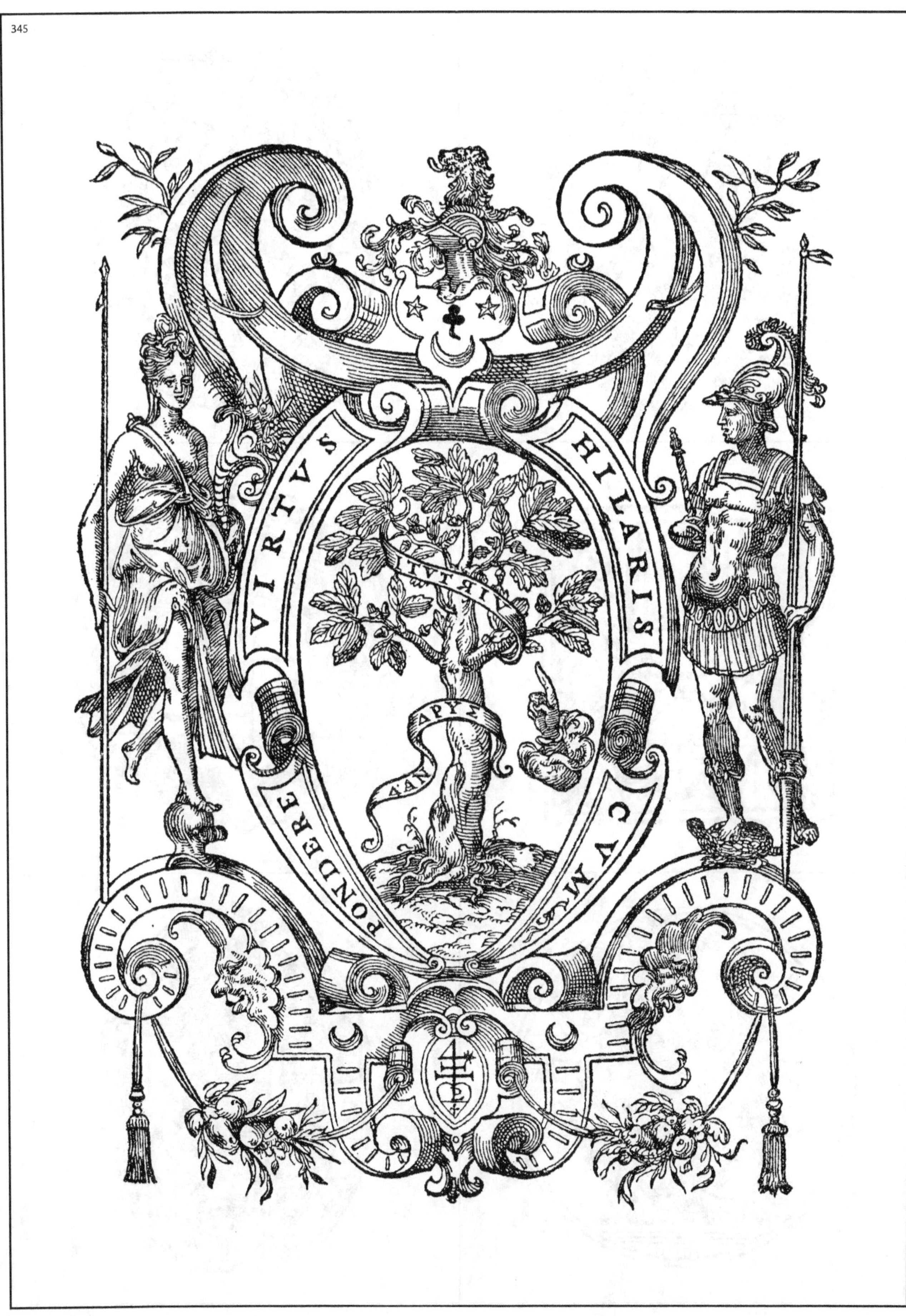

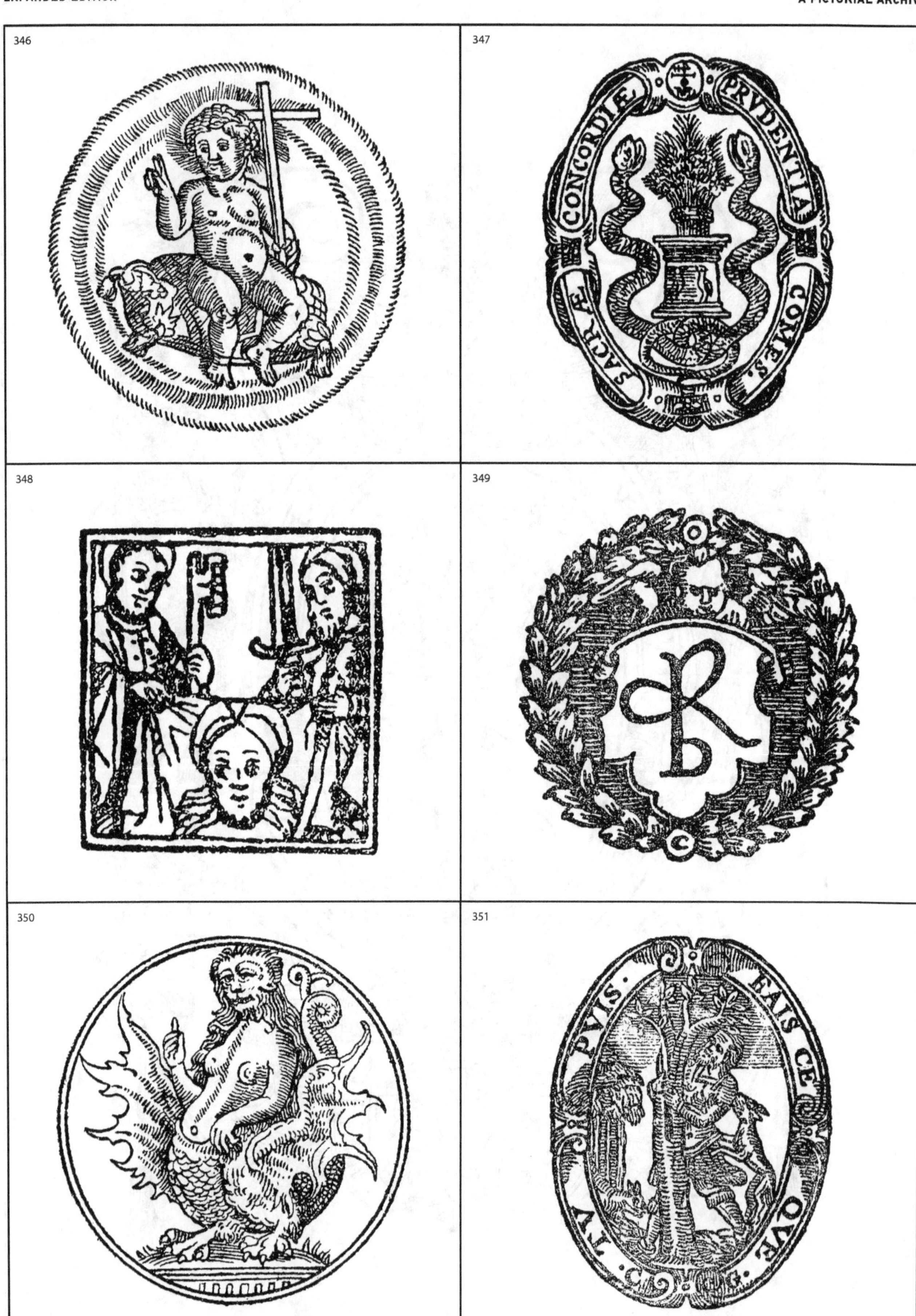

352

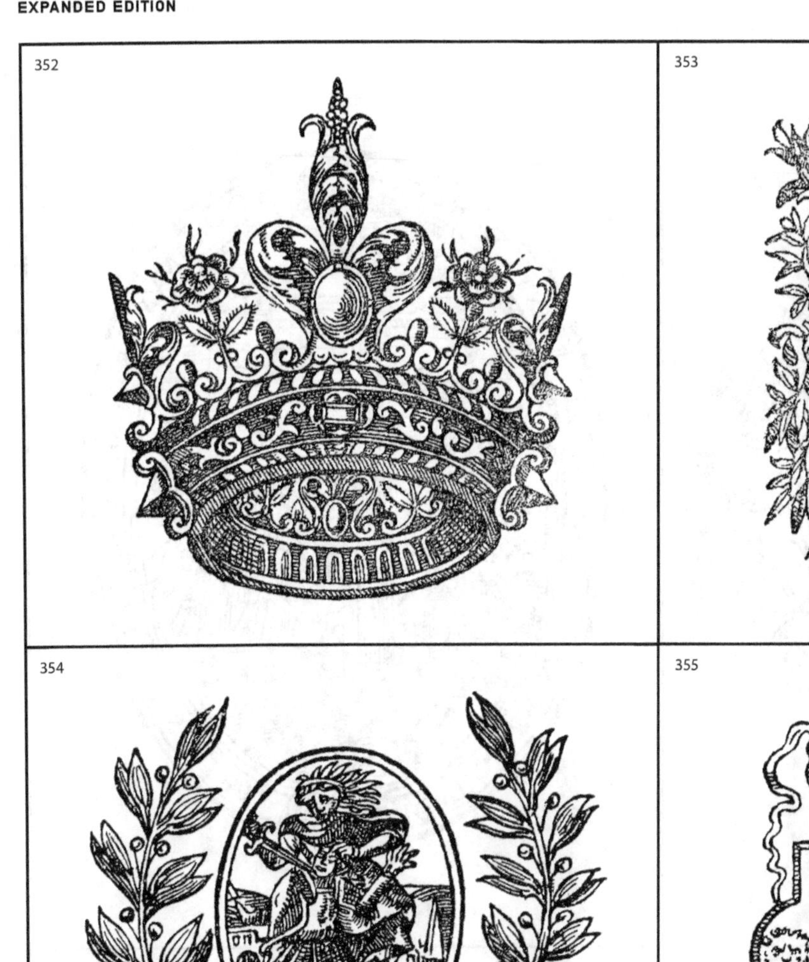

353

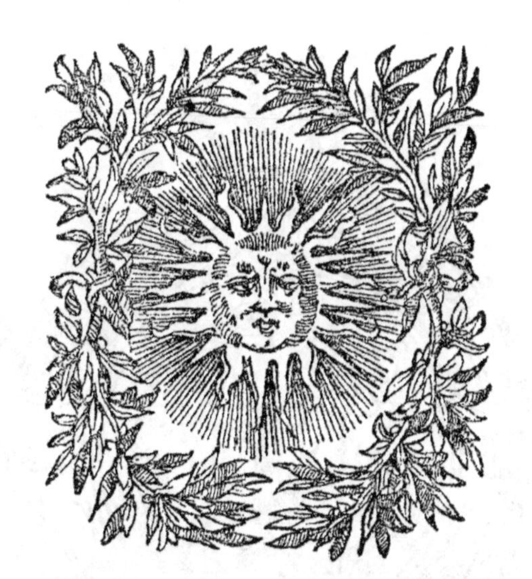

354

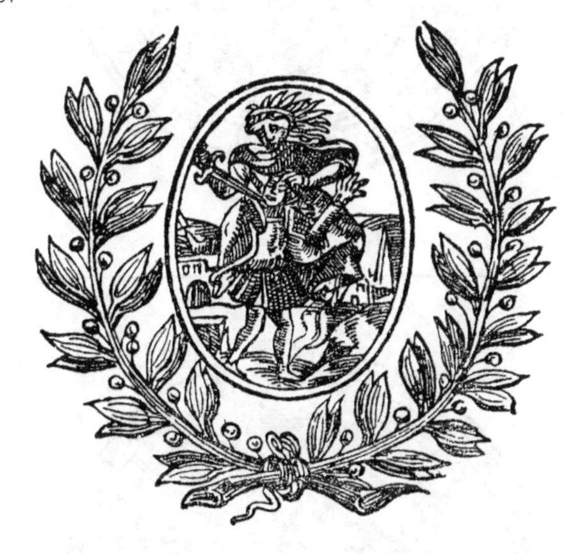

355

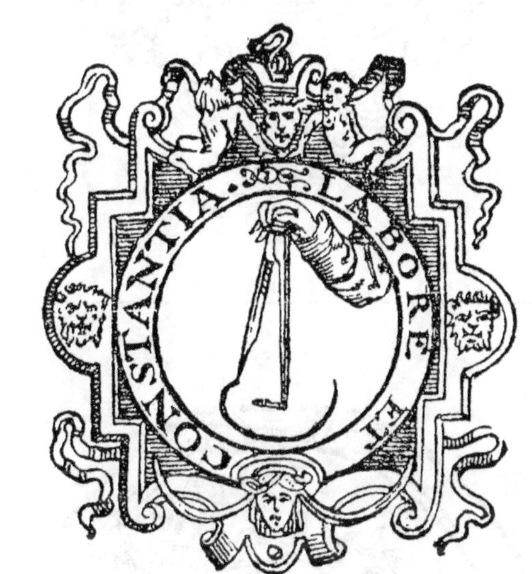

356

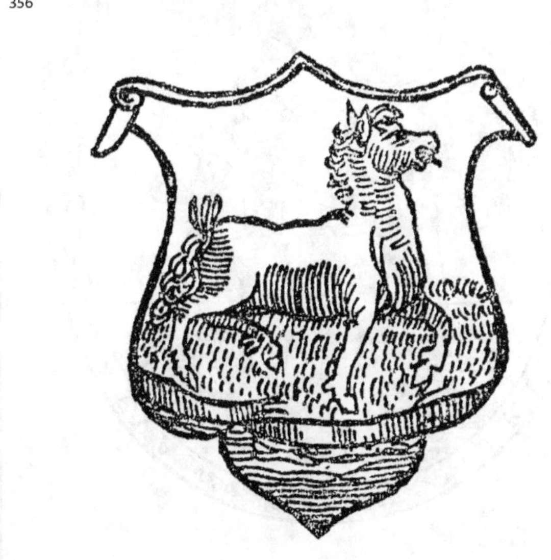

357

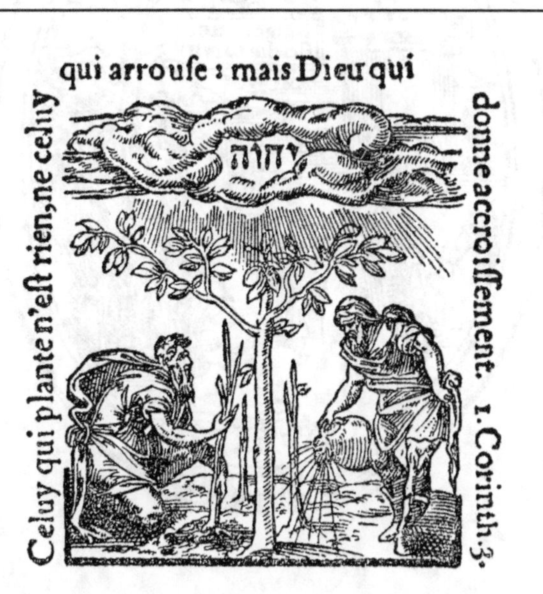

358

359

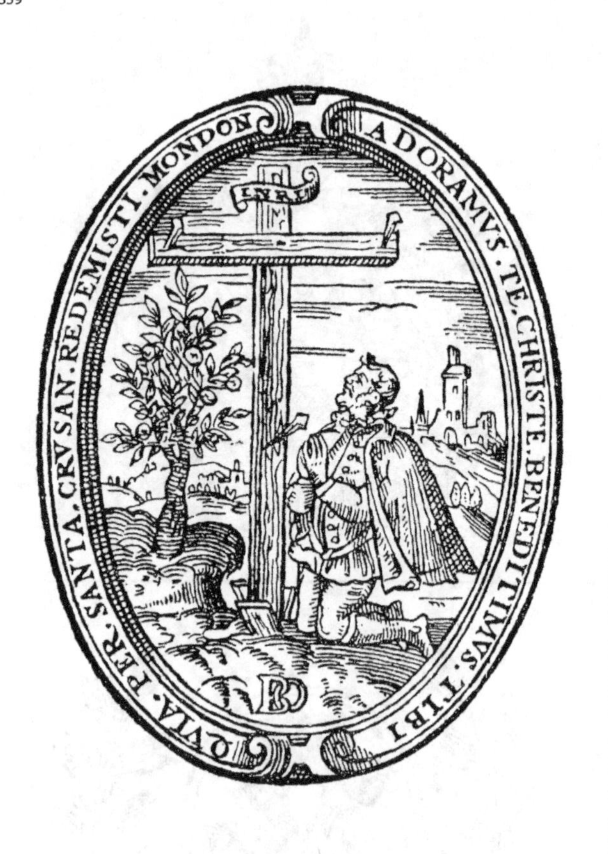

360

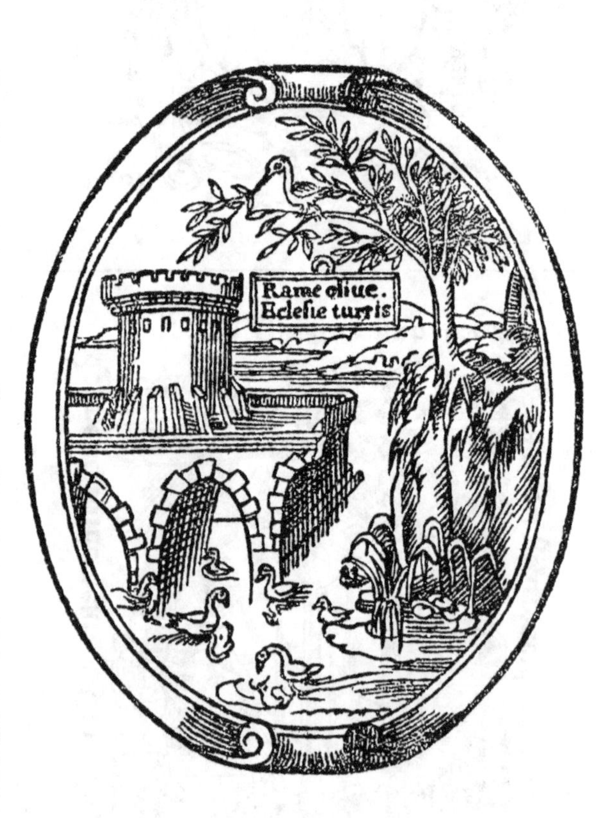

361

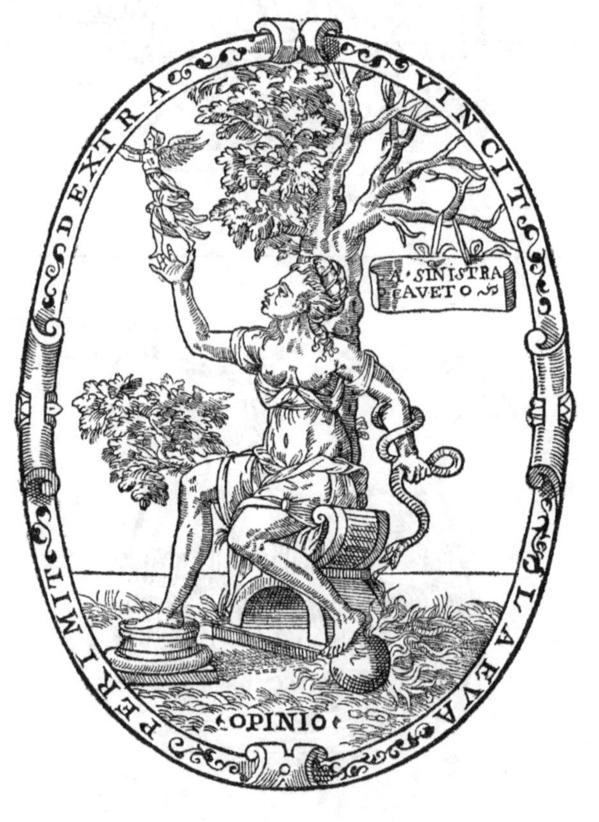

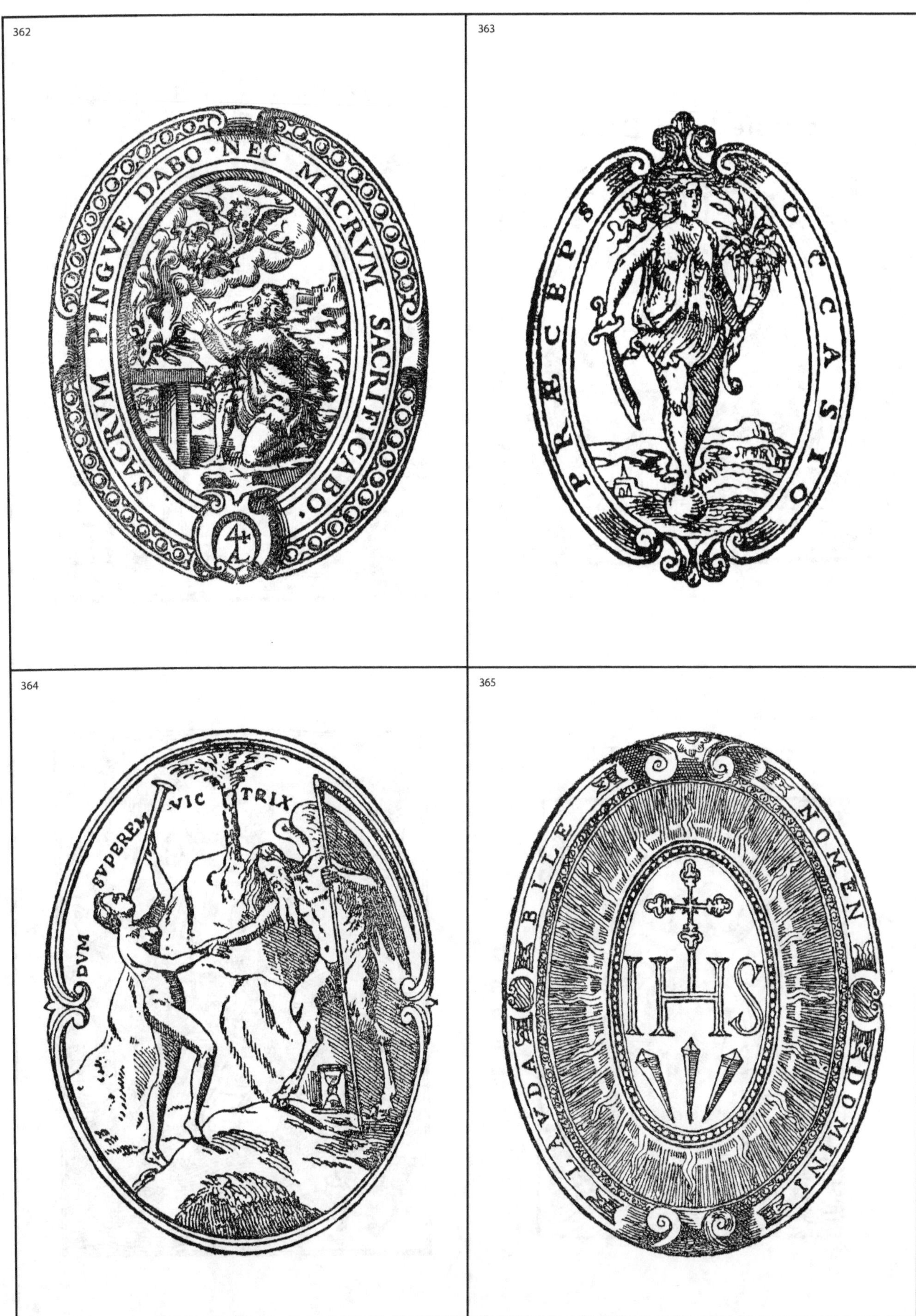
362
·SACRVM PINGVE DABO·NEC MACRVM SACRIFICABO·
363
PRÆCEPS OCCASIO
364
DVM SVPEREM VIC TRIX
365
LAVDABILE NOMEN DOMINI

SYMBOLS & EMBLEMS

366

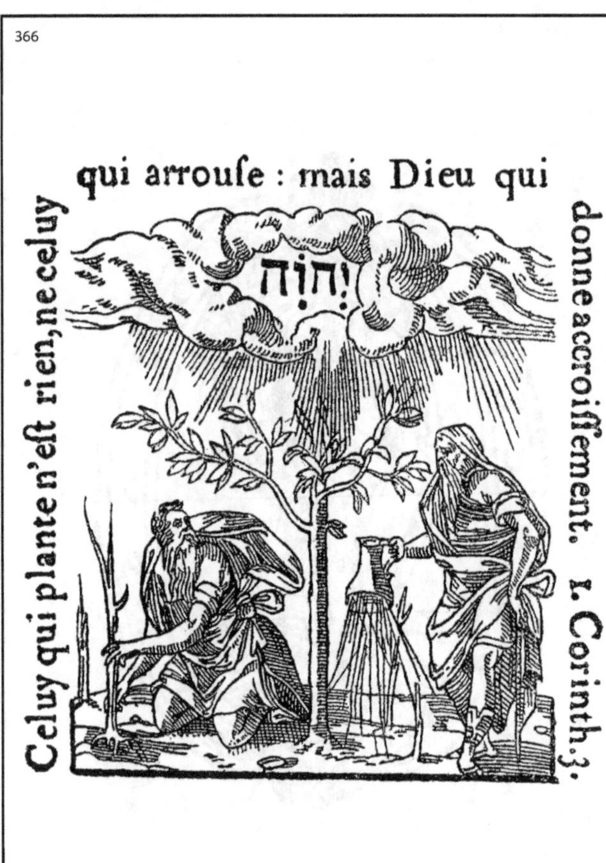

367

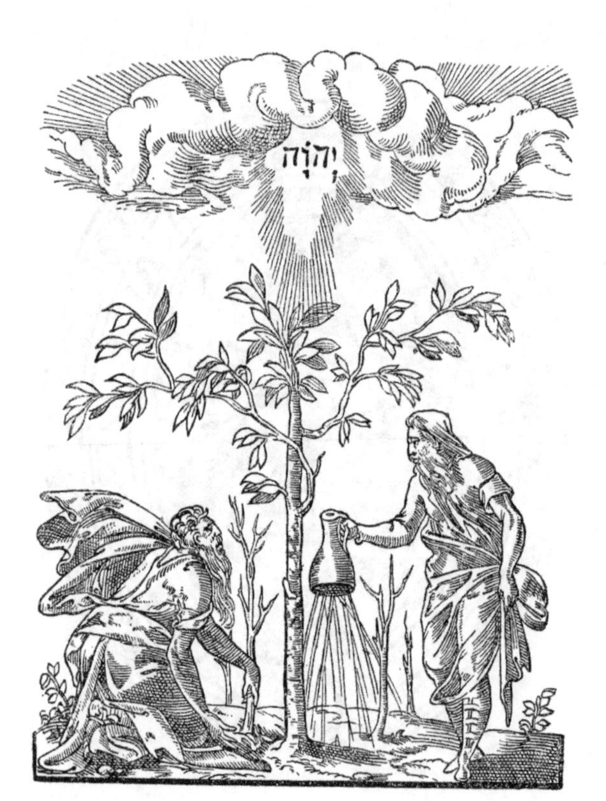

368

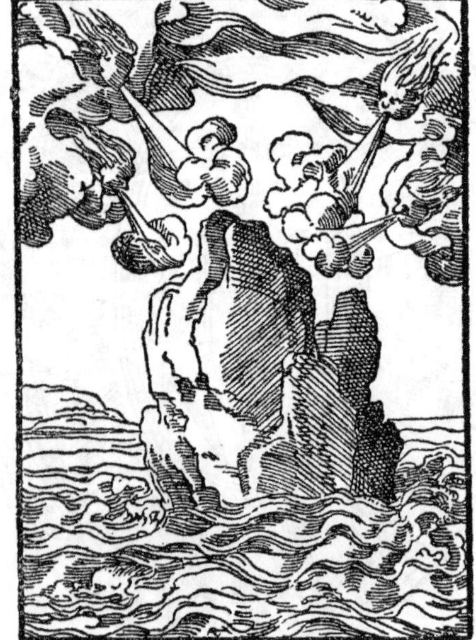

369

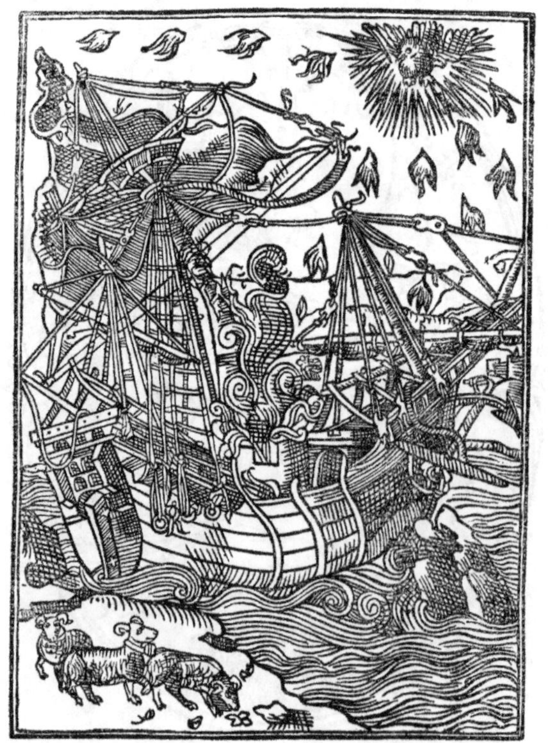

370

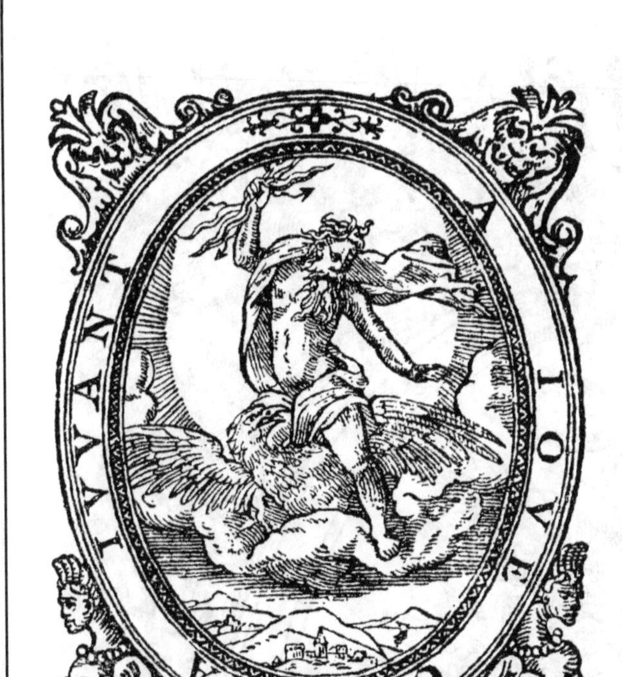

371

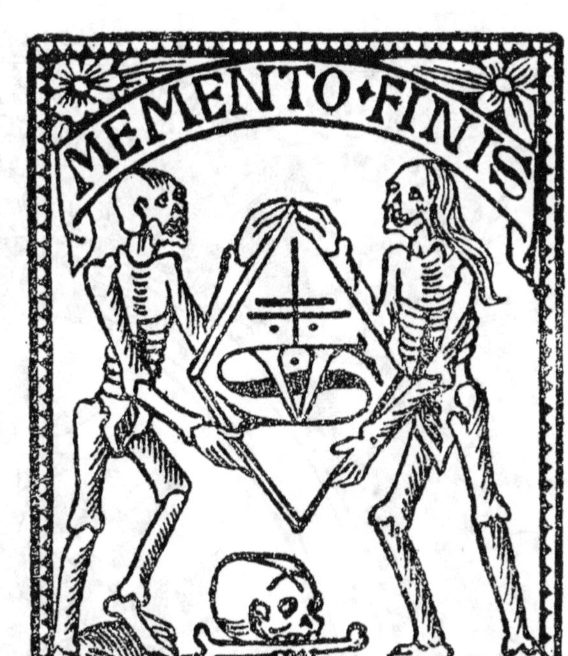

372

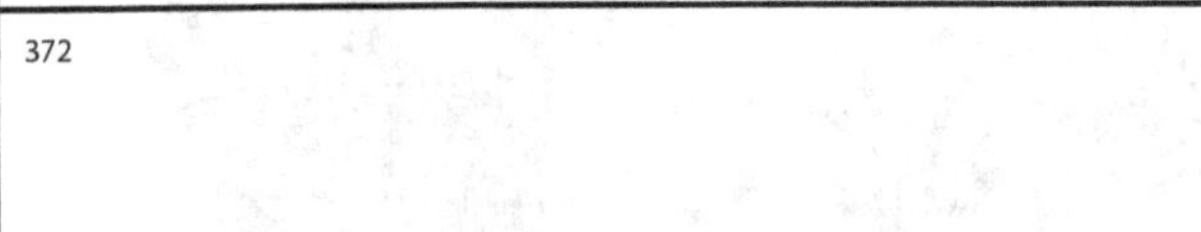

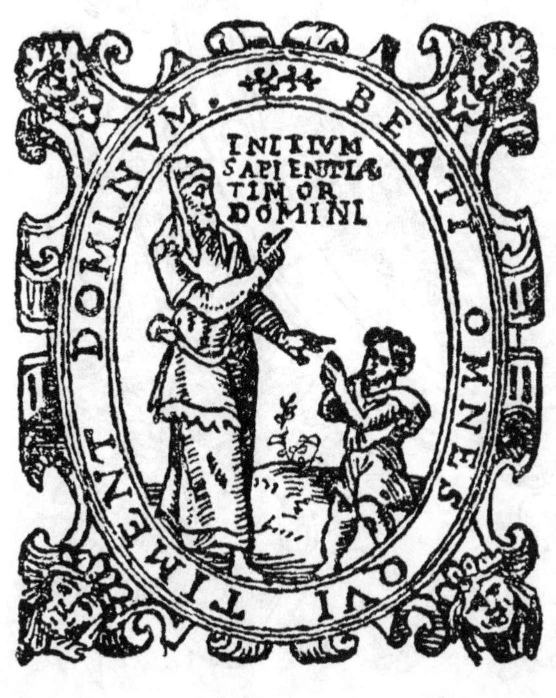

373

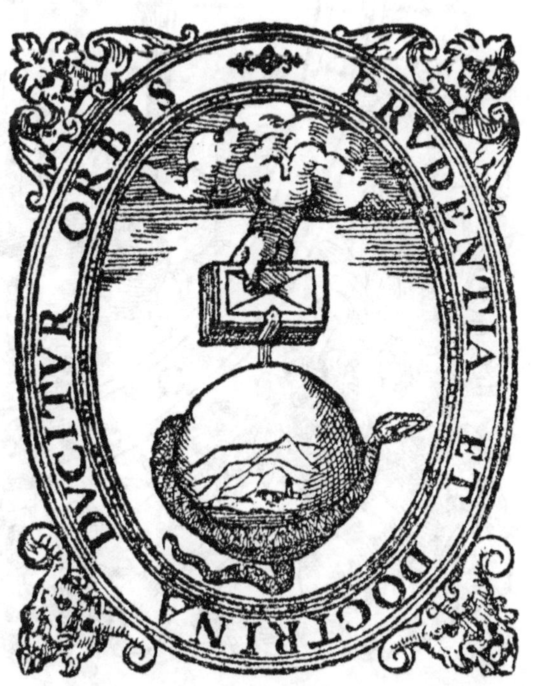

374

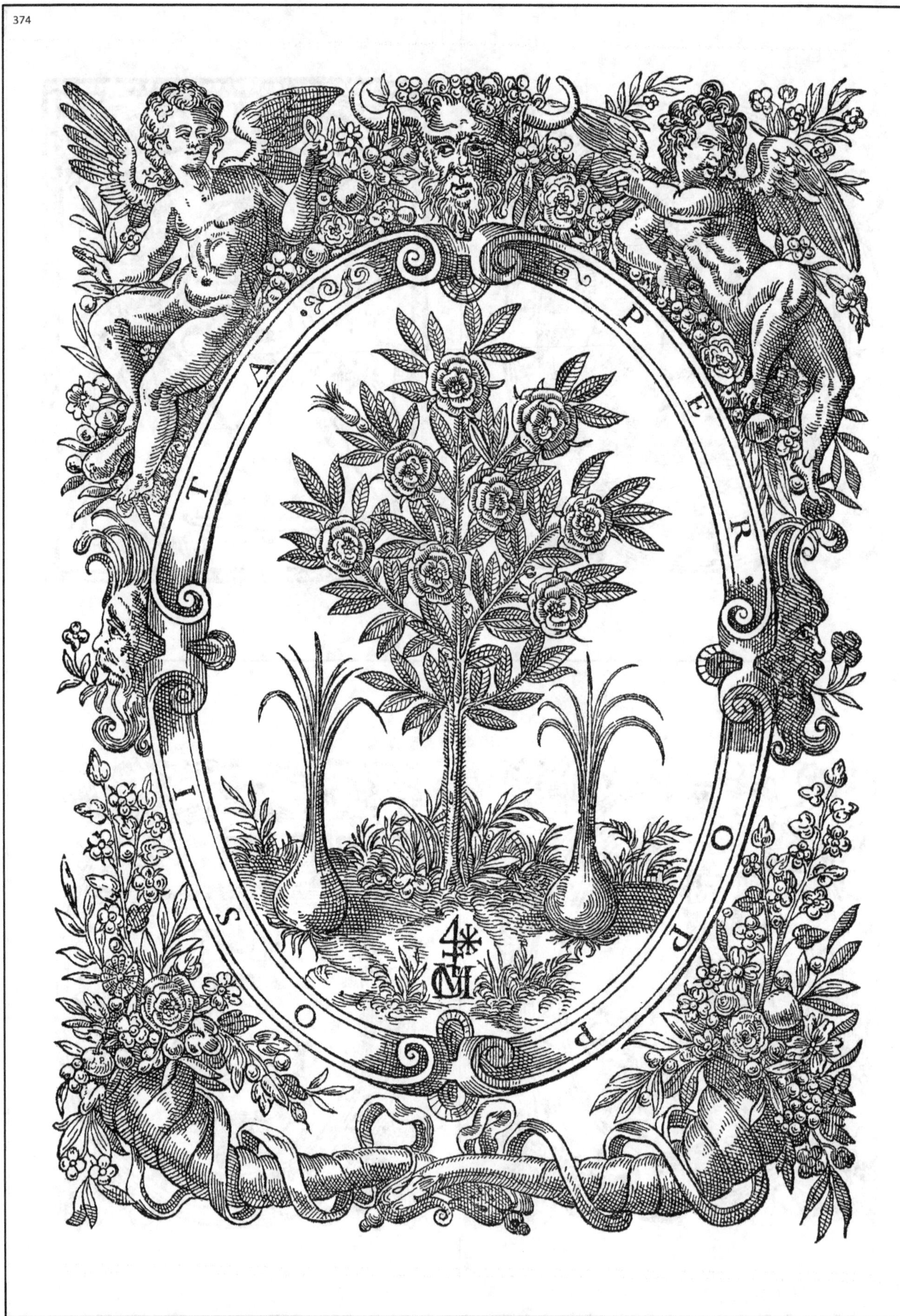

375

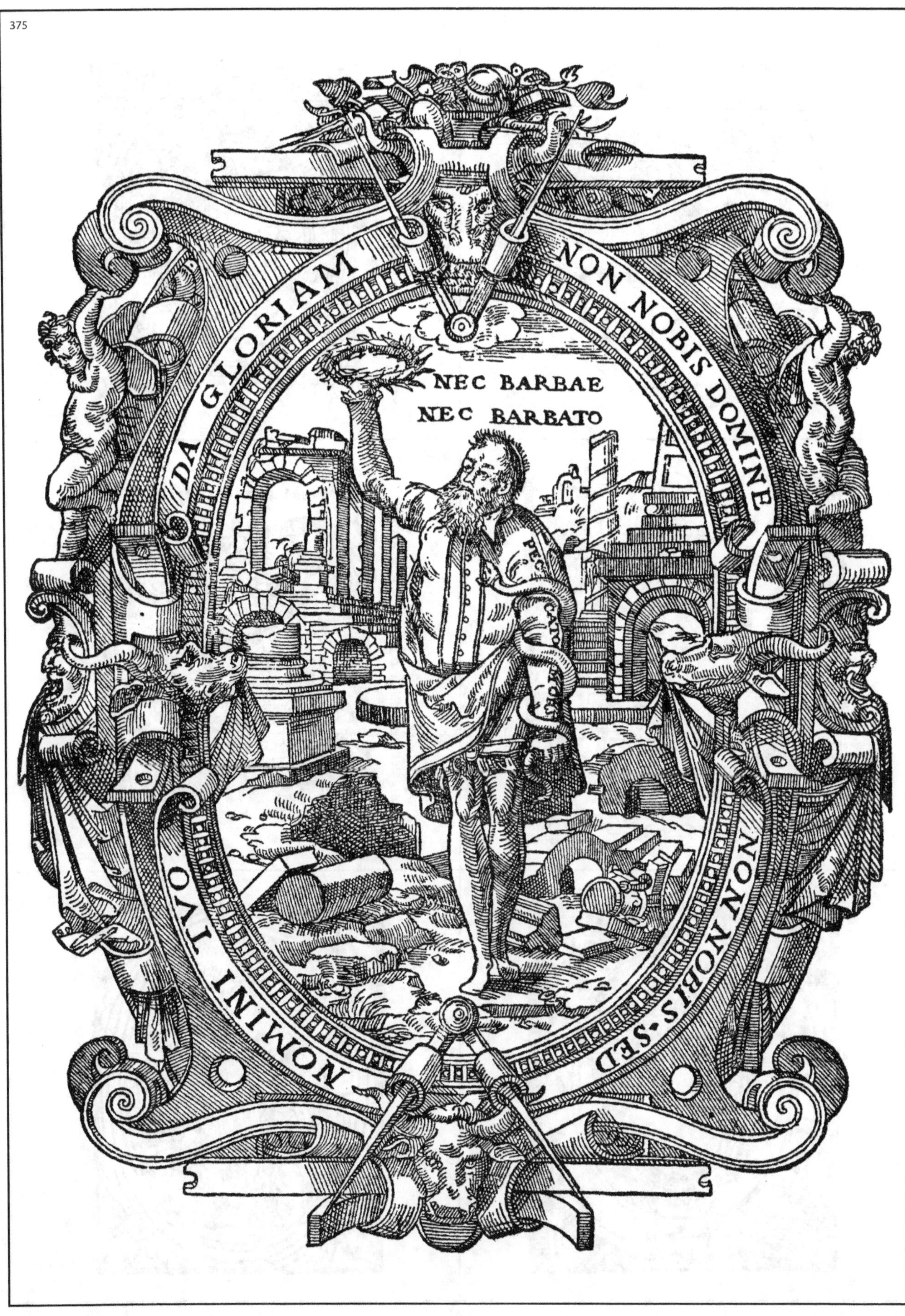
DA GLORIAM
NON NOBIS DOMINE
NEC BARBAE
NEC BARBATO
NOMINI TVO
NON NOBIS SED
PEC

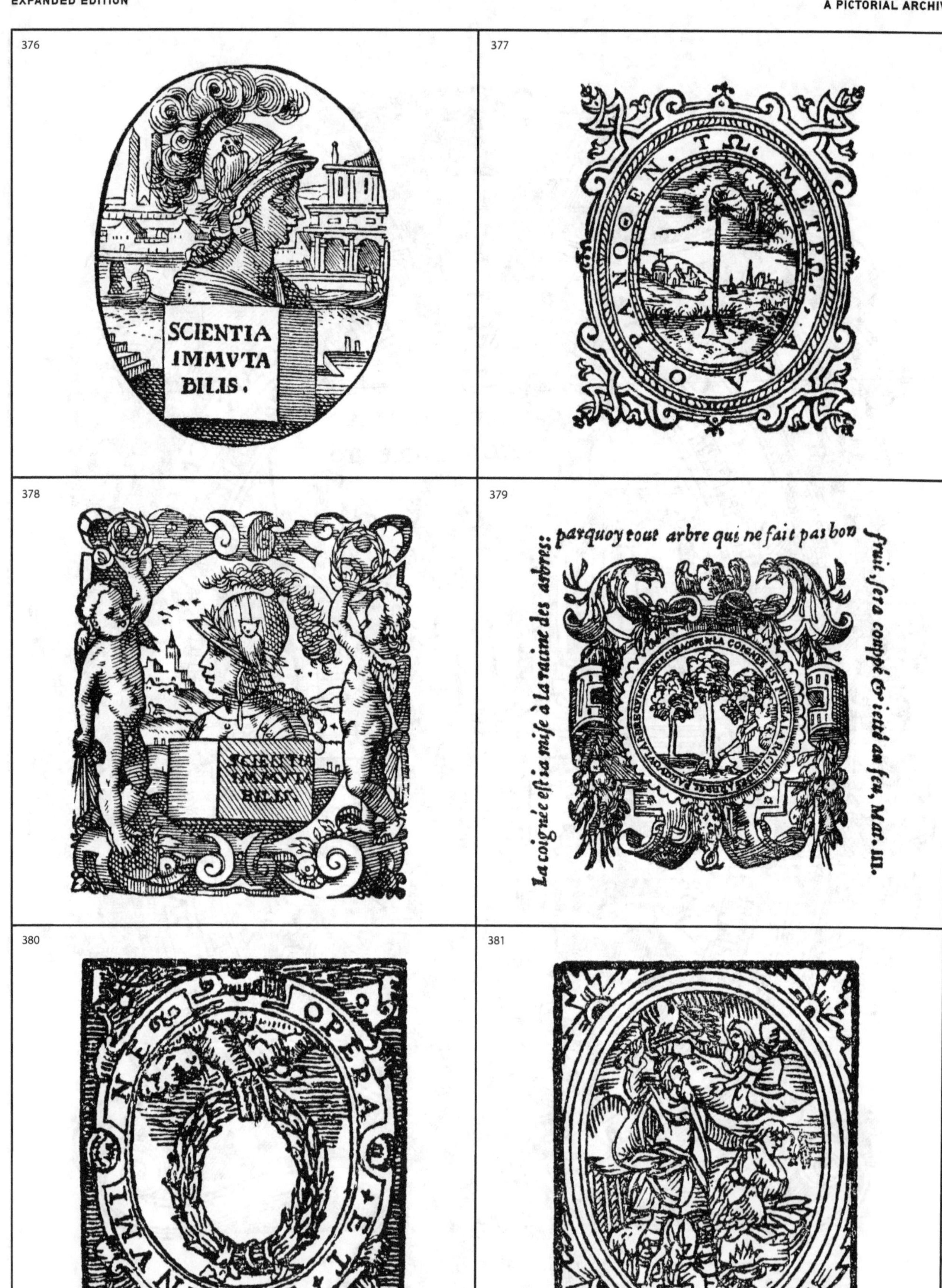
376
SCIENTIA
IMMVTA
BILIS.
377
378
379
parquoy tout arbre qui ne fait pas bon
fruit, sera coupé & ietté au feu, Mat. III.
La coignée est ia mise à la racine des arbres:
380
OPERA
381

382

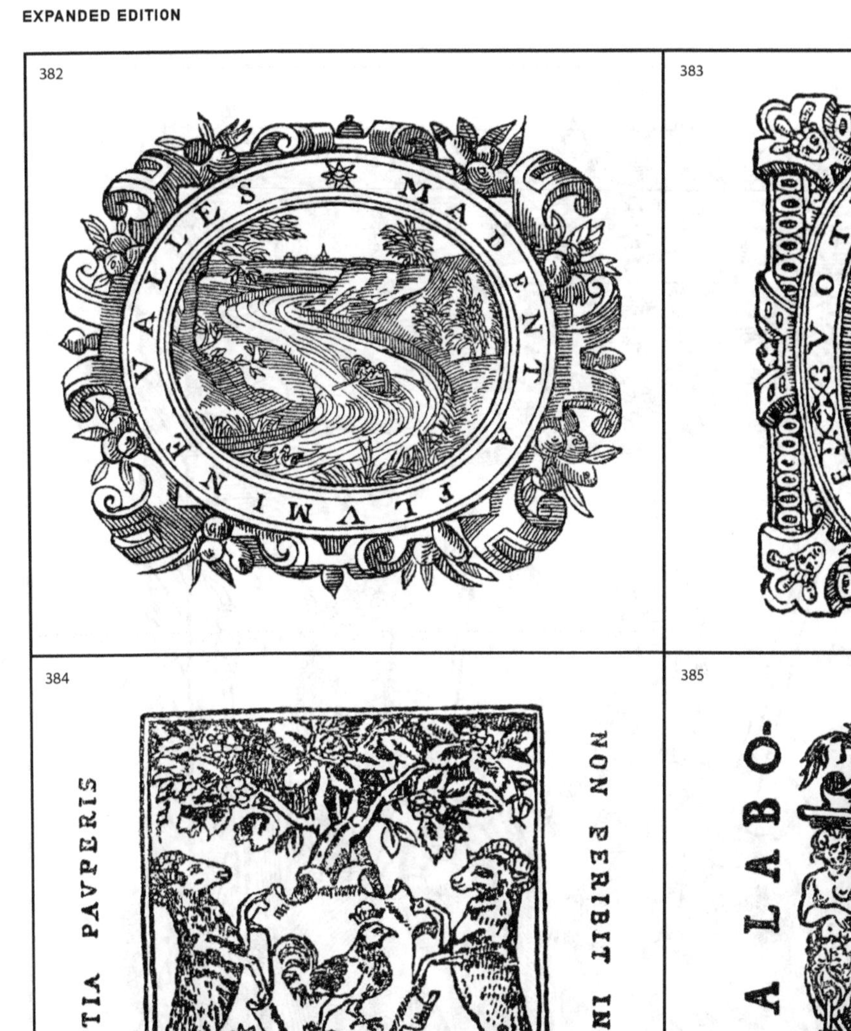

383

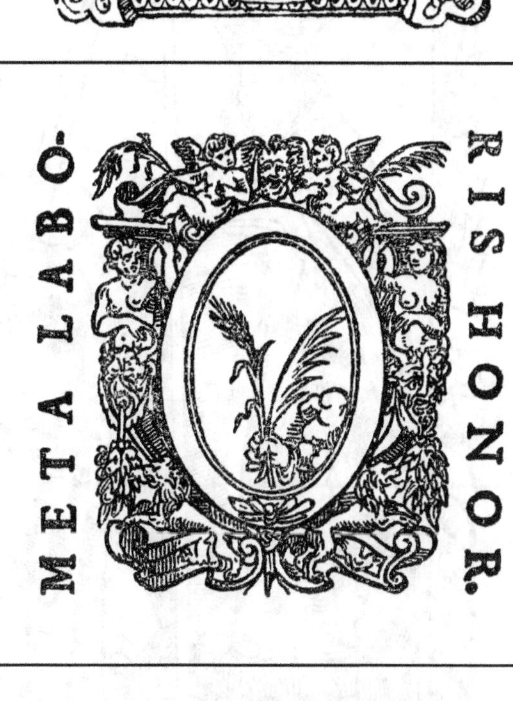

384

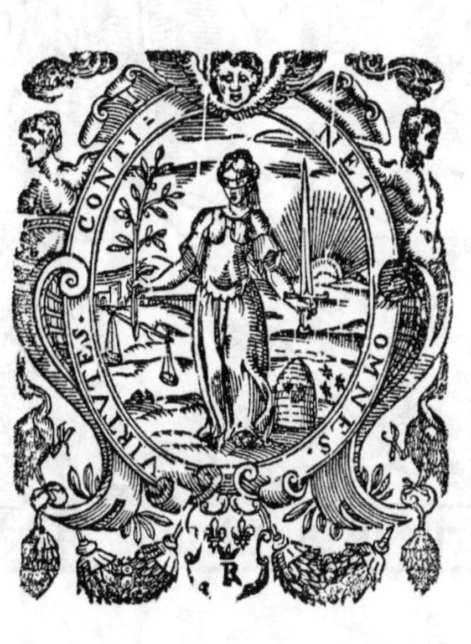

385

META LABO-

RIS HONOR.

386

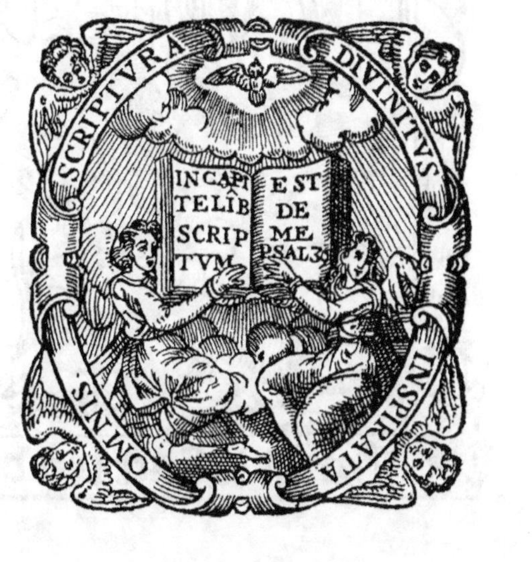

387

388

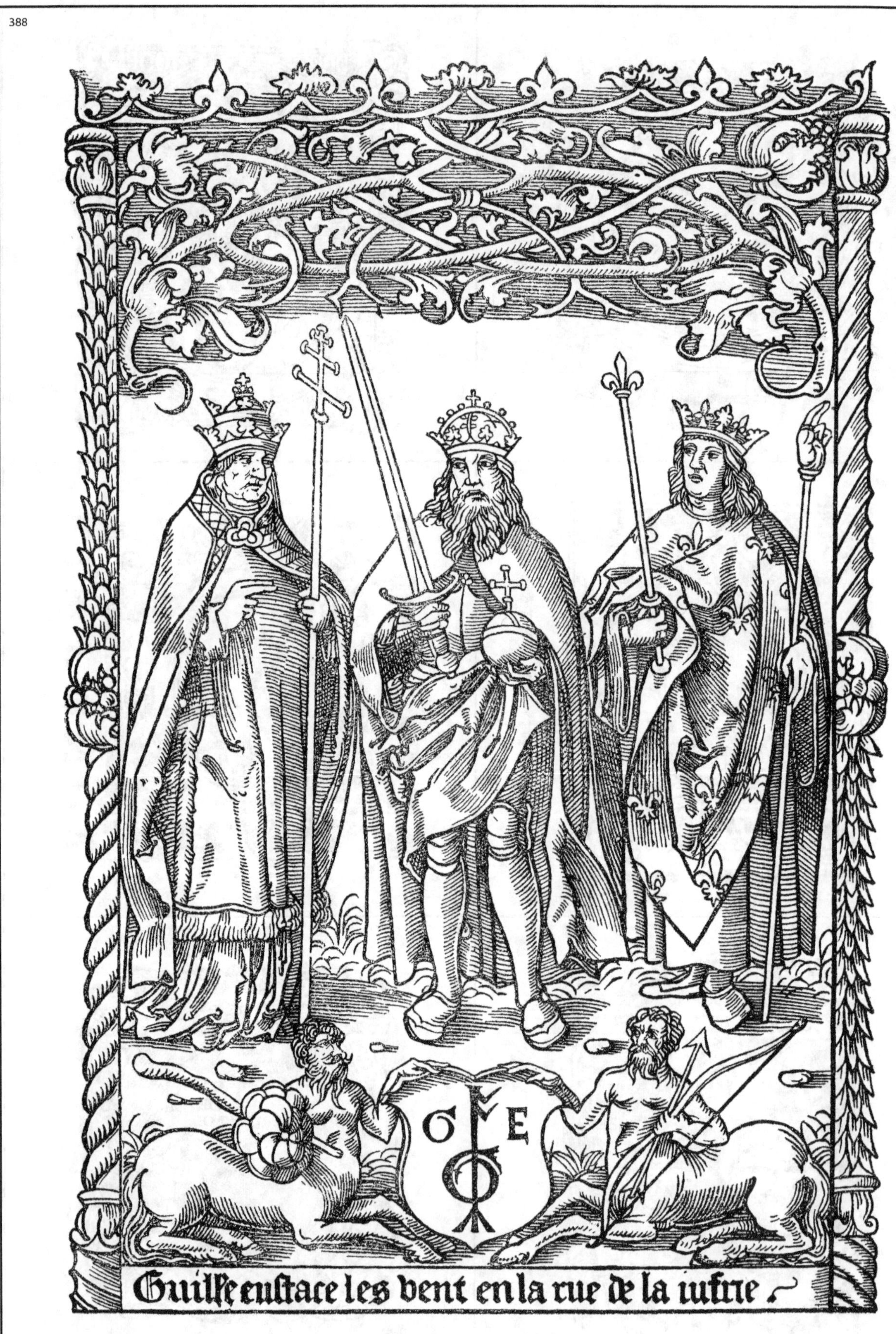

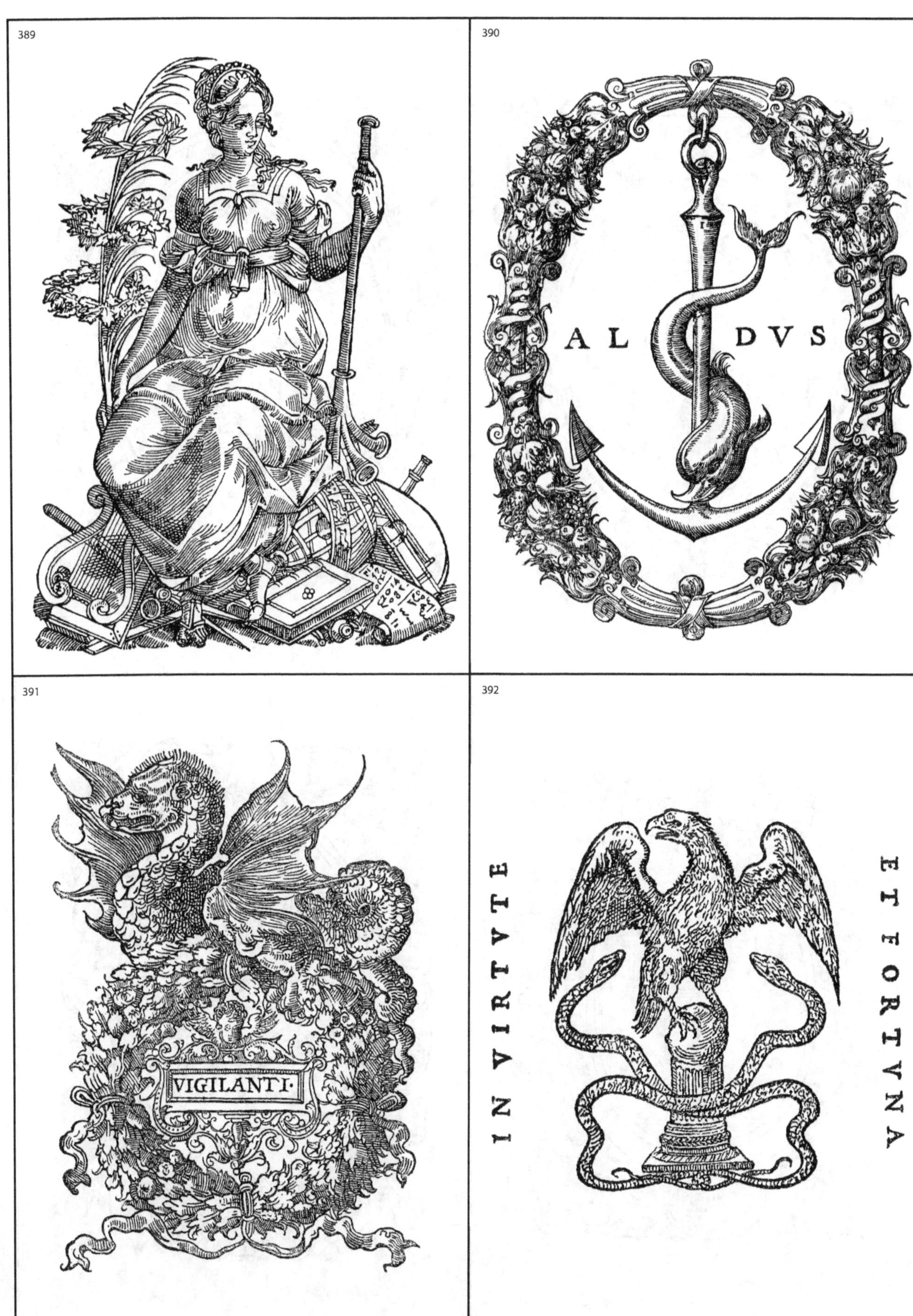

389

390
AL DVS

391
VIGILANTI·

392
IN VIRTVTE
ET FORTVNA

393

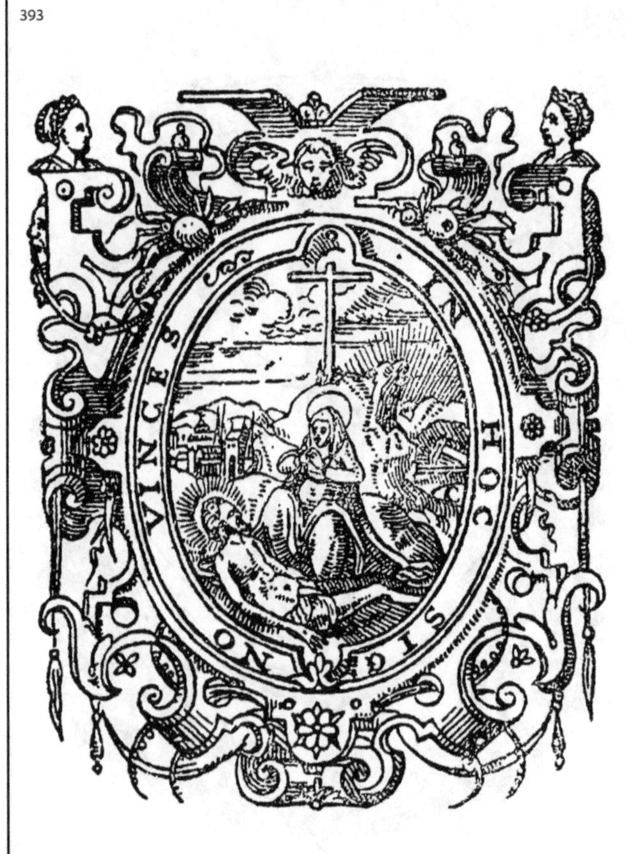

394

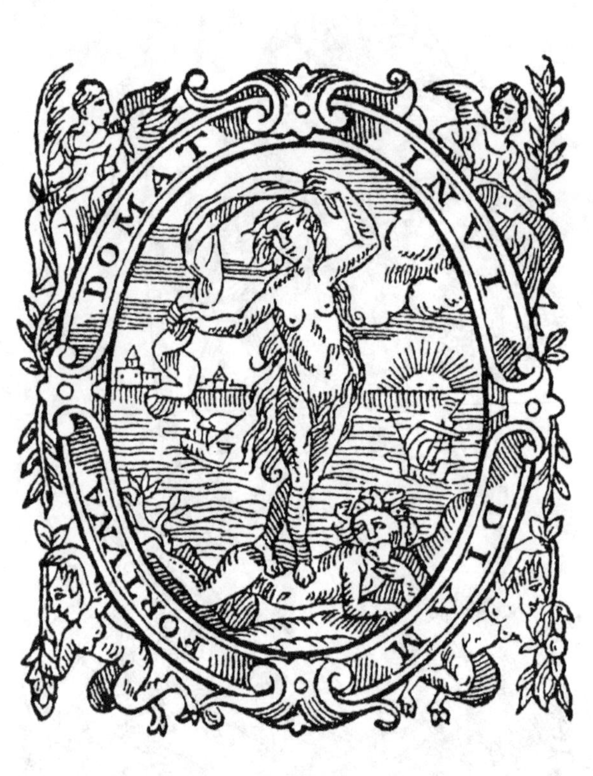

395

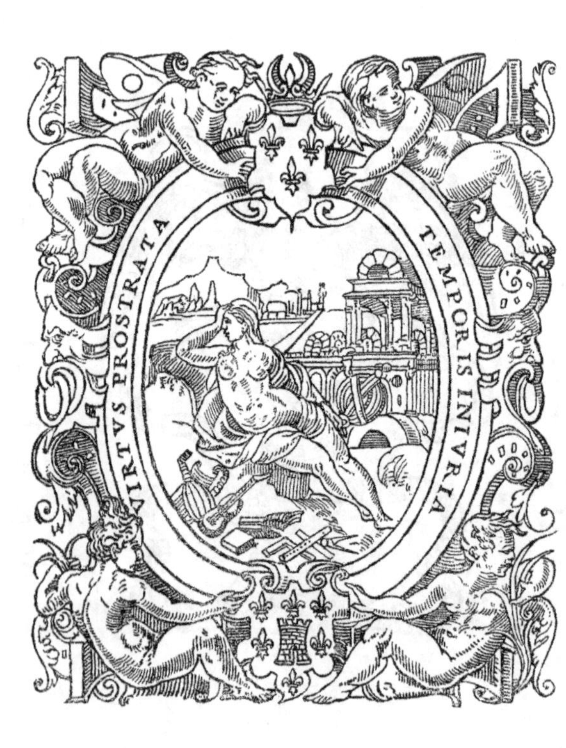

396

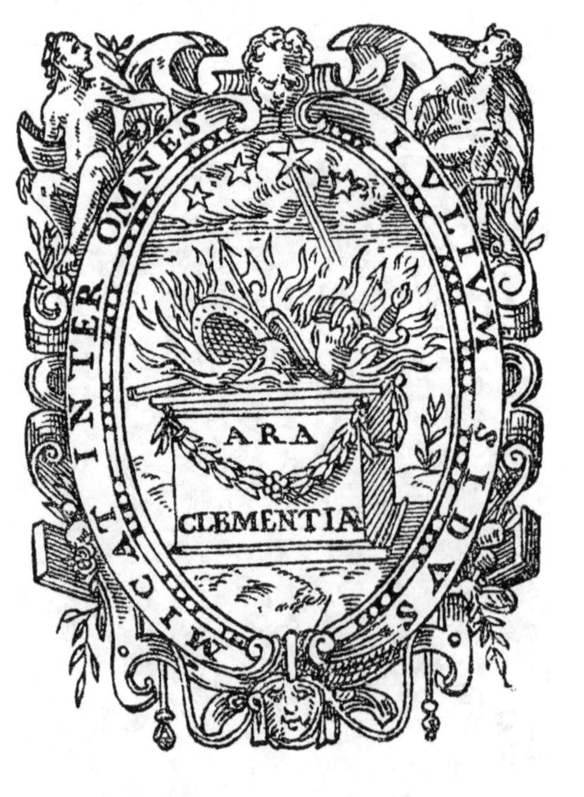

397

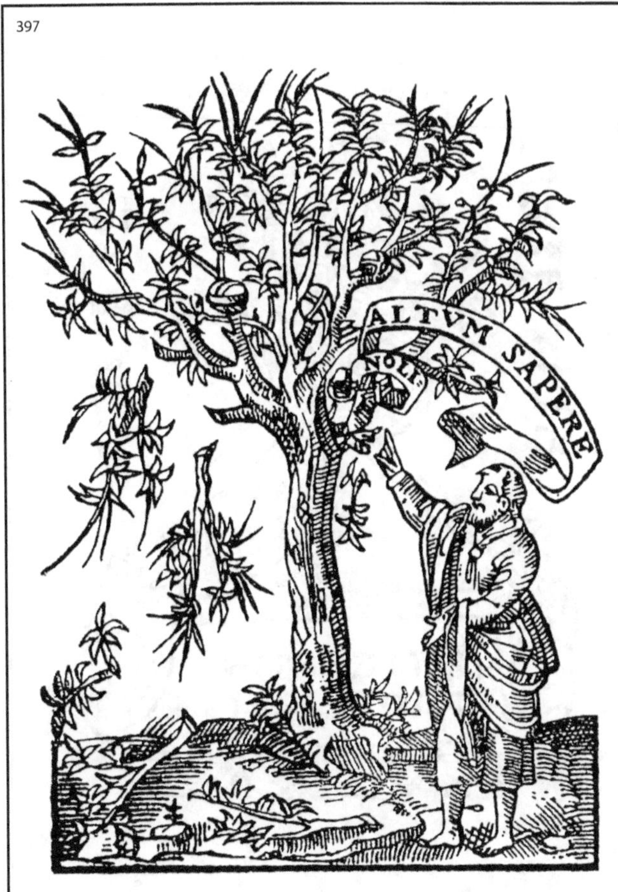

398

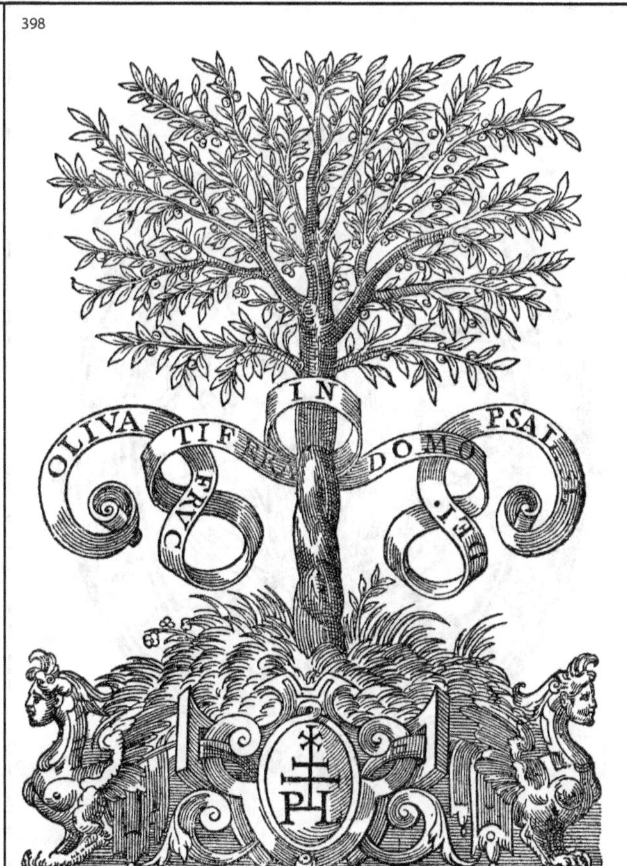

399

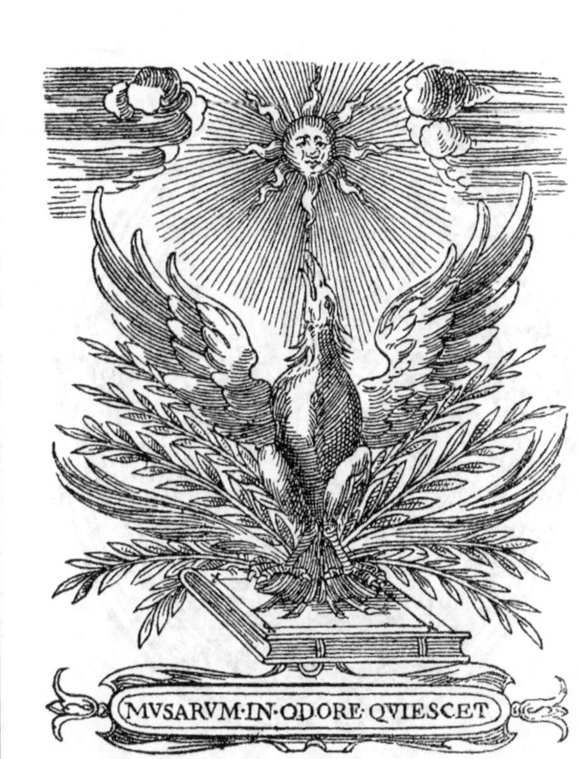

400

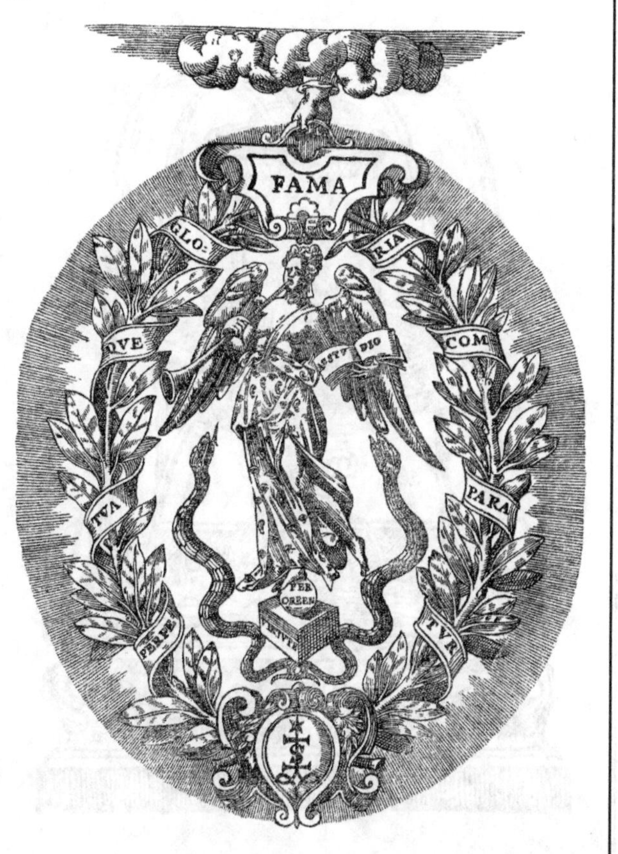

401

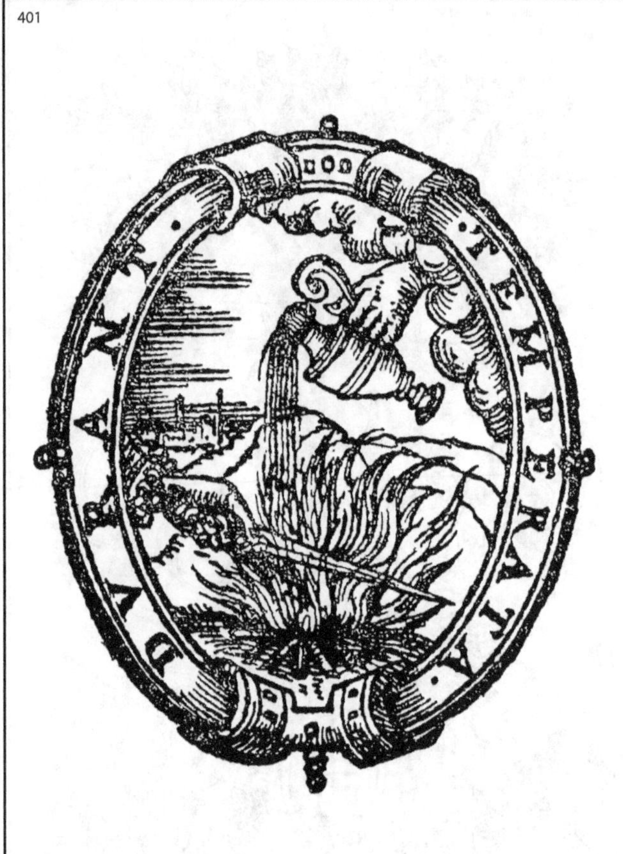

402

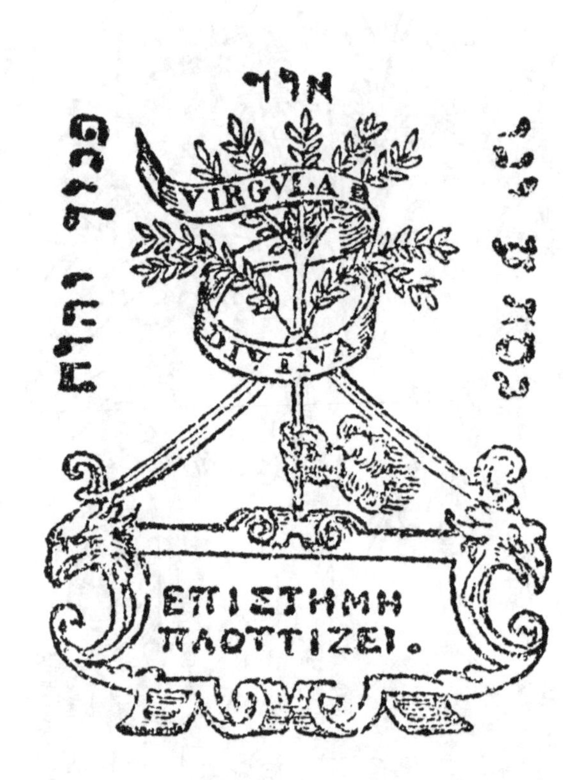

403

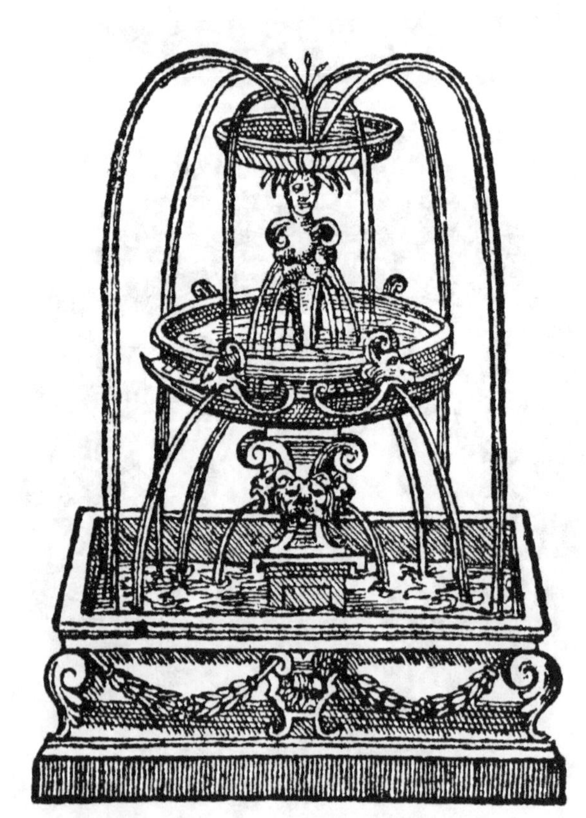

404

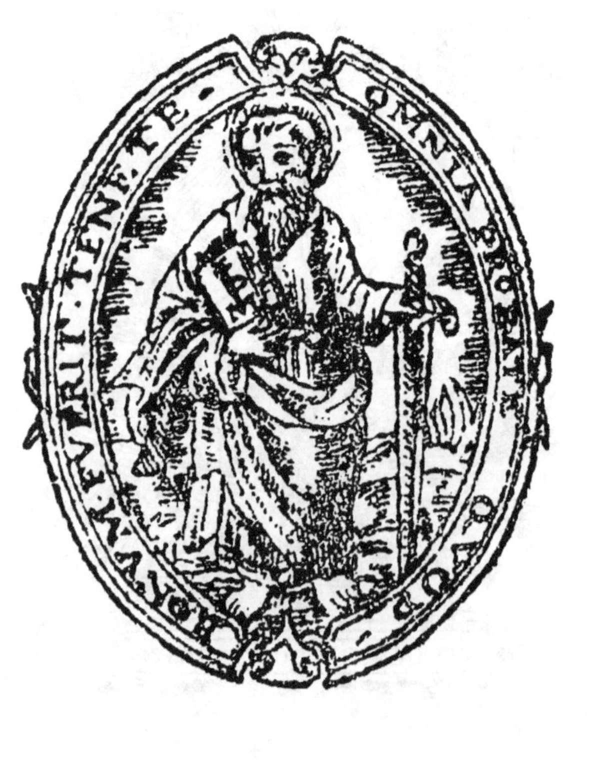

405

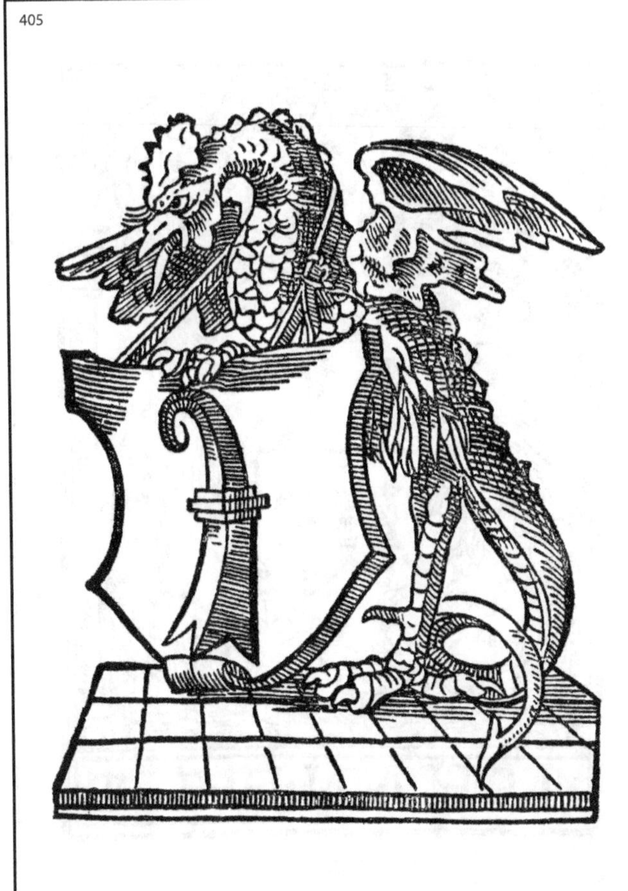

406

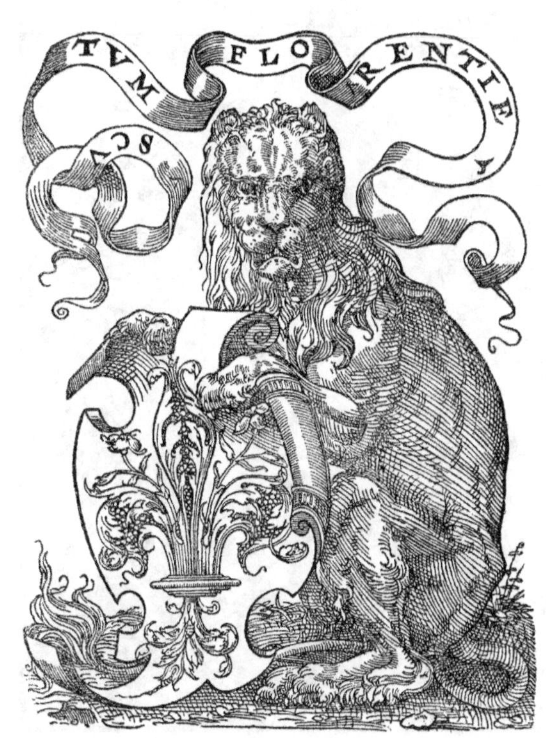

407

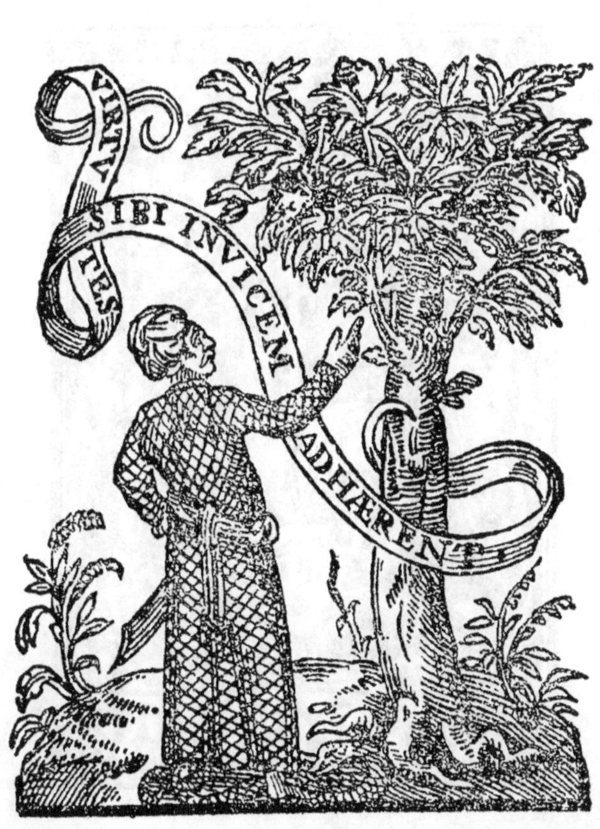

408

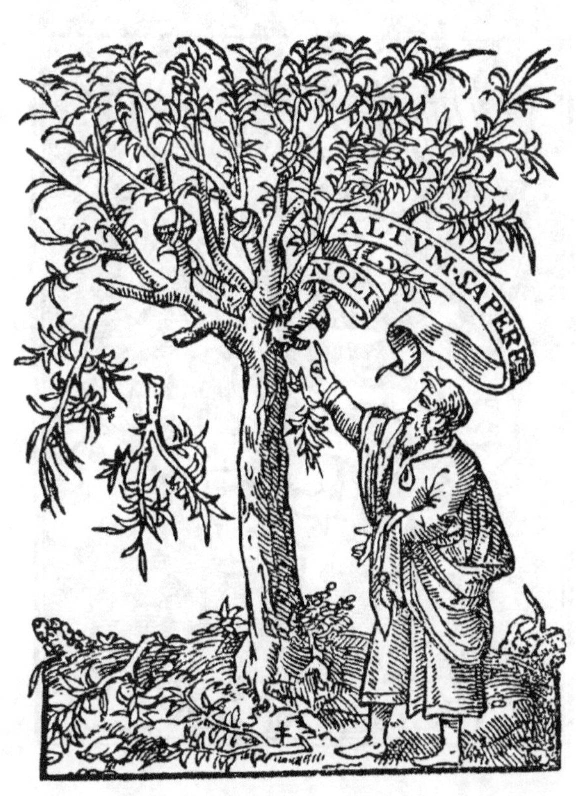

409

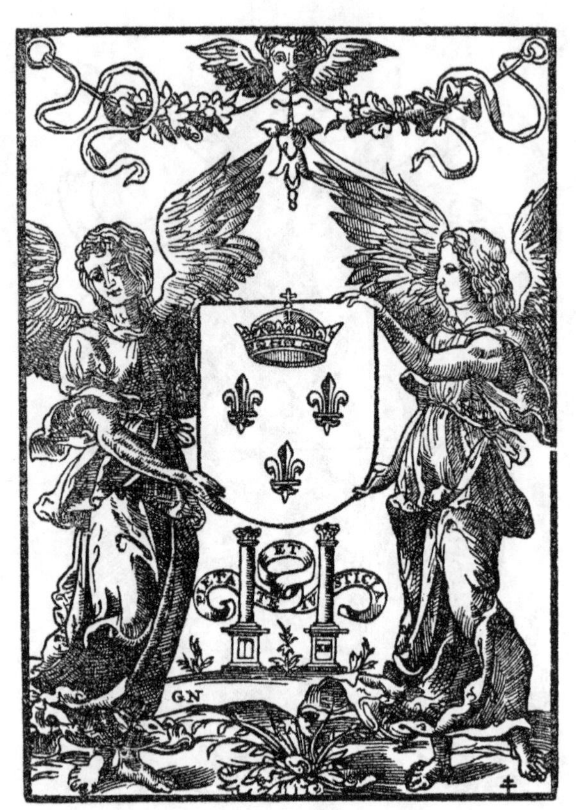

410

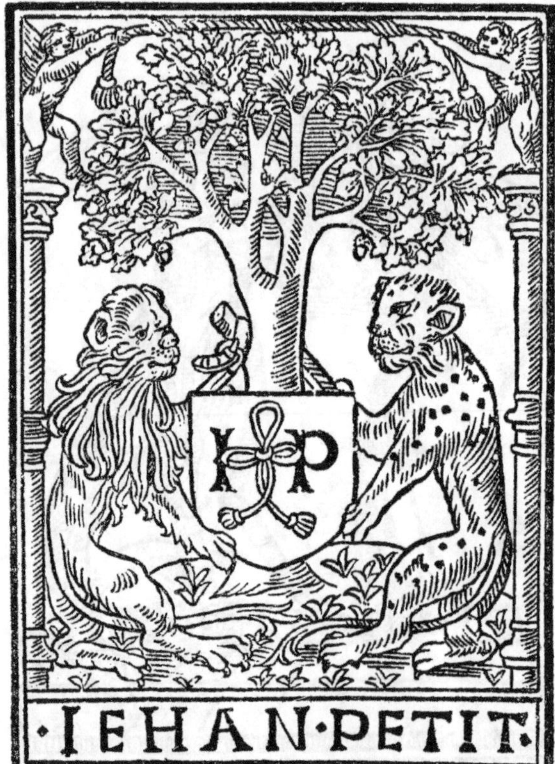

411

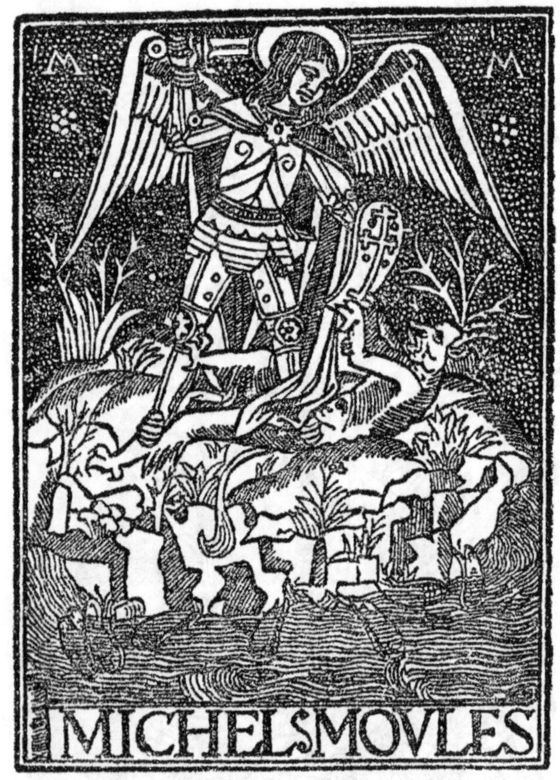

412

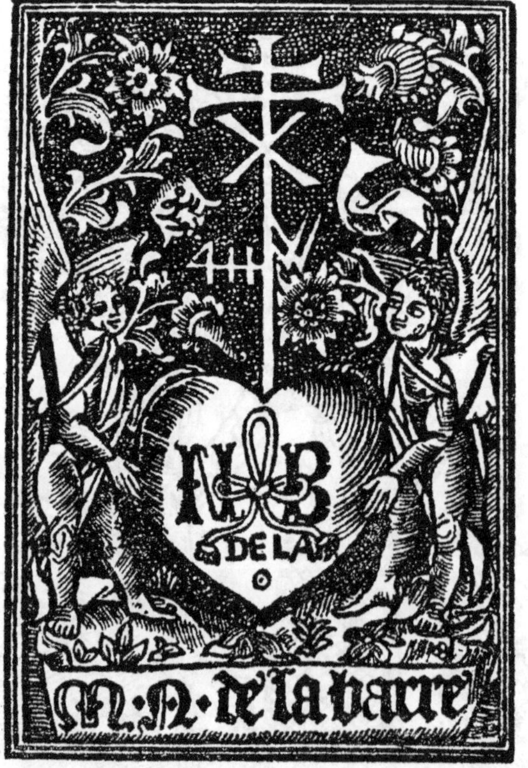

413

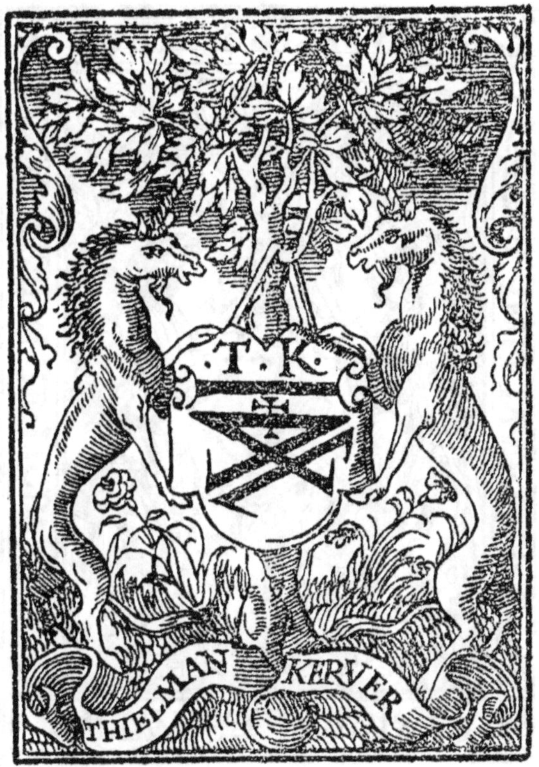

414

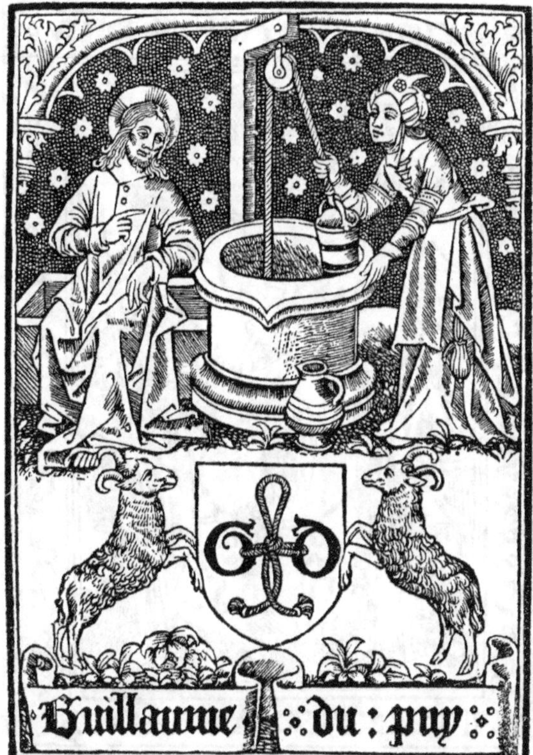

415

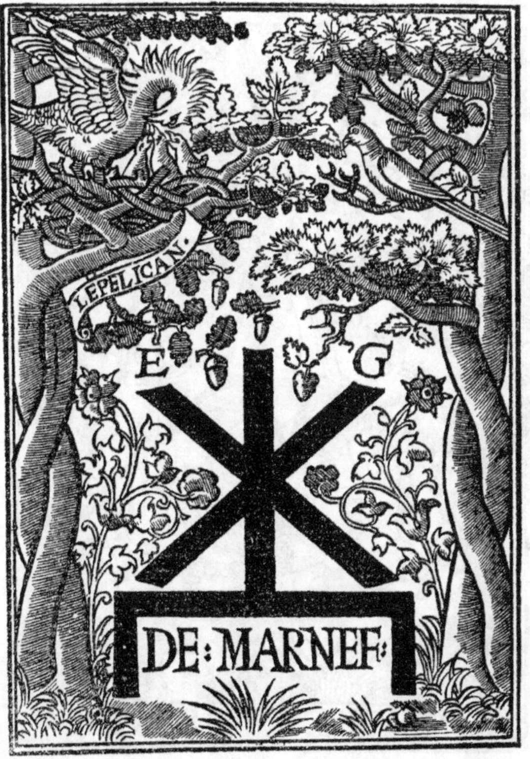

416

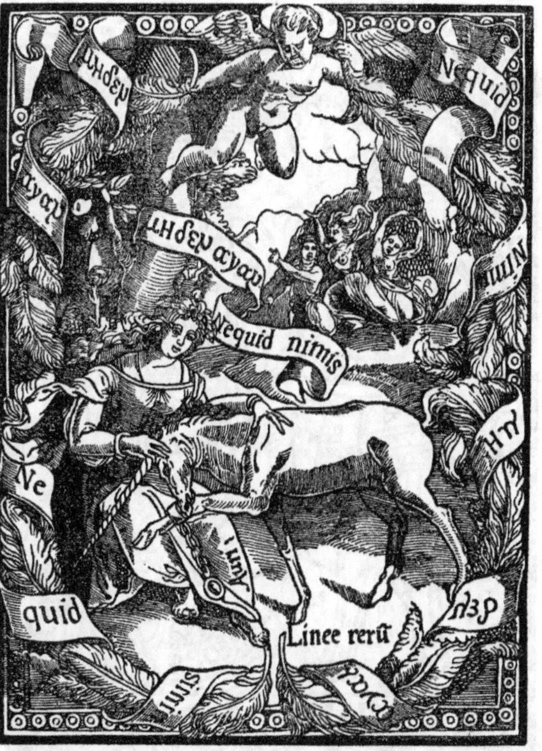

417

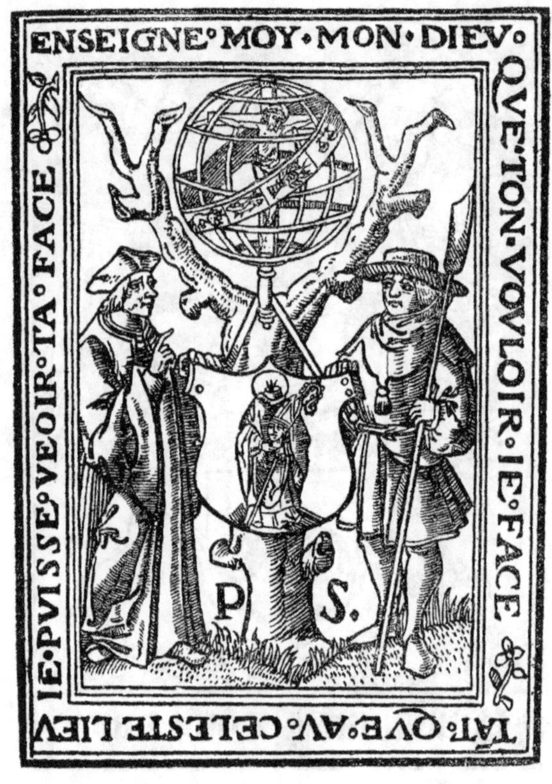

418

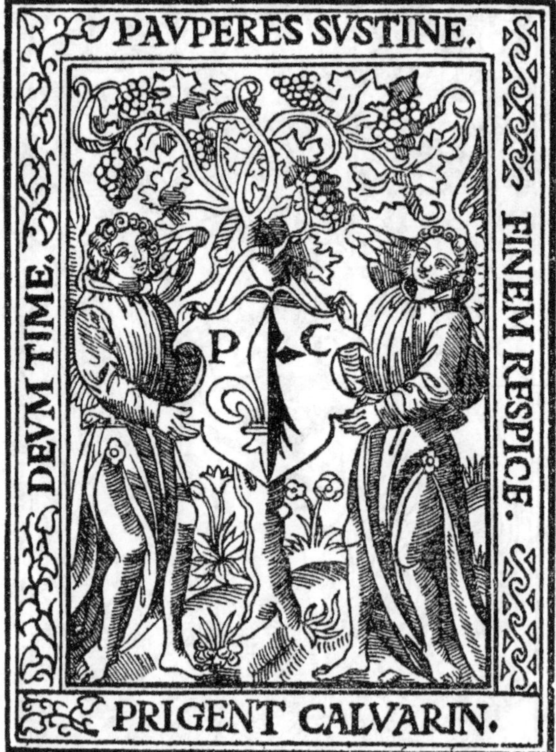

419

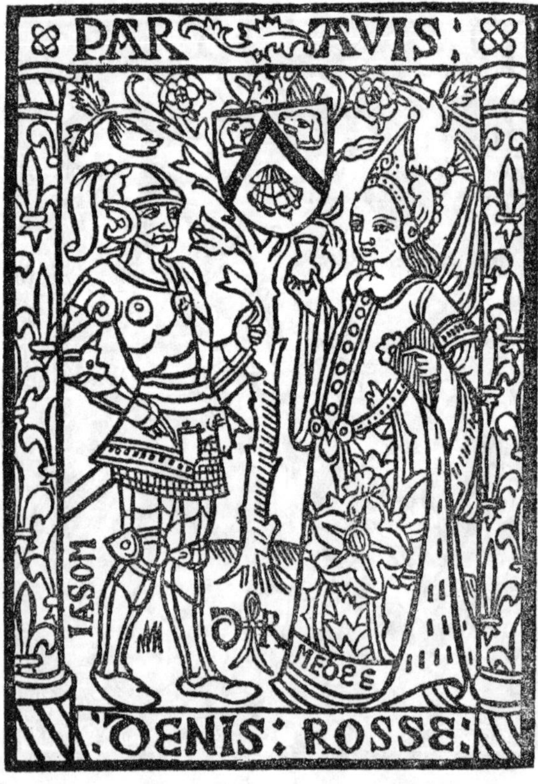

420

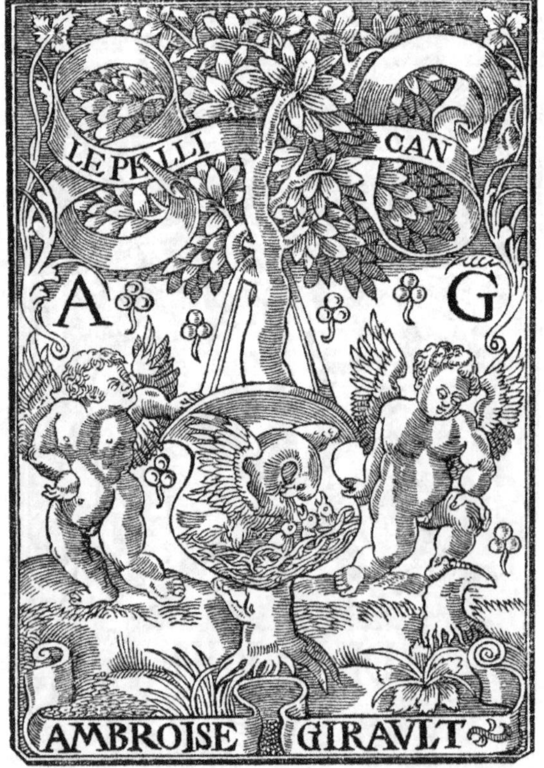

421

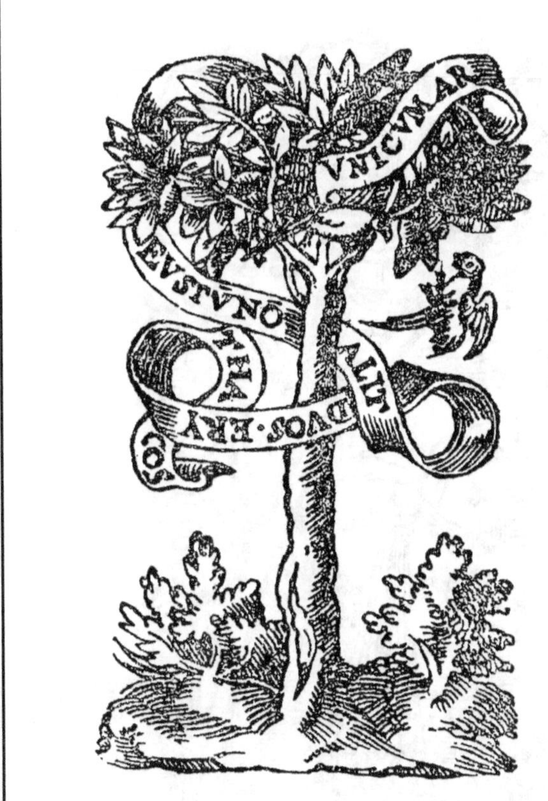

422

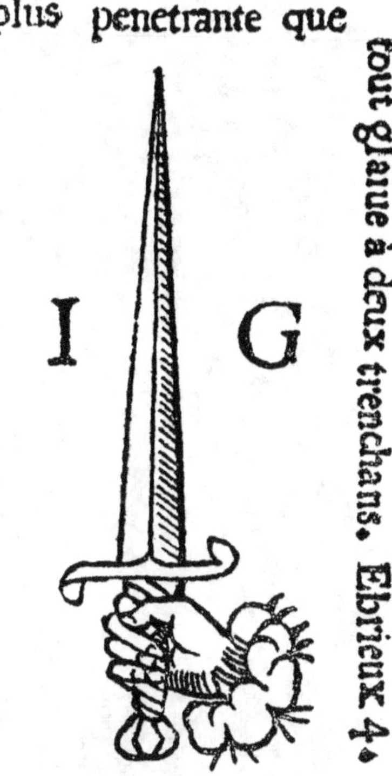

423

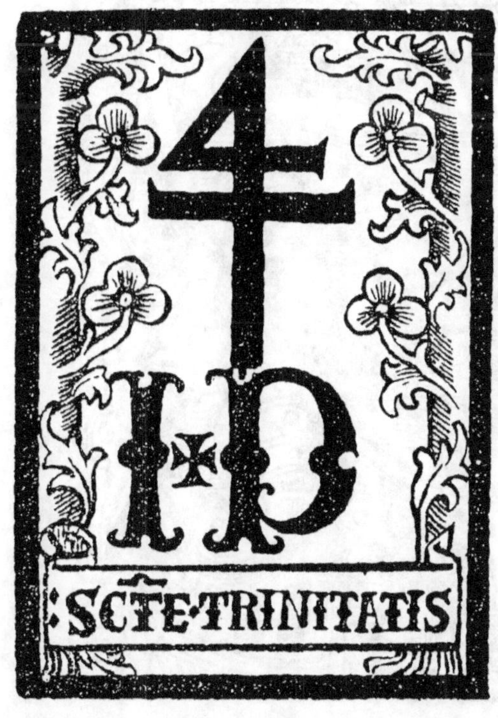

424

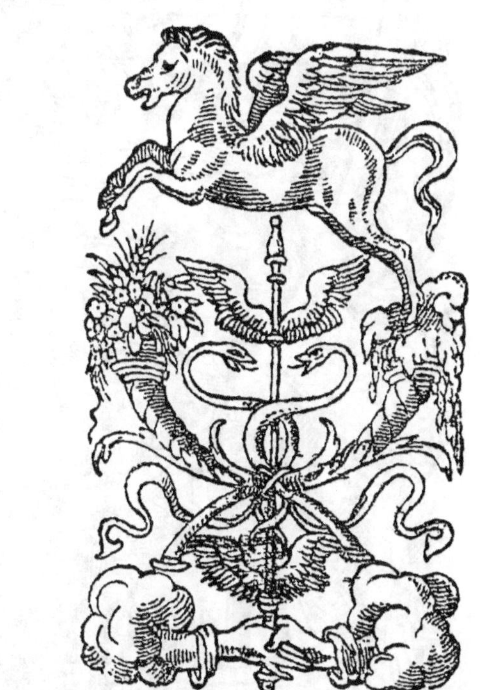

425

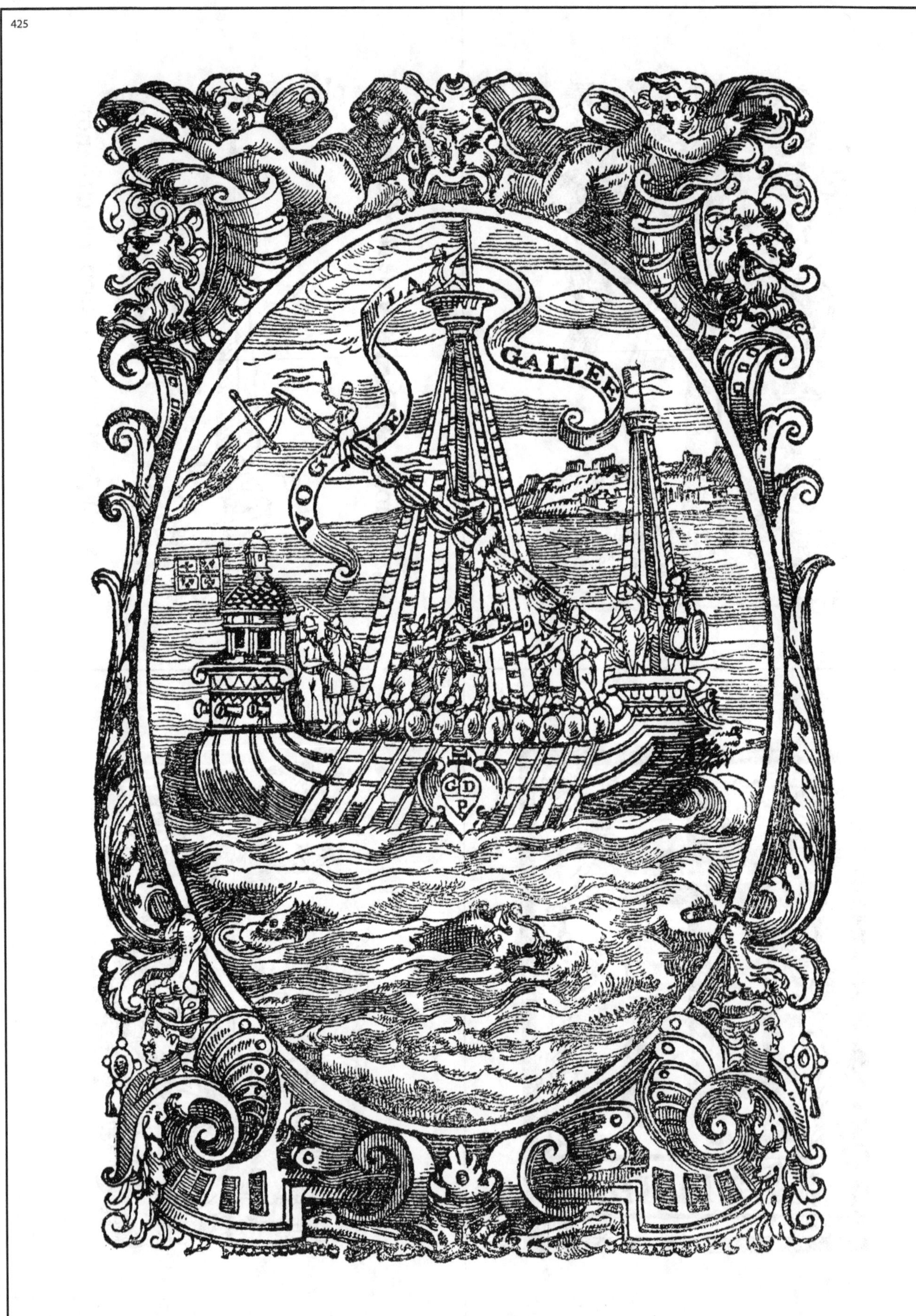

426

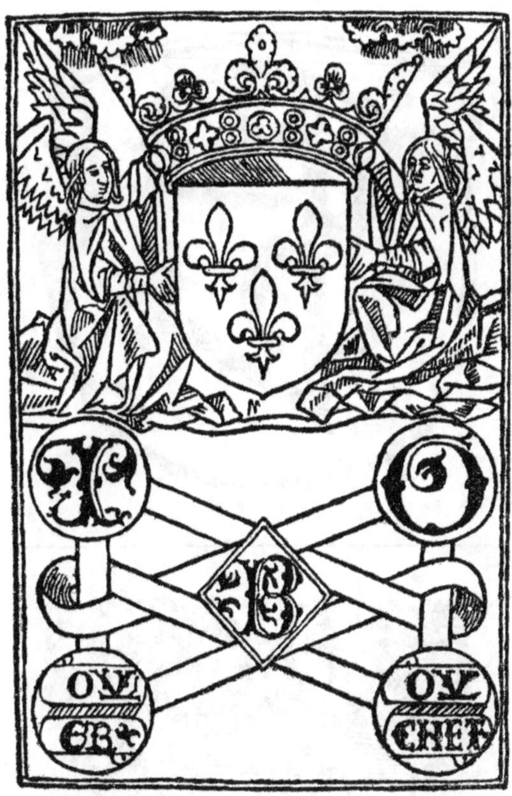

427

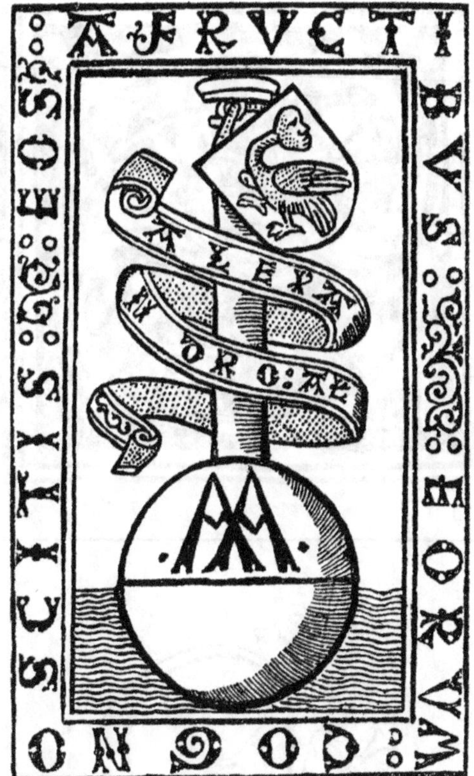

428

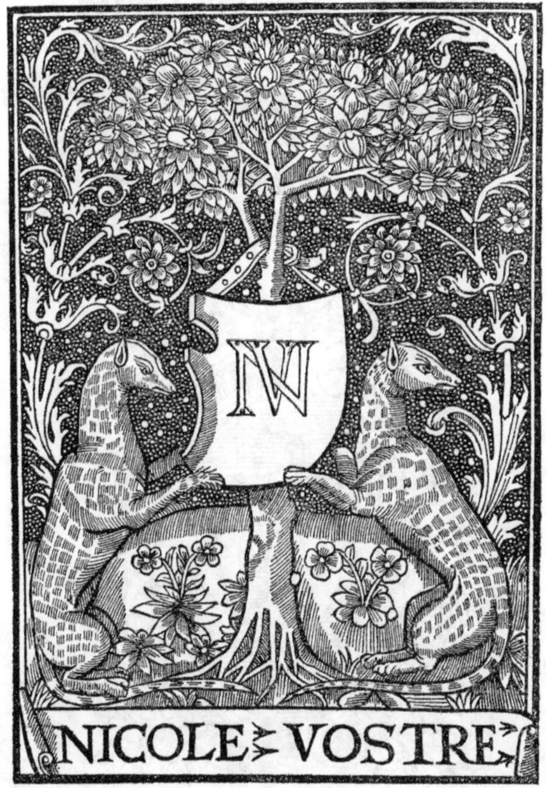

429

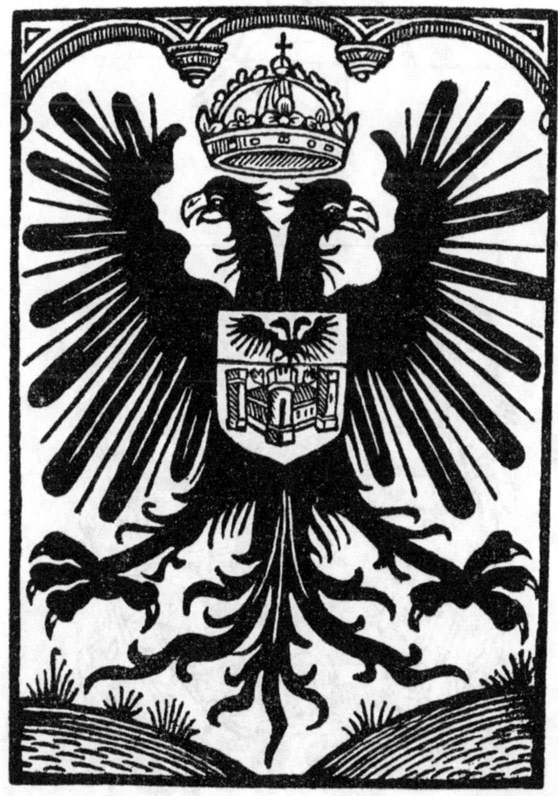

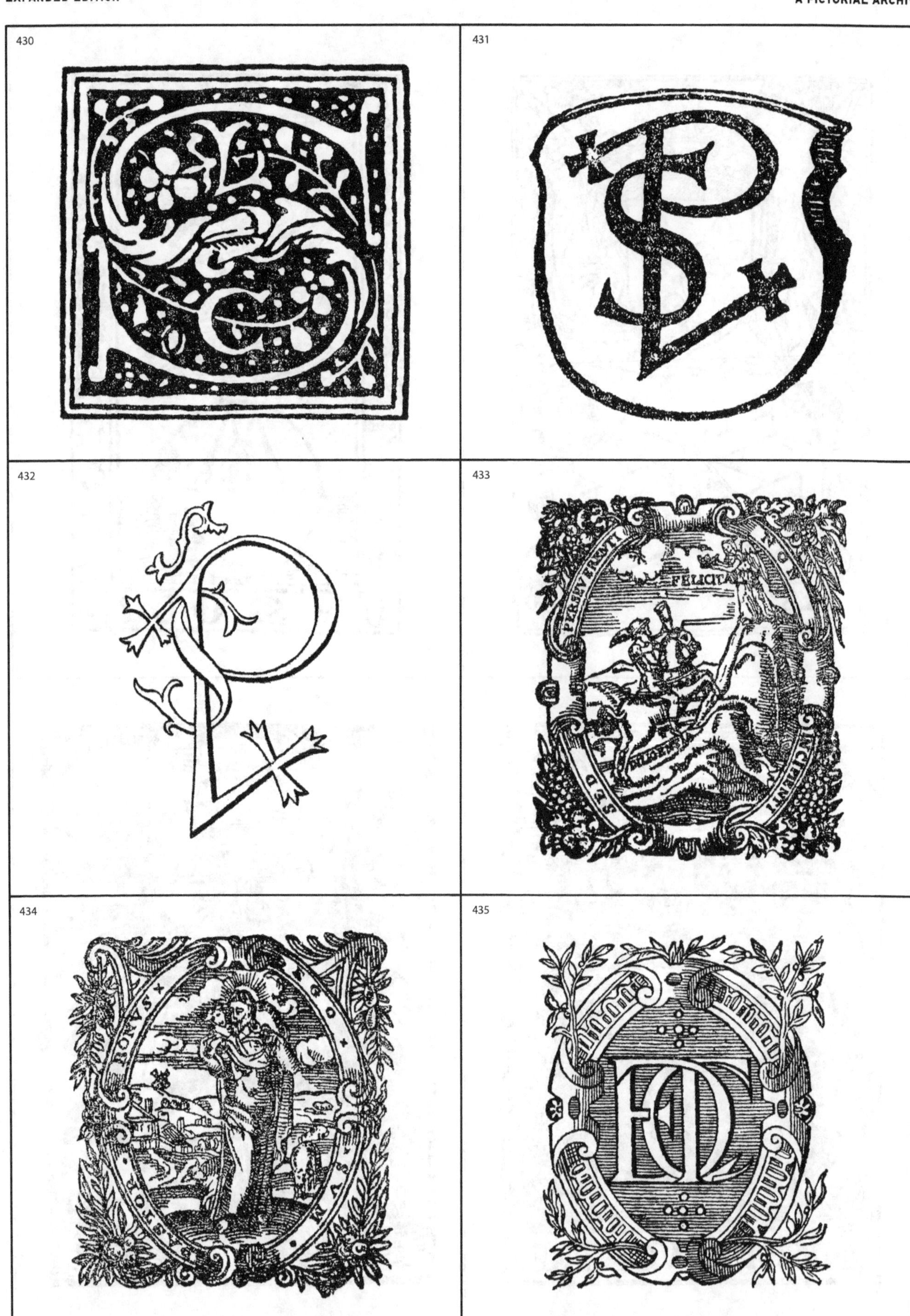

430

431

432

433

434

435

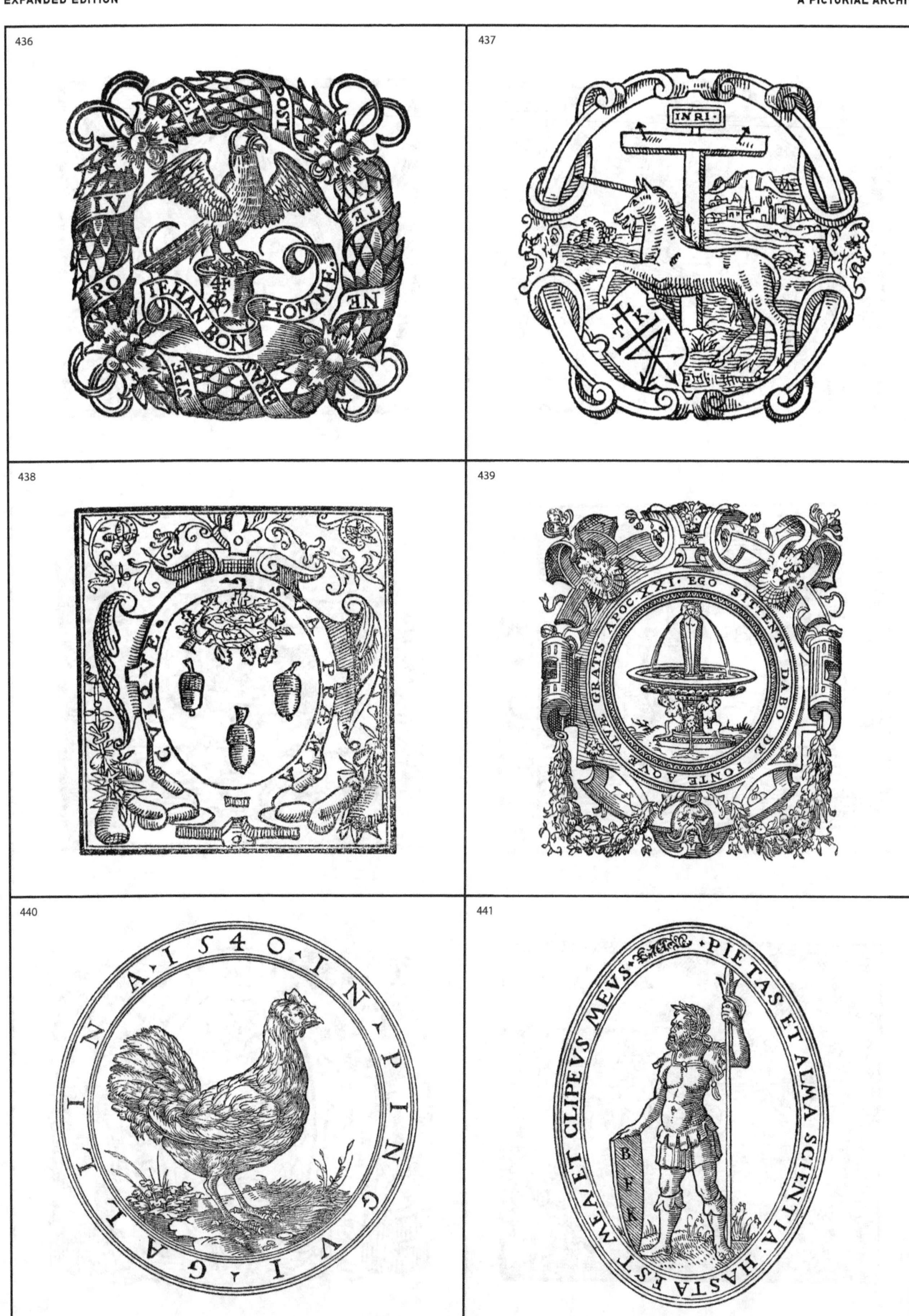

442

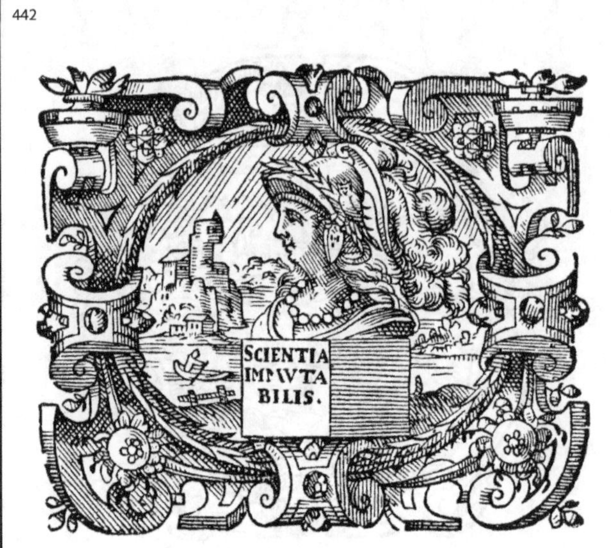

443

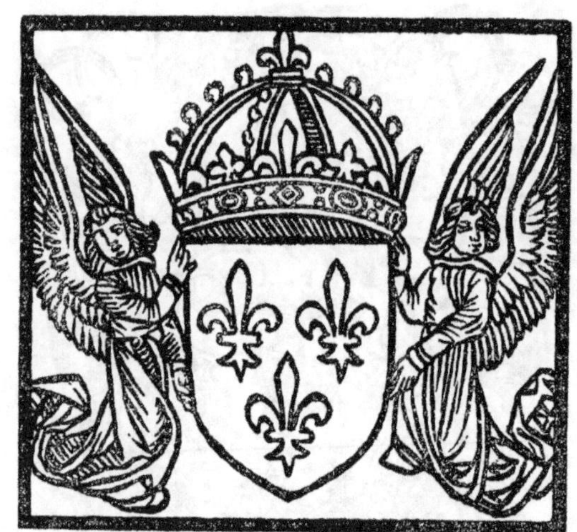

444

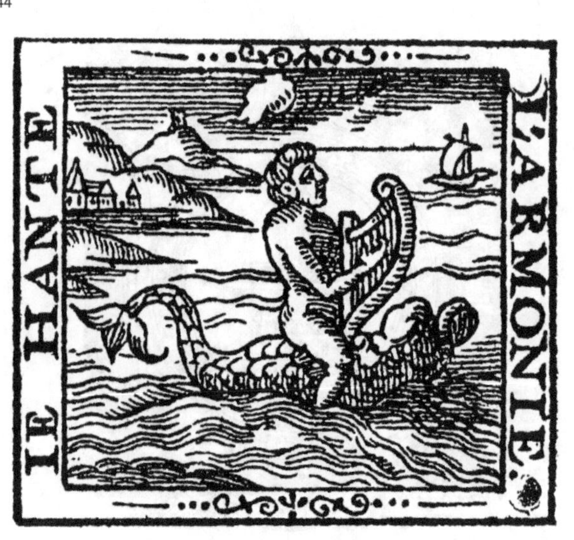

445

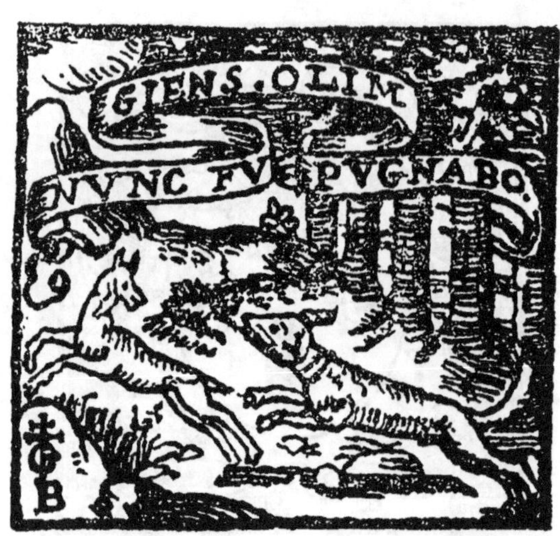

446

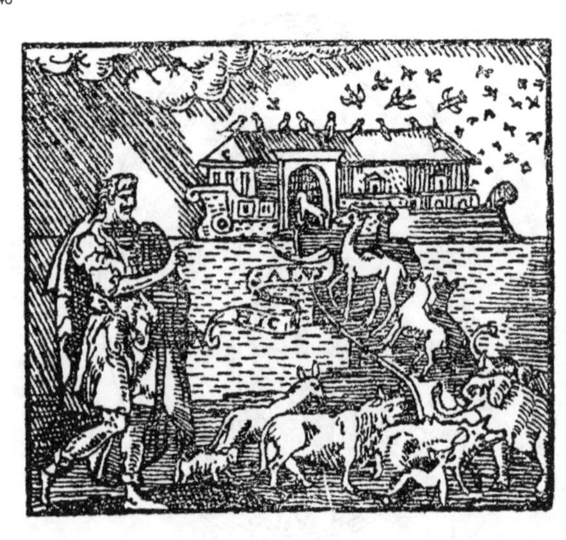

447

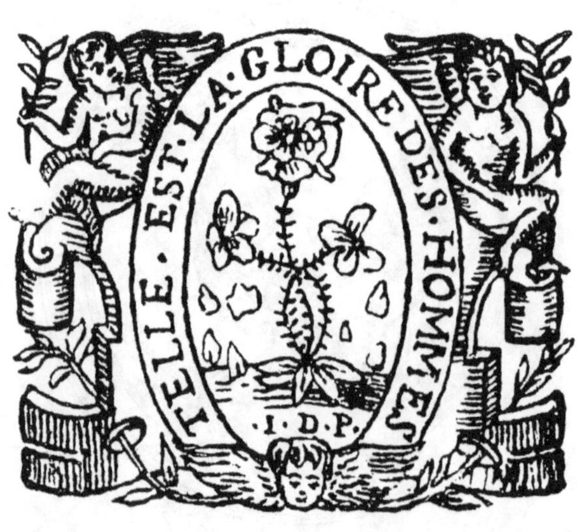

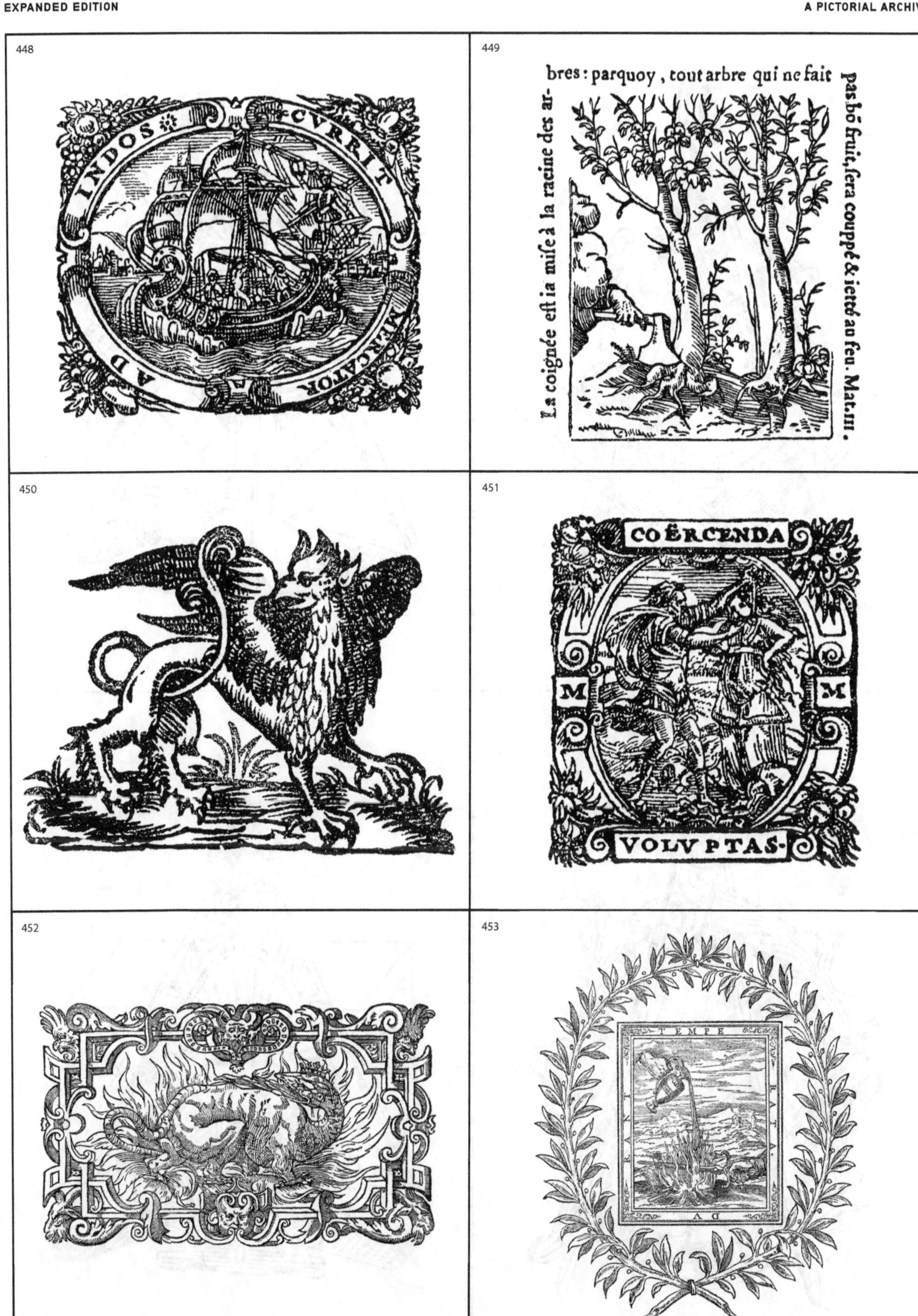

448
CVRRIT · AD INDOS · MERCATOR ·

449
bres : parquoy , tout arbre qui ne fait
pas bõ fruit, fera couppé & ietté au feu. Mat.III.
La coignée est ia mise à la racine des ar-

450

451
COERCENDA
M M
VOLVPTAS·

452

453
TEMPE

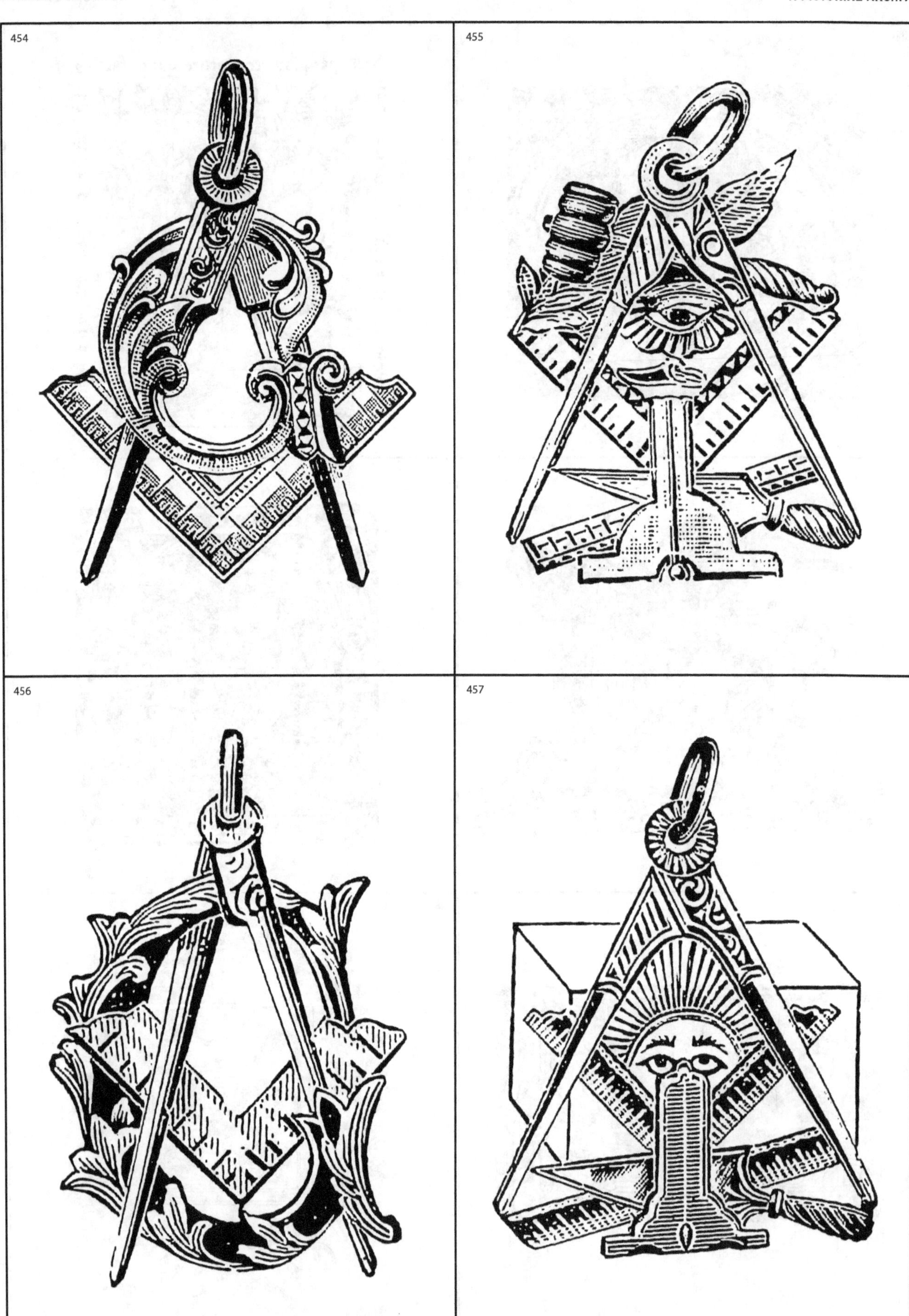

454

455

456

457

458

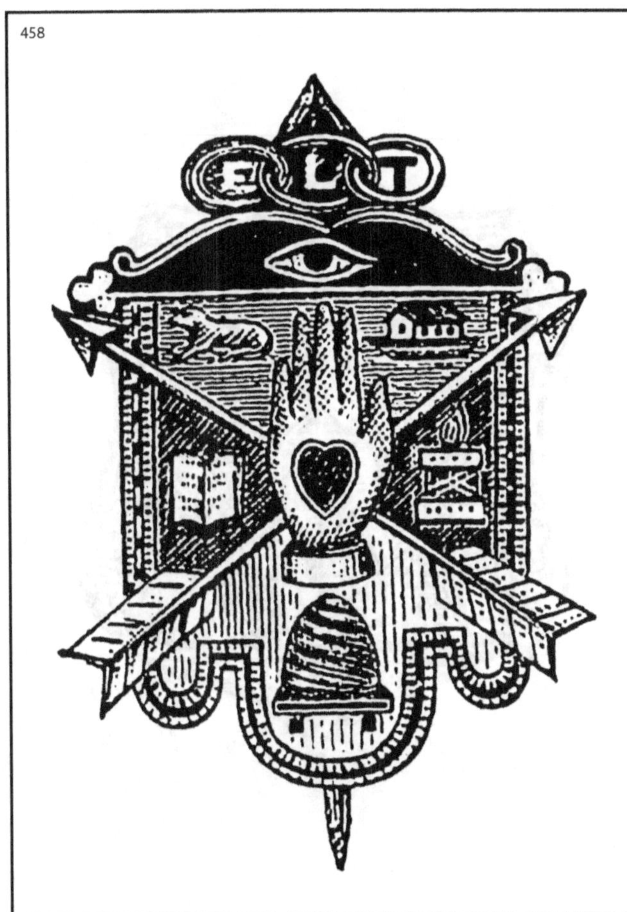

459

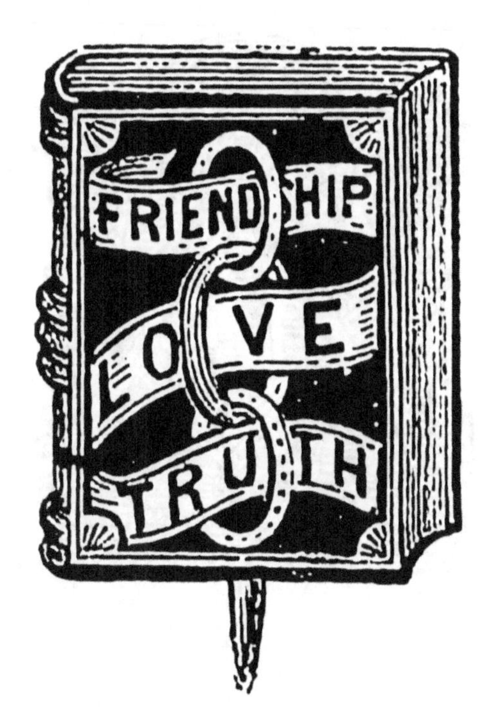

460

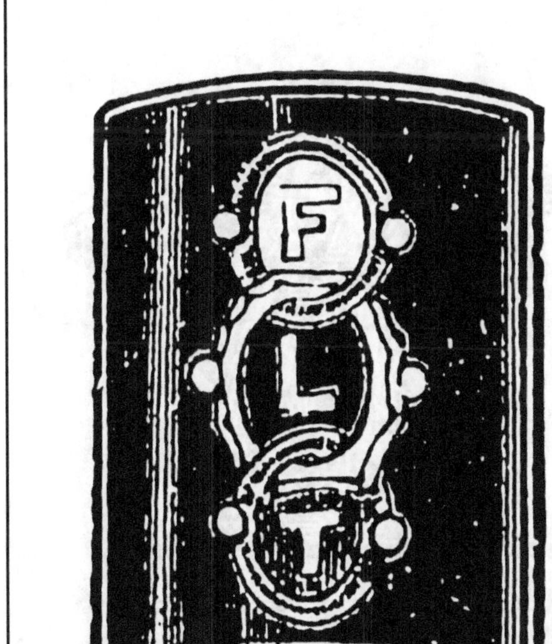

461

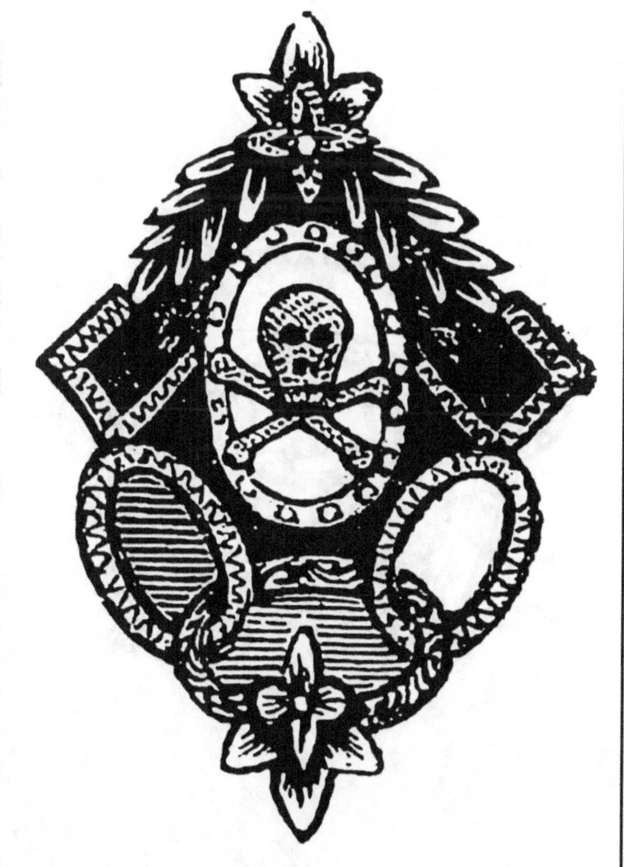

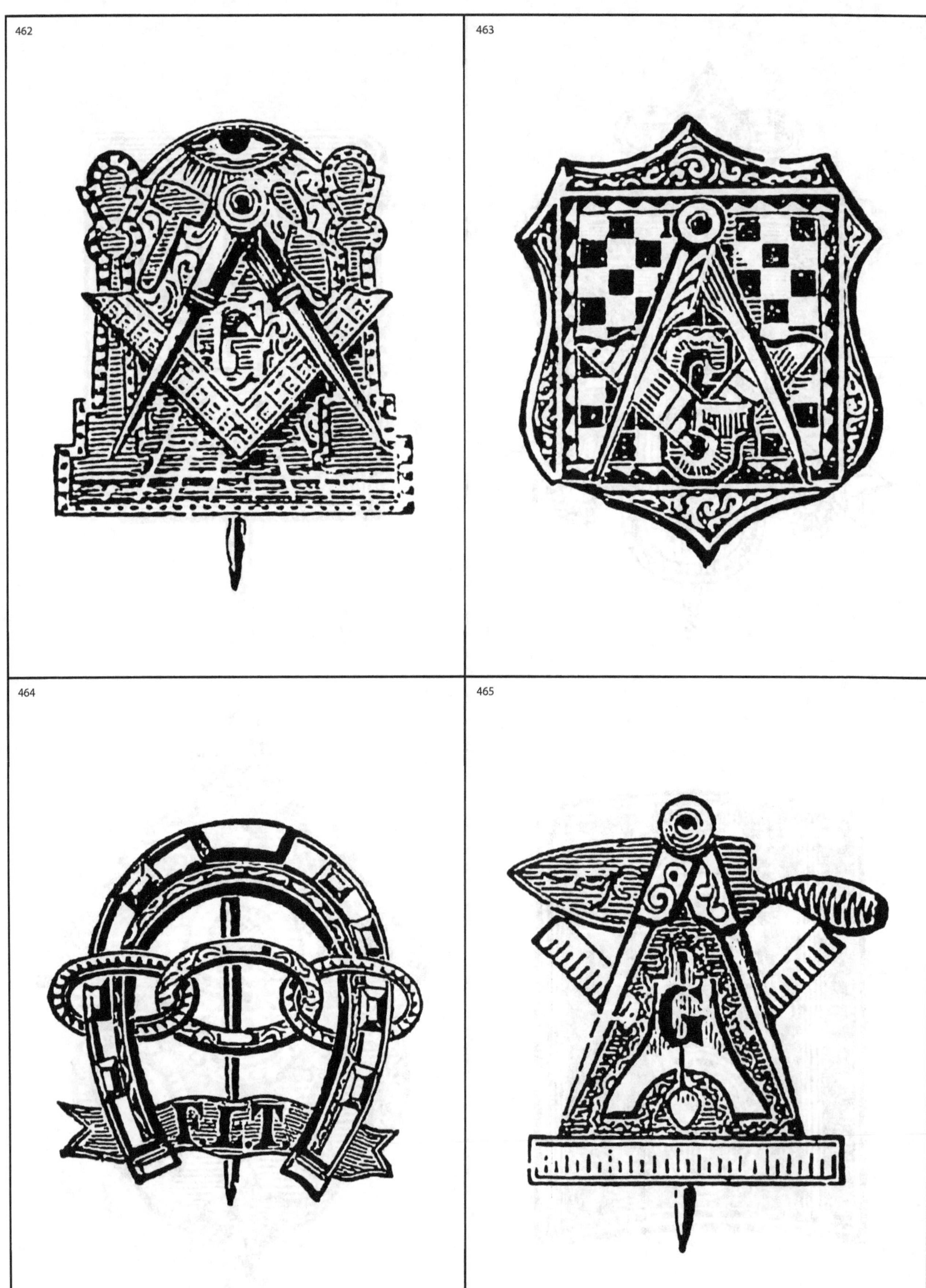

462

463

464

465

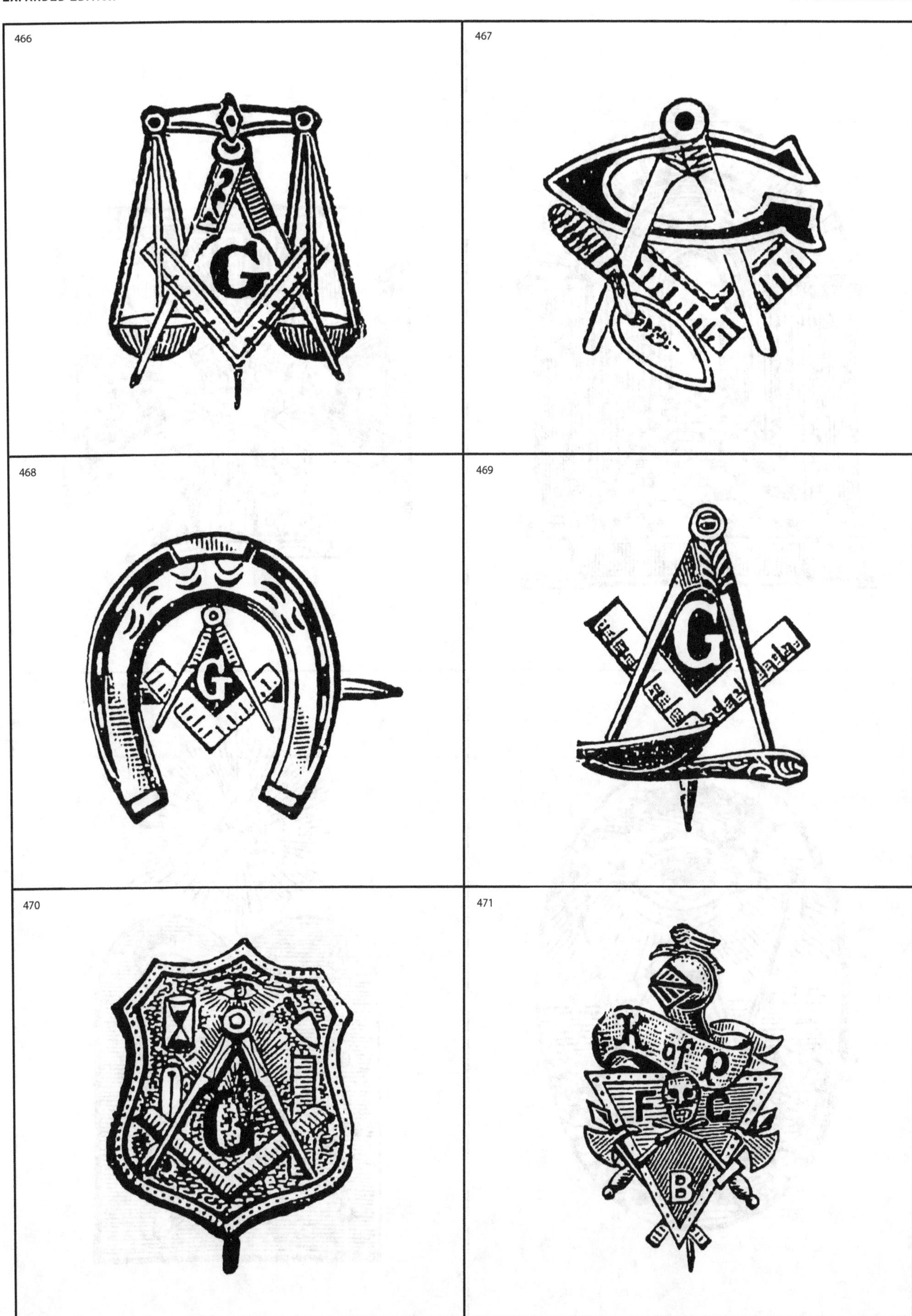
466
467
468
469
470
471
K of P
F C
B

472

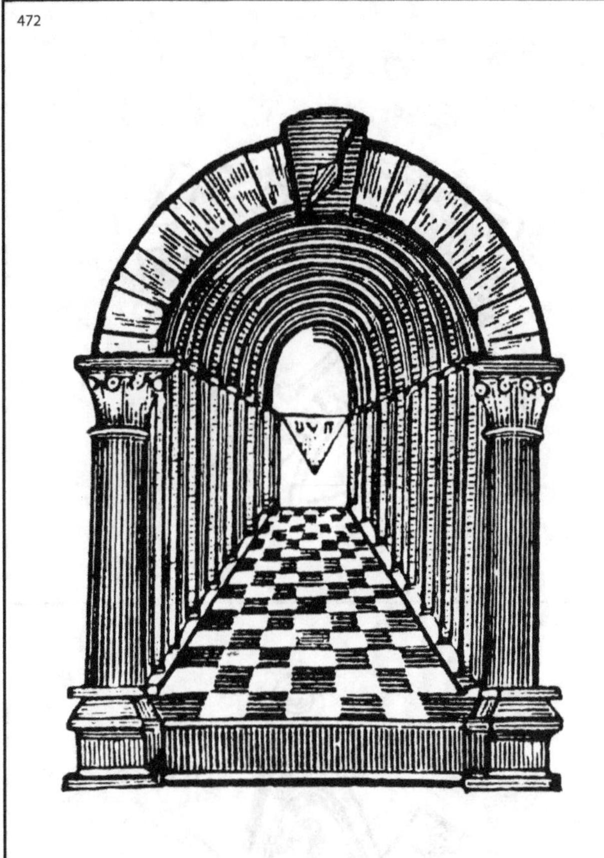

473

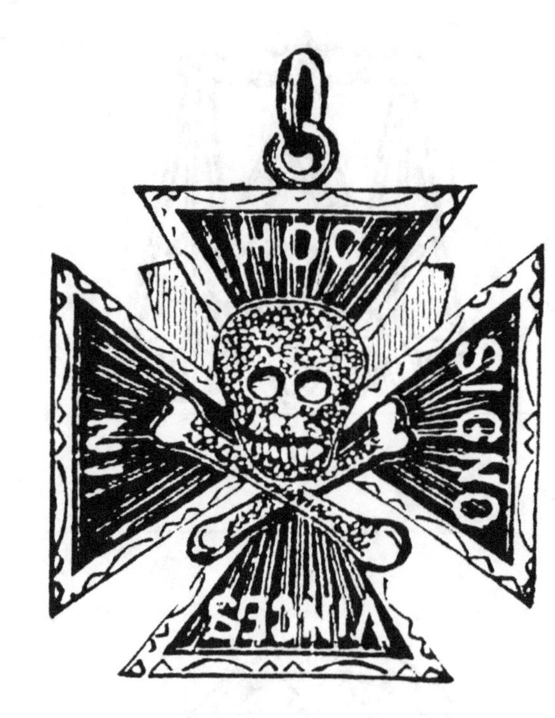

474

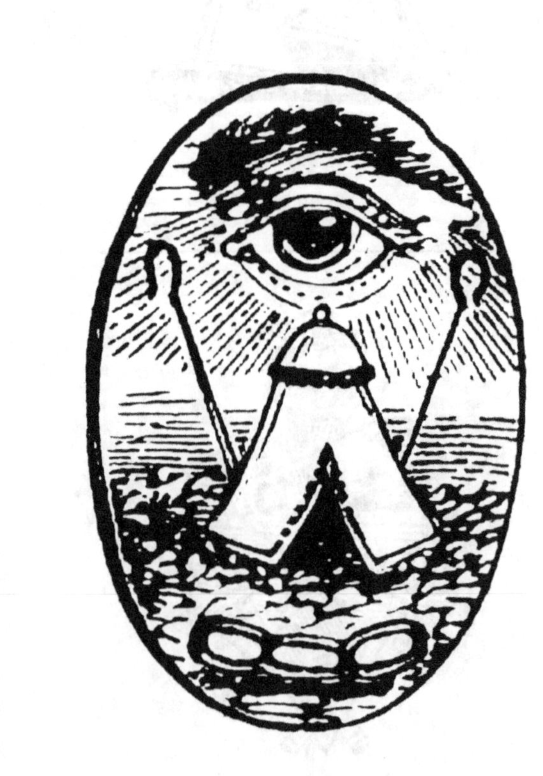

475

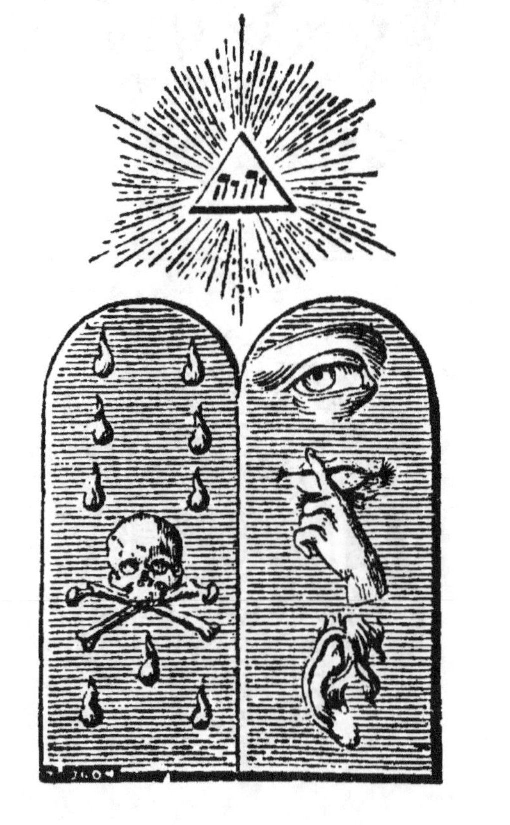

476

477

478

479

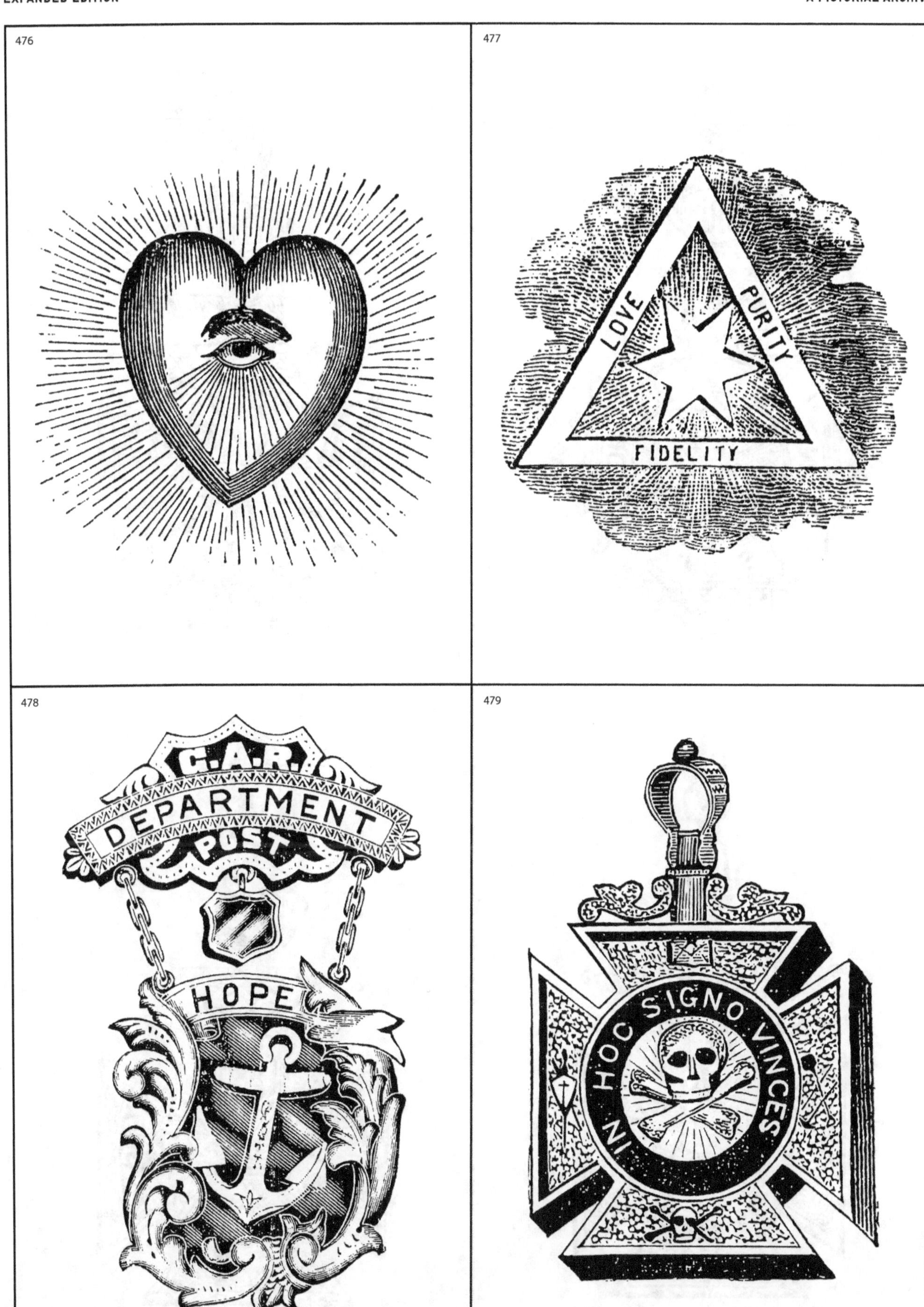

480

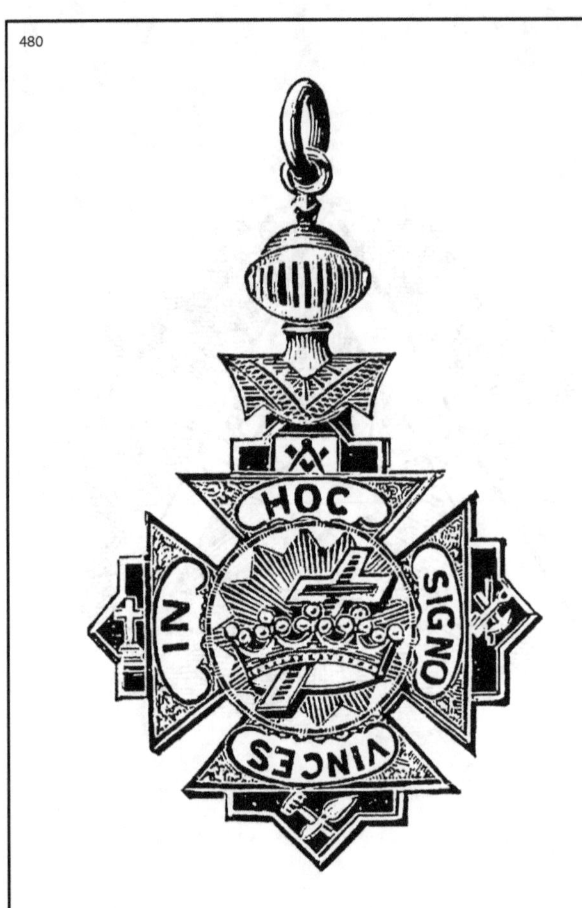

481

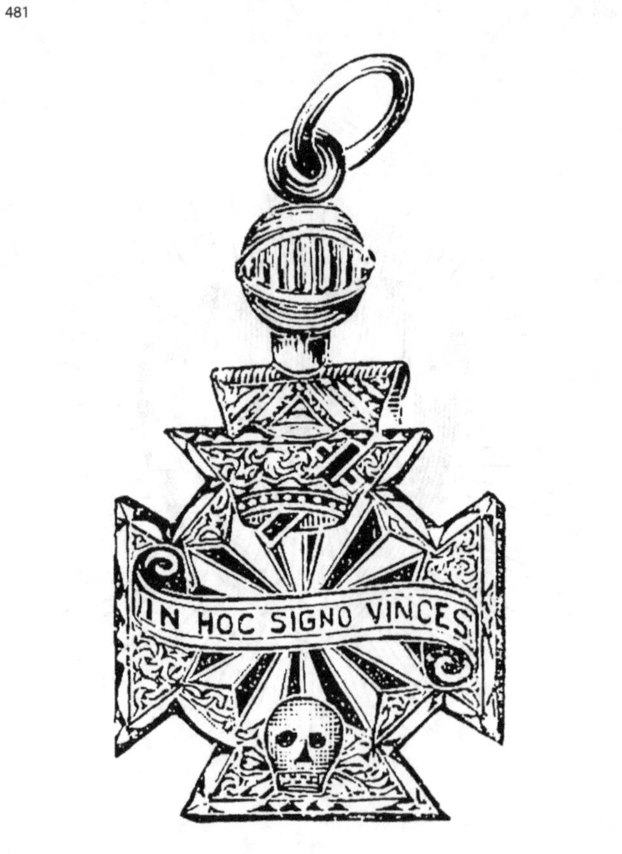

482

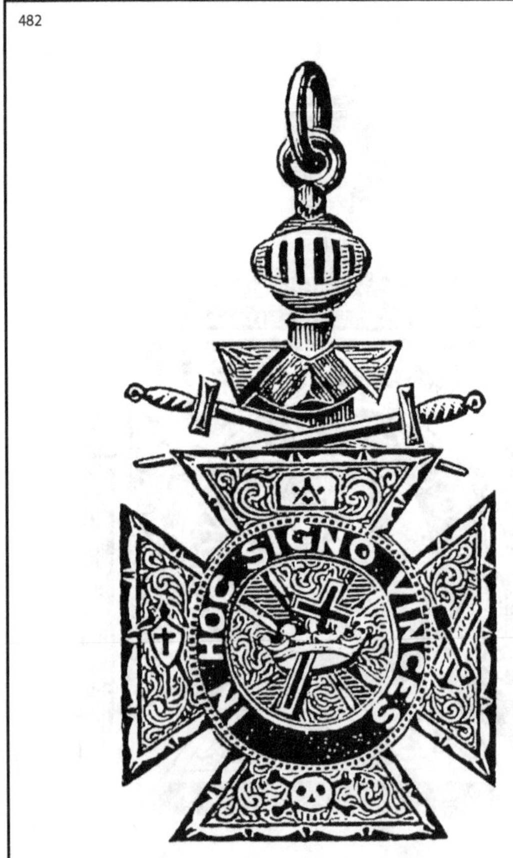

483

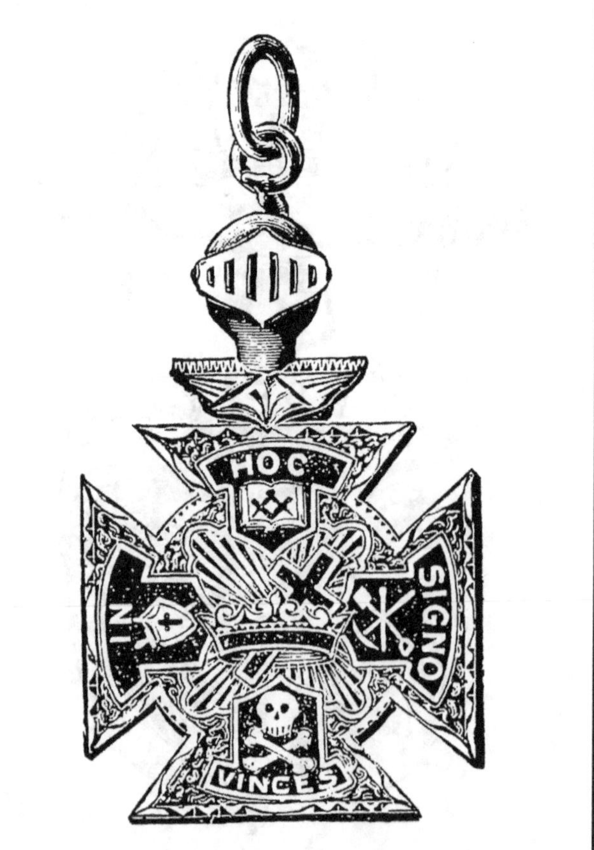

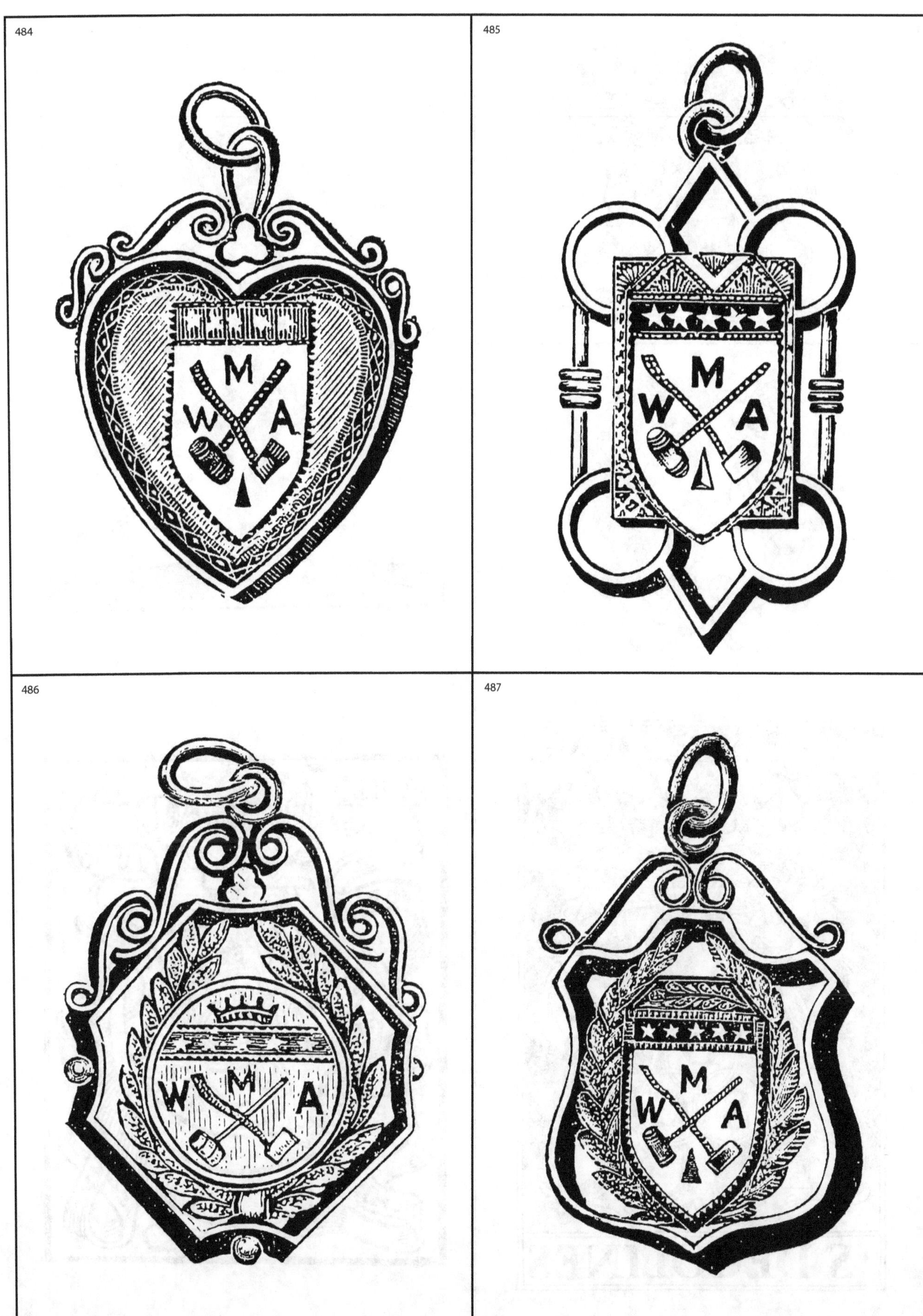

484

485

486

487

488

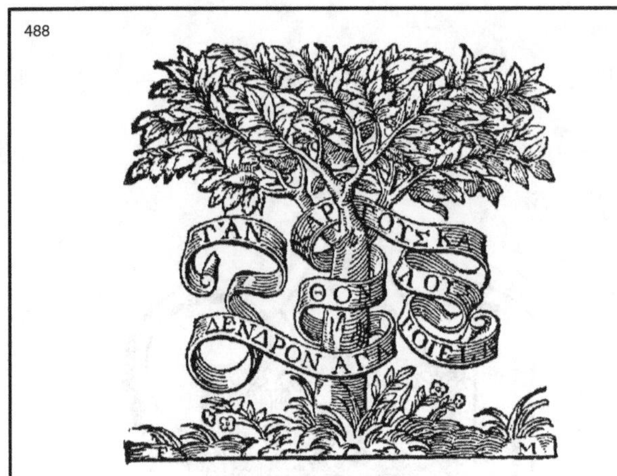

490

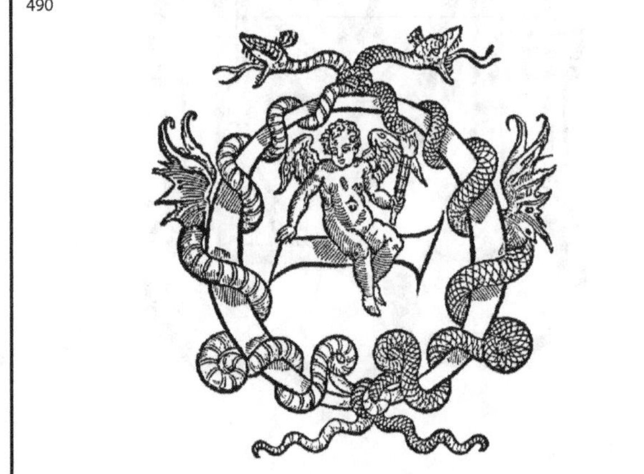

489

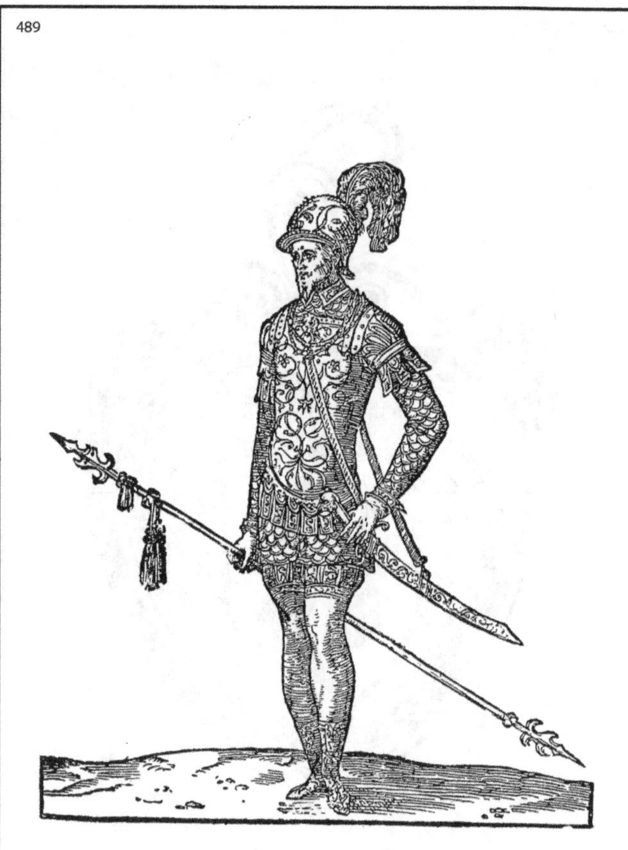

491

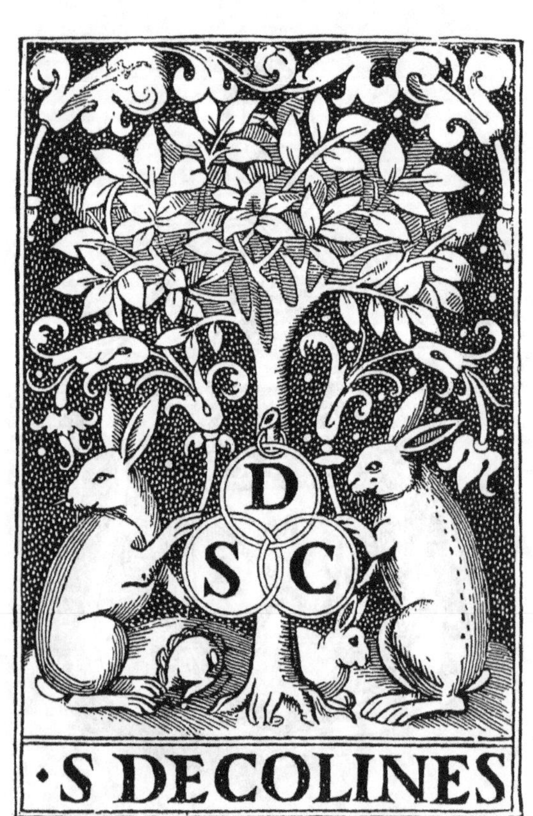

492

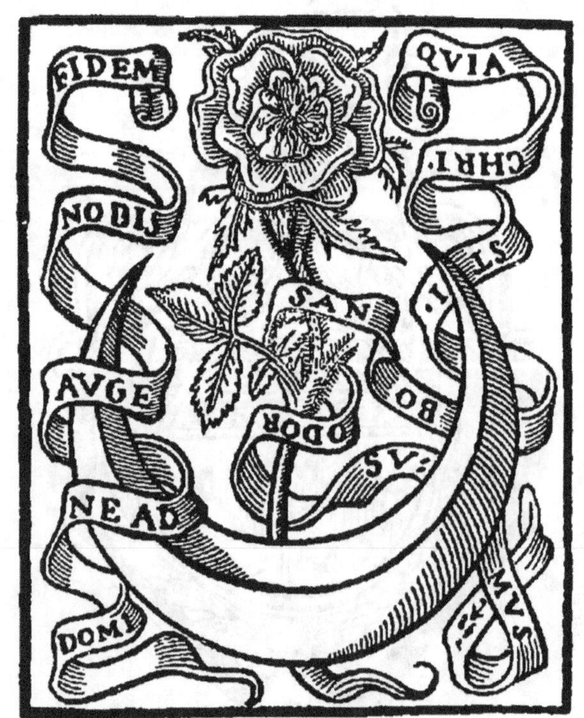

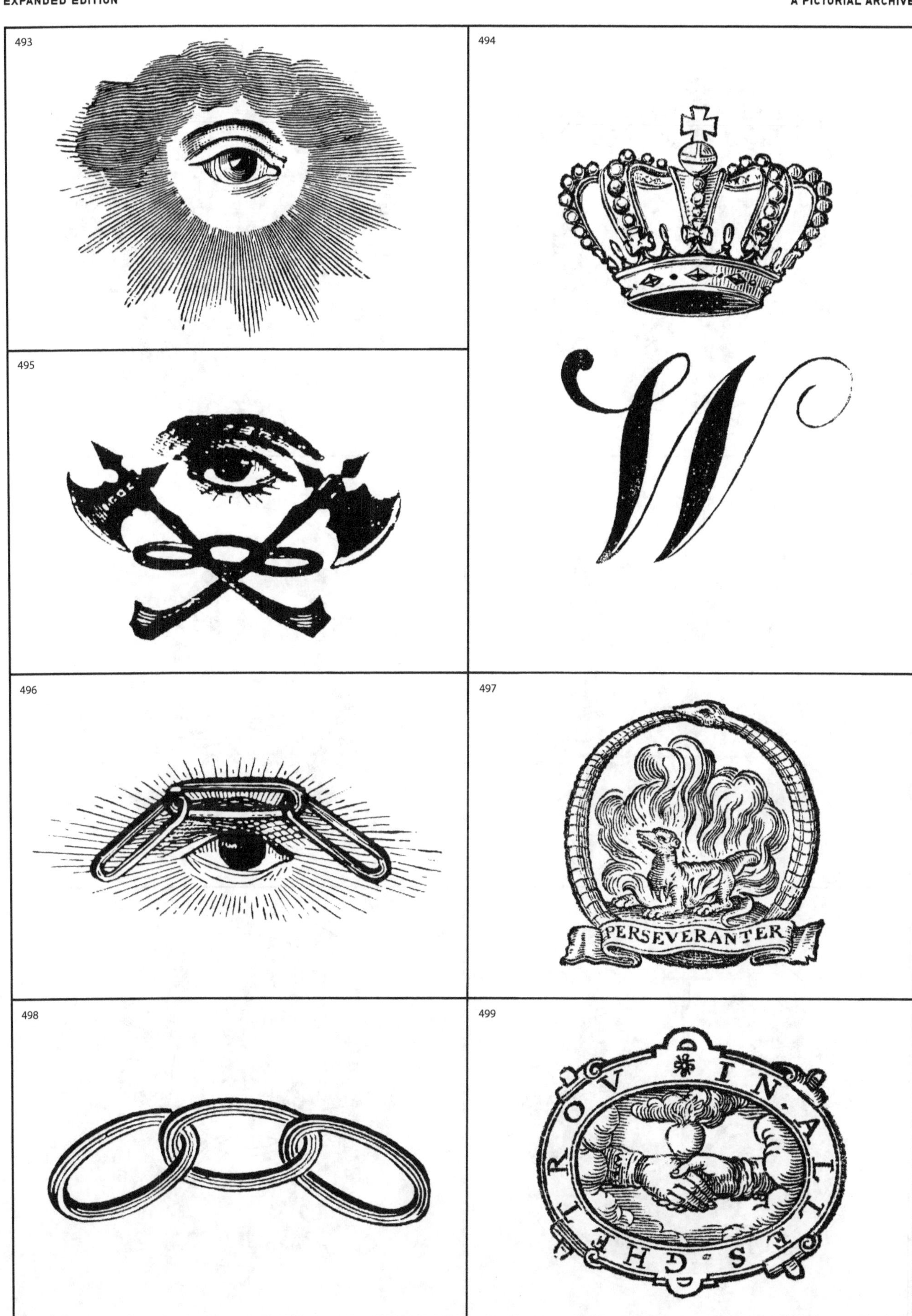
493
494
495
496
497
PERSEVERANTER
498
499

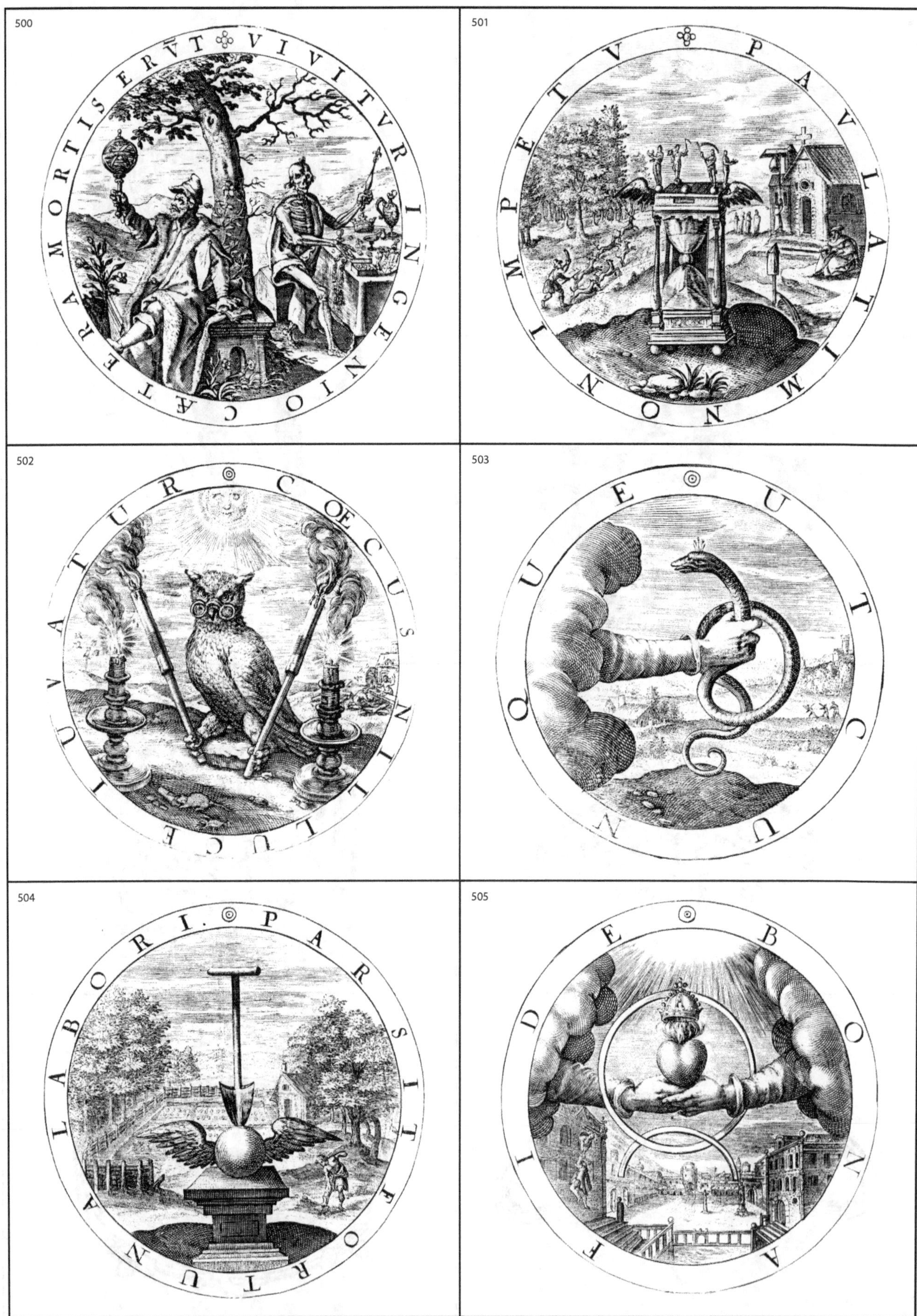

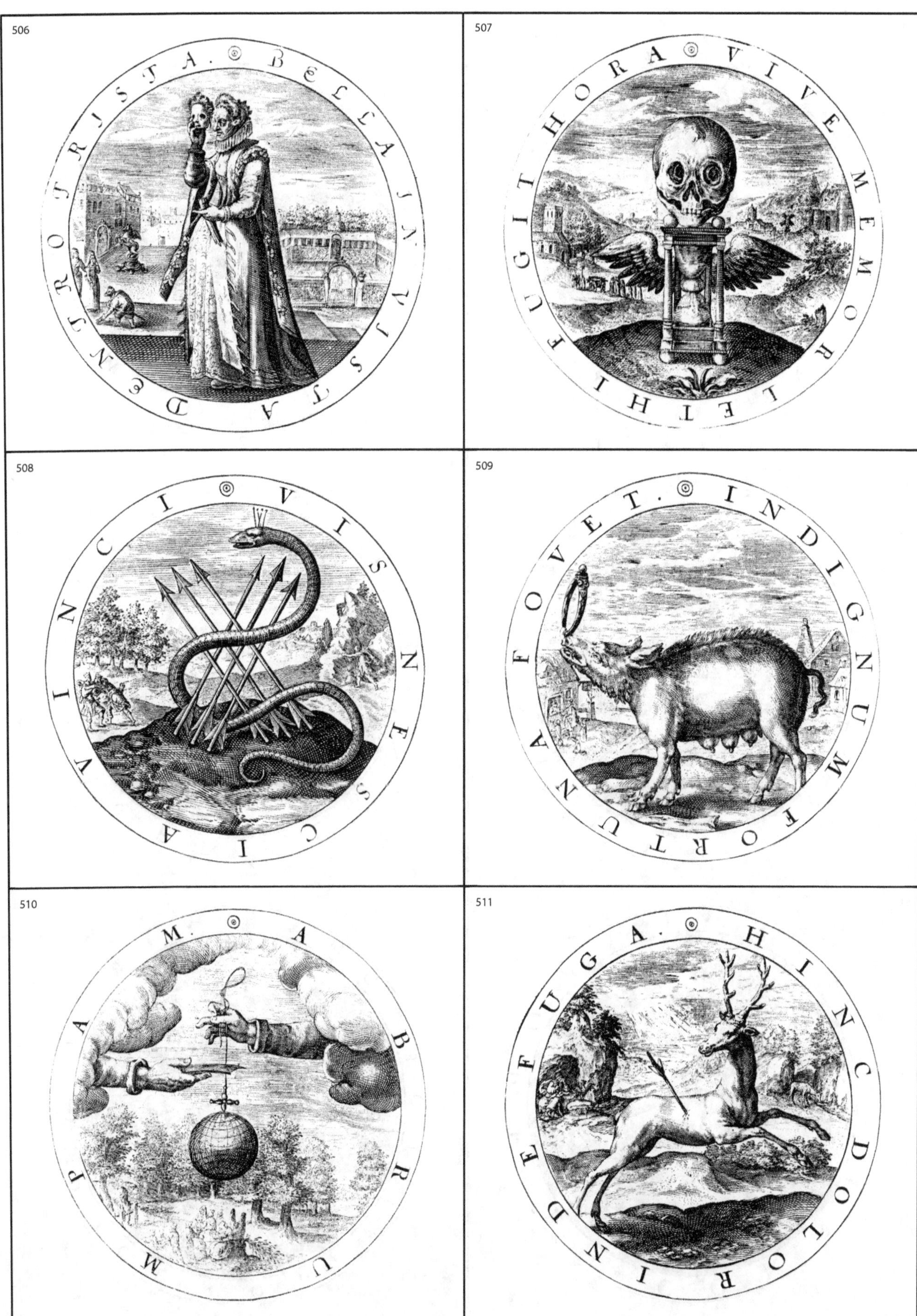

506
507
508
509
510
511
SYMBOLS & EMBLEMS

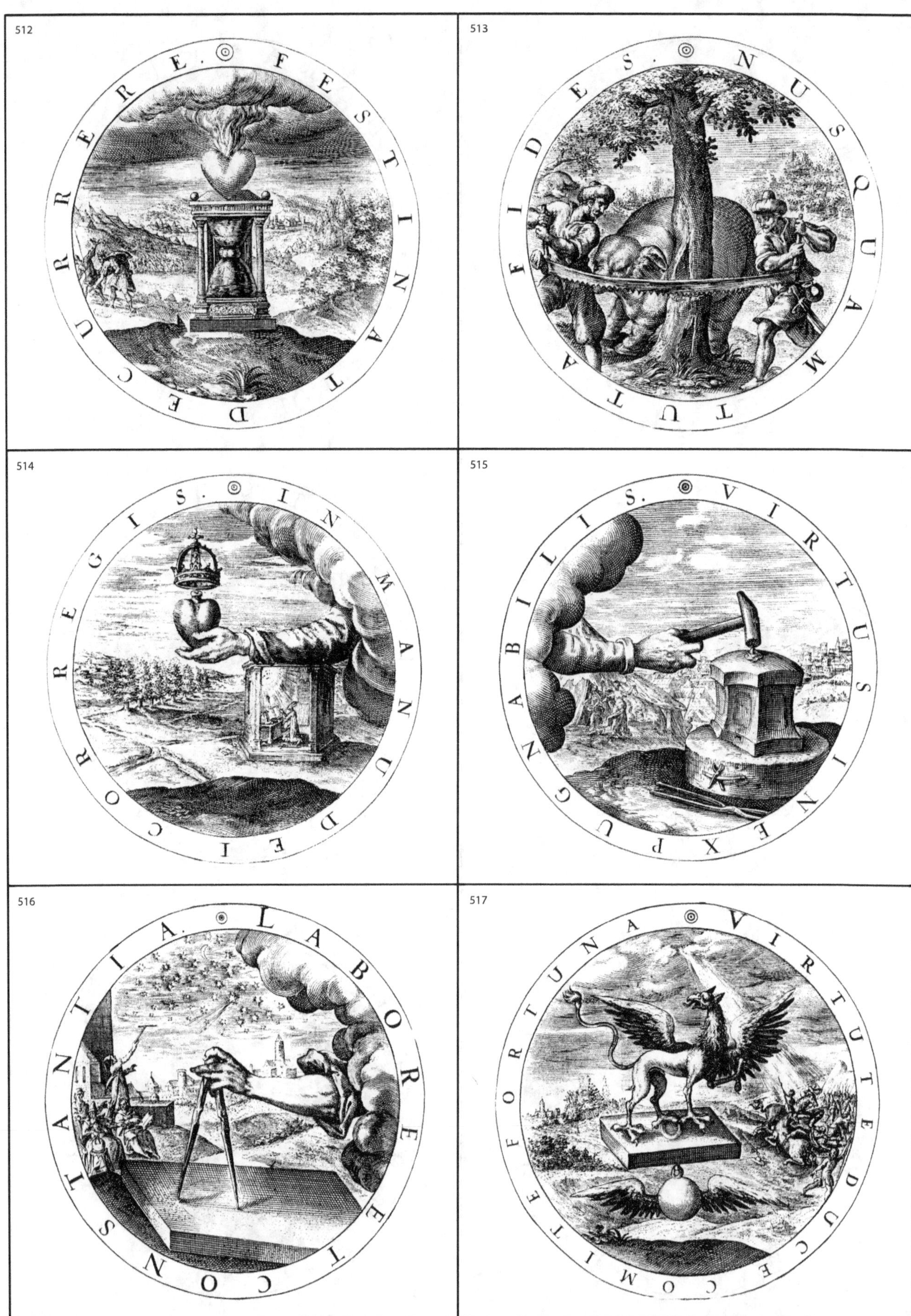
512
FESTINA LENTE CURRERE DECURE

513
FIDES NUSQUAM TUTA

514
REGIS IN MANU DEI CORE

515
VIRTUS INEXPUGNABILIS

516
LABORE ET CONSTANTIA

517
VIRTUTE DUCE COMITE FORTUNA

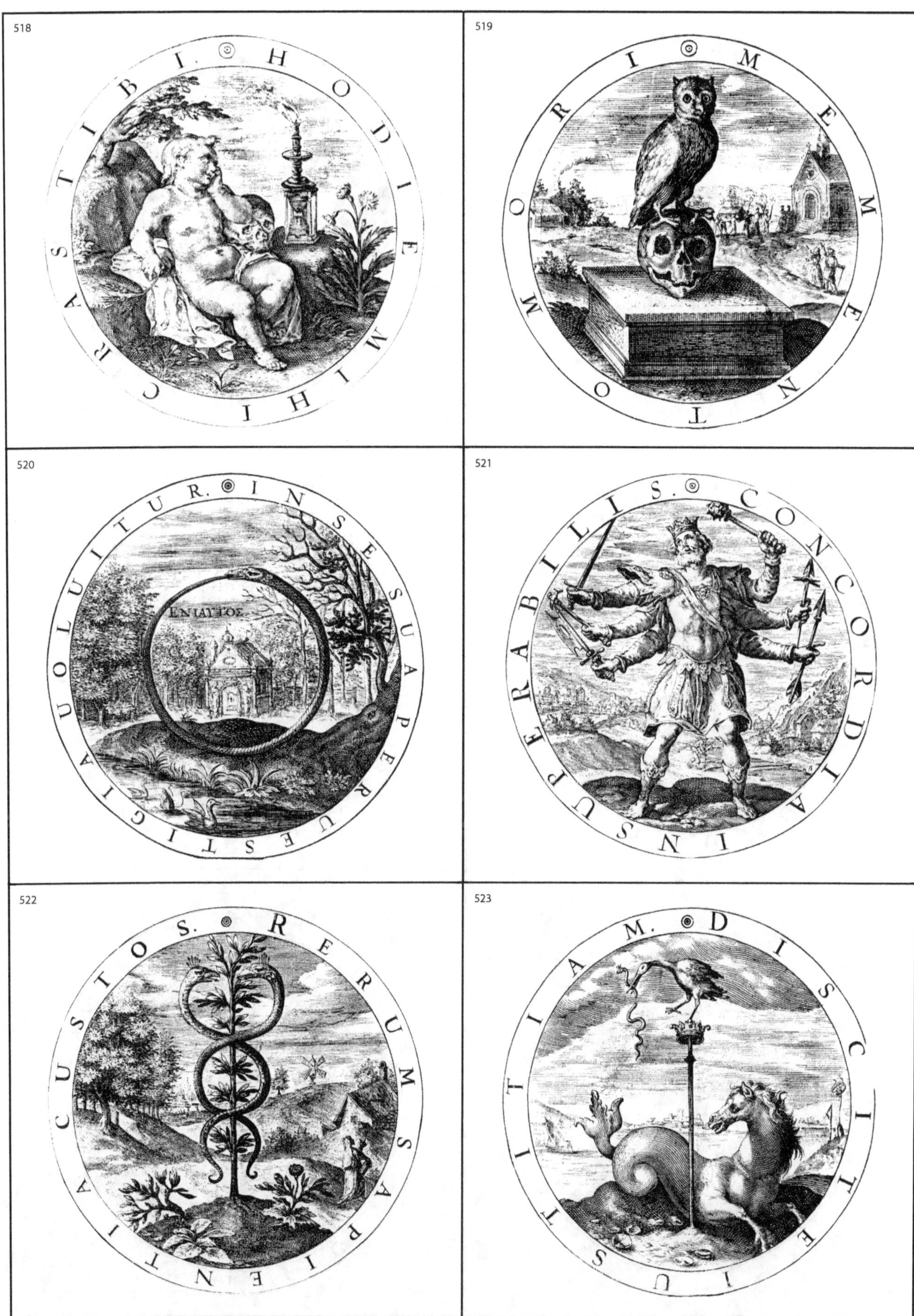

518
HODIE MIHI CRAS TIBI

519
MEMENTO MORI

520
INSE SUA PER VESTIGIA VOLVITUR. INS
ΕΝΙΑΥΤΟΣ

521
CONCORDIA INSUPERABILIS.

522
RERUM SAPIENTIA CUSTOS.

523
DISCITE IUSTITIAM.

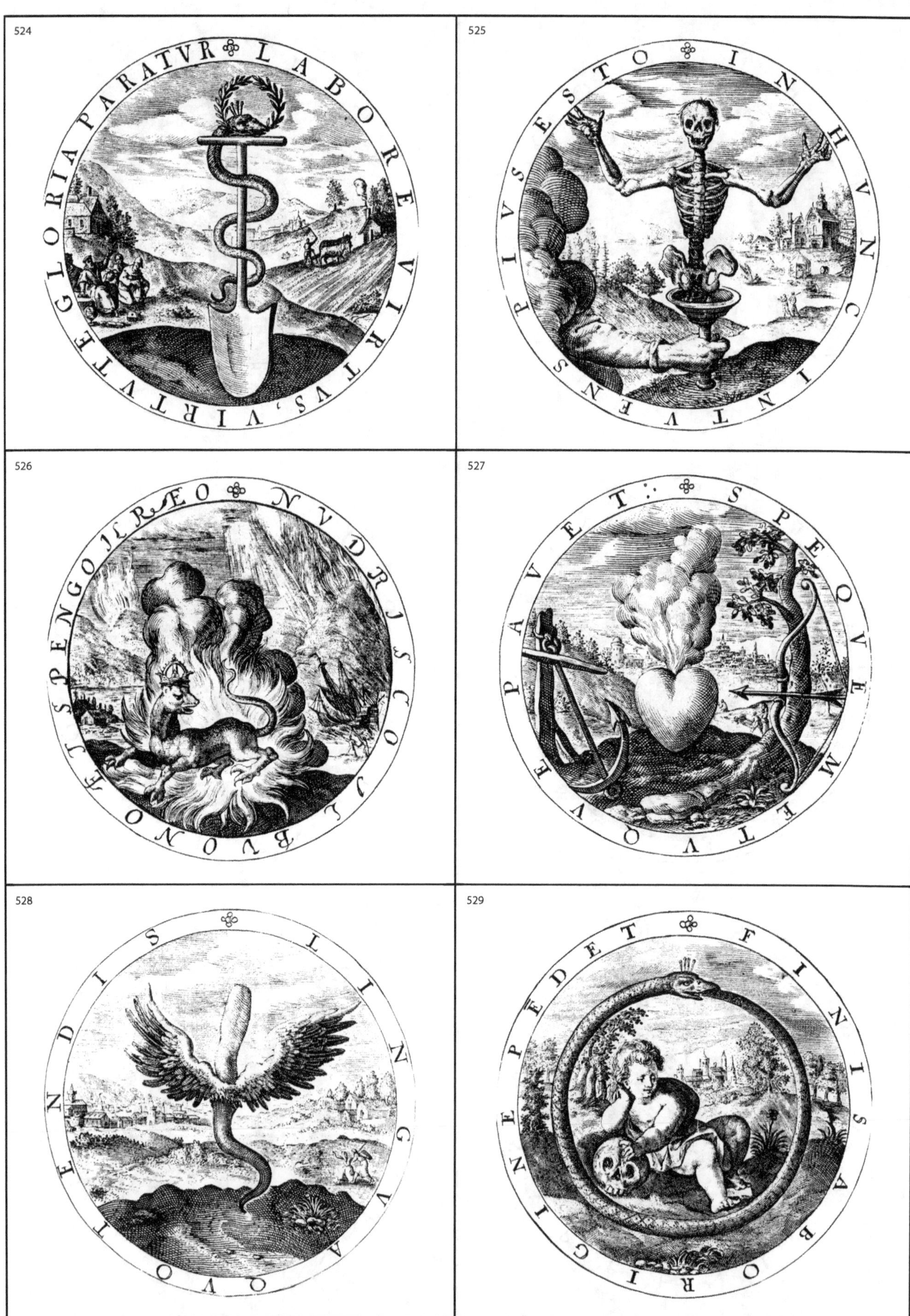
524
GLORIA PARATVR LABORE VIRTVTE VIRTVS
525
IN HVNC INTVENS PIVS ESTO
526
NVDRISCO ET ESTINGVO SPE
527
SPEQVE METVQVE PAVET
528
LINGVA QVOVENDIS
529
FINIS AB ORIGINE PEDET

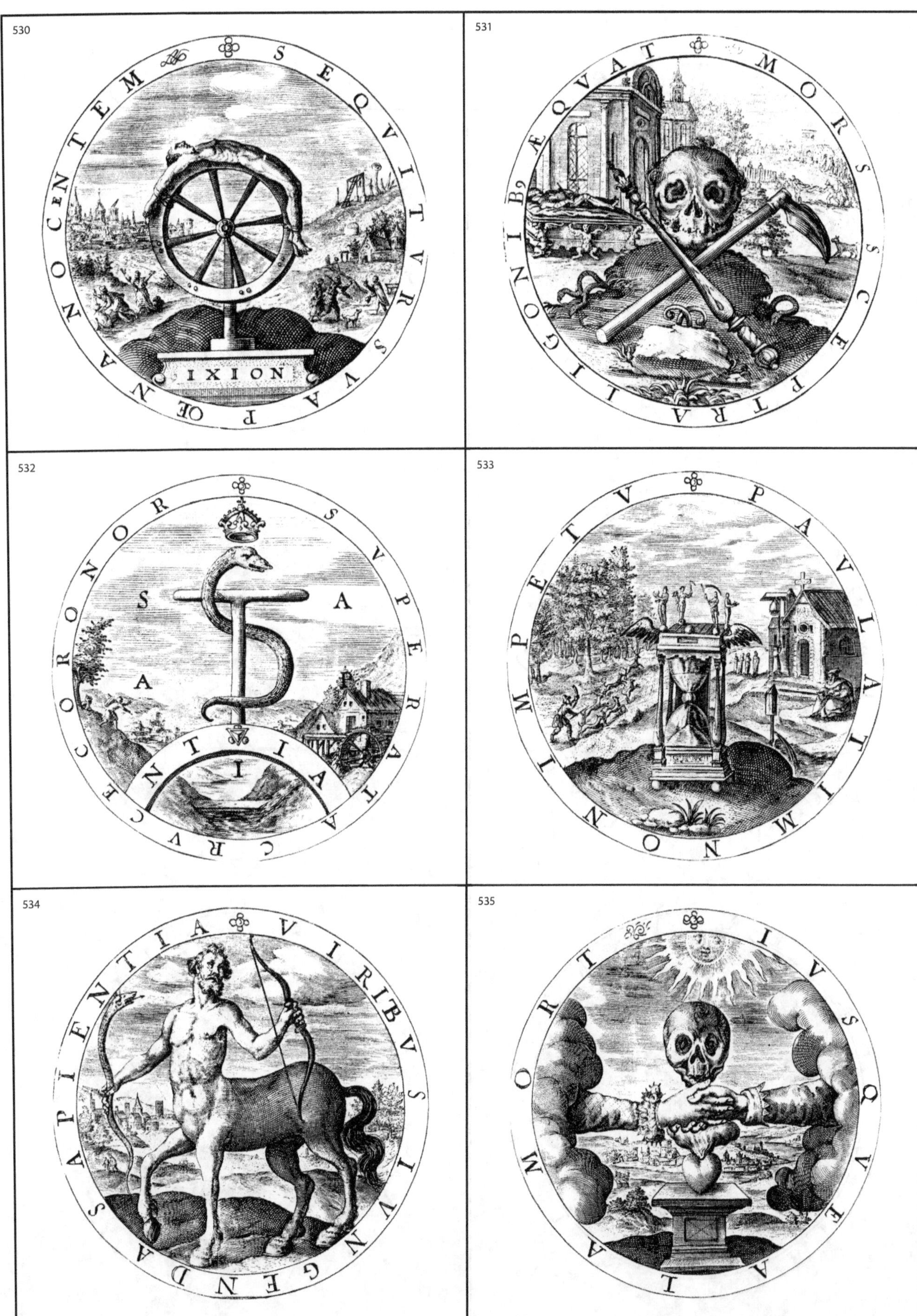

530
SEQVITVR SVA POENAM OCENTEM
IXION

531
MORS SCEPTRA LIGONIB AEQVAT

532
SVPERAT CRVCE CORONOR
SAPIENTIA

533
PAVLATIM NON IMPETV

534
VIRIBVS IVNGENDAS SAPIENTIA

535
IVS QVE MORTALIA

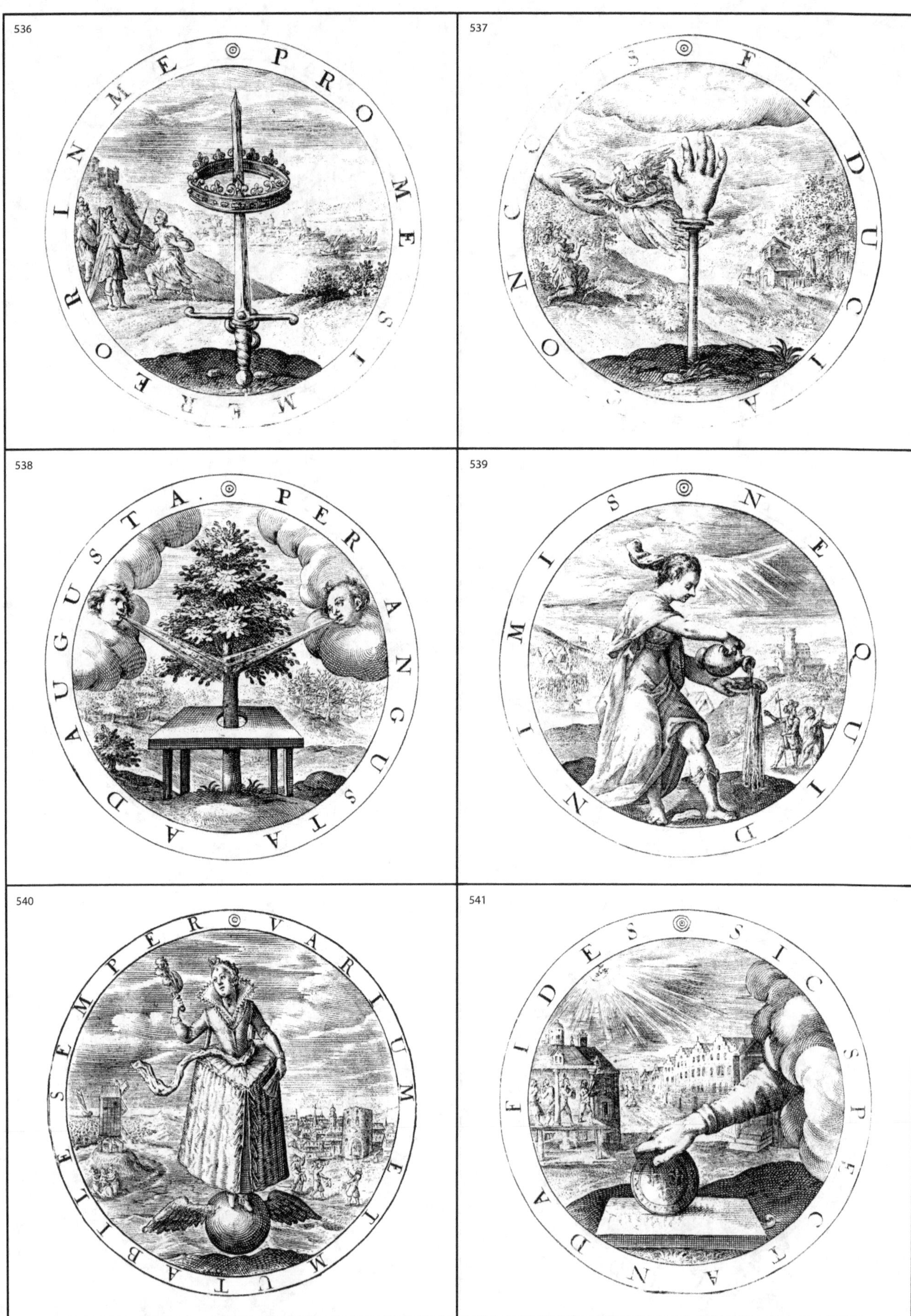

536
IN ME PROMESIMERAEOR
537
CONCS FIDUCIAS
538
AUGUSTA PER ANGUSTA AD
539
MIS ONE QUID NIMI
540
SEMPER VARIUM ET MUTABILE
541
FIDES SIC SPECTANDA

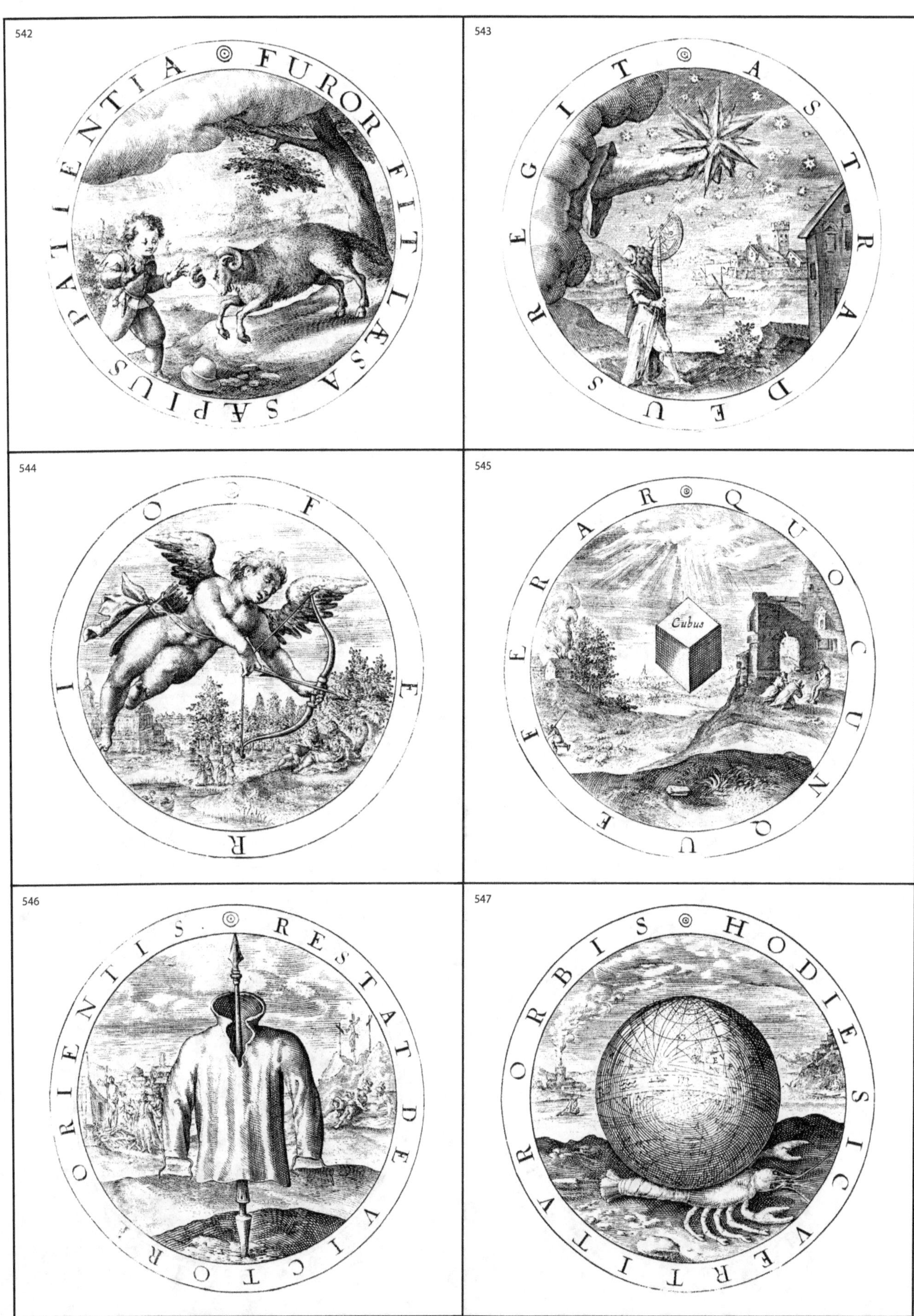

542
FUROR FIT LÆSA SÆPIUS PATIENTIA

543
ASTRA REGIT DEUS

544
FERIO

545
QUOCUNQUE FERAR
Cubus

546
RESTAT DE VICTORIA ORIENTIS.

547
ORBIS HODIE SIC VERTITUR

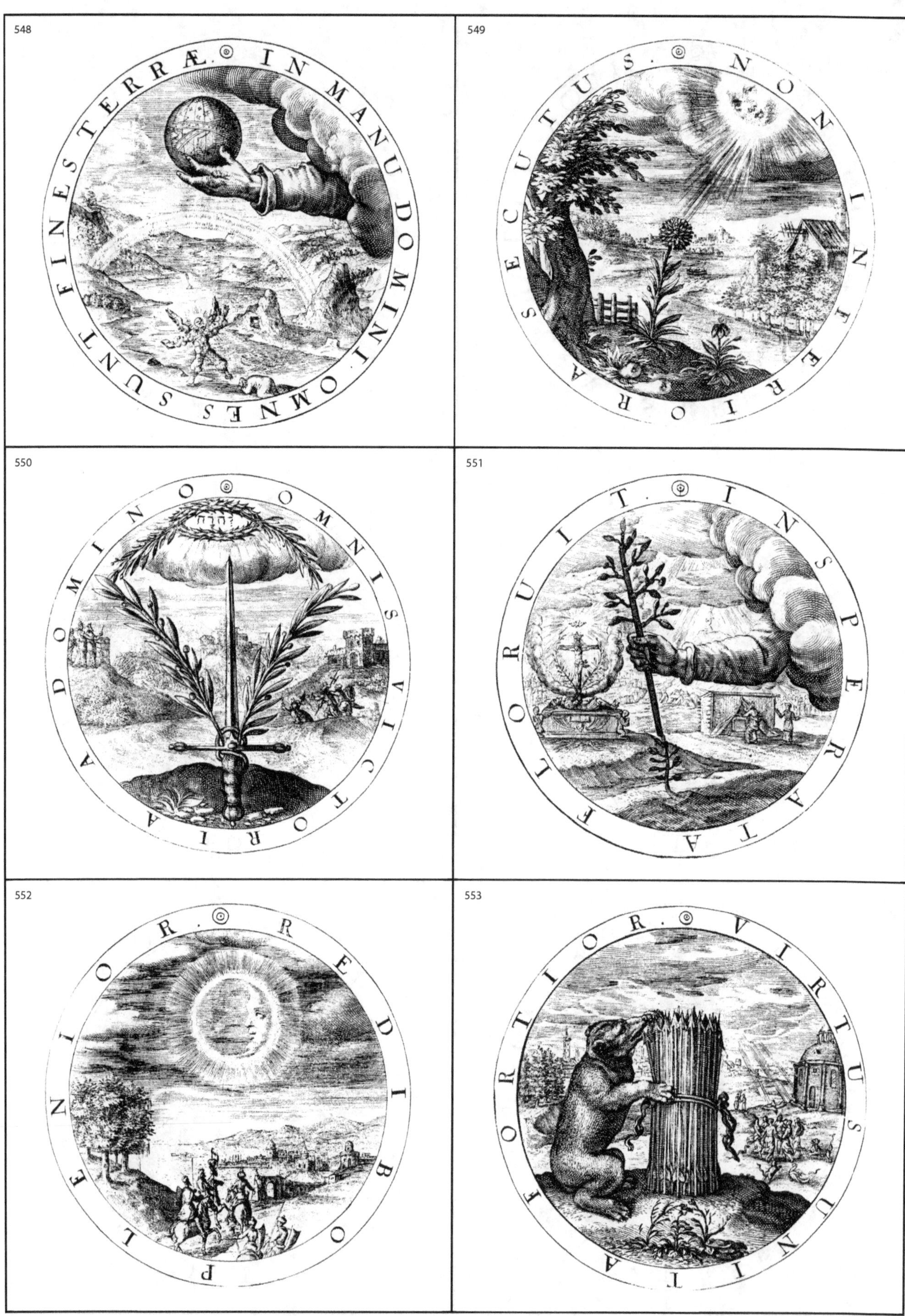

548
FINESTERRÆ · IN MANU DOMINI OMNES SUNT

549
SECUTUS · NON INFERIORA

550
A DOMINO OMNIS VICTORIA

551
INSPERATA FLORUIT

552
PLENIOR · REDIBO

553
VIRTUS UNITA FORTIOR

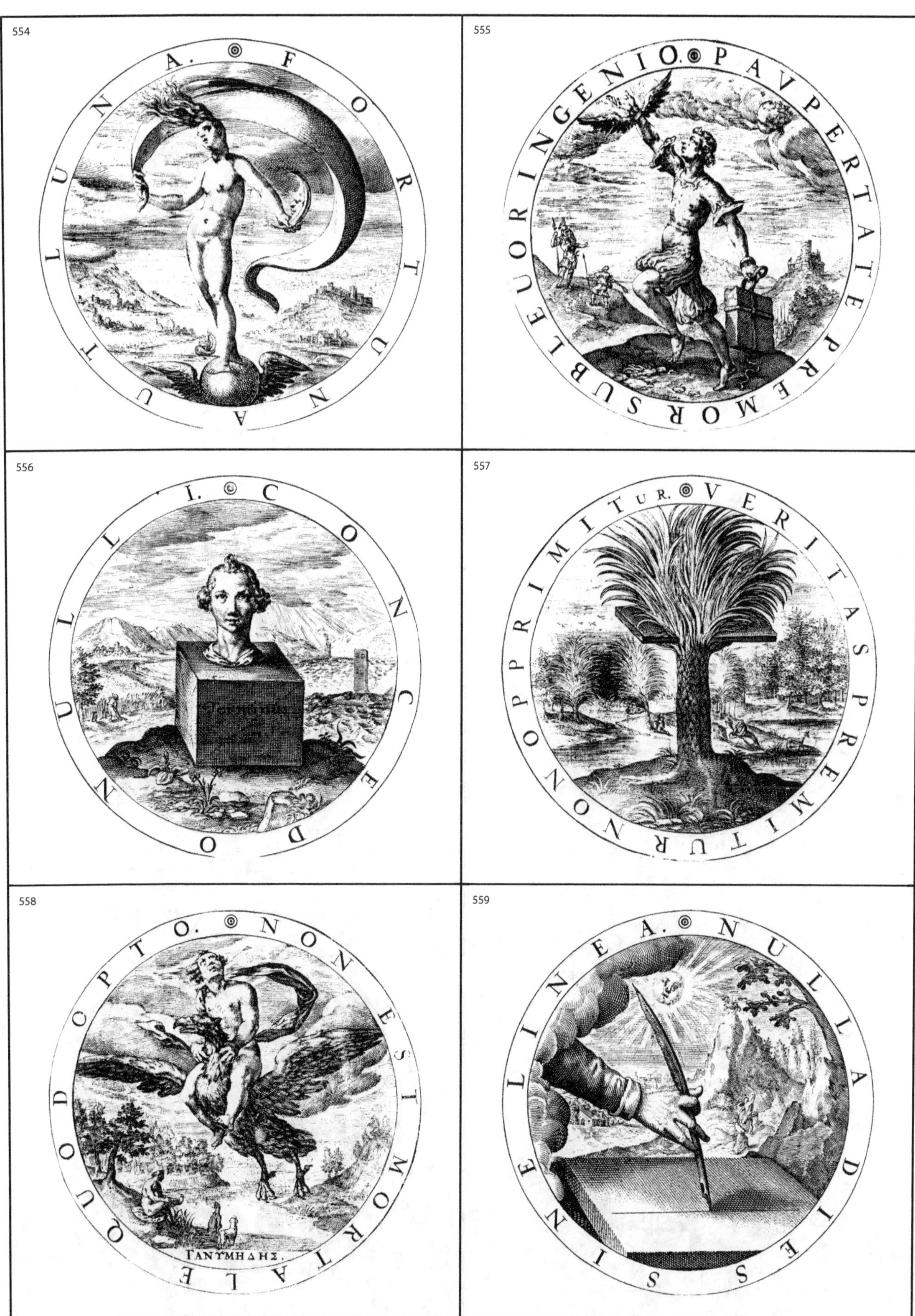

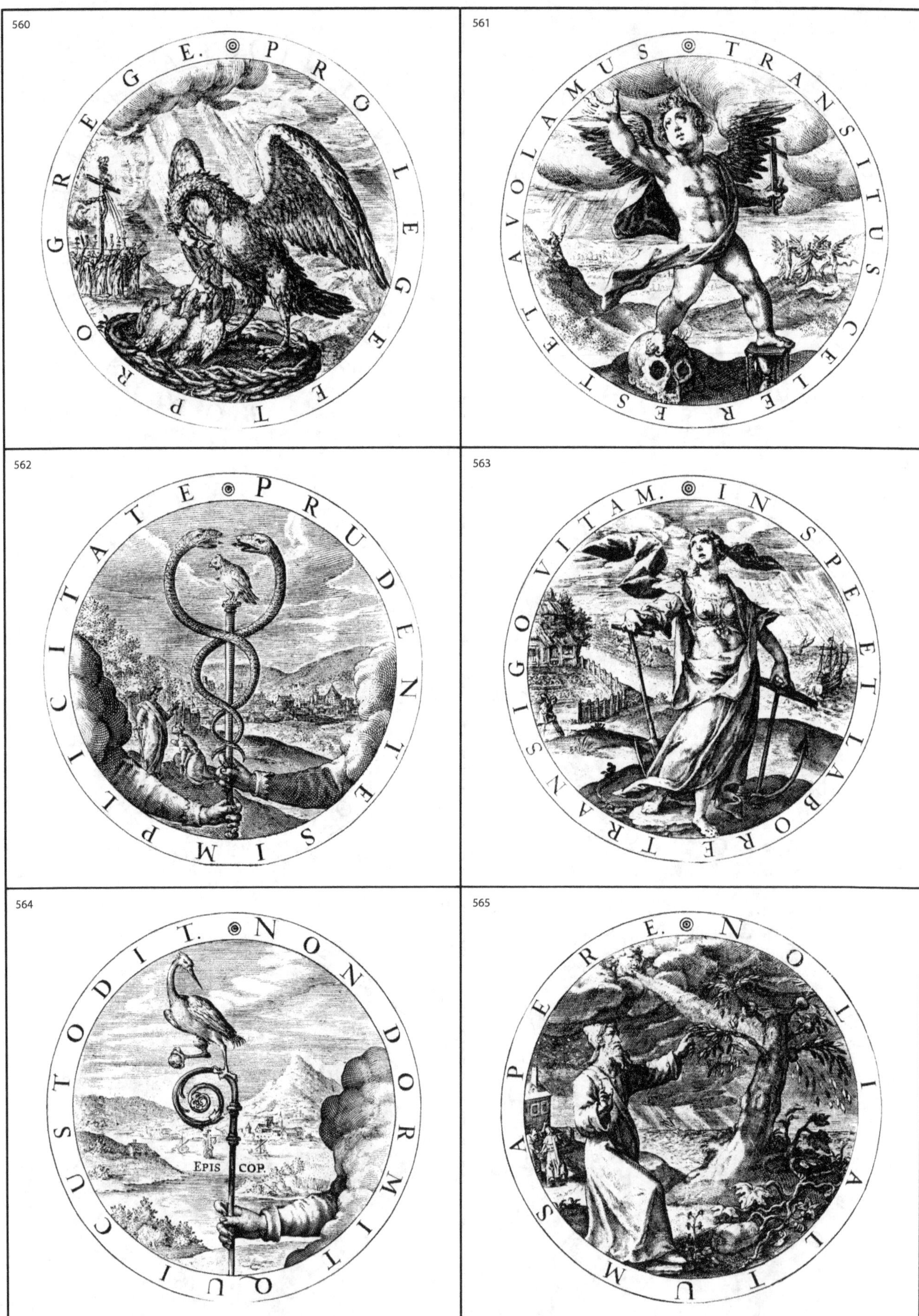

560
PRO GREGE. PRO LEGE ET PRO

561
TRANSITUS CELER. ESTET AVOLAMUS

562
PRUDENTES IMPLICITATE SIMPLICI

563
IN SPE ET LABORE TRANSIGO VITAM.

564
NON DORMIT QUI CUSTODIT.
EPISCOP.

565
NOLI ALTUM SAPERE.

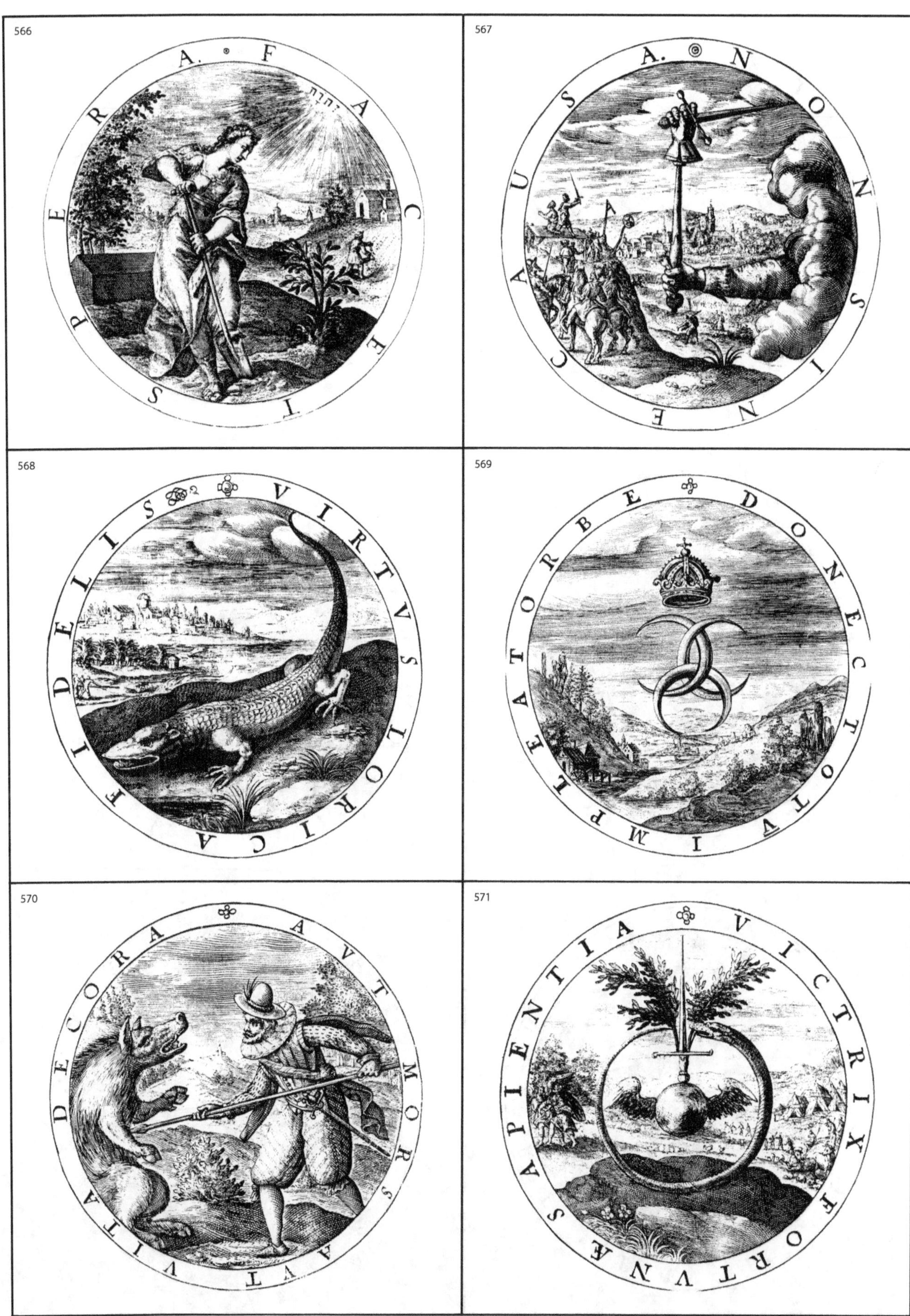
566
A. FAC
SPERA IPSE

567
A. NON SINE CAUSE

568
VIRTUS IORICA FIDELIS

569
DONEC TOTVM IMPLEAT ORBE

570
AVT MORS AVT VITA DECORA

571
VICTRIX FORTVNÆ SAPIENTIA

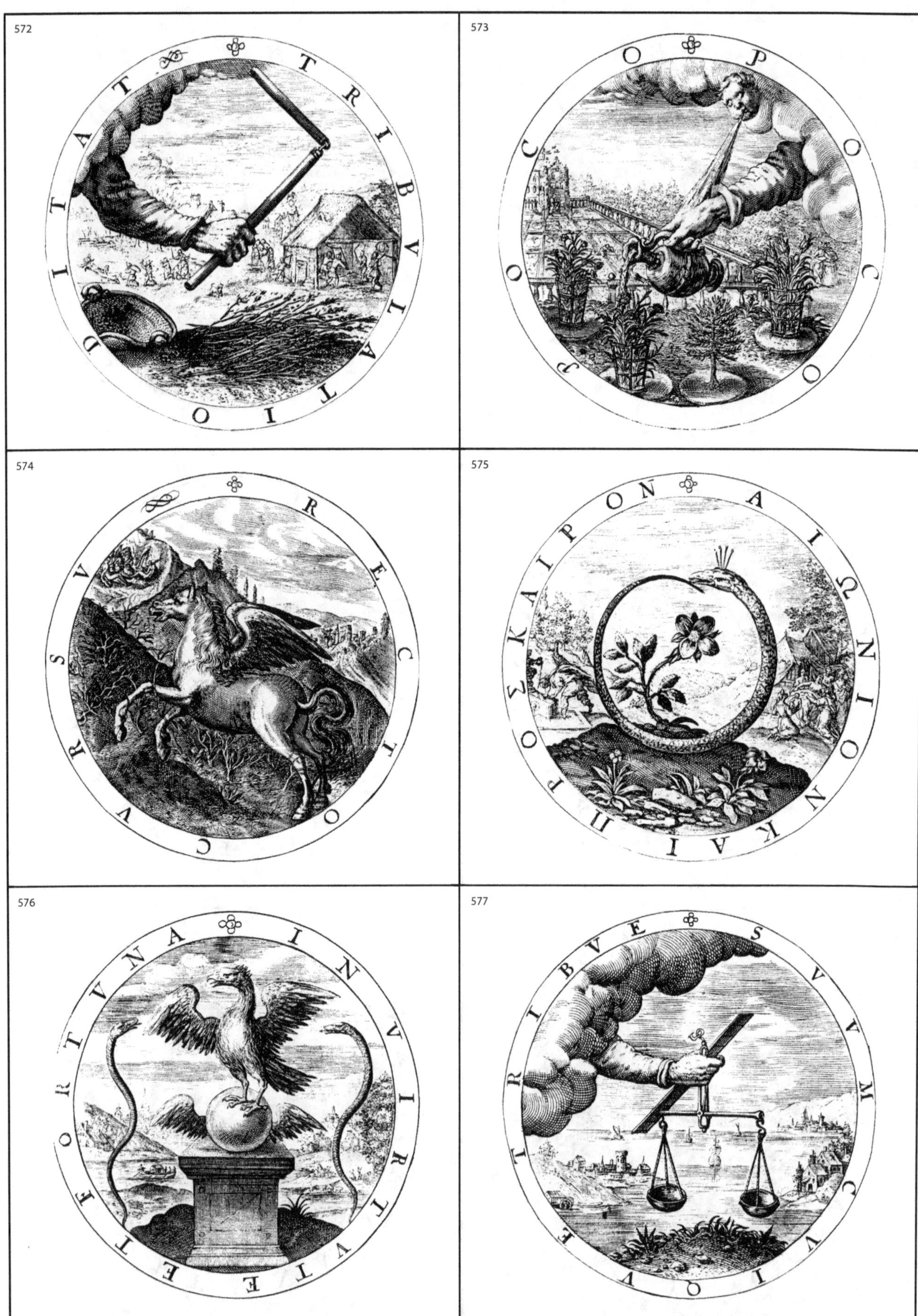

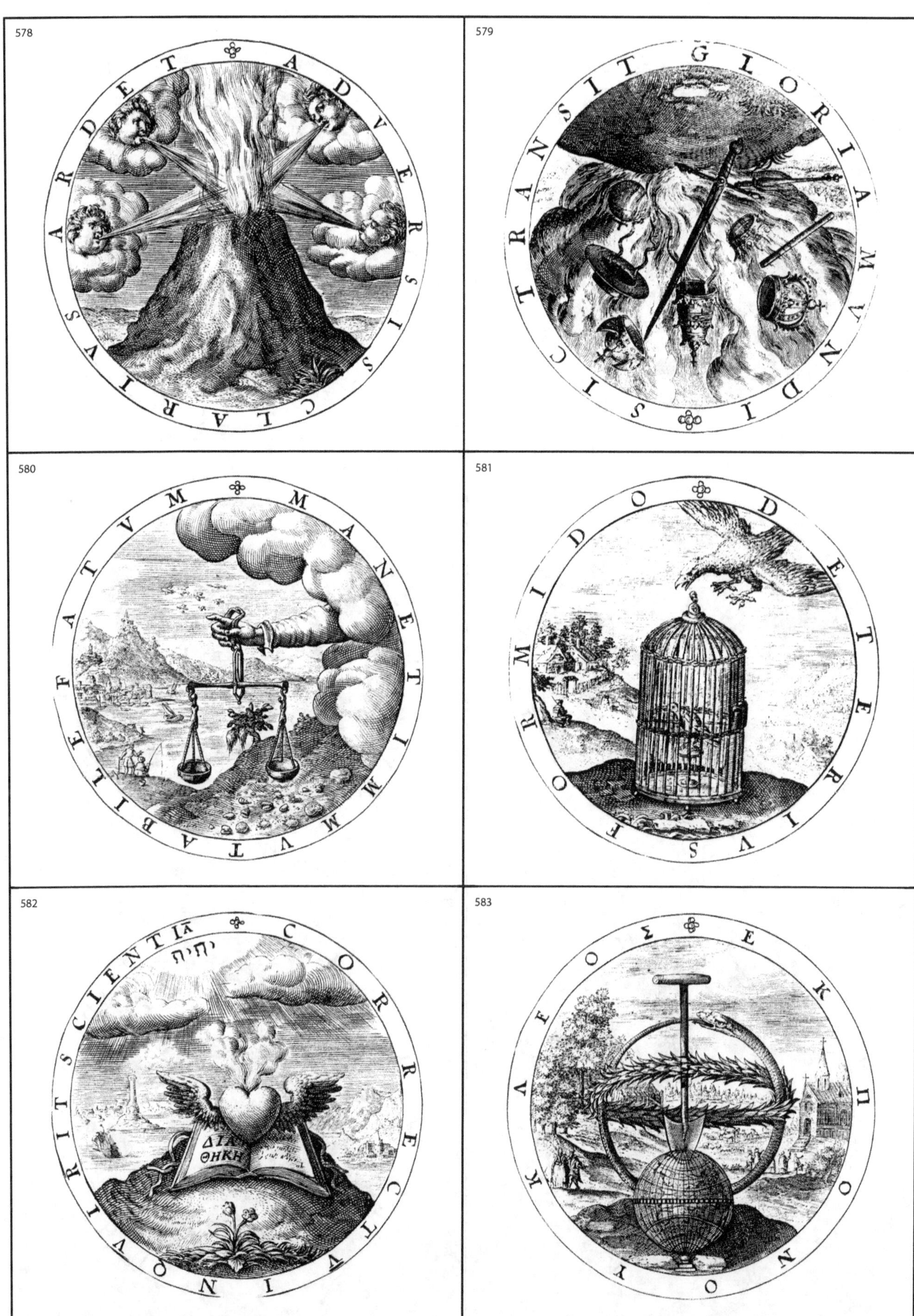

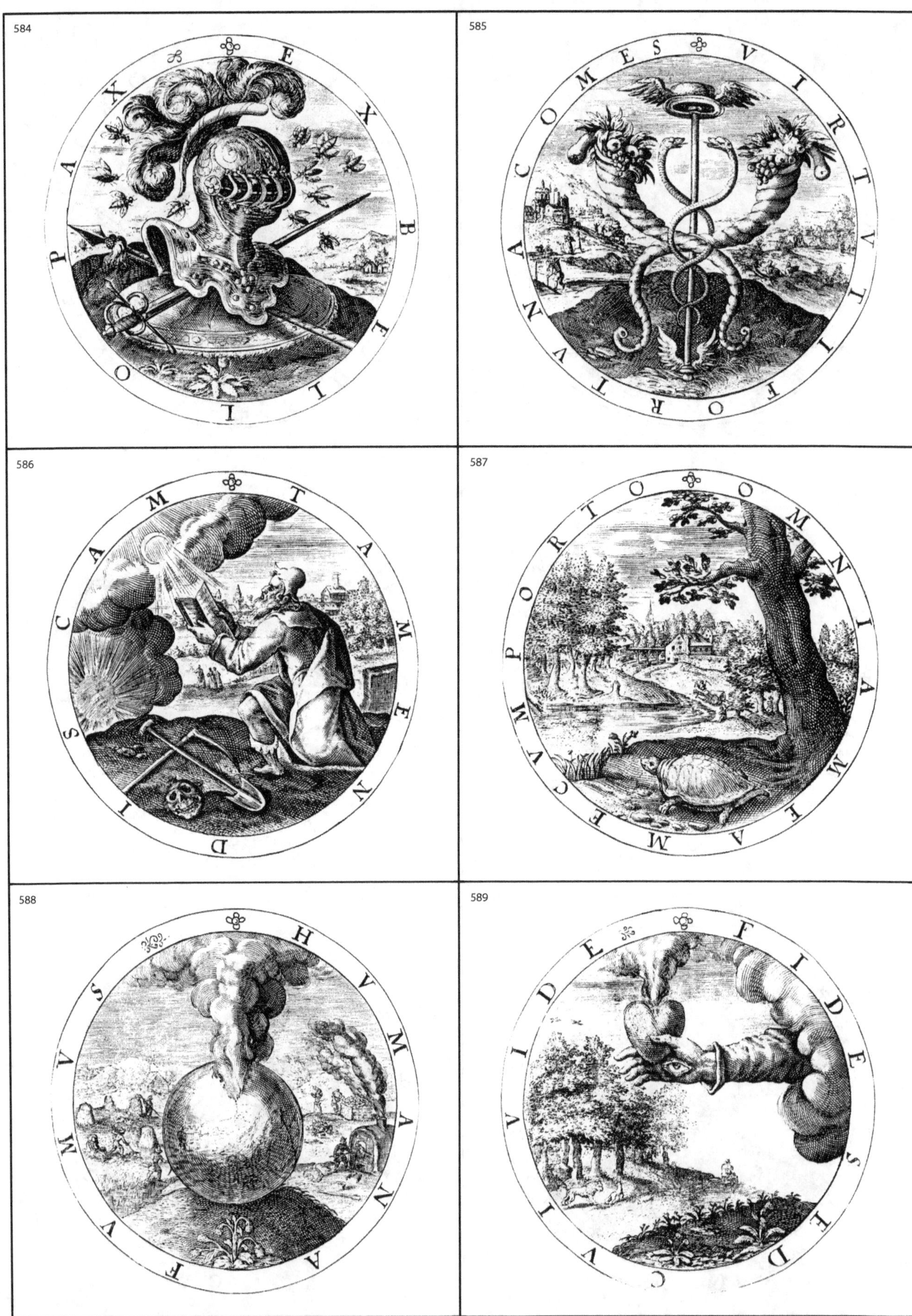

584 585 586 587 588 589

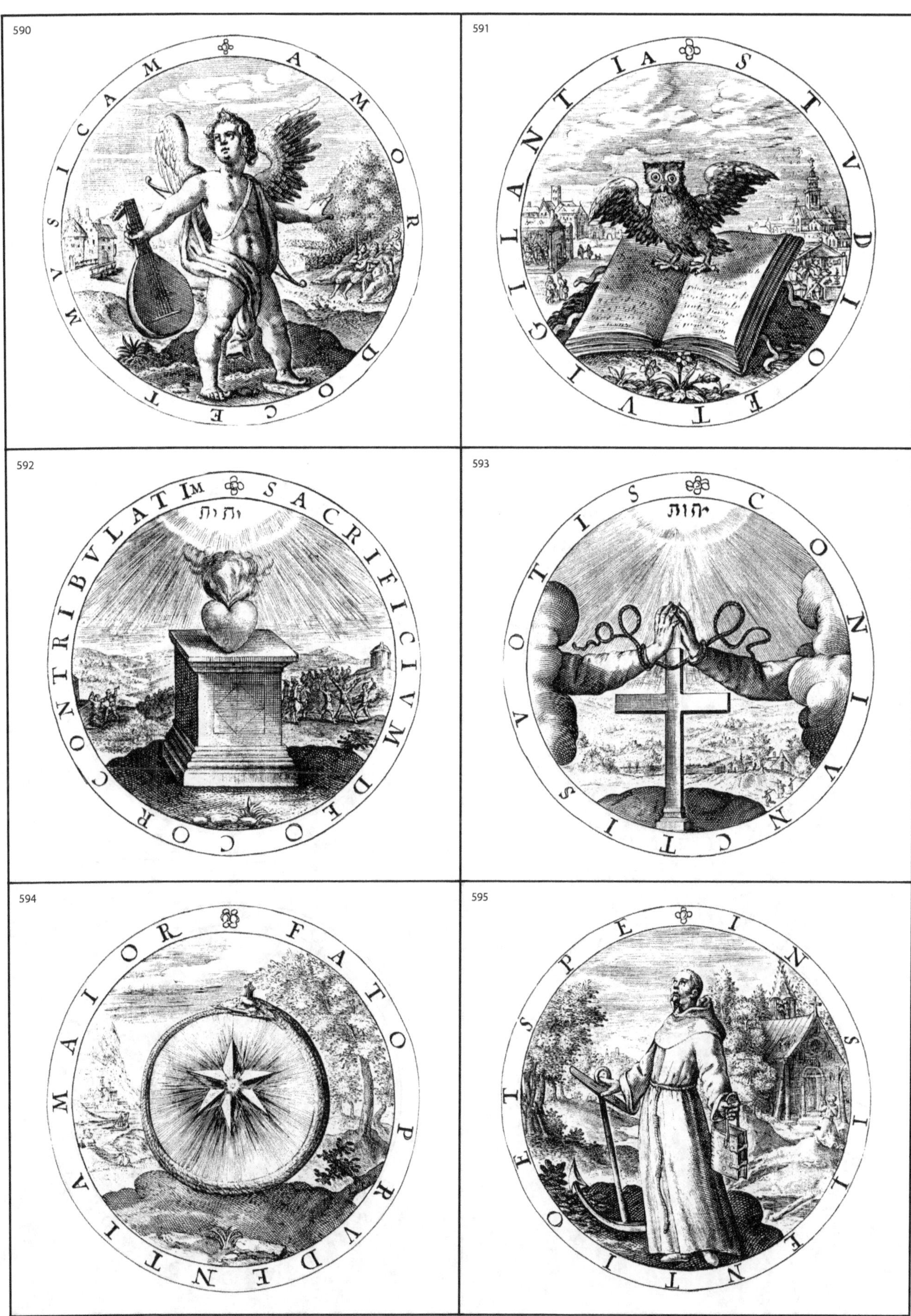

590
AMOR DOCET MVSICAM ET

591
STVDIO ET VIGILANTIA

592
SACRIFICIVM DEO COR CONTRIBVLATIM

593
CONIVNCTIS VOTIS

594
FATO PRVDENTIA MAIOR

595
INSPE ET SILENTIO

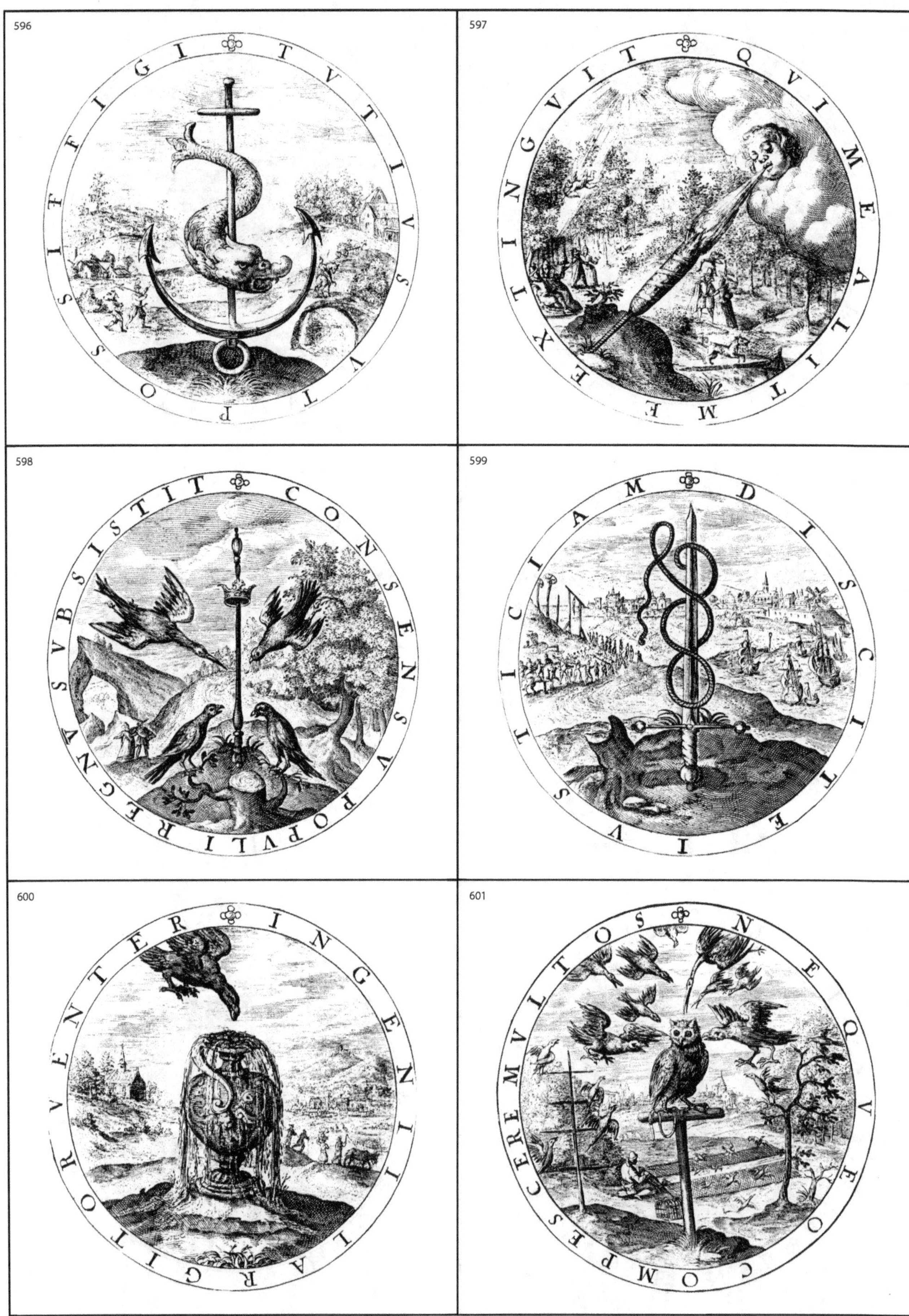

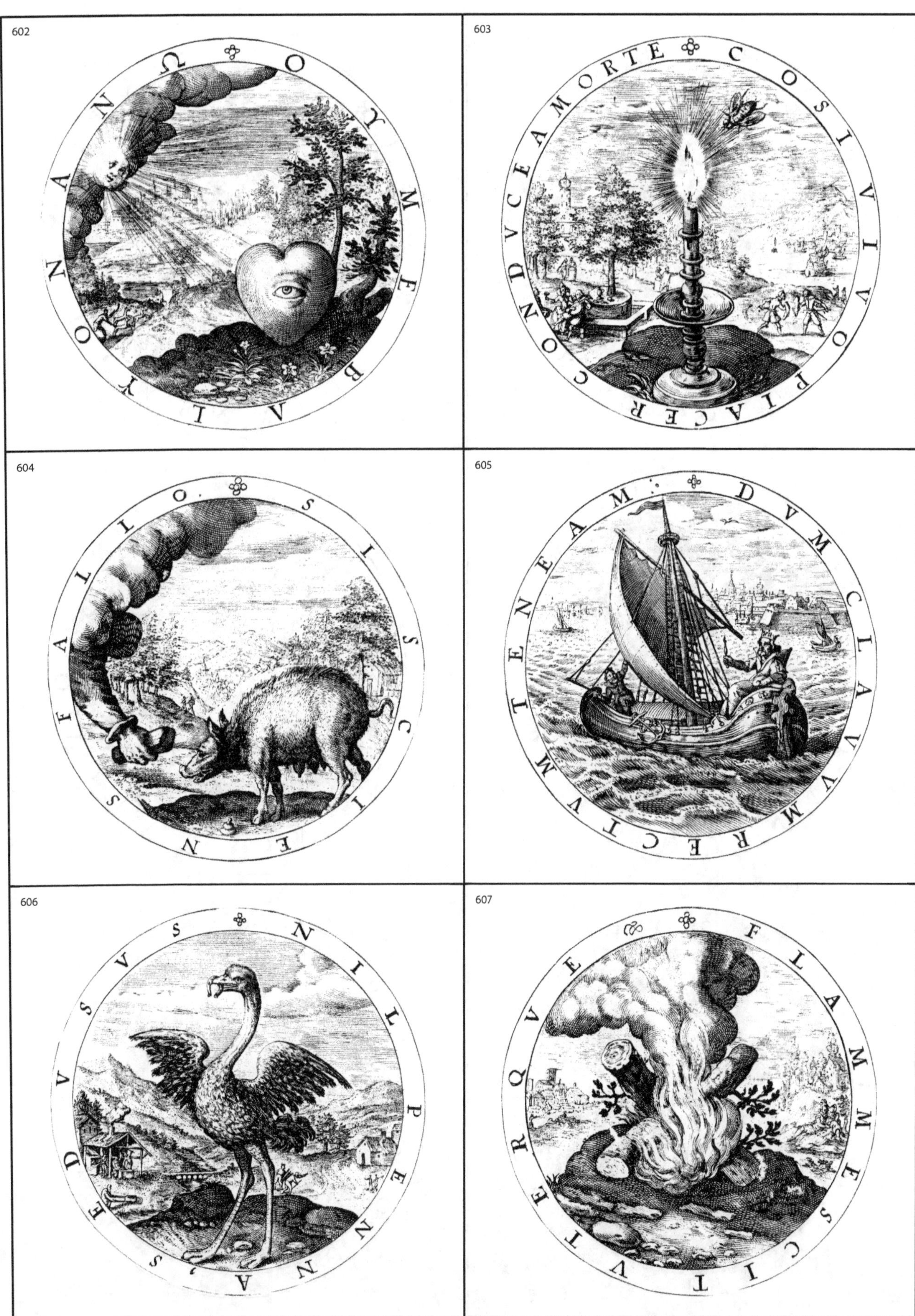

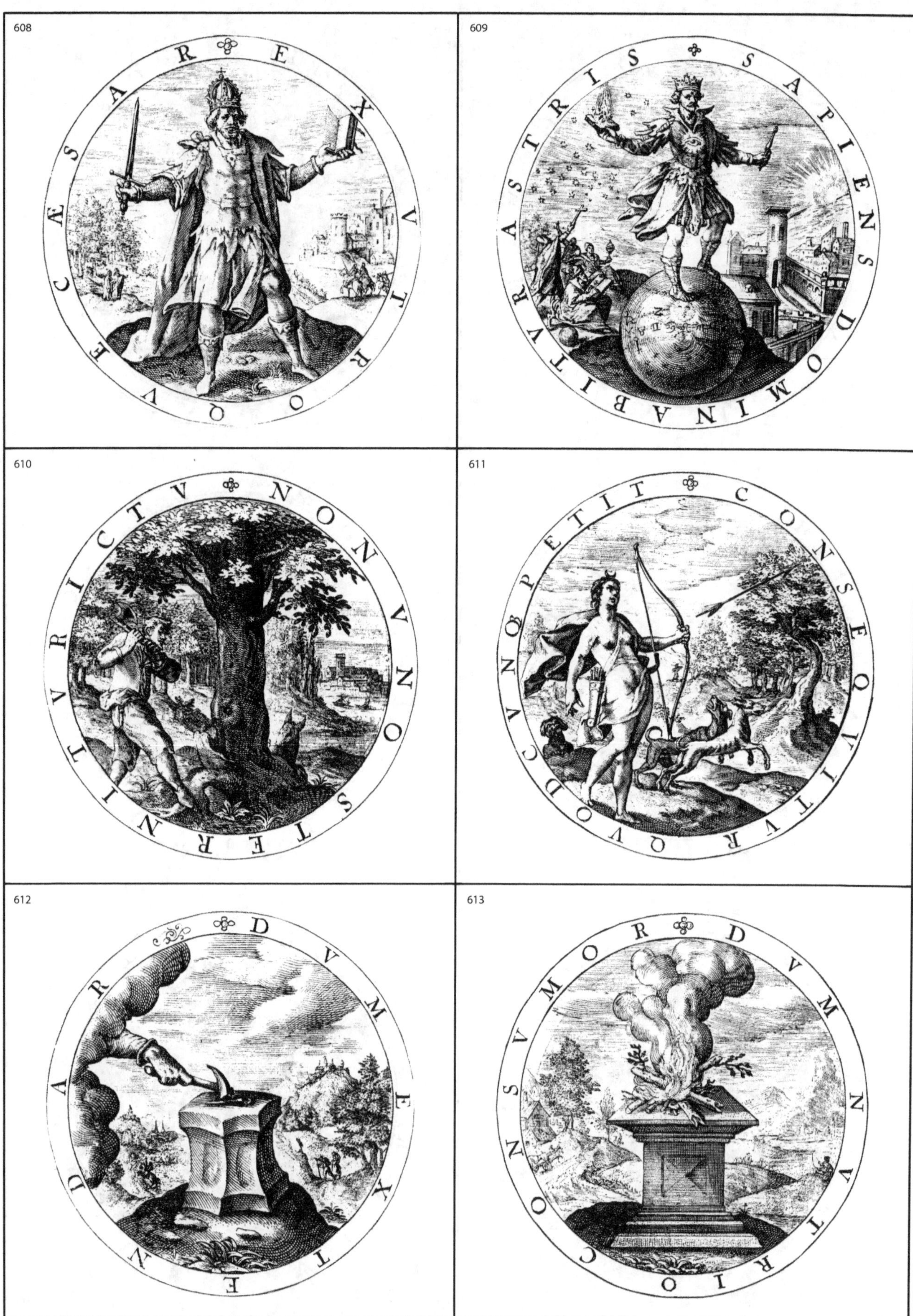
608
REX VTRO QVE CÆSAR
609
SAPIENS DOMINABITVR ASTRIS
610
NON VANO STERNITVR ICTV
611
PETIT CONSEQVITVR QVOD NON
612
DVM EXTREND AR
613
DVM CONSVMOR VTRIO VANT

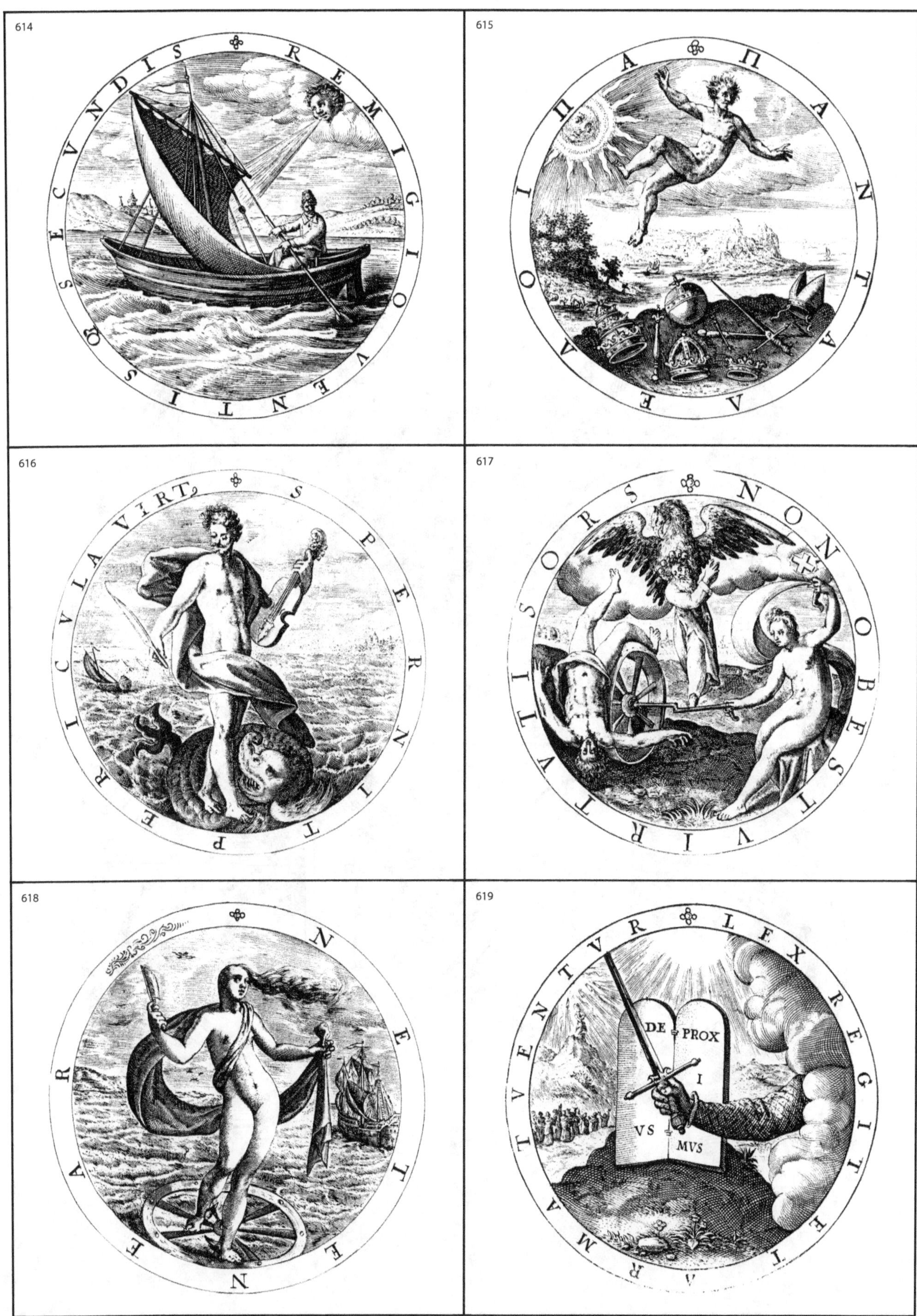

614
615
616
617
618
619

620

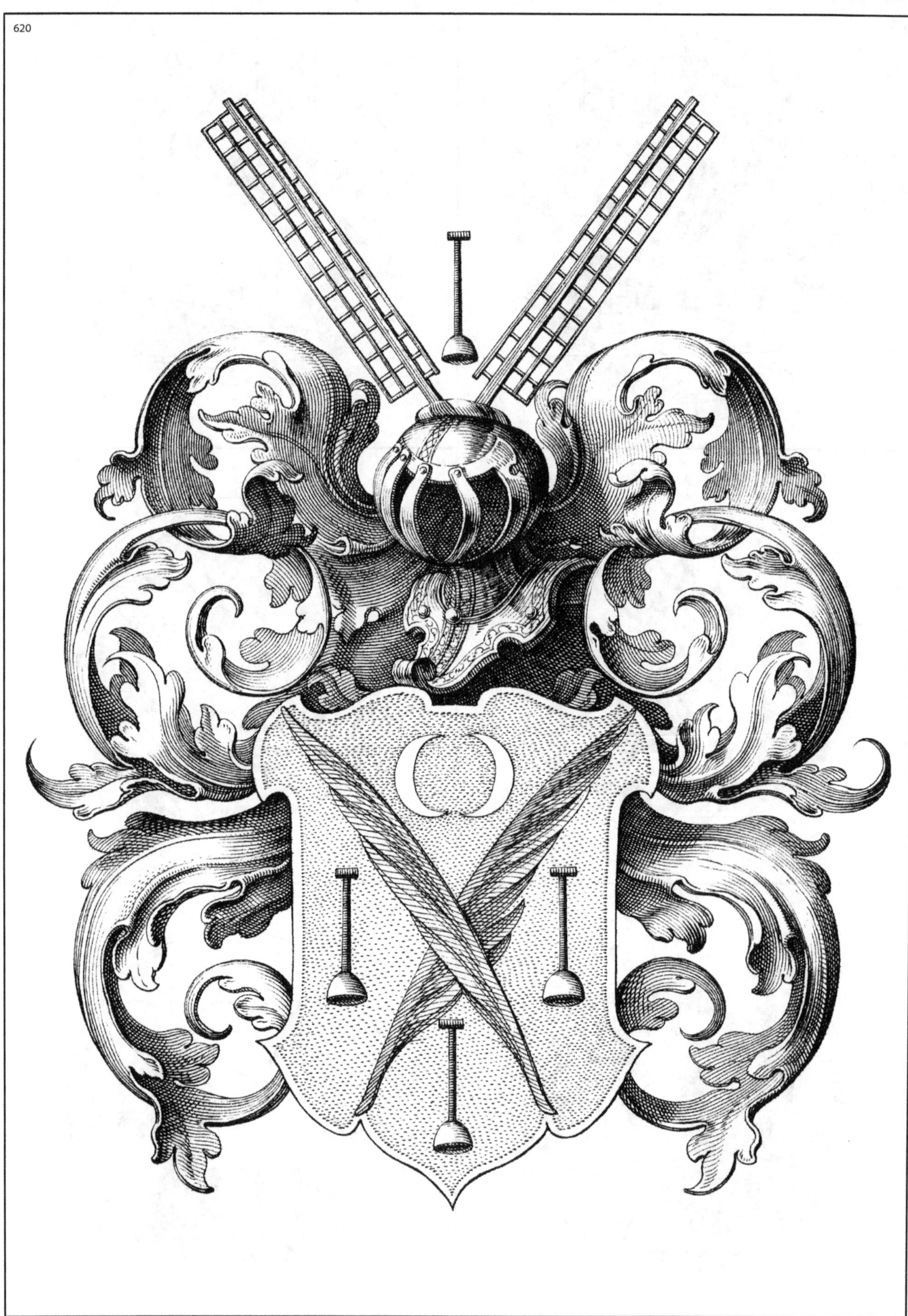

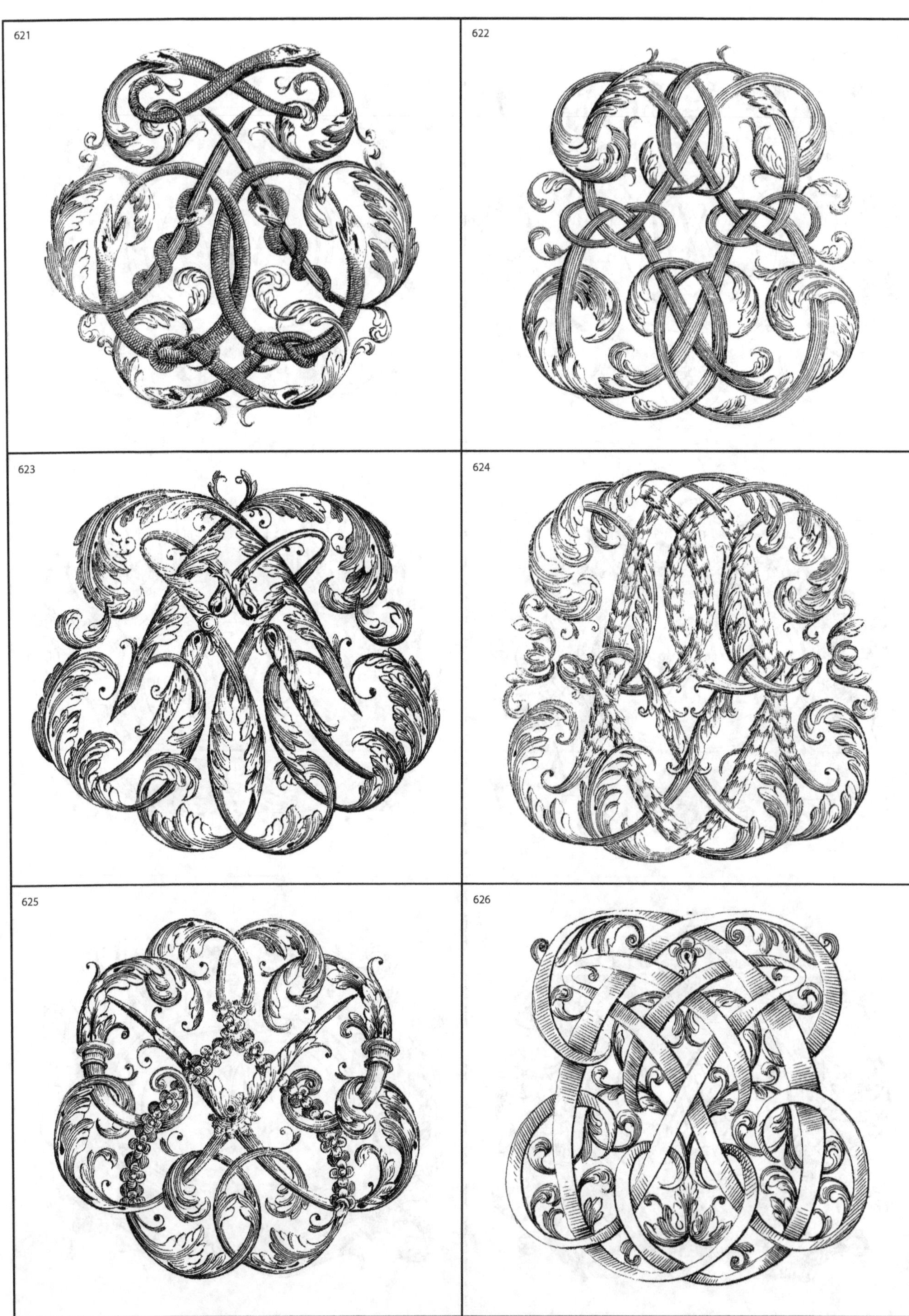

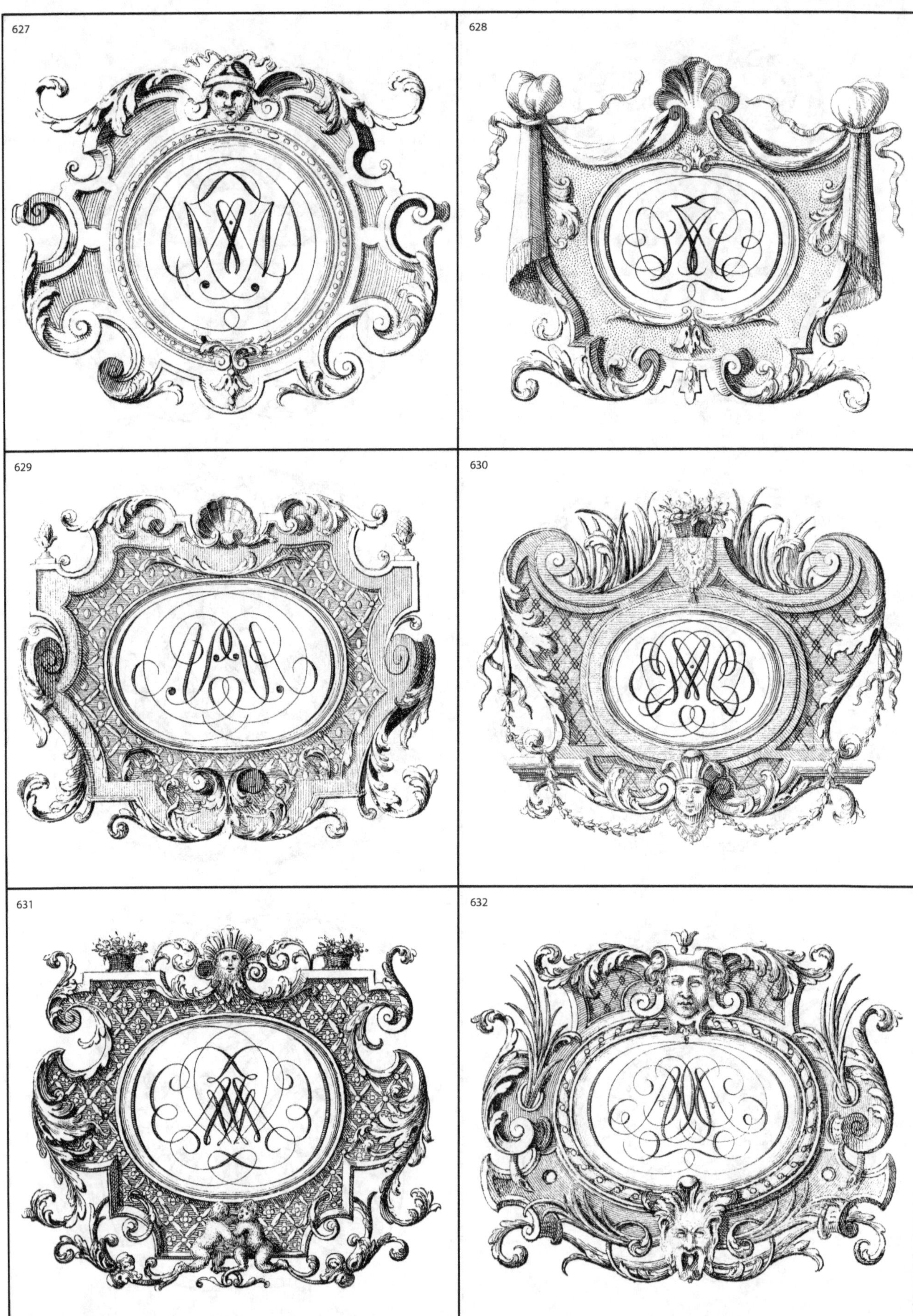

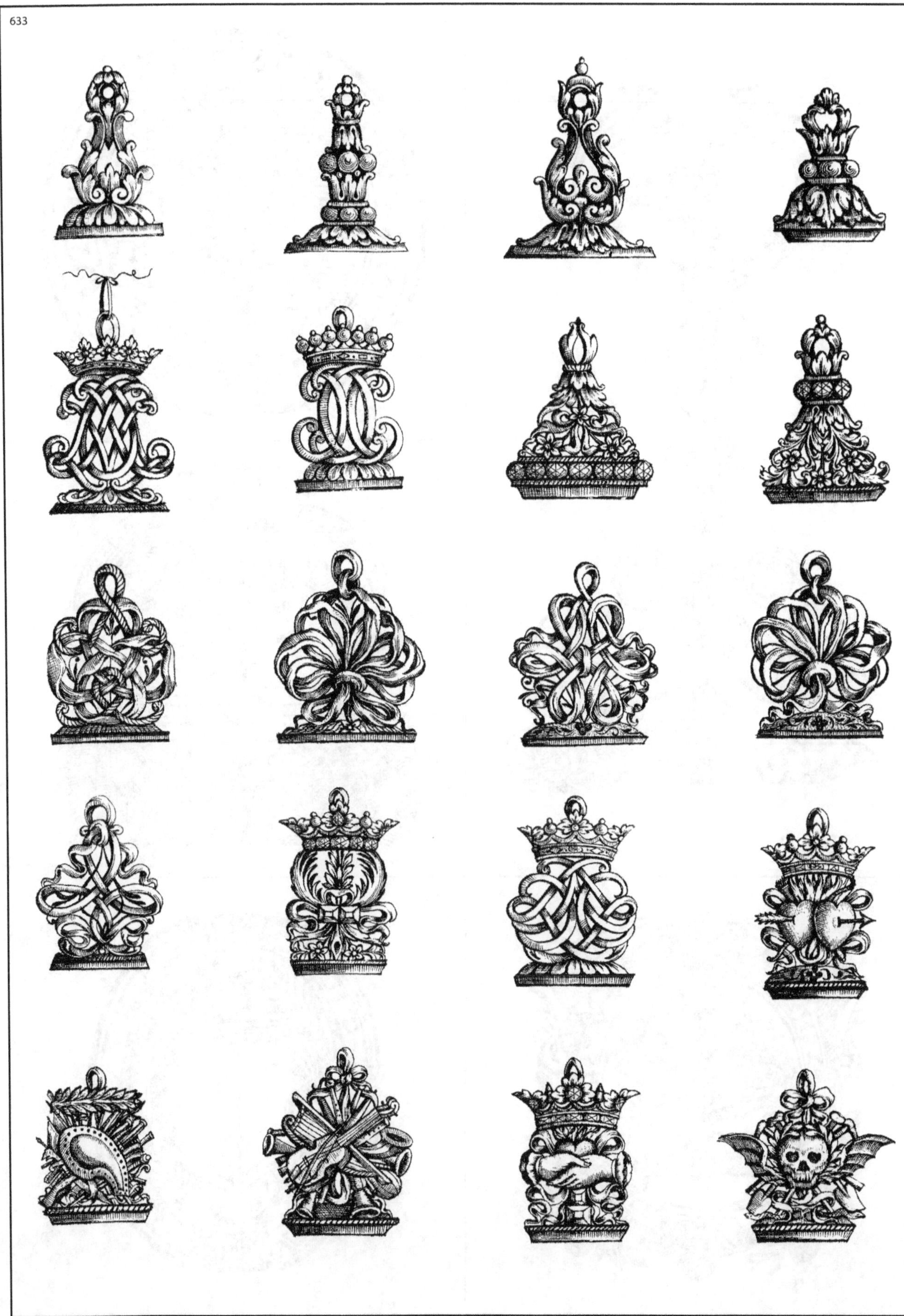

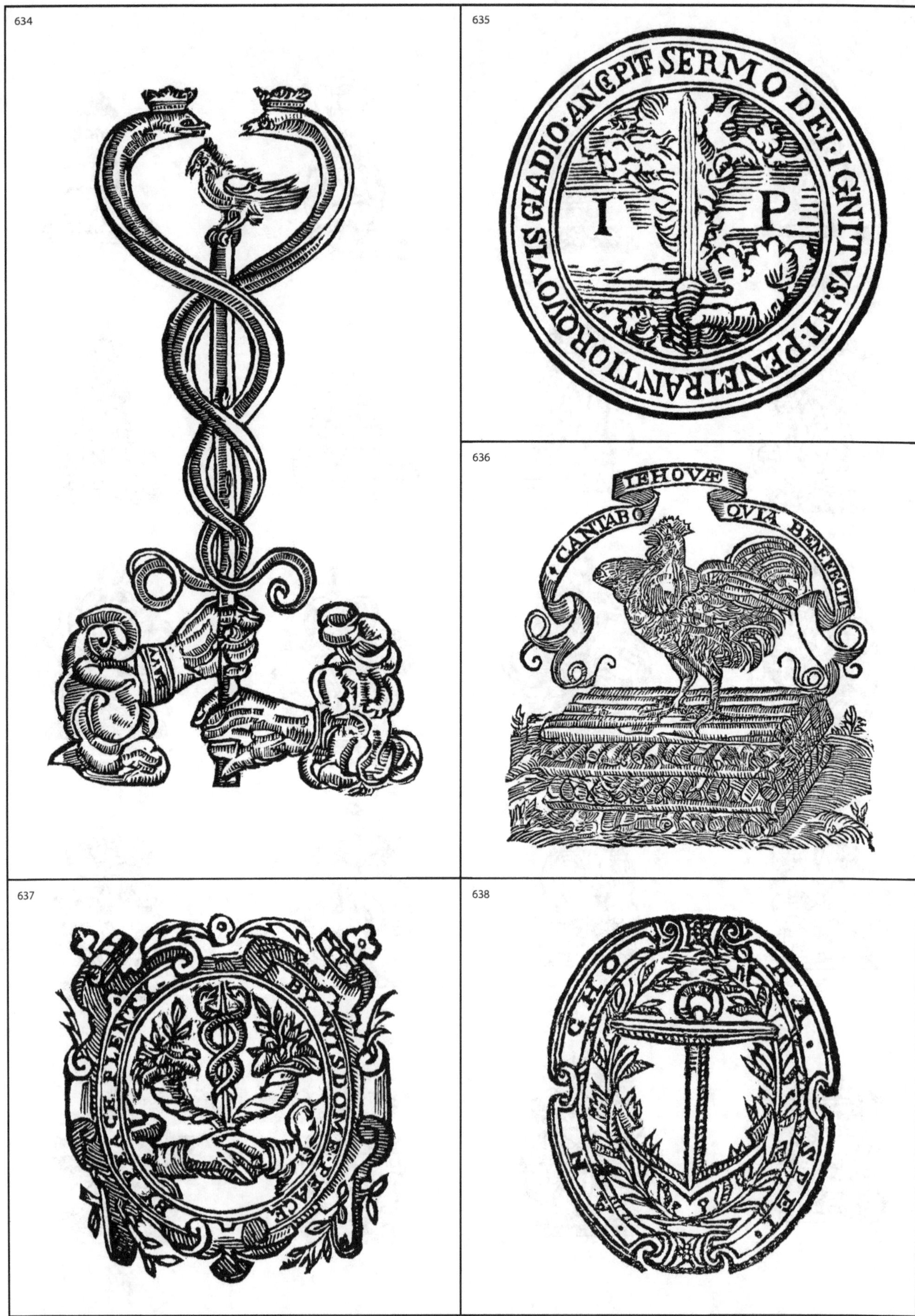

634
635
INCIPIT SERMO DEI IGNITVS ET PENETRANTIOR QVOVIS GLADIO
I   P
636
IEHOVÆ
CANTABO   QVIA BENEFECIT
637
638

639

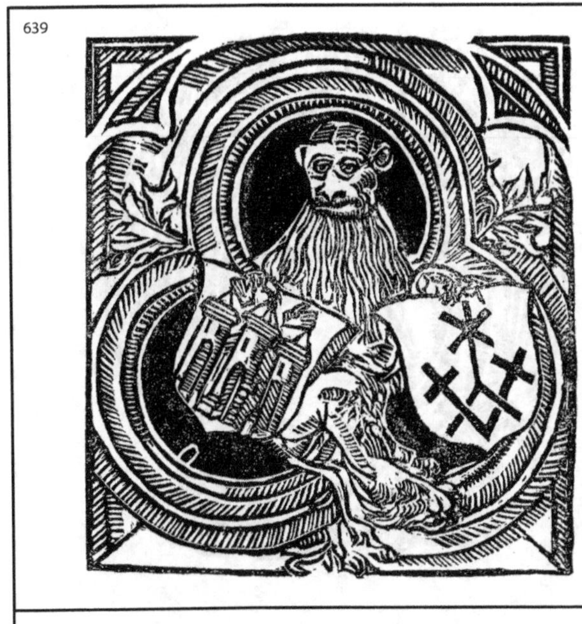

640

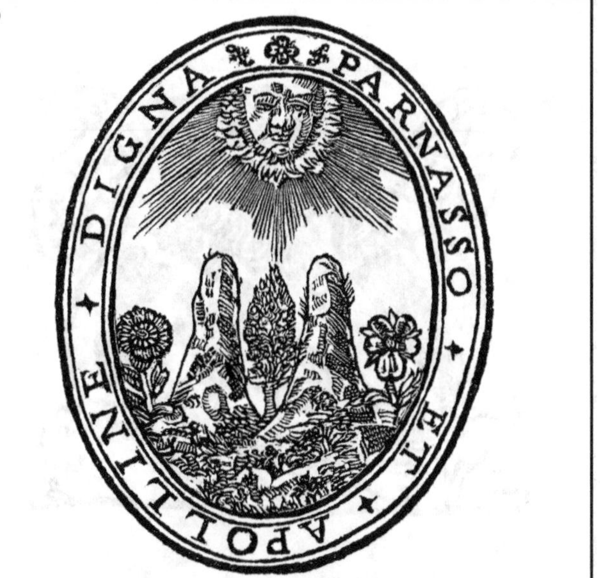

641

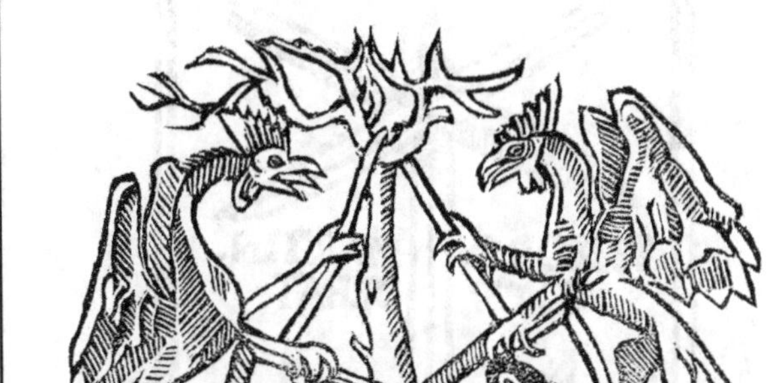

642

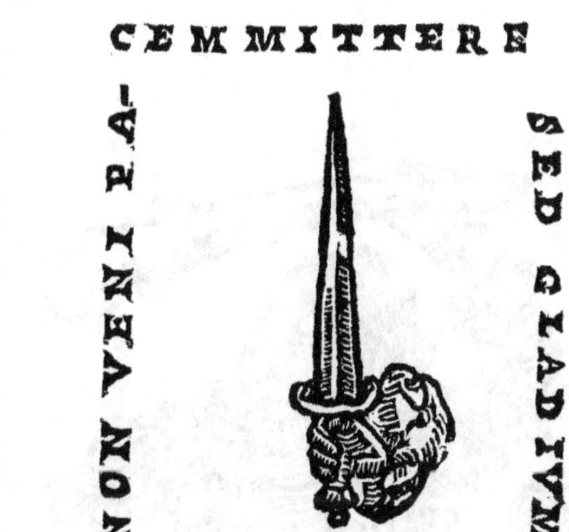

643

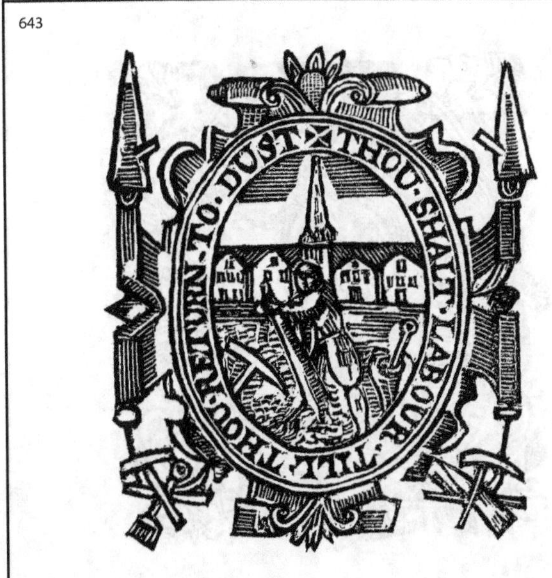

644

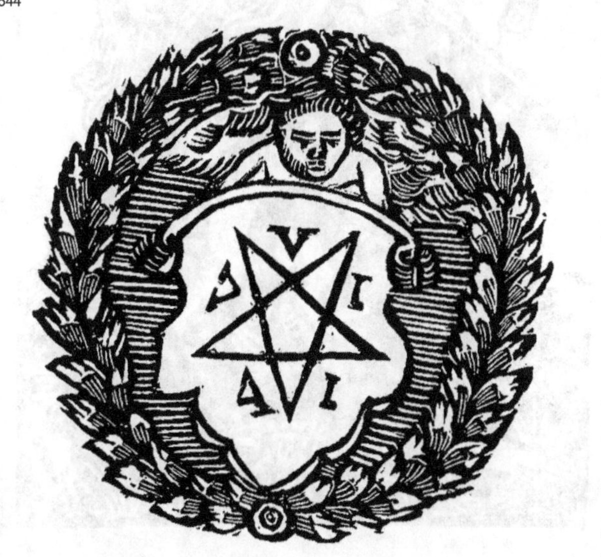

645

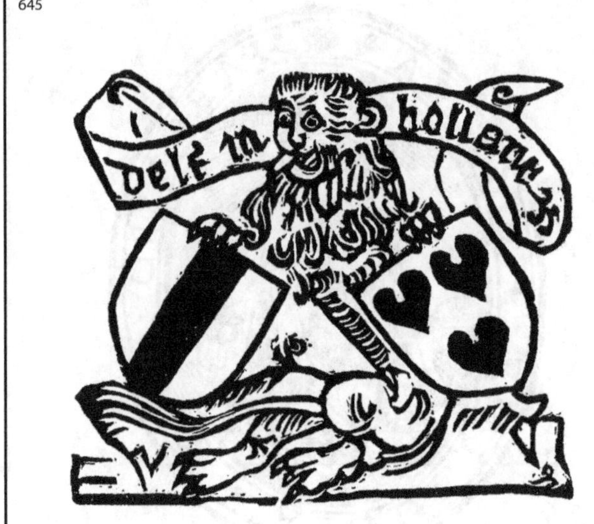

646

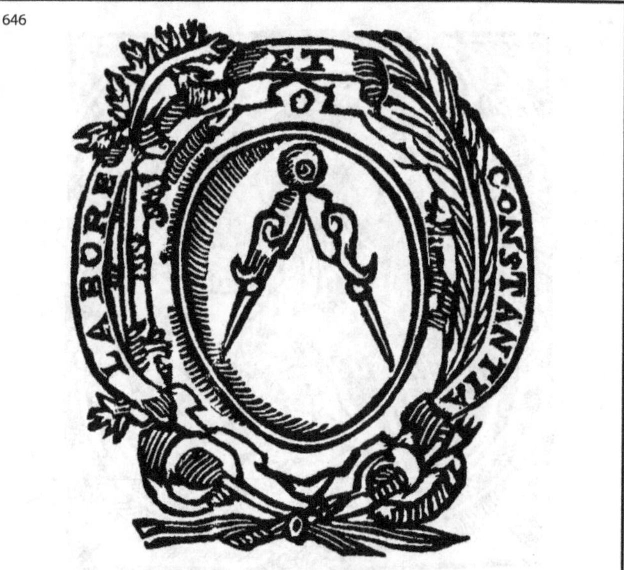

647

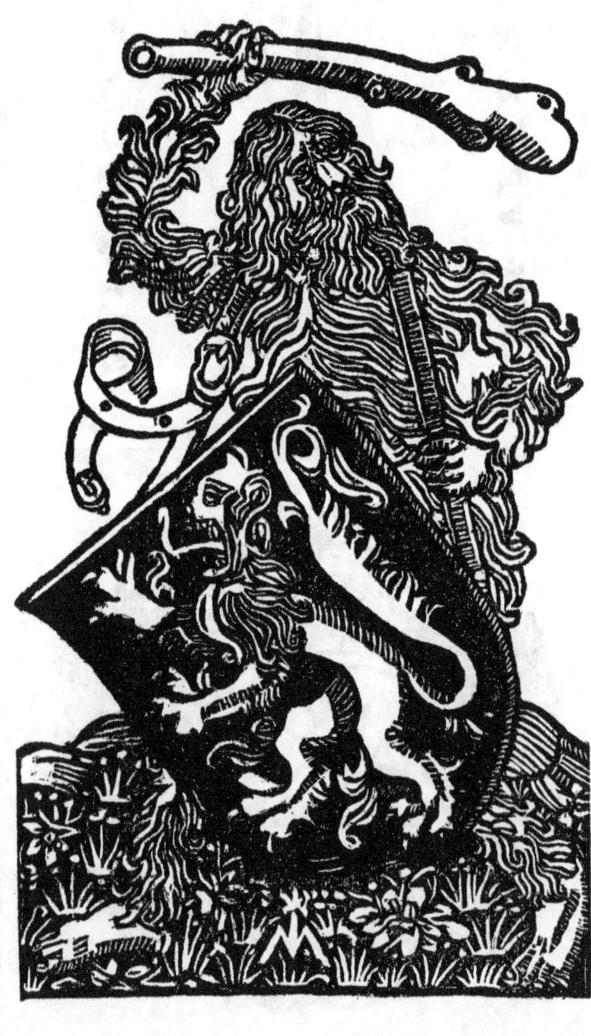

648

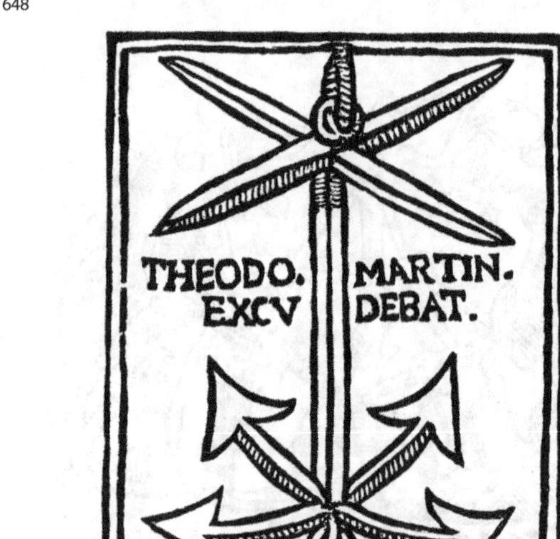

649

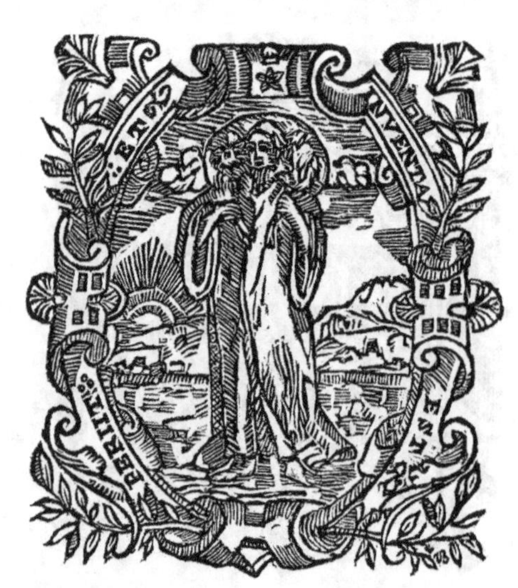

650

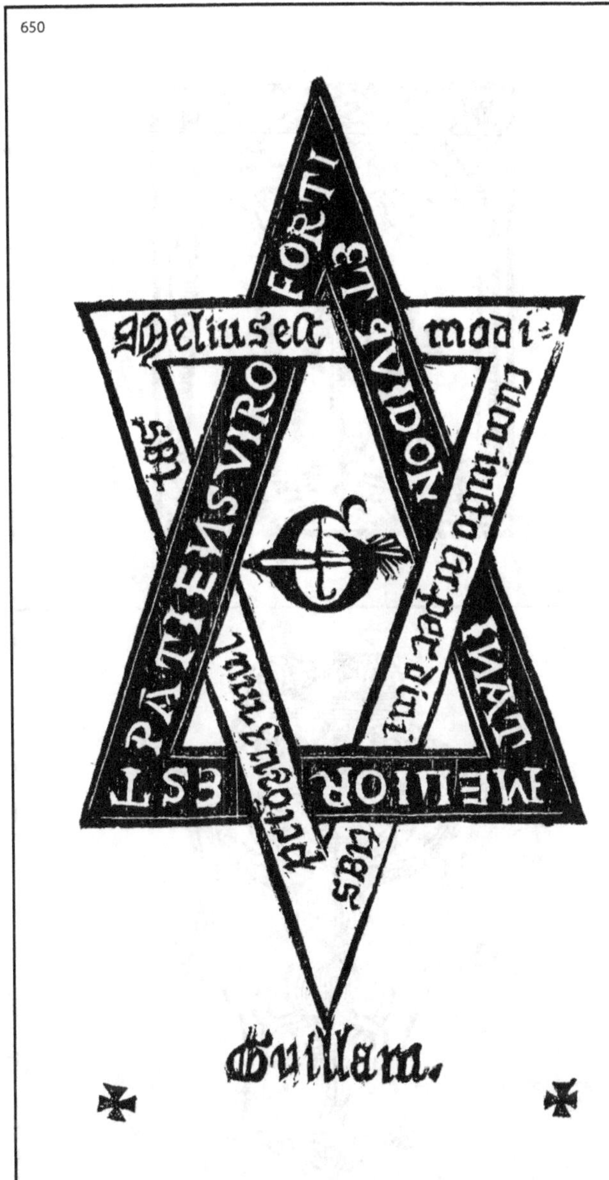

651

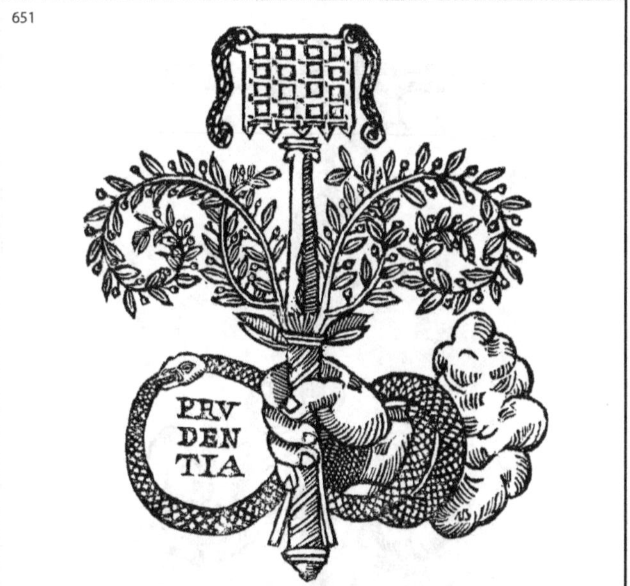

652

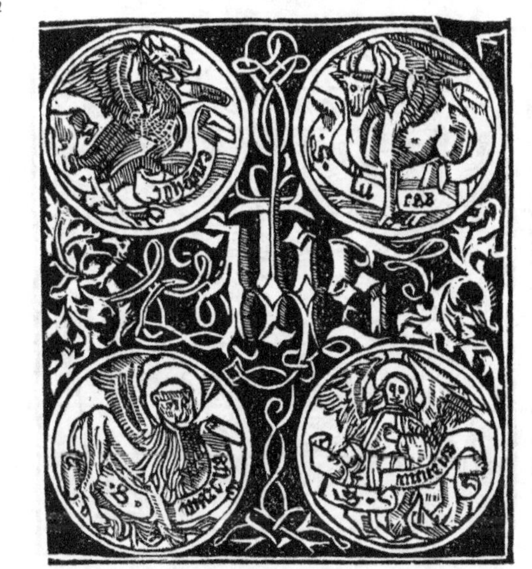

653

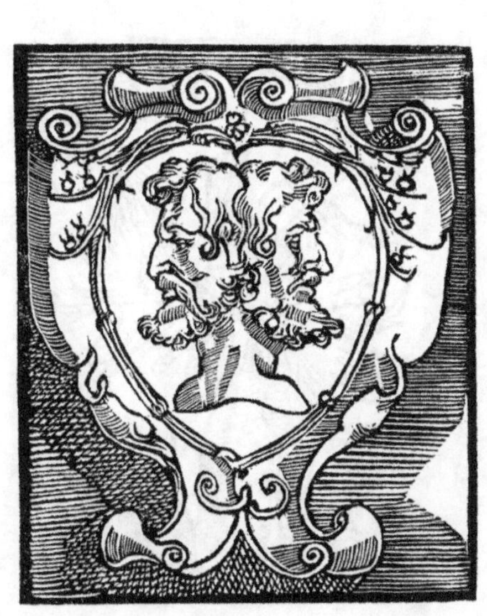

654

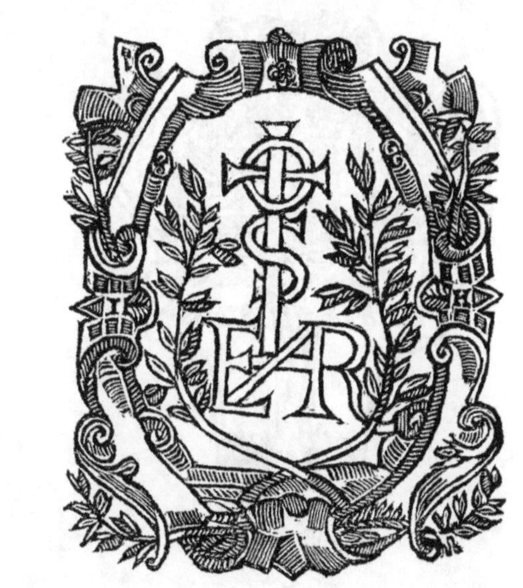

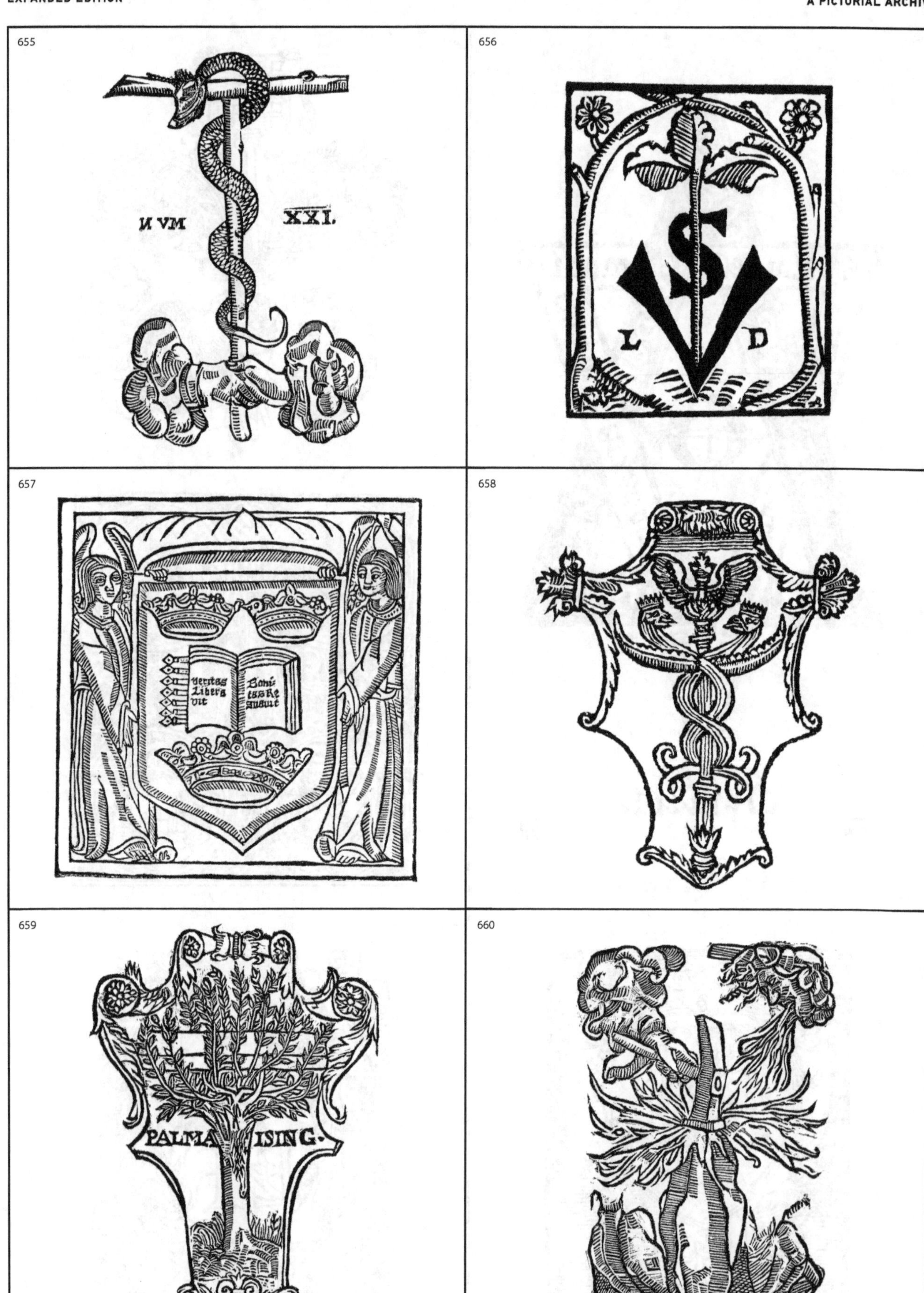

655

656

657

658

659

660

661

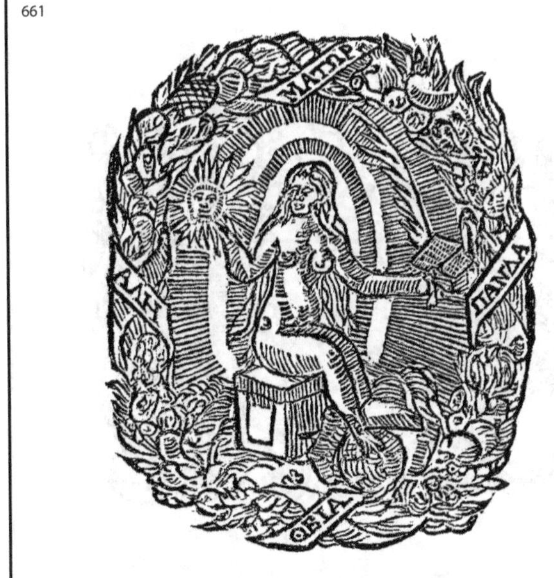

662

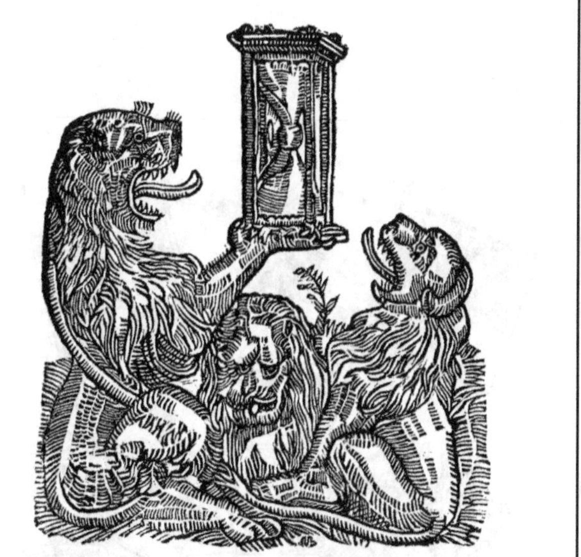

663

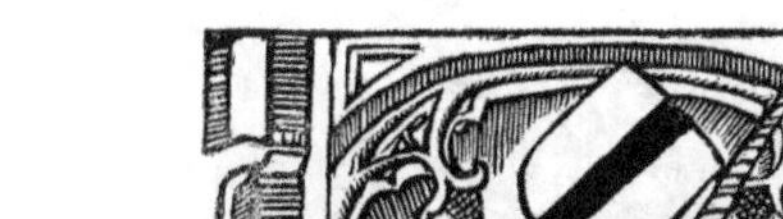

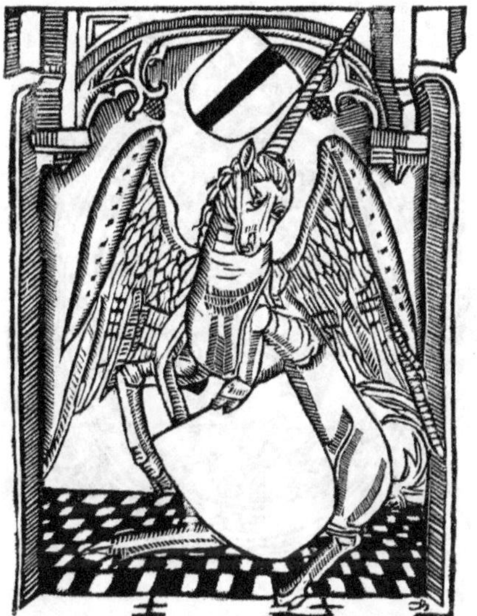

664

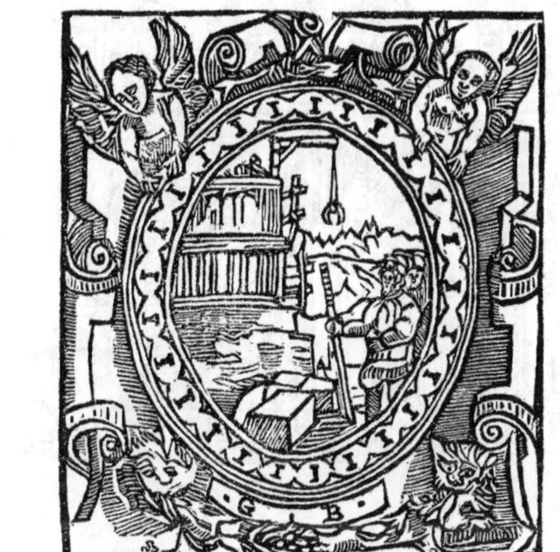

665

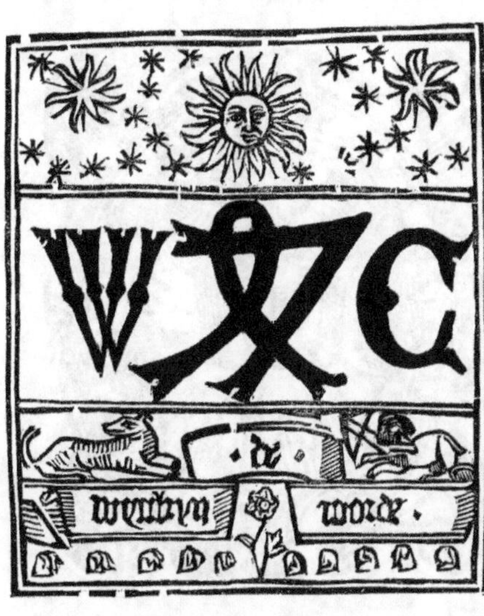

666

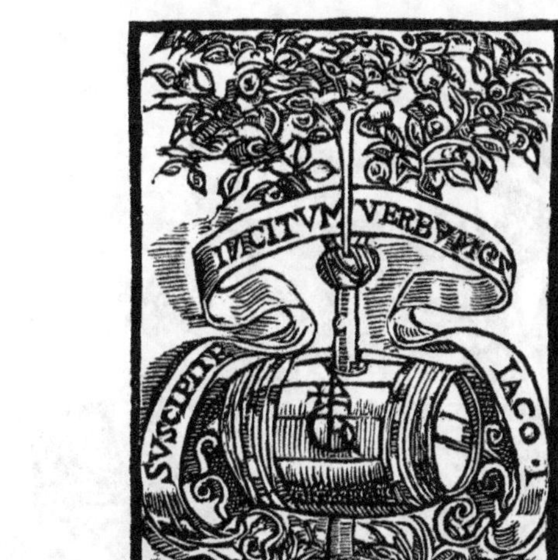

667

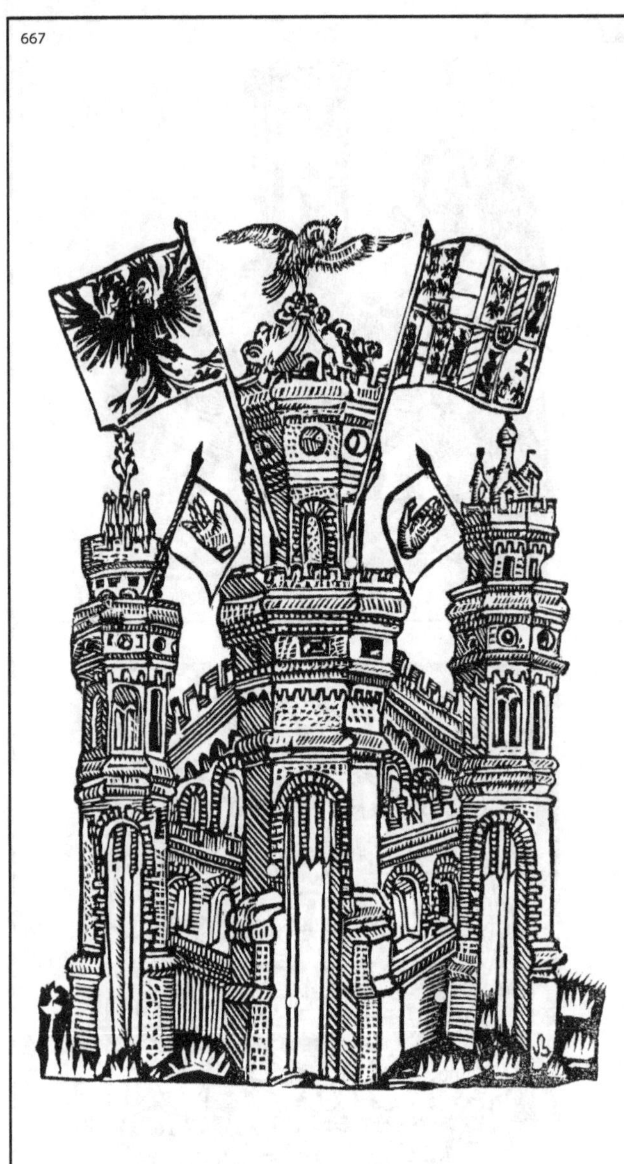

668

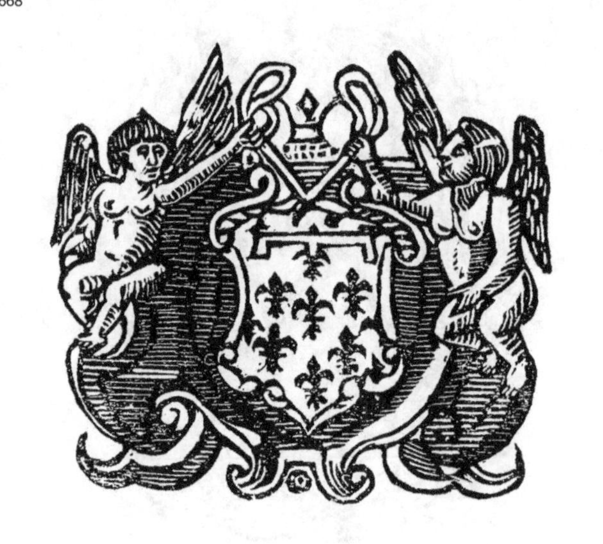

669

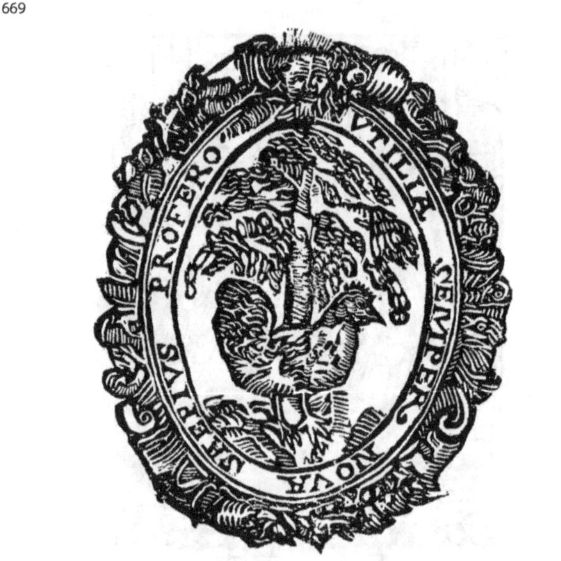

670

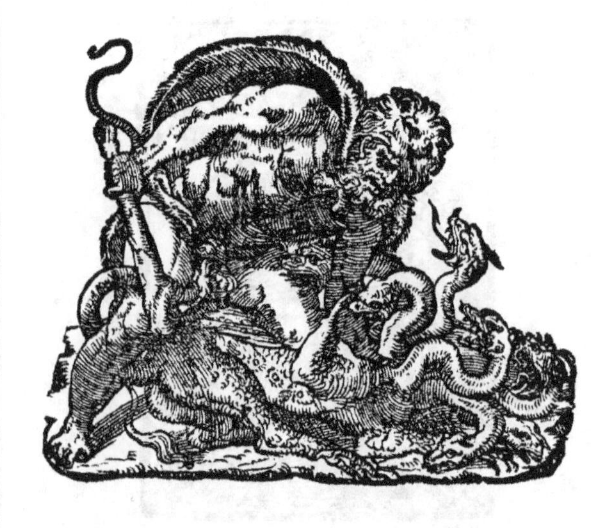

671

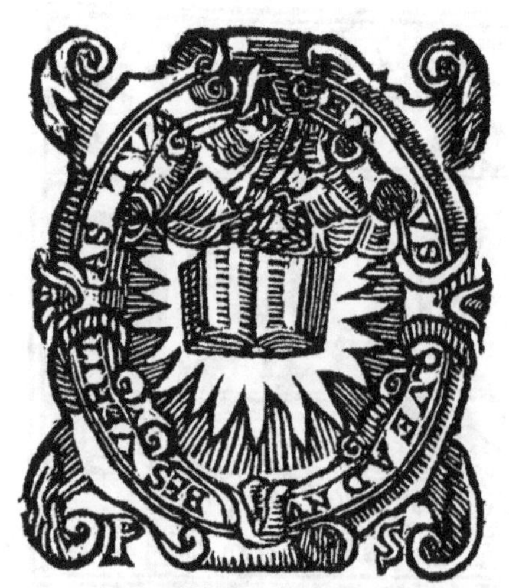

672

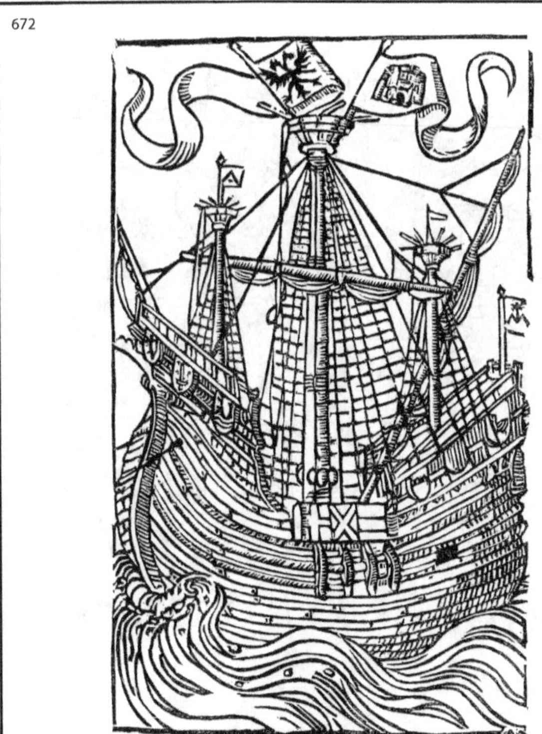

673

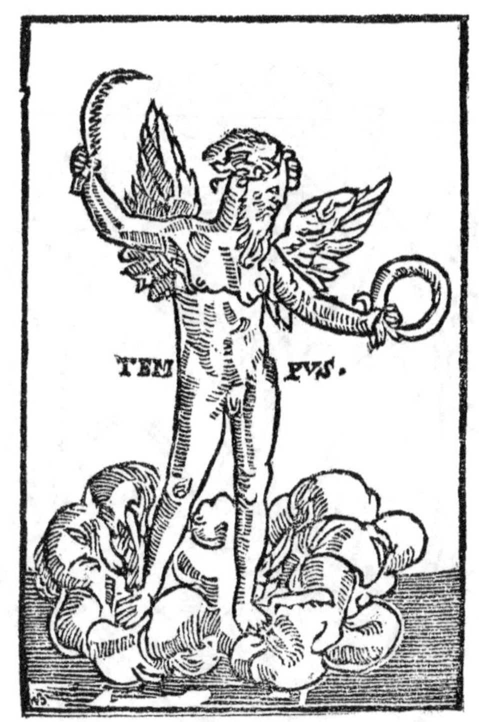

674

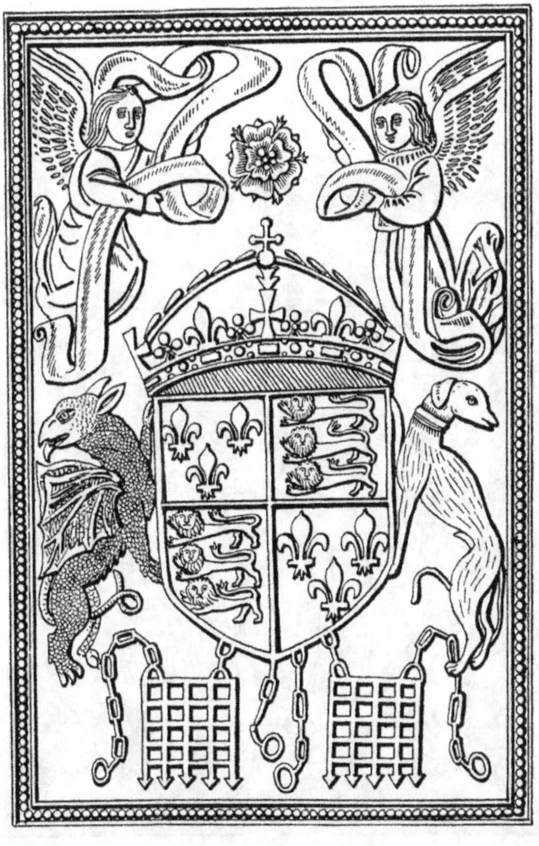

675

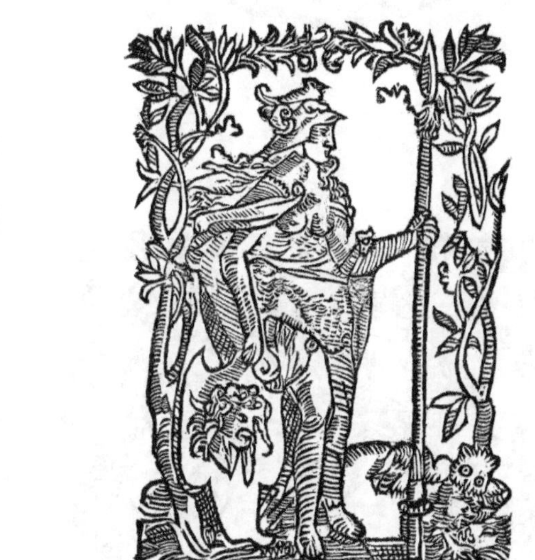

676

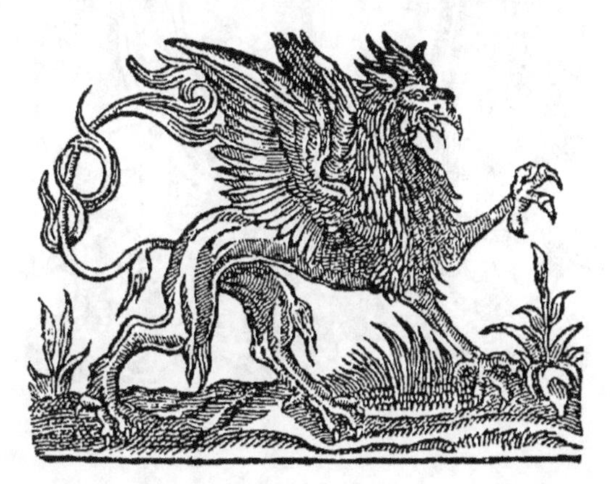

677

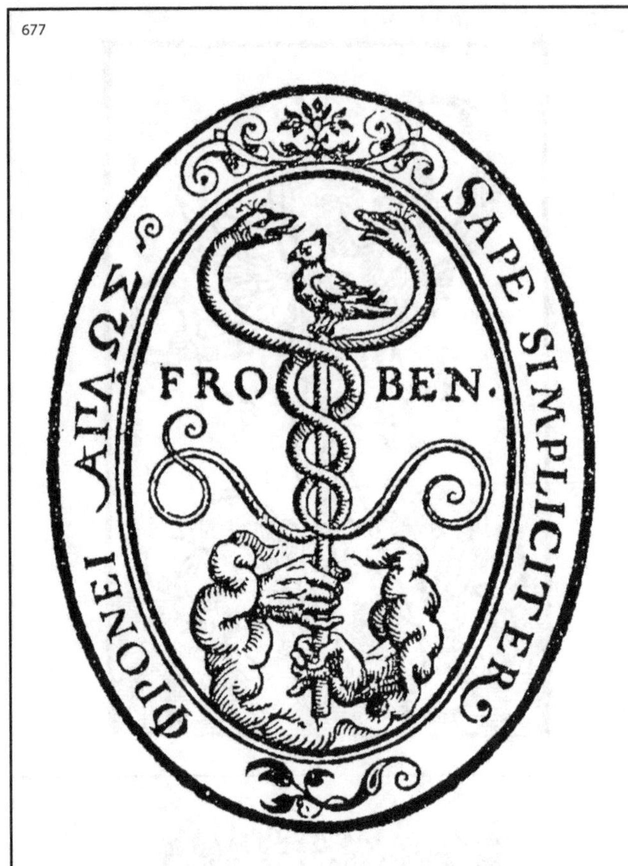

678

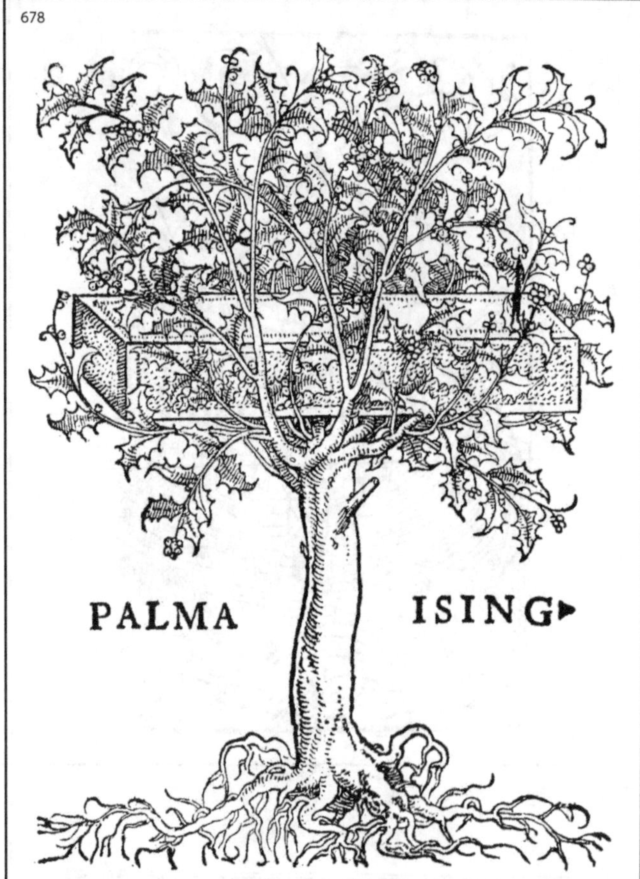

679

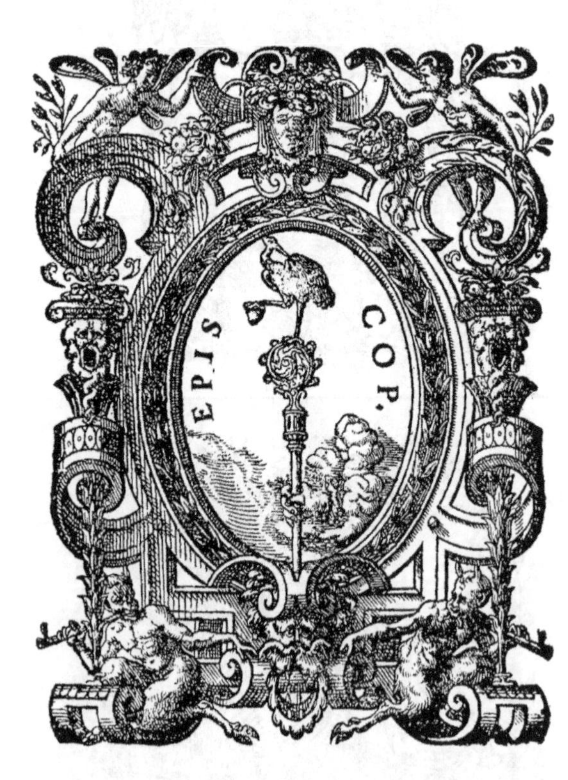

680

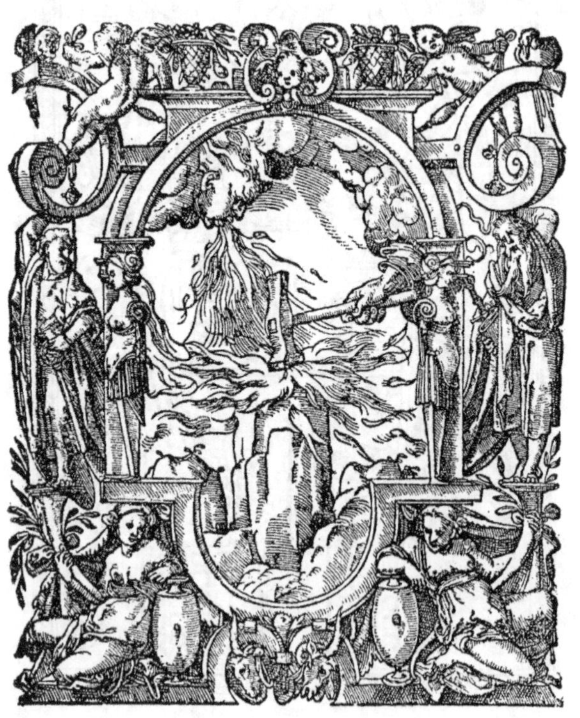

681

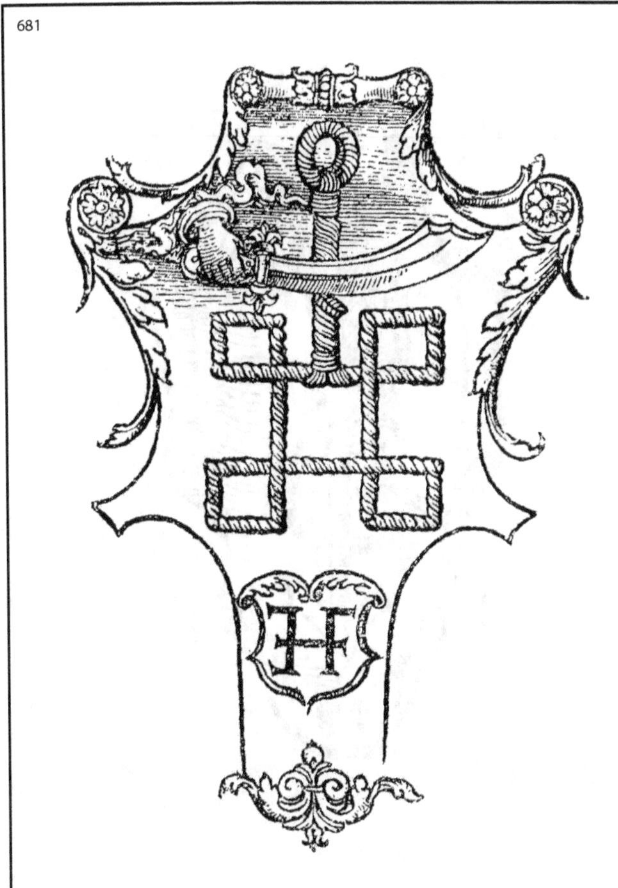

682

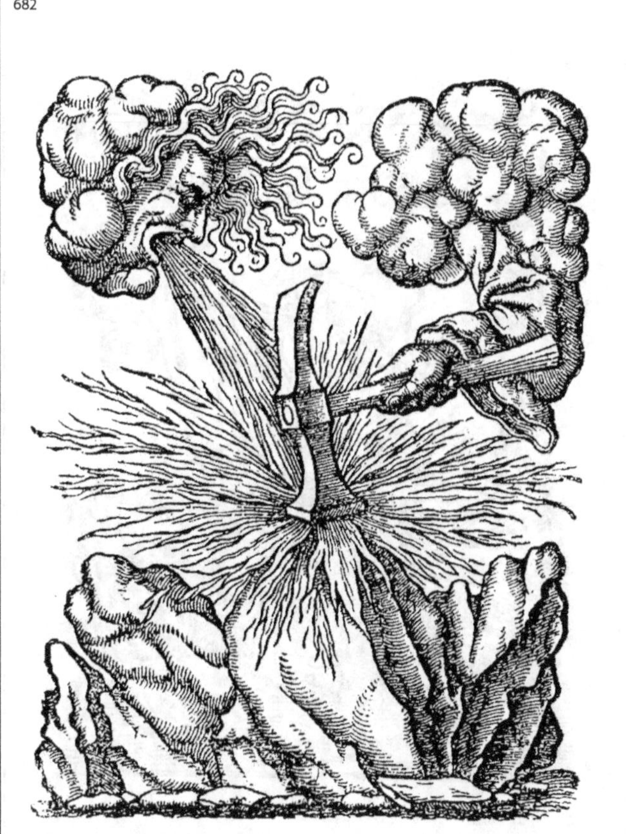

683

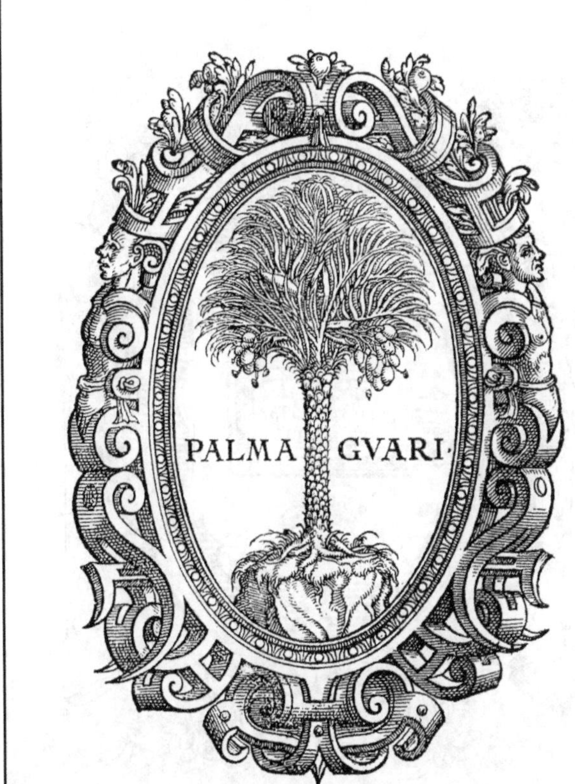

684

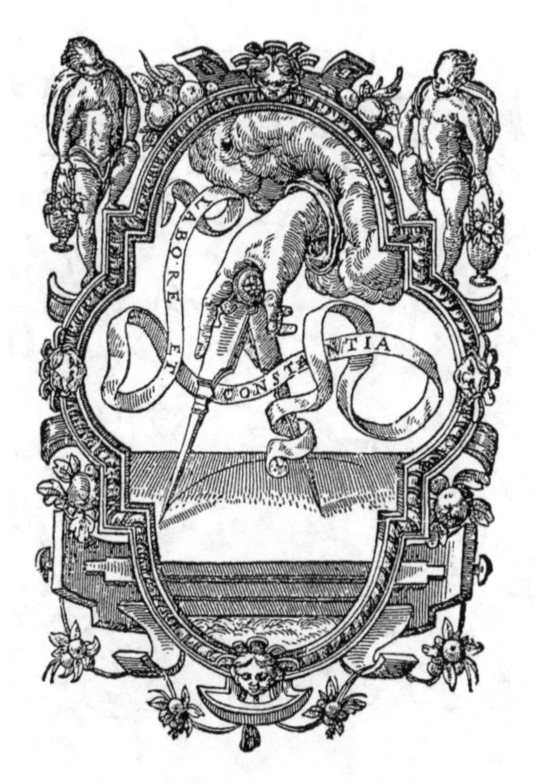

685

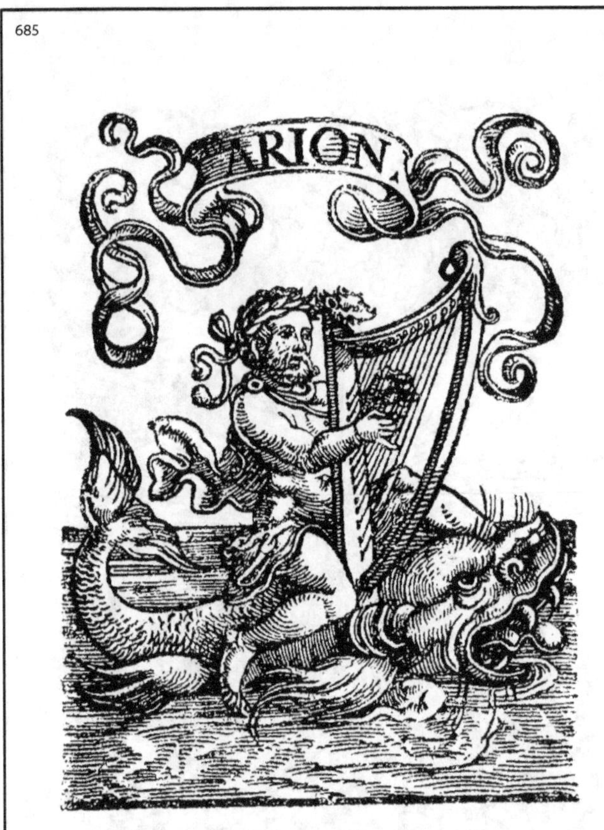

686

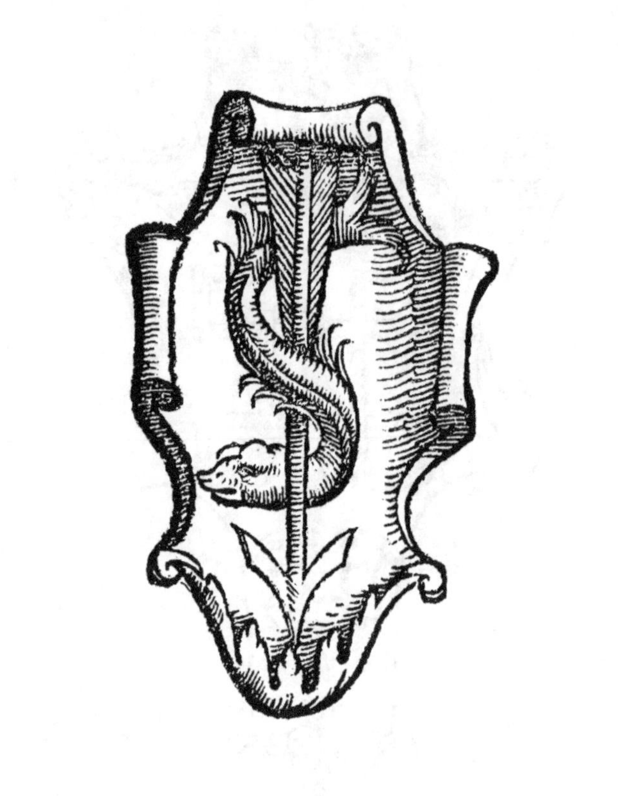

687

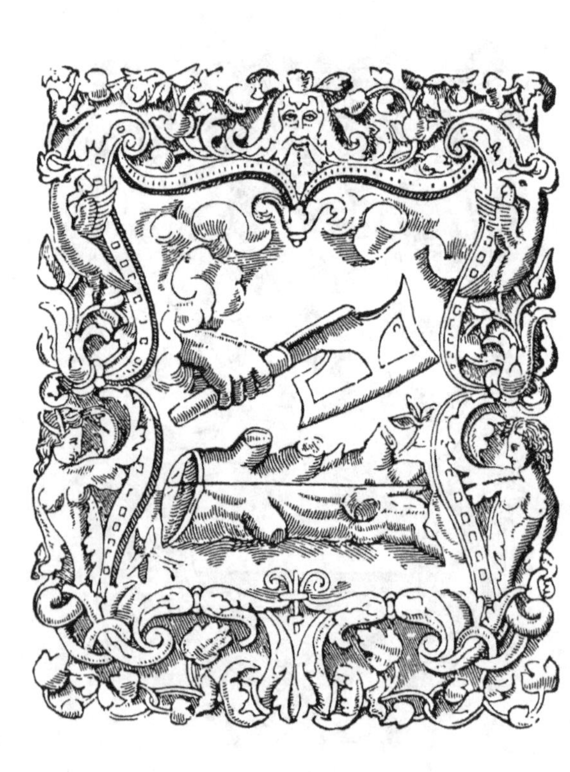

688

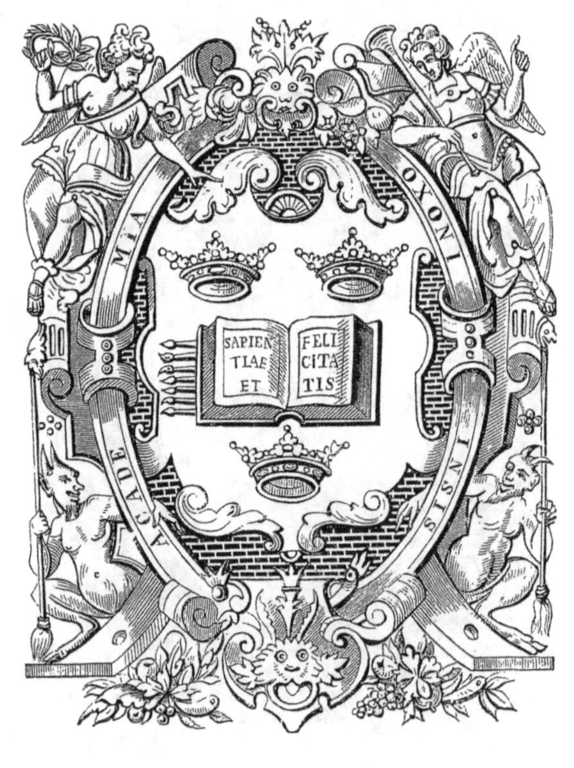

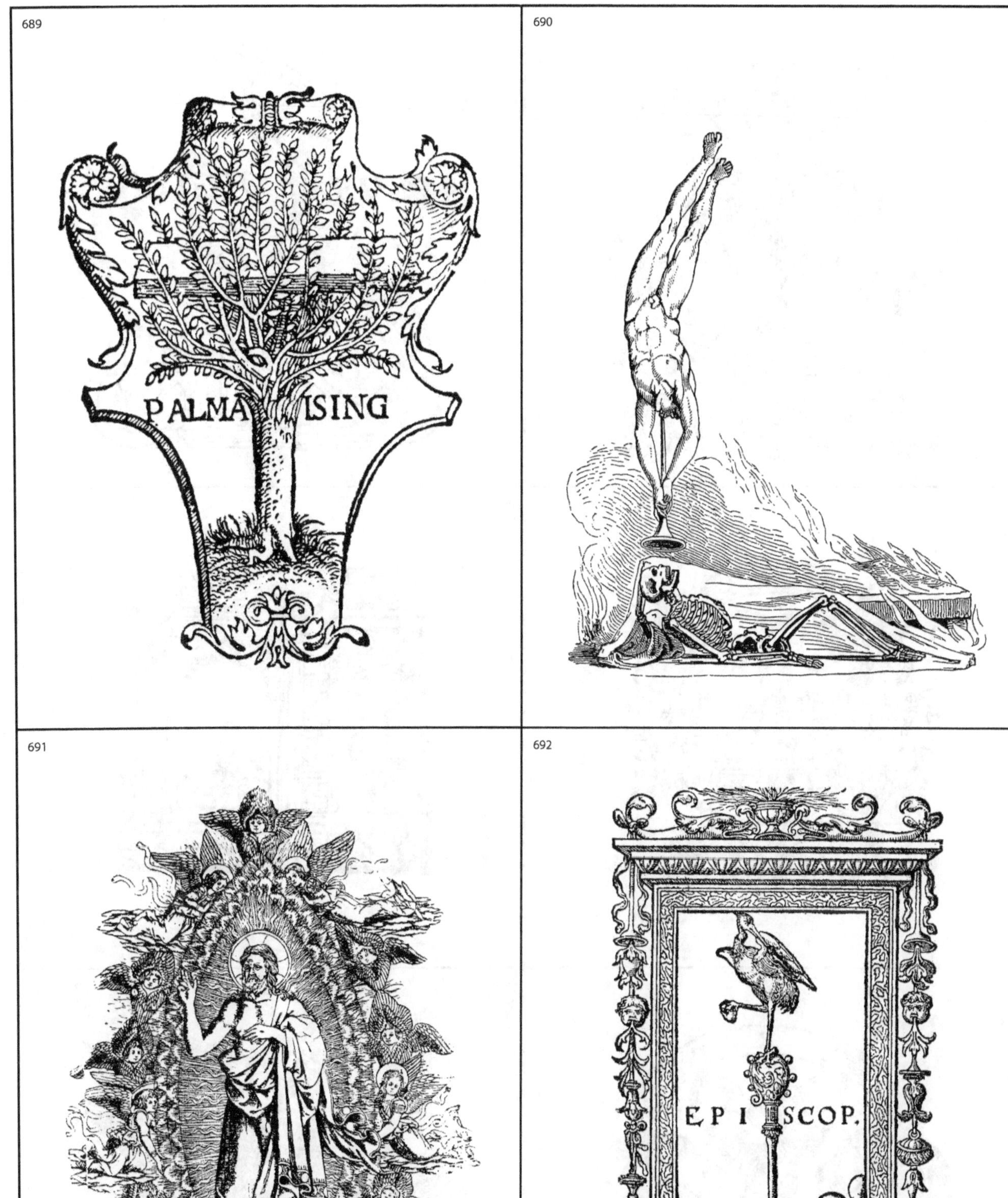

PALMA RISING
EPISCOP.

693

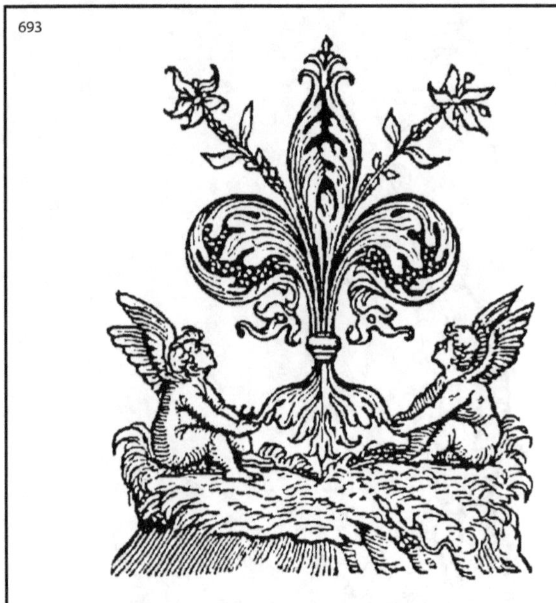

694

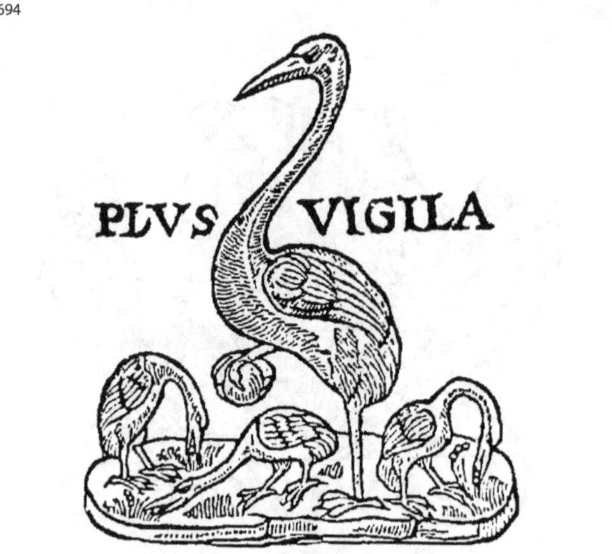

695

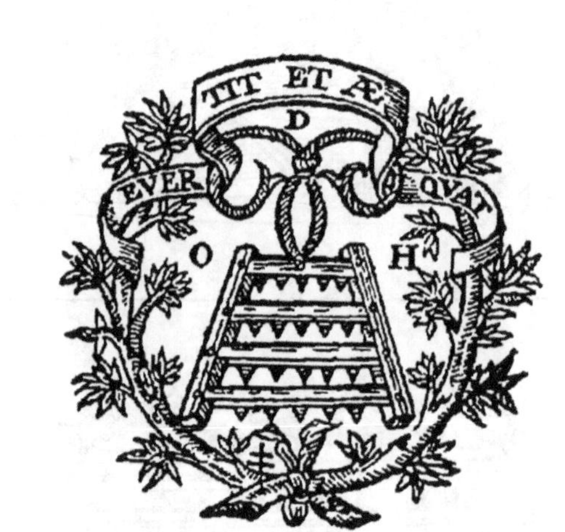

696

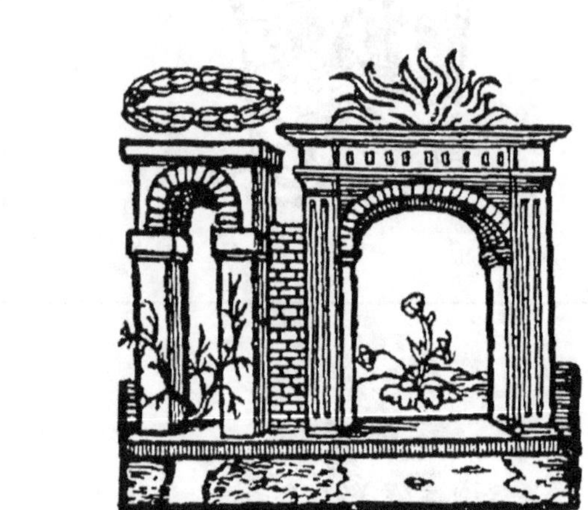

697

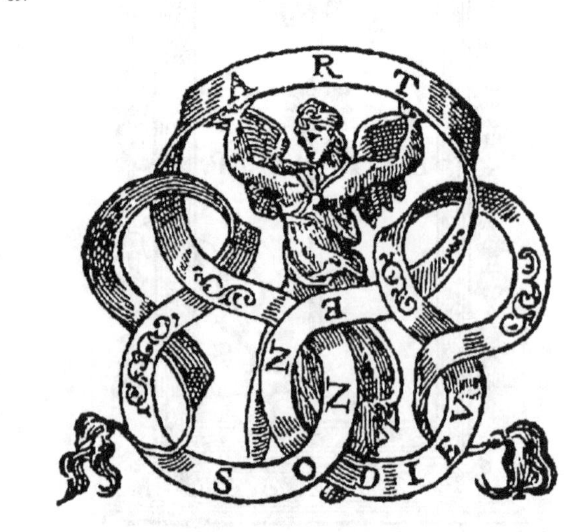

698

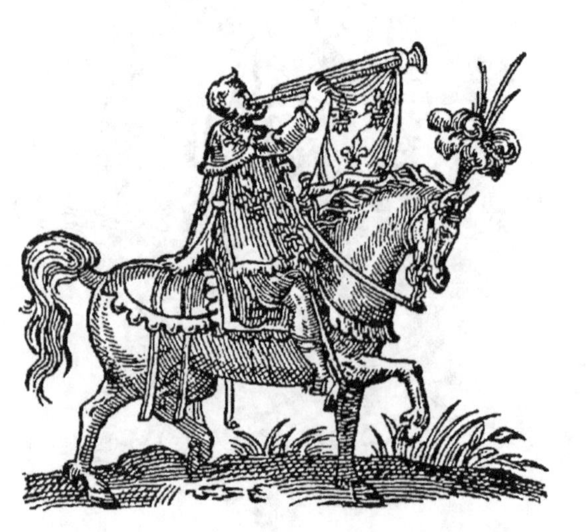

699

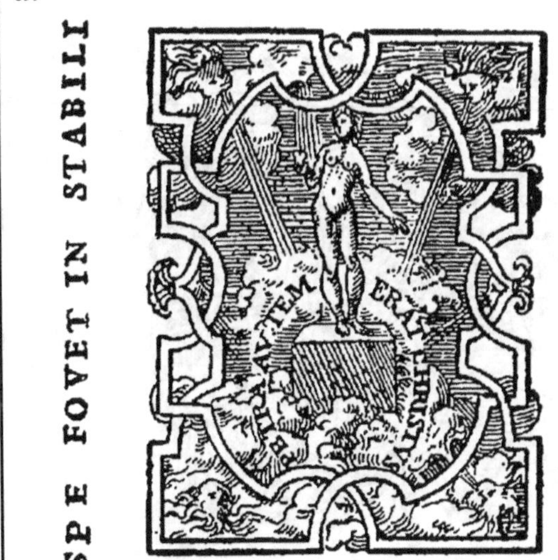

700

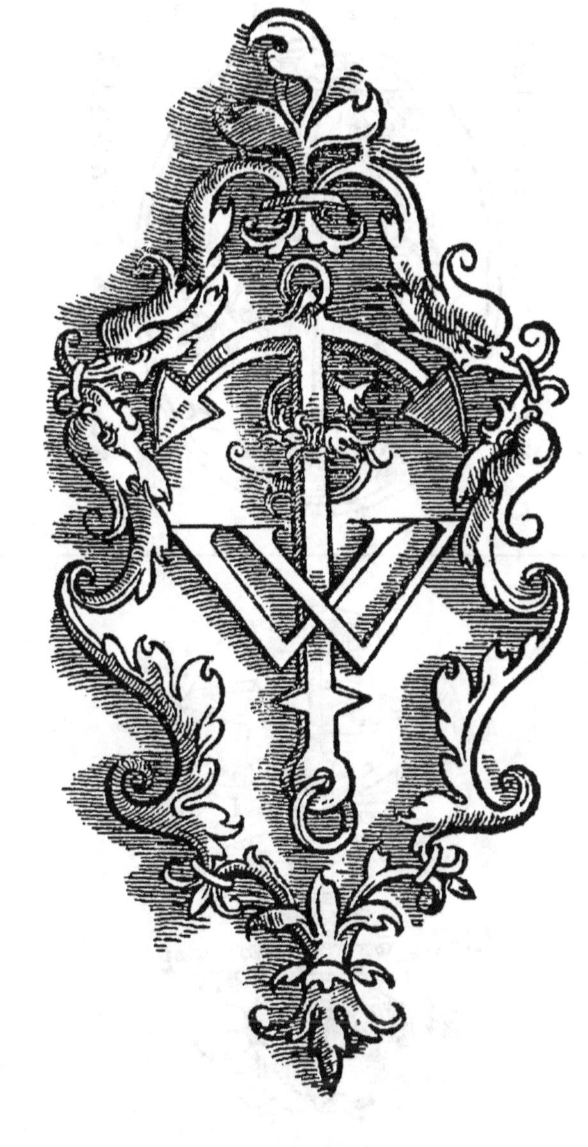

701

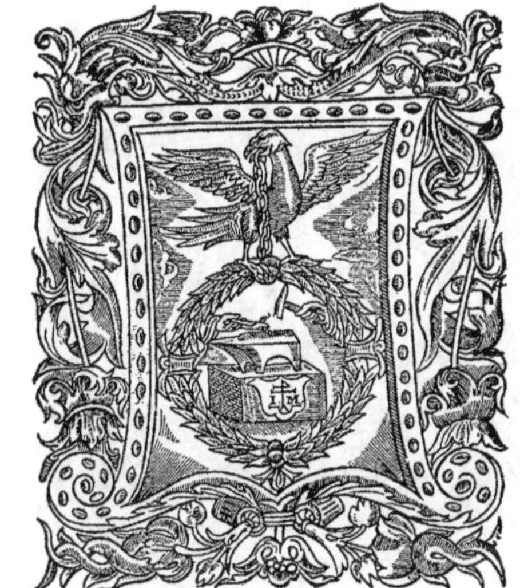

702

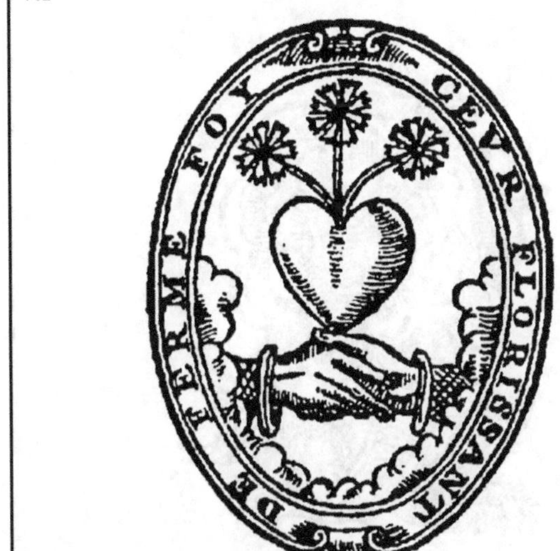

703

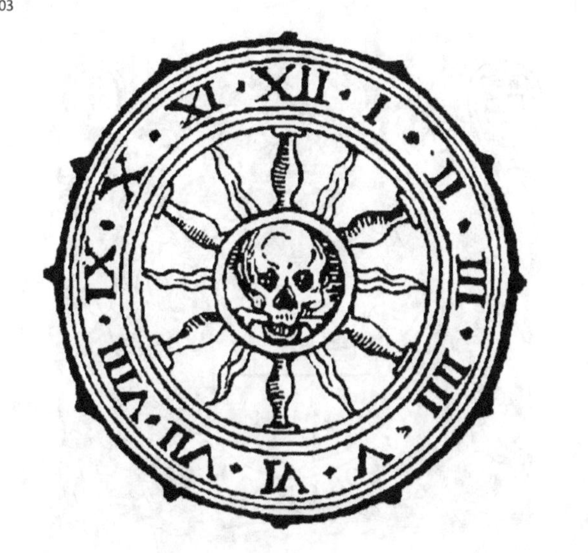

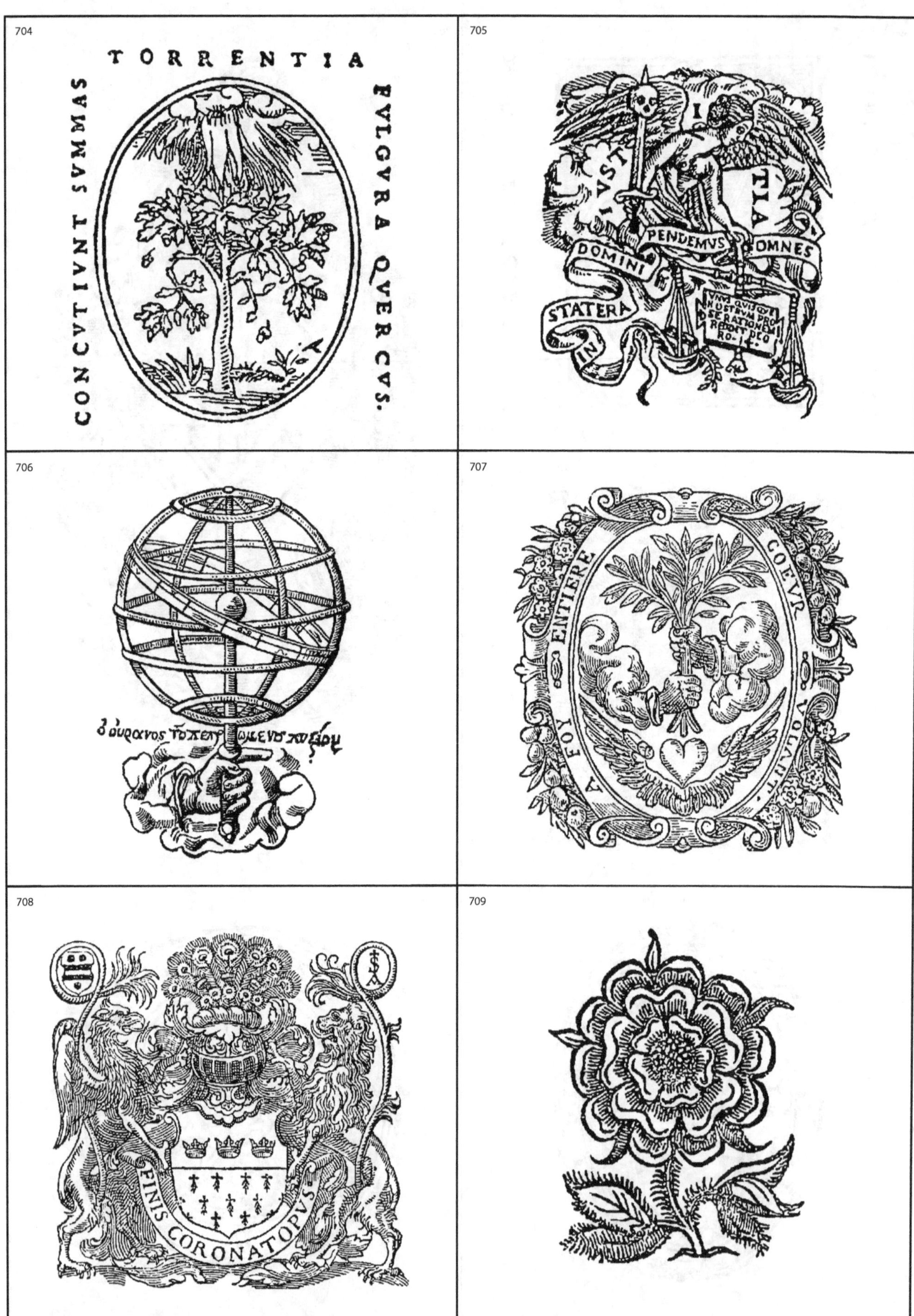
704
TORRENTIA
CONCVTIVNT SVMMAS
FVLGVRA QVERCVS.

705
IVSTITIA
DOMINI
PENDEMVS OMNES
STATERA IN

706

707
A EOY ENTIERE COEVR VOVLANT

708
FINIS CORONAT OPVS.

709

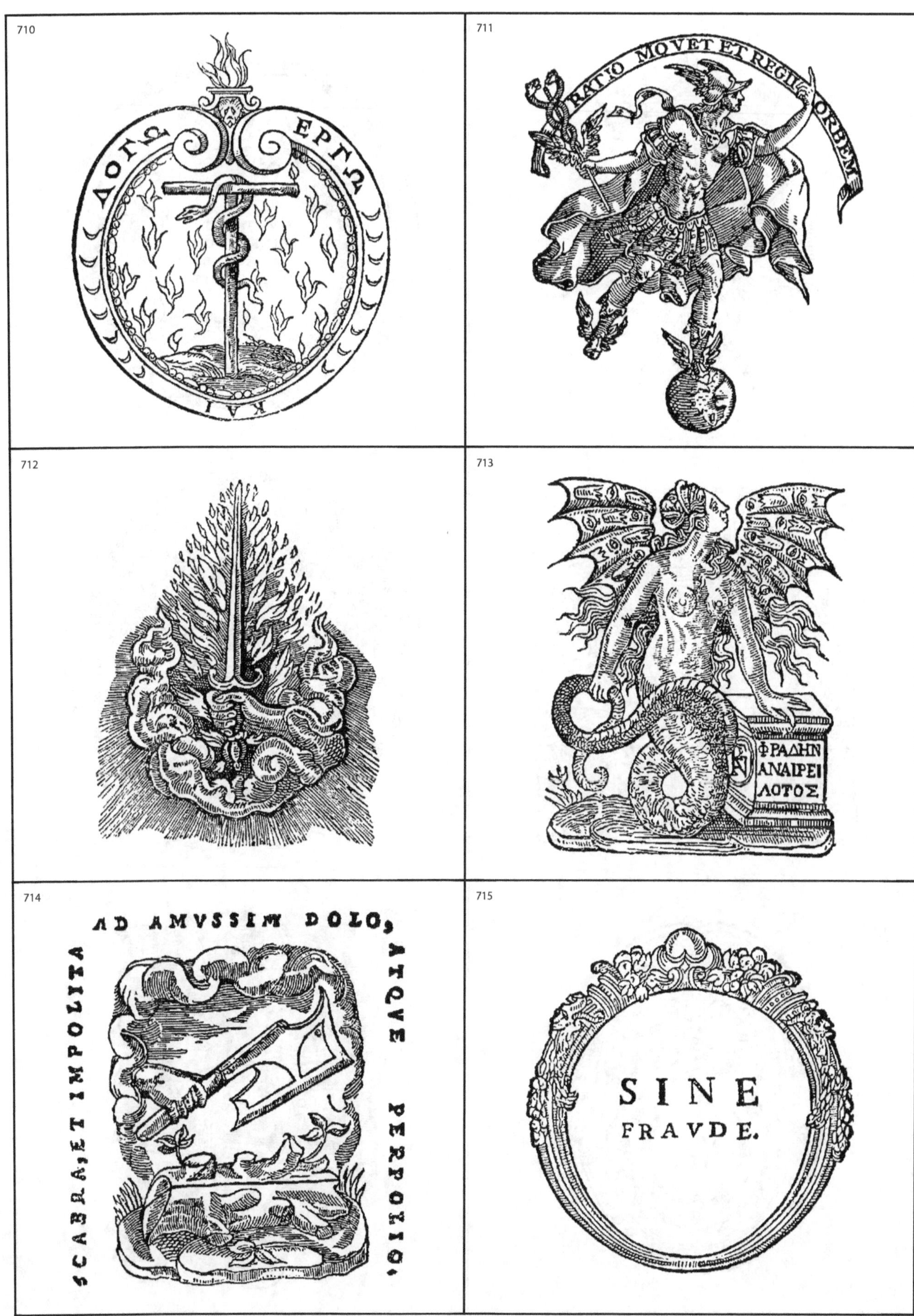
710
ΔΟΓΩ   ΕΡΓΩ
711
RATIO MOVET ET REGIT ORBEM
712
713
ΦΡΑΔΗΝ ΑΝΑΙΡΕΙ ΛΟΤΟΣ
714
AD AMVSSIM DOLO,
SCABRA, ET IMPOLITA
ATQVE PERPOLIO.
715
SINE FRAVDE.

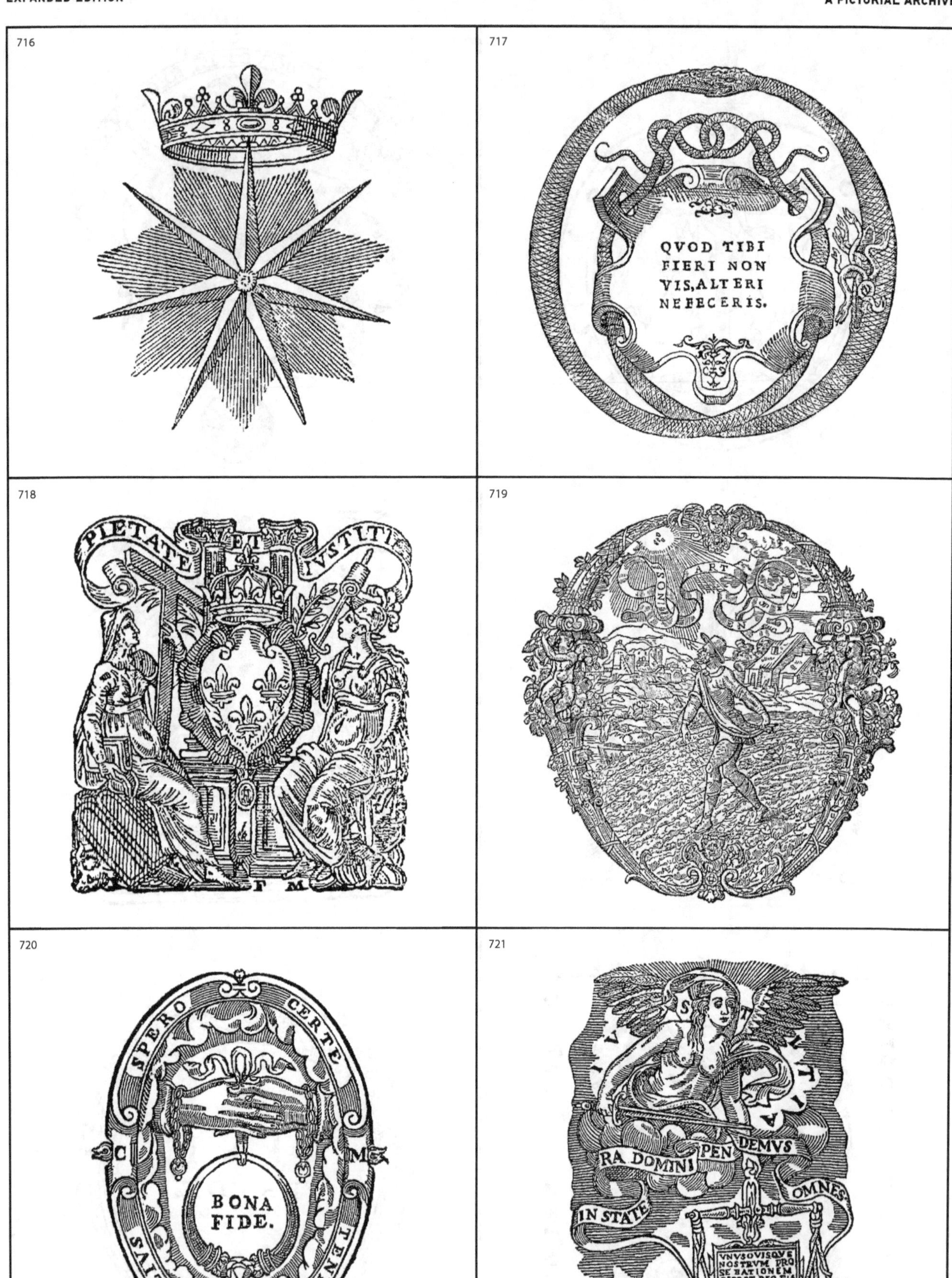
716
717
QVOD TIBI
FIERI NON
VIS, ALTERI
NE FECERIS.
718
PIETATE ET IVSTITIÆ
719
720
SPERO CERTE
BONA FIDE.
MELIVS TENEO
721
IVSTITIA
RA DOMINI PENDEMVS
IN STATE OMNES

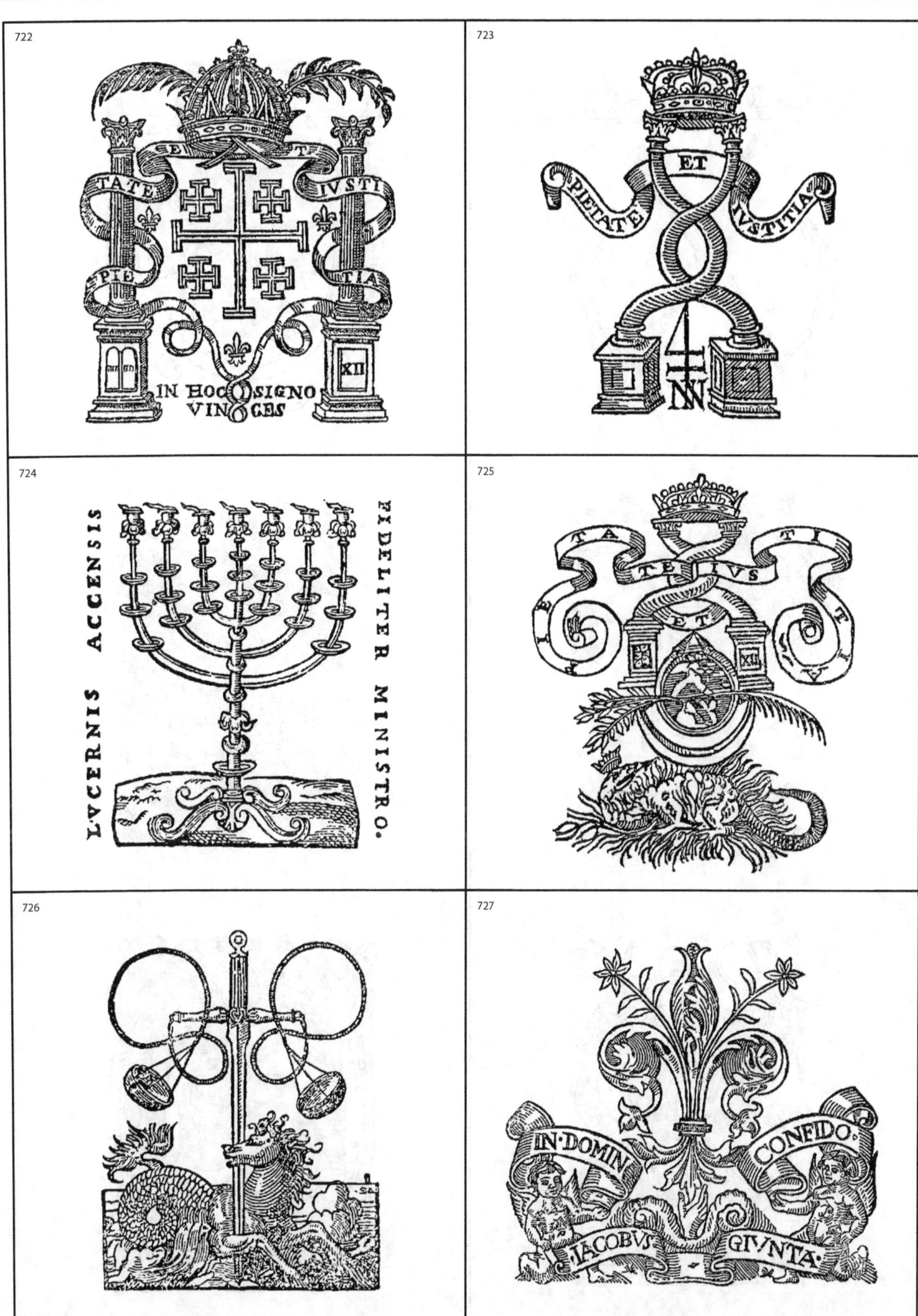
722
ET
TATE
IVSTI
PIE
TIA
IN HOC SIGNO
VINCES
XII

723
ET
PIETATE
IVSTITIA
NN

724
LVCERNIS ACCENSIS
FIDELITER MINISTRO.

725
ETA
TI
TE IVS
ET
XII

726

727
IN·DOMIN
CONFIDO·
IACOBVS
GIVNTA·

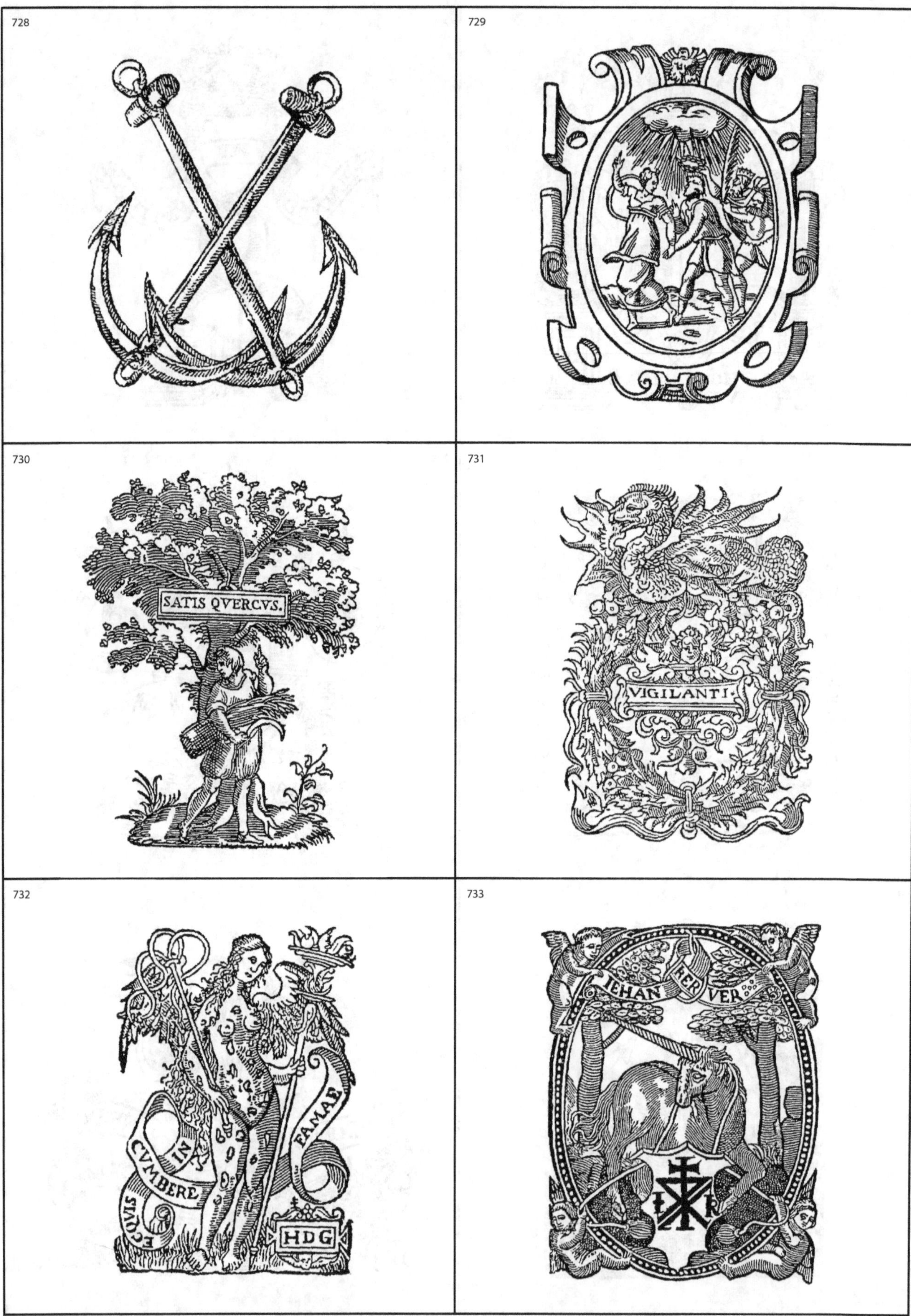

728
729
730
SATIS QVERCVS.
731
VIGILANTI·
732
CVMBERE
FAMAE
EQVVS
HDG
733
IEHAN   VER

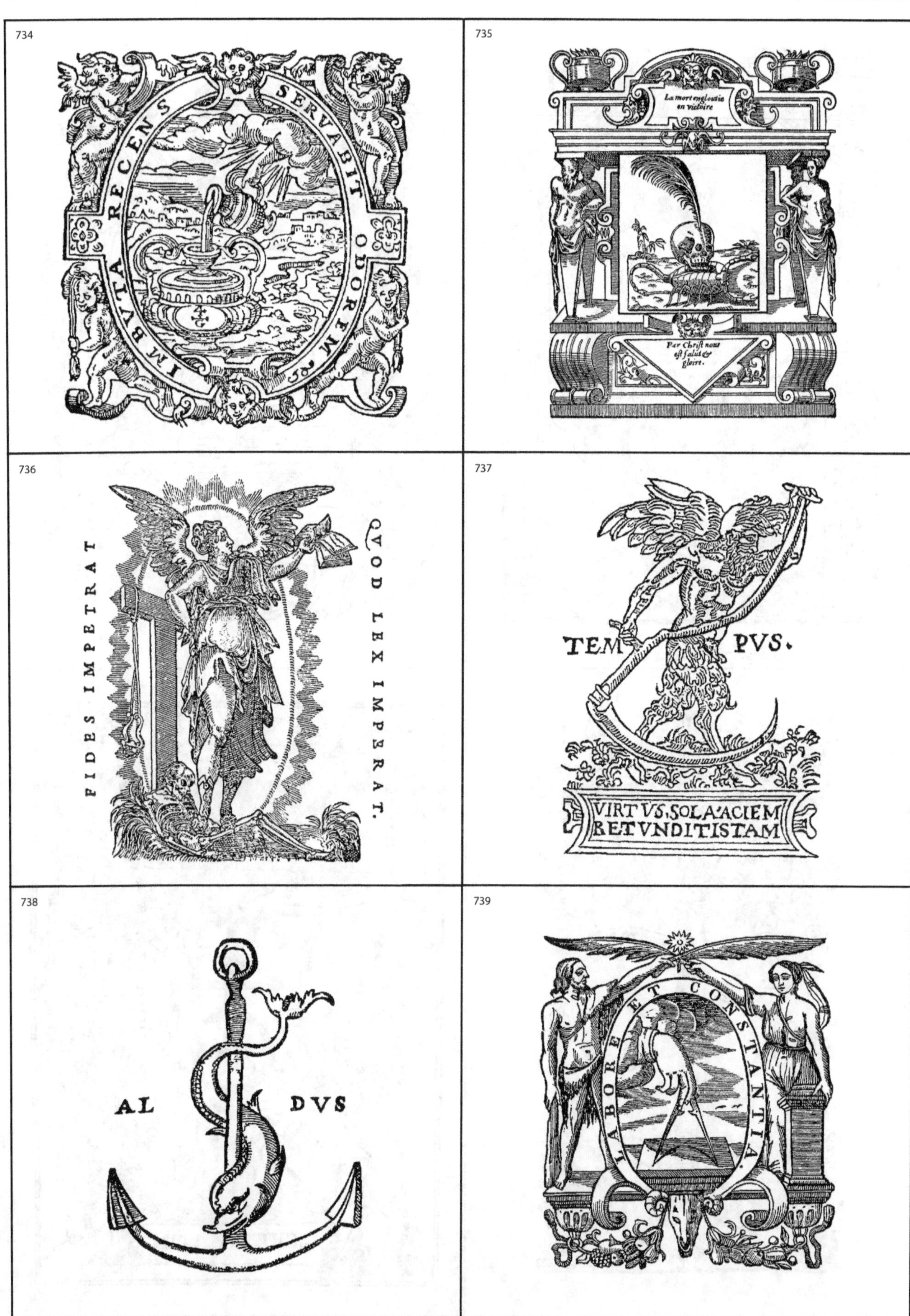

734
IMBVTA RECENS SERVABIT ODOREM

735
La mort engloutie en victoire
Par Christ nous est salut & gloire.

736
FIDES IMPERAT
QVOD LEX IMPERAT.

737
TEM PVS.
VIRTVS SOLA ACIEM RETVNDIT ISTAM

738
AL DVS

739
LABORE ET CONSTANTIA

740

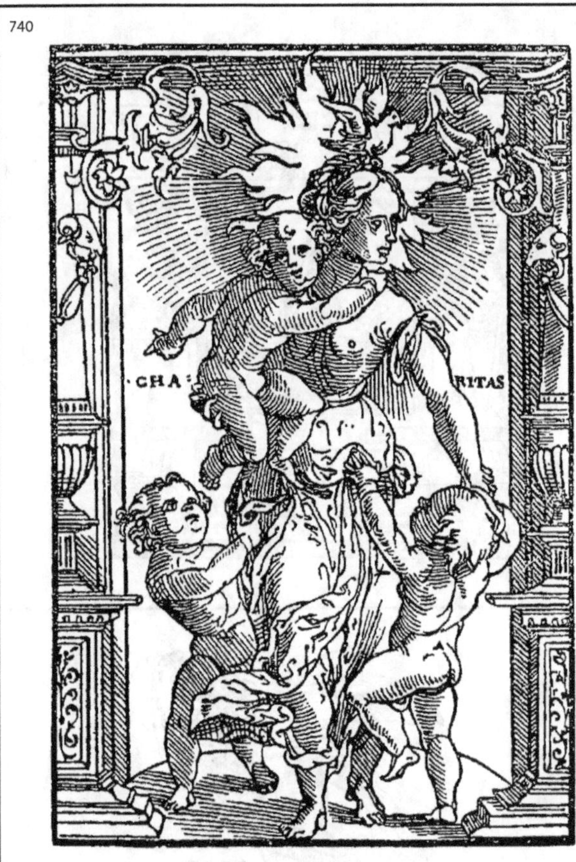

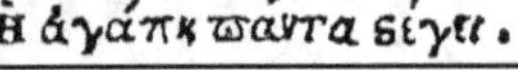

741

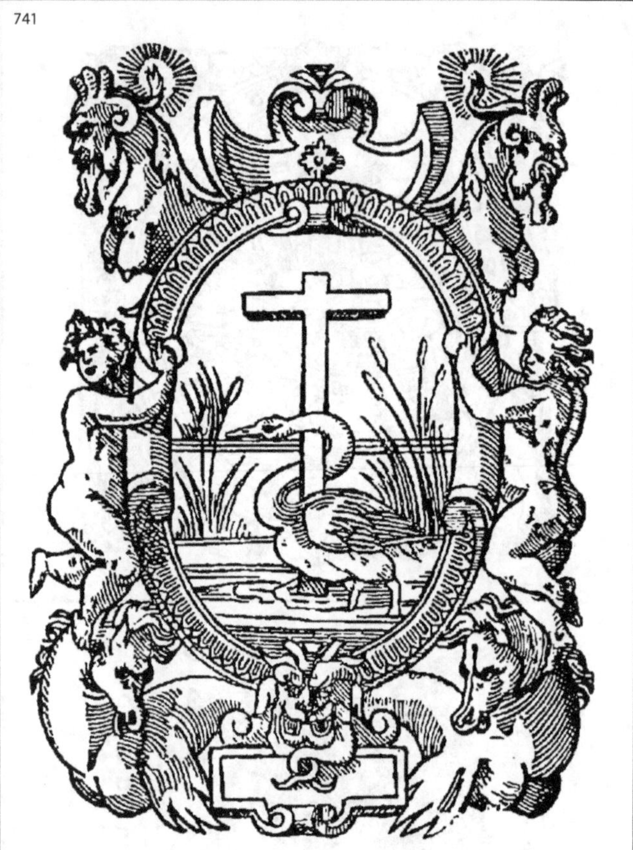

742

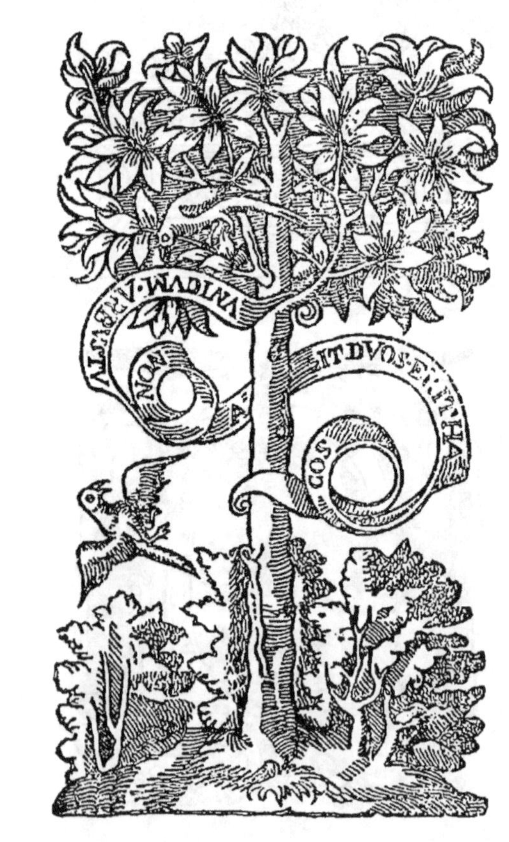

743

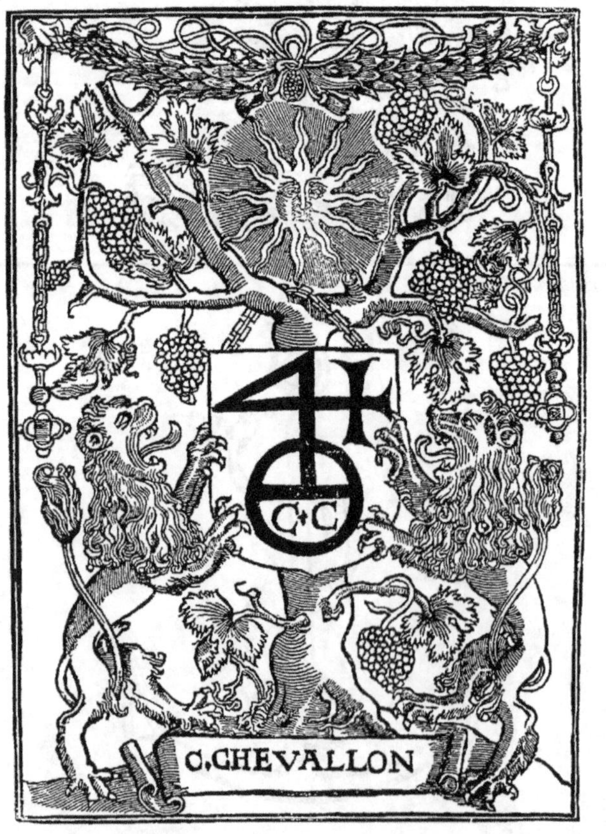

744

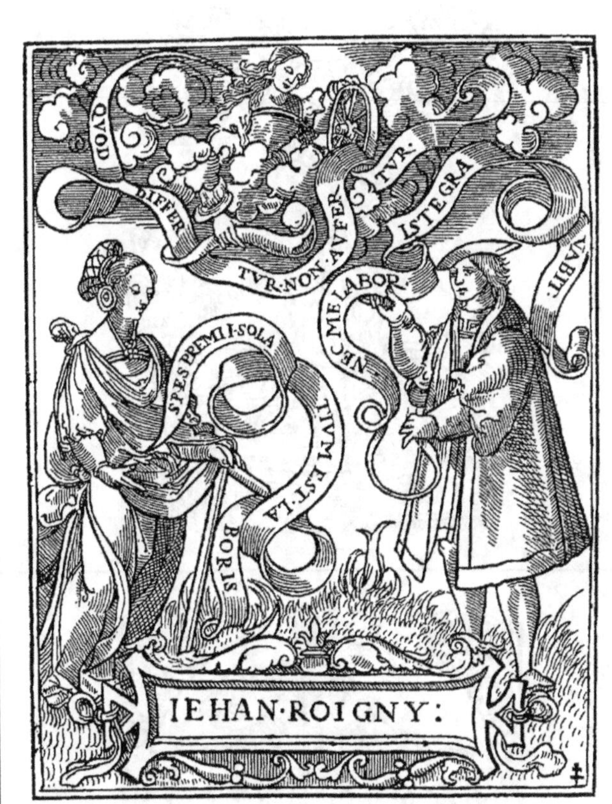

745

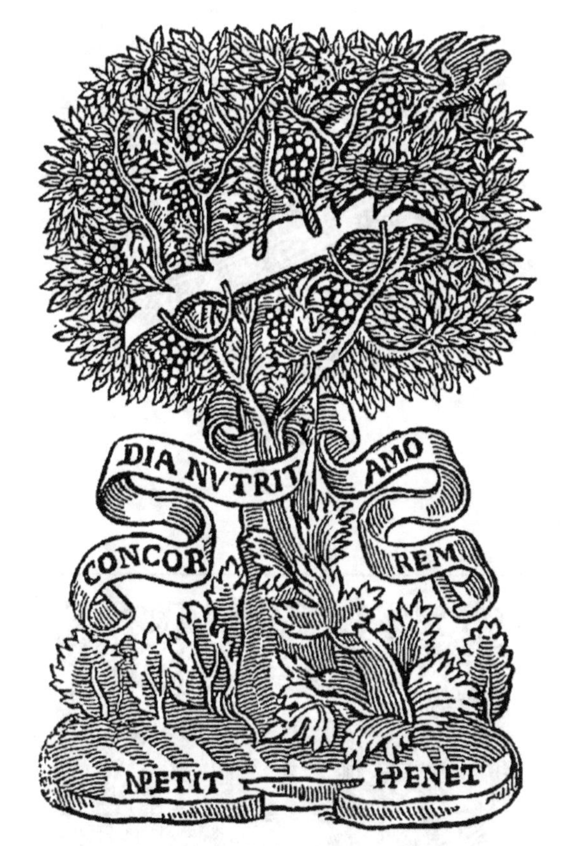

746

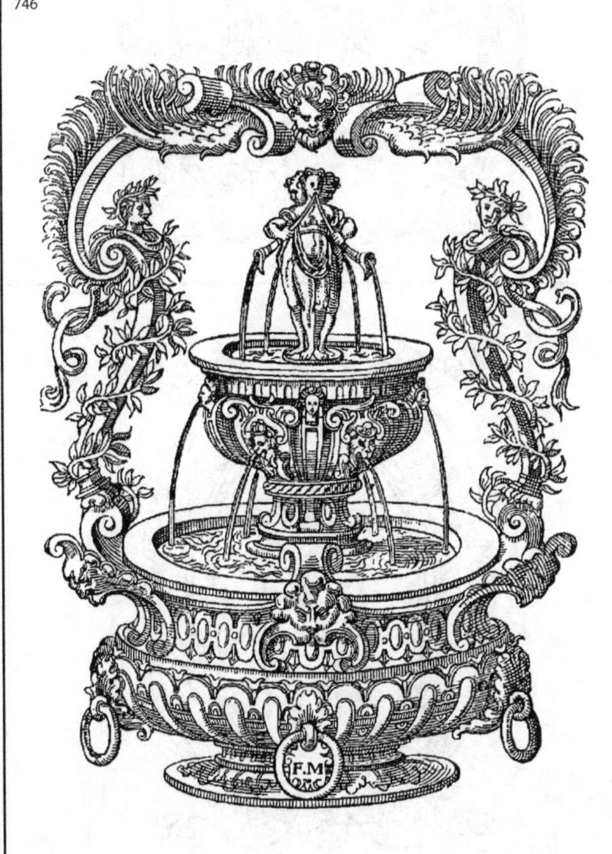

747

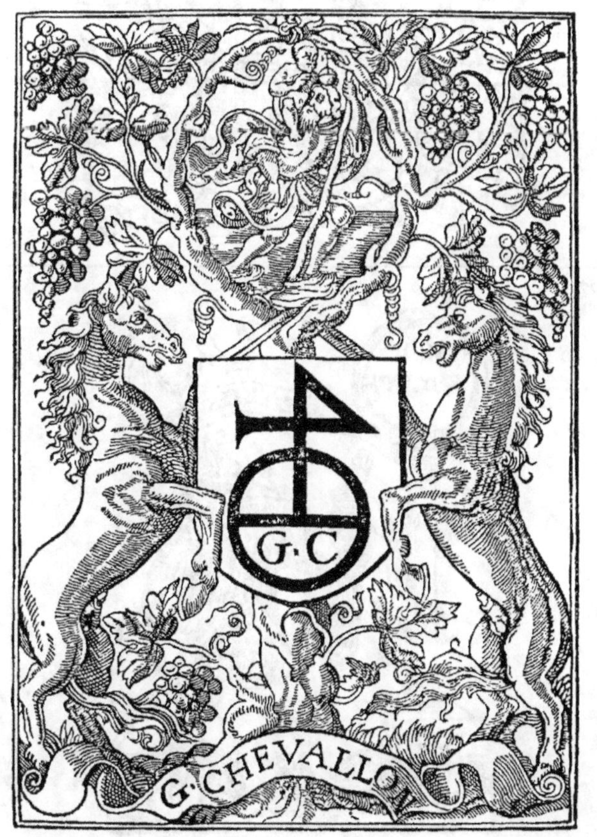

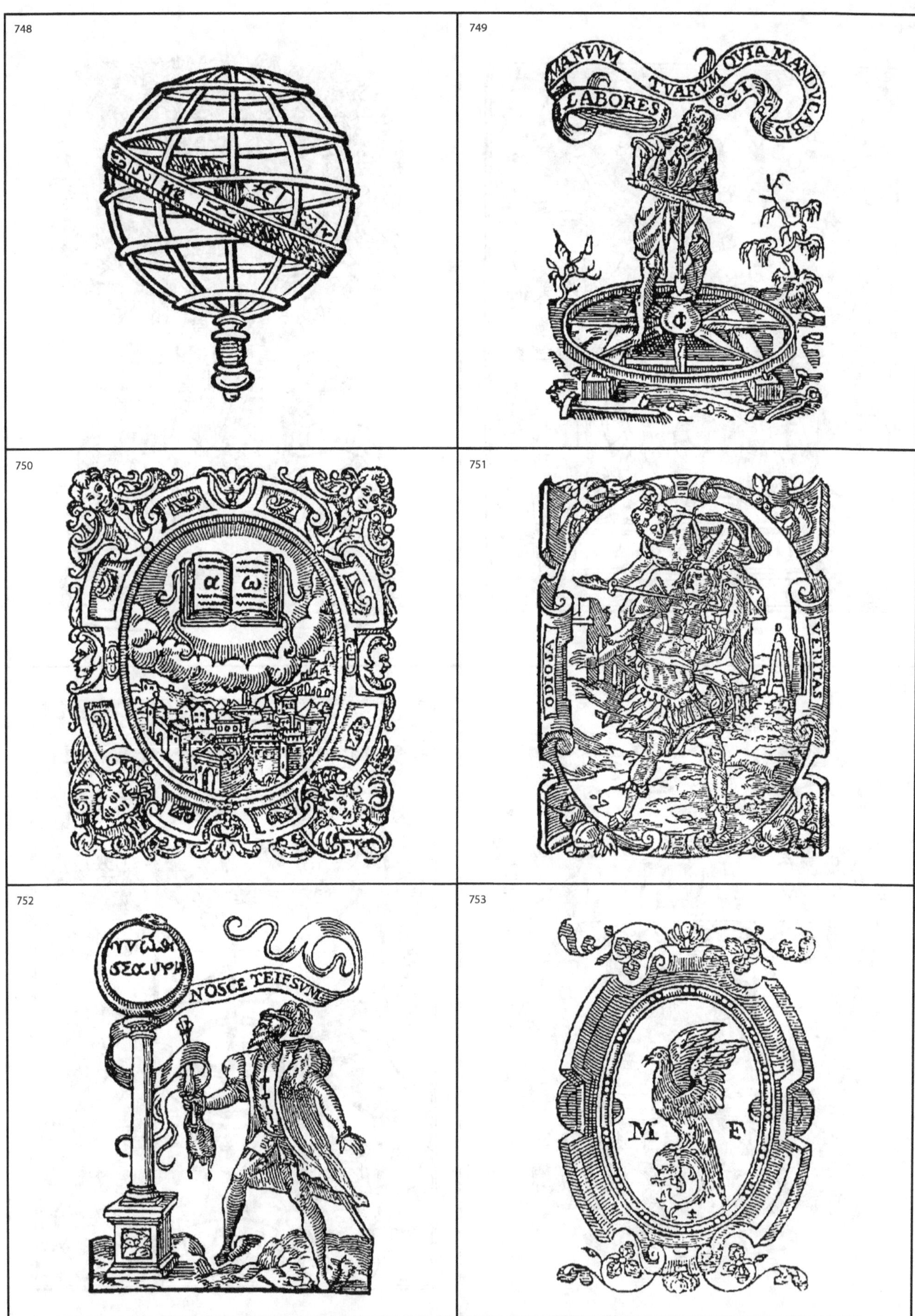

748
749
LABORES TVARVM QVIA MANDVCABIS MANVM 128
750
751
ODIOSA   VERITAS
752
NOSCE TEIPSVM
753
M   E

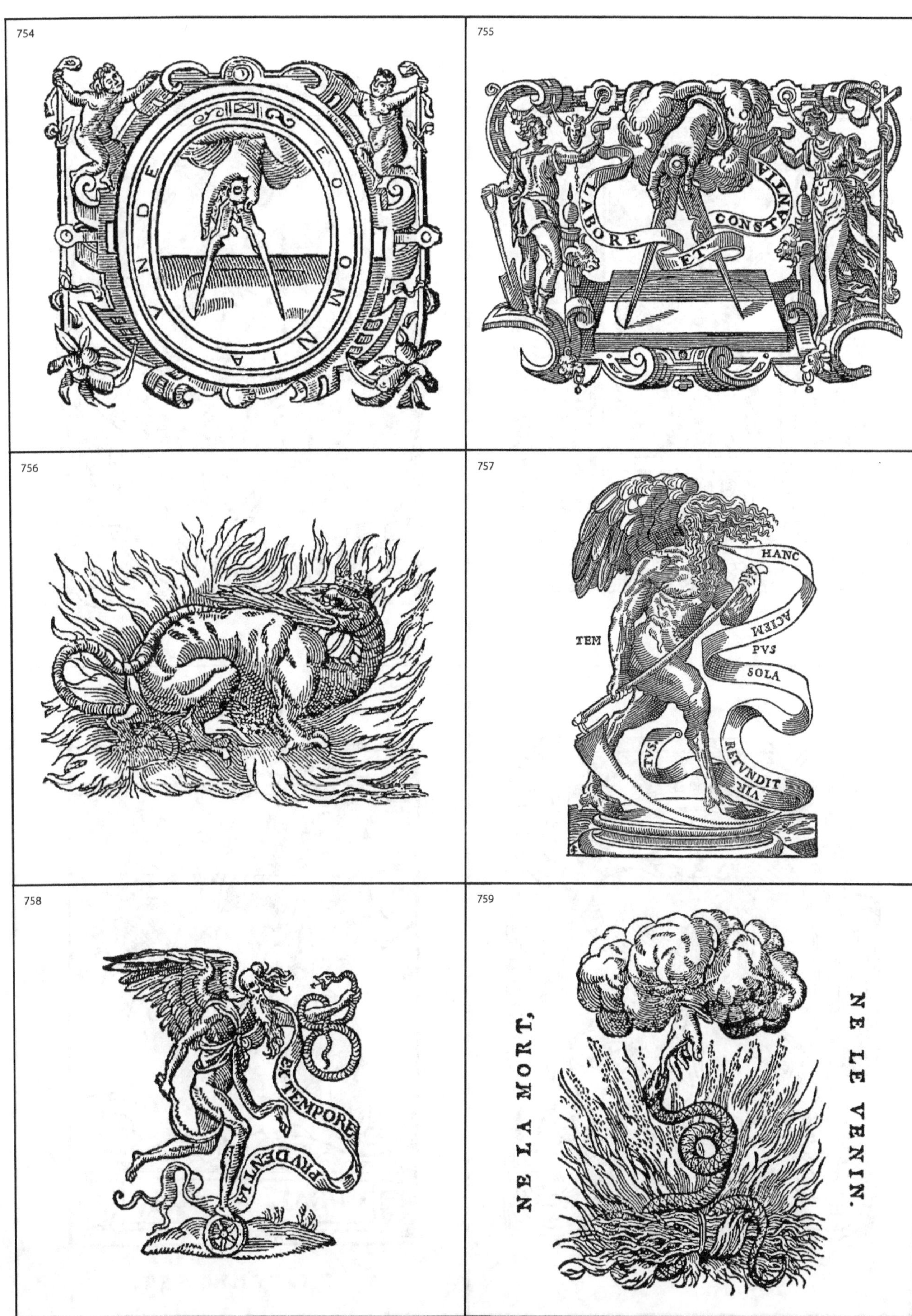

754
755
756
757
LABORE
ET
CONS
VIIN
HANC
ACIEM
PVS
SOLA
TEM
TVS
RETVNDIT
VIR
758
EX TEMPORE
PRVDENTII
759
NE LA MORT,
NE LE VENIN.

760

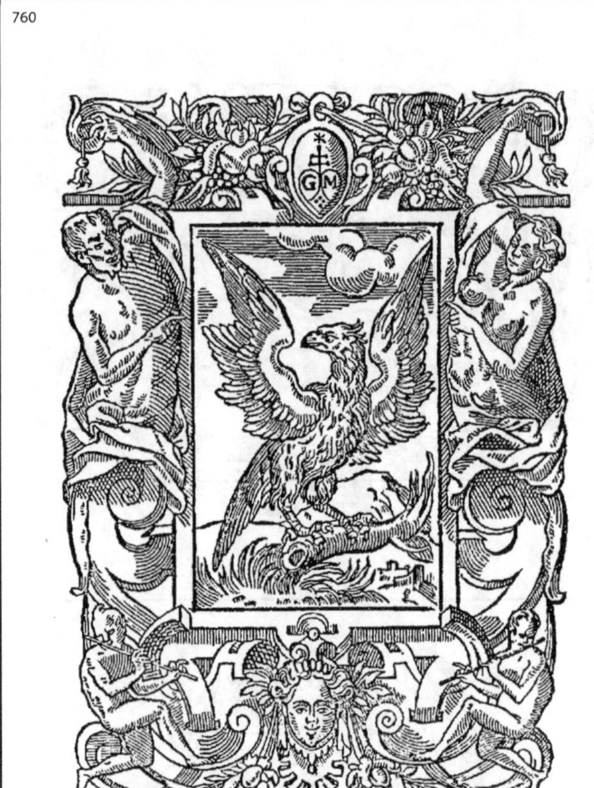

761

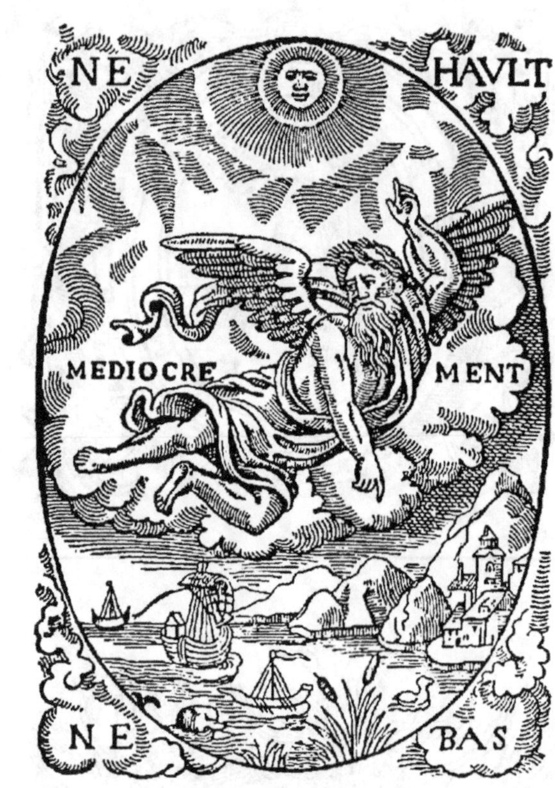

762

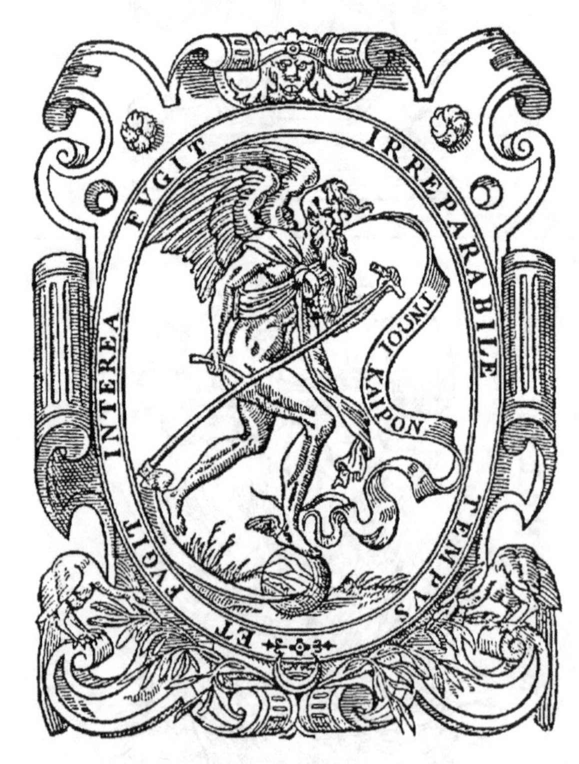

763

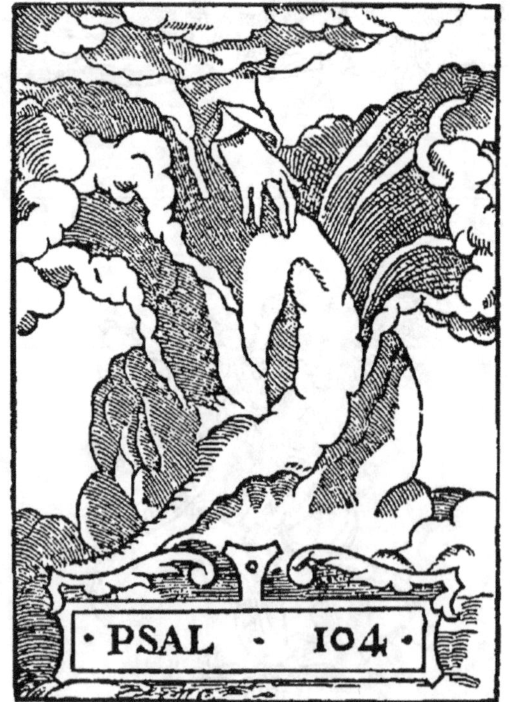

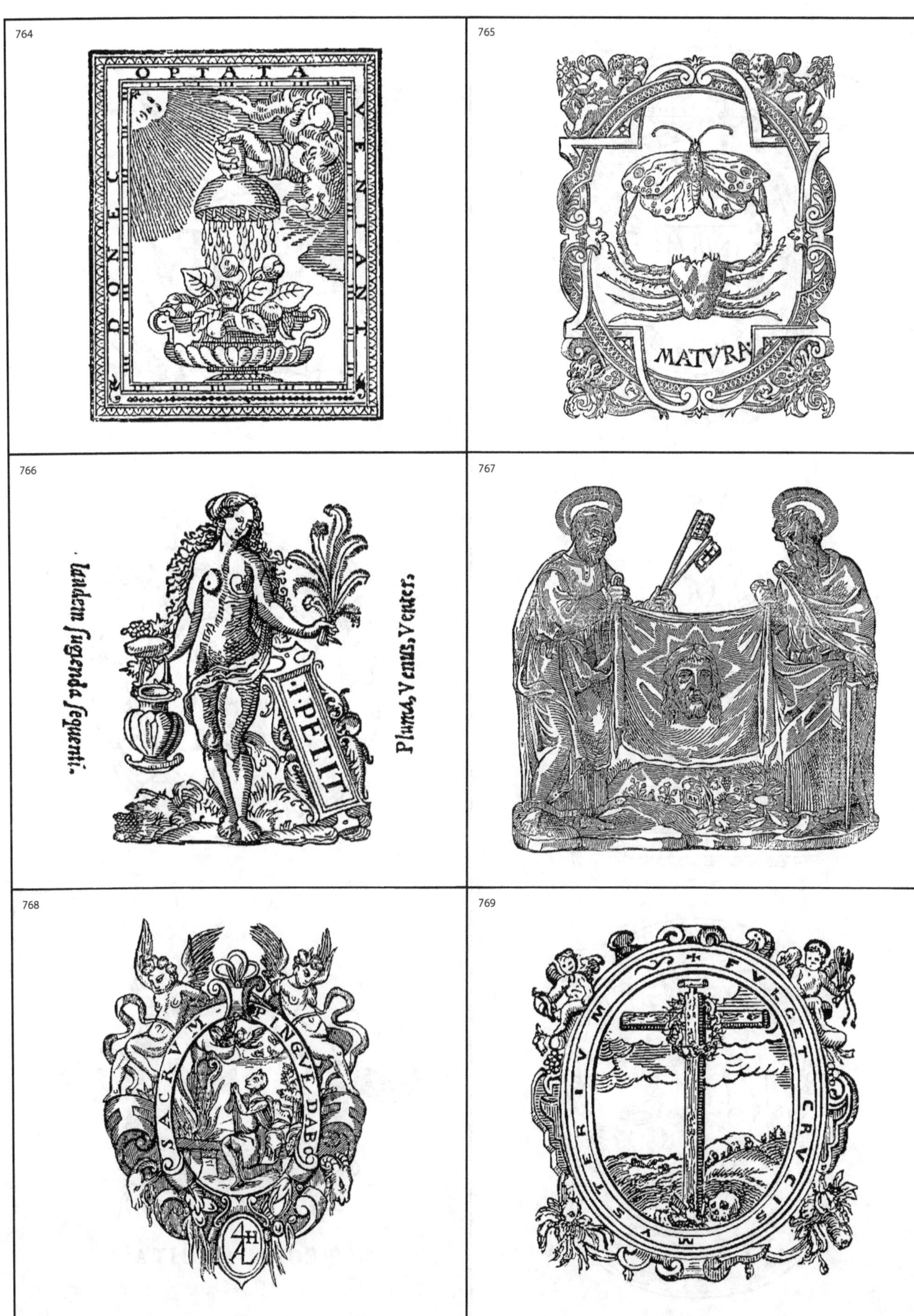
764
OPTATA
DONEC VENIANT

765
MATVRA

766
laudem fugienda sequenti.
I.PETIT
Pluma, Venus, Ventus.

767

768
SACRVM PINGVE DABO

769
MYSTERIVM FVLGET CRVCIS

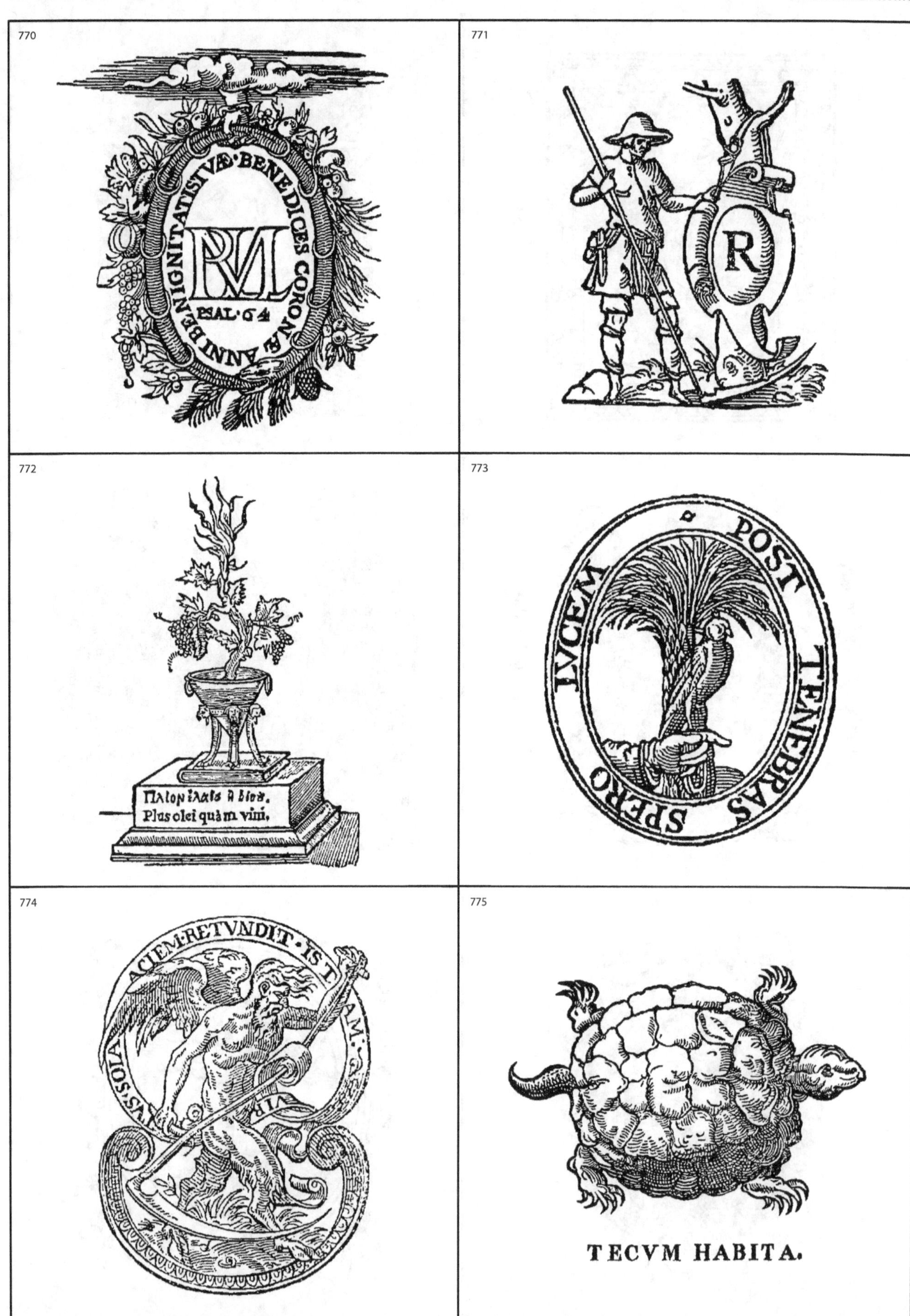

770
BENEDICES CORONÆ ANNI BENIGNITATIS TVÆ
PVL
PSAL·64

771
R

772
Πλέον ἔλαιε ἢ βίου.
Plus olei quàm vini.

773
POST TENEBRAS SPERO LVCEM

774
ACIEM·RETVNDIT·IST·IAM·
VIRTVS·SOLA

775
TECVM HABITA.

776

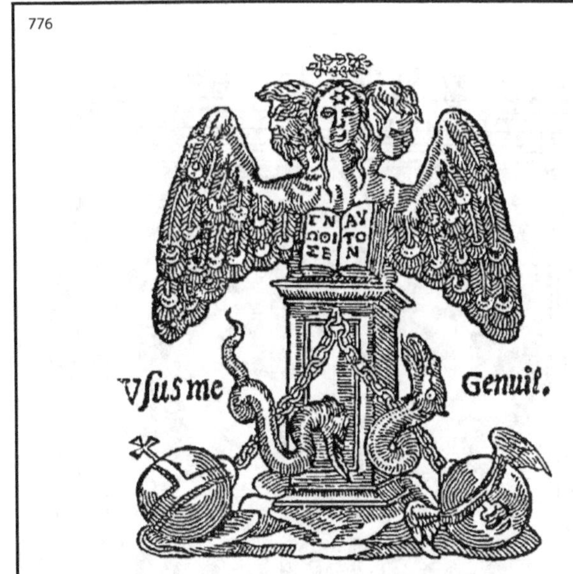

778

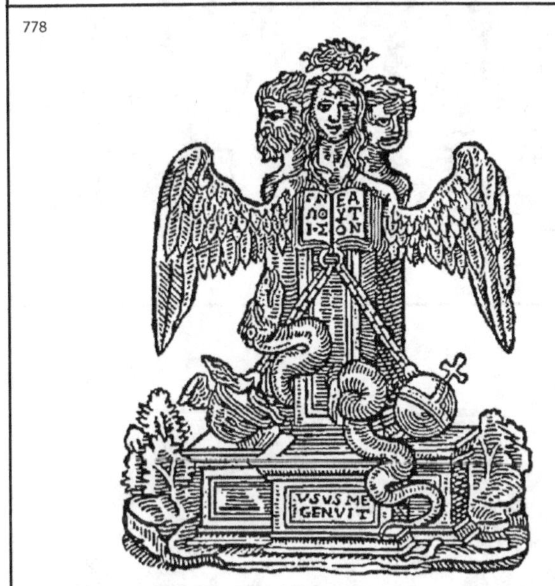

777

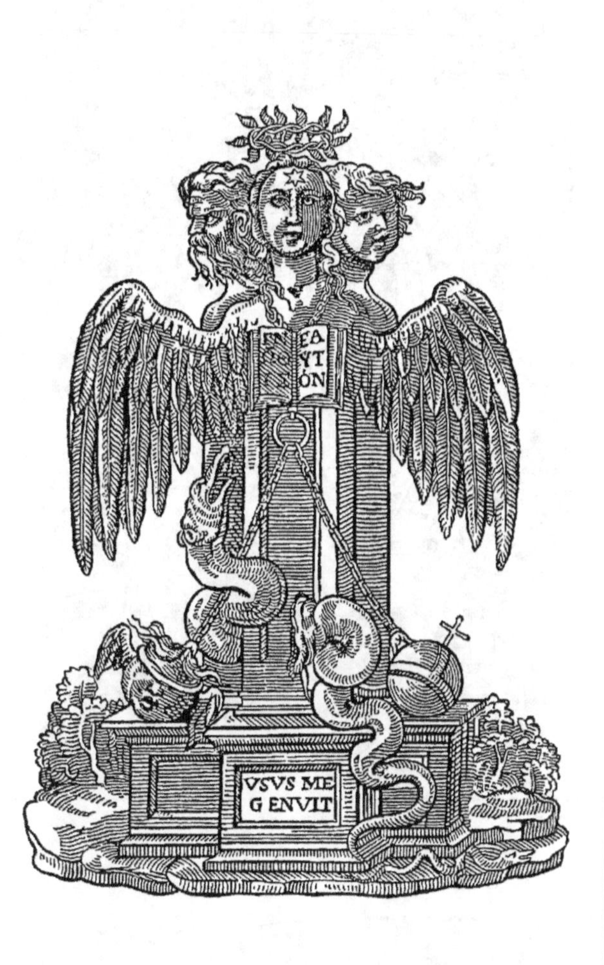

779

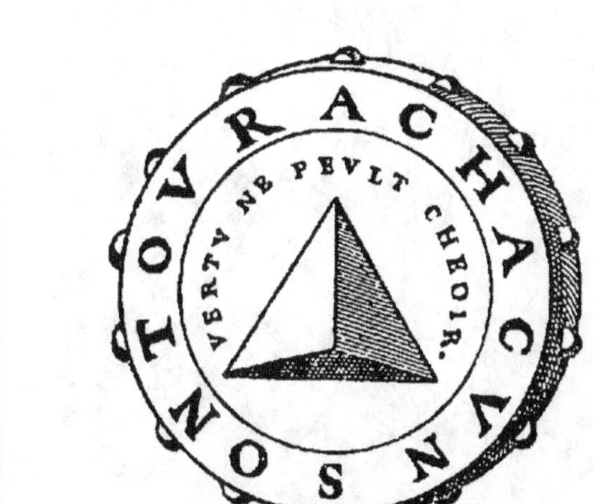

780

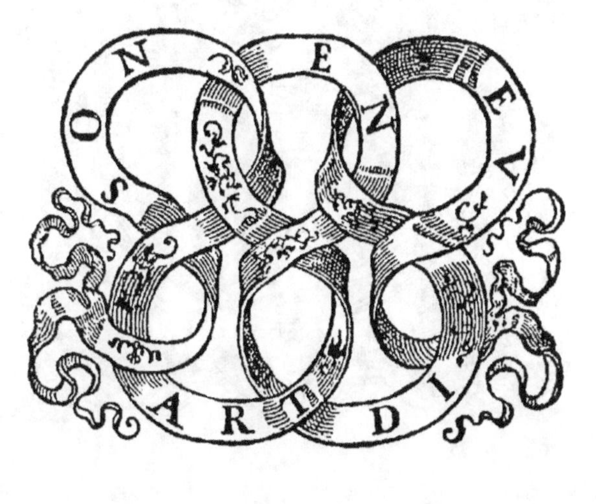

781

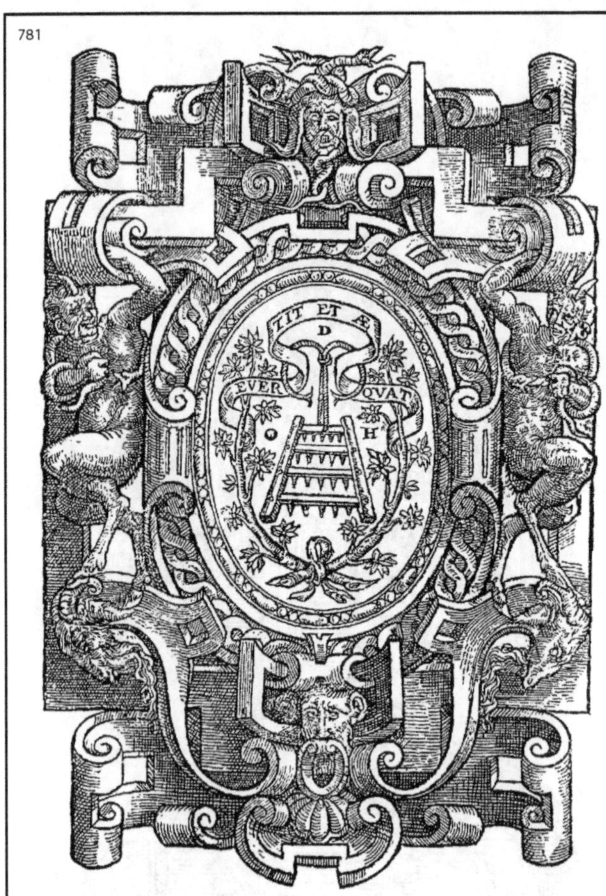

782

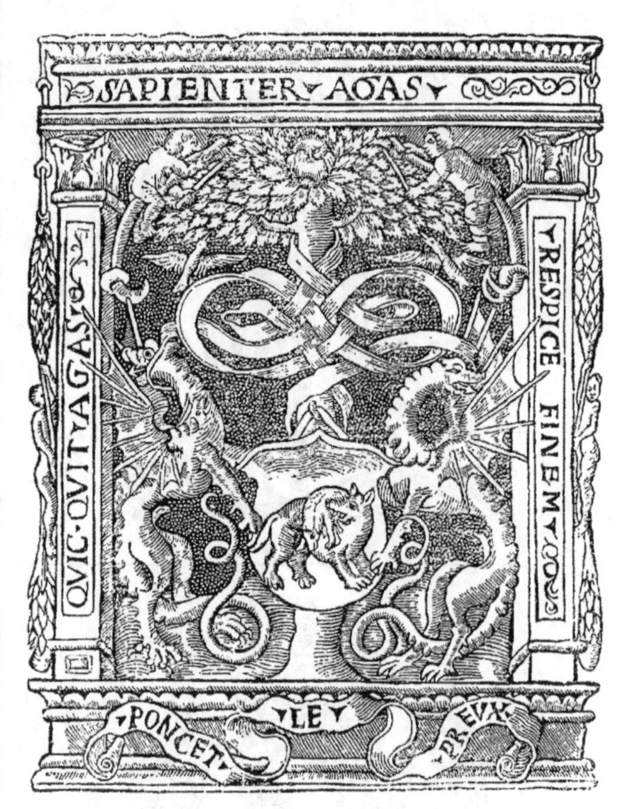

783

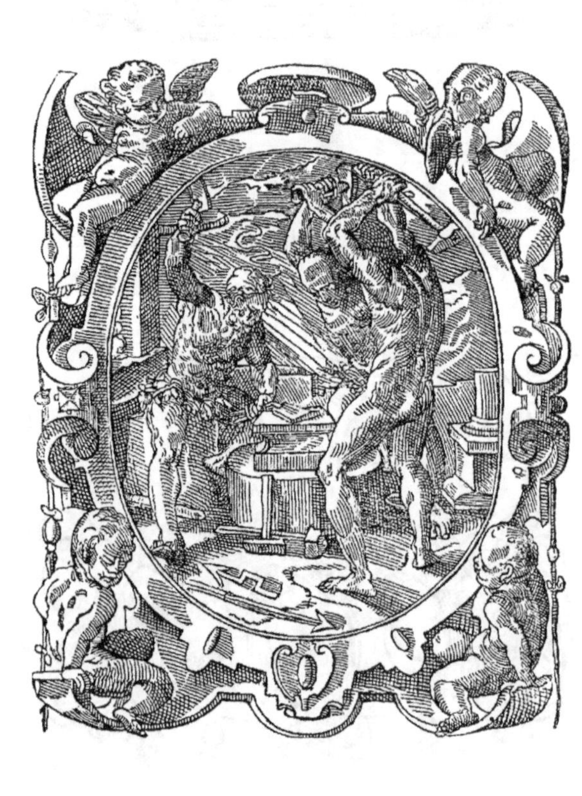

784

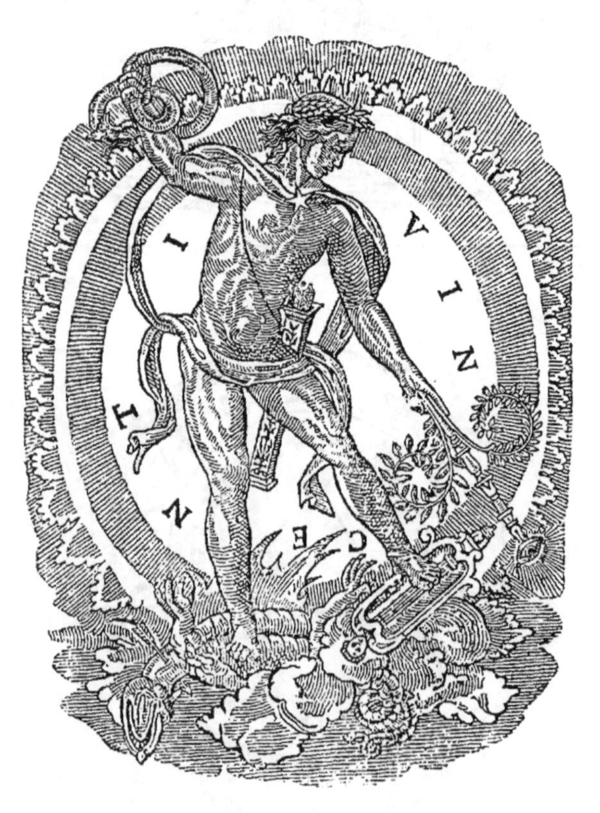

785

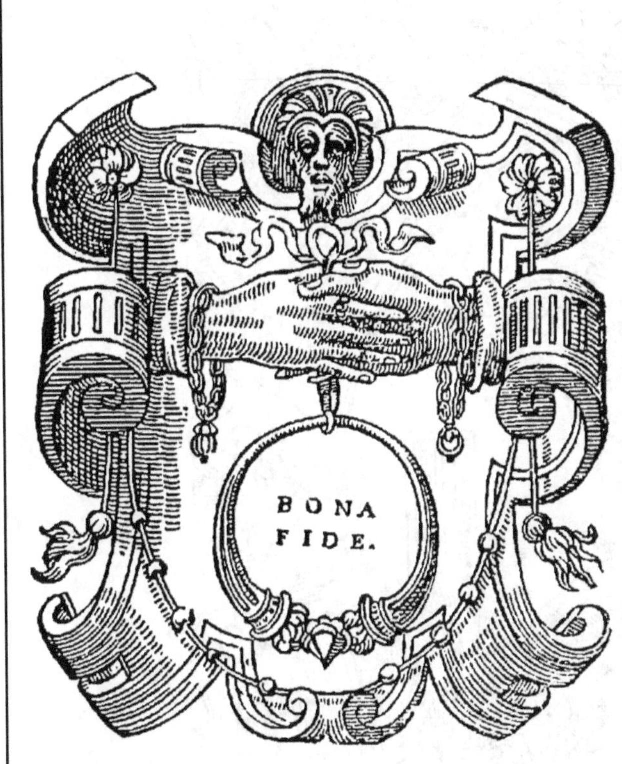

786

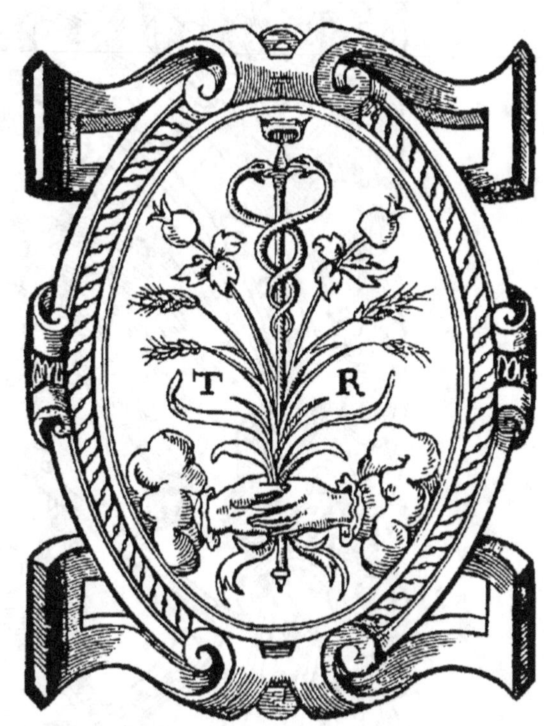

787

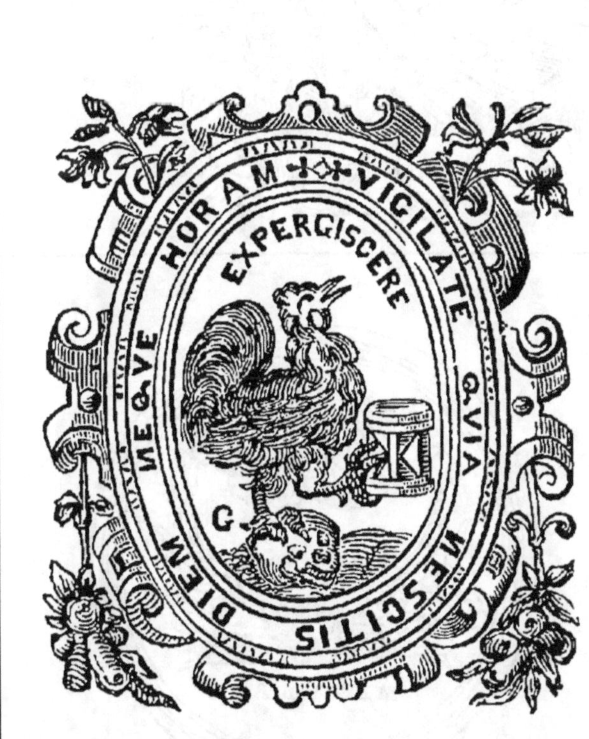

788

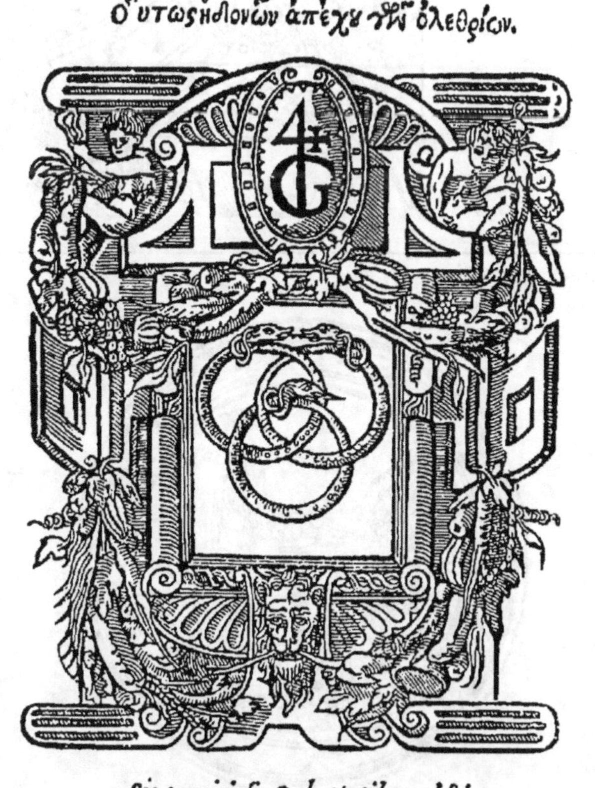

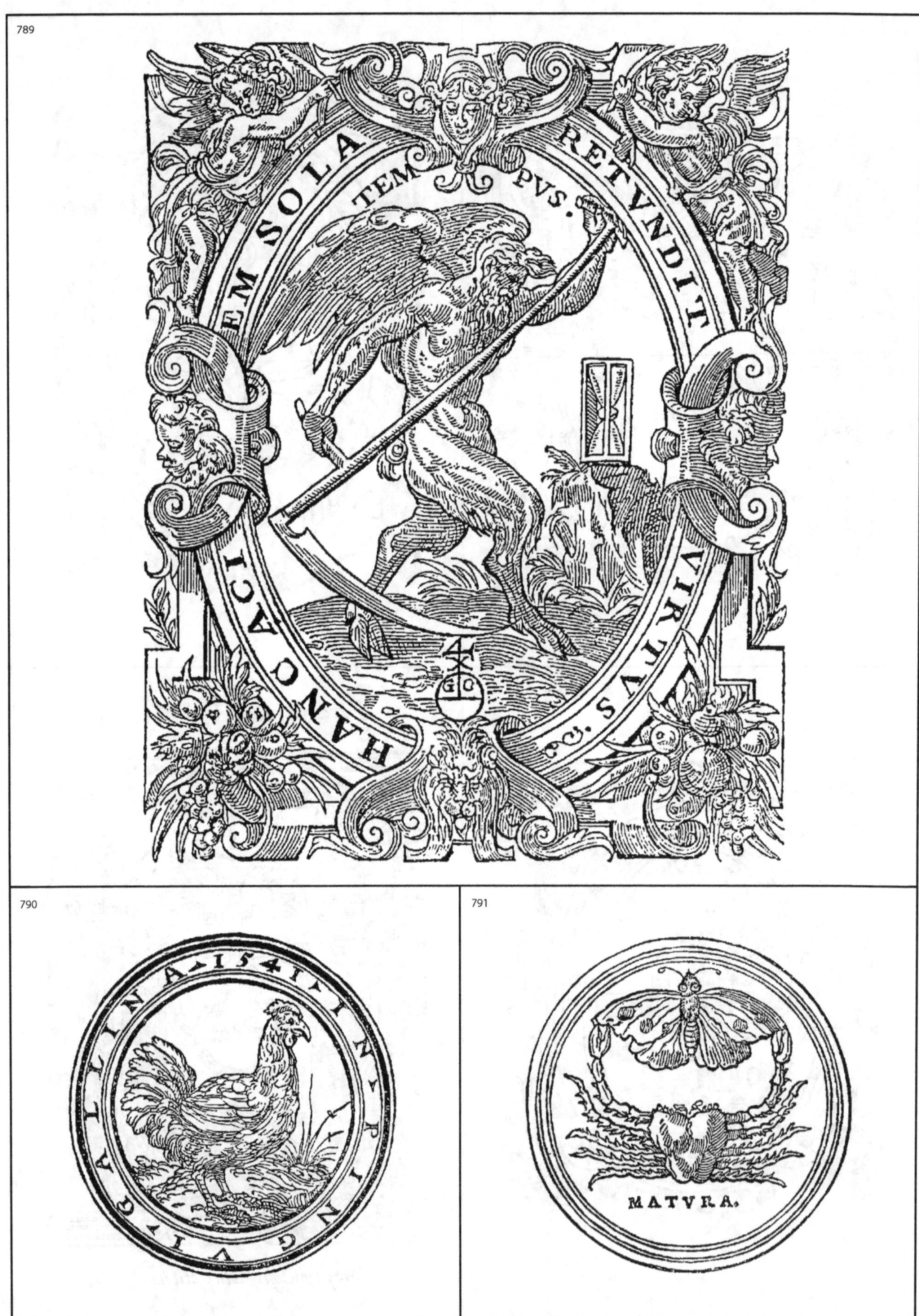
789
EM SOLA
TEM PVS RETVNDIT
HANC OCI
VIRTVS
790
IN A·1541·IN
GVIL GALL
791
MATVRA.

792

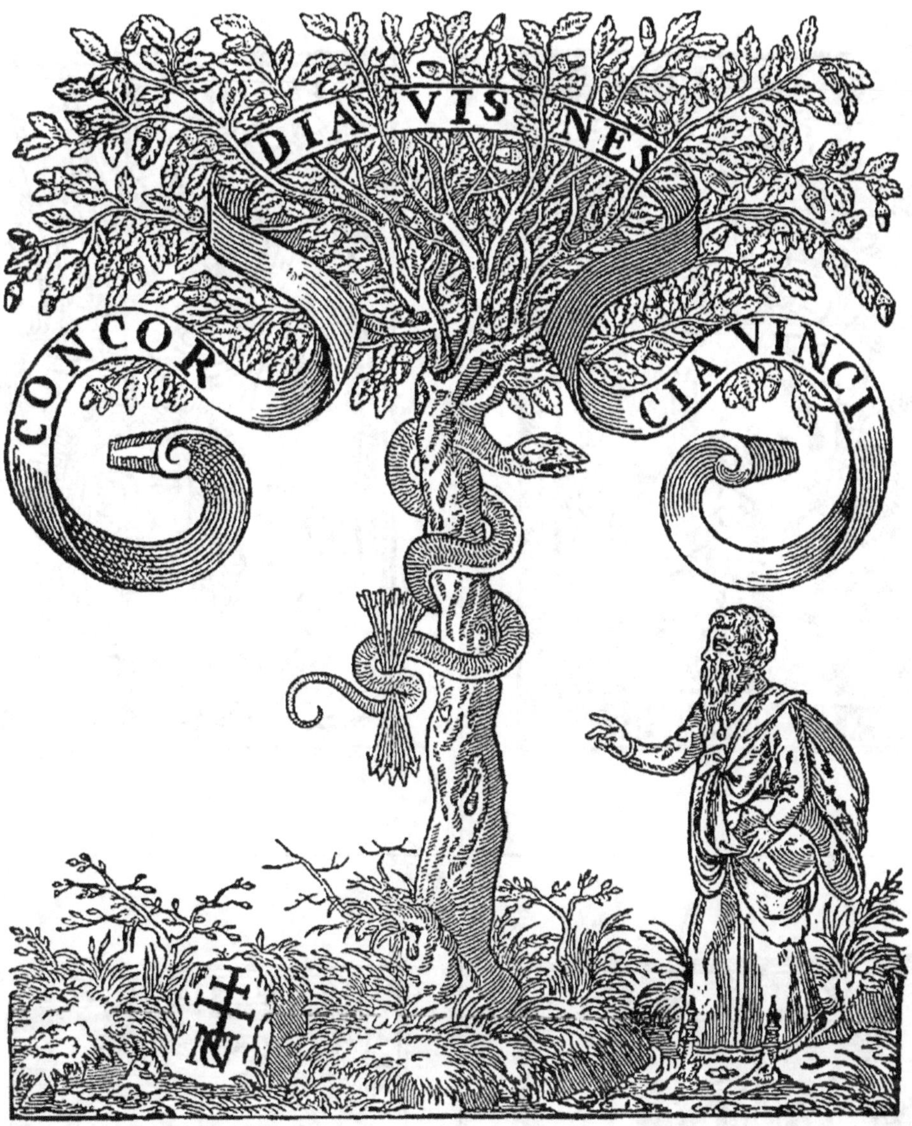

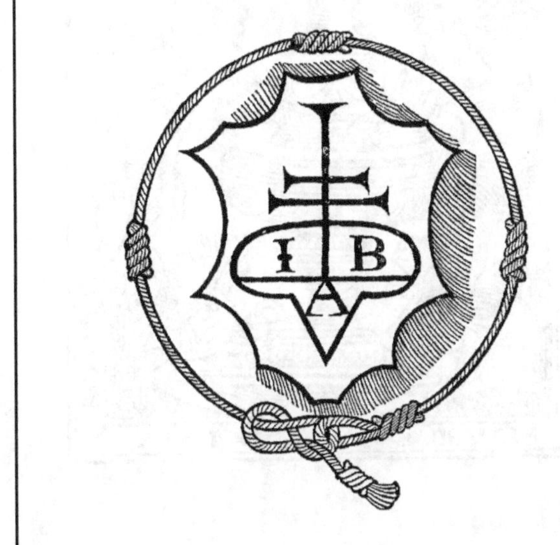

793

794

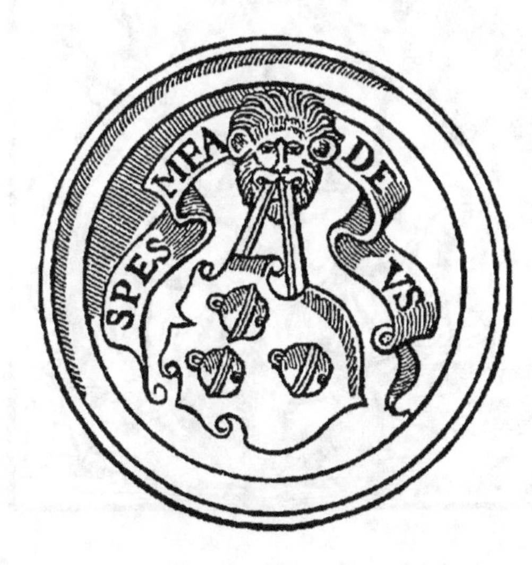

795

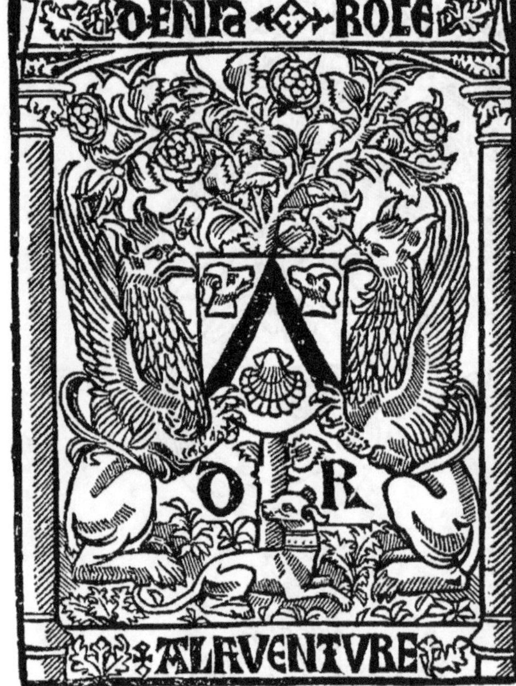

796

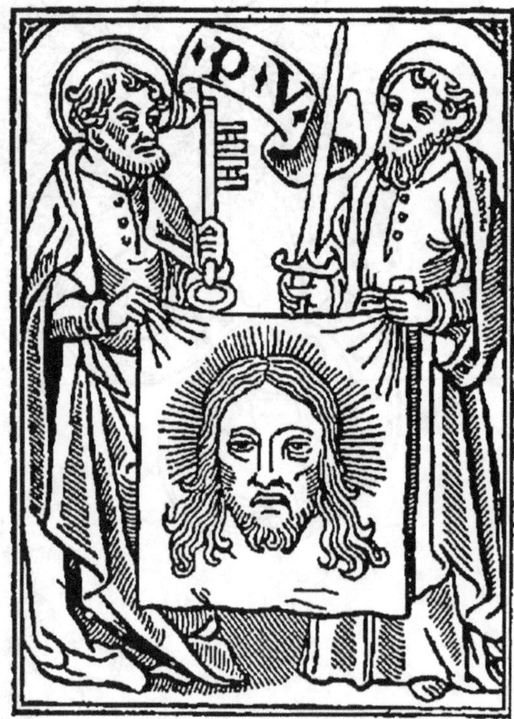

797

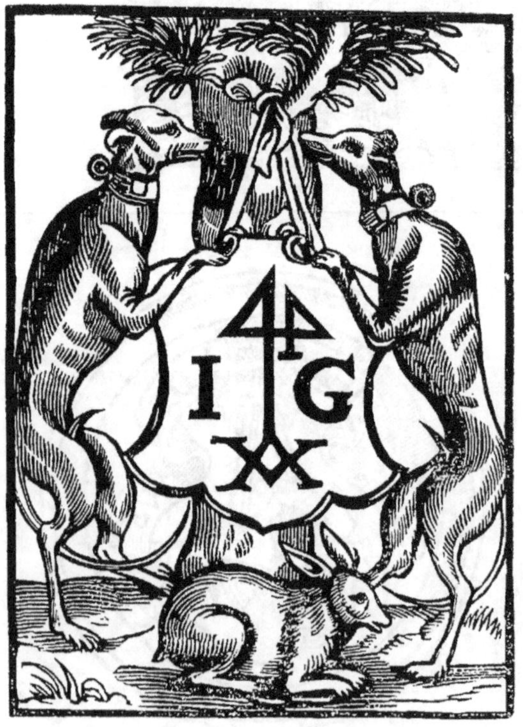

798

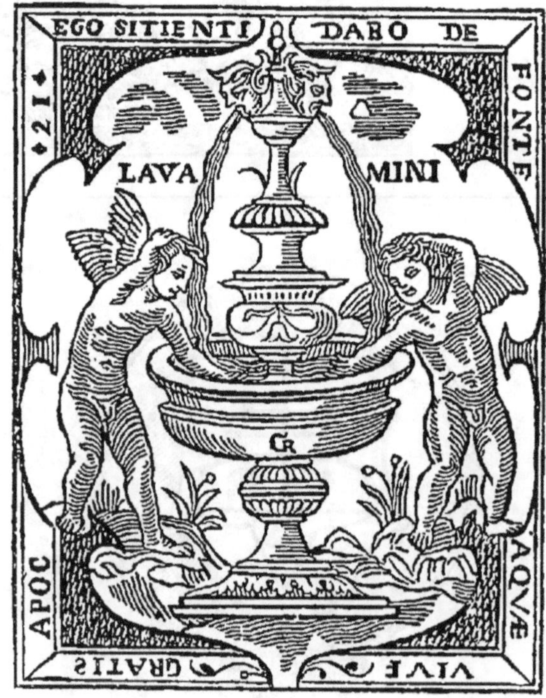

799

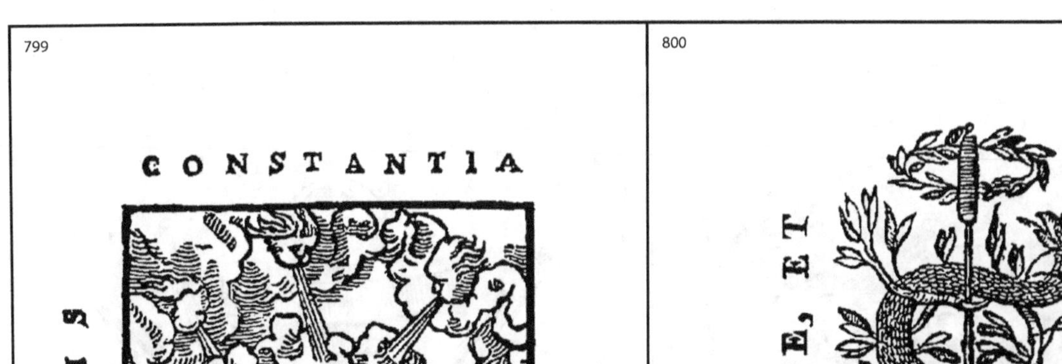

800

801

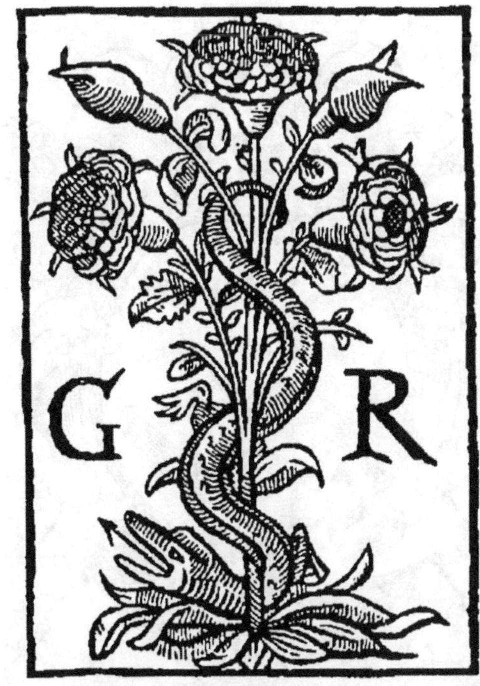

802

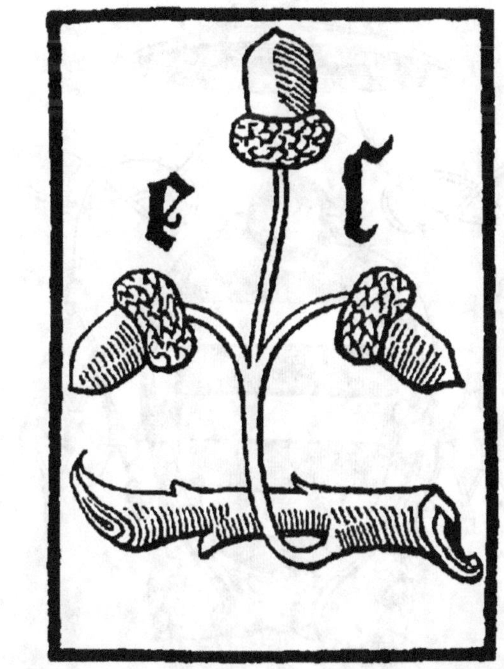

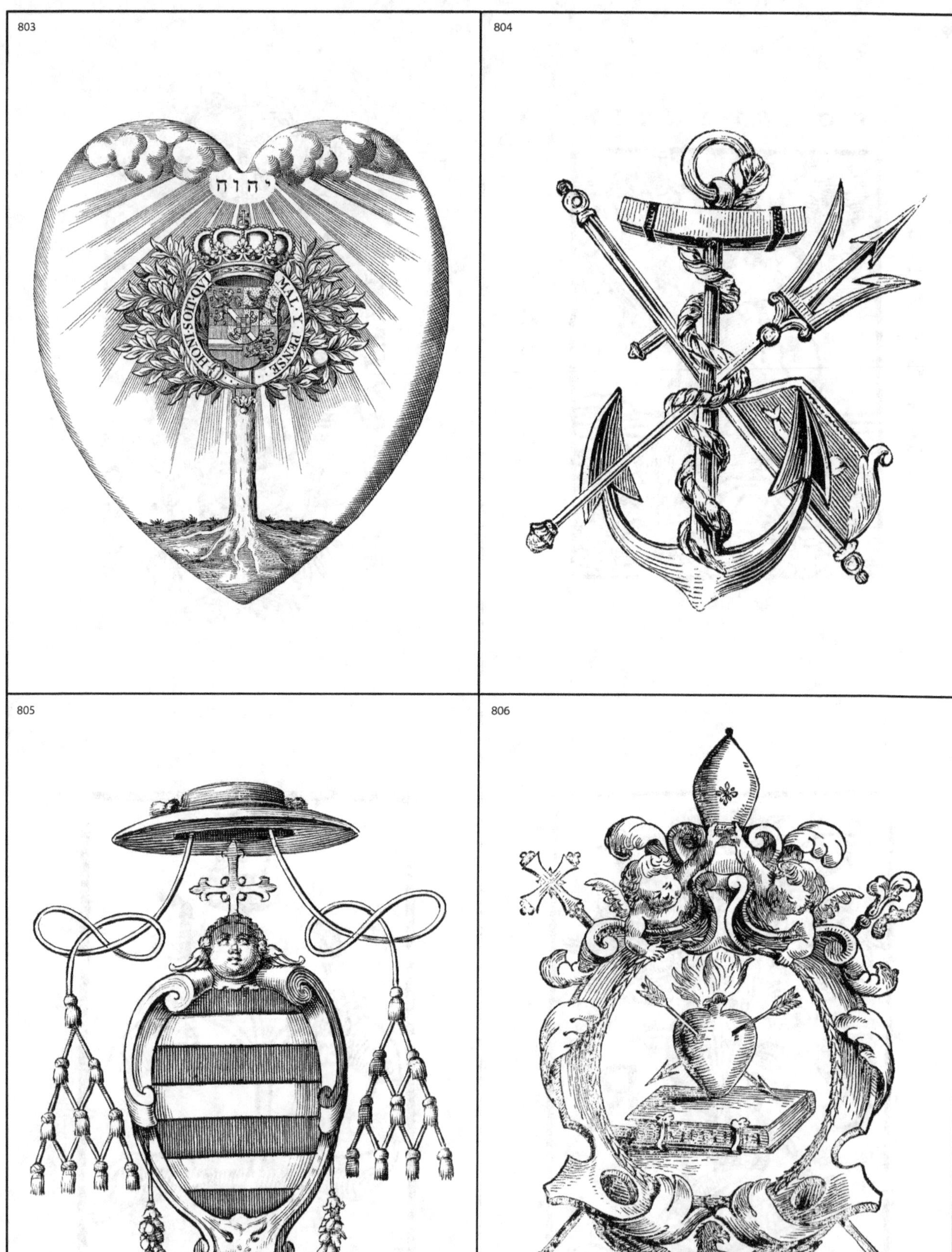

807

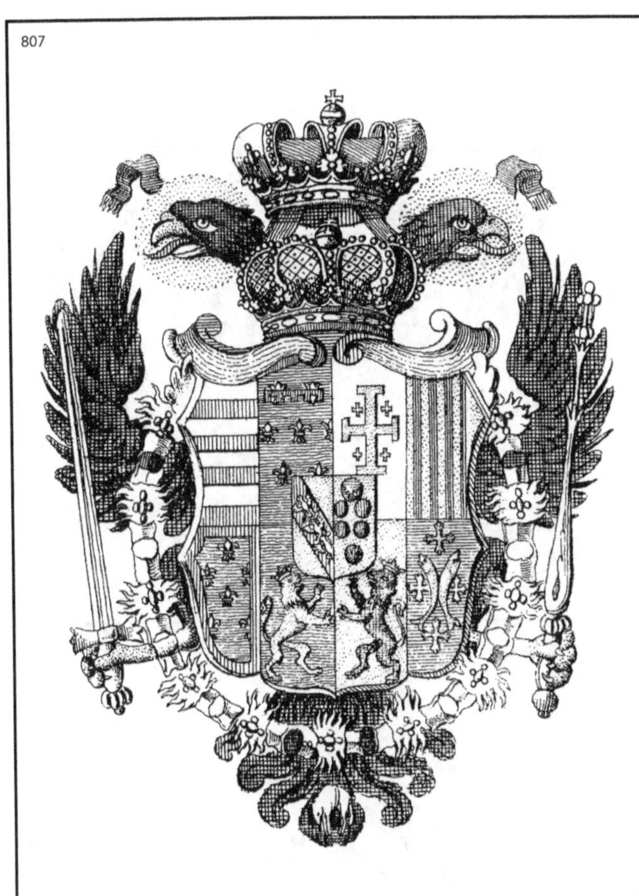

808

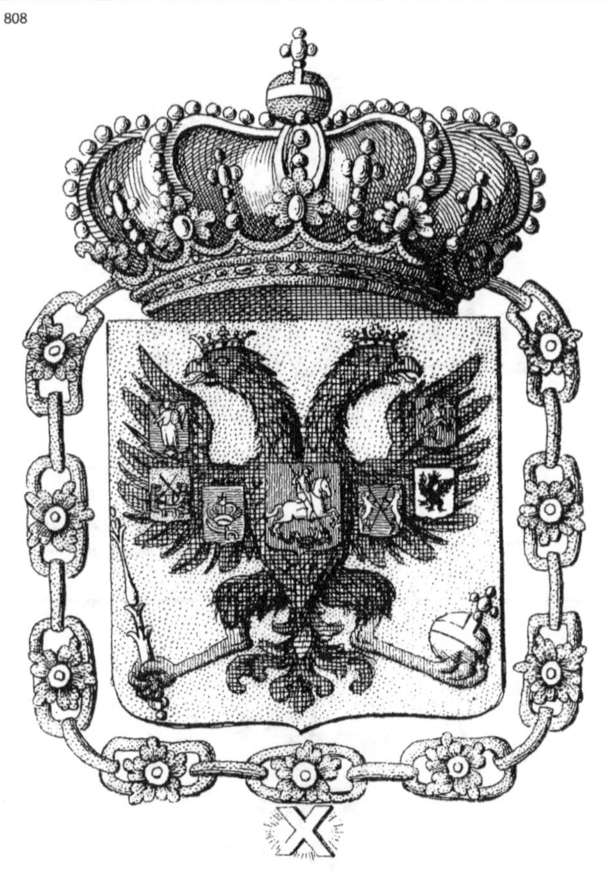

809

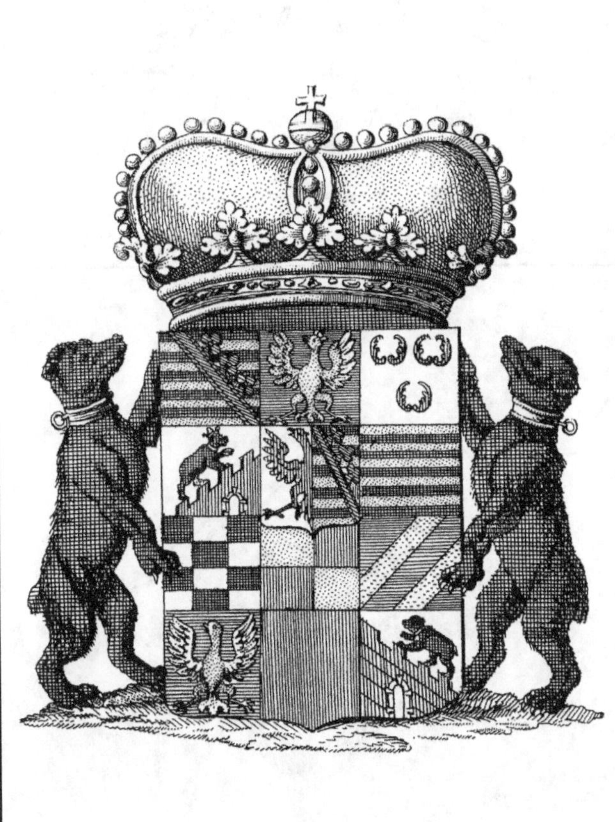

810

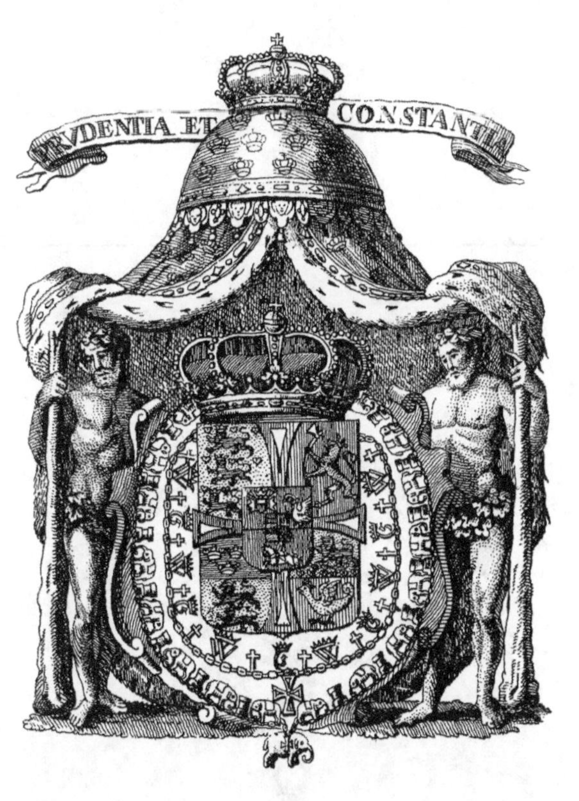

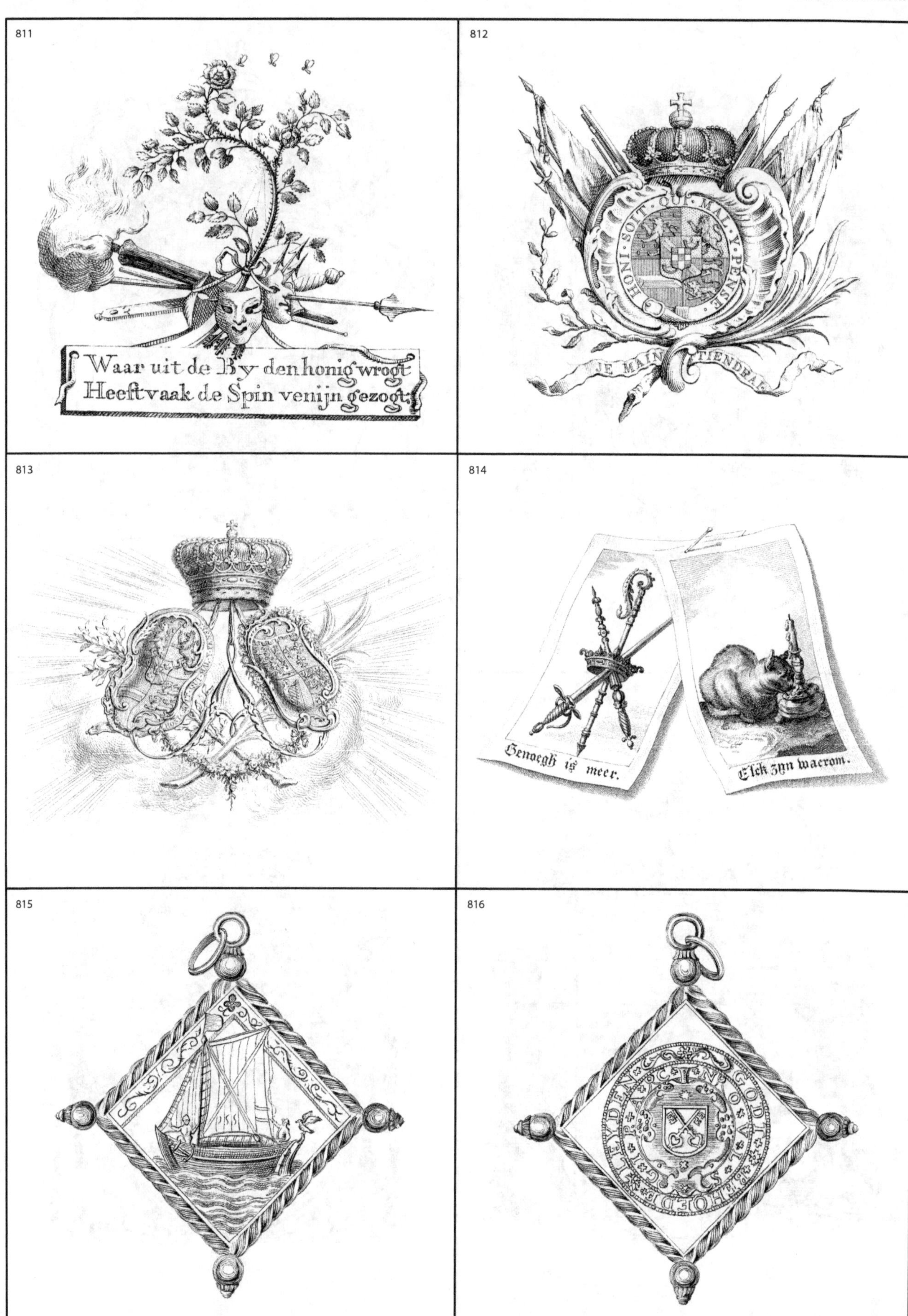

811

Waar uit de By den honig wrogt
Heeft vaak de Spin venijn gezogt.

812

HONI · SOIT · QUI · MAL · Y · PENSE

JE MAIN TIENDRAE

813

814

Genoegh is meer.

Elck zyn waerom.

815

816

817

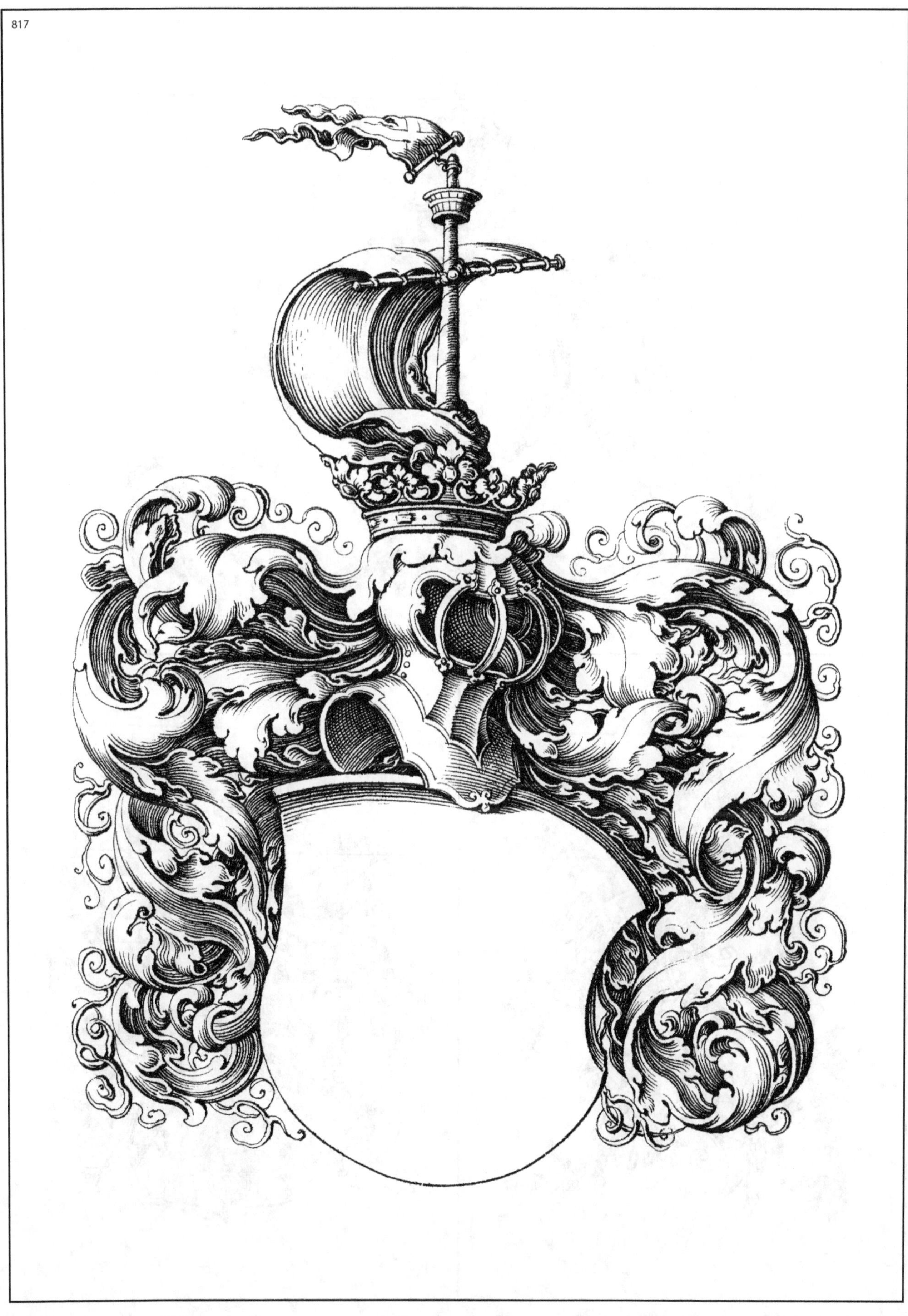

818

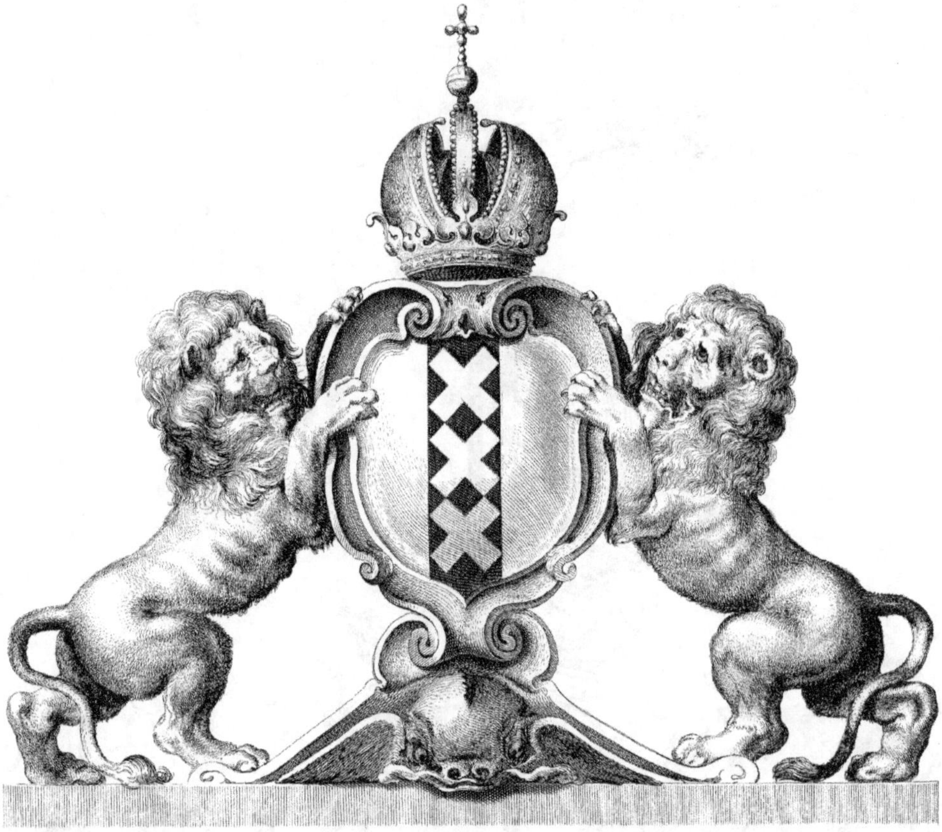

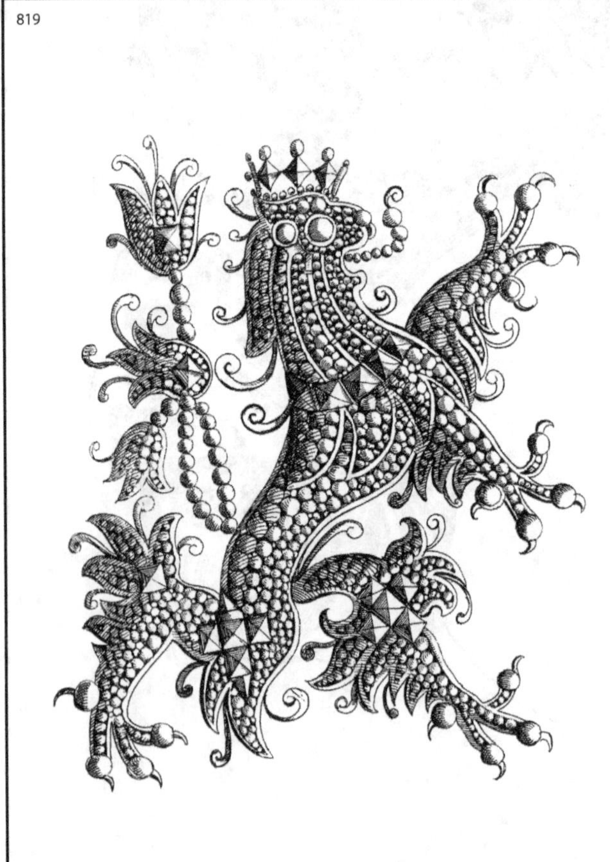

819

820

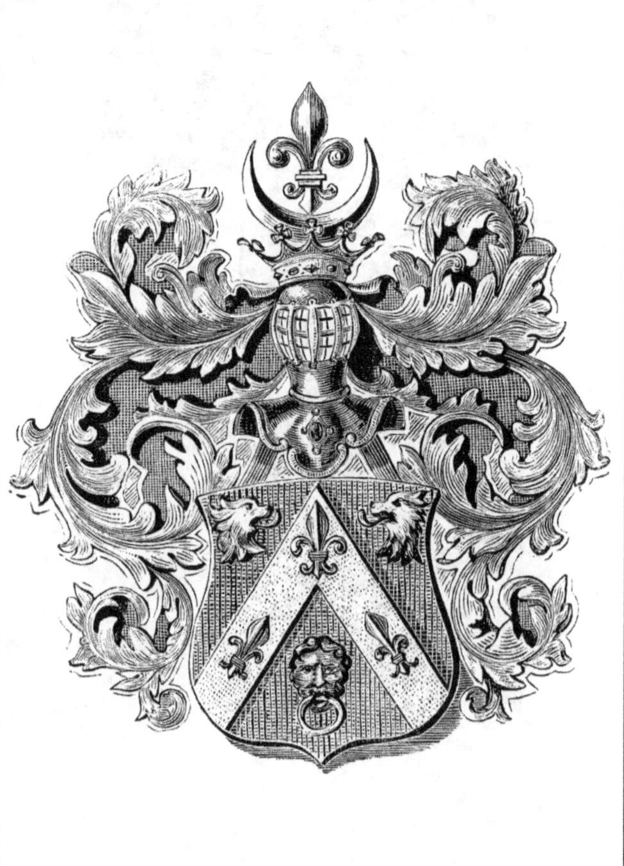

821

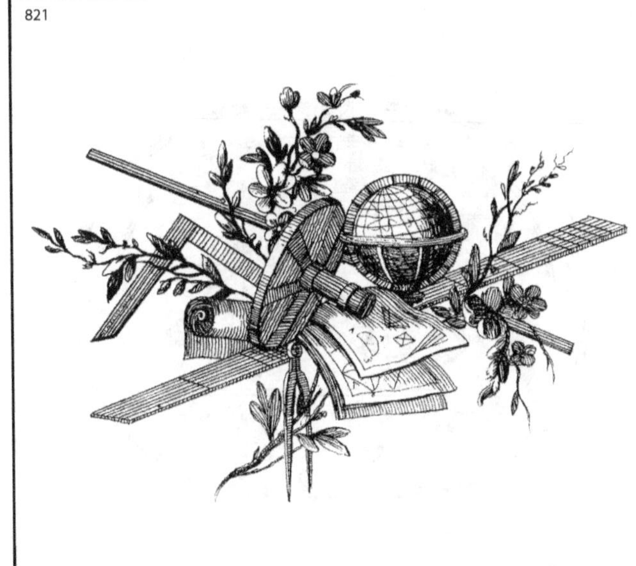

822

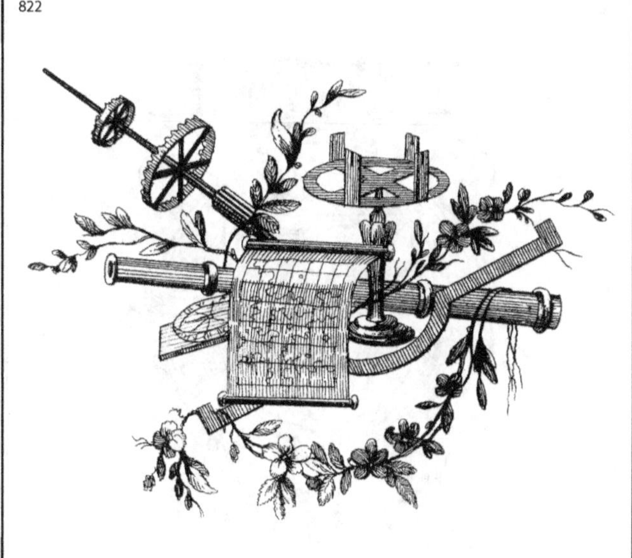

823

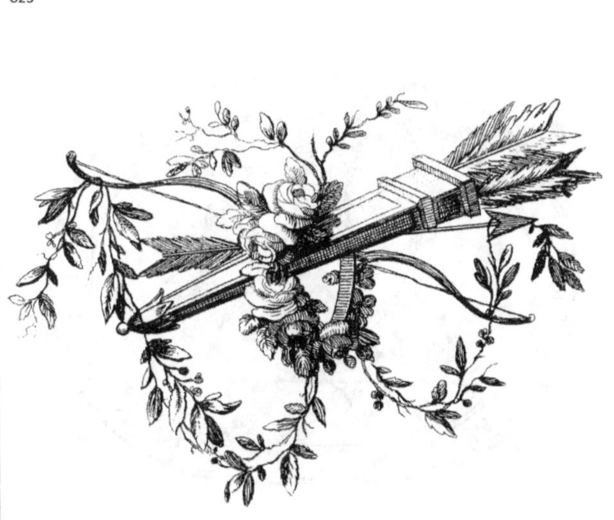

824

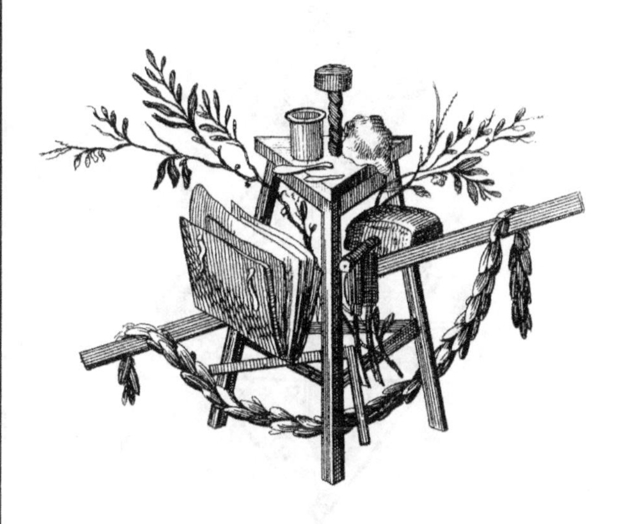

825

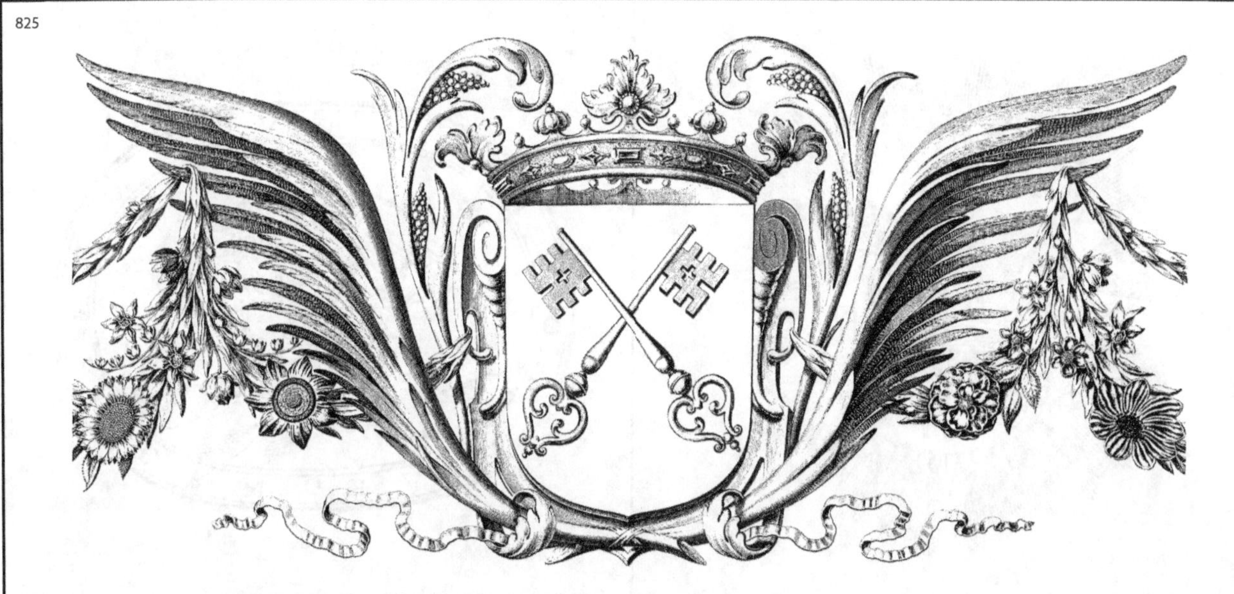

SYMBOLS & EMBLEMS

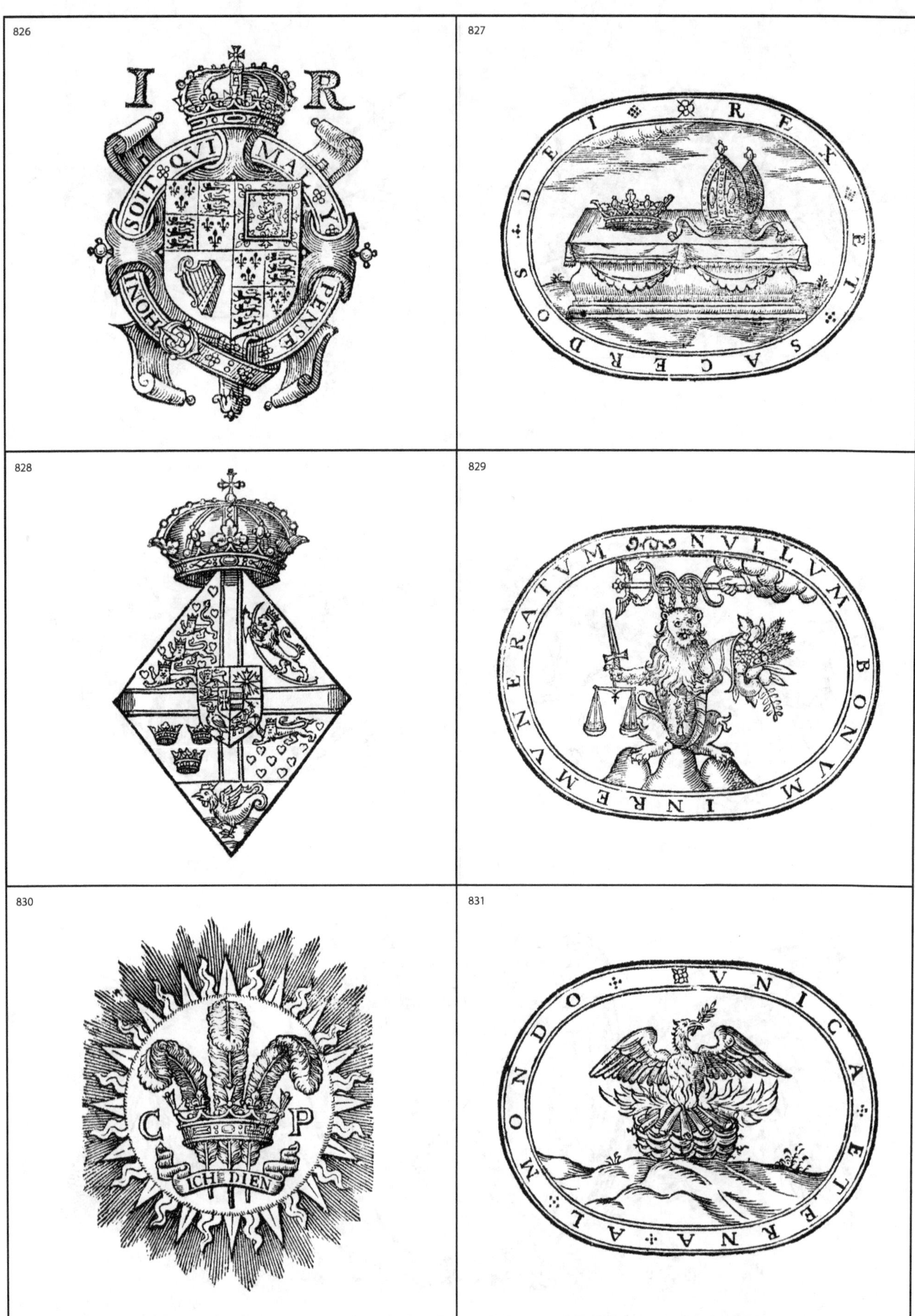

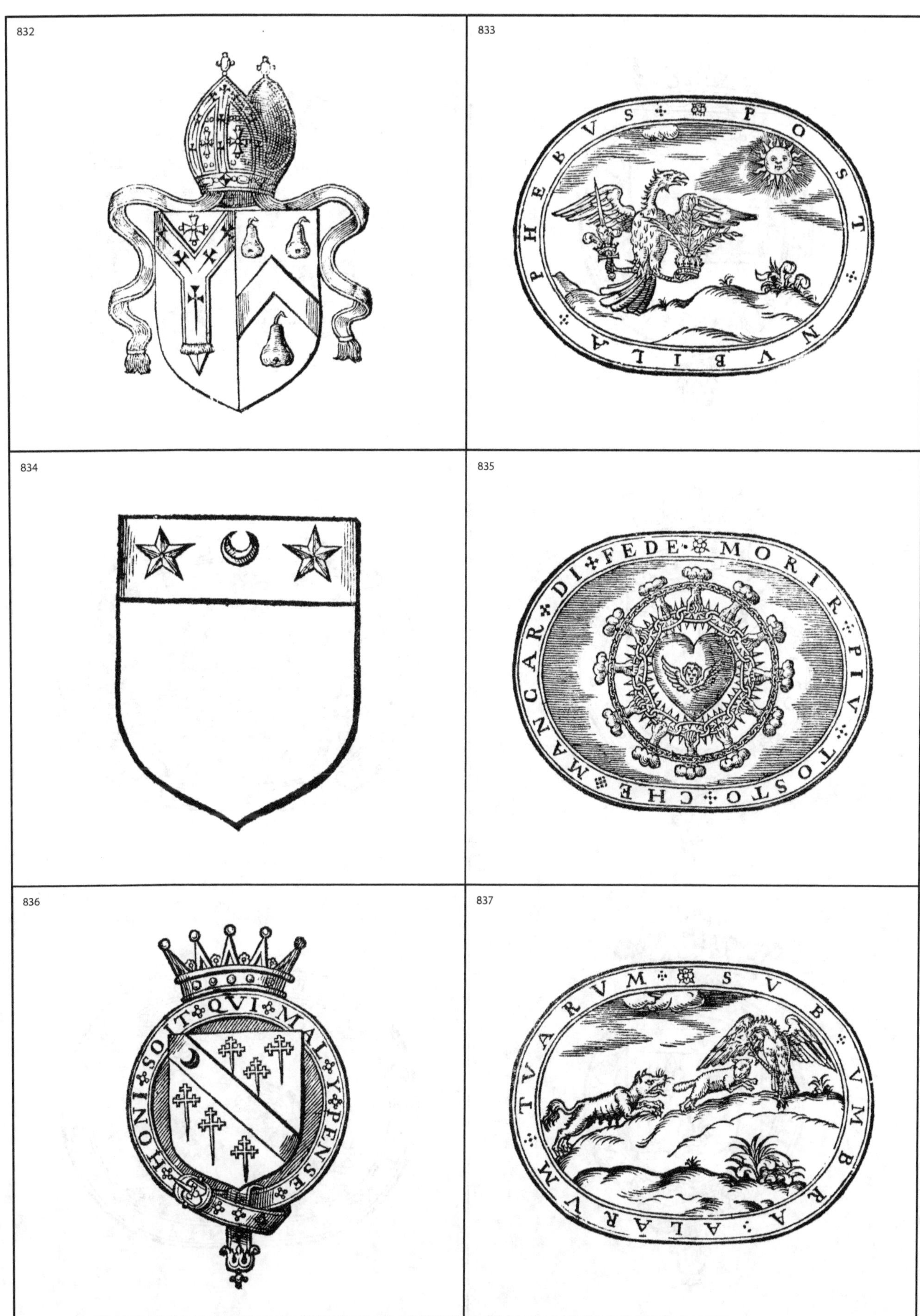

832

833

834

835

836

837

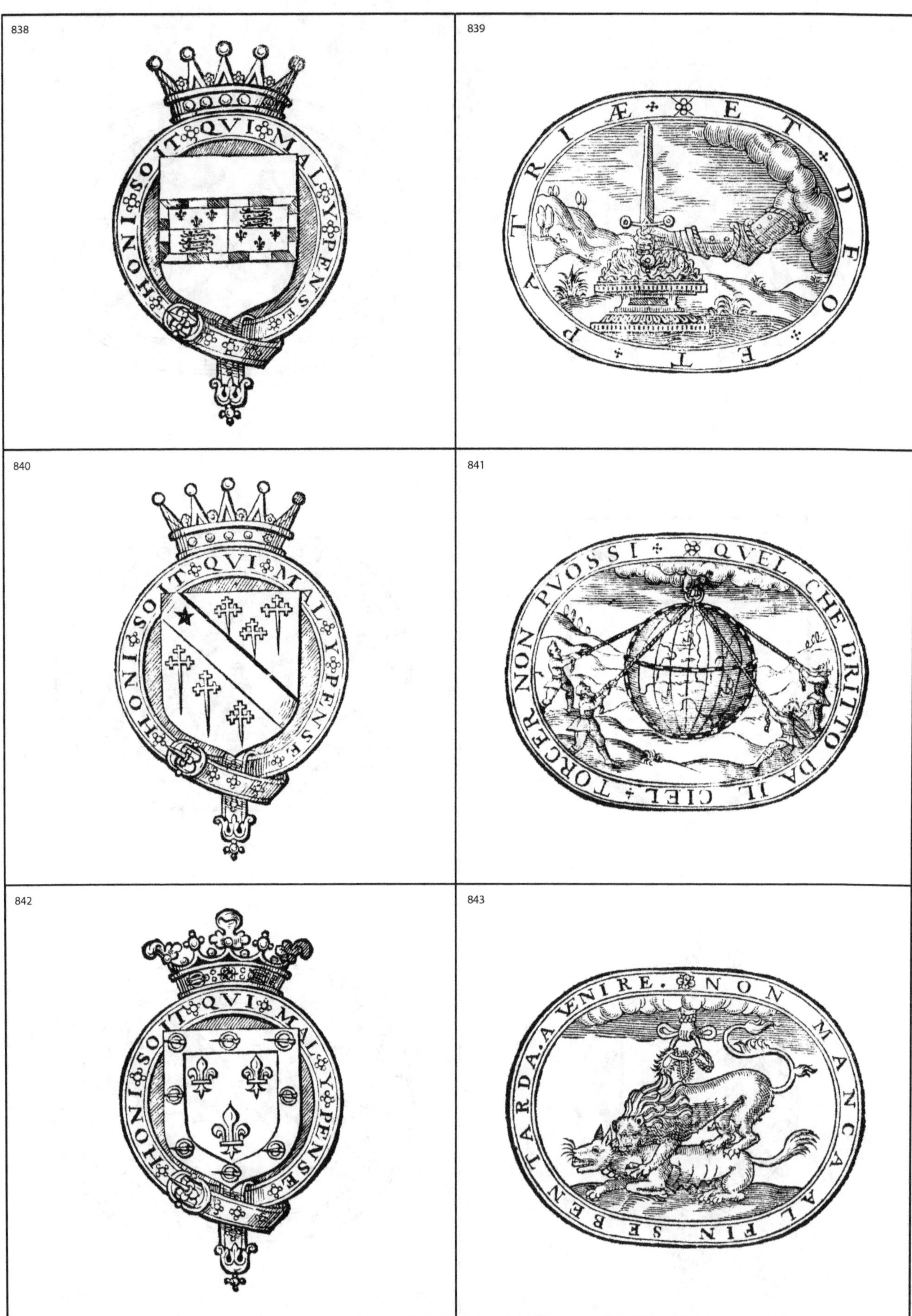

838

839

840

841

842

843

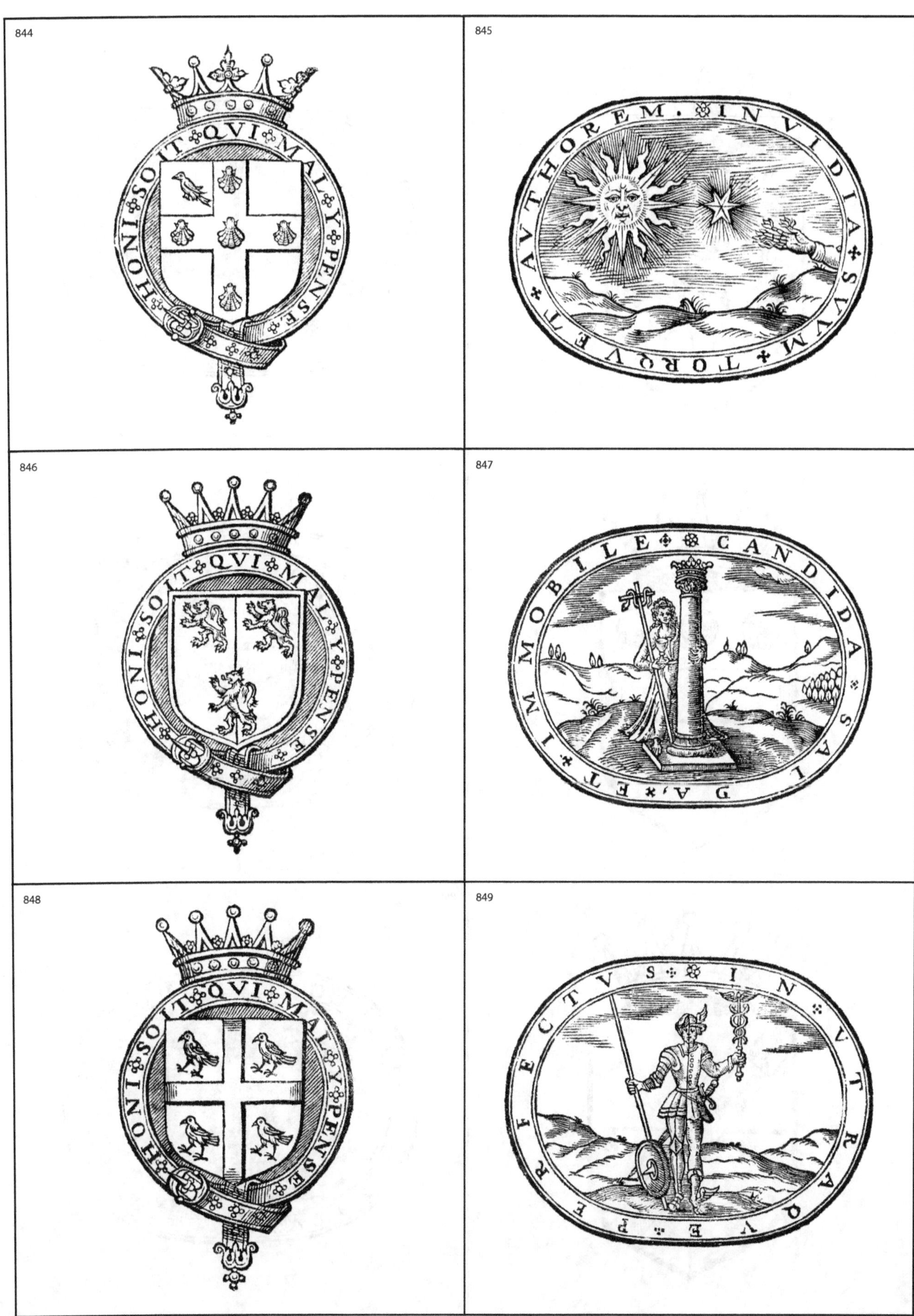

850

851

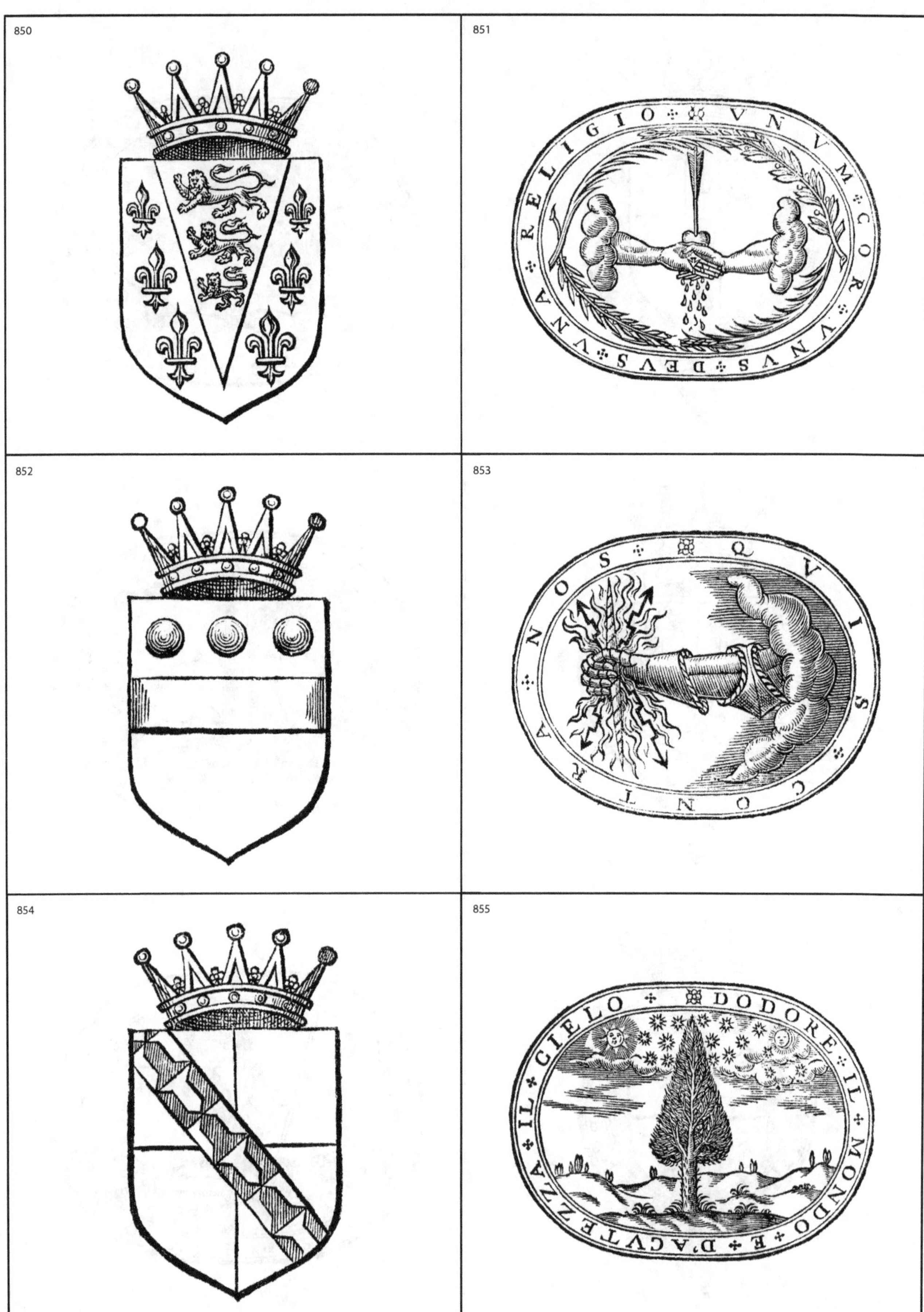

852

853

854

855

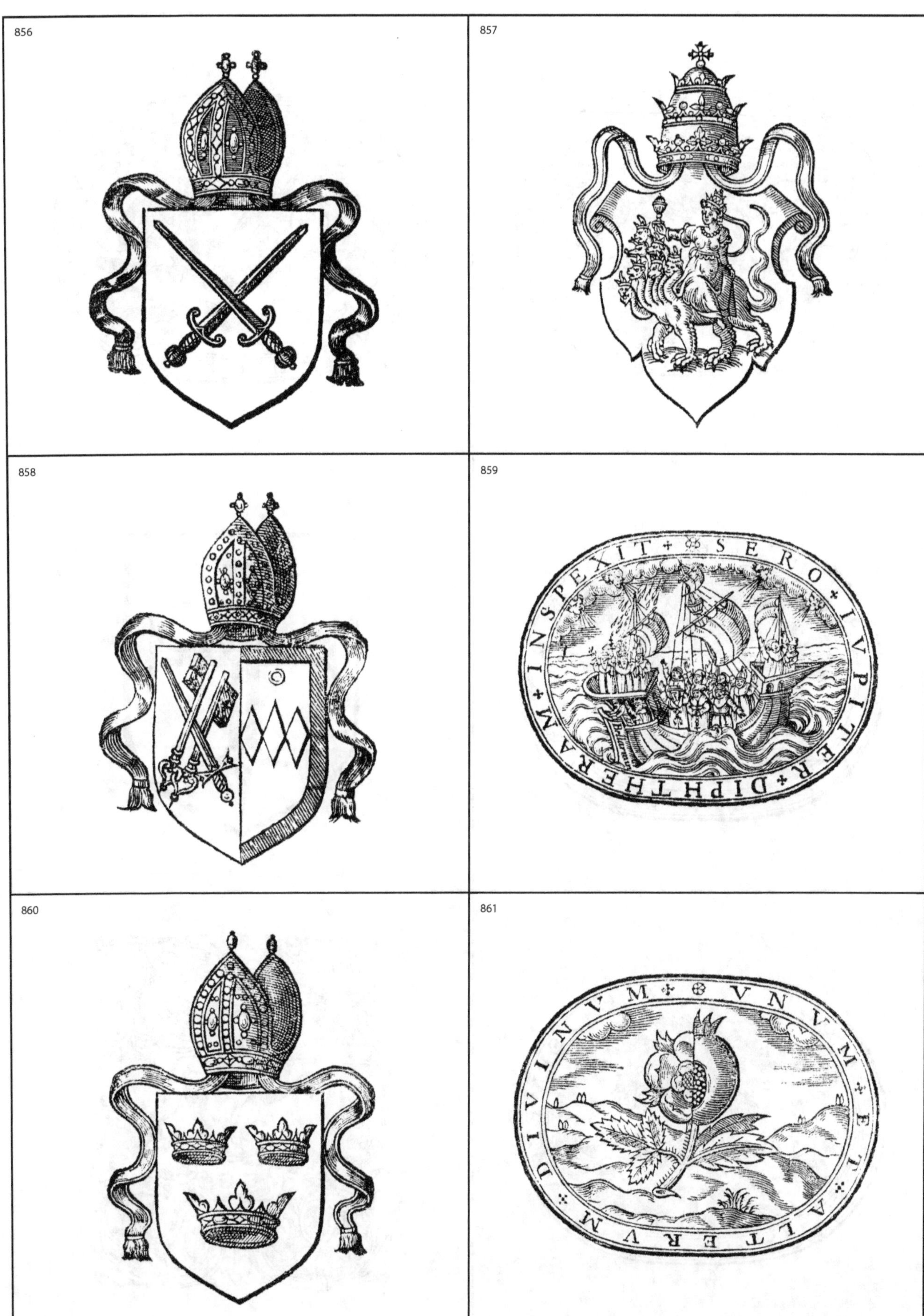
856

857

858

859
INSPEXIT ✦ SERO ✦ IVPITER ✦ DIPHTHERAM ✦

860

861
DIVINVM ✦ VNVM ✦ ET ✦ ALTERVM ✦

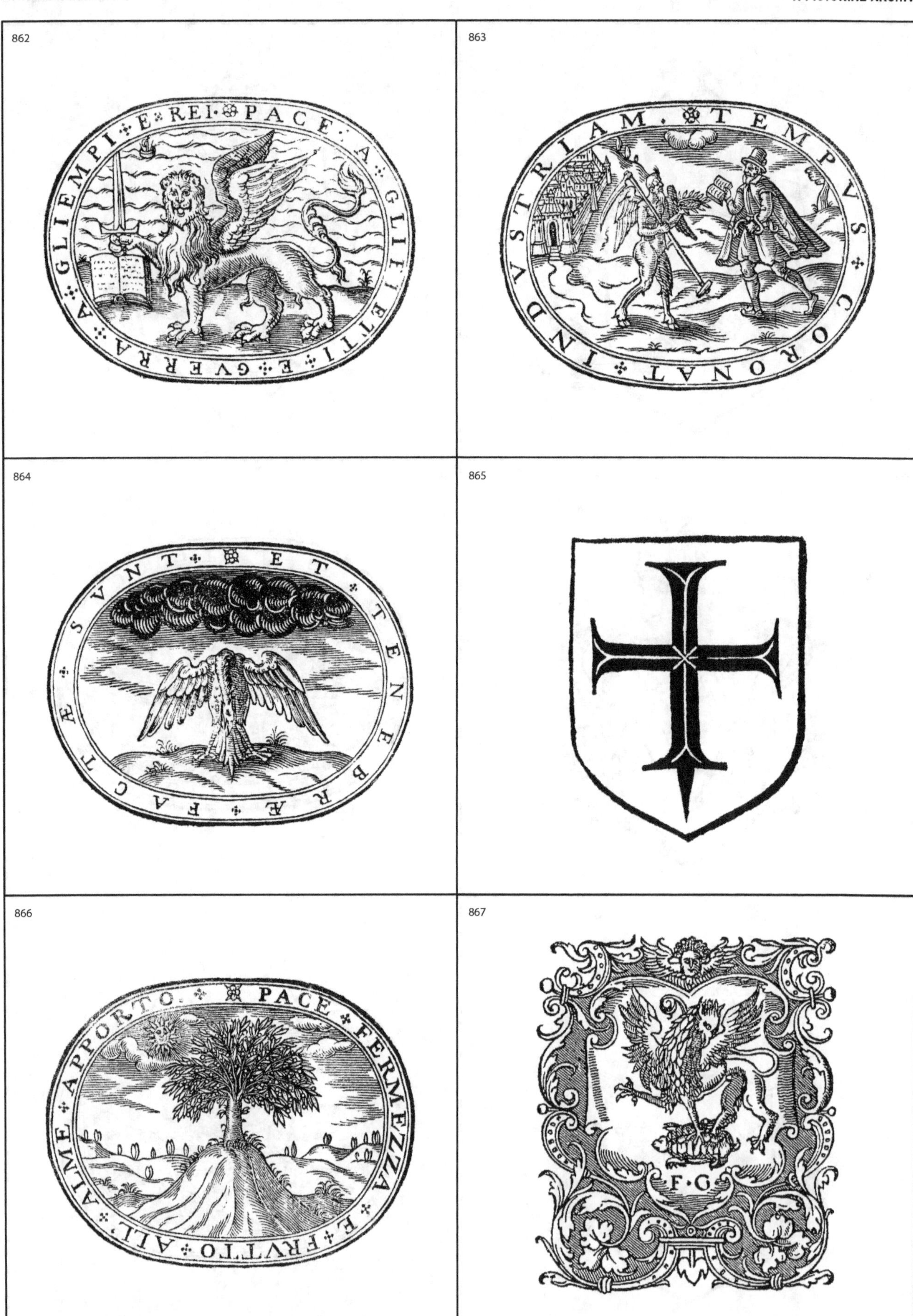
862
863
864
865
866
867
F·G

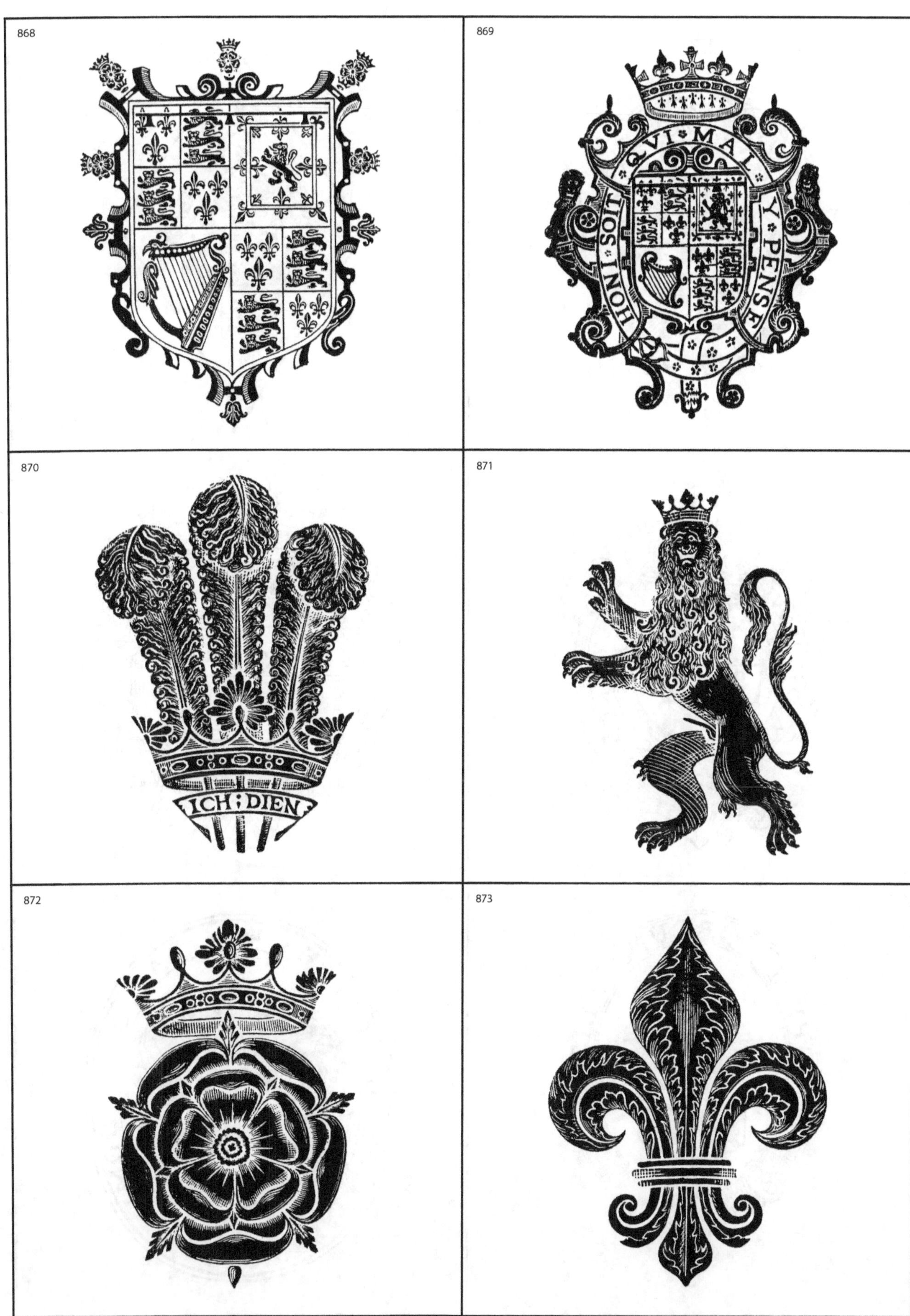

868
869
870
ICH · DIEN
871
872
873
QVI · MAL · Y · PENSE
HONI · SOIT

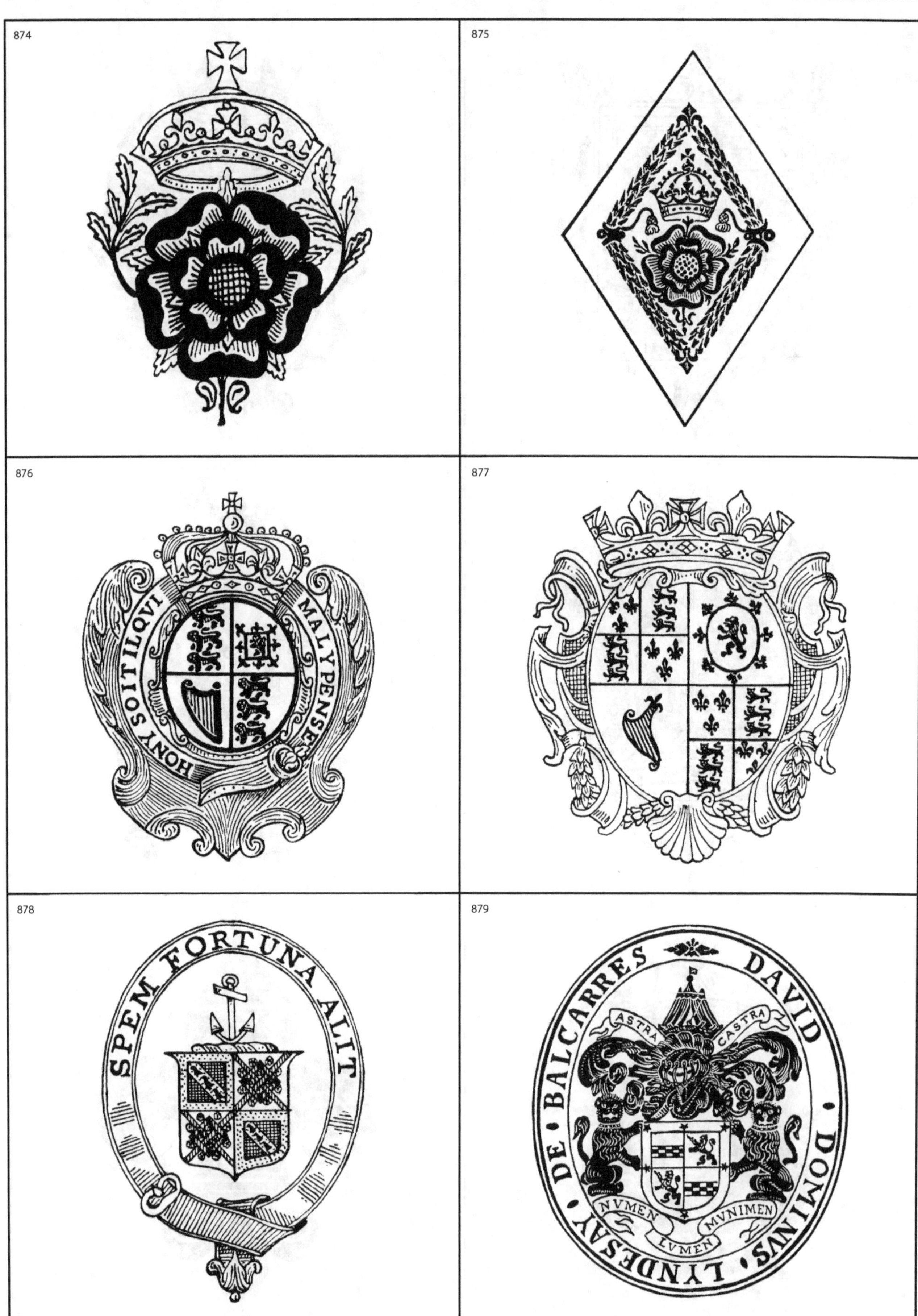
874
875
876
HONY SOIT ILQVI
MALY PENSE
877
878
SPEM FORTUNA ALIT
879
ASTRA
CASTRA
DE · BALCARRES
DAVID
NVMEN
MVNIMEN
LVMEN
LYNDESAY · DOMINVS

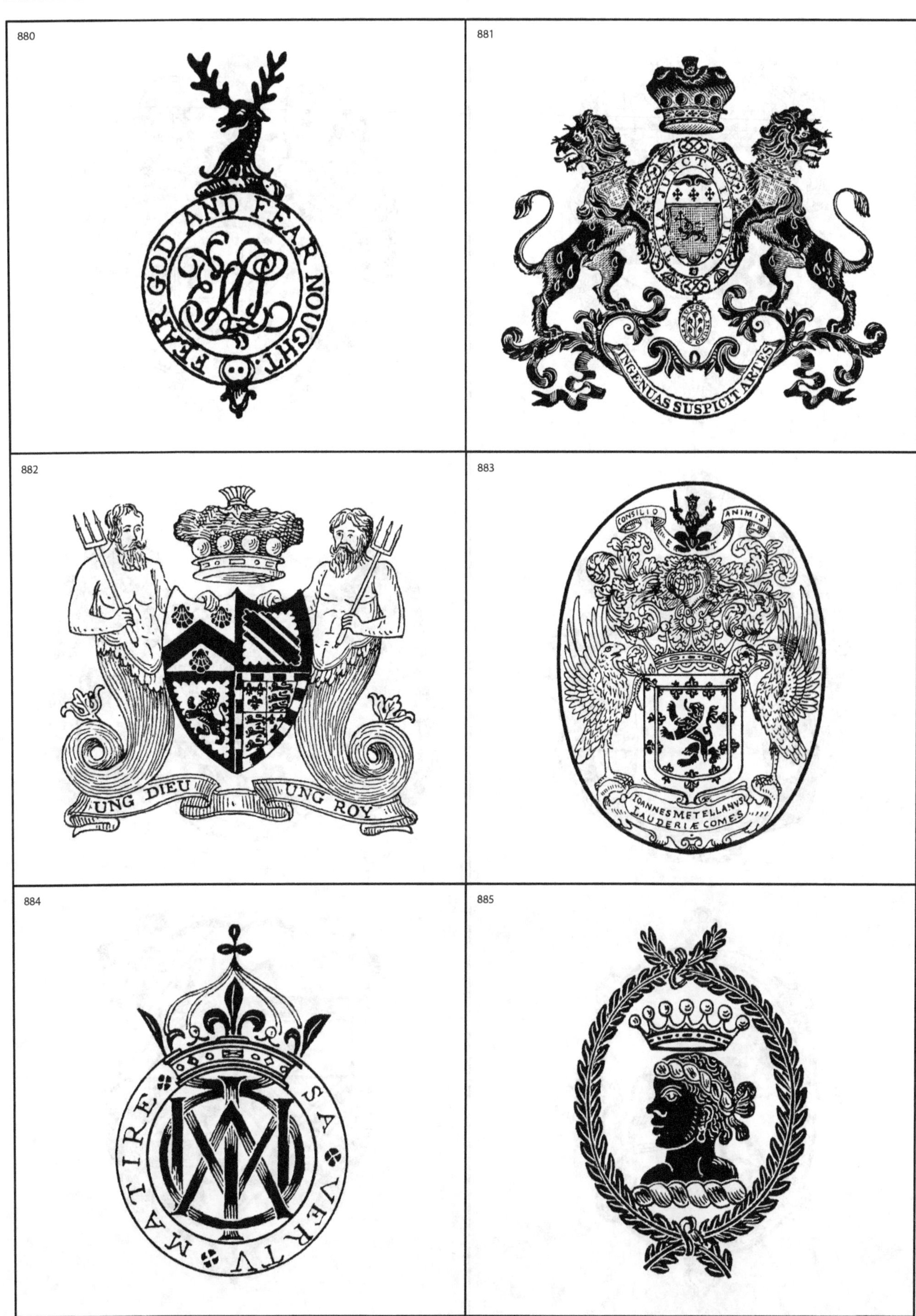
880
881
882
883
884
885
FEAR GOD AND FEAR NOUGHT
INGENUAS SUSPICIT ARTES
UNG DIEU UNG ROY
CONSILIO ET ANIMIS
IOANNES METELLANVS LAUDERIÆ COMES
SA VERTV MATIRE

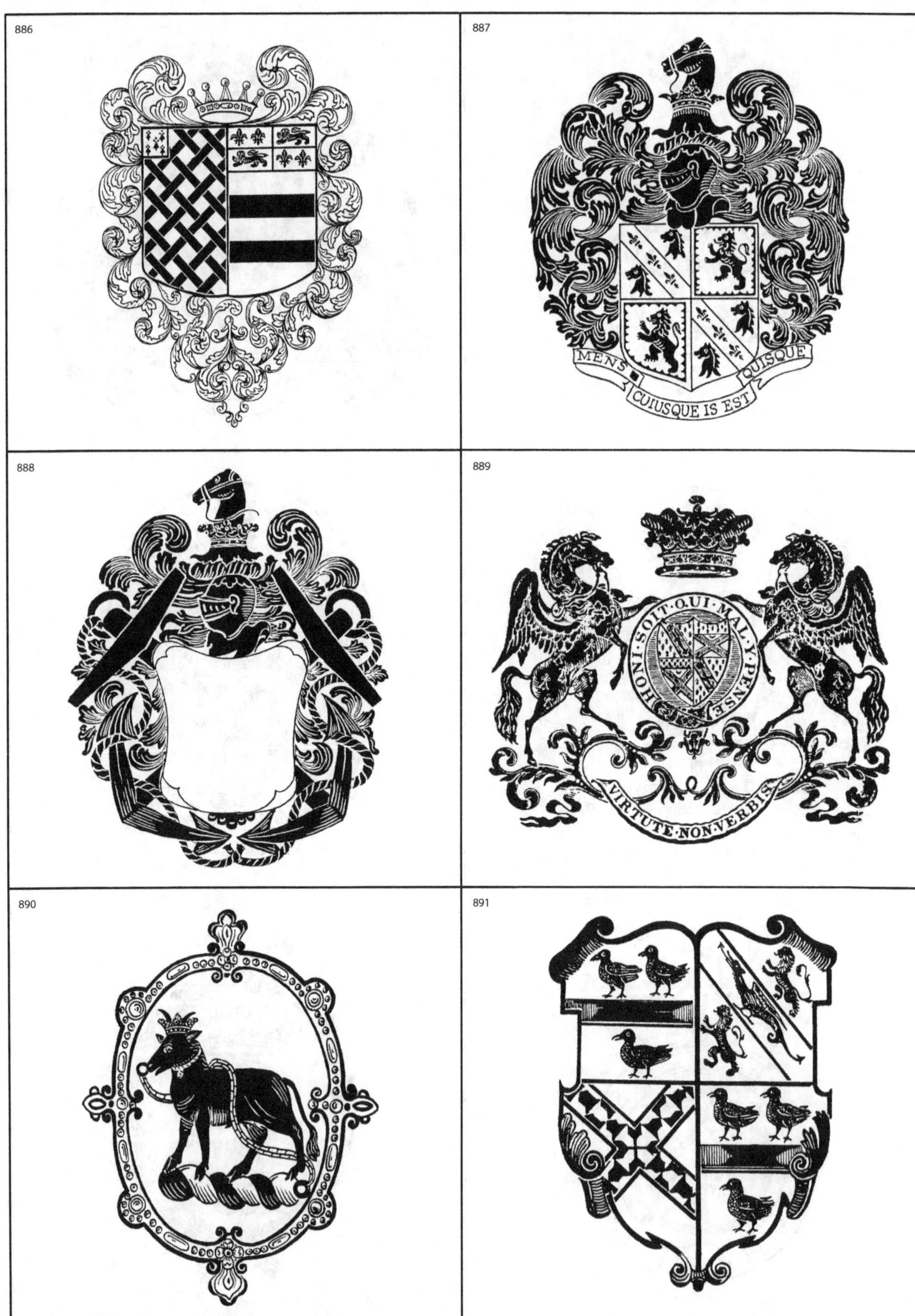

886
887
MENS CUIUSQUE IS EST
888
889
HONI SOIT QUI MAL Y PENSE
VIRTUTE NON VERBIS
890
891

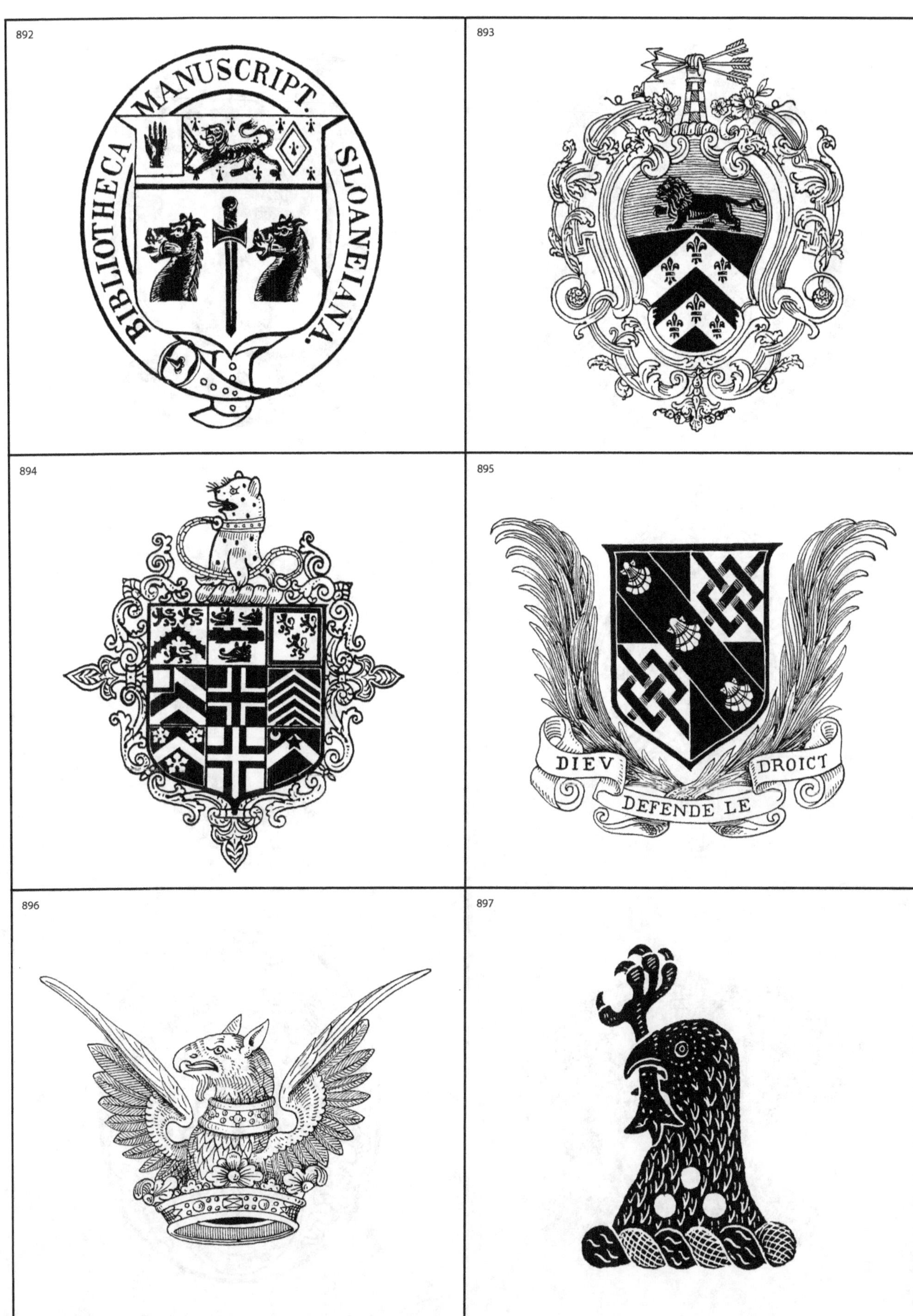

892

893

894

895

896

897

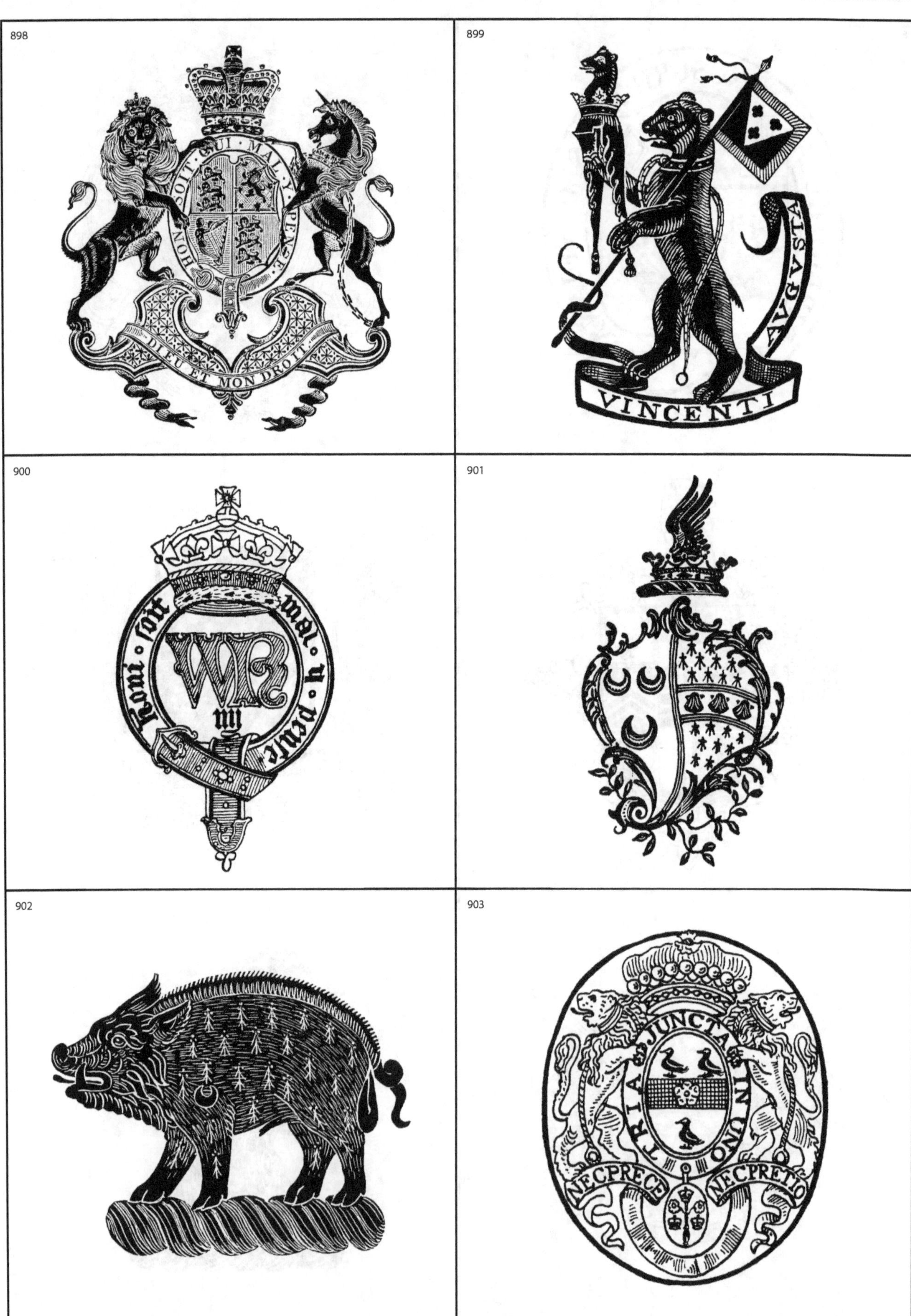
898
899
VINCENTI
AVGVSTA
900
901
902
903
NECPRECE   NECPRETO
JUNCTA

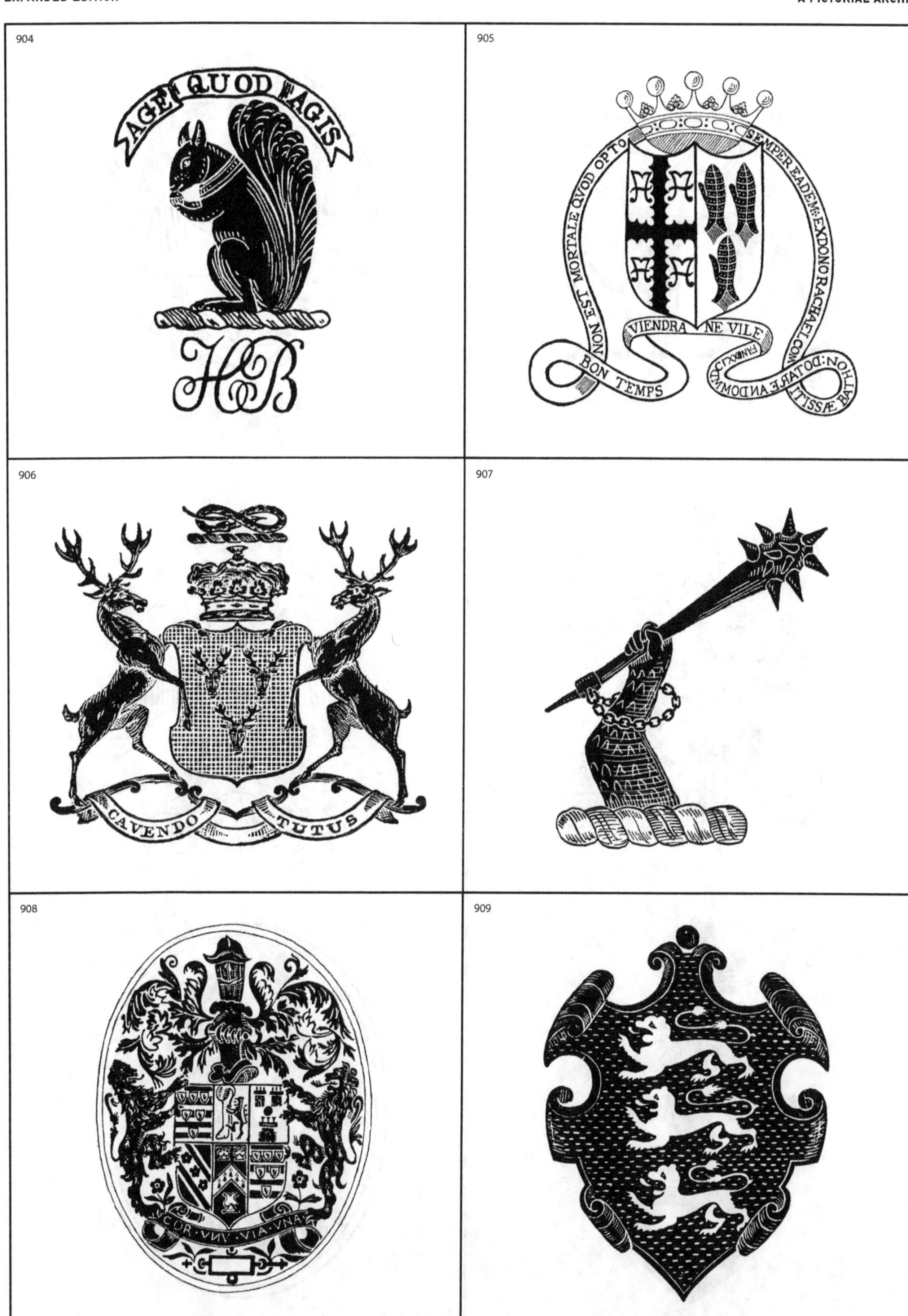

904
AGE QUOD AGIS
HB

905
NON EST MORTALE QUOD OPTO
SEMPER EADEM: EX DONO RACHAEL COM:
VIENDRA NE VILE
BON TEMPS

906
CAVENDO TUTUS

907

908
UN COR UNA VIA UNA

909

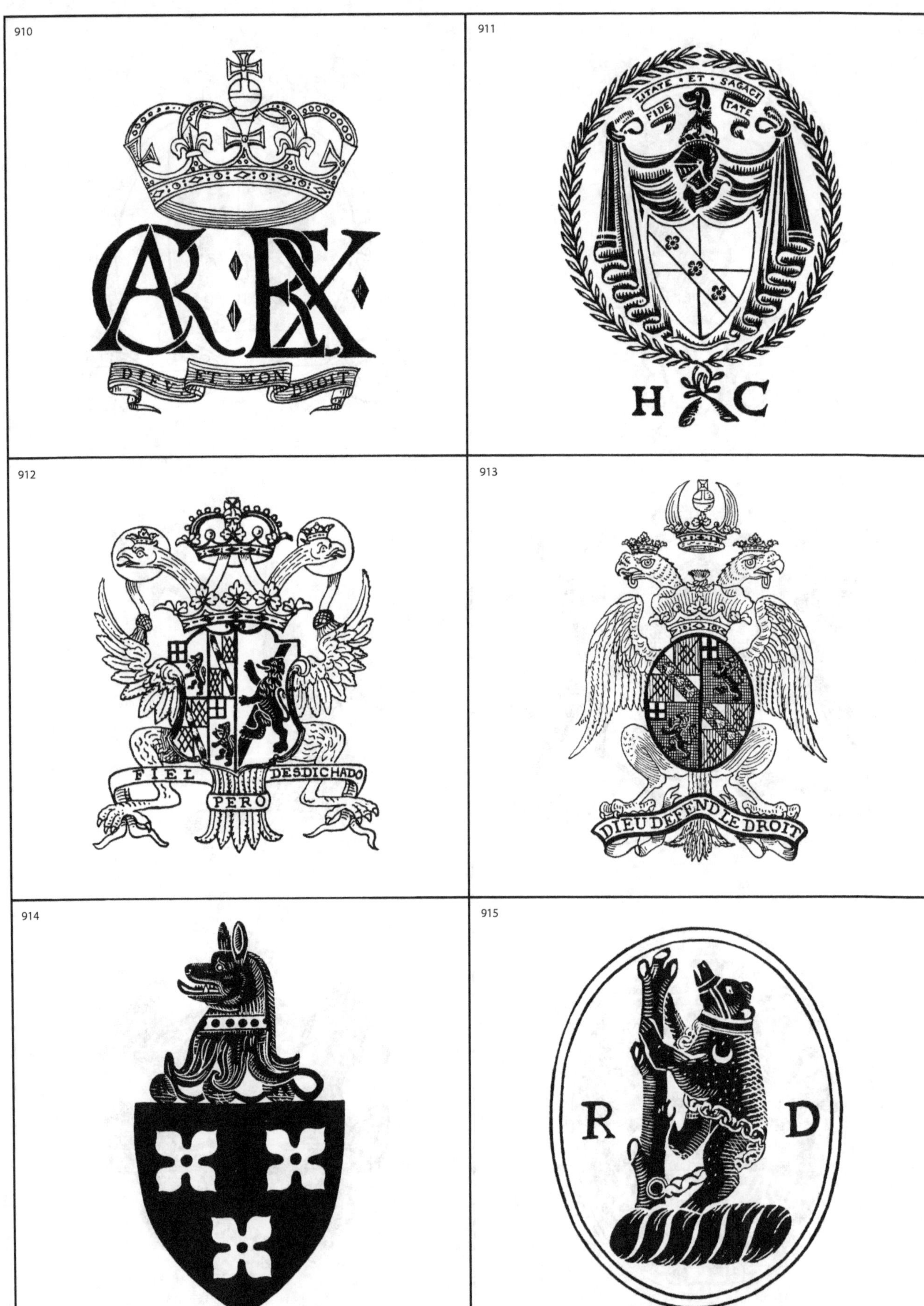
910
911
912
913
914
915

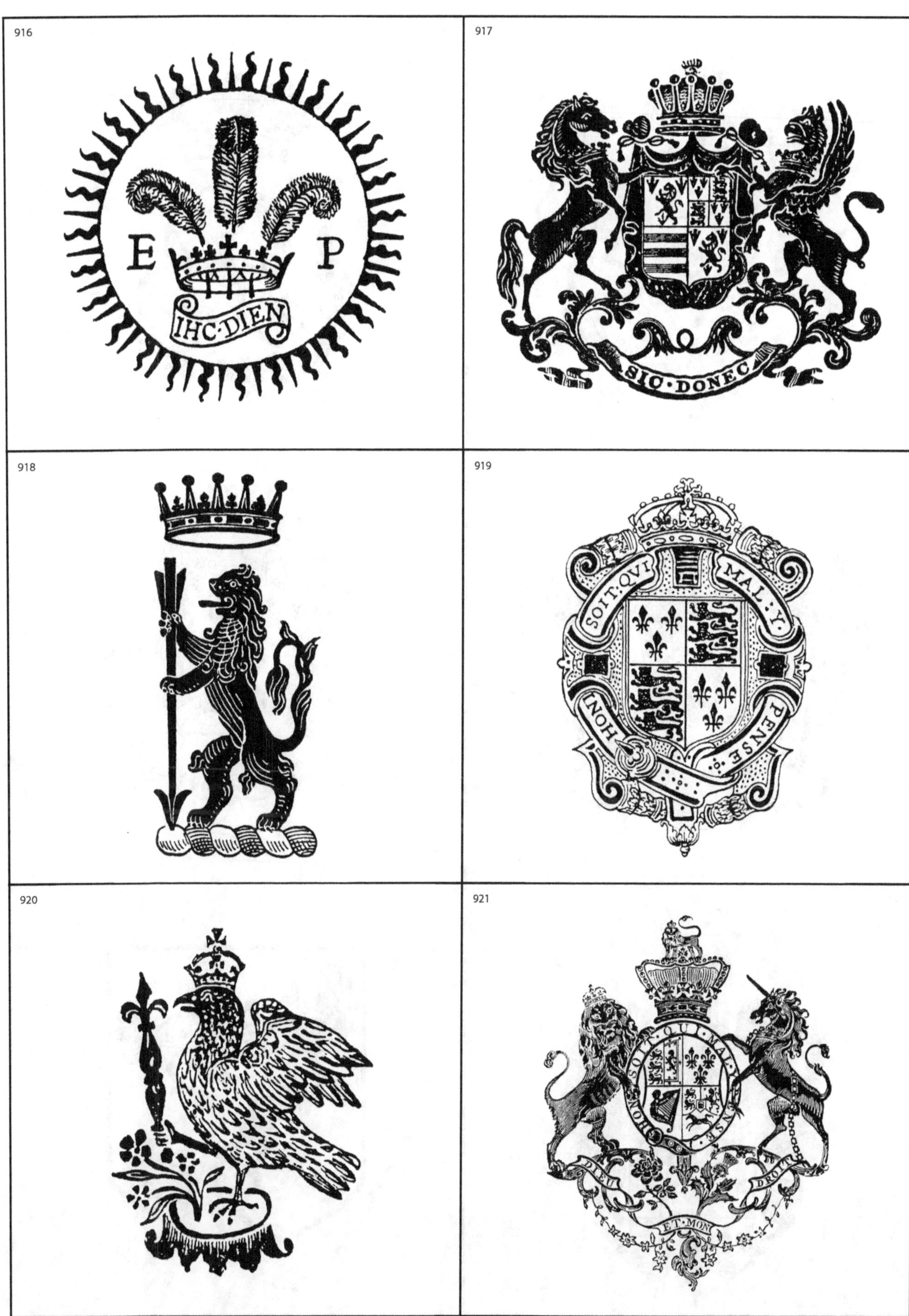
916
917
918
919
920
921
IHC·DIEN
SIC·DONEC
SOIT·QUI MAL·Y·PENSE·
HONI
DIEU ET·MON DROIT

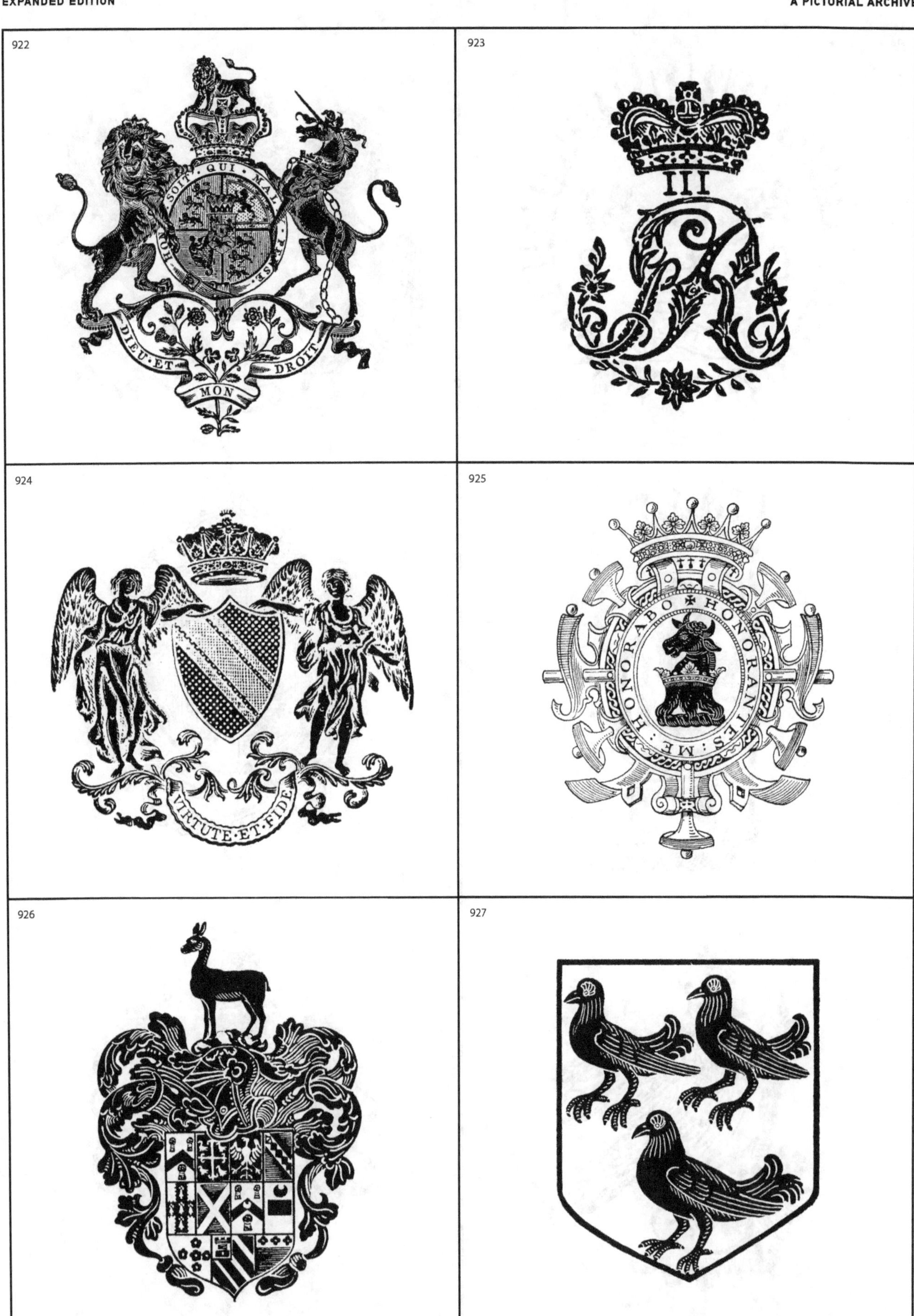

922

923

924

925

926

927

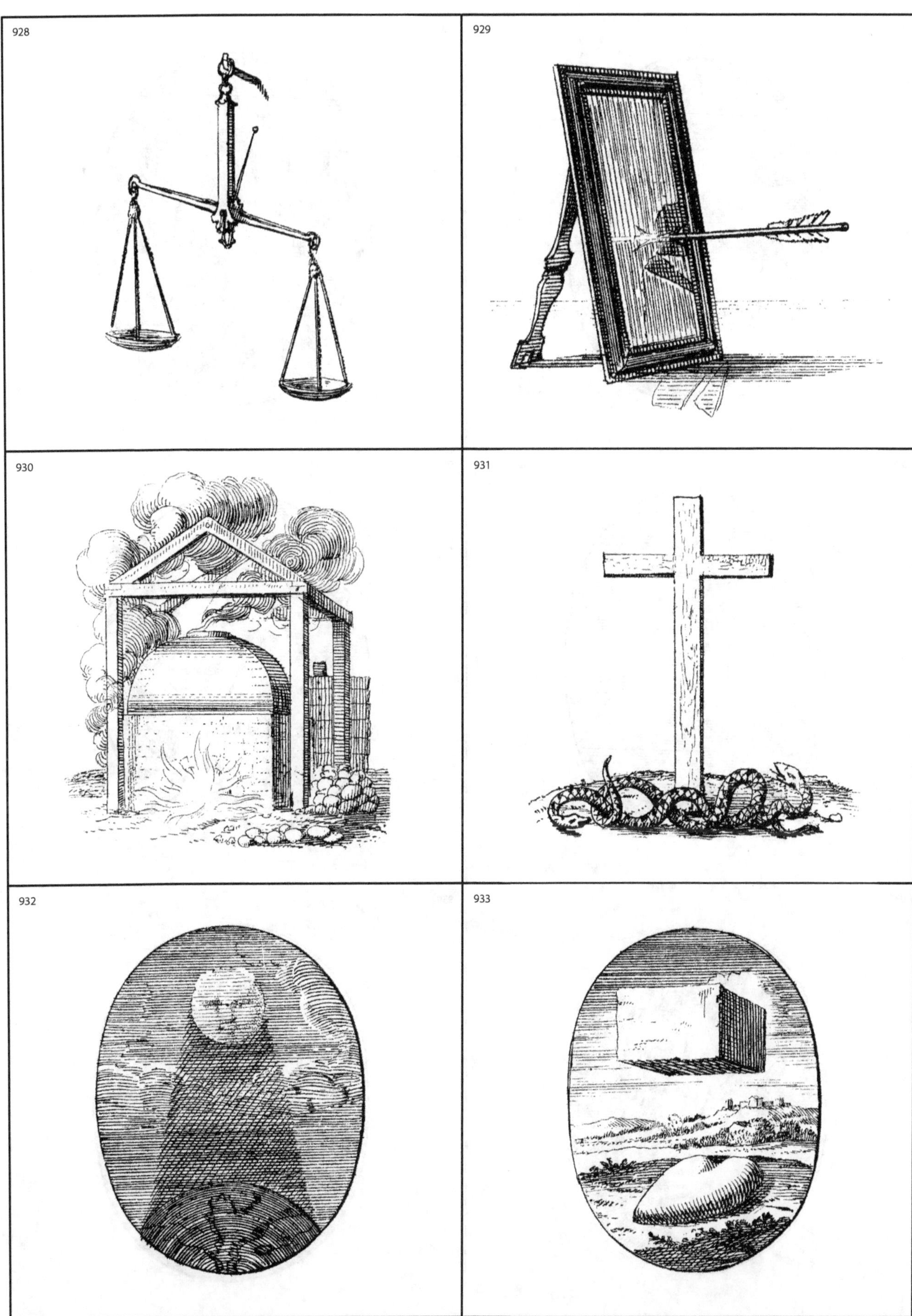

928

929

930

931

932

933

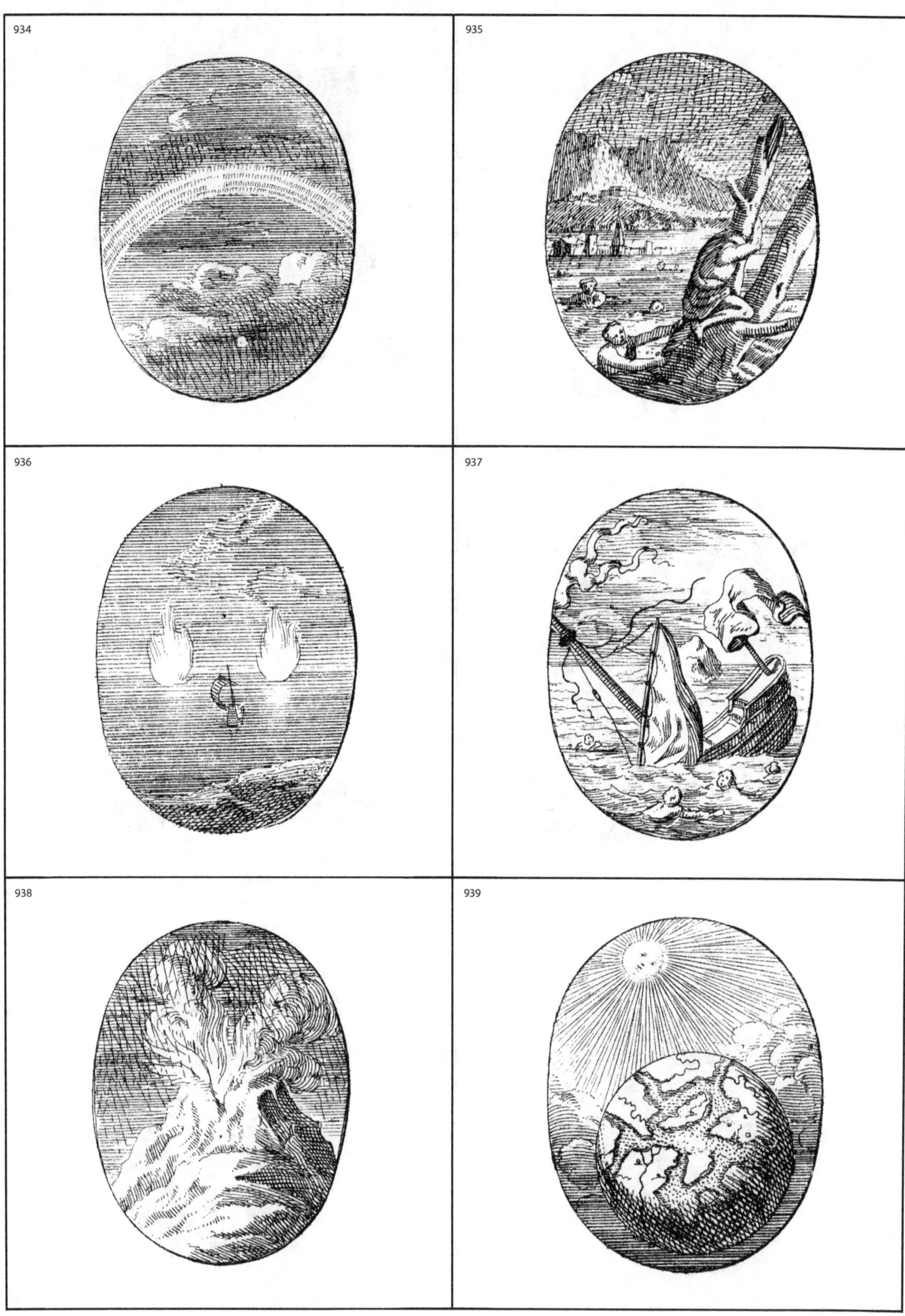

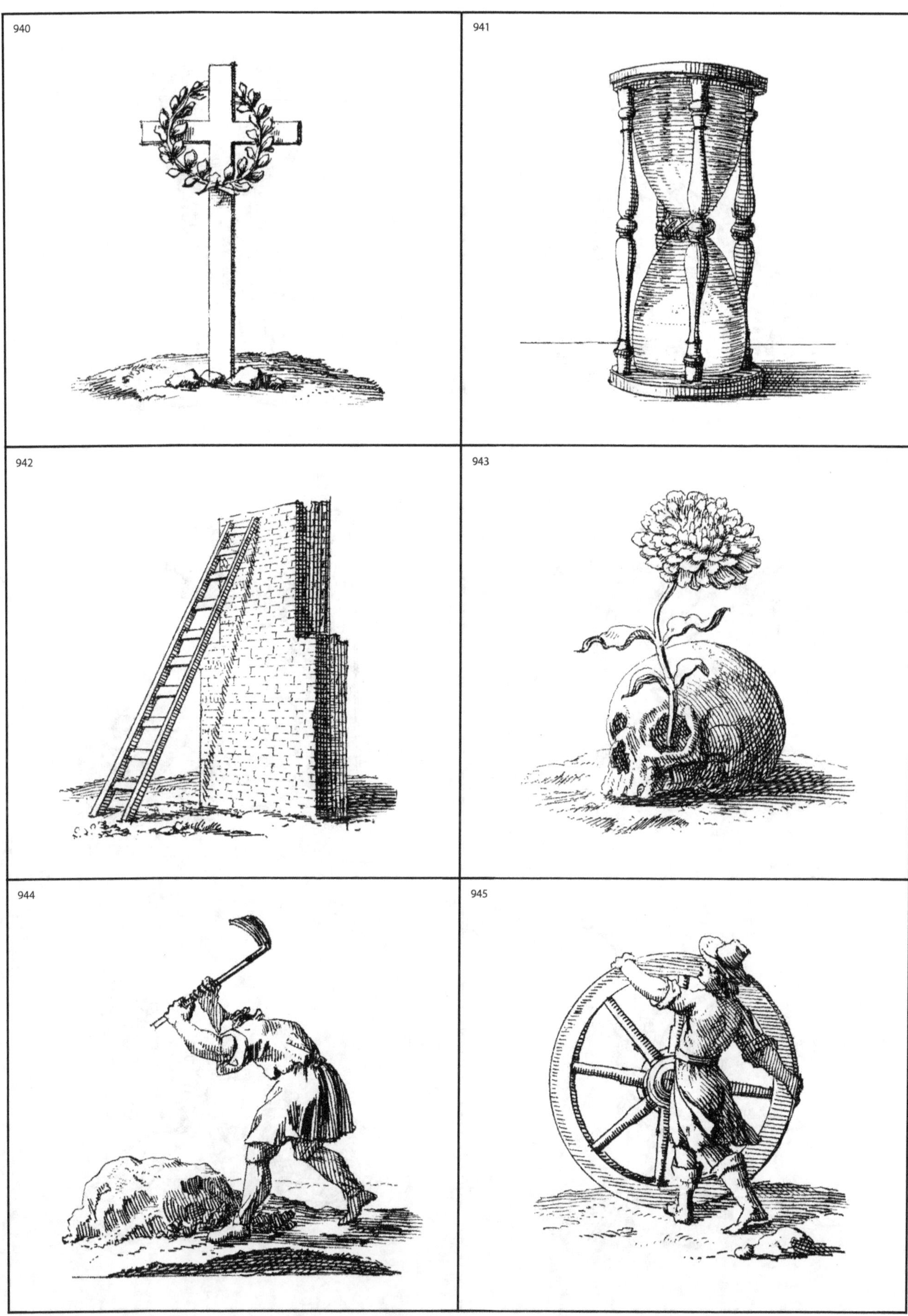

940

941

942

943

944

945

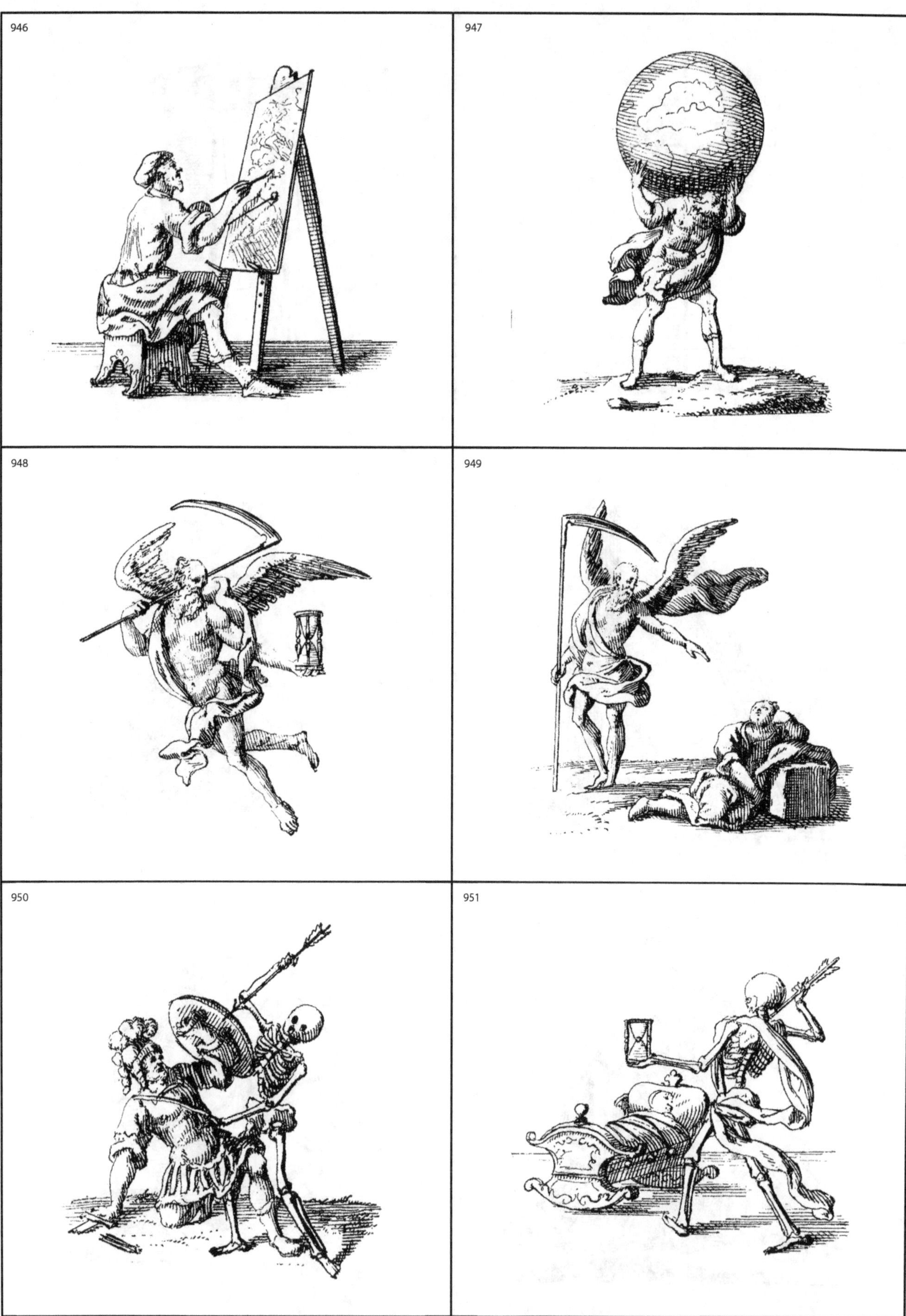

946

947

948

949

950

951

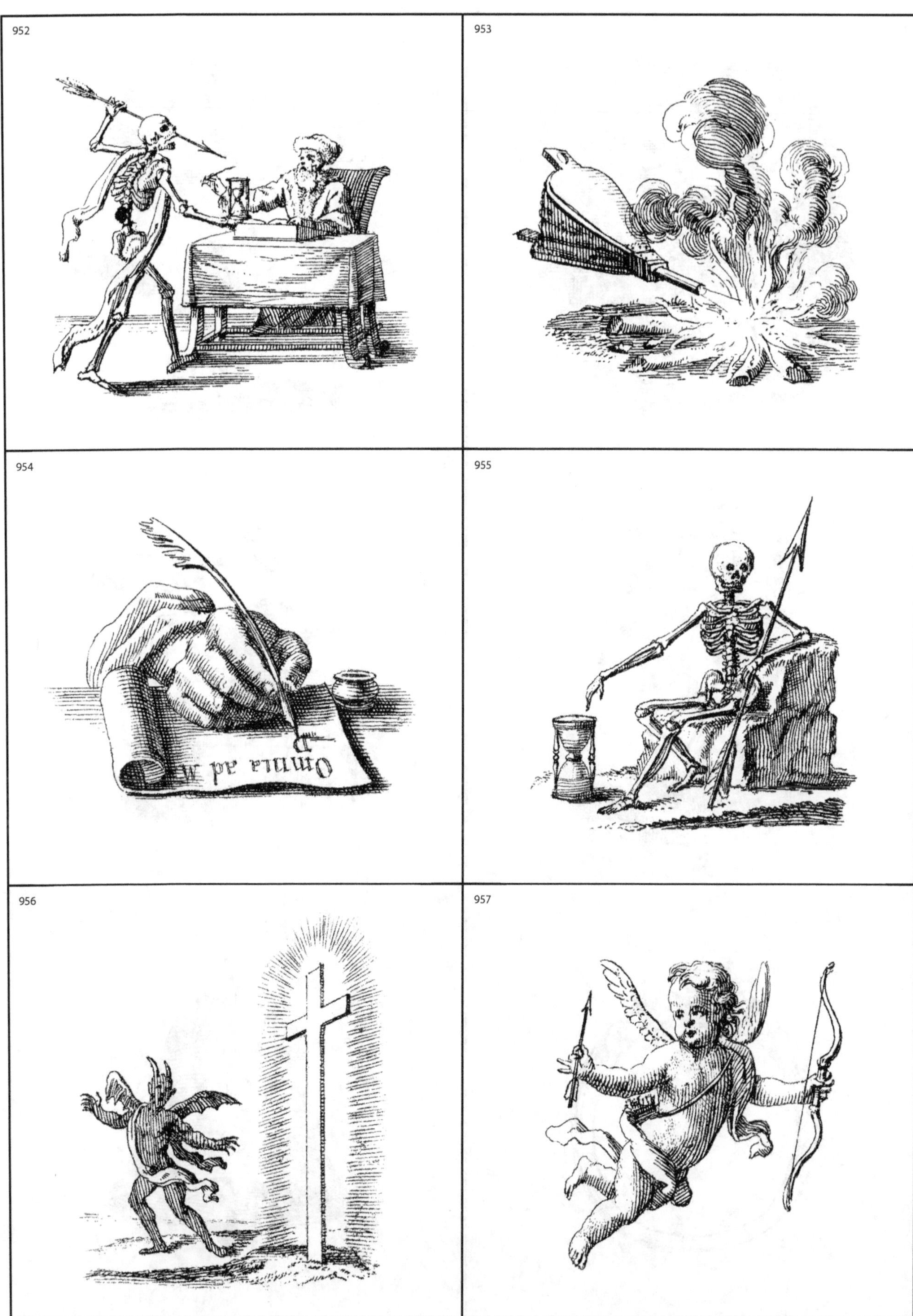

952

953

954

955

956

957

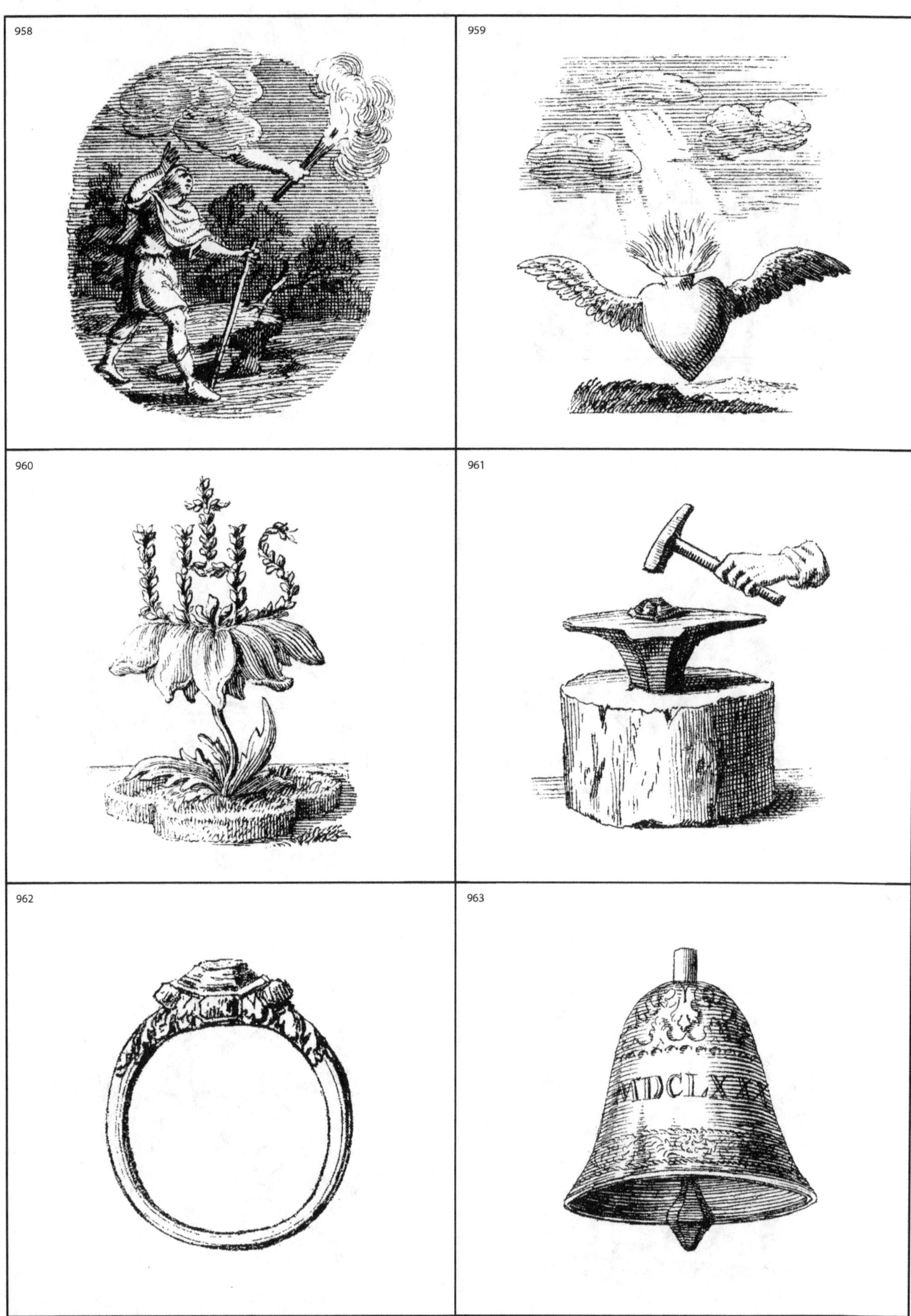

958

959

960

961

962

963

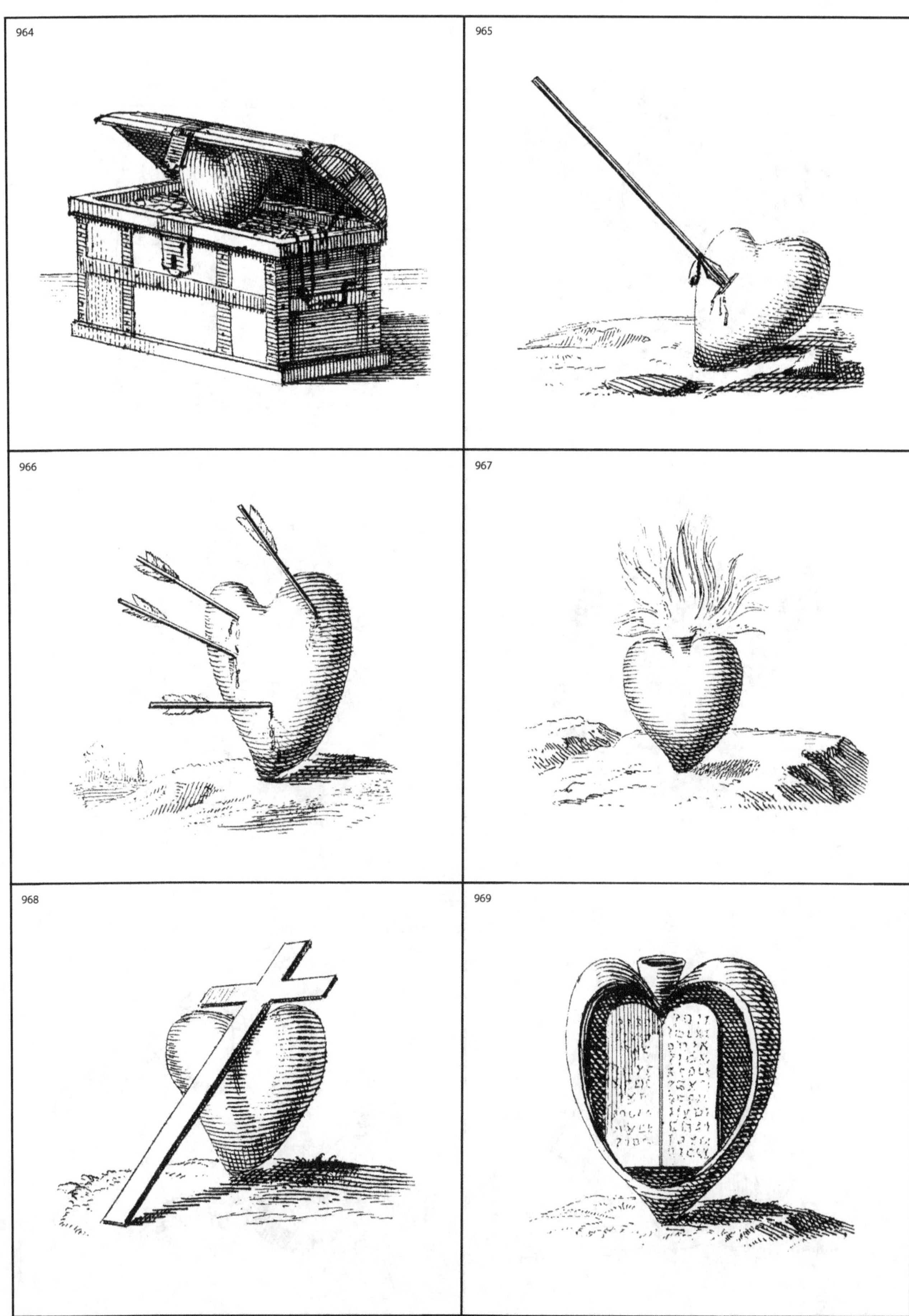

964

965

966

967

968

969

SYMBOLS & EMBLEMS

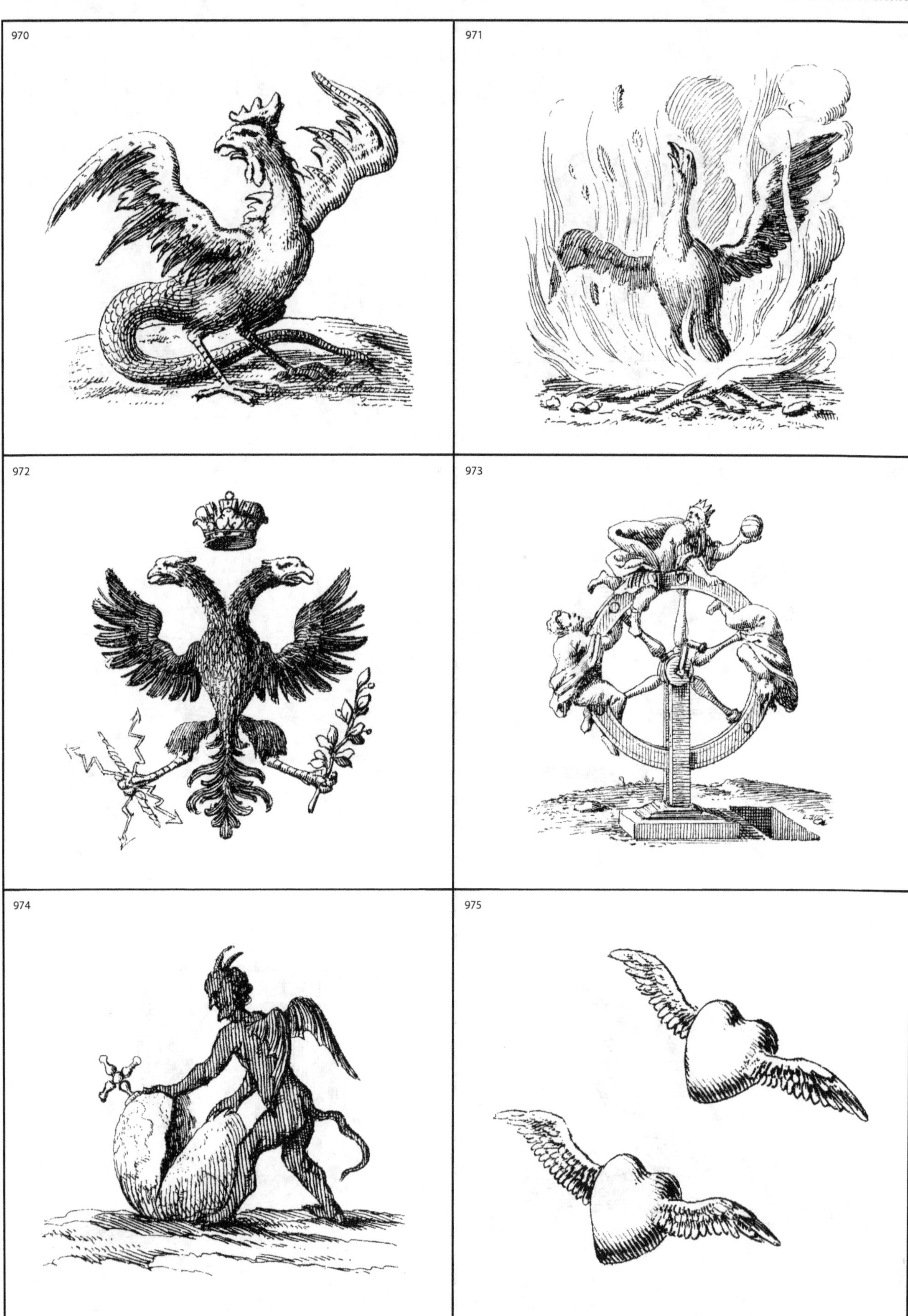

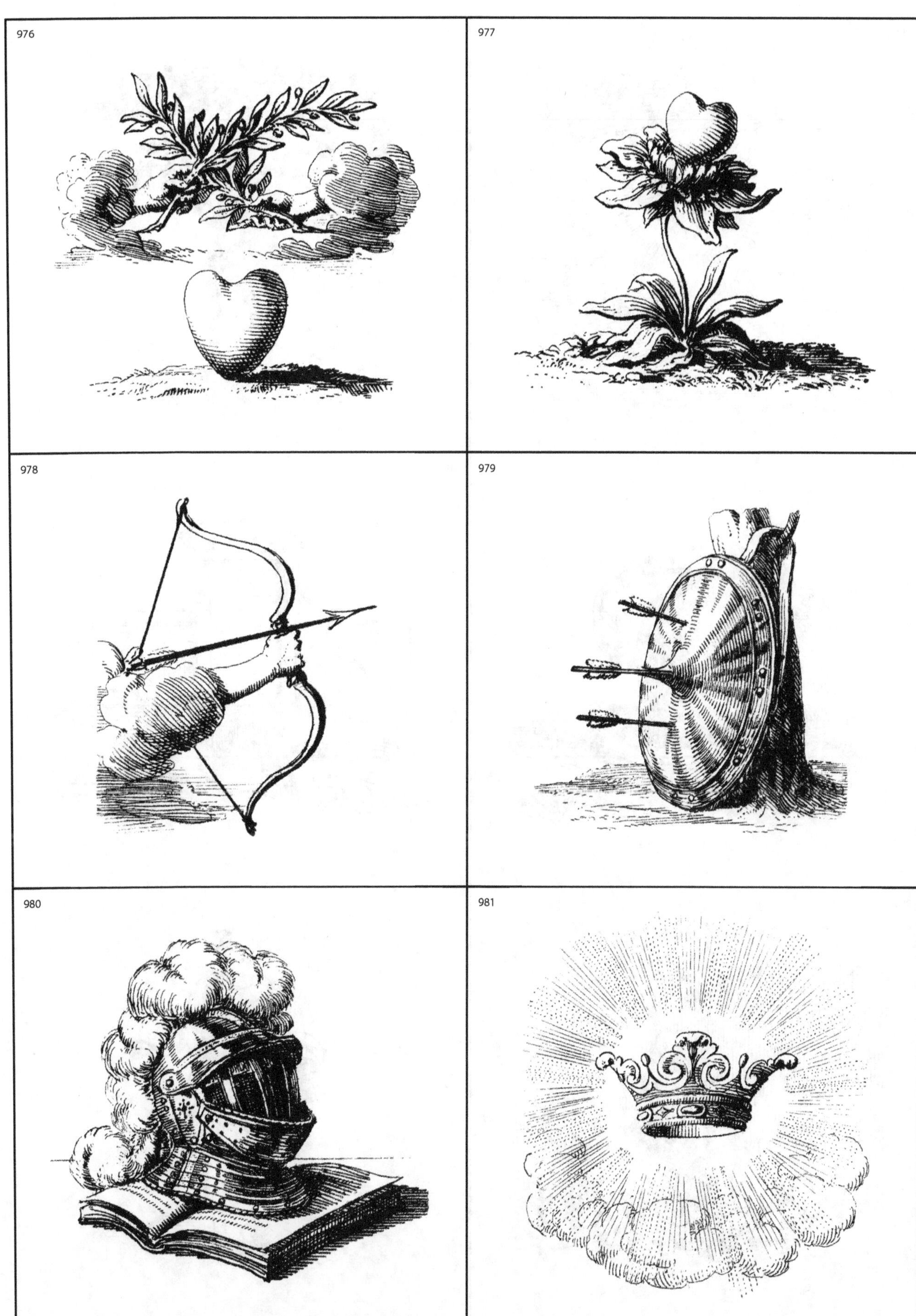

976

977

978

979

980

981

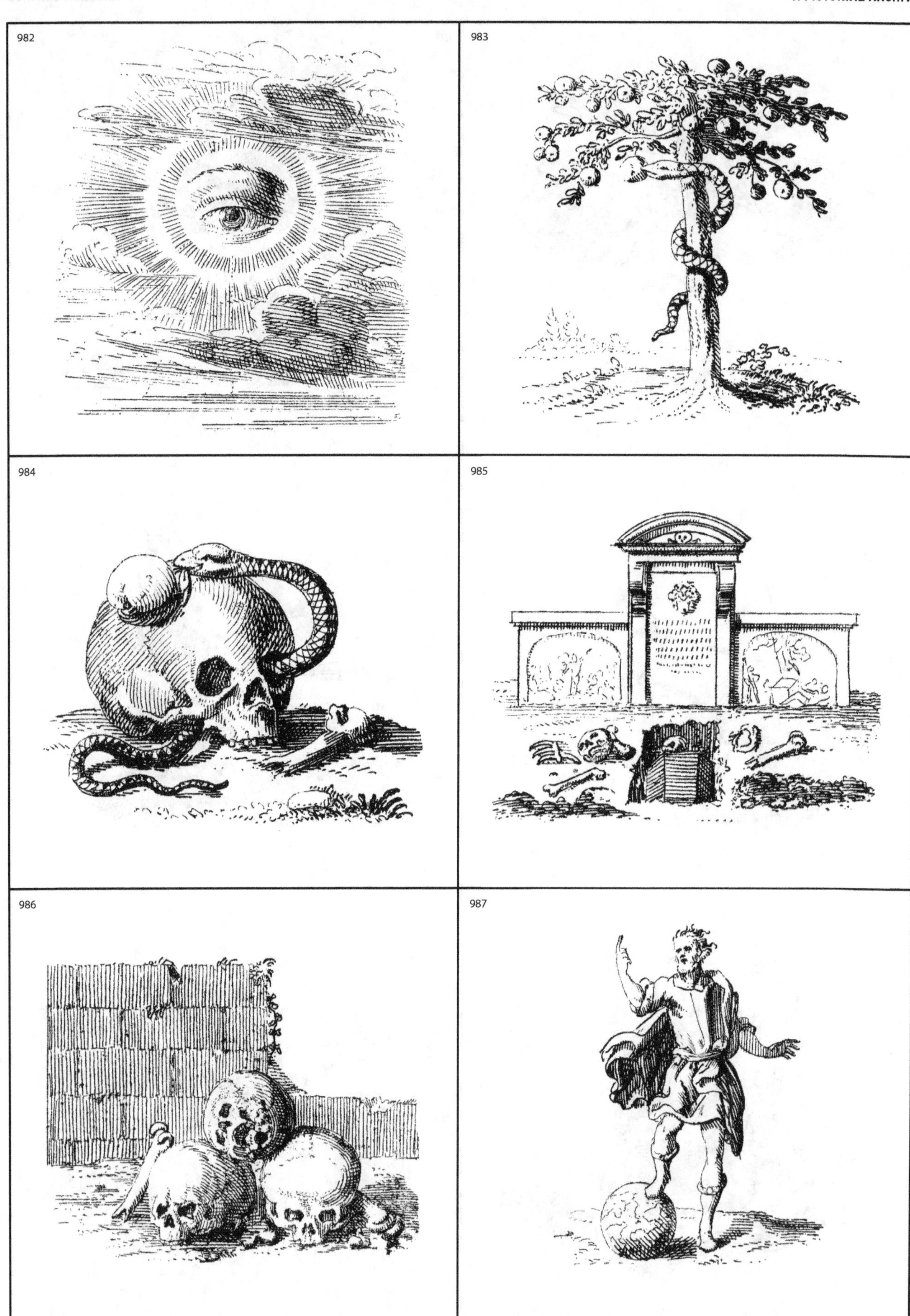

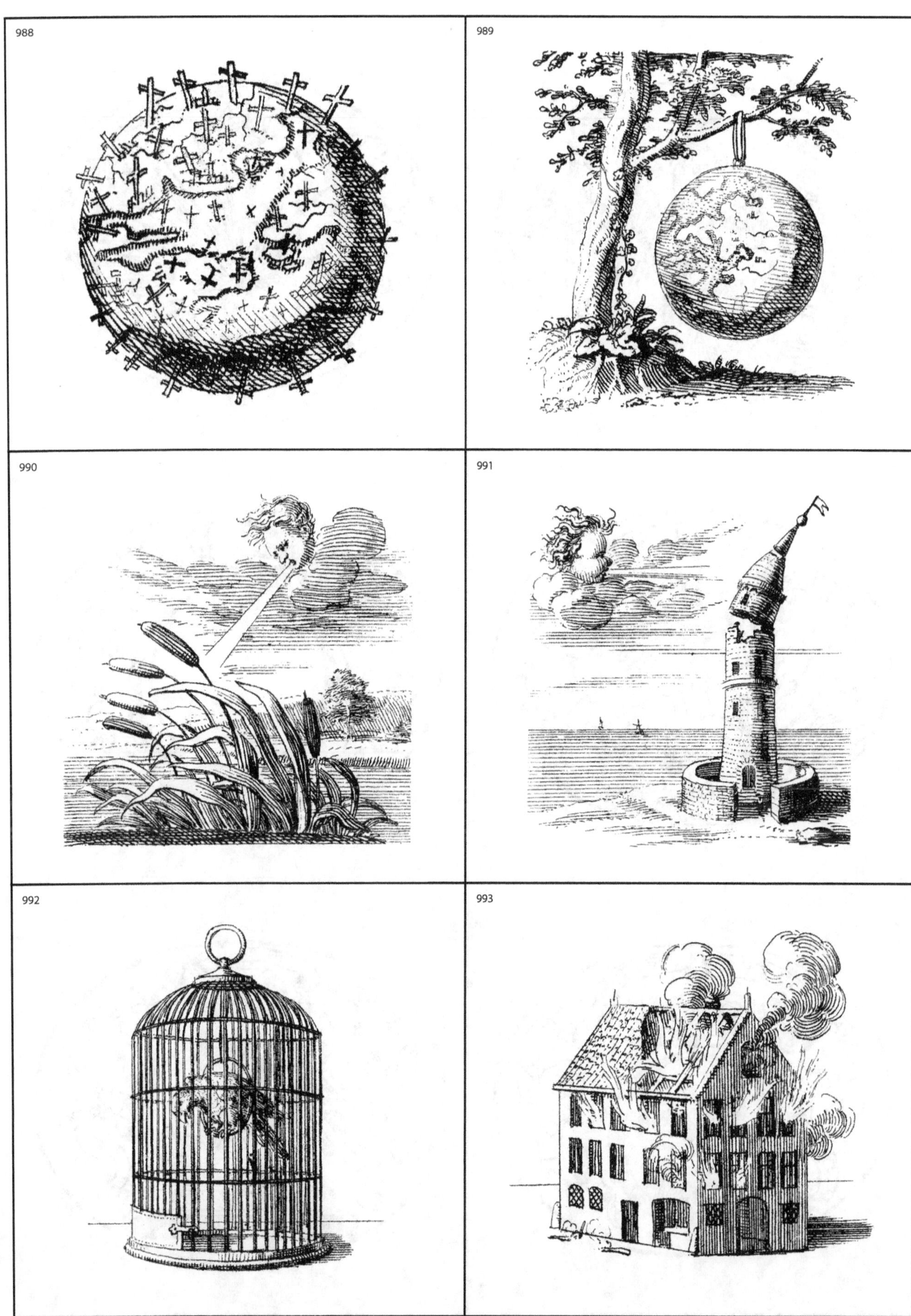

988

989

990

991

992

993

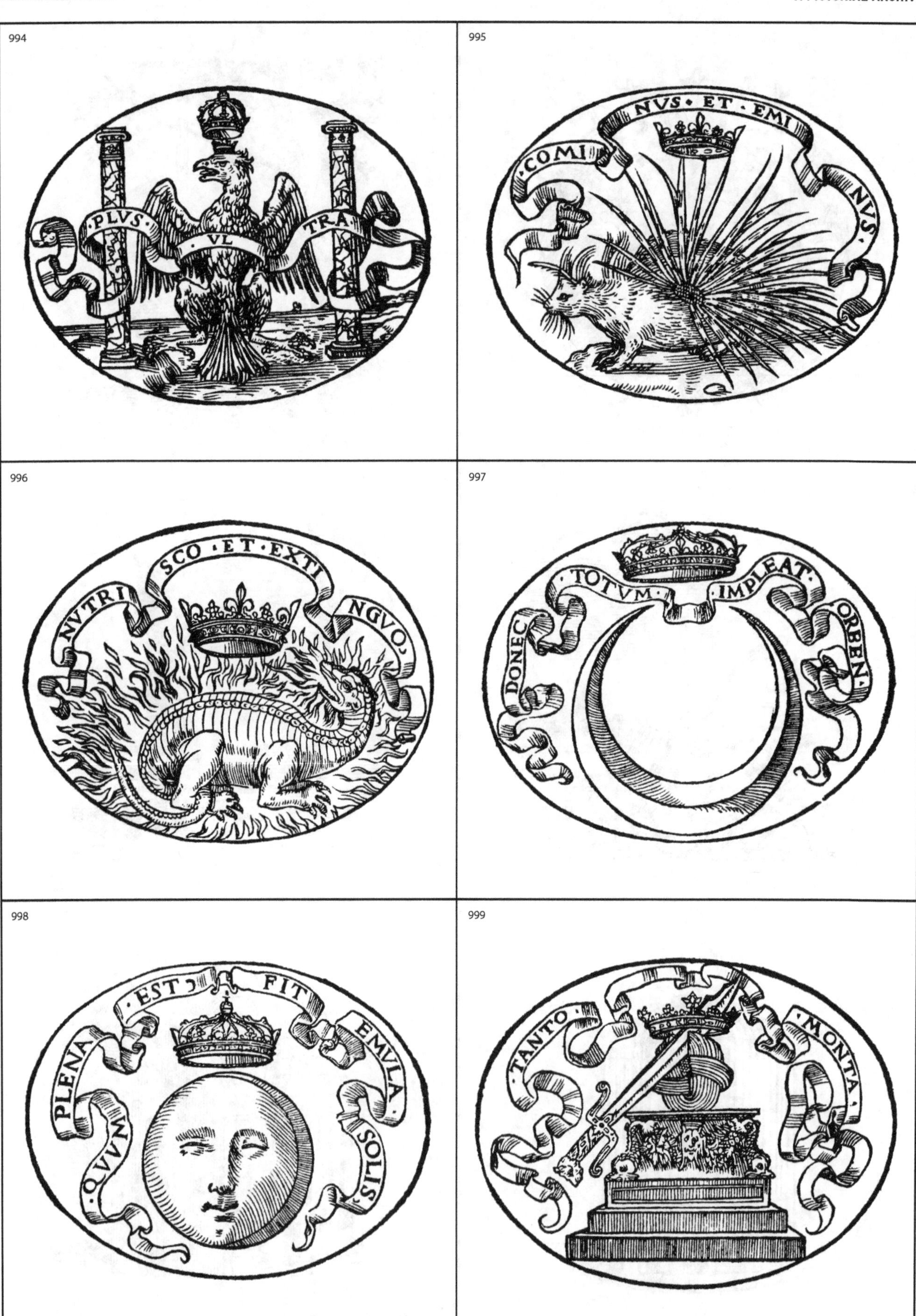
994
PLVS VL TRA

995
COMI NVS · ET · EMI NVS

996
NVTRI SCO · ET · EXTI NGVO

997
DONEC TOTVM · IMPLEAT · ORBEN

998
PLENA · EST FIT EMVLA SOLIS QVVM

999
TANTO MONTA

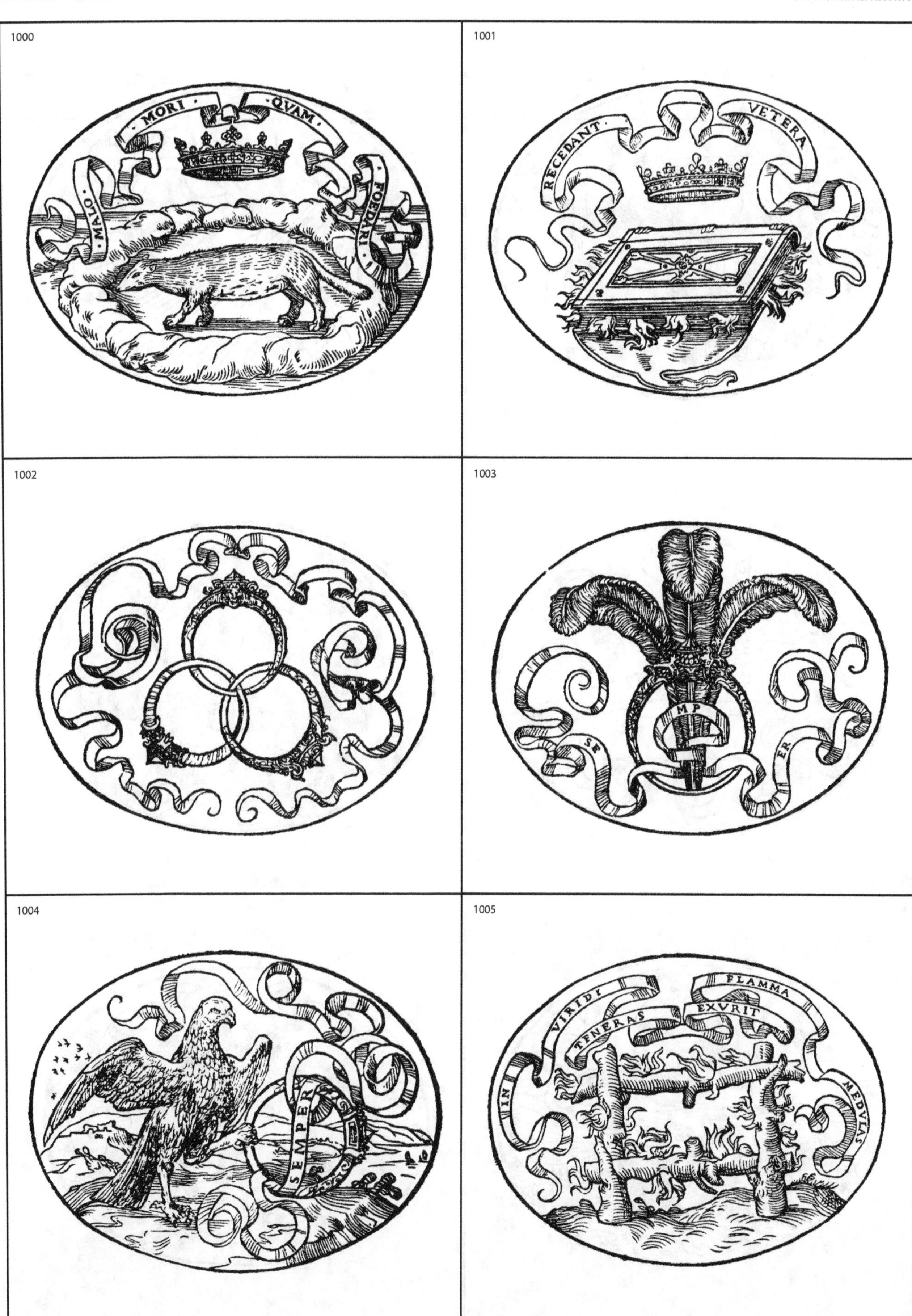
1000
· MORI · QVAM ·
· MALO ·
· FOEDARI ·

1001
· RECEDANT ·   VETERA

1002

1003
SE   MP   ER

1004
SEMPER

1005
IN VIRIDI   FLAMMA
TENERAS   EXVRIT
MEDVLLAS

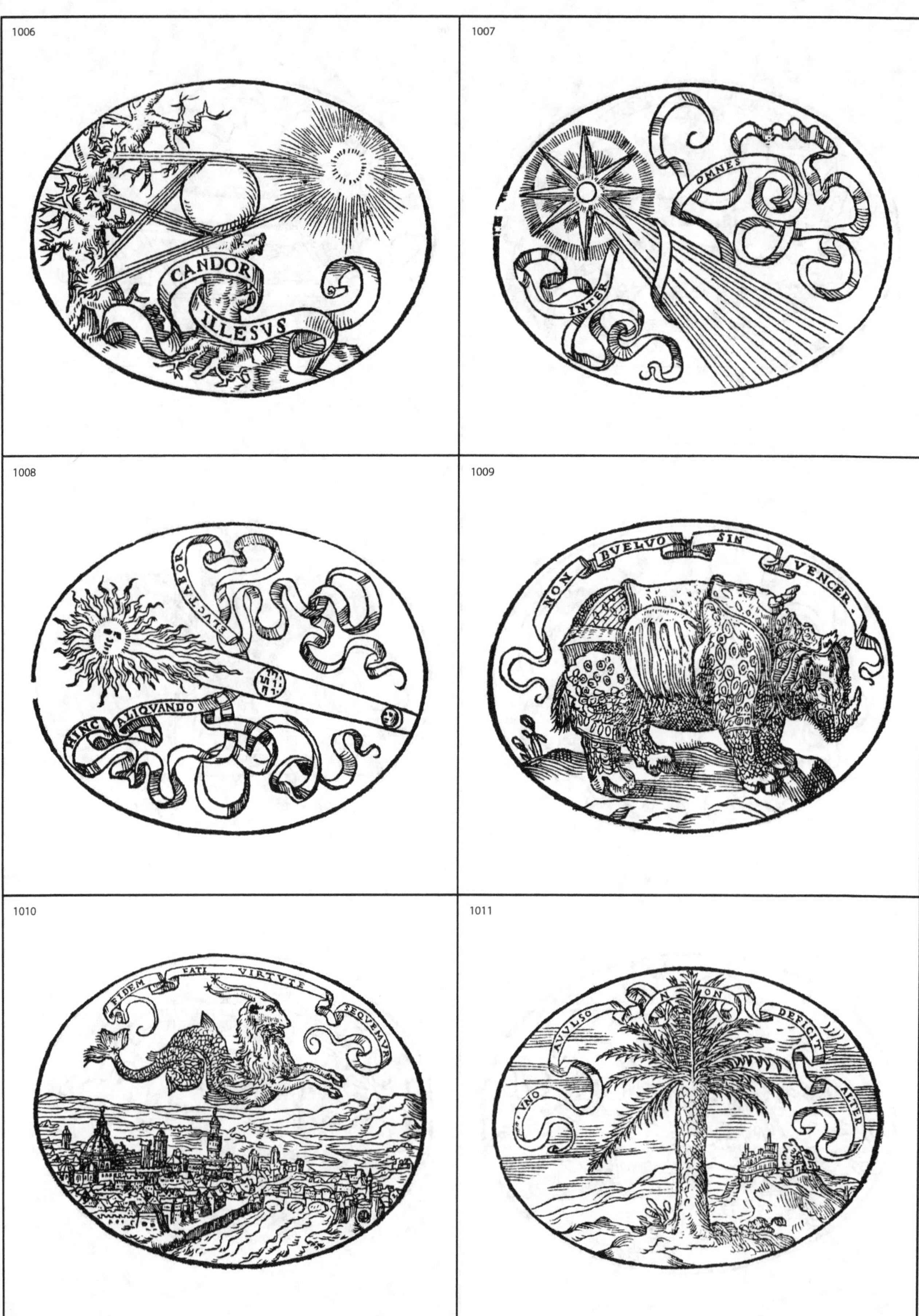
1006
CANDOR
ILLESVS

1007
OMNES
INTER

1008
LVCTABOR
HINC ALIQVANDO

1009
NON BVELVO SIN VENCER.

1010
FIDEM EATI VIRTVTE SEQVEMVR

1011
NON
AVVLSO DEFICIT
VNO ALTER

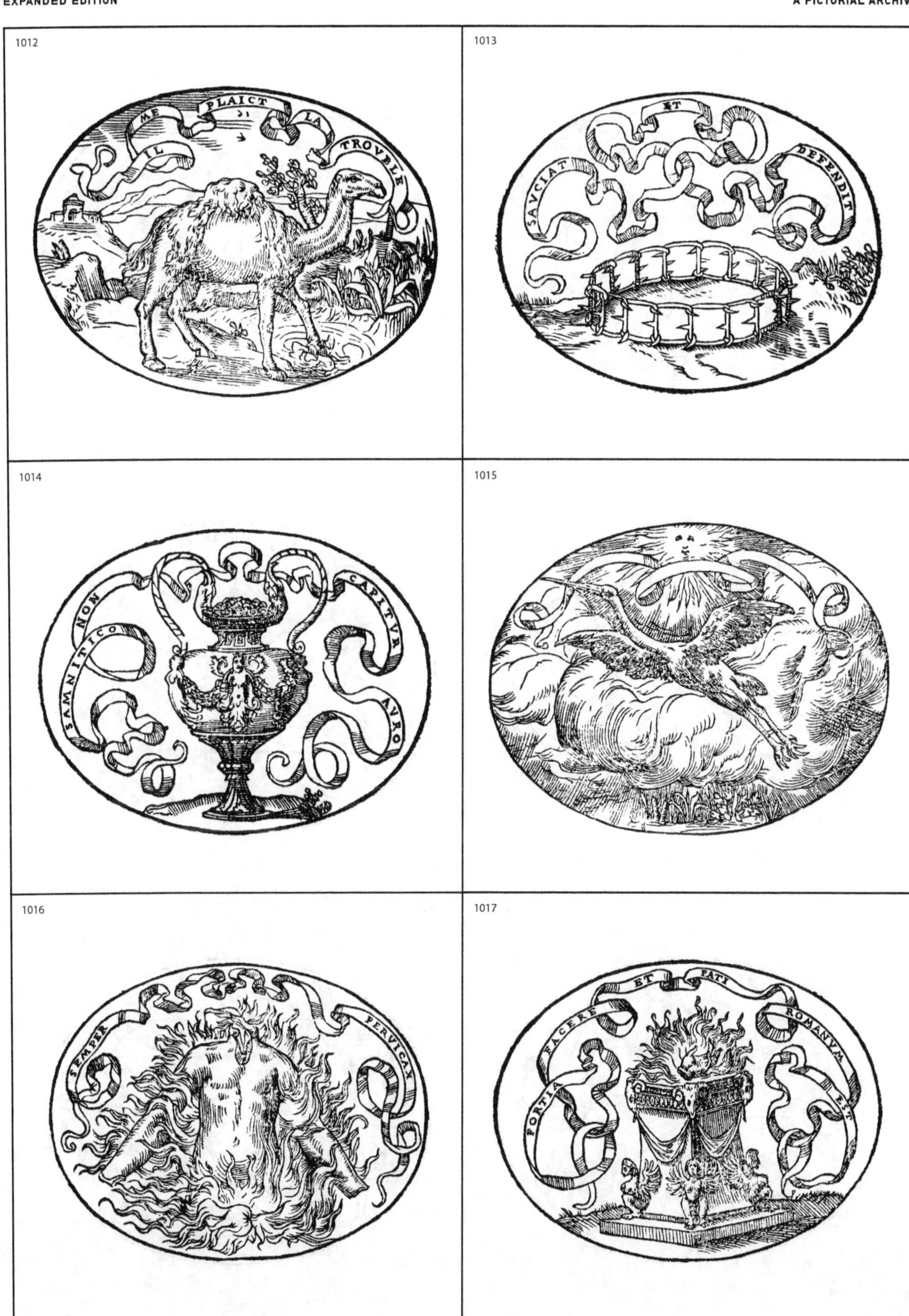
1012
ME PLAICT LA
IL
TROVBLE

1013
ET
SAVCIAT
DEFENDIT

1014
NON
SAMNITICO
CAPITVR
AVRO

1015

1016
SEMPER
PERVICAX

1017
ET PATI
FACERE
ROMANVM
FORTIA
ET

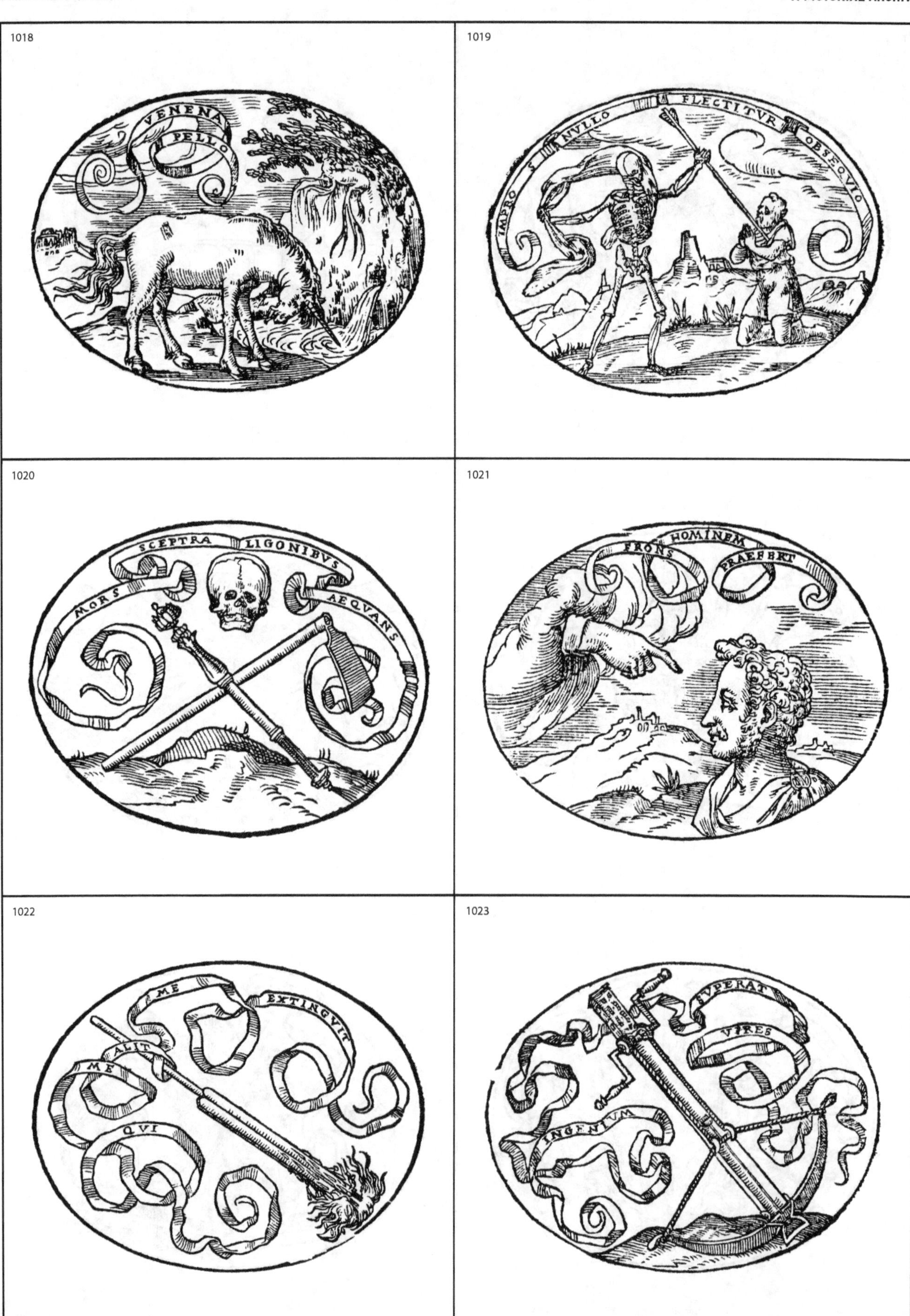
1018
VENENA PELLO

1019
IMPRO S NVLLO FLECTITVR OBSEQVIO

1020
SCEPTRA LIGONIBVS
MORS AEQVANS

1021
FRONS HOMINEM PRAEFERT

1022
ME EXTINGVIT
ALIT
ME
QVI

1023
SVPERAT
VIRES
INGENVM

1024

1025

1026

1027

1028

1029

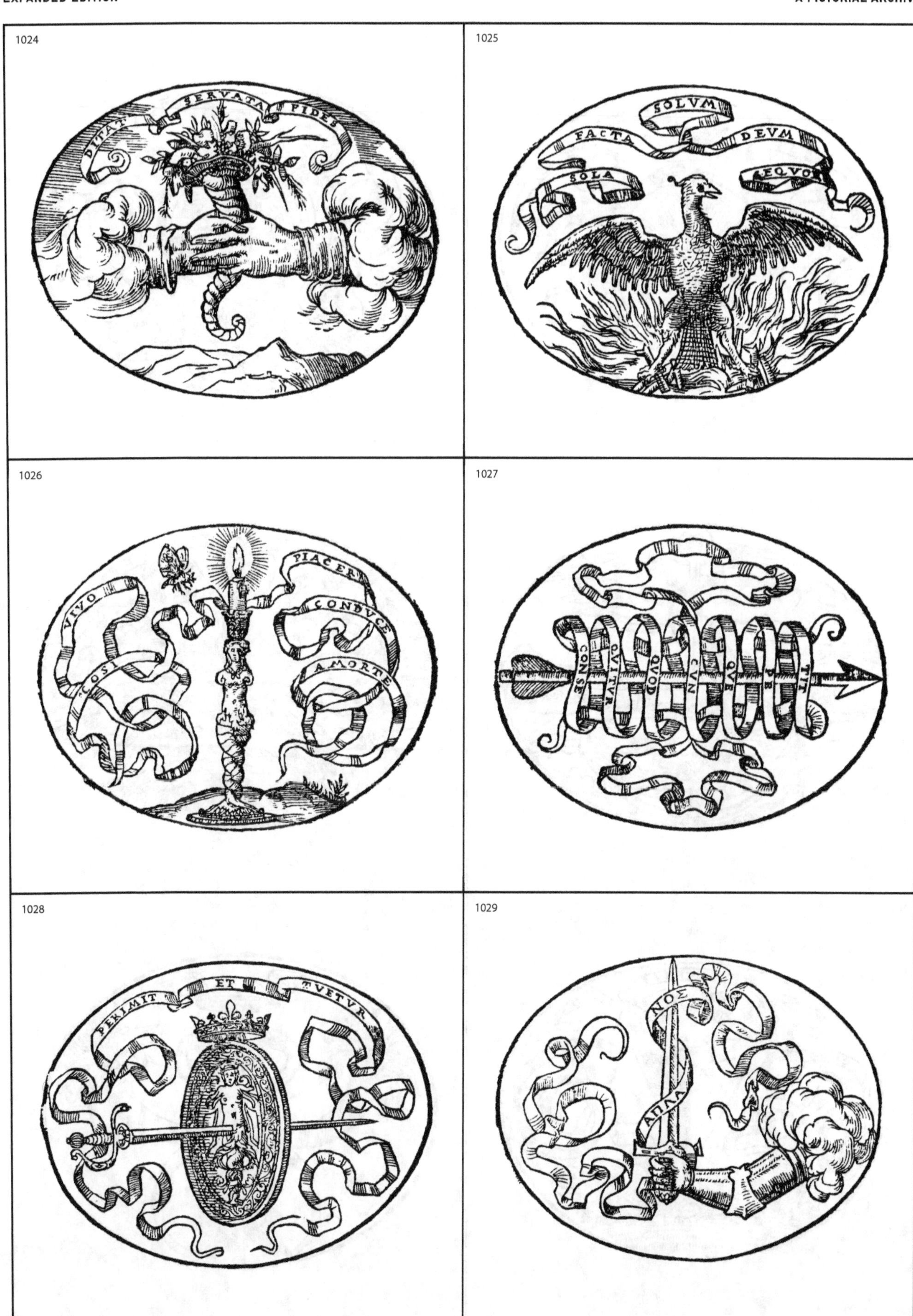

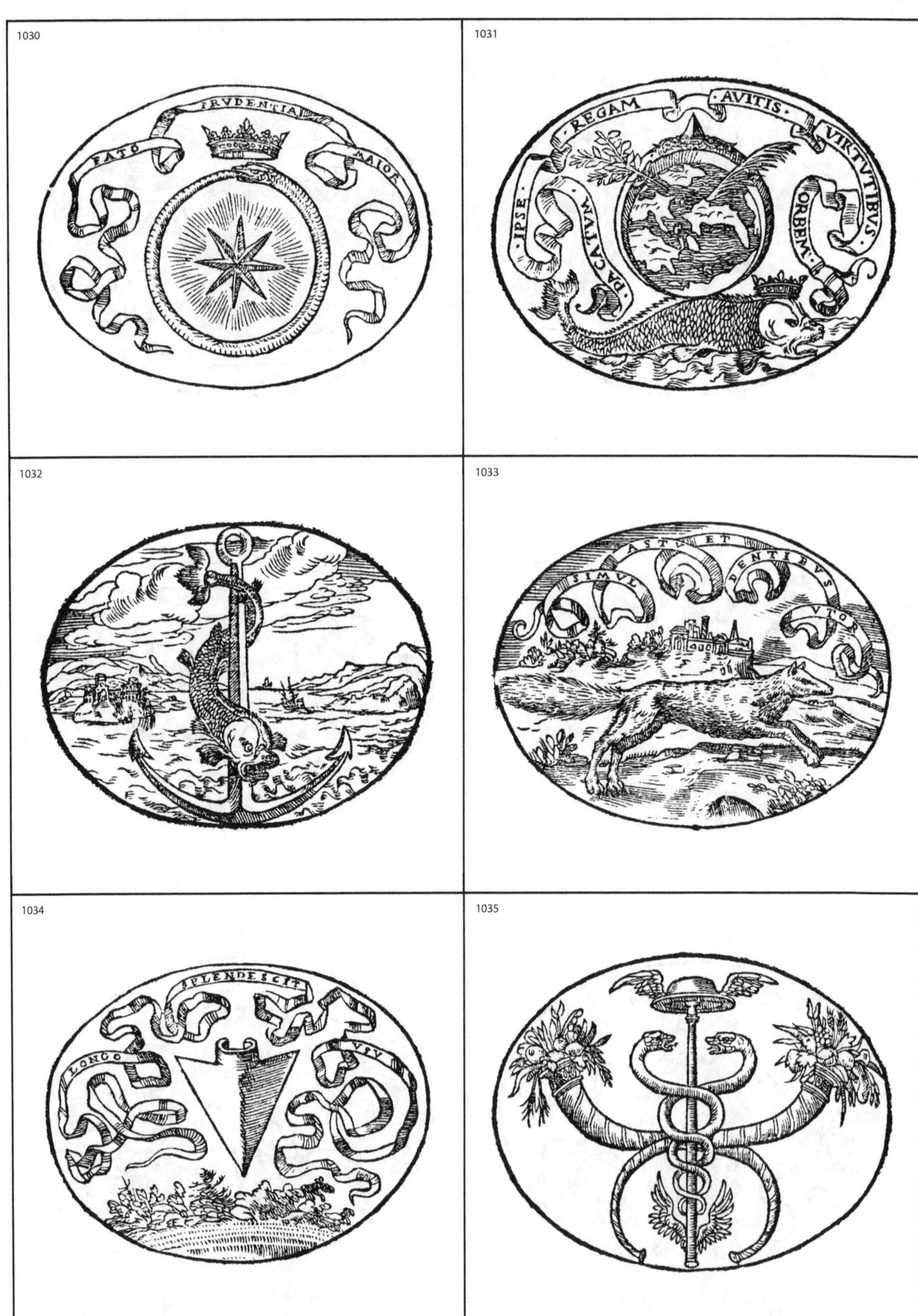

1030
PRVDENTIA
FATO
MAIOR

1031
REGAM
AVITIS
IPSE
VIRTVTIBVS
PACATVM
ORBEM

1032

1033
ASTV ET
SIMVL
PENTIBVS

1034
SPLENDESCIT
LONGO
VSV

1035

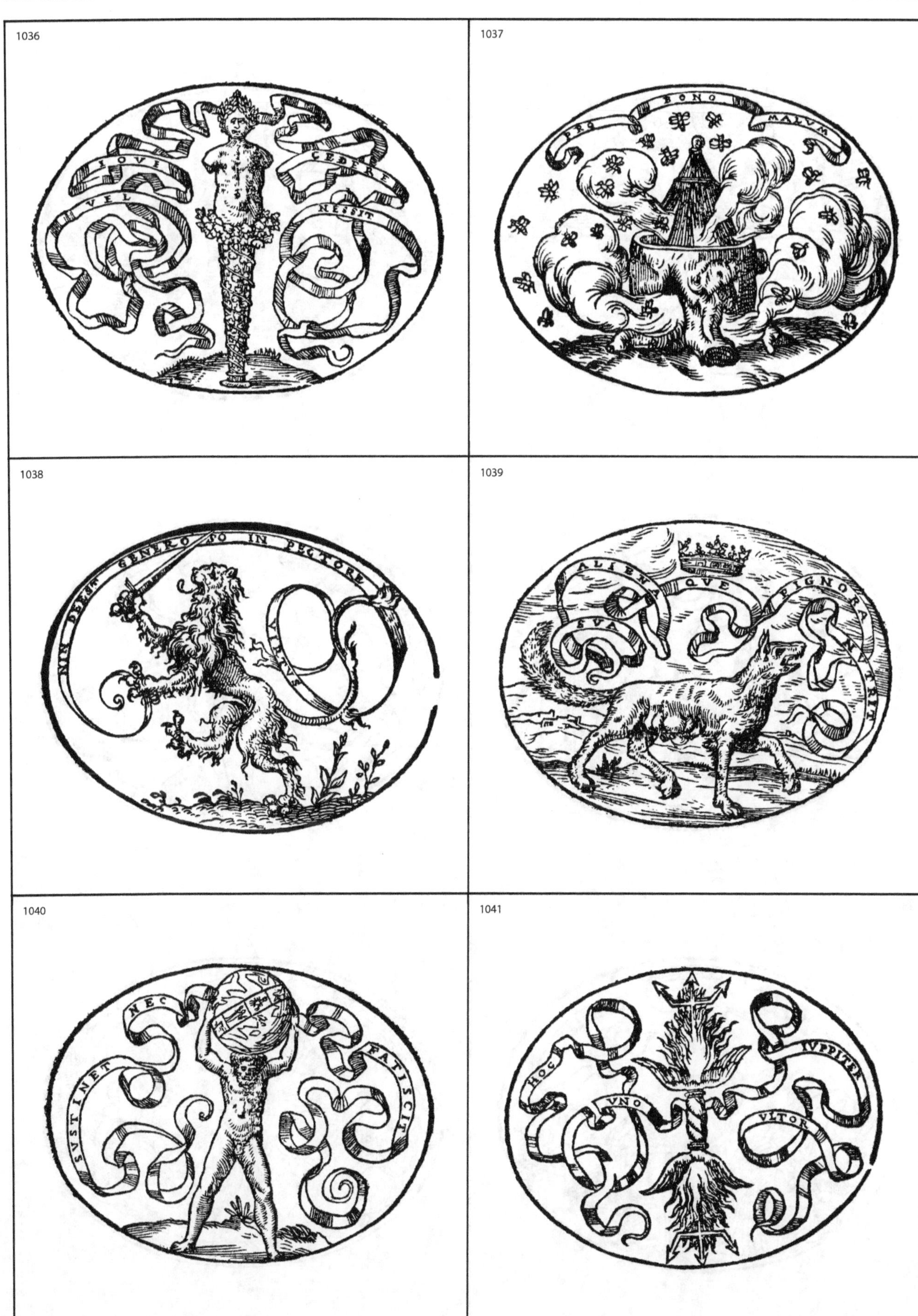

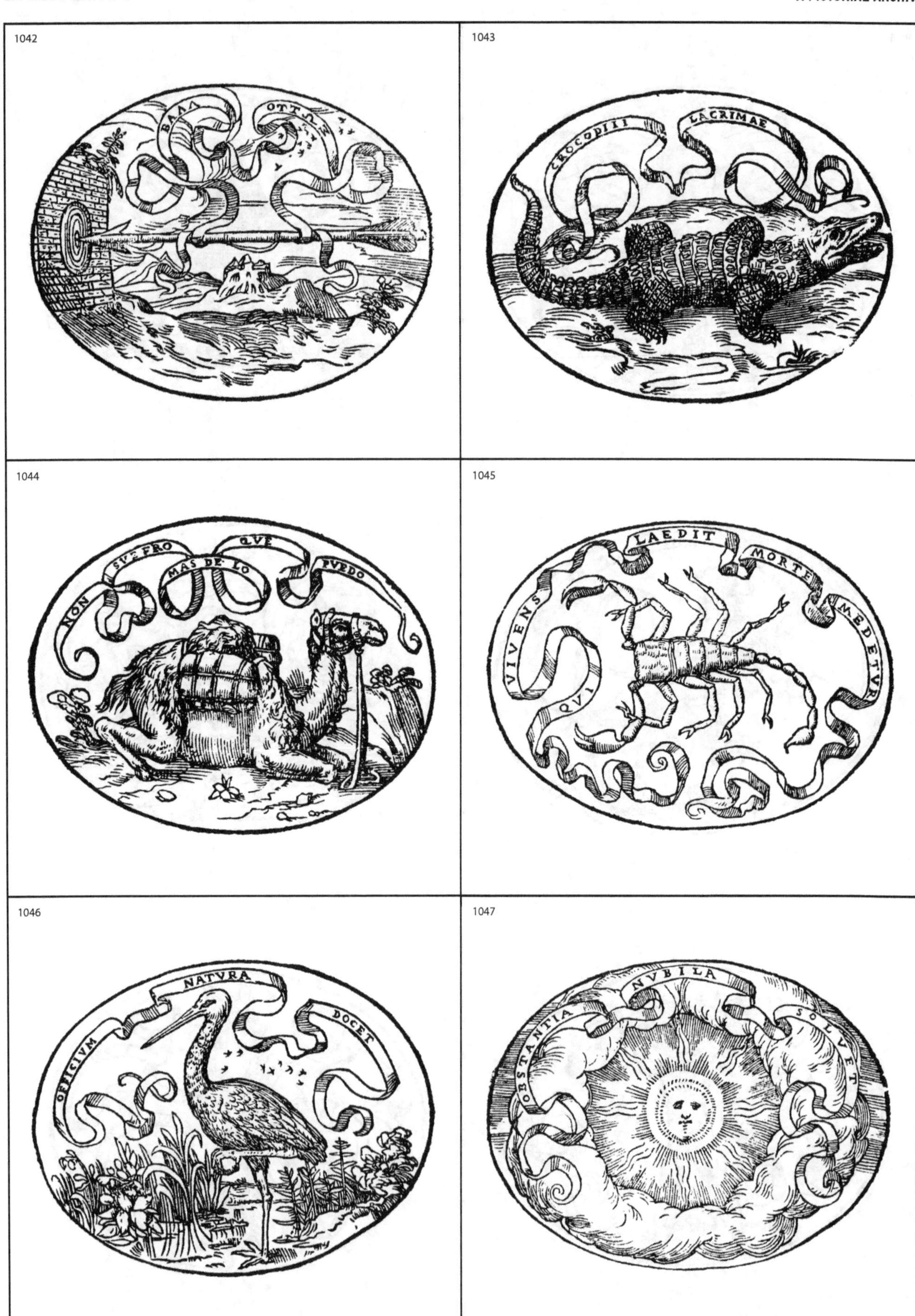
1042
BALA OTTA

1043
CROCODILI LACRIMAE

1044
NON SVFFRO QVE MAS DE LO PVEDO

1045
LAEDIT MORTE VIVENS QVI MEDETVR

1046
NATVRA OFICIVM DOCET

1047
OBSTANTIA NVBILA SOLVET

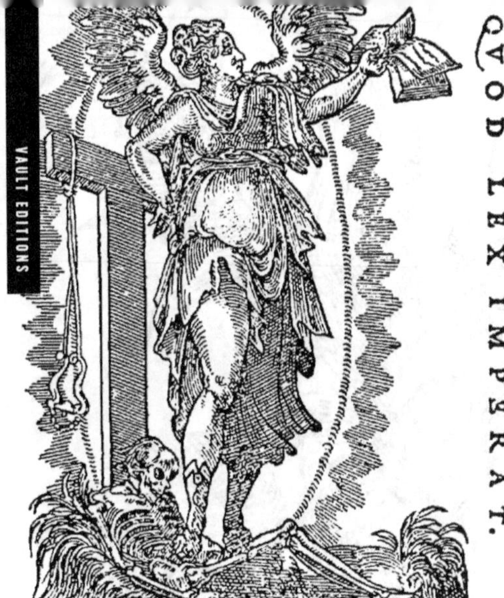

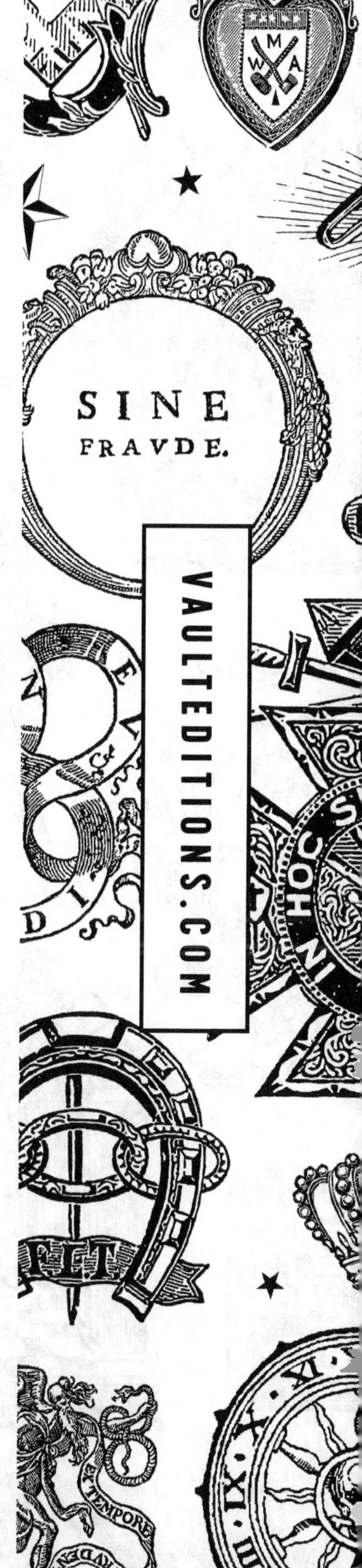

DOWNLOAD YOUR FILES

All images featured in this book are available to download as high-resolution files, ready for use in your creative projects. To access your files, visit the link below and enter the password provided.

The files are provided in high-resolution JPEG formats, suitable for both print and digital use. Each image has been individually restored and cleaned to ensure the finest possible quality,

preserving the detail and character of the original works while making them ready for modern creative applications.

Download yours now and get creating!

STEP ONE

Enter the following web address on a desktop or laptop computer in your web browser.

vaulteditions.com/pages/vlicd

STEP TWO

Enter the following password to access the download page:

vlicd2846292386

STEP THREE

Follow the prompts to access your high-resolution files.

CONTACT

For technical support, please email:
info@vaulteditions.com

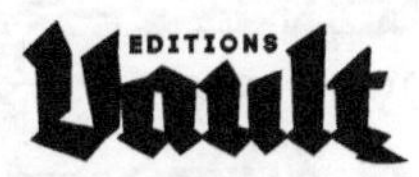

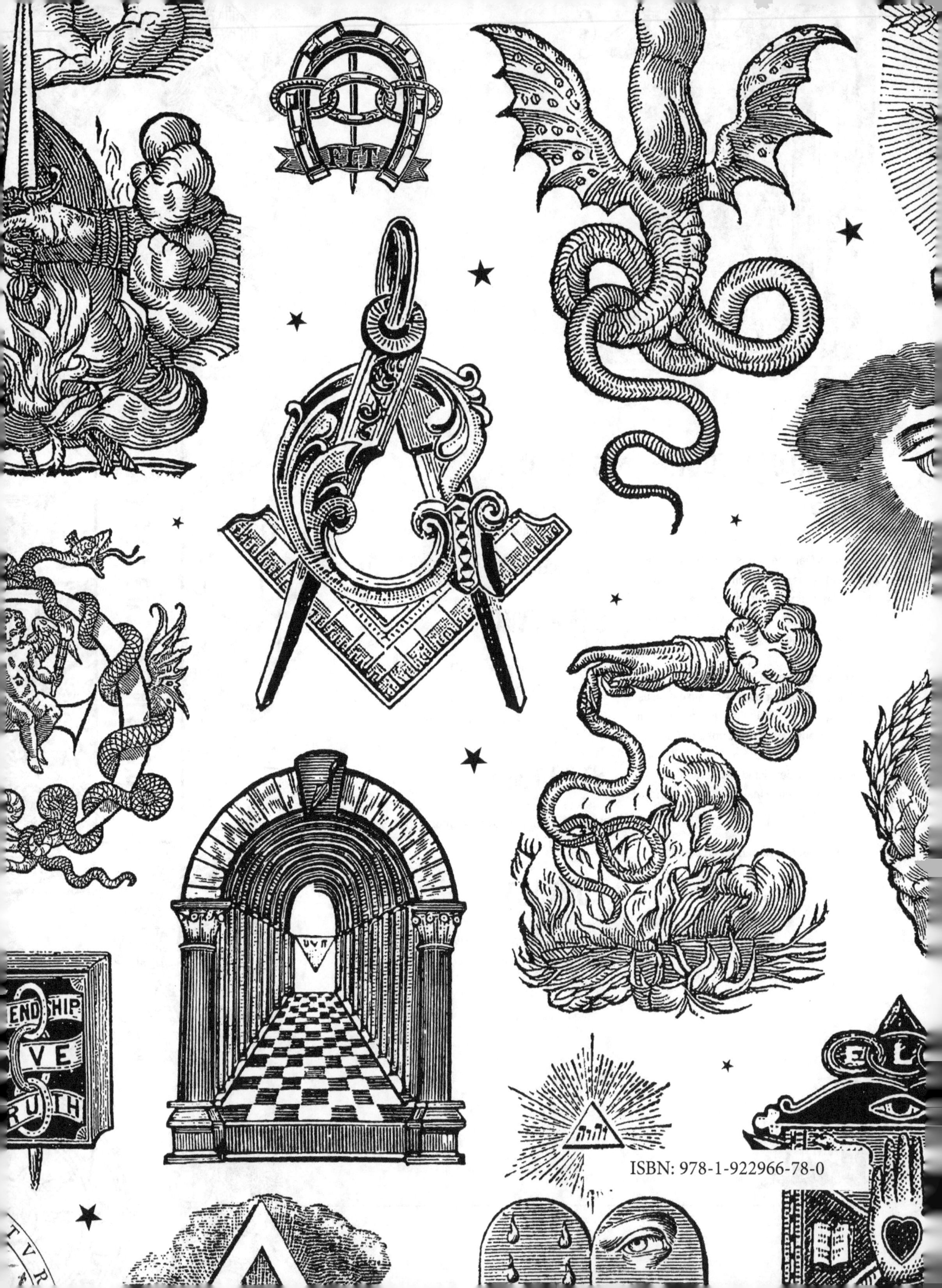

ISBN: 978-1-922966-78-0